AMERICA'S HANDYMAN BOOK

AMERICA'S HANDYMAN BOOK

SECOND REVISED EDITION
A BASIC DO-IT-YOURSELF GUIDE
TO THE REPAIR, MAINTENANCE,
AND IMPROVEMENT OF THE HOME

by the staff of
THE FAMILY HANDYMAN
Magazine

CHARLES SCRIBNER'S SONS
New York

All photographs and diagrams in this book have appeared in *The Family Handyman* magazine. Many of the photographs were provided originally by the following manufacturers:

Adjustable Clamp Co.
Alsco, Inc.
American Plywood Association
American Walnut Manufacturers
   Association
Armstrong Cork Co., Inc.
Babock & Co.
The Borden Co.
Black & Decker Manufacturing Co.
The Celotex Corp.
Chicopee Manufacturing Corp.
The Dow Chemical Co.
Du Fast Inc.
The Forsberg Manufacturing Co.
Marlite Wallpanels
Monsanto Chemical Co.

The National Plastic Products Co.
Owens-Corning Fiberglas Corp.
PPG Industries
Red Devil Tools
Reynolds Metals Inc.
Skilsaw Inc.
Structural Clay Products
   Institute
Sylvania Electric Inc.
Synchro Corp.
Union Carbide & Carbon Corp.
U.S. Expansion Bolt Co.
Western Wood Products
   Association
The Wiremold Co.

Library of Congress Cataloging in Publication Data

Main entry under title:

America's handyman book.

  Includes index.
  1. Dwellings—Maintenance and repair—
Amateurs' manuals. I. Family handyman.

TH4817.3.A43   1979   643'.7   79-17955
ISBN 0-684-10147-5

Design by Elaine Golt Gongora

3 5 7 9 11 13 15 17 19   F/C   20 18 16 14 12 10 8 6 4

ACKNOWLEDGMENTS

I would like to acknowledge the invaluable contributions of *The Family Handyman* Magazine staff who contributed to the first edition, including Arnold Abramson, publisher; Dorothy Sheehan, assistant to the publisher; Morton Waters, editorial director; and Franc L. Roggeri, art director. I also wish to thank the editorial staff that supervised the revised edition, including Gene Schnaser, editor; Paula Smith and Gary Branson, associate editors; Lura LaBarge, technical editor; Arnold Romney, contributing editor; Terry Redlin, art director; and Ron Chamberlain, associate artist.

Others who helped see the second revised edition to its completion include Ashley Pennebaker, Richard Day, Mike McClintock, Mort Schultz, Sue Sheppard, Lorn Manthey, Monte Burch, Tom Philbin, and George Smolik.

Howard Jones, Publisher
The Family Handyman Magazine

The editors of *The Family Handyman* Magazine are grateful to the following manufacturers and associations for their assistance in compiling the second revised edition:

Armstrong Cork
American Society of Heating, Refrigeration and Air Conditioning Engineers
Association of Home Appliance Manufacturers
BernzOmatic Corp.
Black & Decker Mfg. Co.
Bostick Co.
Chevron USA
GAF Corp.
General Switch Inc.
Genova
Glidden Coatings and Resins

Gries Reproducing Co.
Halo Lighting
Johns-Manville Corp.
Kool-O-Matic Corp.
Leviton
Masonite Corp.
McGraw-Edison
Northern States Power Co.
Owens-Corning Fiberglas Corp.
Rockwell International
Sears, Roebuck & Co.
The Stanley Works
Swingline Corp.
True Temper Corp.

CONTENTS

INTRODUCTION

As technology accelerates, the majority of Americans are forced into career specialization to make a living. The days are gone when, by virtue of your occupation, you could hope to "embrace all knowledge and parts thereof." In fact, our world has become so specialized that the simple phrase "do it yourself" has taken on a distinct and unique meaning in our vocabulary.

In one sense, "do it yourself" reflects a historic attitude of Americans, who traditionally pride themselves as a people possessing an abundance of initiative and self-reliance. But in another sense it represents a protest against the restrictions of specialization, of standardization and mechanization, of red tape and high prices. It is often easier to do it yourself, when you can, and usually much more economical, exciting, and rewarding.

The early colonial homesteader serves as an outstanding example of a man forced by necessity into mastering a variety of skills. He was a literal "jack of all trades," and the craftsmanship with which he handled his simple tools and materials is attested today by the value placed on the rare products still in existence from his crude workbench. An authentic object of early Americana is now a treasure, not only because of its antiquity and inherent good workmanship, but also because it was handmade. There is an intrinsic value associated with work done using one's own hands that sets it apart, makes it exclusive and not merely a duplicated item rolled off an assembly line, given a stock number, and stacked alongside others exactly like it.

In the 1800s, miscellaneous work and odd jobs fell to the lot of men called handymen. Sometimes they were itinerant and made their living as they traveled about the countryside. Some of them made word-of-mouth reputations for themselves and built tidy little businesses. But as times changed so did occupations. As industry grew, the demand for specialized skilled labor increased, and gradually the handyman became just a memory of the horse-and-buggy days. Homeowners were able to call on the services of a variety of tradesmen: carpenters, plumbers, electricians, painters, gardeners, or masons, plus a wide range of experts on such subjects as fireplaces and chimneys, floors, doors and windows, insulation, siding, and so on.

In the late 1940s, as a result of World War II, prices and labor costs boomed. Further, there was a woeful lack of adequate and suitable housing for the exploding population. Young couples, in their desperation for shelter, were buying or renting homes that were too small for their growing families. Builders, in a seller's market, too often put the absolute minimum into their houses, and the problem of repairs was ever present.

As it became difficult, if not impossible, for many millions of homeowners to afford the cost of outside help, the term "do it yourself" emerged. At first it carried a note of banter, as if the very idea were somewhat outlandish. Possibly it was, for a people so long unused to the idea . . . and, further, they didn't know how to do it themselves. They had no how-to information with which to begin. How many knew how to build in shelves, expand storage space, add rooms in an attic, fix a sagging floor, or mend a leak in a roof? Who could clean out a chimney, pour concrete, or paint a house?

Sensing a new market, tool manufacturers began to produce light-duty stationary and portable power tools, heretofore made primarily for heavy industry. First came a popular version of the ¼" electric hand drill, followed immediately by a list of accessories that made it one of the most versatile tools ever conceived. Realizing that a full workshop of stationary power tools would be beyond the average homeowner for reasons of cost as well as lack of space, toolmakers evolved a series of combination tools, the first being a table saw – drill press – lathe with a common source of power. There soon followed a combined table saw and jointer, and again accessories appeared to increase their versatility. A precision instrument in industry, the radial arm saw, was brought out in a version especially for the new "home handyman." It too became a combination tool with the addition of many conversion accessories.

Other manufacturers began to prepare products suited for use by the amateur. Prepasted and trimmed wallpapers appeared on the market; new paints, easy to work with and quick drying; prefinished wallboard panels in standard sizes; complete window and door assemblies, ready to install; a variety of floor and wall tiles of all sizes and shapes, easy to cut and work with; new, fast-acting adhesives; lumber in standard sizes. These are but a few of the many new products that gave momentum and incentive to the idea of "doing it yourself."

But as some manufacturers assembled directions for the use of their products, the language of professionals was used and the homeowner became bewildered. He faced problems concerning his house and property for which he knew no answers and had no ready, easily understandable source of how-to information.

One of these homeowners was Arnold E. Abramson. He and his growing family had just moved into an early eighteenth-century colonial home, and the needed repair and restoration work seemed overwhelming. Thus, acutely aware of the problem, he began to develop in his mind the idea of a publication that would devote itself exclusively to the guidance and instruction of the growing members of baffled, nonexpert homeowners. Gradually the nucleus of a staff was gathered for a new magazine called *The Family Handyman*. A rare few were found who did have the "how-to" at their fingertips; then came the writers who could interpret the technicalities into simple, everyday language; and, finally, the artists who could further condense complexities into drawings and diagrams relatively easy to understand. *The Family Handyman* was thus born and shortly became the most popular magazine in the do-it-yourself field.

From the first issue, in January 1951, the emphasis in assembling the magazine has been on simple, step-by-step language. No effort has been spared to maintain this clarity to guide the homeowner handyman in the use of tools, the selection of materials to use, the best way to do a job. Step-by-step photos abounded in every issue; line drawings and diagrams explained such intricacies as rabbeting, dadoing, wiring, furring out a wall, and hanging a door.

After 29 years of publishing, the original formula for the homeowner-handyman reader has changed little. *The Family Handyman*'s editorial content can still be divided into three major categories: a) preventive maintenance that prolongs the life of the home; b) repairs that eventually become necessary; and c) improvements that increase the comfort, convenience, and value of the home. This is the basis on which the first edition of *America's Handyman Book* was assembled in 1961 and revised in 1970.

In the years since the first edition, there has been a tremendous growth in the do-it-yourself field. Today a journeyman construction specialist will command a daily fee of $120 to $200 or more. The cost of hiring a two-day home repair job done might easily exceed the monthly mortgage payment. As professional construction rates increase, manufacturers of materials ranging from paint to plumbing are aiming their products at the do-it-yourselfer, with ease of application their chief goal. Easily soldered copper pipes have replaced iron, which had to be threaded and installed with expensive fittings. Plastic pipe, which can be easily cut and joined with solvents, replaces cast-iron drain pipes, which had to be joined with oakum and melted lead. These and hundreds of other products are being purchased in increasing quantities by the family handyman.

Since the original edition of this book was published, energy has become an increasing concern of the homeowner. In past years, efforts to limit home energy consumption consisted mainly of trying to keep utility bills in line with those of the neighbors. Today extensive research is under way to find methods of making the home more energy efficient. Reducing energy consumption has become the number-one goal for most owners of homes. This revised edition summarizes in depth what you can do to cut your energy bills.

There are two areas to consider in the cost of home ownership. The first is the initial cost of the home. There is little you can do about increases in land, material, and labor prices. The second is the cost of owning and maintaining the home. Here there is great opportunity for you as a homeowner to control expenses. The best of new and old techniques and materials has been incorporated in this revision.

The Family Handyman Magazine

1

HOW TO: PLAN TO CUT ENERGY COSTS · WEATHERPROOF
YOUR HOME · CHOOSE INSULATION MATERIALS · INSTALL
HOME INSULATION · SELECT AN INSULATION
CONTRACTOR · INSULATE PIPES, DUCTS, HEATERS ·
INSTALL VAPOR BARRIERS · PROVIDE ADEQUATE VENTING ·
CHOOSE AND USE CAULKING AND WEATHERSTRIPPING
MATERIALS · MAKE HEATING AND COOLING SYSTEMS
EFFICIENT · REDUCE ENERGY USED BY APPLIANCES · BUY
PRODUCTS THAT HELP SAVE ENERGY

HOME ENERGY

The bulk of this book is designed to help you save money by showing you how to take care of your home so that it lasts longer and how to save on improvements and repairs by doing more yourself. But another opportunity to save money has become increasingly important recently — home energy.

Energy is a manufactured commodity like most other products, subject to the laws of supply and demand. Since the winter of 1973–1974, Americans have become painfully aware of the fact — mainly through higher and higher home energy bills — that energy supplies are no longer unlimited.

Domestic reserves of fossil-fuel resources cannot be increased, and energy from alternative sources is still remote. Wind, geothermal, and solar energy sources are not expected to offer much relief for twenty to twenty-five years. Other less exotic alternate sources such as coal gasification, tidal power, bioconversion, ocean thermal differences, and solid waste are still too expensive to be practical. Only nuclear power appears to show promise in the near future, if environmental considerations are worked out.

The homeowner plays a significant role in energy consumption. Today about 40 percent of all energy consumed in the United States is used for transportation, 30 percent is used for products, and 30 percent is used in the home. Of the 30 percent used in the home, about 42 percent is consumed for space heating and 14 percent for air conditioning. Heating and cooling alone account for 17 percent of the overall energy drain in this country.

This chapter covers what you can do to reduce your home energy needs, not only by weatherproofing your home by insulating, weatherstripping, caulking, and so on, but also by showing you where you may be wasting energy and money without even knowing it.

HOW TO PLAN TO CUT ENERGY COSTS

Energy conservation is both a challenge and an opportunity for the homeowner. Studies on test homes show that a typical American family may be able to cut its fuel bill by close to 50 percent by making a few economical home improvements. To give you an overall look at the possibilities, the American Society of Heating, Refrigeration and Air

Conditioning Engineers provides the following checklist of forty-six steps you can take, based on initial cost.

Some steps cost little or nothing, some are modest in cost, and others require substantial investment. The payback of some steps may surprise you; the entire list can help you line up priorities for your own energy conservation program.

CUTTING ENERGY COSTS

No-cost measures

Step	Cost	Annual Savings	Comments
Turn down thermostat, especially at night or when house is unoccupied; keep lower than you used to.	0	A 5°F reduction from 10 p.m. to 6 a.m. saves 6% to 11%.	Savings depend on weather; this is one of your biggest chances for savings.
Close unused rooms; do not heat or cool them.	0	Depends on size of area closed off	If kids are away at college, this saving will add up.
During winter open drapes and shades to let sun in; close at night to keep heat in; during summer close to keep sun out.	0	Can reduce heat gain up to 50%	Too many variables to give exact savings
Close damper in fireplace when fire is out.	0	Worthwhile but not quantifiable	Closed flue keeps heat in and cold air out.
Reduce hot water thermostat to 140°F if you have a dishwasher; otherwise set at 120°F	0	$10 to $90	Savings depend on size of temperature reduction, cost of energy, and type of heater.
Keep doors and windows closed when possible; turn off unneeded lights, TV, radio; open refrigerator and freezer as briefly as possible; dress appropriately.	0	Worthwhile but not quantifiable	Common sense goes a long way.
Take shower, not bath.	0	$20 to $80	Bath consumes twice as much hot water.
Fill washer, dishwasher, avoiding partial loads; use warm wash and cold rinse on washer.	0	$20 to $65	Depends on type of water heater and cost of energy
Avoid no-frost regrigerators; be sure to defrost manual models regularly	0	You'd save 40% by changing to manual model.	Operating cost of frost-free model @ 5¢ per kilowatt hour: $83; manual: $50
Use oven to cook more than one dish at a time.	0	Difficult to calculate	
Turn off dishwasher when it reaches the drying cycle.	0	Small	Open door and let nature do the drying.
Avoid TV sets with "instar feature, or add a switch between set and the wall socket.	0	Worthwhile	These sets have current running through some circuits even when turned "off."

Studies of test homes show how a typical homeowner may be able to cut fuel bills nearly 50 percent in some cases. Furnace tune-ups, lower thermostat settings, furnace cleaning and servicing, installation of storm windows, and insulation of ceilings are steps showing high payback per dollar invested. Source: Chevron U.S.A.

Step	Cost	Annual Savings	Comments
On electric ranges, keep reflector below heating element clean.	0	Varies	Clean reflectors improve efficiency.
Dry clothes in consecutive loads without interruption.	0	Small	Don't let dryer cool before you dry next load.
Turn dryer off as soon as clothes are dry, or leave them damp for easier ironing.	0	Varies	Some people let it run longer than necessary.
Keep lint screen of dryer clean.	0	Small	Remove lint after each load.
Use light colors on walls, carpets, furniture, and drapes.	0	Worthwhile but not quantifiable	Light colors reflect light, so you can use less illumination.
Buy appliances on the basis of original cost, plus operating expenses over the entire life of the appliance.	0	Varies, but is likely to be substantial	An item with a higher first cost may be a better buy if its operating cost over (say 10 years) is low.

Step	Cost	Annual Savings	Comments
In gas systems, turn off furnace's pilot and gas supply in warm weather.	0	Worthwhile	For safety, your gas company should do this.
Turn up air conditioner thermostat to 78°F or 80°F	0	Substantial	Each increase of 1°F saves 3 to 5% of energy used.
Reduce load on cooling system by cutting use of appliances during heat of day.	0	Worthwhile	Appliances generate heat.
Clean air conditioner filter frequently.	0	Worthwhile	This measure can bring 10% gain in efficiency.
Cut out unnecessary and purely decorative lights.	0	Varies	It takes ½ pint of oil to generate the electricity used by a 100-watt floodlight in 10 hours.
Avoid long-life lamps except in inaccessible places.	0	Varies	Long-life lamps use more electricity.

Moderate-cost measures

Step	Cost	Annual Savings	Comments
Have heating system cleaned and adjusted every fall.	$35 to $75	10%	A dirty furnace wastes energy.
Clean permanent furnace filter regularly; replace throwaway filter every 60 days.	Clean: 0 Replace: $2 to $3	Hard to measure	If this chore is omitted for a long period, you'll pay for it.
Install aluminum foil behind radiators.	$1 to $2	Hard to measure	This homemade reflector sends heat back into room.
Weatherstrip doors and windows; caulk sills, seams, cracks, and so forth.	Depends on size of living unit	10% or more	Breaks in the exterior let cold in and heat out or vice versa.
Fix leaky faucets, especially hot water.	Up to $25	$8 to $35 a year	Leaks can waste 600–6,000 gallons a year.
Shade your air conditioner.	Varies	Worthwhile	
Use kitchen, bathroom, and attic exhaust fans sparingly.	Small	Hard to measure	Expel heated air in winter, cooled air in summer.
Make sure refrigerator and freezer door gaskets are air-tight.	New gasket costs up to $30	Up to 50% of operating costs	
Select a window air conditioner that is properly sized and with a high "Energy Efficiency Ratio."	Varies	Substantial	Read the yellow and black "Energyguide" label to determine the EER rating on the model you are considering.
Substitute fluorescent for incandescent lights where possible	Varies	75%	A 25-watt fluorescent tube has the light output of a 100-watt incandescent bulb.

Step	Cost	Annual Savings	Comments
Be sure damper in fireplace closes tightly; replace if necessary.	$10 to $50	Substantial	If damper doesn't work, much costly heat will go up chimney.
Have your air conditioner cleaned and lubricated during fall or winter.	$20 to $40 for each unit	If unit is dirty, saving will be substantial	Without cleaning, appliance loses 10 to 27% of efficiency; servicemen offer low rates in off-season.
When buying new appliances, watch for energy-saving features.	Little	Small	Every little bit helps

Higher-cost measures

Step	Cost	Annual Savings	Comments
In a central air-conditioning system, use air economizer, which shuts down compressor and circulates outside air when it is cooler.	$100 to $150	Will save 20% to 30%	
Install storm windows and doors; keep them in place in summer.	$20 and up per window	15%	You'll recover the cost in energy savings in a few years.
If storm windows are too expensive, tape a sheet of plastic over each window.	$5 per window	15%	If you rent, plastic may be the solution.
Install insulation in attic, walls, floors. Consult your utility for data in your area.	Varies	20% or more (could be as much as 50%)	You'll recover cost in a few years (sooner if you do it yourself).
Install awnings, sun screens, and so forth to protect windows and doors.	Varies	Can cut solar heat gain up to 80%	Awnings should be designed so they won't trap hot air in window area.
Plant appropriate shrubbery or trees around house.	Varies	Substantial	Forms windscreen
Plant deciduous trees strategically.	Varies	Substantial	They'll shade house in summer; allow sun to warm it in winter.
Consider heat pump, especially if house is heated and cooled by electricity.	$2,000 to $4,000, depending on home	Varies, but can be substantial	Gives year-round climate conditioning, convenience, cleanliness.
In a centralized cooling and heating system, insulate ducts at least 1½".	Varies; $200 or more	As much as 25%	Important if ducts run through uninsulated attics or crawl spaces

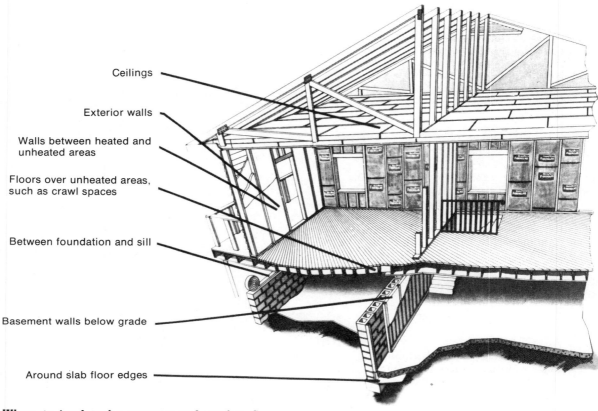

Ceilings

Exterior walls

Walls between heated and unheated areas

Floors over unheated areas, such as crawl spaces

Between foundation and sill

Basement walls below grade

Around slab floor edges

Where to insulate for economy and comfort. Source: Owens-Corning

HOW TO WEATHERPROOF YOUR HOME

The largest single energy expense in running your home is keeping it heated and cooled. The primary way to save on heating and air conditioning costs is with insulation. Just by installing proper attic insulation you can cut your heating and cooling fuel consumption substantially. You can have your insulation done by a professional contractor or, with a certain amount of know-how, you can do the job yourself.

Incomplete and conflicting statements abound concerning the saving of home energy. Check your plans with more than one "expert" before deciding on a course of action. Start your program by setting aside one hour to conduct an energy audit on your own home. Taking along a flashlight, pencil, and note pad, make a thorough inspection from top to bottom. Your inspection is likely to reveal some major energy-saving opportunities.

Before spending money to save energy, use as many no-cost and low-cost methods available to you as possible. Next use your home energy survey to start plugging major energy leaks.

R value numbers are used to describe the relative effectiveness of different types of insulation: the higher the R number, the better the material will resist heat loss and heat gain. Any material with an R value greater than R-2 per inch is considered an insulating material. As an example, brick (about R-0.2 per inch) and wood (approximately R-1 per inch) are not considered insulation materials, even though many people think they are.

R values are determined by laboratory testing (rather than by in-use testing in actual homes). Their purpose is to provide you with a design guideline. R values help you determine how much insulation of a particular type you need to get the performance you want. All insulation packages now have R value information on the labels, because of a 1979 rule by the U.S. Federal Trade Commission.

In most situations, the R value per inch is not

important. If one insulation material has a lower R value per inch than another, you can buy additional material to achieve the total R value you want. If you want to add R-19 to your attic, for example, compare the prices of different materials on the basis of *the cost per square foot of R-19*. Although you may need more of one material or less of another, you will usually find that the cost is similar for equal R values.

How much insulation your home should have depends on your climate and your fuel costs. In general, the higher your fuel costs and the colder your climate, the more you need. To get an idea of how much insulation you should add to combat current heating costs, call your local gas or electric utility. Ask what their minimum insulation recommendations or requirements are for new homes in your locale. Michigan Consolidated Gas Company, for instance, is recommending that homeowners in the Detroit area insulate their attics to R-44. You will want to bring your insulation levels up to current standards — or higher, since fuel costs are continuing to rise.

HOW TO CHOOSE INSULATION MATERIALS

There are a number of different materials available to insulate your home, including fiberglass, cellulose, mineral wool, vermiculite, and various

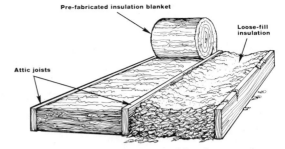

Blanket insulation is prefabricated by the manufacturer into uniform densities or R values. It's easy to install — you simply unroll and lay in place. Loose-fill insulation is machine or hand poured to achieve the desired R value. Source: Owens-Corning

plastic foams. These insulation materials are available in different forms:

Blankets are rolls of insulation designed to fit between joists or rafters that are on either 16″ or 24″ centers. Thickness varies from 1″ to 12″. Blankets come with or without vapor-barrier backing.

Batts are similar to blankets, but are cut into 4′ or 8′ lengths. These are easy to use if you're going to install insulation yourself.

Loose-fill insulation is either poured or blown in. Loose fill can be either of fiberglass, cellulose, or rock wool.

Foam insulation for homes may be the liquid type

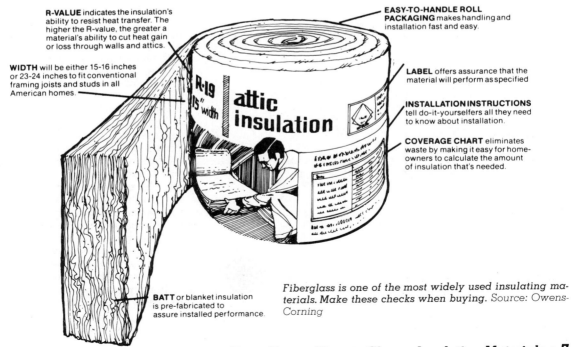

R-VALUE indicates the insulation's ability to resist heat transfer. The higher the R-value, the greater a material's ability to cut heat gain or loss through walls and attics.

WIDTH will be either 15-16 inches or 23-24 inches to fit conventional framing joists and studs in all American homes.

EASY-TO-HANDLE ROLL PACKAGING makes handling and installation fast and easy.

LABEL offers assurance that the material will perform as specified

INSTALLATION INSTRUCTIONS tell do-it-yourselfers all they need to know about installation.

COVERAGE CHART eliminates waste by making it easy for homeowners to calculate the amount of insulation that's needed.

BATT or blanket insulation is pre-fabricated to assure installed performance.

Fiberglass is one of the most widely used insulating materials. Make these checks when buying. Source: Owens-Corning

R-VALUES OF DIFFERENT KINDS OF INSULATION

	R/Inch	R11	R19	R22	R30	R38	R44
			Inches Needed For				
LOOSE FILL MACHINE BLOWN							
Fiberglass	R2.3	5	8.5	10	13	16.5	19
Mineral wool	R3.125	3.5	6	7	9.5	12.5	14
Cellulose	R3.4	3	5.5	6.5	8.8	11	13
LOOSE FILL HAND POURED							
Cellulose	R3.4	3	5.5	6.5	8.8	11	13
Mineral wool	R3.125	3.5	6	7	9.5	12.5	14
Fiberglass	R2.3	5	8.5	10	13	16.5	19
Vermiculite	R2.1	5.5	9	10.5	14	18	21
BATTS OR BLANKETS							
Fiberglass	R3.14	3.5	6	7	9.5	12.5	14
Mineral wool	R3.14	3.5	6	7	9.5	12.5	14
RIGID BOARD							
Polystyrene beadboard	R3.5	3	5.5	Rigid board materials not used in these thicknesses.			
Extruded polystyrene (Styrofoam brand)	R5	3-2	5-3.5				
Urethane or isocyanurate	R6.2	2	3	*Manufacturers state R value for UF foam is about R4 to R4.3. However, UF foam shrinks after application, reducing R value. HUD says the average 6% shrink reduces R value 28%, so R4.3 should be R3.			
Fiberglass	R4.0	3	5				
LIQUID FOAM							
Urea-formaldehyde (UF foam) R3*		3.5	4				

This chart can be used to determine how much insulation you need to add to obtain the R value recommended in your area. Based on data found in the 1977 ASHRAE Handbook of Fundamentals (except UF foam, as noted above).

(made of urea formaldehyde) or the semirigid board type (made of urethane, isocyanurate, or polystyrene). In liquid form it can be injected into the walls. The board type can be applied directly to wall studs.

HOW TO INSTALL HOME INSULATION

Fiberglass represents the bulk of insulation sales. It's available in batts, blankets, or as loose fill in a wide range of R values. It may have a fac-ing material of paper (kraft) or aluminum foil. Installing batts or blankets can be an easy do-it-yourself project that even an inexperienced home-owner can accomplish in a weekend.

The only tools required are a sharp knife, a straightedge, a rule, and a pair of work gloves and safety glasses. Installation is simply a matter of measuring the area to be insulated, cutting the material to fit, and laying it in place between the home's structural framing members.

1.

2.

3.

4.

Insulating unfloored/unfinished attics. **Step 1.** *Lay temporary flooring and hang worklight. Leave insulation in packages until you're ready to use it.* **Step 2.** *Insulation should extend far enough to cover top plate, but shouldn't cover eave vents; if necessary, install baffles at inside of the eaves.* **Step 3.** *Begin laying insulation blankets at outer edge of the attic; work toward the center area of the house.* **Step 4.** *Fill space between chimney and wood framing with unfaced fiberglass insulation. Keep insulation 3" from recessed light fixtures.* NOTE: *If the R value in your climate calls for a second layer, and the cavity has been completely filled, place the additional layer of unfaced insulation directly on top of the existing material, either parallel to the joists or at right angles.* Source: Owens-Corning

FIRST STEP – MEASURE The first step in installing batts or blankets is to measure how much material will be needed. This involves measuring the length and width of the area to be insulated and multiplying these two dimensions to determine the square footage of material required.

After calculating the square footage, next determine how wide the insulation should be. Since insulation is usually installed between joists or studs, you will discover the space between these members almost always measures a constant 22½" or 14½", depending on local building codes and the age of the dwelling. Studs and joists are installed on either 24" or 16" centers in virtually all conventional homes. Therefore, the typical home-insulation project will require a material that is designated either 24" to 23" or 16" to 15" in width.

After determining the required square footage and width, the final step is to determine the proper insulation thickness or R value, and whether a vapor barrier will be needed.

If the area is already insulated but is not up to modern standards, which might be the case with an attic, then unfaced insulation – insulation without a vapor barrier – should be used. If there is no existing insulation, a material faced with either a kraft paper or aluminum-foil vapor barrier should be installed.

If you are not certain of the proper R value, ask your local utility or insulation supplier for advice in selecting the right R value for your climate and the part of the home to be insulated.

The following is a step-by-step, do-it-yourself guide to insulating six critical areas of the home

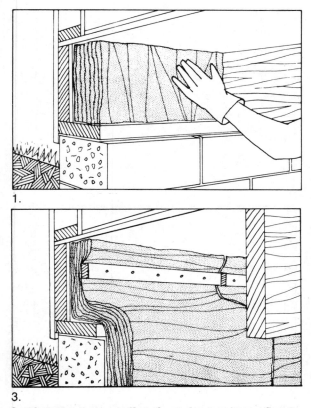

1.

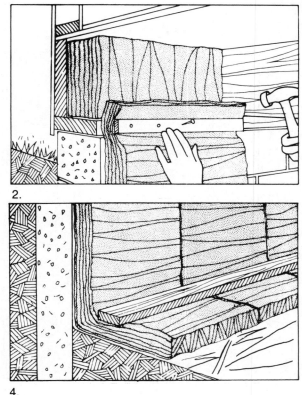

2.

3.

4.

Insulating masonry walls in heated crawl spaces. **Step 1.** *Measure and cut small pieces of insulation to fit snugly against the band joist.* **Step 2.** *Using longer furring strips, nail strips of insulation to the sill. The strips should be long enough to cascade down the wall and extend 2' along the ground into the crawl space.* **Step 3.** *On walls* *running parallel to the joists, it isn't necessary to use separate pieces of insulation for the band joist.* **Step 4.** *After the insulation has been installed, lay sheets of polyethylene film under the insulation and over the entire floor area. Use 2×4 studs or rocks to help hold the insulation in place.* Source: Owens-Corning

against winter heat loss and summer heat gain: (a) unfloored, unfinished attics; (b) finishing attics to living areas; (c) walls between heated and unheated areas; (d) basement walls; (e) floors above unheated crawl spaces; and (f) masonry walls in heated crawl spaces.

INSULATING UNFLOORED, UNFINISHED ATTICS
This is a popular do-it-yourself project. Begin by laying a piece of temporary flooring; a plank or section of ½" plywood should suffice. Leave the fiberglass insulation in the bags or rolls in which it came until you're ready to use it, since insulation is packaged in a compressed state and will expand once the package is opened.

Start laying the insulation at the outer edges of the attic and work toward the center. This allows more headroom for whatever cutting and fitting procedures are required. You might find that a

long-handled push broom will prove helpful in extending the insulation to the edges of the attic, which you may not be able to reach without it.

Lay in the long runs first and place the leftovers aside for filling up the smaller spaces later. Where you encounter wiring, push the insulation under. Be sure to butt each individual section of insulation tightly up against the adjacent piece for a complete barrier to heat.

Be careful when you extend the insulation to the edges of the attic that you don't block the flow of air from eave vents—if your home has them. You might even find it useful to install baffle boards at the inside of the eaves to keep from blocking these vents.

The space between the chimney and wood framing should be filled with an unfaced material. If you're installing insulation with a vapor barrier,

1.

2.

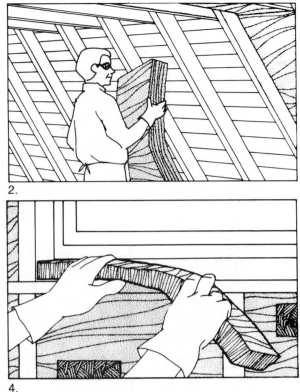

3.

4.

Insulating finished attics. **Step 1.** *Construct knee walls along sides of attic and collar beams at desired ceiling height.* **Step 2.** *Install blanket insulation between rafters and collar beams. The vapor barrier should face in toward warm-in-winter area of the house.* **Step 3.** *Use sepa-* *rate pieces of insulation for rafters and collar beams, since a continuous piece may result in gaps.* **Step 4.** *Install insulation in end and knee walls. Stuff leftover pieces in the small spaces around window frames.* Source: Owens-Corning

simply tear off the facing. IMPORTANT: Be sure to keep insulation a minimum of 3″ from recessed light fixtures to avoid the possibility of fires.

If you are reinsulating over existing insulation and the joist cavity is already filled with the original material, place the new layer at right angles to the joists for a particularly snug thermal barrier.

INSULATING FINISHED ATTICS If you want to convert your attic to living space, insulating the new wall and ceiling area is another priority project. After you've constructed the knee walls along the sides of the attic and collar beams at the desired ceiling height, you're ready to insulate.

Install the batts between the collar beams and rafters with the vapor barrier facing in toward the warm-in-winter side. Use a separate piece of insulation for these areas, since trying to fit a continuous length of insulation where beams and rafters meet could result in hard-to-fill gaps. Finally, again being sure the vapor barrier faces in, install insulation in end and knee walls. Stuff leftover pieces around window framing.

INSULATING WALLS Insulating walls between heated and unheated spaces in an existing home is usually a job for a professional contractor, since the stud cavities are not accessible. Exceptions are those cases where an exterior wall has been left unfinished, as with walls between a house and an attached unheated garage. Here insulation can be installed in the stud cavity — with the vapor barrier facing toward the warm-in-winter side of the wall.

INSULATING BASEMENT WALLS Insulating basement walls can save a surprising amount of energy. To insulate these walls, begin by installing a framework of furring strips or studs to the masonry surface. Nail the bottom plate directly to

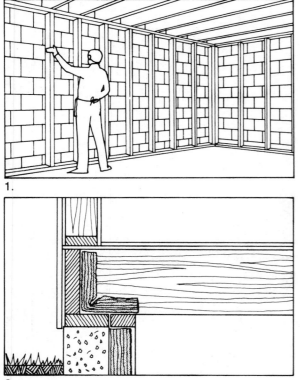

1.

2.

3.

4.

Insulating basement walls. Step 1. *Install framework of furring strips or studs to masonry walls, either 16″ or 24″ on center.* **Step 2.** *Install insulation between furring strips or studs. Staple flange on insulation facing to framing* members. **Step 3.** *Cut pieces of insulation to fit in band joist between top plates and subfloor.* **Step 4.** *Cover installed insulation with desired wall finish. Do not leave faced insulation exposed.* Source: Owens-Corning

the floor and the top plate to the joists above. The furring or studs can then be nailed to this framework, either 24″ or 16″ on-center.

Install the insulation between the studs much the way you would insulate an above-grade wall. If you're using a faced material, staple the flange on the facing to the strips or studs, with the facing toward the warm-in-winter side of the wall. If you're using an unfaced material, install a separate vapor barrier, such as polyethylene film or foil-backed gypsum board.

Be sure to cut a separate piece of insulation to fit the band joist between the top plate and the subfloor. Once the insulation is installed, paneling or other wall finish can be applied directly to the framing members.

INSULATING FLOORS ABOVE UNHEATED CRAWL SPACES This step can help prevent uncomfortable drafts and energy loss. Slip insulation batts between the floor joists with the vapor barrier fac-

ing up toward the warm-in-winter side; the insulation will remain in place temporarily. Begin at one end of the wall and install wire mesh (chicken wire works nicely) perpendicular to the floor joists to hold the insulation in place permanently.

In lieu of wire mesh, use "tiger teeth" or crisscrossed wire strung between nails to secure the insulation. Be sure the insulation fits snugly up against the band joist and overlaps the bottom plate.

INSULATING MASONRY WALLS IN HEATED CRAWL SPACES Insulating these walls is also worthwhile. Begin by measuring and cutting small pieces of insulation to fit snugly against the band joist. Using longer furring strips, nail vertical lengths of insulation batts to the sill. Make sure the lengths of insulation are long enough to cascade down the wall and extend 2 feet along the ground into the crawl space.

On walls that run parallel to joists, it is not nec-

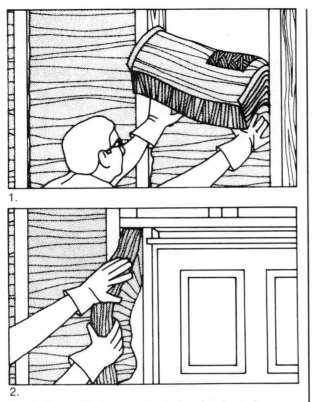

1.

2.

Insulating walls between heated and unheated spaces.
Step 1. *Wedge insulation between wall studs. The vapor barrier should face the warm-in-winter side of the wall.* NOTE: *Do not leave faced insulation exposed.* **Step 2.** *Use scraps to fill in cracks and small areas around door and window frames.* Source: Owens-Corning

1.

2.

3.

Insulating floors above unheated crawl spaces. Step 1. *Slip insulation blankets between floor joists with vapor barrier facing up toward house's heated area.* **Step 2.** *To keep material permanently in place, install wire mesh, "tiger teeth," or criss-crossed wire over joists.* **Step 3.** *Be sure insulation fits snugly against the band joist and overlaps the bottom plate.* Source: Owens-Corning

essary to cut separate header strips. Simply use longer pieces of insulation nailed with furring strips directly to the band joist. After the insulation has been installed, lay a polyethylene film under the insulation and the entire floor area. Use old boards or rocks to help hold the insulation in place on the ground.

IMPORTANT: Always provide good lighting, and when handling insulation, make sure all skin areas are covered. Use gloves and a breathing mask. Keep in mind that blown insulations, as well as foam, are usually best installed by professional contractors. However, it is not impossible to blow in insulation yourself.

Cellulose fiber insulation material is made by processing, then chemically treating, wood pulp derivatives. In recycling the wood, the cellular structure of the wood fiber is maintained, trapping tiny dead air cells. The resulting material can be

Polystyrene foam board. Extruded polystyrene rigid foam board can be used to insulate masonry walls, concrete floors, ceilings, and interior walls. It is light and easy to cut, but walls must be covered with 1/2" gypsum board to reduce fire hazards. *Photo by Dow Chemical U.S.A.*

Blow-in insulation. Loose-fill insulation can be used in the attic, as well as blown in wall cavities. Wall installations are more difficult, and you may want to consider using a professional insulation contractor. *Source: Owens-Corning*

blown into the stud spaces of your walls, filling in around the plaster keys, conduit, pipes, nails, and so on. It can also be blown in to fill the voids between the joists in your attic floor.

You will find the insulation is sold by the bag at lumber yards and home center stores as well as through contractor/dealers. Whether or not you purchase your own blow-in insulation or hire a contractor, look for a brand that is listed by Underwriter's Laboratory for fire resistance and meets federal specifications regarding nonsupport of animal and insect life.

Specific application techniques can vary from one house to another. Your supplier may have an application manual available. If you can operate a portable drill, hammer in wood plugs, sand each plugged area smooth, and repaint it, you already have most of the skills necessary.

With the manual to guide you, the next step is to rent blowing equipment. Operation of the machine is not that complicated. Rent scaffolding too, if you don't own or can't borrow sufficiently safe means of reaching the top portions of all your exterior walls.

The key to a successful job is thorough preliminary planning. Understand your house and how the application applies to it specifically. Ask your dealer to help you figure the number of bags of insulation you'll require. Buy batt insulation (for

stuffing) at the same time, and purchase enough wood plugs to fill all the drilled holes, plus a few extra. Check that color-matching paint is available for the touch-up needed.

INSTALLING STYROFOAM Extruded polystyrene rigid foam board (Styrofoam TG brand insulation) is lightweight and, with reasonable skills and common carpentry tools, can be installed by the homeowner. It has interlocking tongue-and-groove edges, and is available in 3/4" and 1" thicknesses. For fire-safety reasons, building codes say that Styrofoam-brand insulation (and other plastic insulations) must not be left exposed. Any material with a flame-spread rating of 200 or less may be used to finish the wall: either 1/2" gypsum wallboard or plywood thicker than 1/2" will meet this requirement.

To install Styrofoam insulation on masonry or standard interior walls, measure the area to determine how many square feet of insulation you need. You'll need mastic in cartridges, a caulking gun, 1/2" gypsum drywall, drywall tape-and-joint compound, 2"-wide wood nailer strips, drywall nails, and masonry nails or common nails, depending upon the wall material.

Prepared wall surfaces must be clean and dry, and baseboards or moldings must be removed. The finished wall will be thicker, so you should decide how you want to treat window or door frames — for

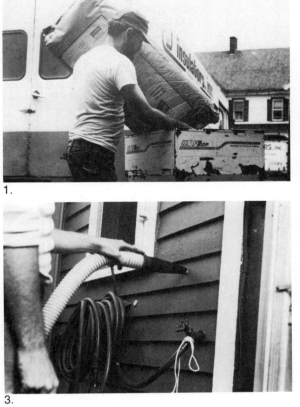

1.

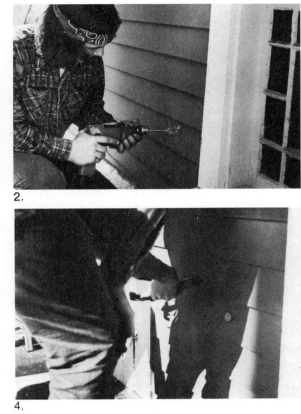

2.

3.

4.

Cellulose fiber insulation blown into wall cavities. **Step 1.** *Bagged cellulose fiber insulation is fed into the hopper, where it is blown through a long flexible hose.* **Step 2.** *Holes are drilled into stud spaces.* **Step 3.** *Each open stud*

space is filled. Wood plugs are used to close holes. **Step 4.** *Plugs are hammered in tightly, sanded smooth, and re-painted to match house.* Photos by Lura LaBarge

example, type of edging or trim. Wood nailer strips then should be installed continuously along the top and bottom edges of the walls, around un-trimmed window and door edges, and any place you intend to hang heavy draperies, bookcases, wall lamps, or such.

Cut the Styrofoam boards to fit around all sur-face projections, such as windows or electrical out-lets. This can be done with any sharp knife. Apply mastic according to instructions on the cartridge and press the Styrofoam firmly against the wall. Finish with the proper application of gypsum board.

For ceiling application the procedure is similar, except joists must be located instead of installing nailer strips. Extra-long nails also must be used to help hold the insulation board to the ceiling while the mastic is curing.

Concrete floors can be insulated in the same

way by installing a waterproof coating and a series of furring strips. Instead of covering the Styrofoam with drywall, use a protective subfloor surface of 1/2" exterior grade plywood. Generally, installation brochures are available through the manufacturer or your supplier.

HOW TO SELECT AN INSULATION CONTRACTOR

There can be a number of reasons to consider a contractor. In some cases he can actually save you money. He has the proper tools and knowledge and often buys insulation in large quantities of either carload or truckload lots. He can therefore place insulation at a lower per-foot cost than the individ-ual. And in times of shortages a contractor who has been in business for years may have easier access to insulation.

Selecting an insulating contractor. There are often good reasons to use a professional insulation contractor. Besides being trained to do a good job, established contractors have access to insulation for lower prices and in fact may be able to install it at a lower cost than you can yourself. Photo by Owens-Corning

Try to find a reputable contractor who will install high-grade insulation that meets R value requirements and who will do so for a reasonable price. One way a reliable contractor can be found is by seeking out an old established firm. It is reasonable to assume that a business that has survived over time has dealt fairly with its customers. Another way is to check with your local lumber or home-care center. If they are not in the business of installing insulation, they will recommend a reliable contractor because the dealer puts his own credibility on the line when he directs his customers to another business.

Many nationwide catalog and department stores sell and install insulation. You thus have the same recourse for guarantee of the insulation that you would have when buying another product from these firms.

Whichever approach you take, ask the contractor for written specifications for the job. He will then specify the type and brand of insulation he will use, the R value of the finished job, and a firm charge for the job. Get it all in writing. When the job is finished, check to be sure you got the type and brand of insulation you asked for, at whatever thickness required to achieve the desired R value.

When making payment to the contractor, ask for a lien waiver. This is a form that will serve as a receipt for you, and a guarantee that the contractor paid his supplier for the insulation he installed. If there is any doubt in your mind that you didn't get what you paid for, ask the contractor for an expla-

nation. If his explanation is not satisfactory, you may take action through the courts, the Better Business Bureau, or the consumer protection services of your state.

IMPORTANT: It's always a good idea to check with such agencies before employing a contractor, to see if there are any complaints against him. Also, remember that filing legitimate complaints helps weed out unscrupulous contractors.

HOW TO INSULATE PIPES, DUCTS, HEATERS

Other places to insulate include water pipes, ducts, and even your water heater. If any or all of these are in unheated spaces, there's no question you'll save energy dollars. Even if your basement is finished off, it will pay. While heat radiating from the water heater, ducts, or pipes is not "lost" during the heating season, it may affect adversely your cooling bills in summer.

Insulate pipes that pass through walls (if you're building or remodeling and pipes are accessible) or through any unheated space. The same is true of heating ducts or pipes passing through attics.

If you have radiant (baseboard) hot-water heat, insulate the loops that connect the panels from room to room. You will find on the basement side that these feeder pipes may be from 2' to 10' or more long; and you're trying to hold 180° F of heat there (as opposed to hot water piping, which should be 120°F to 140°F). Also consider insulating cold water pipes running through the basement. This will prevent moisture from condensing and dripping on the floor, when humid summer air in the basement meets the cold pipes.

FINISH THE JOB   Three important considerations when insulating your home include proper installation of vapor barriers, provisions for proper ventilation, and use of landscaping to help lower energy bills.

HOW TO INSTALL VAPOR BARRIERS

Vapor barriers are used to prevent moisture from penetrating the exterior walls and causing such problems as peeling paint and mildew on exterior siding. Vapor barriers also provide a barrier against exfiltration of warm air. Moisture allowed to pass into insulation will lower its R value. The rate of passage of moisture through a wall is called the perm factor. A standard of efficiency of 1 perm or less for vapor barriers is considered acceptable.

This efficiency can be achieved with 2 to 4 mil polyethylene plastic sheeting, or aluminum foil/kraft paper–faced insulation batts. Assuming a proper job is done installing barrier-faced batts,

INSULATING WATER HEATERS

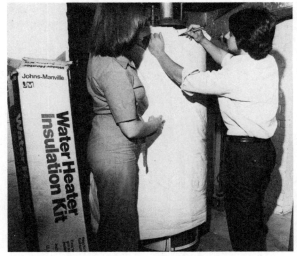

1. *Wrap insulation blanket around heater. Mark at overlap for circumference of heater. Cover should be cut so that plate and vent(s) at bottom of gas heater are not covered.*

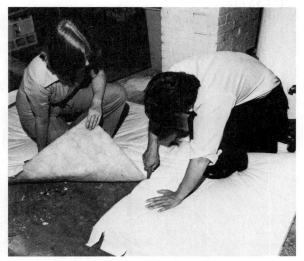

2. *Cut for fit around circumference of heater, and for length from top to bottom of heater. Note tabs on insulation at bottom of photo; these are to fasten at top edge of heater.*

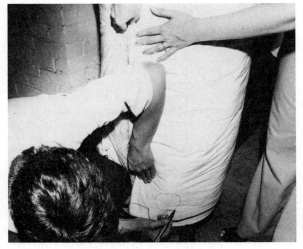

3. *Holding blanket in place, mark the location of the vents, controls, and faucet drain on bottom of water heater. Then cut the insulation away here.*

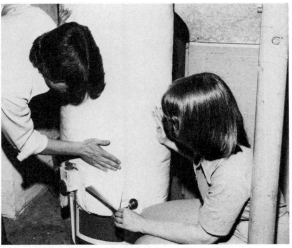

4. *Insulation in place. Note that vents, covers, controls, and drain are not covered. Use a protective insulator for the top of electric heater tanks; don't install on gas heaters. Photos by Johns-Manville Corp.*

foil/kraft-faced batts can be as efficient as polyethylene plastic.

In practice, polyethylene plastic sheets are more commonly used. Another form of vapor barrier is aluminum foil–backed gypsum board panels. The foil backing must not be torn or pulled away while the panel is being handled and cut, or the value of the backing as a vapor barrier will be destroyed.

Until recently, the theory was that only outside walls would include a vapor barrier. However, tests have shown that vapor barriers in the ceilings, as well as exterior walls, are desirable.

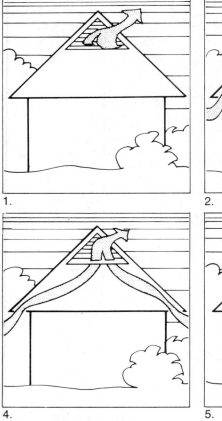

1.

2.

3.

4.

5.

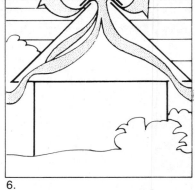

6.

Attic ventilation. *FHA attic vent requirements: For attics with a ceiling vapor barrier, ventilate with 1 square foot of vent area for each 300 square feet of ceiling. For attics without a ceiling vapor barrier, ventilate with 1 square foot of vent area for each 150 square feet of ceiling.* NOTE: *Ridge, roof, or gable vent must be at least 3' above eave vents.* 1. *With vapor barrier: 1 square foot of gable vent for each 300 square feet of ceiling. Install one half in each end of gable.* 2. *With vapor barrier: 1 square foot of roof or ridge vent and 1 square foot of eave vent for each 600 square feet of ceiling.* 3. *With vapor barrier: 1 square foot of gable vent and 1 square foot of eave vent for each 600 square feet of ceiling.* 4. *Without vapor barrier: 1 square foot of gable vent and 1 square foot of eave vent for each 300 square feet of ceiling.* 5. *Without vapor barrier: 1 square foot of gable vent for each 150 square feet of ceiling. Install one half in each end of gable.* 6. *Without vapor barrier: 1 square foot of roof or ridge vent and 1 square foot of eave vent for each 300 square feet of ceiling. Vent sizes must be adjusted for screening, louvers, and rain or snow shields.* Source: Owens-Corning

HOW TO PROVIDE ADEQUATE VENTING

Venting is important in weatherproofing your home. Any enclosed portion of the house that is not heated requires venting, including attics, soffits, or overhangs around the perimeter of the house, and crawl spaces under the house.

To remove moisture in any of these areas, a free flow of air should be maintained. This requires inlet vents to allow fresh air in, outlet vents to allow inside air to escape. An example of this is using vents under soffits or eaves, allowing a free flow of air to vents on the roof, at or near the ridgeline. Other examples would be using vents or louvers at both ends of a gable, or at both ends of a crawl space in areas of the house that are unexcavated.

Venting of the attic space is necessary in all seasons. Heat should not be trapped above the insulation in the attic, or damaging moisture may be caught along with it. The single exception to this advice is the closing of vents under a crawl space. There, moisture levels are lower in winter, and a partial closing of the vents will still allow moisture to escape, while lessening the flow of cold air under floors.

In summer, attic temperature can build to levels of 150° F or more if the space is not properly vented. By providing venting to the outside, air of ambient temperature will also enter. Thus, on a 90° F day, attic temperatures can be lowered from 150° F to near-ambient, or 90° F levels, and a considerable savings on air-conditioning costs results. It may even allow natural cooling of the home on all but the hottest days. Venting methods and installation procedures are covered more thoroughly on pages 58–63.

HOW TO CHOOSE AND USE CAULKING AND WEATHERSTRIPPING MATERIALS

Even the most inexperienced do-it-yourselfer can caulk and weatherstrip. All you need are some relatively inexpensive materials, a few tools you may already own, and some time. By doing these two jobs, you'll be sealing drafty leaks to keep cold air out and warm air in.

CAULKING Caulking offers a high return on investment. A number of different caulking materials are available. The list includes the polysulfide, polyurethane, and silicone caulks, which are considered to be among the best available. Suitable options are the latex caulking compounds; these are higher priced but last longer.

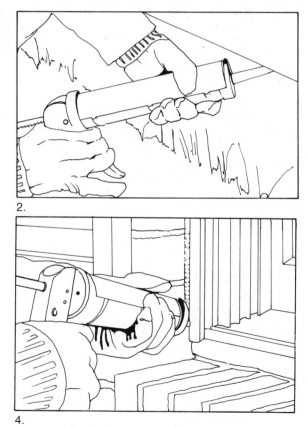

1.

2.

3.

4.

Caulking. 1. Of the caulks and sealants available, the preferred types are polysulfide, polyurethane, or silicone. 2. Use narrow strips of fiberglass insulation to fill large cracks. Finish the job with caulk, carefully applied, to seal tightly to surfaces on either side of crack. 3. Extra-long cracks can be filled fast with caulk in rope form. Use your fingers, paint stick, putty knife, or large screwdriver to force it into cracks. 4. Caulking bead should overlap both sides for a tight seal. If necessary, use a wider bead to make sure caulk adheres to both sides. *Illustrations by Ron Chamberlain*

Warm-air leaks are often common around windows, doors, and mudsills where masonry and wood construction join, and pipes carrying utility services into the house. Count the number of doors and windows in your home, and compute the footage of cracks to be caulked. Allow about 20 running feet for each door and average-sized window. Four or five tubes of caulk will do the average-sized house. The actual quantity needed will depend on how well the house is presently caulked.

Also check the perimeter of the house from the inside (in the basement or crawl space), looking toward the outside. If you see light coming in, you know there's a crack and cracks mean heat loss. Some of them can be quite sizable. If so, you can augment the tube caulk material with caulk in rope form, which is useful where you have long wide cracks to seal.

Caulk along the mudsill where exterior siding meets the masonry foundation. Often large cracks are found here. If a crack is too large to be filled with a 3/8" bead of caulk, you can stuff it with fiberglass insulation, pushing it well in with a screwdriver or putty knife, then seal over the insulation with the caulk.

Caulk well at the corners where door and window trim meet the siding. Don't neglect the underside of these areas, such as under the door sills. At the same time, caulk holes in siding where gas, electrical, or water service pipes pass through.

Also caulk wherever siding meets brick or stone veneer, or fireplace chimneys. The general rule

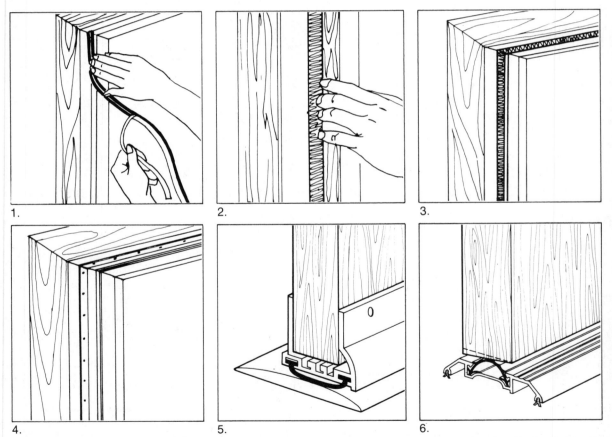

1.   2.   3.

4.   5.   6.

Door weatherstripping. *Types of door weatherstripping include: 1. Adhesive-backed foam strips that install on inside face of door jamb; 2. Wood-backed foam stripping; 3. Rolled vinyl stripping with aluminum channel back; 4. Spring metal stripping; 5. Door shoes that attach to bottom of outside doors; and 6. Vinyl bulb thresholds that require door to be removed and beveled. Door sweeps can be metal, vinyl, or fiber extensions; attach to bottom of doors.* Source: Owens-Corning

here is that when two different materials meet, the joint should be caulked. A good time for caulking and sealing is just before repainting your house. In this way you can cover the white (standard) caulk with your paint color. If your house doesn't need painting, don't delay the caulking procedure. Caulks are now made in a number of colors and wood tones to blend with almost any type and color of siding.

WEATHERSTRIPPING DOORS AND WINDOWS
Weatherstripping also offers high return per dollar spent. Spring metal weatherstripping is highly durable for use around doors or basement windows, and the cost is very low. Adhesive-backed foam or wood-backed foam stripping are easily installed, but both lack durability. Their low price makes frequent replacement feasible. Another stripping material available is rolled vinyl with an aluminum channel backing. Though not attractive, it is durable and easy to install.

When weatherstripping, don't neglect to fit door shoes to the bottoms of outside doors. These are made of a metal strip with a vinyl or felt compression strip. The purpose of a door shoe is to seal the crack between the bottom of the door and the door sill. It is attached to the inside face of the door with screws. There are metal/vinyl door shoes available that slide over the bottom of the door and attach with screws on both sides. These are durable, but they are a bit more difficult to install, since the door must be removed to install them.

Many windows of recent vintage have felt or

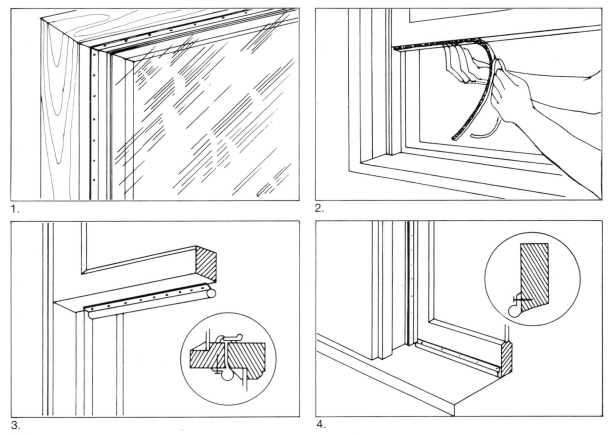

Window weatherstripping. 1. *Thin spring-metal weatherstripping can be tacked into place by opening sash and sliding strip between sash and top and bottom channels. A full-width strip is attached to the upper sash's bottom rail. 2. Adhesive-backed foam strips can be installed on all types of windows where there is no friction. 3. Rolled vinyl should be attached the full width of sash's bottom rail on double-hung windows. 4. Casement and tilting windows can be weatherstripped so vinyl rolls compress when the window shuts.*

foam vinyl weatherstripping that slides into slots cut in the wood sash. Such stripping is easily replaced.

Check the weatherstripping in your house at least at the beginning of each heating season. The metal spring stripping will in time tend to fold inward and fail to spring back against the door when it's closed. If the stripping is not torn or bent, it can be sprung outward by running a screwdriver inside the V of the strip and spreading it until it's wide enough to fit snugly against the edge of the closed door.

SHADING

Shading your home can also stack up dollar-saving benefits. Leafy, deciduous trees, evergreens, hedges, vines, or a wall trellis around your home offer excellent, inexpensive shading during summer and spring months. Awnings can also help. They work best on west windows because they block the sun in summer when it is hot and overhead, but let it in during the winter when it's lower on the horizon. Reflective screens also reduce solar heat and glare more than 50 percent before it ever reaches the glass. Screens create an air blanket of insulation that makes them especially attractive. Reflective screens and films are rated with a shading coefficient number: the lower the number, the better. The highest recommended number is .55.

HOW TO MAKE HEATING AND COOLING SYSTEMS EFFICIENT

With high fuel costs, it makes good sense to make sure your home is tight, as well as to do all you can to get your furnace and air conditioning equipment adjusted to operate at peak efficiency. **HEATING COSTS** Heating costs can be reduced several ways. Besides using adequate insulation, caulking, weatherstripping, ventilation, and humidity levels, you can start by lowering the thermostat in winter to 68° F or lower. For every degree above 68°F, you use 3 percent more energy. For additional savings, you can set your thermostat back 5°F or more at night. An automatic setback thermostat can do the job for you (see chart).

You can also open the drapes during winter days to let the sun warm up your home, and close them at night to keep the heat in. Always close doors to rooms not in use.

Furnace tune-ups on an annual basis can cut another 5 percent off your heat use. Furnace filters should be checked monthly and changed or cleaned when necessary. If your furnace is not adjusted properly it will work harder and use more fuel to get the results you want.

THERMOSTAT SETBACK SAVINGS

CITY	HEATING-Night set back 10°F	COOLING-Day set up 5°F
ATLANTA	15%	10%
CHICAGO	11%	16%
DALLAS	15%	8%
LOS ANGELES	16%	20%
MINNEAPOLIS	9%	9%
PITTSBURGH	11%	10%
ST. LOUIS	12%	10%
SEATTLE	12%	9%

This chart shows fuel savings possible with setback thermostats. Savings listed are for heating with a 10° night setback, and for cooling with a 5° day set up (5 A.M. to 4 P.M.). Additional savings are possible by setting back thermostat when families are away from the home. Source: Honeywell.

A complete tune-up requiring special equipment to test CO_2 levels and exhaust stack temperatures should be done by a qualified heating expert. His inspection should also cover nozzle angle and condition, electrode length and corrosion, possible cracks in porcelain electrode insulators, and other fine points; if left unattended, they could cause a furnace to shut down. Routine maintenance by the homeowner can help keep the furnace operating near peak efficiency.

There is a great variety of heating systems and fuels used. The most common are forced air or hot water systems (powered by gas or oil), or fully electric systems. The heat produced is measured in Btu's (British thermal units). One Btu is the amount of heat energy required to raise the temperature of one pound of water by one degree Fahrenheit. A Btu rating is usually stamped on the furnace name plate, but this can be misleading. For instance, a furnace with a gross input listing of 100,000 Btu's can be expected to deliver about 80,000 Btu's, making it roughly 80 percent efficient.

The efficiency of fuel furnaces depends largely on the level of maintenance in the following areas: proper burner adjustments; clean and properly adjusted nozzle and jet openings; clean fuel and air filters; clean ducts and pipes; and a clean and properly lubricated blower or circulator.

Fuel-burning furnaces need enough air to assure that all the fuel is burned cleanly. Lack of air keeps the fuel from burning completely and can produce excessive soot and carbon monoxide fumes. Too much air overcools the combustion process and carries too much heat up the flue. Improper air flow can cut furnace efficiency by as much as 50 percent. As a guideline, the adjustable air intake should be opened until the flame is smokeless and then closed slightly to produce just the beginning of smoke in the flame.

On a gas furnace the flame should appear bright blue close to the burner. An air-starved flame is yellowish. A pale, blue-white flame is a sign of too much air. A sliding collar, or, on some models, a dial mechanism, can be adjusted to open or close an air hole at each burner until the flame burns a bright blue. The burners also should be free of carbon and soot deposits.

On an oil furnace the fuel is pressurized at the furnace pump, sprayed as a mist mixed with air, and ignited by a set of electrodes. The fuel from the supply tank must be clean to avoid clogging. The fuel is passed through a filter before reaching the furnace. Disposable paper filters or sediment bowls should be cleaned periodically using compressed air or clean fuel oil. Care should be taken not to damage the fine mesh screens. Be sure to shut off the main fuel valve to the furnace before opening either the drain plug on the filter or removing the entire base of the unit for cleaning.

The nozzle-electrode assembly must be removed from the firebox for cleaning of the jet and nozzle and inspection of the electrode gap, which is usually 3/16″. Remember, all work on the furnace should be done after the appropriate fuse or circuit breaker has been removed or shut off.

Improper combustion can lead to excessive soot and carbon deposits in the flue as well as clogged air filters. Although in most cases this results in inefficient operation, the deposits, particularly along horizontal sections of the flue pipe that connect to vertical runs, can build up and become ignited by the furnace flame causing a severe "puff back" of furnace fire that could escape into the room.

Many flues have a clean-out door at the base where deposits accumulate. Individual sections of the pipes can be disconnected to inspect and clean the line closer to the furnace.

The efficiency of the delivery system can also be increased by an annual cleaning of the blower fan. On most units a squirrel-cage fan is used. The individually angled blades along the perimeter of the cage can become clogged with dirt, grease, and lint, which should be removed with a brush and soapy water.

The efficiency of belt-driven fans can be lost if the belt is too loose. You should be able to deflect it about an inch. Replace it if it's cracked or shows other signs of wear. Keep a second belt on hand for emergencies. When cleaning the fan, check the motor too, dry-brushing away any dirt from the casing to make sure that the ventilation slots are not blocked.

Since there is no combustion in electric furnaces, many of the maintenance problems common in fuel-burning furnaces do not apply. Heat is generated directly from current that passes through a series of resistance wires and is delivered either by a fan through ducts, or, in the case of electric baseboard heaters, directly into the room.

With no exhaust cycle the only problem is to keep the air that circulates inside the furnace or around the baseboard units as clean as possible. For this reason many electric furnaces are used in conjunction with air purification systems. Filters should be inspected regularly and the heat-radiating fins on baseboard units should be vacuumed to increase air flow efficiency.

Electric furnaces draw large amounts of power and are costly to operate. This must be balanced against their cleanliness and high efficiency.

Be sure to check any fireplaces in the home. Conventional fireplaces can allow more heat to escape than they add. Be sure to close dampers tight when you are not using your fireplace. Check the dampers from time to time because they can warp and become loose. (But make sure a gas log fireplace is properly vented.) Metal, wood, or glass fireplace doors can close off the hearth when not in use to cut down on heat loss. A number of prefab fireplace designs, as well as a host of accessories, are available to help update older, inefficient fireplaces.

AIR CONDITIONING COSTS Air conditioning costs can account for half or even more of your summertime energy bill. You can shave these costs with adequate insulation, ventilation, and humidity control, as well as other steps.

For example, you can set the thermostat in summer on 78° F. For every degree cooler, your air conditioner uses 5 percent more energy. (See chart, page 24). You can keep out the sun's heat by closing drapes, curtains, and blinds. Thermal drape linings, window treatments, awnings, and shade trees, as well as light color roofs will also help drop air conditioning needs. If you plan on buying air conditioning equipment, be sure you understand energy efficiency ratings (EER, covered later in this chapter).

Before summer starts it is especially critical to see that your air conditioner operates near peak efficiency. Most room air conditioners have a foam or mesh filter mounted inside the removable access panel. Clean it with warm water and detergent to remove dust and dirt.

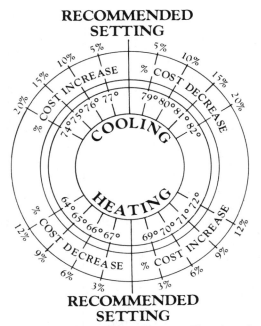

Thermostat settings for air conditioning. This chart shows the cost of keeping room temperatures above or below the cooling setting of 78°F (based on A/C design temperature of 95°F). Generally, for every degree cooler than 78°F, your air conditioner will use 5 percent more energy. Source: Northern States Power

Appliance use. Home laundering uses energy for water heating, washing, drying, and ironing, all of which can be done with less energy by using energy-efficient models and energy-saving techniques. *Photo by Whirlpool Corporation*

The evaporator coil usually cleans itself with water that condenses on it. For a thorough cleaning, use compressed air from your shop compressor or vacuum cleaner to blow dust off the coil, and to avoid getting the motor or controls wet. The condenser is normally protected on the outside of the unit by a metal screen.

It is also important that the fan motor and blades are kept clean. Modern units may have sealed bearings that do not require regular oiling, but on older motors a few drops of oil should be added for smooth operation.

Central air conditioners should be cleaned in the same way. There the evaporator coil is usually located at the furnace and the condenser coil outside the house, with copper tubing transferring the refrigerant back and forth. Similar maintenance should be performed on heat pumps.

Before winter arrives, prevent cold air leaks by covering up the outside of window and wall air conditioning units. It is best to remove window units before it gets cold; you'll be able to seal the window more tightly. With central air conditioning units, wrap ductwork in any exposed areas, such as the attic or garage, with mineral wool fiber in-sulation material and wire. Don't forget the central air conditioning condenser unit located outside. Before winter comes, protect the machine with a heavy-duty plastic cover to prevent damage from snow or ice.

HOW TO REDUCE ENERGY USED BY APPLIANCES

APPLIANCE OPERATING COSTS Appliance operating costs can be reduced by buying modern, more energy-efficient models. Besides being better insulated, newer models use energy-saving designs incorporating microprocessors. These replace electromechanical and solid-state controls on dishwashers, washers, dryers, and microwave ovens. A microprocessor is a solid-state electronic device that is programmable, and produces predetermined outputs to operate a product. Microprocessors allow greater control of the functions of any appliance, and make instant "decisions" that save energy. Since they have no moving parts, maintenance is minimal when compared with mechanical controls.

Look for the ENERGYGUIDE labels when you are shopping for new appliances. Because of a law passed by Congress, the U.S. Department of Energy and the Federal Trade Commission have developed these labels to give you better information on how much it will cost to operate many of the appliances that you may buy for your home.

These labels are first appearing on central furnaces, room air conditioners, water heaters, dishwashers, clothes washers, refrigerator-freezers, and freezers. Eventually you will find them on central air conditioners and on all heat pumps.

For current information on ENERGYGUIDE labels and how they can help you make better buying decisions, write to the U.S. Department of Energy, Appliance Labeling Program, Washington, D.C., 20545.

The following are tips that can help you stretch energy dollars used by appliances:

REFRIGERATION An unexpected energy eater could be your refrigerator/freezer. Here are a few ways to beat the cost of keeping things cool.

Keep it clean. Defrost the freezer when the ice is 1/4" thick to keep refrigerator and freezer motors from working overtime. Vacuum the condenser coils located at the bottom or behind your unit three or four times a year.

Organize. Most people don't think about it, but a lot of cold energy escapes every time you open the refrigerator door. So organize your refrigerated food items so that you can find them easily.

Keep your refrigerator away from heat sources. You may be wasting some cooling efficiency if your refrigerator or freezer is located next to your stove or a heating vent.

Set the refrigerator control. The temperature control should be set between 38° F and 40° F. Check with an outdoor thermometer left on a middle shelf overnight. Set the freezer compartment at 0° F.

Avoid two refrigerators. Two is one too many, especially if you're using one to cool a couple of six packs in a hot garage. A standard 14 cubic foot partial frost-free refrigerator/freezer could be costing you $80 a year to operate.

Buy efficiently. When buying a new refrigerator, choose the correct cubic footage for your size family. Frost-free model refrigerators/freezers and side-by-side models with full-length freezer units do use more energy. Shop and buy the most efficient unit possible.

WATER HEATING Your water heater is another big energy user, and can account for up to 15 percent of your energy bill. Besides insulating the exterior of the heater, here are other ways to save money.

Set water heater at 140°F. That's a medium setting if your water heater is not numbered. This applies if you have a dishwasher. Otherwise, set to 120°F.

Shower vs. bath. A shower can use less water by far. Cut the water you use for showers in half with a flow restricter. It's an inexpensive device found at your hardware store.

Use cold water. Wherever you can, use cold water instead of hot—for example, in the garbage disposal, rinsing dishes before putting them in the dishwasher, in the coffee pot.

Fix drips. A leaky hot water faucet dripping one drop per second can add up to 200 gallons a month. That's water you pay to heat going down the drain.

WASHERS/DRYERS Here again, hot water is a big energy user. It's not difficult to learn to use your washer and dryer efficiently.

Full loads. You'll save energy and money by washing and drying full loads. Try to avoid the small, "Hurry, I-need-it-now" wash-and-dry cycles.

When to use cold water. For best results, follow the manufacturer's washing instructions provided with the garment. However, rinsing clothes in cold water is very energy efficient and effective.

Short cycles. If your washer has a timer, use the shortest cycle possible. Regular clothes need only an 8 to 10 minute wash. Overdrying may cause shrinkage, and wrinkles and clothes will wear out faster.

Remove the lint. Make your dryer's job easier by cleaning the lint filter after every use.

LIGHTING A single light bulb is a small user of energy, but the total required may be large. One 100-watt incandescent lamp produces more light than two 60-watt lamps, so use larger but fewer bulbs when possible.

Suit needs to the task. Conserve by using 3-way bulbs or dimmer switches. Light-colored walls and furniture reflect more light, as do lamp shades that have a flat white liner.

Fluorescent lights. These hard-working energy savers provide five times the light for the same amount of electricity. If you plan to remodel in the kitchen or bath, replace incandescent lighting with fluorescents.

Outdoor lights. If you need outdoor lighting for safety and security, investigate low voltage systems.

RANGES/OVENS The meals prepared, what you cook in, and how you cook can make a difference in your energy budget. Here are tips:

Preheating. Although cooking directions often tell you to preheat the oven, it has been found that preheating time is a waste of energy. Just set the oven to the designated temperature and put your dish into the oven immediately.

Keep it clean. A clean range is an efficient range. A yellowish gas flame indicate burners need cleaning (or adjusting). A blue flame is a sign of an efficiently operating burner.

FIGURING ELECTRICAL NEEDS

This chart will give you an idea of the power draw of various appliances and cost. Example costs are based on an average of 4½¢ per kilowatt hour (October through May) and 5¢ per KWH (June through September). Your average KWH costs may be higher. *Source: Edison Electric Institute & Northern States Power.*

	Average Wattage	Average Hours of Use Per Month	Average KWH Per Month	(Oct.-May) Average Cost Per Month at 4½¢ Per KWH	(June-Sept.) Average Cost Per Month at 5¢ Per KWH	Your Cost
LAUNDRY						
Clothes dryer — electric	4,856	17	83	$3.74	$4.15	____
Clothes dryer — gas (electric usage cost)	300	17	5	.23	.25	____
Iron	1,008	12	12	.54	.60	____
Washer, automatic	512	17	9	.41	.45	____
Washer, non automatic	286	22	6	.27	.30	____
Water heater, quick recovery	4,500	110	500	22.50	25.00	____
COOKING AND REFRIGERATION						
Broiler (countertop)	1,436	6	8	.36	.40	____
Electric fry pan	1,196	13	16	.72	.80	____
Microwave oven	1,450	14	20	.90	1.00	____
Range/oven (self cleaning oven add 25¢ a month)	3,000	41	123	5.54	6.15	____
Refrigerator (12 cubic feet)	300	250	75	3.38	3.75	____
Refrigerator (frost-free — 12 cubic feet)	330	316	105	4.73	5.25	____
Refrigerator-freezer (partial frost-free — 14 cubic feet)	350	350	123	5.54	6.15	____
Refrigerator-freezer (side-by-side — frost-free — 19 cubic feet)	500	360	180	8.10	9.00	____
Freezer (upright — frost-free — 15 cubic feet)	440	333	147	6.62	7.35	____
Freezer (chest type — 15 cubic feet)	341	292	100	4.50	5.00	____
(Upright models lose more cold air when the door is open, thus they can use up to 25% more electricity than chest type models.)						
KITCHEN						
Blender	386	3	1	$ .04	$ .05	____
*Coffee maker (Standard percolator type — 2 pots per day)	900(4)	9(300)	20	.90	1.00	____
*Coffee maker (drip type — 2 pots per day)	1,550(5)	9(300)	30	1.35	1.50	____
Dishwasher	1,201	25	30	1.35	1.50	____
Toaster	1,146	3	3	.14	.15	____
Crockery cooker	100	120	12	.54	.60	____
HOME ENTERTAINMENT						
Radio	71	101	7	.32	.35	____
Stereo	109	83	9	.41	.45	____
Television — black and white (tube type, 160-watt)	160	182	29	1.31	1.45	____
Television — black and white (solid state, 55-watt)	55	182	10	.45	.50	____
Television, color (tube type, 300-watt)	300	183	55	2.48	2.75	____
Television, color (solid state, 200-watt)	200	183	37	1.67	1.85	____
(TV sets with instant-on features, add $1.00 per month.)						

	Average Wattage	Average Hours of Use Per Month	Average KWH Per Month	(Oct.-May) Average Cost Per Month at 4½¢ Per KWH	(June-Sept.) Average Cost Per Month at 5¢ Per KWH	Your Cost
MISCELLANEOUS						
Blanket	177	69	12	.54	.60	———
Clock	2	730	1	.04	.05	———
Vacuum cleaner	630	6	4	.18	.20	———
*Garage door opener						
(Controller on continuously)	230(2)	2(720)	15	.68	.75	———

*These appliances operate at higher wattages for short periods; lower wattages for continuous amounts of time ( ).

You may be using some of your appliances only at certain times of the year. When this happens, the average cost of running that appliance can best be computed on a per-hour-of-use basis.

	Cost Per Hour Of Operation
Air conditioner (room 8,000 BTU)	
*EER 6	6½¢
*EER 7	5¾¢
*EER 8	5¢
Air conditioner (central 30,000 BTU, 2½ ton)	
*EER 6	25¢
*EER 7	22¢
*EER 8	19¢
Auto engine heater (750-1500 watts)	3.5¢-7¢
Battery charger (120 watts)	½¢
Dehumidifier (200-600 watts)	1¢-3¢
Electronic air filter (60 watts)	⅓¢
Filter pump — for swimming pool (800-1,000 watts)	4½¢-5½¢
Furnace fan or circulator (300-800 watts)	1½¢-4¢
Humidifier — w/o heating element (120 watts)	½¢
Oil burner (450 watts)	2¼¢
Roof and gutter cable (7 watts/foot)	4½¢ per 1,000 watts
Supplementary electric heaters (1,000-2,500 watts) 300-750 hours per heating season)	4½¢ per 1,000 watts
Vaporizer (700 watts)	3¢
Motors (power tools, vent fans, and so forth)	4½¢ per hour

*You can get a rough idea of the Energy Efficiency Ratio (EER) of your present air conditioner by finding the label (usually inside the front cover) and looking for the BTUs and watts. The EER equals the BTUs divided by the watts. The higher the EER, the better. NOTE: The EER ratings you find on the yellow and black ENERGYGUIDE labels on new air conditioners are calculated by a more complex procedure and will be a bit more accurate.

Home lighting varies throughout the year; more is used in winter. However, rates are often higher during summer. These figures are an average for year-round use.

	Average Monthly Kilowatt-Hours
Five-room house	50
Six-room house	60
Eight-room house	80
Post light (dusk-to-dawn operation with 100-watt light bulb)	35
Christmas decorations (Interior)	60

Plan all-oven meals. Bake compatible foods together, such as pot roast with carrots, onions, and potatoes, with baked apples for dessert. Everything cooks at the same time and temperature.

Microwave ovens. Cooking foods for an average family of four, using a microwave oven, is four times as energy efficient as conventional cooking. There is no preheating and no wasted heat given off into the kitchen, and little humidity for your air conditioning system to remove.

No peeking. Every time you open the oven door, you lose 25°F or more of heat. Use a timer and be patient.

Pots and pans. Match the size of the pot to the size of the burner to prevent excessive heat loss. Use tight-fitting covers. Trapped steam cooks foods quicker.

Leftovers. Both gas and electric ovens retain heat from 15 to 30 minutes. An electric range top element stays warm for 3 to 5 minutes. Use that free heat to warm up desserts or rolls or to crisp crackers.

Plan outdoor meals. In the summer, cook outside. It's fun, saves energy, and keeps the house from heating up.

SMALL APPLIANCES Small appliances work harder and for a lower cost than the major appliances. Use them whenever it's practical. Other tips:

Pull the plug. Coffee pots, broilers, and electric skillets are all efficient energy users. But don't forget to turn them off when you're through using them.

Substitute. Smaller crock pots, electric fry pans, and electric broilers for cooking smaller meals are more efficient than using your oven. Use any of these when it makes sense.

Vacation time. While you're on vacation, give your energy bill a break too. All it takes is a few extra minutes before you leave home. During the summer, if you're leaving for an extended period, switch the air conditioner off. If you're going to be gone for a month or more, turn your refrigerator off, clean it thoroughly, and prop the door open.

If you have a gas water heater, turn the thermostat to its lowest setting. Turn your electric water heater off at the circuit breaker. When you return, run some water from a hot water faucet to make sure there is water in the heater before you turn it back on.

Get a timer to turn inside lights on for short periods of time, instead of leaving lights on continuously.

APPLIANCE USE COSTS Saving electrical energy begins by understanding how electricity is measured, and knowing how much electricity appliances use. The kilowatt hour is used by utility companies to measure the amount of electricity used in your home. A kilowatt hour (KWH) is 1,000 watts used for one hour. If you burn a 100-watt light bulb for 10 hours, you use one KWH. If you use a 1,000-watt appliance continually for one hour, you would be using one KWH.

Your electric meter records the usage of kilowatt hours. It can easily be read from left to right on the dials. Record the number that each dial point has just passed (the lower number). On the dials shown, the reading is 17251. If you read the meter a month later and the reading is 17737, the difference between the two readings would be 486. That's the number of kilowatt hours used between the dates of the two readings.

Meter readings. *Electricity use is measured by kilowatt hours. The reading on these dials is 17251; if the next reading is 17737, the difference is 486. This is the number of kilowatt hours used.* Source: Northern States Power

The chart on pages 26 and 27 will help you figure electrical charges for your home. Space is provided to figure your own usage. Keep in mind that your life-style, as well as the size of your family and style of your home, all can influence monthly electrical charges.

HOW TO BUY PRODUCTS THAT HELP SAVE ENERGY

We have discussed some good ways to reduce your home's energy needs. Other steps you can take include experimenting with various products on the market designed to cut energy use. Here are some examples.

DOORS AND WINDOWS

Storm doors and windows help provide dead air space, which makes air movement difficult. In general you can expect to cut heat loss 50 percent with storms. When buying storm doors and windows, check the products' air infiltration rate. In the storm door/window industry, you may find units that allow as high as 4 cubic feet per minute of air infiltration. However, better units keep air infiltration rates as low as .05 cfm. If you have double-glazed windows, or regular windows with storms, you can also add plastic storms from the inside of the house using commercially available kits.

Replacement windows and doors with good thermal efficiency normally can be ordered to the exact size needed. They often incorporate new and more efficient weatherstripping systems that greatly reduce heat loss. Insulated doors of metal provide insulation and weatherstripping that stops from 2½ to 6 times more energy loss than conventional wood entrances. In many cases no storm door is needed for such replacement doors.

If you are replacing windows and have a choice, position them to take advantage of solar heat. To get more sun, position windows—especially large ones—facing south.

Water conservation equipment was discussed under "Water Heating" earlier in this chapter.

SAVING HEAT

Wood-burning heating equipment available can cut home heating costs substantially. Wood is a

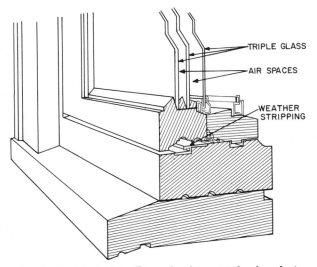

Triple-glazed window. *Example of new triple-glazed window construction. Wood or metal sash has thermal break to prevent condensation.* Source: Northern States Power

Wood heating equipment. *Installation of newer energy-efficient prefab fireplaces, as well as wood stoves, and heat savers in older fireplaces can provide a supplementary source of heat to cut energy bills.* Photo by Rochester Institute of Technology

renewable resource, and new fireplaces, stoves, and heaters are especially designed to extract more heat from wood burned. When buying wood-burning equipment, keep in mind that a wood fire needs more attention than gas, oil, or electric furnaces. Wood requires extra labor to cut, split, and haul; storage room is needed, and you have to feed the fire manually. If you have a fireplace, you may be able to improve its efficiency with a number of newer heat-saving accessories, such as glass doors and chimney caps.

Automatic vent dampers are devices that close off a chimney when a burner isn't running, thus cutting down the amount of heated air that normally escapes up the chimney. It's the same idea as the manually operated damper on a fireplace.

A government summary of studies on vent dampers shows savings mostly between 7 percent and 31 percent on fuel bills, and it is estimated that vent dampers have the potential of reducing national oil and gas use for space heating by at least 10 percent. The energy-saving potential for your particular furnace, boiler, or water heater depends on several factors, including design and initial cost of the damper, type, location, size and age of the heating appliance, and the size of your annual heating bill.

Although used in Europe since 1932, automatic dampers are a relatively new development in the United States, and there naturally has been some concern over their safety. But industry standards and certification procedures have been established by the American Gas Association (AGA) and Un-

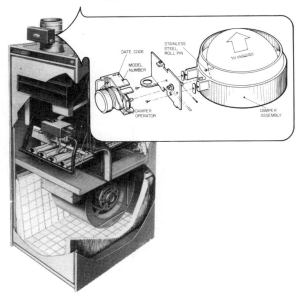

Automatic vent damper. *Reduces heat loss up the chimney when the burner isn't running. Check local codes for acceptance and details of installation.*

derwriters Laboratories (UL), and local code acceptance of the devices is increasing.

Both AGA and UL specify that automatic vent dampers must be installed by a qualified contractor. Costs (installed) should run from $150 to $250.

This will be lower for gas, higher for oil.

Two basic types of dampers are currently available in the United States. Most are electrically operated and triggered by either a motor or a solenoid. Mechanically actuated dampers are controlled by fuel gas pressure in the main burner delivery line.

Be sure to check local codes thoroughly before having an automatic vent damper installed.

HUMIDIFIERS Humidifiers in many cases can let you use a temperature setting as much as 3°F lower without affecting the comfort level in your home.

Air becomes drier as it is heated. Suppose you heat air having a temperature of 10°F and a relative humidity of 70 percent to 72°F. At 72°F the ability of that air to hold moisture is increased by over 300 percent. In other words, when you heat 10°F, 70 percent relative humidity air to 72°F, the relative humidity is only 6 percent, which is extremely dry. Yet the relative humidity of air in the average American home during the heating season is not much more than this. It averages out to be 13 percent, twice as dry as the air in the Sahara (26 percent), and seems to contribute to catching cold.

One way of telling whether the humidity level is too low is to conduct the "ice cube test" in your living room. On a typically cold day when your heating system is operating, put three ice cubes in a glass, add water, stir, and wait three minutes. If moisture (or condensation) doesn't form over the glass, the indoor humidity level is too low.

Humidifiers are available as small tabletop models (commonly called room vaporizers), portable floor models, and central units that are attached to a forced hot-air heating system. A central system humidifier works by evaporating or spraying fine drops of moisture into the air flowing through the heating system. The furnace fan circulates the humidified air through the home.

A central system humidifier can be used only with a forced hot-air heating system. When buying, check for an ARI (Air Conditioning and Refrigeration Institute) symbol of certification. If your home is equipped with hot water, steam, or electric heating, and there is a need for humidification, one or more portable floor units must be used.

OTHER ENERGY SAVERS

Duct boosters are another way to get more from the heat your furnace produces. Boosters improve heat transmission in older, gravity-feed furnaces or modify heat distribution in forced hot-air furnaces. The unit is simply a fan driven by a small electric motor which fits into the duct from the furnace to the area you want to heat.

Obviously, a straight run of pipe would allow the most efficient air movement between the furnace and a cold room. The pressure loss in a 90° elbow, with a 3' run of pipe, would equal about 23' of duct. Two 45° elbows, with a 3' run, would equal only 13 linear feet, offering less resistance to flow.

A duct booster installation works as well with a standard forced air furnace as it does with the gravity type. Connect the booster to the register, or install it in the duct to improve heat circulation to cold rooms.

Thermostatic radiator valves, also called nonelectric heating control valves, are available for installing in any hot water or two-pipe steam heating system. The valves effectively control the heating medium in a room, a loop, or a zone for both fuel savings and increased comfort.

Zone control valves prevent overheating to provide substantial fuel savings and, if desired, the temperature setting can be locked or limited. Such valves give 100 percent shutoff, protect against freezing, and provide a check valve so that the heating system need not be drained for repair. Usually these are best selected and installed by a qualified heating contractor.

Automatic timers for electric water heaters can cut power needs for heating water by 50 percent or more. Electric water heaters rank second only to home heating and cooling systems in energy consumption. Units automatically turn the water heater on and off, according to time periods you set. By restricting operation to when hot water is normally needed (two hours in the morning and two hours in the evening), power use drops while the average family still gets ample hot water.

Motorized flue dampers can also capture heat otherwise wasted from heating units. They are available on newer furnaces or can be bought separately. Vent dampers mount to the flue of the furnace and automatically open and close when the thermostat calls for heat. The automatic flue damper is capable of saving up to 16 percent on a season's heating bill.

It cuts the operating cost of an indoor furnace by improving year-round utilization efficiency in two ways. First, closing the flue when the furnace isn't operating prevents indoor air from escaping up the chimney. Second, closing the flue immediately after the flame shuts off traps the heat stored in the heat exchangers, preventing it from escaping up the chimney and requiring less time for warm-up when the thermostat calls for heat. Some automatic dampers are motor driven to the closed position and have a safety switch that prevents the fuel valve from operating unless the vent is fully open.

Heat pumps are available that both augment furnace heating and air conditioning. The heat pump is a heat transfer device that moves heat into the building from the atmosphere outside during cold weather. Using a heat pump, you will gain more heat than the electricity costs to make the transfer, down to near 0° F. In summer, the heat pump moves the heat from inside your house to the outside air, thus providing air cooling.

New burners for both conventional oil and gas furnaces are available as replacement items. These are better engineered to provide more efficient combustion.

Thermographic scanners are available that will give a picture graph readout of hidden leaks in the home. The larger units with picture readouts are priced beyond the budget of the homeowner. You can hire an expert to provide a picture graph of your house for a small fee. Many will do a "before and after" reading to show you areas where caulking, insulation, or other measures are needed.

Further methods of conserving energy are being monitored by colleges, the government, and private industries. Data are being fed into the U.S. Department of Energy on all alternative energy possibilities, plus the best construction techniques and methods are being developed at a fast pace. To stay abreast of the latest in energy conservation practices, write the U.S. Department of Energy, Washington, D.C. 20545.

2

HOW TO: DETERMINE YOUR HEATING NEEDS · MAINTAIN
YOUR HEATING SYSTEM · INSTALL A HUMIDIFIER ·
CURE TOO MUCH MOISTURE · SELECT AND
INSTALL PROPER VENTING · INSTALL CENTRAL AIR
CONDITIONING · MAINTAIN YOUR AIR CONDITIONER ·
MAINTAIN YOUR FIREPLACES

HEATING AND COOLING SYSTEMS

Homeowners often take the operation of the furnace for granted. If your furnace is relatively new and was installed by a top-notch professional, you can get by with this attitude for perhaps two to four years, but by that time you will be paying more for fuel than you would if the system were properly maintained.

The truth is that the furnace is like any other appliance in your home. It needs regular maintenance, periodic adjustment, cleaning, filter changes, and other attention to operate efficiently.

HOW TO DETERMINE YOUR HEATING NEEDS

Start with the furnace itself. It is factory rated to burn fuel and deliver heat at a definite rate. The measuring unit is the British thermal unit: the amount of heat energy necessary to raise the temperature of one pound of water one degree F. The furnace output of Btu's is indicated either on the nameplate or in the manufacturer's catalog.

The manner in which heat is transferred from the furnace to the rest of the house will determine how much of the furnace's capacity you can utilize. If you have steam heat, or hot water with a circulating pump, or hot air delivered by blower, you can expect 80 percent utilization. If you have gravity-fed hot water or hot air, and no circulator, heat is more difficult to control. Left to the action of nature's laws, both hot air and hot water rise at slower speeds and consequently lose more of their heat on the way to distant points. Because of this lower efficiency, fewer gravity systems are being produced each year, and heating contractors will usually give bids only on a forced hot-air or forced hot-water replacement system.

Chart 1. EXPECTED LOW TEMPERATURES FOR KEY CITIES

	Degrees (Fahrenheit)		Degrees (Fahrenheit)
Atlanta	+10	Louisville	0
Baltimore	+10	Memphis	0
Birmingham	+10	Miami	+35
Boston	0	Milwaukee	−15
Buffalo	−5	Minneapolis	−20
Charleston	+15	New Orleans	+20
Cheyenne	−15	New York	0
Chicago	−12	Oklahoma City	0
Cleveland	0	Omaha	−10
Dallas	0	Philadelphia	0
Denver	−10	Pittsburgh	0
Detroit	0	Phoenix	+25
Fargo	−25	Portland, Me.	−5
Helena	−25	Portland, Ore.	+10
Houston	+20	Salt Lake City	−10
Indianapolis	−10	San Francisco	+35
Jacksonville	+25	Seattle	+15
Kansas City	−5	St. Louis	−5
Los Angeles	+35	Washington, D.C.	0

Some of the heat delivered to the rooms by the furnace is lost through windows, doors, walls, ceilings, and floors. The speed with which the heat is lost is determined by the construction and insulation of the house. The materials used and the way in which they are put together can mean the difference between an overworked furnace, high fuel bills, and chilly rooms, or an economical heating system that provides comfort efficiently. Heating engineers have worked out a table of temperatures in key sections of the country during a normal winter. Pick your location on Chart 1 (Expected Low Temperatures for Key Cities) and make a note of the temperature listed for your area.

Since you probably wish to maintain your home's heat at about 68° F, where the numeral in Chart I is minus, *add* that figure to 68° F. Where the figure is above zero, *subtract* the figure from 68° F. This is the "temperature factor." For example, in Chicago, the temperature factor is 68 plus 12, or 80. To determine the "heat loss factor," measure your house—the outside length and width, basement height above and below the ground, and then the height of room walls. Use these figures to determine the ground area your house occupies and the area of all exterior walls less windows and doors. You'll also need the area of all flat roofs and attic floors, plus interior walls adjoining unheated porches.

Imagine a house located in Chicago with the temperature factor of 80, with a furnace rated at 100,000 Btu's, forced-draft hot air, and therefore delivering 80,000 Btu's. The house foundation is 5' below grade, 2' above grade, with a concrete floor. The walls are wood frame, asbestos shingles on tar paper over wood sheathing, with lath and plaster inside. The ceiling is plaster, over which there is a floored attic without ventilation but with 2" of insulation between joists. There are two outside doors, each 6' 6" by 3'. There are three windows 2' 4" by 3' 10" and six windows 3' by 5' 2".

From these measurements, the various dimensions of the house can be determined. Referring to Chart 2, multiply the various area totals by the heat loss factor found under the temperature factor column—in this case, all under the column marked 80. The completed calculations follow:

HEAT LOSS FACTOR

Ground area	864 sq. ft.	× 2	1,728
Foundation below grade	600 sq. ft.	× 5	3,000
Foundation above grade	240 sq. ft.	× 56	13,440
Ceiling with no heat above	864 sq. ft.	× 9	7,776
Exterior walls less openings	797 sq. ft.	× 24	19,128
Openings	163 sq. ft.	× 36	5,868
Total			50,940

And from Charts 3 and 4:			
Running feet door cracks	44 ft.	× 160	7,040
Running feet window cracks	160 ft.	× 34	5,440
Total			12,480
Grand Total			63,420

Since the heat loss is now determined to be 63,420 Btu's, and the furnace provides 80,000 Btu's, that furnace is not overloaded, nor is it even working at its full capacity. However, if the attic were unfloored and ventilated and the windows and doors were without weatherstripping or storm sash, the picture would change considerably. The ceiling figure would become 42,336 instead of 7,776. The window and door figure from the crack chart would become 6,283 instead of 5,440. This would give a total heat loss of 98,823 Btu's—more than the furnace could produce. The house would be cold and fuel bills high.

Chart 2. HEAT LOSS FACTOR

Building material	Temperature factor (Fahrenheit)								
	40	50	60	65	70	75	80	85	90
DOORS AND WINDOWS									
without storm sash or weatherstripping	45	57	68	73	79	85	90	102	113
with storm sash	30	38	45	49	53	56	60	64	68
with storm sash and weatherstripping	18	23	27	29	32	34	36*	38	41
WOOD SIDING									
tarpaper, wood sheathing, wood lath, plaster	10	13	15	16	18	19	20	21	23
tarpaper, wood sheathing, 1/2" gypsum lath, plaster	8	10	11	12	13	14	15	16	17
tarpaper, wood sheathing, 3 1/2" insulation, lath, plaster	4	5	5	6	6	7	7	8	8
no insulation, wood lath, plaster	40	50	60	65	70	75	80	85	90
composition siding on wood siding, tarpaper, wood sheathing, wood lath, plaster	8	11	13	14	15	16	17	18	19

*All figures starred have been extrapolated from other figures.

(Continued)

Chart 2. HEAT LOSS FACTOR (continued)

Building material	Temperature factor (Fahrenheit)								
	40	50	60	65	70	75	80	85	90
WOOD SIDING									
tarpaper, wood sheathing, 1/2" insulation board, fiberboard or plasterboard	8	10	11	12	13	14	15	16	17
tarpaper, wood sheathing, 3/8" gypsum board finish	10	13	16	17	18	20	21	22	23
tarpaper, wood sheathing, 3/8" plywood interior finish	12	12	14	16	17	18	19	20	22
STUCCO SIDING									
wire lath, wood sheathing, tarpaper, wood lath, plaster	12	15	18	20	21	23	24	26	27
hollow tile, wood furring, lath, plaster	10	13	16	17	18	20	21	22	23
ASBESTOS SHINGLE SIDING									
over tarpaper, wood sheathing, lath, plaster	12	15	18	20	21	23	24*	26	27
8" BRICK WALL									
bare wall	20	25	30	33	35	38	40	43	45
brick, furring, lath, plaster	12	15	18	20	21	23	24	26	27
brick, furring, 1/2" insulation lath, plaster	9	11	13	14	16	17	18	19	20
12" BRICK WALL									
bare wall	10	12	14	16	17	18	19	20	32
furring, lath, plaster	14	18	22	23	25	27	29	31	22
furring, 1/2" insulation, lath, plaster	8	10	11	12	13	14	15	16	17
8" CONCRETE BLOCK WALL									
furring, lath, plaster	13	16	19	21	22	24	26	27	29
furring, 1/2" insulation, lath, plaster	10	12	14	16	17	18	19	20	22
CEILING BELOW ATTIC									
unfloored, ventilated	24	30	37	40	43	46	49	52	55
unfloored, unventilated	14	18	21	22	24	26	27	29	30
unfloored, unventilated, 2" insulation between joists	5	7	8	8	9	10	10	11	12
unfloored, unventilated, 3 1/2" insulation between joists	4	5	6	6	7	8	8	8	9
floored, ventilated, no insulation	11	14	17	18	20	21	22	24	25
floored, unventilated, no insulation	9	11	13	14	15	16	17	18	19
floored, unventilated, 2" insulation between joists	5	6	7	8	8	9	9*	10	11
CEILING—NO ATTIC									
plaster, lath, sheathing, roofing	13	16	19	20	22	23	25	26	28
plaster, lath, 1/2" insulation, sheathing, roofing	9	12	14	15	16	17	18	19	20
plaster, lath, 2" insulation between joists, sheathing, roofing	5	7	8	8	9	10	10	11	12
plaster, lath, 3 1/2" insulation between joists, sheathing, roofing	4	5	6	6	7	7	8	8	9
BASEMENT									
8" concrete below grade	2	2	3	3	4	4	5*	5	5
8" concrete above grade	28	35	42	46	49	53	56*	60	63
8" concrete block above grade	22	28	34	36	39	42	45	48	50
8" cinder block above grade	17	21	25	27	29	32	34	36	38
12" concrete above grade	23	29	35	38	41	44	46	49	52
CONCRETE BASEMENT FLOOR	0	0	1	1	1	1	2	2	2
CONCRETE SLAB—NO BASEMENT									
slab unheated	2	2	3	5	7	8	10	12	13
ENCLOSED PORCH									
unheated, wood siding exterior wall, no insulation, plaster inside	12	16	19	20	22	23	25	26	28
same wall but with insulation	7	9	11	11	12	13	14	15	16

*All figures starred have been extrapolated from other figures.

Chart 3. TO DETERMINE NUMBER OF RUNNING FEET OF CRACKS IN DOORS AND WINDOWS

Opening Height	Opening widths									
	1'8"	2'	2'4"	2'8"	3'	3'4"	3'8"	4'	4'4"	4'8"
3'10"	12.7	13.7	14.7*	15.7	16.7	17.7	18.7	19.7	20.7	21.7
4'6"	14.0	15.0	16.0	17.0	18.0	19.0	20.0	21.0	22.0	23.0
5'2"	15.3	16.3	17.3	18.3	19.3*	20.3	21.3	22.3	23.3	24.3
5'10"	16.7	17.7	18.7	19.7	20.7	21.7	22.7	23.7	24.7	25.7
6'6"	18.0	19.0	20.0	21.0	22.0*	23.0	24.0	25.0	26.0	27.0
7'2"	19.3	20.3	21.3	22.3	23.3	24.3	25.3	26.3	27.3	28.3
7'10"	20.7	21.7	22.7	23.7	24.7	25.7	26.7	27.7	28.7	29.7

Example: if window is 3'10" high and 2'4" wide, result is 14.7 (starred) running feet of crack for one such window. Add up total of all cracks in all doors and windows, then multiply total by heat loss factor from Chart 4.

Chart 4. ADDED HEAT LOSS FACTOR

	Temperature Factor (Fahrenheit)								
	40	50	60	65	70	75	80	85	90
WINDOWS									
double-hung wood sash, not weatherstripped or without storm sash	28	25	42	45	50	53	57	60	65
double-hung wood sash, weatherstripped or with storm sash	17	20	25	28	30	32	34*	36	38
double-hung metal sash, no weatherstripping or storm sash	52	65	75	85	90	95	105	110	120
double-hung metal sash, with weatherstripping or storm sash	25	30	35	37	40	45	50	55	60
casement windows, metal or wood	35	45	55	60	65	70	75	80	85
DOORS	80	100	120	130	140	150	160*	170	180

Multiply figures obtained from Chart 3 by these heat loss factors. Note that doors are not indicated as weatherstripped or otherwise. Frequency of door use upsets this calculation. Figures shown are average under all conditions.

Since the furnace in the sample house has nearly 17,000 Btu's to spare, more rooms may be added and heated by its present furnace. This may be done, for instance, by finishing the attic or enclosing and heating a porch. Properly insulated, the finished attic would have a lower heat loss than it has now, and actually less burden would be placed on the furnace.

HOT AIR SYSTEMS Although your thermostat may read 70°F (generally the most comfortable room temperature), the room may still feel chilly. There are four factors in hot air heating systems that may cause uncomfortable chilliness even though the heating system seems to be operating efficiently.

Air temperature is usually controlled by a thermostat. Once you set the thermostat at a fixed figure, your furnace should deliver air warmed to that degree to the site of the thermostat. However, if the thermostat is located in a hot spot, the corners of the room may become cold and uncomfortable.

Air velocity is as important to room comfort as is air temperature. The human body tries to maintain its temperature at 98.6°F, and with a room temperature of 70°F, excess body heat is carried away by air in motion. When the surrounding air is too cold, the skin contracts its pores slightly in order to prevent rapid internal heat loss and, as a result, a chill is experienced. The speed of air around your body, therefore, has much to do with your comfort.

Outer wall temperature, if cold, takes heat from the air around your body. Place your hand on the outer wall of your home some cold winter day. If your furnace hasn't warmed it, you can be sure that it will be absorbing heat from the exposed parts of your body.

Relative humidity is as important to room comfort in the winter as in the summer. When the amount of moisture in the air drops below 30 percent of saturation, body moisture is lost through the skin too rapidly and you become chilled even though the thermometer may read as high as 75°F. At the

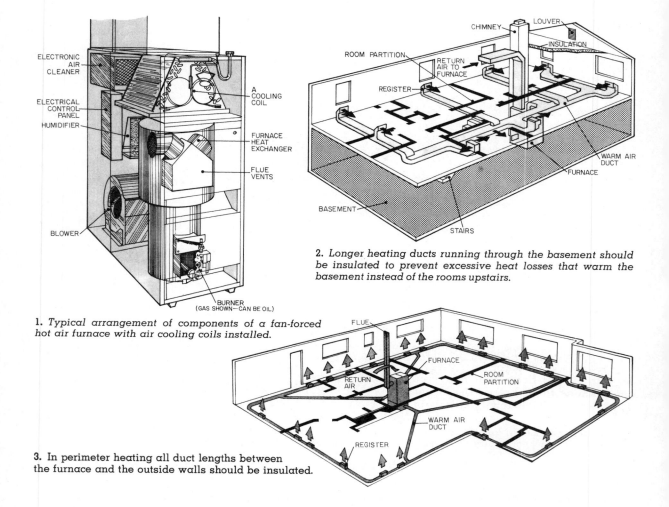

1. *Typical arrangement of components of a fan-forced hot air furnace with air cooling coils installed.*

2. *Longer heating ducts running through the basement should be insulated to prevent excessive heat losses that warm the basement instead of the rooms upstairs.*

3. In perimeter heating all duct lengths between the furnace and the outside walls should be insulated.

same time, your house will suffer from excess drying—the floors will develop cracks between boards as they shrink, the windows will rattle in their frames, and gaps will appear between sections of wood trim. If the relative humidity figure exceeds 60 percent, however, the moisture of your body can't evaporate readily and you will feel uncomfortably warm, even with the temperature at 70°F. Your house will likewise suffer—from damp walls, sweating windows, and swelled and warped woodwork. About halfway between these two extremes is the point at which to set your humidity controls.

Properly installed, the hot air heating system should have the furnace centrally located in the basement or floor, which keeps the hot air ducts at minimum length. The perimeter type of heating system, generally considered the most efficient

arrangement, calls for locating the registers in series along outside walls near the baseboard. Air is delivered into the room from all angles, eliminating unwarmed areas. Cold air return ducts are located on inner walls at ceiling height. Thus there is no return flow of cold air across the floors. From the standpoint of economy, this arrangement is expensive to install since the ducts are longer and, because these ducts are quite likely to pass through cold areas under the floor, they must be insulated to conserve hot air.

Older systems, with a centrally located furnace, provided ducts running through interior walls to near-ceiling level; the register's fins directed warm air to outer walls, down which the warmed air flowed, then back across the floor. As a rule, the area about 2' above the floor remained much colder than the rest of the room. Where return ducts were placed at baseboard level on inner walls, this was inevitable. When the return-flow ducts were placed along outer wall baseboards, the cold air flowing down outer walls, and particularly walls with large window areas, was picked up before it could flow back across the floor, eliminating much of this discomfort.

Common complaints in hot air heating systems and their cure are specified in the following checklist of common complaints. The major flaws in warmed air heating systems, and their elimination, include the following:

Lack of steady heat flow. When the furnace is oversized it tends to fire infrequently, and areas far from the heat source may cool too much before newly warmed air is delivered. Such areas are alternately hot and cold. Use a thermostat with a heat anticipator, which controls not only room temperature but the on-off cycles of the furnace as well. By setting the control at more frequent operating intervals, but at lower temperatures, the room temperature will become more stable and comfort will increase. Excessive on-off cycling decreases furnace efficiency since fuel is burned more completely in a furnace that has warmed up during longer burn periods.

Hot upper floors, cold lower floors. Ducts run to upper floors in straight lines from the furnace, warming upper floors first and providing more heat than for floors below. The homeowner's tendency is to close the upper registers in an attempt to force the heat through the lower ones. Instead, however, the ducts hold trapped hot air in the walls, which become heated in consequence and are, in effect, hot air registers in the full height of the walls. Proper control can be achieved in a damper at the first floor level, just above baseboard registers. When this damper shuts off the flow of air to upper floors at the right location, the lower floors receive more heat. At the same time, a top-of-the-stair air break, such as modern folding doors or a screen, will slow down the flow of warmed air from lower floors to the upper one, thus helping to keep the lower floors warm.

Dirt and dust buildup. This results from several causes—infrequent cleaning of ducts, dirt on blower fan blades and filters, and register leaks. Periodic cleaning of ducts, fan blades, and filters is sound economy as well as a cure for the dirt. A clogged filter will even cause the blower to operate erratically. Change the filter, particularly if it has been in service for a few months. If you have no immediate replacement filter, vacuum the old one and use it temporarily. The fiberglass type is generally recommended. It should be replaced at least once during each heating season.

Registers or grilles should be vacuumed every six weeks during the heating season; failure to do so will result in a sizable accumulation of dust. Air leaks from the bases of registers can be overcome by removing the register, gluing a strip of felt around the base, and replacing the register tightly

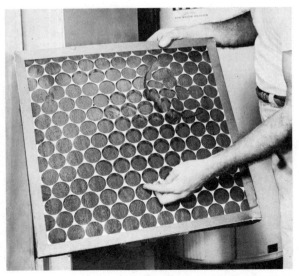

Hot air systems require some special attention. Filters need periodic checkups, as they tend to become clogged with dust, lint, and sometimes soot. The surface can be brushed clean, but filter replacement is inexpensive.

After periods of furnace shutdown, be sure to vacuum registers before starting up blower system. Otherwise you may be unpleasantly surprised with a cloud of dust.

in its mounting. (Foam rubber may be used in place of felt.) Diffusion-style registers also help to avoid this condition since the air is directed to all parts of the room.

CHECKLIST OF COMMON COMPLAINTS in Hot Air Heating Systems and Steps toward Correcting the Faults

High fuel bills
a. Oversize furnace for size of house.
b. Excessive fuel being fed to furnace. Reduce jet on oil burners, reduce heat extractors where stack temperatures are within safe limits of manufacturer's specifications.
c. Controls out of calibration. This requires factory checkup.
d. Blower belt slipping. Apply belt dressing or replace.
e. Blades of blower dirty. Shut down system and clean.
f. Intake filters plugged. Shut down system and clean or replace.

Rooms too hot
a. Thermostat improperly located. Relocate.
b. Air delivery system not balanced. Adjust (or install and adjust) volume dampers behind supply registers.
c. Thermostat incorrectly set.

Noisy operation
a. Ducts of lightweight metal. Require stiffening to prevent vibration.
b. Inner casing of furnace loose. Shut down, investigate, and tighten bolts.
c. Blower troubles: belt too tight causing vibration; motor cable rubbing on fan or cabinet; blower not properly centered in cabinet opening; bearings in need of oil; pulley warped or bent; static electricity jumping from wheel to cabinet; end play in shaft. Tape up loose cables; tighten cabinet nuts, replace defective parts, adjust thrust collars to take up the end play of shaft.
d. Motor trouble: motor not rubber mounted; base fasteners loose; pulley not tight on shaft; bearings worn; speed incorrect. Remount motor on rubber, tighten motor down, tighten pulley, replace poor bearings, adjust speed up or down slightly.

Insufficient heat
a. Controls improperly set.
b. Dirt on heating surfaces. Shut down system and clean.
c. Insufficient return air. Check baffles on all registers, remove dirt from ducts.
d. Filters plugged. Shut down and clean or replace.
e. Check blower for: slipping belt; belt too tight causing overloaded motor to cut out; dirty blades; blower running backwards; defective motor; blower too small for house.
f. Check thermostat for: correct location; calibration; correct type for controls used.
g. Loose wires. Locate, tape joints. Check and tighten wire nuts with fuse off.
h. Close fireplace damper.

Heat loss through ducts. Heat will be lost (as much as 25 percent) through duct metal where the ducts pass through cold areas on their way to registers. Even the longer ducts passing through a basement area should be insulated to prevent undue heating of the basement at the cost of cold rooms upstairs.

Also, heat from uninsulated pipes discharged into basement air is a frequent cause of wet walls when the hot air, touching cold basement walls, loses its moisture by condensation. Where ducts pass through open crawl spaces, they definitely should be well insulated. Heat also travels up through outside walls to the attic unless these wall spaces are well sealed. In perimeter-type hot air heating, all duct lengths between the furnace and outer walls should be insulated.

Some gravity systems can be improved by relocation of ducts. Older installations placed the duct registers directly above the furnace floor or baseboard level. When registers are located higher on the wall, the rising air increases its speed as it mounts higher in the duct. This draws air into the furnace faster, and swifter circulation results. Also, the warmed duct distributes radiant heat into the walls and then into the rooms as supplementary heat. The improvement in heating efficiency is well worth the cost of the additional lengths of duct.

HOT WATER SYSTEMS Hot water heating is cleaner than warmed air heating and can be better controlled to meet weather changes than steam heat, but not so well as forced air heat. With automatic gas, oil, or stoker-fed furnaces, the forced-feed type of hot water system can be fitted with other automatic controls so that the entire heating system can be ignored for weeks at a time.

Basically, hot water heating divides into two types of systems: gravity-fed, or the "open" type; and force-fed, or the "closed" type. (Exception: Some

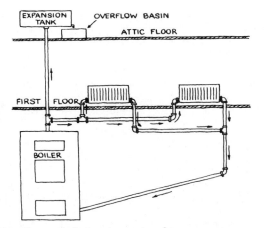

"Open" gravity hot water system has an open expansion tank that is located in the attic of the house.

gravity systems may also be "closed.") If you aren't sure which type you have, check the following points of difference, through which your own type can be determined. Then consider the advantages of one over the other, with a view toward obtaining the most heat for the least cost and bother.

"Open" gravity-fed system. Here's how a system of this type works:

1. Water temperatures. In this system, the maximum safe water temperature is about 180° F. When heated, water expands, and to take care of the increased mass of water in a gravity-fed system, an expansion tank—open to the air— is provided at the system's top, usually in the attic.

2. Circulation. Since warmed water rises exactly as does warmed air, water in the gravity-fed system rises through pipes as it is heated by the furnace. When it reaches the radiators, it gives off about 20° F of its temperature, and the cooled water then flows downward through return-flow pipes to the furnace for reheating.

3. Controls. Since the property of heated water to rise is the only means of getting hot water to rooms over the furnace, a sudden drop in outside temperature means that the boiler must first heat a large mass of cold water. The delay could mean a well-chilled house before warmed water reaches the more distant rooms. Thermostats can be set manually to start the furnace operating at will, or "anticipatory" thermostats set outside the house to start it working when exterior temperatures drop below a predetermined figure. Even with these, there is the wait until the boiler has heated a sufficient mass of water to a degree where circulation begins.

4. Pipe sizes. Since the volume of heated water is important where the temperature of the water circulated is relatively low, gravity-fed systems usually start with a 3″ diameter main line, with 1″ riser pipes to radiators. Return pipes from radiators, where used, are of the same size and feed back into 3″ return mains.

Force-feed system. The following is how this type of system works:

1. Water temperature. Since the force-feed system is "closed," the water in it may be put under pressure. The usual pressure of 20 pounds permits raising the water temperature above the usual boiling point (the boiling point being automatically raised along with the pressure).

Water temperatures of 240°F are not uncommon, yet no steam pressure is created by this method. Therefore, it is evident that the water delivered to radiators takes more usable heat with it. Instead of an open tank at the top of the system to take care of water expansion—which would prevent putting the water in the system under pressure—a sealed tank is provided. This is first filled with air, which is compressed by expanding water.

2. Circulation. On the closed-type system, a small motor-driven pump forces heated water from the boiler through the system on demand of the thermostat, which controls the motor in most cases. Since the water can be heated to a much higher degree, it carries more heat. Whether or not all of its heat is lost, the water is forced through the radiator back to the furnace. In consequence, if sufficient heat has been delivered to the rooms, the water that returns to the boiler is still hot enough to need little fuel consumption to keep it at a desirable temperature for heating purposes.

3. Controls. Most gas-fired boilers are operated so the pump and gas burner run simultaneously from the thermostat. But in some force-fed systems, the thermostat controls the circulating pump and

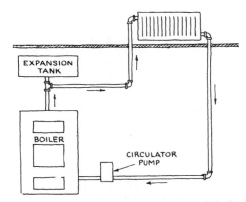

Forced circulation hot water system has a closed expansion tank with water under pressure.

water temperature controls the firing of the boiler. This may be manually set (as explained later), but the general principle is that, as cold water returns to the furnace, an aquastat causes the furnace to fire to reheat the water. When the water is heated to the desired temperature, the aquastat shuts off the furnace. If the furnace itself becomes overheat-ed, it will shut down in response to the high-limit switch.

4. Pipe sizes. Since more heat is carried by the water under pressure, a smaller pipe is possible. Main line pipes of 1½" diameter are usual, with ½" riser pipes to radiators. Returns are the same size.

Where water is forced through the system, several methods of return are possible. The various systems are known as the one-pipe return, two-pipe direct return, and the two-pipe reverse return.

The first one-pipe systems had the main line and the radiators in a single line without risers or returns to each radiator. The first radiator—the one nearest the furnace—got the most heat, and those farther along the line received progressively less. From the last radiator, water returned directly to the furnace for reheating. This one-pipe system has since been modified so that each radiator has its own riser and return connected to the main line. Baseboard radiators and in-line convector systems are adaptations of this improvement.

In the two-pipe direct return system, water from the first radiator is the first returned, and this would be the hottest water with the least consumed heat, whereas the last radiator returns its cooled water last and thus places an added load on the boiler. Fuel consumption is higher, and the rooms are not evenly heated. To offset this problem, the reversed return system was introduced. In this type of installation, water from the first radiator is sent to the return pipe but continues along the line of flow, picking up equally cooled water from each in turn, then returning all to the boiler. All radiators are equally heated, and the boiler has an evenly balanced load at all times. Fuel bills are smaller.

The following are some controls and control adjustments that can be used to increase the efficiency of hot water systems. They result in even heat, lower fuel consumption, and more control of a well-managed heating plant:

1. In mild weather, set the water temperature control at 80°F to 90°F by means of the aquastat. To do this and to take advantage of the fuel saving, a separate hot water heater (domestic use) should be used. Combination boiler/water heater units are not as efficient. Otherwise, excess fuel is burned to heat hot domestic-use water, and the remaining heat goes up the flue.

2. Have the high-limit switch adjusted by your serviceman to provide brief but more frequent on-off cycles. This will provide a temperature better regulated to exterior temperatures in seasons of quick change.

3. Establish a two-pump system for two-story and ranch-style homes. Any part of the house you

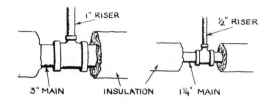

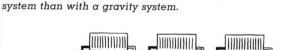

Pipe sizes — gravity and forced circulation
Since more heat is carried by water under pressure, a smaller-sized pipe can be used with a forced circulation system than with a gravity system.

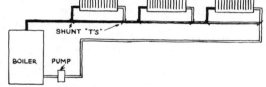

Early one-pipe systems with a single feed to each radiator were inefficient until special shunt T-connections were developed.

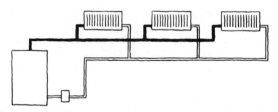

The two-pipe direct return system, while an improvement over the old one-pipe method, nevertheless resulted in high fuel consumption and uneven heating.

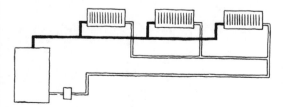

The two-pipe reversed return system permits the furnace to operate with an evenly balanced load at all times; all radiators are heated equally.

Closed hot water systems are equipped with overhead pressure tanks that frequently become waterlogged and thus are unable to develop pressure for higher temperatures. To remedy this, attach hose to tank, drain, close valve, and remove hose. Generally the tank should be half full of air and half full of water at 160°F.

want heated above normal can be kept at a higher temperature without overheating the rest of the house. You can take full advantage of sun heat on the protected sides of the house with this system. Zone your own home with this dual-pump system.

4. In extremely cold weather, increase pressure in the closed system. Pressure may be increased to 20 pounds, delivering more heat to radiators.

Hot water systems will not work properly unless the correct water level is maintained. To find the correct level, fill the system until the expansion tank is half full and all the radiators properly vented. Notice the black arrow on the boiler gauge. This arrow, which shows what the water level actually is, should rest over a red arrow which shows what the water level should be. Whenever the black arrow reading falls below the red arrow level, the reducing valve should automatically replenish the water supply. If it doesn't, check the valve. If you need to add water, do it slowly until the black arrow is returned to its correct position. Vent the radiators a week later to release air that will have been driven out of the new water.

When water is heated, the air is driven from it and, having no place to go in a closed system, it follows the flow to a point where, in bubble form, it can remain—in the tops of radiators, as a rule. These radiators remain cold because the air prevents them from filling with hot water. Check the pipes leading to the radiators. If the pipes do not

run parallel to the joists and the risers are not perpendicular, air can become trapped and efficiency is cut. Further, as water flows through pipe, it meets resistance from the rough interior pipe surface, rough fittings, and the length of the pipe itself. Short-turn elbows, which present a two-thirds greater resistance to smooth water flow, can be replaced with long-bend elbows. The more resistance presented, the more time it takes hot water to reach radiators. Hot water pipes should be insulated between the boiler and the radiators to prevent needless heat loss along the way. The insulation will pay for itself in one season.

The regular venting of radiators is a routine job in the operation of a hot water system. Use automatic vents that open to release air and close as water touches them. Otherwise, radiator valves that need manual attention must be checked and bled, if needed, every few weeks. In a properly installed system, this should not be a problem.

STEAM HEAT Steam, a mixture of hot air and hot vapor, rises through pipes even more rapidly than does hot air or hot water. When water is heated enough to turn it into steam, pressure is created by expansion. There is a limit to the pressure a home heating boiler can stand. To insure that this limit is never exceeded, every steam boiler is provided with a safety valve set to open and release excess steam when the safety limit is reached. Safety valves on home heating systems are usually set to open, or blow off, at 15 pounds per square inch of pressure. Most are of the "pop" type. The valve pops completely open at 15 pounds per square inch of pressure and remains completely open until a predetermined lower pressure is reached, when it closes again.

Many safety valves have a test lever, which opens the valve manually. It is a good idea to check this at least once a month during the heating season. If the valve will not open and release steam or if it continually leaks steam, it is defective. Do not tamper with this valve or try to repair it. You can save yourself a repair bill by simply unscrewing the valve and replacing it with a new factory-set one. Don't tamper in any way with the inside mechanism or try to put it back in working order. Before removing it, shut down the boiler and let it cool. Many safety valves are fitted with a seal so that the setting cannot be changed.

Steam boiler try cocks are used to determine the water level in the boiler. The proper water level is midway between upper and lower cocks, so you should get water out of the lower one, steam out of the top. These cocks become clogged with rust and water sediment, but they can easily be cleaned by unscrewing the handle all the way out, then inserting a narrow wire in the valve opening and into the boiler. Do this job, of course, when the system has been shut down long enough for the boiler to cool.

The gauge glass is the most convenient way to check the water level, but it is not so reliable as the try cock method. If the gauge glass and try cocks do not agree, the try cocks, when known to be clear, are correct. The bottom connection between boiler and gauge glass may be stopped up when the gauge is half full, and thereafter it will remain half full—even when there is not a drop of water in the boiler! Clean the gauge glass cocks in the same manner as the try cocks. The glass itself may be cleaned by removing it and washing with a strong ammonia solution. To remove the glass, turn off the gauge cocks, then remove the nuts at each end of the glass. Then raise or lower the glass to free one end. In replacing the glass, use regular glass-gauge washers. Lampwick packing is not as satisfactory.

ROOM THERMOSTATS Thermostats are generally used to control central heating appliances. Most common are wall-mounted thermostats, which are actually a special kind of electric switch, opening or closing an electric circuit, to open or close a fuel valve or actuate fans or pumps. Thermostats generally operate on house voltage stepped down by a transformer.

Thermostatic control, which transmits room temperature to the boiler and regulates it accordingly, saves you countless trips to the basement. Clock thermostats may be obtained that automatically reduce the temperature when you go to bed and turn up the heat at the time you like to get up in the morning.

Such automatic devices need more controls than just a thermostat to handle emergencies. Suppose, for instance, that the thermostat called for more heat and there was no water in the boiler. To handle this emergency, you would find, near the gauge glass, a low-water cutout. This is float-operated and designed to stop burner or stoker operation any time the water in the boiler drops below a safe level. This device is connected to an automatic water feeder, which admits water as needed to the boiler. Except for a flushing once a month to remove sediment, it is best left alone.

Again, since no automatic firing device should be allowed to heat a boiler to the point where the safety valve can blow, a pressuretrol or pressurestat should be installed. These controls are operated by the steam or water pressure in the boiler and set to cut out at about 4 pounds of steam pressure. They should not be tampered with, as they are generally factory set. Replacement by a professional is necessary when these controls are out of order.

Suppose the thermostat calls for heat on an oil burner and the oil is sprayed into the fire box but fails to ignite. A dangerous amount of oil may be sprayed in, then ignited, and an explosion could result. To prevent this hazardous series of events, a stack switch is mounted on the smoke pipe or flue door. When the burner starts, the stack switch has from 15 to 45 seconds (depending on local regulations) in which to heat up. If it fails to heat, the burner operation is halted and will stay stopped until the cause of failure is located and corrected. Similarly, if a gas pilot goes out, the main burner won't come on until the pilot is relit and the red safety button is pushed.

RADIANT HEAT Radiant heating systems eliminate registers, ducts, radiators, and convectors. Instead, hot water tubing (or, less frequently, electric heating cable) is concealed in the floor, in the walls or in the ceiling. Radiant heating is accepted by the Federal Housing Authority and all building codes in new homes.

In the case of hot water radiant heating systems, the tubing (almost invariably flexible copper tube) is run back and forth in rows from 6″ to 12″ apart. Water from a standard hot water boiler is reduced in temperature to a maximum of 90°F to 120°F and circulated continuously through the tubing. A mixing valve controlled by the thermostat regulates water temperature. Where tubing is placed in a concrete floor, the floor itself is warmed first and heat rises from it.

Servicing the boiler system for the concealed radiation system requires the same procedure as for any hot water boiler. The radiation pipes, which are embedded in concrete or buried in walls, are first pressure-tested to be sure they are leakproof, and only a major defect in the slab could cause a leak. Maintenance of both radiant heating pipes and radiant electric cables is virtually nil.

CONVERSION TO BASEBOARD RADIATION One obvious advantage of the baseboard radiator is that it's hardly noticeable, particularly when painted to match its surroundings. No pipes or valves show, floor space is saved, and the space under windows is available for any use you wish to make of it. This is a decided advantage where long, low picture windows have been installed. Floor-length drapes may be used, and there is more freedom in placing furniture.

Baseboard radiation is efficient from the technical point of view. The old, high radiator warmed a cold wall in a concentrated area only, and the walls to each side remained cold. Long, low radiators were an improvement, but the baseboard radiator covers the entire outside wall with a blanket of warm air.

Tests have shown that even when the outside

Figure A. *The two-pipe system, the origin of baseboard heating, can be used with steam as well as a gravity hot water heating system.*

Figure B. *Units are built to be coupled closely. Standard close-nipples are concealed when sections are joined and covered.*

Figure C. *Single-pipe finned convector hangs on hooks. It requires forced-feed hot water supply and delivers maximum heating.*

temperature is at zero, baseboard radiation warms a cold wall from floor to ceiling with a variation of less than 3°F. To heating engineers, this means efficiency and low fuel cost, but to the homeowner it means comfort plus economy. The heat is not concentrated near the ceiling, and the floors are warm.

As seen in Figure A, with a cast-iron radiator designed primarily for hot water or either forced flow or gravity flow, the system may be used for steam heat as well. A two-pipe steam system needs a supply and a return line. If your present steam radiators have a two-pipe arrangement, you can use baseboard radiators, but if it is only one pipe, it is better to forego the idea, since furnace conversion is too costly to warrant the change. Not so with hot water. You may use a baseboard radiator with any hot water system.

Don't try to mix different types of radiators. Each type has different characteristics. The water flow

rates, the heat transfer mechanism, the use of parallel or series circuits are all different. Unless all the radiators are the same, the system can't be well engineered.

The so-called R panel type (Figure A) delivers radiant heat primarily. Less than half the heat output is by convection, that is, by the circulation of hot air. The R panel becomes warm and sends out heat rays of the same type put out by electric heaters. The wall becomes heated to a height of about 5' and the wall itself becomes a radiant panel. In short, much the same type of heat is obtained as from pipes concealed in walls or floors.

The RC panel type (Figure B) heats primarily by convection through the fins. This type delivers about 60 percent more heat than does the R type.

The heating element shown in Figure C consists only of a finned copper pipe. It is not a radiator and can be used only with a forced-flow hot water heating system. In operation, hot water pumped from the boiler heats the finned pipe. Air enters around the pipe through openings at the bottom of the baseboard, passes over the heating element, and comes out warm at the top. Sizes range from 8" to 10" high and from 2" to 2½" thick. Lengths are in units of 6', 8', and 10'.

Depending on the manufacturer, the front baseboard panel is held in place by a snap device, either to a continuous back panel or to a series of small brackets. One combines in a single clip the holder for the heating element and a snap-on bracket. (See Figure C.) In all cases, the front panel portion is easily removable, allowing inspection and cleaning.

Normally, only the outside walls of a room are equipped with baseboard radiators.

Wall preparation for all types of mountings is much the same. The wooden baseboard molding is first removed and the plaster, if any, is patched and smoothed. Mark the location of studs. If the floor is not finished to the plaster line, fill the joint with molding strips. It is essential, of course, that a home be insulated for this type of heating.

Piping, valves, and fittings are the same as for ordinary radiators. Long lengths of panel are assembled on the job by means of push nipples and assembly clamps provided by the manufacturer. Since the panels expand about ⅛" for every 10' when hot, make floor openings for pipe connections to the main line to accommodate this expansion (slots are better than holes). Cast-iron panels may be fitted with adapters for copper pipe and, conversely, finned copper-tubing types may be fitted with adapters to connect with steel pipe.

The final problem is the determination of how many feet of baseboard radiation will be needed. This figure is based on how much heat is lost from

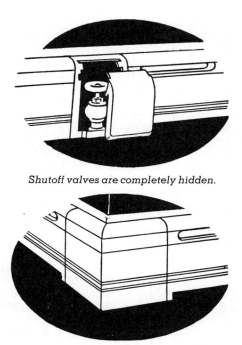

Shutoff valves are completely hidden.

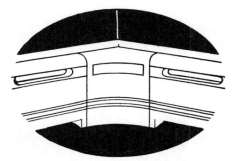

Corner plates make a continuous line.

Outside corners are fully protected.

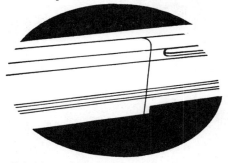

False fronts hide gaps between radiators.

the room through windows and doors, lack of insulation, glass window area, thickness and nature of the walls, storm sash, and location of the room in relation to the rest of the house. The old radiator will help you in this calculation. Make a complete description of its size, number of sections, and tubes, and consult your heating expert. He will know the amount of radiation received from the old radiator, and that will tell how much is needed from the new installation. If the room has been altered, as by the addition of a picture window, this factor must also be taken into consideration in the new calculations.

HEAT PUMPS Another heating system coming into wider use is the electrically powered heat pump. It is basically a reversible refrigeration system that provides cool air in summer as well as warm air in winter. Most units have an auxiliary electric heating element that switches on automatically when the outside temperature drops too low for efficient heat production, normally around 20° F. There are two basic types: the single unit system, which has both coils outside the house and an air duct to carry the heated or cooled air inside; and the split system, which has one coil inside connected to the fan and ducts with tubing joining it to the outside coil.

You can think of it simply as a compressor with two heat exchangers. When refrigerant fluid is compressed, heat can be extracted from it. When it expands, heat is absorbed. Consumers who are facing high utility costs for electrically heated homes will, in a moderate climate, gain substantial savings. Again, these savings must be weighed against installation costs (generally higher than fuel burning units) in the $1,000 to $1,500 range.

HOW TO MAINTAIN YOUR HEATING SYSTEM

There is much the homeowner can do to insure full value from each fuel dollar. Any heating system will lose as much as 20 percent of its efficiency if it is forced to work below par. Rust, soot, lack of air, and insufficient oil on moving parts will all contribute to a costly reduction in heat output. Maintenance may often be a task involving only a few moments' time. As simple a matter as vacuuming convectors and registers will step up efficiency immediately.

RADIATORS With the coming of autumn and the starting up of the heating system, there are sometimes problems of radiators that won't heat, radiators that knock and hammer, and radiator valves that spit, sputter, and dribble. Fortunately, repairs are not difficult, nor are special tools required. Indeed, most of the repairs can be made without any tools at all.

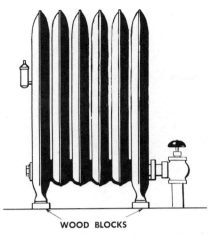

WOOD BLOCKS

Wood blocks under radiators aid return flow to boiler, cure knocks, and promote radiator efficiency.

For example, suppose you have a steam radiator that will not heat. First, make sure the radiator valve is turned on. If it is, the trouble is almost sure to be in the air valve. This valve does two things: it allows the cold air in the radiator to be pushed out by the steam coming up from the boiler, and when the steam hits the valve, the rise in temperature automatically closes the valve to keep steam from escaping into the room.

If the air valve is stuck (because of rust, grit, or corrosion), no air can escape, steam cannot enter, and the radiator is airbound. To remove rust and grit, first close the radiator shutoff valve, and manually unscrew the air valve by turning it counterclockwise. Shake the valve vigorously—this may loosen rust—then try to blow through its threaded end. If air passes through, reinstall the valve; if not, boil it in a strong solution of washing soda and water for about twenty minutes. You can put the valve back on the same radiator to see if it works, but a better test is to put the valve on a radiator that is heating well. If this radiator continues to heat, fine; if not, obviously the valve is defective and will have to be replaced.

You have, in the exchange, installed the good air valve in the radiator that formerly would not heat up. If this radiator still does not heat—and you know now that the air valve is all right—the radiator is probably waterbound. To remedy this, put small blocks of wood about an inch high under the radiator legs farthest away from the shutoff valve. Make sure the radiator is at least level, and preferably tilted slightly toward the shutoff valve. This will not only allow the radiator to heat but will cure the hammering noise it probably has been making. If the hammering continues, put blocks under all four legs, but make sure the radiator is level.

Sometimes an air valve will sputter steam and water. Once again, try it on another radiator. If the valve still allows water to escape, the thermostatic device inside the valve is broken and the valve will have to be replaced.

If a radiator heats slowly, or only after all other radiators are hot, the air valve has too small an opening for the escape of air. You can buy an air valve with an adjustable opening and set the opening wide enough so that the radiator heats along with the others. The greater the distance between radiator and boiler, the wider the opening should be. With several of these adjustable valves, the system can be balanced so that all radiators heat equally, or for that matter, some radiators can be regulated to heat before others.

Do not try to balance a steam system by partly closing the radiator shutoff valves, as this is likely to cause hammering. Keep steam radiator valves completely open or completely shut. Loosening of parts in the shutoff valve will also prevent a radiator from heating properly. Shut off the furnace and let it cool before taking a shutoff valve apart to see if it is working.

Radiator valves sometimes leak around the packing nut. Tighten the nut a couple of turns. If it still leaks, shut off the valve and allow it to cool. Unscrew the packing nut and slide it up on the valve shaft. Wind some valve packing, which you can buy in any hardware store, around the shaft under the nut. Be sure to wind the packing in the same direction (clockwise) in which you are going to turn the nut when it is tightened. Then tighten the nut and turn on the valve.

Hot water radiator valves also leak around the packing nut. Their repair is the same as for a steam valve, except that the water in the hot water

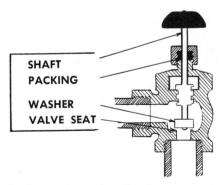

SHAFT
PACKING

WASHER
VALVE SEAT

Leaking radiator shutoff valves can easily be mended with a wrench and a length of valve packing.

Hot water radiators must be bled at intervals to remove air cushion that retards flow of hot water.

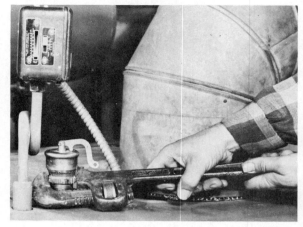

1. *Dirt, rust, scale, and water sediment in the bottom of your boiler mean that it takes longer to warm up. Begin the tune-up by removing safety valve on boiler, loosening it with a pipe wrench.*

system must be drained until its level is below the valve you want to fix. Unlike steam valves, hot water shutoff valves need not be fully open or closed. They may be used as throttling valves to regulate the amount of heat to each radiator. The entire system should be balanced in this manner to favor those radiators that do not heat enough and to cut down on those that are too hot.

Hammering in steam pipes is caused by water trapped in pipes no longer having enough slant back toward the boiler. This happens most often in old houses because of settling of the floors, sagging beams, or the rotting away of pipe hangers and supports. The cure is to locate the low section where water can collect, then raise the pipe just enough to restore proper pitch. Since only a little movement of the pipe is needed to trap water, by the same token only a little movement is needed to correct it.

BOILERS A rumbling noise in the boiler itself, surging noises in the pipes, or an unsteady water line in the glass are all signs that the boiler water is dirty. To drain the boiler, let the fire go out and the boiler cool so that rust and sediment in the water can settle to the bottom. Turn off the cold water feed valve to the boiler. If you're not sure which valve it is, find where the cold water pipe enters your home and trace it to the boiler. Probably you'll find a shutoff valve just where the cold water pipe is attached to the boiler.

Keep one eye on the water gauge on the side of the boiler. There is one with all systems except a closed hot water heating system using an expansion tank. When water in the glass gauge shows the boiler is half full, shut off the feed valve. If you have a hot water heating system with an expansion tank, close the valve from the system to the

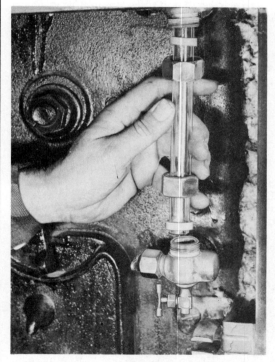

4. *Water gauge glass may become rust-coated inside and conceal water-level line. To clean, remove top and bottom nuts and washers, pull glass up, then out at bottom. Clean with brush.*

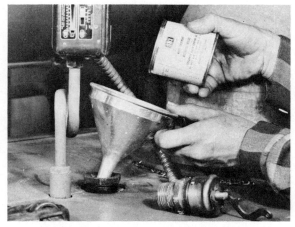

2. Next, catch water drained through clean-out faucet. Use a pail or run a hose to drain. Flush boiler by pouring more water into valve opening at top. Continue until water flows out of the boiler clear.

3. After shutting faucet, pour in water conditioner or a boiler-cleaning compound. Most of these compounds also inhibit rust. For best results, follow carefully instructions of the manufacturer of the brand you choose.

5. Boiler fins become caked with soot, which acts as insulation and causes heat loss. Remove door, scrape soot off fins with brush, then pick up dislodged soot with vacuum.

6. Hose-type vacuum attachment will serve to reach far corners. Soot also indicates poor burner adjustment and incomplete combustion.

7. Oil burner motors need periodic attention—a few drops of oil for bearings and removal of dust and fine ash from armature. Apply high-grade machine oil to cups.

8. Smoke pipes may fill with soot and fine ash or rust scale. This impairs draft and causes heat loss. A vacuum hose does the clean-up job without creating a messy basement.

OIL BURNER CHECKLIST

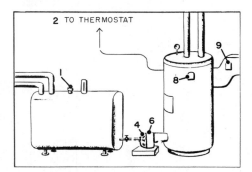

If an oil burner fails to operate or operates poorly, there are several trouble spots a homeowner can check. The numbers in the sketch correspond with illustrated steps.

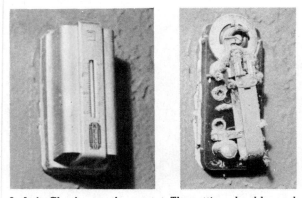

2. Left: Check your thermostat. The setting should equal the thermometer reading. Someone may have turned down the setting and forgotten to put it back. Of course, if the thermostat is on a warm inner wall, the temperature will be comfortable; outer areas of the house will always be cool by comparison.

3. Right: Shut off the electric current at the main fuse box. Then open the thermostat by removing the screws that hold on the cover. If you find dust like this, no doubt the thermostat has been prevented from working. Blow out or remove dust with a fine bristle brush. There is no point in calling a serviceman.

1. Check your fuel oil tank. It might be empty. Even if the gauge shows oil in the tank, it might be stuck. Remove the cap and check quantity with a thin stick or dowel. There should be about 3" or more to maintain the proper flow.

4. Your furnace needs air to burn. Air is taken in through openings of this housing. A screw loosened by vibration may close the air intake. Adjust, while the furnace is burning, until the flame is clean, bright, and smokeless. Next time your serviceman calls, he can make an accurate adjustment, but meanwhile the furnace will operate.

---

tank. Then open the drain valve on the bottom of the tank and let the water out. Leave the drain valve open for an hour or two and then close the drain valve and reopen the valve connecting the system with the tank. Remember, open this valve when you're finished draining the tank; it must be open before you start the system working.

While draining a rust-filled boiler is always recommended, excessive draining and refilling is not always the wisest policy. Heating water liberates

minerals that then cling to the inside of boiler and pipes, clogging them. Where the water is known to be heavily mineralized, it is better to avoid draining and refilling and instead to use a rust-inhibitor chemical in the boiler water. Chemical treatment of the water can cover the entire system with a protective coating on inside surfaces of boiler and pipes and eliminate mineral buildups.

AUTOMATIC BURNERS Automatic heating equipment, owing to its complexity and the need

5. *The large nut opposite the oil intake covers the fuel control valve. If the nut is tight, forget it. The trouble is elsewhere. If loose, remove by hand and adjust the set-screw this nut covers—while the furnace is operating—until you have a large, clear flame. Have this adjusted and tightened correctly on the next call of your serviceman.*

6. *Check the oil flow. You may have plenty of oil, but it's not getting to the furnace. On top of the blower unit pump there's a cap firmly held down with a series of six or eight nuts. Shut off the burner switch first, then remove these nuts and lift off the cap. There's a gasket between the cap and the pump.*

7. *With the cap off, you can lift out the twin filters that screen dirt from your oil supply. There is usually grit from the oil and rust scale from the inside of the tank. You'll see it coating the filter and preventing free flow of oil. Rinse the filter in clean oil or kerosene and replace filter, gasket, and cap.*

8. *An aquastat controls water temperature of steam and water systems. You can look into this with current off by removing the cover and blowing out dust. Check the tilting lever to see that both mercury switches operate freely. If set too low, the aquastat may be preventing a supply of properly heated water from being delivered, even if the furnace works well. Setting should be about 180°F.*

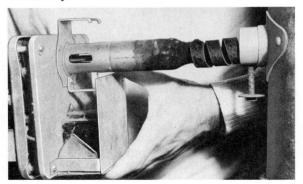

9. *Inside view of stack switch. This keeps furnace shut down when smoke pipe is too hot for safety. Coil curls and uncurls as temperature changes, thus operating furnace. Smoky fires coat coil with soot and prevent proper action. Clean away soot with kerosene. Switch will not turn furnace on if stack is too hot—you'll have to wait from 5 to 30 minutes for stack to cool to see if switch is working correctly.*

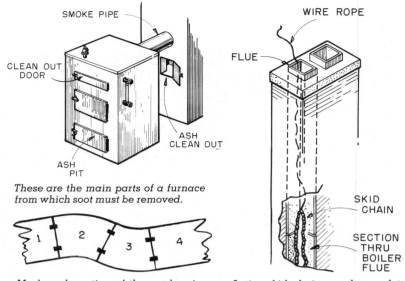

Soot must be cleaned out of furnace and smoke pipe for more efficient home heating. Examine the smoke pipe to check for holes; any found must be sealed by soldering, or else the entire pipe must be replaced. Clean pipe with a brush, and after it is replaced, make certain that joints at chimney and furnace are sealed. Use asbestos cement to assure a perfect seal; apply with trowel.

These are the main parts of a furnace from which soot must be removed.

Mark each section of the smoke pipe so you can put it together afterward.

A tire skid chain can be used to remove soot.

for expert adjustment, is better tended by a professional. A homeowner can prolong the life of his heating equipment by cleaning dust, dirt, and lint from fans and motor housings, and by oiling motors periodically with S.A.E. 30 oil. An oil burner is a carefully adjusted mechanism, and usually repairs must be made by a serviceman. However, there are a number of things a homeowner can do and should know about that might eliminate the necessity for calling in outside help.

Oil burner nozzles should be checked and cleaned once a year, as the passage of fuel at high pressure widens the small jet orifices and eventually delivers a greater quantity of oil than required. This results in fuel loss and, furthermore, produces a poor flame. A smoking chimney is a sign of this trouble if you have an oil burner.

Gas burners require little attention as a rule. Gas alone will not burn until air is present. The gas burner merely mixes air with gas in proper proportion and passes it to the igniter. Observe the flame now and then. It should burn blue. Yellow tips on the flames are a sign of not enough primary air. In this case, the air shutter is not open enough to make the flame blue. Too much air will cause a lifting flame or flashback ignition inside the burner.

SUMMER SHUTDOWN With a little care at the time you close down your heating system for the summer, you can stretch the life of your heating equipment. First, clean thoroughly. With a wire

brush, scrape all heating surfaces exposed to the fire until completely free of soot, ash, or residue. It is the combination of sulfur in soot and moisture in the air that seriously damages heating equipment during the shutdown period. Pick a time soon after a rain when the soot is still damp. Shut all the dampers and drafts to avoid a face full of soot. The dampers and drafts are marked on some heating units. Clean the chimney and the ash cleanout; then the smoke pipe.

Before you begin to take apart the smoke pipe, mark the joint of one pipe on the other with a thin stripe of paint (automobile touch-up paint dries quickly). These stripes will be guide marks when the pipes are reassembled later. You might even number the sections if there are many elbows and varying lengths. Take the pipes out into the backyard on a windless day. Use a stiff brush attached to a long handle and scrub them with soapy water or detergent. This will prolong the life of the pipes, since removal of soot prevents damping during the summer, a process that quickly rusts holes from the inside out. Stand the pipes in the sun to dry. When they are reinstalled, open the stove damper—but only after soot has been removed from the furnace—to let the wind blow through to keep them dry.

If your heating plant is made of steel instead of cast iron, coat the cleaned surfaces with lubricating oil. Thoroughly clean out the fire pit with a vacuum cleaner. Clean the inside with a wire

TENDING THE BOILER

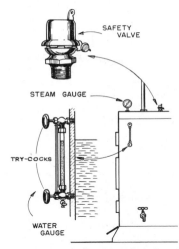

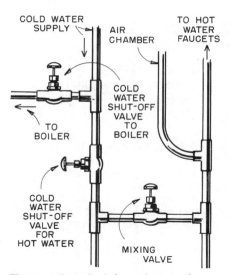

Water gauge on side shows height of water in boiler. Drain cock at bottom permits easy flushing of tank.

This is a "map" of the valves in the usual closed hot water heat system, showing what each valve controls.

brush, then leave the ashpit door slightly open for ventilation.

Refill oil tanks after the furnace has been turned off for the summer. This reduces to a minimum the exposed areas of tank walls, preventing formation of rust scale due to condensation of air moisture on the cold metal. At the same time, protect the tank bottom (where such accumulated moisture invariably settles) against pinhole leaks by introduction of a can of auto gas-line antifreeze (alcohol) annually. Tanks to be buried in the ground outside the house should be treated in this manner and painted on the outside surface with bituminous coatings before burial. Indoor oil tanks may be painted as a protection against rust.

When daily heat is no longer needed, pick a mild day to have the boiler drained.

The hot water system should be left filled with water right up to the expansion tank. If for any reason the system has been drained and refilled, the furnace should be fired long enough to raise the water temperature close to the boiling point (about 180°F minimum) to eliminate gases found in fresh water. Such gases can start corrosive action very quickly.

The steam boiler, which is usually filled with water only to the halfway mark on the gauge glass, should now be completely filled. Close all radiator valves and raise the water level to the very top of the system. Be sure the water level is lowered in the fall when you fire up the boiler again. (Put a

note on the fuel valve as a reminder to adjust the water level.) If you have a mixing valve to cool the very hot water you use at the faucet in the winter, see if it's still open. As your boiler will not be operating over extended periods of time for a while, you'll probably partially (or even completely) close this valve as warmer weather comes. Be sure to check this mixing valve, or else you might have cool water instead of hot in spring and summer.

All boiler accessories, regardless of the kind of fuel used, should be left in good working order. Oil the door hinges after brushing. Clean the dampers the same way. Clean or replace the gauge glass on steam systems.

During the summer, it is best to cut off all electric power to the automatic heating systems. You can do this by either throwing the main control switch, if you have one, or by removing the proper fuse from its box on or near the furnace. If you plan to be away from the house for a prolonged period of time, the best insurance is to shut off the gas entirely, including the pilot light, so that a chance breakage and resumption of service won't fill your utility room with gas.

MIDWINTER MAINTENANCE House heating costs being what they are, homeowners should do all they can to maintain furnaces and hot water heaters in the best operating condition. It is a more than comforting thought, in the warmth of the home, to know that what can be done has been done—at no cost and for little time.

THERMOSTATS Thermostats are the nerve centers that help to control house heating systems. In normal use, they need only be set to the temperature wanted — thereafter, they will start the furnace when the room temperature drops to about 2° below the setting. In time, however, some of the older regulators collect dust and grit that affect their entire operation. They must be cleaned, particularly on forced hot air systems that move large volumes of air and, therefore, dust.

First, remove the metal housing by taking out the small set screw, located either at the top or the bottom of the unit. With the inner works exposed, carefully dust everything with a soft brush (a camera lens brush is good), paying particular attention to two metal strips installed in parallel. The one strip with the free end expands and contracts according to the temperature and contains the electric contacts that make or break the electric circuit to the heating unit.

These strips must be free of dust and clean to do their job. If necessary, *lightly* wipe the strips with a soft cloth to remove any stubborn dust. It is not a good idea to vacuum a thermostat, because the force of the suction may harm the works. It doesn't hurt, however, to hold the vacuum nearby, to pick up the particles dislodged by the brush.

The thermometer in the housing is not connected to the thermostat in any way. All it does is tell you the temperature at that wall position.

FURNACE The first thing to do is clear the area around the furnace. Vacuum the furnace's sides with a brush attachment. Vacuum all the connecting pipes, the pipe hangers, the valves, and the deck around it. If the dust sticks to the surface, wipe it clean.

With everything cleaned up, take time to acquaint yourself with the following:

1. Locate the manual fuel shutoff valve. This will be found (on gas-fired units) on the black supply pipe leading into the furnace. The handle will be in line (open) with the direction of the pipe. If there is ever any cause to suspect escaping gas (natural gas is odorless, but a chemical is added in order to make it detectable), simply turn the handle until it is at a right angle to the pipe, cutting off the supply. The gas utility servicemen can then be called to investigate.

2. Facing the furnace, examine all the tubes leading to the burner area at the base. Using a small, adjustable wrench, tighten all the nuts that couple the tubes to the furnace itself (these will be the pilot line, thermocouple, and vent tube), assuring that they are not loose. Bad fittings will cause detectable gas leaks and allow sediment to partially clog the tube's opening, impairing operation.

3. Find the red push button. Then read the lighting instructions. Familiarize yourself with the pilot and the "off" and "on" positions of the main gas valve.

4. Turn the furnace on to observe the flame pattern. (The thermostat setting might have to be raised.) All ribbon burners should have the same flame height and the same inner cone height. Gas flames should not contact the metal heat exchange areas. Any rust or debris on the burners should be vacuumed off.

5. Clean and examine all electric motors (motors for blowers or for line circulating pumps). Find the oil cups (little spring-loaded caps cover them) and apply the motor manufacturer's recommended amount of No. 10 oil in each. This is an extremely important maintenance step.

6. Examine the vent that goes from the furnace to the chimney. This should be sound, both where it rests on top of the furnace and where it goes into the chimney — with no breaks, tears, or spaces.

WATER HEATER The same general maintenance approach can be taken with the water heater. Tubing fittings must be firm; all surfaces should be free of dust buildup; the air shutter should be adjusted for the best flame, as described above; the vent connector should be secure; and sludge should be drained, as needed.

VARIOUS SUPPLEMENTARY HEATING APPROACHES Many houses have one or two rooms that have always been hard to heat. The central heating system that can evenly heat every single corner is rare indeed. Houses where a room has been added or a porch enclosed may need heat. Now there are two ways to approach these problems. Usually the addition of supplementary heat was the only consideration. With rising fuel costs, the best economic choice may be to reduce the heat loss rather than add supplementary heat. Insulating the ceiling, caulking, and adding storm windows and storm doors all help shrink the heat loss. The energy-saving approach must be considered carefully and thoughtfully, because of the rapidly rising cost of energy. Reducing energy needs now will pay off during the years the heating equipment is used. Reducing room heat losses could help balance heat distribution systems.

There are many situations where supplementary heat is the most reasonable solution. Sporadic or intermittent usage would be the best applications. For any heating jobs, be sure to contact a number of both heating and insulation contractors. You may be able to use the best ideas from each. There are many possible approaches to solving heating problems; a compromise that provides good heating and low energy cost is the goal.

The wide variety of auxiliary heating units

makes it imperative that the potential buyer first know just what they are and how they're used. Some are portable, but some require installation. In some instances, outside help may be necessary for installation. Floor or wall space available must be considered, as well as the decorative scheme of the room. Some units burn fuel; others use electricity.

Although electrical units are frequently the easiest to install, requiring no supply pipes that can be difficult to run in a finished house, they do use the most costly fuel. The cheaper installation, say opposed to adding another loop to your hot water system, should be weighed against the long-term fuel costs.

Built-in electric heaters come in many shapes and sizes, with and without fans, timers, and other refinements. Individual units are often thermostatically controlled, or a series of units installed in a room may be controlled by one thermostat. Some heaters include a light for dual-purpose installations and many have a fan for better distribution of warmed air. There are types that recess between wall studs; others are surface mounted. Some, which require no floor space, have add-on features for continuous baseboard installations.

Clean heat is available wherever electrical wiring can be run. In older houses, electrical units may be installed on existing walls or built in as part of a remodeling job. In a newly built wing, they might be used to augment an overloaded central system. In existing houses, they can be strategically located to provide that extra heat needed to dispel morning chill or to warm the newly finished basement.

Built-in units are generally designed for quick and simple installation. While wiring is within the range of some electrically minded handymen, some local codes prohibit them from doing it. Most manufacturers recommend installation by a professional electrician, regardless of the code requirements. Special wiring may be needed if the unit uses a 220-volt line.

A console heater (also known as a circulator heater) is the successor to the old coal- or wood-burning stove. It is automatic and engineered to circulate as well as radiate heat. In oil-fired units, kerosene or No. 1 fuel oil can be piped from an outside storage tank or fed from one at the back of the unit. Installation is quite simple. The manufacturer's instructions cover the critical part of the job—provision of proper venting to insure complete combustion, correct operation of the controls, and safe removal of combustion products.

Similar to the oil-fired models but often preferred in areas where clean-burning natural or LP gas is available, vented gas room heaters are manufactured in many sizes and styles. Fully automatic and available with optional blower features, their prices vary. Installation is more likely to require professional help, at least for the gas line connection, which calls for an experienced pipe fitter. Certain rules on venting and clearance to combustible material must be followed to insure safety as well as compliance with warranty provisions. Ignoring the rules is dangerous. Failure to remove all the products of combustion is hazardous to the occupants.

Frequently thought of as a primary heat source, a floor furnace can provide excellent supplementary heat, though its use is limited to rooms over basements or crawl spaces because of the depth of the unit. Its chief advantage lies in the fact that it is space saving, and it has a relatively low initial cost. Installation is quite simple, requiring an opening in the floor and framing to support the unit. By doing this part himself, the homeowner saves a substantial part of the installation cost. Automatic temperature controls and electric ignition are some useful accessories. Other units, floor furnaces in every sense, require baseboard space. They're especially useful in hall or partition locations, for they can be installed to provide heat at baseboard level to two rooms.

Recessed wall heaters also possess space-saving advantages over the typical space heater and are the most popular type of supplementary heating device. Versatile and comparatively easy to install, they fit standard 16" stud spacing and project only a little into the room. Gas of one type or another is the fuel used. Most units can be converted by the dealer from one to the other, should this become necessary.

Even on vented gas heaters, the installation procedure is not too complicated, thanks to prefabricated wall vents especially developed to remove combustion products safely.

Venting and running of gas lines must comply with local codes and are jobs for the experienced gas-heating man. Framing for the heater and the finish work may be done by the family handyman. Check with your dealer first.

HOW TO INSTALL A HUMIDIFIER

Adding moisture to heated air in the winter protects furniture from coming unglued and also reduces static electricity shocks. However, humidification requires significant amounts of energy. Each pound of water needs over 1,000 Btu's to change into water vapor, and moisture can only be added to air as water vapor.

It is difficult to maintain adequate humidity levels. Since most homes average about one air change per hour, the indoor and outdoor air are

INSTALLING A HUMIDIFIER

1. Furnace plenum showing opening where old humidifier was removed.

2. Plenum stiffener plate installed over larger opening with screws.

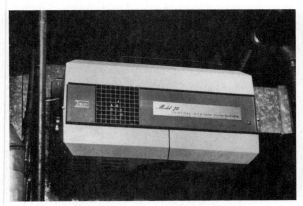

3. New humidifier is hung on stiffener plate.

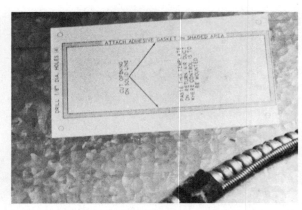

4. Paper template for humidistat is pasted on return air duct.

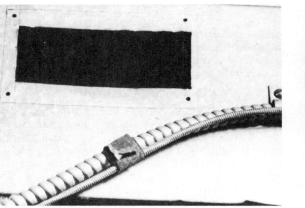

5. Opening for humidistat is cut, using snips and small saw.

6. Foam strips act as gasket at edge of plenum hole.

7. *Remove cover of humidistat. Fasten with screws over the hole.*

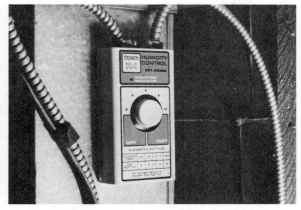

8. *Humidistat cover replaced. Left wire goes to humidifier, right to power.*

9. *Old water supply valve eliminates need for saddle valve installation.*

10. *Water supply tube goes over top of humidifier to reservoir valve.*

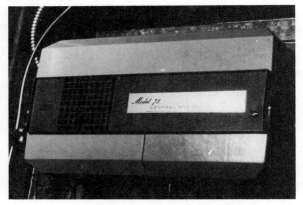

11. *Finished installation showing water tubing and wire from humidistat.*

constantly being exchanged. During the winter, cold outside air can hold little water vapor. The air flowing through the house picks up the moisture and takes it outside. This is why air in houses tends to be drier in cold weather. Evaporation of water is an energy-consuming process, and it tends to decrease room temperature unless heat is added through increased energy consumption in the heating system.

TYPES OF HUMIDIFIERS How to add moisture depends on the kind of heating system you have. In warm air heating systems, you can easily attach a humidifier to the cold air return duct or the plenum, the sheet metal box on top of the furnace from which all the ducts branch out. Follow the manufacturer's installation instructions.

The atomizers feed a fine spray or mist through a tiny nozzle or by means of a whirling metal disk or moving belt into the warm air plenum or cold air return duct. This moisture is then distributed throughout the house by the warm air ducts. However, water hardness is often a problem with these units because they can become clogged with lime scale and require frequent attention if your water is not softened.

The evaporative type may have fiberglass wicks or a spongelike pad that evaporates water into the warm airstream. The most efficient and popular variant of the evaporative type has a revolving drum covered with a spongy plastic material. Driven by a small electric motor, the drum dips into a small water reservoir, which receives its supply from a $1/4''$ copper tube connected to the nearest cold water pipe. The level in the reservoir is kept constant by a float valve. The moisture picked up by the slowly turning drum evaporates from its spongy cover in the moving air that passes through the humidifier.

If your home is heated by steam, electricity, or hot water, there are humidifiers that are not attached to the heating system. These look like wood cabinets with a fine furniture finish and can be used in your living or dining room without looking conspicuous. They have reservoirs to be filled every day or can be connected to a water supply. Usually they are operated by an electric motor and may spin off a very fine mist, or they may have a fan that blows air against a revolving belt or drum that dips into a reservoir.

Humidifiers are sized according to their water output. An average house of seven to eight rooms, with about 16,000 cubic feet of space, needs a unit that provides approximately $1/2$ gallon per hour to maintain a relative humidity of about 35 percent at 72°F. (Relative humidity is the percentage of moisture in the air at a certain temperature compared with the total amount the air can absorb at the same temperature.) A larger house, with ten to fourteen rooms and a 30,000 cubic foot area, would require a unit with an output of 1 gallon per hour.

A typical installation can be handled in three separate phases. The first is the attachment of the humidifier, a big plastic box, to the plenum. Also included in this first step is the attachment of a small humidistat to the cool air return duct. (A humidistat regulates the amount of moisture added to the warm air by sensing the relative humidity in the air just before it is distributed by ducts to the various rooms of the house.)

The second step is adding the electrical wiring, and third is connecting the water supply to the humidifier. After shutting off the furnace, cut a rectangular opening in the plenum, which is covered with a steel plate called a plenum stiffener, supplied with the humidifier. The humidifier will then hang from this plate. Following the manufacturer's instructions, use a pair of aviation snips and a small metal-cutting saw to cut the openings, using the plate as a template. A paper template may be provided instead. The wiring is very simple, but if you are not familiar with this type of work, do not handle it.

A typical water-pipe connection uses a saddle valve, which consists of a clamp that can be attached to the nearest cold water line, a small brass valve with its own shutoff handle, and a connection for the copper tubing. To tap the water pipe, the water supply must be shut off and a small hole drilled into the pipe, unless a self-piercing valve is supplied. A rubber washer between the pipe and the valve prevents leaks when the clamps are tightened around the pipe.

Next, the copper tubing is inserted into the brass valve compression nut and then the nut is tightened to hold the end of the tube in place. The other end of the tubing is inserted into the humidifier's float valve and fastened with a nylon compression nut turned by hand only. (The float valve regulates the level of water in the reservoir.)

Now the water supply may be turned on and the saddle valve opened to allow the reservoir to fill. The humidifier's switch is turned to "on," a drum with a cover of foam plastic turns in the reservoir, and the small blower forces moist air into the plenum via a round opening in its stiffener.

HOW TO CURE TOO MUCH MOISTURE

The problem of excessive moisture in the home is more complicated than that of not enough, and the methods of solving it are more varied. Too much moisture in this case means excessive water vapor in the air, which appears as condensation. Other signs include rust on tools and iron and steel objects; heavy, unpleasant odors in confined places; and mildew on clothing, upholstery, drapes, and painted surfaces. The cure is usually ventilation, insulation, heat, or a combination of these.

CONDENSATION The surest sign that you have too much moisture in the house in winter is condensation on the windows. If there is a great deal of condensation on the windows so that they really drip, you can be pretty sure that the relative humidity in your home is well over 40 percent.

If you have gas heating equipment, the sudden appearance of condensation on windows might indicate the venting system is plugged. Warm air coming out of the draft hood is also an indication. Call your serviceman immediately.

Don't be panicked by a sudden cold snap: When outside temperatures drop more than 20°F from the day before, the windows will be colder and more moisture will condense under those conditions.

If you have storm windows and the condensation is on the house window, you can be certain that your storm windows are not working, the most likely cause being that the storm windows are too loose. On a windy day enough wind gets past the cracks around a storm window to move the air in the dead air space between the storm and house windows. When this happens you lose the insulating value of the dead air space because the air is no longer "dead." You can easily fix this by caulking around the storm window and tightening the screws that hold it in place.

If you do not open the windows during the winter, seal the cracks around the sash with a rope-type caulking that will not harden and can easily be removed in the spring. If you would like to keep them movable, put additional weatherstripping around the sash.

KITCHEN MOISTURE It may surprise you, but kitchens, or rather the cooking and washing of dishes that goes on there, are a great source of moisture in a home. The steam and water vapor that rise from pots on the range and from a sink full of dishes in hot water are enough to put 2 pounds of water into the air of a house in the form of vapor.

Close the kitchen door and open the window over the sink a bit to allow the steam and vapor to escape. Better yet, turn on your kitchen exhaust fan while the cooking and dishwashing go on. An exhaust fan will suck out not only cooking odors but also the water vapor that arises from the cooking pots on the range.

LAUNDRY AND BATHROOMS Very few bathrooms have exhaust fans, yet this room also generates a great deal of moisture, which could be handled most easily by a fan.

The utility room used as a laundry is another place that raises the level of humidity in the home. A washing machine gives off 2 or more pounds of water vapor per load, and a dryer adds another 1½ pounds. The best solution to this problem is to vent the dryer to the outside and to install an exhaust fan near the washing machine.

THE DAMP CLOSET If the closet has an outside wall, see if it is colder than the others. If it is, the trouble may be caused by lack of sufficient insulation behind this wall. In that case, warm, moist air in the house may be condensing its moisture on the cold wall. The remedy here is to insulate the back wall.

If you don't have a cold wall, ventilation may be the simplest cure. To test this, leave the door of the closet open for several days. If this seems to help, install a louvered door, which will permit air to circulate in and out of the closet.

MOISTURE IN BASEMENTS Most basements are hard to keep dry. Sometimes the trouble is caused by soil moisture that infiltrates the concrete or cement block basement walls under hydrostatic pressure and then stays in the air as water vapor. The cause may also be an outright leak at the point where the wall meets the floor, or it may seep through weak mortar joints between the cement blocks. In such cases you may not necessarily have big pools of water on the floor, but a slow seepage that becomes water vapor and makes the basement damp.

The best way to cope with this problem is to dig out weak or crumbling mortar wherever leaks occur, using a cold chisel and hammer. Then plug the openings with hydraulic cement and follow this with a layer of waterproof cement over all the walls.

In winter a gas or electric heater may do a good job of keeping the basement warm and dry, provided that there is no moisture leaking through the walls. Insulating the basement walls and running a heater will give you maximum protection against excess moisture.

The safest and best way to insulate basement walls is to erect a stud wall of 2 × 4s (or 2 × 3s). Treat the studs with a waterproof solution, install insulation batts between them, cover with polyethylene plastic sheeting (stapling the plastic to the studs), and nail plasterboard to the studs.

In summer, even if you have waterproofed your walls and there are no leaks, you may still find the basement damp. This can be caused by warm, moist air condensing on the cool basement walls if they have not been insulated.

Since it is very difficult to ventilate a basement enough to reduce moisture significantly, use an electric dehumidifier after first closing all basement windows and doors. Be sure to empty daily the accumulated condensation gathered by the dehumidifier.

BASEMENT CRAWL SPACES Crawl spaces underneath a house with an earth floor are a source of humidity in a house. The water in the soil forms into water vapor that migrates through the joists and floors into the house. The cure here is to cover the earth with 55-pound roll roofing overlapped at least 3″, or use 4-mil (.004″) polyethylene sheeting. Hold the polyethylene or roll roofing down with bricks or stones. In addition, the crawl space should be properly ventilated. Also, to allow moisture to escape, instead of condensing on the under-flooring above, foundation ventilators or masonry ventilators must be installed. Basementless crawl spaces should have a net free ventilated area of 1/150 of the ground area, except when the ground surface is covered with a vapor barrier. If a vapor barrier is used, the ratio can be reduced to 1/1500.

HOW TO SELECT AND INSTALL PROPER VENTING

ATTIC VENTS If you have a leak in the roof or if you have ice dams building up in your gutters, you will get moisture and dampness in the attic. Obviously, you have to eliminate roof leaks; you can reduce ice damming with proper ventilation.

But you don't have to have leaks to have an attic that is damp and smelly. Most attics have louvered vents at both ends, but they are often too small to provide really adequate ventilation. Moist air penetrates the attic through its vents and water vapor moves through its wooden walls and comes up through its floor from below. Getting rid of this moisture requires providing enough ventilation.

You can make the vent openings at each end of the attic larger and cover them with larger aluminum louvers. If you have no vapor barrier under the attic floor, you should have 1 square foot of inlet and 1 square foot of outlet opening for every 300 square feet of attic ceiling. If there is a vapor barrier under the floor, the same vent area will suffice for every 600 square feet (see page 18).

Other ways of venting the attic include eave, roof, ridge, and cupola vents. Eave vents are simply openings cut into the overhang on opposite sides of the roof, with a metal cover that is placed over the hole.

A ridge vent is a metal cover above holes in the roof on both sides of the ridge. The cover prevents rain or snow from entering but is raised enough above the holes to allow air to escape. Finally, a cupola, which is a small square tower with a copper or zinc roof and wooden louvers on all four sides, can be placed over holes on both sides of the ridge in the center of the roof.

ATTIC FANS On a hot summer day, attic temperatures may easily run as high as 130°F or more. With normal insulation, upstairs bedrooms would register around 100°F, with the downstairs at 90°F. Walls and ceilings absorb the heat, with the result

ATTIC VENT REQUIREMENTS

The total net free area of venting needed is shown in square inches where length and width figures intersect. Charts courtesy FHA and Home Ventilation Institute.

Width (in feet) (Requirements in Square Inches)

Length (in feet)	20	22	24	26	28	30	32	34	36	38	40	42	44	46	48	50
20	192	211	230	250	269	288	307	326	346	365	384	403	422	441	461	480
22	211	232	253	275	296	317	338	359	380	401	422	444	465	485	506	528
24	230	253	276	300	323	346	369	392	415	438	461	484	507	530	553	576
26	250	275	300	324	349	374	399	424	449	474	499	524	549	574	599	624
28	269	296	323	349	376	403	430	457	484	511	538	564	591	618	645	662
30	288	317	346	374	403	432	461	490	518	547	576	605	634	662	691	720
32	307	338	369	399	430	461	492	522	553	584	614	645	675	706	737	768
34	326	359	392	424	457	490	522	555	588	620	653	685	717	750	782	815
36	346	380	415	449	484	518	553	588	622	657	691	726	760	795	829	864
38	365	401	438	474	511	547	584	620	657	693	730	766	803	839	876	912
40	384	422	461	499	538	576	614	653	691	730	768	806	845	883	922	960
42	403	444	484	524	564	605	645	685	726	766	806	847	887	927	968	1008
44	422	465	507	549	591	634	676	718	760	803	845	887	929	971	1013	1056
46	442	486	530	574	618	662	707	751	795	839	883	927	972	1016	1060	1104
48	461	507	553	599	645	691	737	783	829	876	922	968	1014	1060	1106	1152
50	480	528	576	624	672	720	768	816	864	912	960	1008	1056	1104	1152	1200
52	499	549	599	649	699	749	799	848	898	948	998	1048	1098	1148	1198	1248
54	518	570	622	674	726	778	830	881	933	985	1037	1089	1141	1192	1244	1296
56	538	591	645	699	753	807	860	914	967	1021	1075	1130	1184	1237	1291	1345
58	557	612	668	724	780	835	891	946	1002	1058	1113	1170	1226	1282	1337	1392
60	576	634	691	749	807	864	922	979	1037	1094	1152	1210	1267	1324	1382	1440
62	595	655	714	774	834	893	953	1012	1071	1131	1190	1250	1309	1369	1428	1488
64	614	676	737	799	861	922	983	1045	1106	1168	1229	1291	1352	1413	1475	1536
66	634	697	760	824	888	950	1014	1077	1140	1204	1268	1331	1394	1458	1522	1585
68	653	718	783	849	914	979	1045	1110	1175	1240	1306	1371	1436	1501	1567	1632
70	672	739	806	874	941	1008	1075	1142	1210	1276	1344	1411	1478	1545	1613	1680

FHA Chart Chart utilizes 1/300 ratio; double for 1/150 ratio; divide by five for 1/1500 ratio.

An attractive cupola conceals a power ventilator to aid attic venting.

A louvered power vent is installed in the gable of the home and is thermostatically controlled.

POWER ATTIC VENT FAN REQUIREMENTS

Cubic feet per minute (cfm) rating needed for the fan is shown where attic length and width figures intersect in the chart.

	Width (in feet) (Requirements in fan cfm)															
	20	22	24	26	28	30	32	34	36	38	40	42	44	46	48	50
20	280	308	336	364	392	420	448	476	504	532	560	588	616	644	672	700
22	308	339	370	400	431	462	493	524	554	585	616	647	678	708	739	770
24	336	370	403	437	470	504	538	571	605	638	672	706	739	773	806	840
26	364	400	437	473	510	546	582	619	655	692	728	764	801	837	874	910
28	392	431	470	510	549	588	627	666	706	745	784	823	862	902	941	980
30	420	462	504	546	588	630	672	714	756	798	840	882	924	966	1008	1050
32	448	493	538	582	627	672	717	761	806	851	896	941	986	1030	1075	1120
34	476	524	571	619	666	714	762	809	857	904	952	1000	1047	1095	1142	1190
36	504	554	604	655	706	756	806	857	907	958	1008	1058	1109	1159	1210	1260
38	532	585	638	692	745	798	851	904	958	1011	1064	1117	1170	1224	1277	1330
40	560	616	672	728	784	840	896	952	1008	1064	1120	1176	1232	1288	1344	1400
42	588	647	706	764	823	882	941	1000	1058	1117	1176	1234	1294	1352	1411	1470
44	616	678	739	801	862	924	986	1047	1109	1170	1232	1294	1355	1417	1478	1540
46	644	708	773	837	902	966	1030	1095	1159	1224	1288	1352	1417	1481	1546	1610
48	672	739	806	874	941	1008	1075	1142	1210	1277	1344	1411	1478	1546	1613	1680
50	700	770	840	910	980	1050	1120	1190	1260	1330	1400	1470	1540	1610	1680	1750
52	728	801	874	946	1019	1092	1165	1238	1310	1383	1456	1529	1602	1674	1747	1820
54	756	832	907	983	1058	1134	1210	1285	1361	1436	1512	1588	1663	1739	1814	1890
56	784	862	941	1019	1098	1176	1254	1333	1411	1490	1568	1646	1725	1803	1882	1960
58	812	893	974	1056	1137	1218	1299	1380	1462	1543	1624	1705	1786	1868	1949	2030
60	840	924	1008	1092	1176	1260	1344	1428	1512	1596	1680	1764	1848	1932	2016	2100
62	868	955	1042	1128	1215	1302	1389	1476	1562	1649	1736	1823	1910	1996	2083	2170
64	896	986	1075	1165	1254	1344	1434	1523	1613	1702	1792	1882	1971	2061	2150	2240
66	924	1016	1108	1201	1294	1386	1478	1571	1663	1756	1848	1940	2033	2125	2218	2310
68	952	1047	1142	1238	1333	1428	1523	1618	1714	1809	1904	1999	2094	2190	2285	2380
70	980	1078	1176	1274	1372	1470	1568	1666	1764	1862	1960	2058	2156	2254	2352	2450

Length (in feet)

HVI Chart   Chart based on factor of 0.7 cfm air per square foot. Add 15% for dark roofs.

Power roof vent eliminates the need for multiple vents.

Power fan mounts in attic behind wooden louvers, to increase venting capacity.

that even though outside nighttime temperatures drop considerably, indoor temperatures remain uncomfortably high. Not until the early morning hours will the house become comfortable.

A fan installed in the attic lowers the 130°F attic temperature about 30°F, resulting in considerable cooling. An attic fan also provides a constant flow of fresh air. It is well worth its small initial installation and operating costs.

To tell exactly how much ventilation is needed for your house with either the natural or power system, it is necessary to determine the square feet of your attic floor and relate that to the "free area" of the ventilation system you have selected. The free area is the approximate clear or free opening of the ventilator through which air may move. The net free area of the ventilators required for a house employing a natural system of ventilation is normally related to the amount of attic floor space.

ATTICS AND STRUCTURAL SPACES The space ventilated should have a net free ventilated area of 1/150. This means that for each 150 square feet of attic floor space, 1 square foot of free area is required. If certain conditions prevail, this ratio can be reduced to 1/300, or 1 square foot of free area to every 300 square feet of attic floor space. These conditions include: (a) a vapor barrier, such as a polyethylene sheet or insulation batts, with a low moisture transmission rate, installed on the warm side of the ceiling; and (b) at least 50 percent of the required ventilating area provided by ventilators located in the upper portion of the space to be ventilated (at least 3' above the undereaves vents),

with the remainder of the required ventilation provided by undereaves vents.

Structural spaces should include porch roofs, canopies, and any enclosed structural space where condensation may occur. All such areas should be cross-ventilated. Openings should be screened and protected from the entrance of rain and snow.

To find the exact free area needed to ventilate your home properly, find the length of the area to be ventilated in the vertical column of the FHA chart and the width of the area in the horizontal column. The total net free area required, expressed in square inches, is shown where these two columns intersect. (The chart utilizes a 1/300 ratio; double it for a 1/150 ratio.)

For example, suppose the total area to be ventilated is 1,200 square feet, such as in a house 30' × 40'. By looking at the chart, the net free area needed is 576 square inches. If roof or gable end and undereaves vents are used, 50 percent of the 576 square inches, or 288 square inches are required for the roof or gable end vents, and the same amount would be required for the undereaves. This is equivalent to a 1/300 ratio.

If undereaves vents are not used, the above total free area requirement must be doubled. This is equivalent to a 1/150 ratio. Even if your attic area is presently vented, it should be carefully checked to determine whether or not the present vent arrangement is adequate to provide proper ventilation.

PROPER SIZE POWER VENTILATOR The Home Ventilating Institute (HVI), a recognized control agency, certifies air delivery of power attic space ventilators in cubic feet per minute (CFM). HVI standards recommend 10 air changes per hour or a minimum of 0.7 cfm per square foot of attic floor space, plus 15 percent for dark roofs (which absorb more heat).

To determine what size power ventilator is needed to cool your attic efficiently, find the length of

INSTALLING A KITCHEN OR BATH VENT

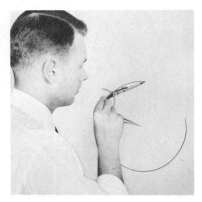

Locate fan in a wall space without obstructions and between studs. Draw circle ⅛" larger than sleeve diameter, at least 1" from either stud.

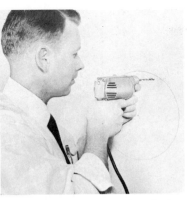

For plasterboard, plywood, and other sawable interiors, drill a series of holes within the circle for a saw starting point. For plaster walls, drill along the circle.

Saw the opening. If the wall is plaster, use ax, chisel, or hammer to break away the plaster. Work a small section at a time to avoid cracking the plaster.

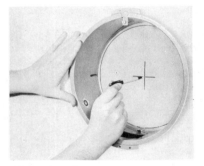

When sheathing is accessible, draw a circle slightly smaller than the inside sleeve on a piece of cardboard. Center the cardboard and mark the center point on sheathing.

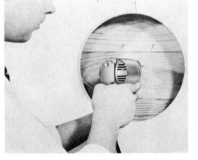

Place a small drill upon the center point marked, and drill a hole straight through sheathing and exterior siding. If exterior is stone or stucco, use masonry drill.

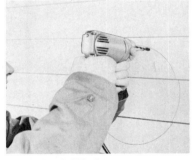

Using the drill hole as a center point, scribe a circle on the exterior siding ¼" larger than the outside sleeve diameter. Then cut along the circle with a saber saw.

Saw the opening. If the exterior is brick or stone, use a hammer and chisel to break away the siding. With rough wiring in, you are now ready to install fan.

Depending on the wall thickness, remove as many sleeve knockouts from the outside sleeve as needed to make room for the outlet box. Be sure current is off!

First assemble the pull chain to the chain on the door. Then take door assembly outside and carefully mount it into the opening on the outside wall.

Here is how the assembly will look at this stage from inside the kitchen. Note how just enough insulation has been removed to make sheathing accessible.

Temporarily slide inside sleeve into place as a way of checking alignment with outer sleeve. With level, make sure outer door is plumb. Tighten corner screws.

Insert inside sleeve, pushing it tight against the outer wall. Bring the cable through the outlet box opening. Tighten screws through openings in the sleeve.

From left to right: The cable is now inserted through the cable clamp and the threaded end of the clamp is inserted through a knockout hole in the outlet box. This is an electrician's job. Next, when outlet is wired, it is inserted into opening in inside

sleeve. Switch-plate receptacle is fastened down with two screws. Thread chain through guide. Now, mount fan-motor assembly by setting the feet of motor-mount bar into slots. Slide to exact vertical position and tighten screws. Screw on cover.

Pull chain to start fan. When you release chain on fan, the door opens automatically and the fan starts. To turn off, pull the chain tight across the catch. Door closes and fan stops.

---

the area to be ventilated in the vertical column of the HVI chart and the width of the area in the horizontal column. The total cfm required is shown where these two columns intersect. For example, in the 30' × 40' house, the power vent unit should be capable of at least 840 cfm.

KITCHEN AND BATH The easiest way to eliminate excessive moisture and heat in the kitchen and bathroom is by using ventilating fans, usually installed in either wall or ceiling. Kitchen fans should be as close as possible to the range, where most of the heat is generated. After selection of the fan, installation takes only a few hours. Before installing the fan, have electrical wiring brought to the point of the opening. Once this is done, follow the photos shown.

CONDENSATION CHECKLIST *In the attic,* water or ice may collect in cold parts of uninsulated,

unventilated areas. Cold metal surfaces (such as vent pipes) may have ice form on them. Icicles will also form on protruding nails in a roof. Install adequate-sized louvers and power attic ventilators.

In the bathroom, make sure you leave the window or door partly open after taking a bath or shower. Ordinary washing, bathing, and such may add several pounds of moisture each day to the air in your house.

In the plumbing, you may find a source of trouble more difficult to locate and control. A leak may form lime salts, which ruin interior wall paint. Also, water from the wet wall may find its way outward and cause exterior paint to blister and peel. Check for any leaks.

In the kitchen, the high humidity from cooking and washing may find its way through exterior walls to ruin exterior paint. Excess moisture in kitchens may be controlled by installing an exhaust fan or vented range hood.

Around the chimney and vents, check for flashing leaks. Damaged brickwork may also allow water to enter the house from the outside. A periodic inspection of this area is a wise precaution.

On the roof, shingles and roofing must be kept in good repair at all times. Shingles should overlap generously or else they will be weak.

At gutters and downspouts, check for clogging by leaves. You will find peeling paint under eaves and around windows frosted on the inside. A poorly drained (or blocked) waterspout will also cause wall dampness and mean costly repair bills.

Near the windows you may find paint failure, too. Rain draining downward behind a poorly flashed window frame will cause damage to paint. Caulk window frames; make sure they fit well. Seal butt ends of siding with paint. Install good flashings at tops of windows.

At the siding, blistering and staining may set in. Do not permit studs or siding to touch the ground. Siding joints must be tight.

On the porch, you may prevent peeling and cracking paint above and below a concrete floor by filling space between slab and siding with caulking compound—and also by painting butt ends of studs and siding.

HOW TO INSTALL CENTRAL AIR CONDITIONING

Most frequently, room air conditioners are installed in a window. There are types to fit every common kind of window—double-hung, casement, sliding sash—by means of special hardware. Many, if not most of these models, are plug-in types that operate on normal house current.

Central air conditioning systems are available in several types. If your house has an existing warm air heating system with ducts of the proper size, it is possible to get a unit that will attach right to the plenum of the warm air furnace and, through them, supply refrigerated air to the entire house. If your house is equipped with another type of heating system, it becomes more difficult and expensive to cool.

In the case of a home with a hot water heating system, for instance, the installation of a central air conditioner means that ducts to carry the cold air must be installed throughout. Often, they must go into the walls, which must be opened, an expensive and time-consuming process.

It is sometimes easier and more economical to air condition a two-story house with two separate machines—one of which is placed in the attic, from where ducts run to the ceilings of the upstairs rooms. The second unit would be placed in the basement, with ducts running up to the first-floor rooms. In this way, most of the installation problems are relieved, but you trade this off against a larger investment in machinery, plus additional wiring that may be required to feed the extra machine.

One major drawback of large air conditioners is the noise they make when running. In central systems, this has been largely overcome by breaking the cooling mechanism into two units. The compressor, driven by a large electric motor, is the noisiest part. It is placed out of doors adjacent to the house. From here pipes run into the cooling unit inside the house. It is this device that does the actual work of cooling as household air is blown across it by a fan.

It is best to have an air-conditioning dealer survey your home to recommend the cooling capacity you'll need. The many factors involved here make it uncertain when done by the homeowner. Each element of the house and its surroundings enters into the calculations. Size, orientation, number of windows and doors, type and thickness of insulation, and so on all are factors in deciding what capacity is needed.

Installing an air conditioner, whether for a single room or for the whole house, requires first that a sufficient supply of electric power is available without overloading the service entrance wiring, or the house wiring itself. This is best determined by a licensed electrician or your local utility company, some of which provide service of this nature.

Central air conditioning may be a luxury that you've thought you couldn't afford. But new do-it-yourself units on the market are changing that picture fast. Now, by buying such a package, and adding a day of your labor, you can have the cool comfort of central air at a pleasantly surprising price.

What does it cost? Depending on the size of your home and where you live, expect to spend between $500 and $650 for the basic unit. Then expect to save between $200 and $300 by installing it yourself. Installation time varies from a few minutes in the case of window units to one day for do-it-yourself central air conditioning units.

Companies that market special central air packages for cost-conscious homeowners offer packages complete with well-organized instructions and backup technicians in case you run into problems. Installation is not difficult. And contrary to what you may have believed in the past, you don't need to be a sheet-metal worker or electrician to do most of the job yourself.

If you follow directions carefully, the only steps it will pay for you to "hire out" include connection

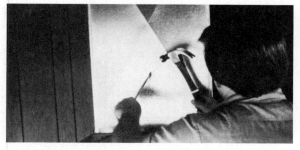

1. *Make starter hole in plenum by driving a screwdriver through the metal.*

2. *Use tin snips or saber saw to cut inspection hole in the plenum.*

3. *Insert a trouble light inside the chamber and measure the height of the duct flanges inside the plenum.*

4. *Score two sets of lines on the plenum, using a level to square the opening. One set of lines should be the size of the coil cover, the other ½" smaller.*

5. *Place the coil cover on the lines, then mark and drill holes that hold bolts to secure cover.*

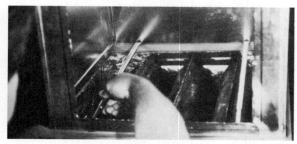

6. *Use snips or a saber saw to cut the square opening (inside lines) in the plenum. Install the adjustable coil rods over the duct flanges. These will support the coil.*

7. *Measure and cut cooling coil baffles to the proper size.*

8. *Install the baffles around the edges of the plenum where the cooling coil will rest. These baffles direct air through the coil.*

9. *Place sealing compound around the edges of the plenum and on edges of the baffles where cooling coil will rest.*

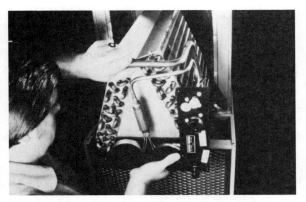

10. *Carefully position the coil so tubing connections are opposite the holes left for them in the coil cover.*

11. *Screw the coil cover in place and connect the precharged tubing to the coil.*

12. *Drain line is installed, routed to nearest floor drain, to drain condensate from the coil.*

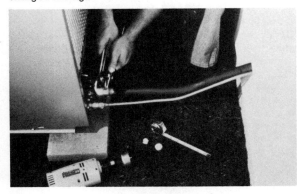

13. *Condensing unit, placed outside the house, is connected to the precharged tubing.*

14. *Complete operation, done in less than a day, can save you from $200 to $300 in labor.*

of the thermostat and hookup from the fuse box to the outdoor condensing unit. A professional electrician can handle both jobs easily and quickly.

Here's what goes into a typical system:

1. *Condensing unit* with a built-in disconnect switch that eliminates the need for a special outdoor electrical box.

2. *Cooling coil,* which fits into the plenum of upflow furnaces. It's designed for compact size and ease of installation.

3. *Preinsulated refrigerant tubing kit,* which includes two lengths of sealed precharged copper tubing and quick-connect couplings. Tubing is extra-heavy to withstand outdoor exposure.

4. *Cooling coil installation kit,* which includes sealing compound, plenum cover, adjustable coil support rods, and air baffles.

5. *Accessory kit,* which includes heat/cool thermostat, leveling legs for condensing unit, and transformer-fan relay assembly.

6. *Installation manuals,* which should be followed carefully.

COOLING NEEDS   First, find the square footage of your home to be air conditioned. Total square feet is multiplied by a temperature zone factor. Next, you measure your furnace plenum, blower diameter, width of wheel, the furnace motor horsepower, and the size and number of branch ducts. All these figures combine to give the size condenser and cooling unit you'll need for maximum cooling.

Many buyers fall into the trap of asking for a unit that's oversized for the house and furnace blower capacity. Bigger, in this case, is not necessarily better. Larger units don't cycle often enough to dehumidify your house effectively. Size the system so that it operates long enough to do a good job of dehumidifying.

The final step before buying is to measure the distance from your furnace to the spot where the condensing unit will be located outside your house. This is to determine the length of pre-charged copper tubing needed to connect the condensing unit and the cooling coil. The condensing unit should be located as close as possible to the furnace, facing away from the house. Distance should not exceed 40 feet.

With these figures in hand, you're ready to contact your dealer, who will specify the correct unit for your home. From there on, you follow step-by-step installation (see photos, pages 64–65) up to connecting the 220-volt electrical hookup. Hiring an electrician for this job will help you make sure local codes are met.

Little maintenance is required to operate the units once they're installed. And they don't have to be removed during the heating season. A thermostat with a heat and cool setting will operate your air conditioner and furnace, but not at the same time. Properly installed, the system will not require recharging or additional refrigerant. If the unit loses refrigerant through a leak in the system, a refrigeration technician can be called to repair the leak and replace the lost refrigerant.

HOW TO MAINTAIN YOUR AIR CONDITIONER

As with furnaces, air conditioners (both central and room varieties) will require a certain amount of maintenance to keep operating efficiently. Of course, proper insulation, caulking, and weatherstripping throughout the house enhance the cooling effect and keep operating costs to the minimum. There are a number of other points that should be attended to.

Keep the filter clean. A dirt-clogged filter can slow down cooling seriously by blocking warm air flow to the cooling apparatus.

Know the type of filter you have before you do any cleaning. (A call to your dealer or a check of the manufacturer's instruction sheet will tell you.) In general, aluminum mesh and plastic foam filters are washable—but aluminum mesh must be coated with a special filter oil for proper functioning. Fiberglass filters should be vacuumed. Fiber filters, common on older air conditioners, should be replaced.

Keep the working parts clean. Before the air conditioner season and at some time during the season, check the fan, motor, compressor, and cooling coils for dust, lint, and so on. If necessary, use a vacuum, being careful to avoid accidental damage. For easier access and a more thorough job, you can usually take the entire mechanism out of the case by removing the few screws that hold it to the air conditioner shell.

Make sure the machine is level. When an air conditioner is installed, a good workman will take great pains to make sure of this. But with time, it can settle out of level. Using a carpenter's level, check the unit from side to side and front to back. Shim it up with small strips of wood where needed. An air conditioner that is not level will interfere with the flow of coolant and not function properly.

Check sealing around the air conditioner. Make sure there are no air leaks around the inside or outside. If there are, cool air escapes and hot air enters. If you have openings inside, a simple way to plug them is with adhesive-backed plastic foam weatherstripping. Outside, use a flexible butyl caulking. Apply heavy beads as needed.

Ventilate the attic. If you've ever been in an uninsulated, unvented attic on a hot summer day, you know what a sauna feels like. Incredibly enough, the temperature in the attic can be 40°F higher than outside air. Ventilating an attic properly will cut air-conditioning costs.

Keep doors of air-conditioned rooms closed. If you don't, the cooled air dissipates into larger areas the air conditioner was not designed to cool.

Get rid of water vapor in bathrooms after showering and washing by opening windows or running an exhaust fan for a short time with the door closed. The same applies to the kitchen when cooking. Ultimately, the water vapor finds its way back to the air conditioners (which also dehumidify air), making them work harder.

HOW TO MAINTAIN YOUR FIREPLACES

The fireplace was once the core of the home. Almost all household activities revolved around it, particularly in winter. Massive, central fire columns, containing a living room fireplace, kitchen cooking fireplace, and Dutch ovens can still be found in some old colonial houses, buried underneath new layers of plaster, wallboard, or paneling.

Over a period of time, these fire columns became impractical and houses were built with smaller, individual chimneys. Until recently, when severe winters, higher fuel costs, and fuel shortages triggered a new interest in them, fireplaces had become an extra in new homes.

Now we've come full circle and fireplaces, both masonry and particularly prefabricated units, are becoming a sound, energy-saving investment. Although the average homeowner is not equipped to build a masonry fireplace, the installation of prefab units, available in an extensive variety of shapes, sizes, and styles, can often be handled without any problem.

Whether you're installing a new fireplace or maintaining an old chimney, certain principles of construction and fire draft remain the same.

HOW THEY WORK Hot air rises and, in the properly functioning fireplace, creates the upward draft that carries off smoke through the chimney. When the smoke backs up from the fireplace into your house, some obstruction is preventing the draft from rising all the way to the top of the chimney—or else something is happening to keep the draft from forming in the first place.

To eliminate persistent smokiness, first check the damper (if any) to make sure that it's open and that it stays open without falling shut. Next, place a small wad of newspaper in the damper opening and light it. If it burns readily and both the small flames and the smoke rise up the chimney, the flue is clear and the trouble lies with the fireplace construction itself. The following are a few of the most likely defects:

1. No damper at all.
2. No smoke chamber or one with unevenly sloping sides.
3. Damper at the back instead of the front.
4. Damper not all the way across the fireplace.
5. Fireplace opening too large for the flue size.
6. No smoke shelf.
7. Chimney top badly located or uncapped.

Start your checkup of the fireplace opening with a ruler. Measure the width, height, and depth and the flue. This will probably mean a trip to the roof. Fireplaces should be made to definitely related proportions as indicated in the fireplace dimension chart. (See next page.)

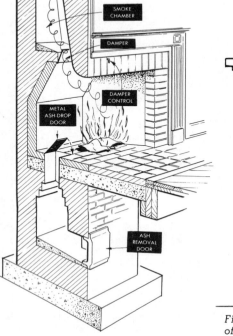

A properly functioning fireplace

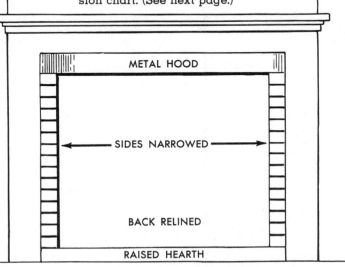

Fireplace dimensions may be adjusted by addition of a layer of brick over the hearth or by adding courses up the sides. (See next page.)

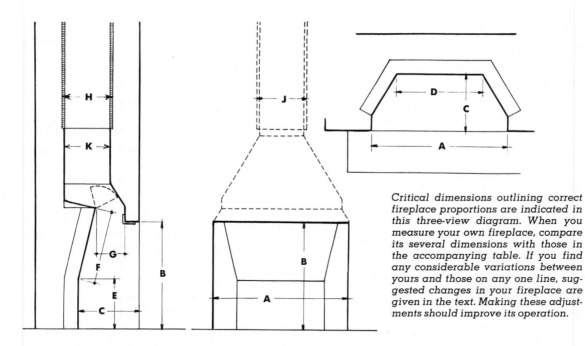

Critical dimensions outlining correct fireplace proportions are indicated in this three-view diagram. When you measure your own fireplace, compare its several dimensions with those in the accompanying table. If you find any considerable variations between yours and those on any one line, suggested changes in your fireplace are given in the text. Making these adjustments should improve its operation.

FIREPLACE DIMENSIONS IN INCHES

	Finished Fireplace Opening							Rough Brickwork		
A Width	B Height	C Depth	D Back	E Vertical Back Wall	F Sloped Back	G Throat		H J Standard Rectangular (outside diameter)		K Flue Lining Round (inside diameter)
26	24	16	13	14	14	$8^3/_4$		$8^1/_2 \times 8^1/_2$		10
28	28	16	15	14	18	$8^3/_4$		$8^1/_2 \times 13$		10
30	30	16	17	14	20	$8^3/_4$		$8^1/_2 \times 13$		10
32	28	16	19	14	20	$8^3/_4$		$8^1/_2 \times 13$		10
34	30	16	21	14	20	$8^3/_4$		$8^1/_2 \times 13$		12
36	30	16	23	14	20	$8^3/_4$		13 $\times 13$		12
40	30	16	27	14	20	$8^3/_4$		13 $\times 13$		12
42	30	16	29	14	20	$8^3/_4$		13 $\times 13$		12
48	33	18	33	14	23	$8^3/_4$		13 $\times 13$		15
54	36	20	37	14	26	13		13 $\times 18$		15
60	39	22	42	14	29	13		18 $\times 18$		18
72	40	22	54	14	30	13		18 $\times 18$		18

DIMENSION ADJUSTMENTS If you discover that the fireplace opening is out of proportion or too large for the flue size, correction is simple. Occasionally a fireplace will not draw, simply because its height is too great. You can check this by holding a board across the top of the face of the fireplace. Slide the board up and down the face a bit to see if this improves the draft. If it does, you can make or have installed a metal hood that will have the effect of permanently lowering the top to the point you found advisable.

Often a fireplace doesn't draw properly because its cubic capacity is too large for its flue; that is, the flue is too small to handle all the hot air flow-

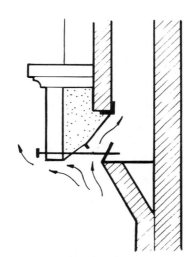

If a damper is placed too low in opening, a metal hood lowering the actual opening by several inches offsets the oversight and restores proper distance between opening and damper location. The hood is attached to fireplace front, the joint completely sealed.

Chimneys require careful maintenance for proper and safe functioning. Make certain there is no loose mortar between bricks. If there is, chip it out with an old screwdriver, wet the surface, and fill with mix (1 part portland cement, 2 parts screened sand, enough water to make mix stiff). Use asphalt roofing compound along flashing.

ing into it. In such cases, experiment with loose brick to decrease the cubic capacity. For example, a layer of firebrick or concrete on the floor of the fire chamber will reduce the vertical dimension, and if you find this eliminates the smoke nuisance, install it permanently. Firebrick may be laid with standard mortar, or a concrete mix may be poured in to the desired level. If the fireplace is too wide, vertical courses of firebrick may be mortared to the side walls of the fire chamber. Point the joints between these bricks with fire clay. A fire-clay mix reinforced with asbestos fibers holds even better. A depth too great (less likely but possible) can be corrected with a course of firebrick mortared to the back wall and on up the slanting wall. NOTE: Whenever adding new courses to old, the old surface must always be soaked first.

THE DAMPER As the sketch of a properly functioning fireplace indicates, the damper should be placed near the front of the fireplace and a smoke chamber above it. From the smoke chamber, the opening narrows abruptly to the flue, and a smoke shelf is usually located at the rear of the flue. This combination of angles and curves creates a good draft. The damper should extend all the way across the top of the fire chamber or smoke will curl out the corners and up toward the mantle. If the damper has been placed too low in the area above the fire chamber, it may be necessary to cover the top of the fireplace opening. Again, a metal hood that is secured to the masonry at each side and sealed across the top may be used.

Always make sure the damper is working properly. Sometimes it becomes loose so that, when you turn the controlling handle to "wide open," the damper door is still partially closed. Scrape away any soot that may have collected at the seat of the damper or on the damper itself and that is thereby narrowing the escape passage. Some dampers are removable. Take yours off if you can; it will make the cleaning job much easier.

THE CHIMNEY Your fireplace may be well designed and the flue properly proportioned, yet it may smoke, owing to the shape or location of the chimney. A chimney should extend at least 2' higher than the highest point on a pitched roof, 3' higher than a flat roof. Insufficient altitude, or trees and buildings in the area around the house, may cause a pileup of wind-driven air around the chimney top. This makes a high-pressure zone that tends to push air down the flue and force smoke back out through the fireplace. It can sometimes be remedied by removal of the tops of neighboring trees or, better still, by extending the chimney upward. You can also cap your chimney with brick and stone (see illustrations), or you can buy a ready-made metal chimney cap. These are available in several styles — a plain metal hood, a weathervane type that swings with the wind, or the rotating kind that contains a bladed turbine activated by the wind. All effectively halt downdraft.

Occasionally examine the exterior of your chimney for weathering of the brick and mortar, resulting in chinks. These can be spotted by wisps of smoke emerging through them. Smoke from a nor-

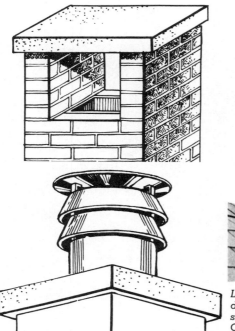

Where chimney draft is poor or downdrafts are common, a masonry cap is a big help, or a metal draft control can be set into the top of the chimney as shown.

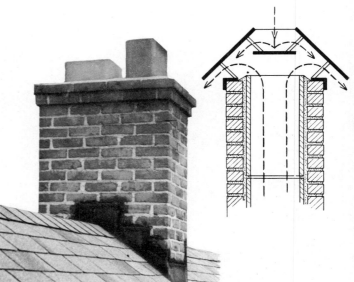

Left: Sometimes the stove or furnace opens into the same flue as does the fireplace. This can cause draft troubles. The fireplace should have a separate flue, as shown in this two-flue chimney. Chimneys can contain up to four flues, which must be walled from each other by at least 8" of brick unless lined with vitrified masonry. Right: Smoke diffuser on chimney diverts downdrafts. Smoke coming up chimney is exhausted out sides, as indicated by arrows.

mal fire should appear only coming out of the chimney above the roof, and any leak elsewhere is a definite fire hazard. It should be repaired immediately. Pick out the old, crumbling mortar, dampen the surface thoroughly, and then apply a strong cement mixture—two parts sand to one part portland cement. After this, the chimney exterior should be coated with a colorless masonry sealer paint to prevent further water absorption by the porous masonry. In this way, water cannot penetrate to plaster inside the house or flow downward to the flue outlets and cleanouts at the base.

Also, go over your entire chimney occasionally, feeling for exterior hot spots with your hand. Any spot too hot for your hand is too hot for your house. Don't try to fix these hot places yourself. They may indicate a broken flue, and the whole lining may need rebuilding. Call in professional help. A loose brick in your fireplace, especially on the bottom, is also a definite fire hazard. Repair it with commercial fire clay or, if it is not available, use a strong cement mixture.

THE FLUE Excessive use of pine or other soft sap

woods will cake a chimney flue with gummy, smoke-borne residue. It clings to the inside of the flue and creates a hard deposit that slowly cuts down the draft and passage of smoke. To remove this residue, attach a length of tire skid chain to a wire or rope and dangle it down the flue from above (on the roof), pulling it up and down rapidly. This will break the deposit loose. The damper, of course, should be tightly closed while this process goes on. If you have no damper, be sure to block the fireplace front until the work is finished. You could use a dampened old blanket, sheeting, or a piece of canvas or plastic for this.

THE FIRE To draw well, a fire must be built not too far forward in the fireplace. Otherwise, the rising hot air simply creates a vacuum in the room, which sucks back the smoke. For this reason, when starting your fire, the opening of a door or window will often provide the necessary initial draft. Once the fire is burning well, it usually can draw in enough air through keyholes and cracks as very few rooms are completely airtight.

Often an initial draft can be created by burning

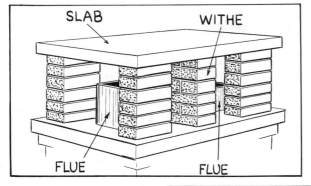

SLAB   WITHE

FLUE   FLUE

One practical way to cap your chimney is to use common brick and a flat slab of stone at least 2" thick (such as flagstone). You may have to hoist the stone up to your roof by rope and pulley. To build the cap, first prepare a mortar of 1 part portland cement, 1 part hydrated lime, 6 parts clean sand. Mix with clean water until mortar is the consistency of bread dough. (The proper ready-mixed mortar, sold by building supply dealers, may also be used—but not fire clay.) Next, erect pillars of brick at each corner, as illustrated. Butter the top of each pillar with a generous ¼" of mortar, then mount your stone. Build the pillars high enough to make each opening under the cap at least as large as the flue opening. If your chimney has two or more flues, a brick wall must be erected on the separation between the flues, carrying this separation or "withe" upward until it meets the flat stone. This in effect gives each flue the separate cap necessary for proper functioning.

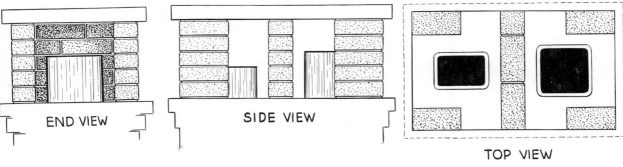

END VIEW   SIDE VIEW   TOP VIEW

a piece of newspaper held up in the fireplace throat as the fire is starting. Andirons, or bricks resting on edge, will permit the draft to get in under the fuel. Start the fire with crushed newspaper or fine, dry kindling, letting it spread to small logs. A large log should be placed behind small logs, well toward the rear wall and with another small log or two burning behind it.

Sometimes a draft can be helped considerably when starting the fire by placing a crinkled sheet of newspaper on top of, as well as underneath, the firewood structure. The burning top paper in effect sucks up air and smoke from the bottom of the pile. And always bear in mind that tightly packed wood forms a mass that blocks the upward movement of the draft and cuts off the oxygen necessary for combustion. Pile your logs with plenty of air space around and between them; these spaces serve as little chimneys conducting the draft to the big chimney.

FIREPLACE CHECKLIST   This list provides things to keep in mind when operating a fireplace.

1. Exercise every care in the repair and mainte-

nance of a fireplace and chimney. Remember, you are playing with fire.

2. If you clean the soot out of the chimney and fireplace once each year, preferably in the fall before you start using them, you should have no soot difficulties.

3. When removing soot or ashes from a fireplace, first wet them down.

4. Remember to test your fireplace on coolish days only. Many chimneys are not designed to draw well except at outside temperatures of less than 50°F.

5. If your heating system is on but the fireplace is not in use, keep the damper tightly shut, otherwise much of the room heat may escape up the chimney.

FIREPLACE HELPERS   While the open-front fireplace has been a standard fixture in many homes for years, it actually provides little more than "inner" warmth. As fire burns in the open-front unit, a warm bank of your home's air constantly moves across the room and into the fire chamber. As the fire heats up, hot, light air is forced up the flue.

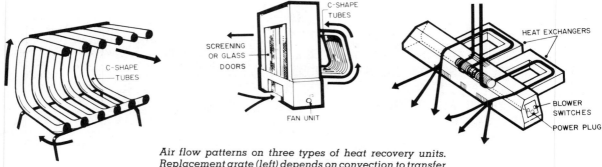

Air flow patterns on three types of heat recovery units.
Replacement grate (left) depends on convection to transfer
heat. Mechanical units (center and right) may have fan
mounted either at bottom or top.

In fact, research shows that close to 12,000 cubic feet of heated room air is drawn up the chimney in any given hour. This has to be replaced with warm furnace air.

Fortunately, new heat savers available retain functionality without costing an arm and a leg. You can turn a conventional open-front fireplace into a real heat producer for as little as $50 or as much as $600 to $700, plus you can save heat without losing that crackling fire atmosphere.

STOP THE DRAFT The first step to saving heat from that fire is to stop the mass exodus of air up the flue. The cheapest route is to add glass doors to the front of the fireplace, which cut the loss of heated room air by up to 85 percent.

Heat recovery units for fireplaces are available in a wide assortment of designs to push heat from wood burned in the fireplace into your home. The cheapest to buy and easiest to install are special hollow-core replacement grates. Some manufacturers say one of these units by itself can double the heat output of the fireplace.

Basically, such replacement grates take advantage of natural convection. Cold air drawn into the opening of the hollow grate is heated at the bottom by the fire and forced out the top. Forced-air grate systems using the same principle, but helping nature along with mechanical blowers, are the next step up.

Units incorporating blowers often involve more than simply taking the old grate out and replacing it with one designed to save energy. However, companies producing such units say units with blowers can boost heat production five times over units without blowers. Blower attachments designed to attach directly to separate hollow-core C-shaped grates are also available.

Blower units have an additional advantage: because the blowers transfer more air, the tubes remain at a much cooler temperature and will last much longer under normal use. Blowers also allow better distribution of heated air. For even better heat distribution, you can turn on the forced-air fan in your existing furnace system (leaving the flame off).

Some units are available with either front screen or glass doors. Glass doors can double the heat output of a blower unit up to 100,000 Btu's per hour, enough to heat a 1,500-square-foot home.

Mechanized fireplace heat-recovery units, however, do not all employ the C-shaped grate design. Some units offer a U-shaped tube configuration with a blower on one end, which simply attaches to the top of your fireplace. Others use double square tube heat exchangers, which also mount inside your fireplace at the top. Installation takes less than a half hour with two self-tapping screws or quick-mount clamps. Fireplace screening or glass doors can be easily added.

Still another way to get more heat is to buy special firebox inserts with glass doors already installed.

If you are planning to install a new prefab fireplace, keep in mind that most already incorporate energy-efficient designs plus accept a variety of accessories that help you use fireplace heat to cut fuel bills.

A relatively simple way to extract more heat from your fireplace is to replace screening with glass doors. Glass doors can earn back their cost, since controlled intake draft reduces wood consumption and also offers safety from flying sparks. Glass fireplace doors are available with heat-tempered glass in a choice of finishes, including baked-on enamel, flat black, polished, and antique brass. The units, available in a wide assortment of sizes, come with glass wool insulation around edges to assure tight fit to brick or other facing.

3

HOW TO: UNDERSTAND ELECTRICAL TERMS • HIRE AN
ELECTRICAL CONTRACTOR • REWIRE YOUR HOUSE •
INSTALL A GROUND FAULT INTERRUPTER • REPLACE A
LIGHT FIXTURE • INSTALL TRACK LIGHTING • INSTALL
DIMMER SWITCHES • INSTALL AND REPAIR DOORBELL
SYSTEMS • INSTALL SMOKE DETECTORS • WIRE MAJOR
APPLIANCES

ELECTRICAL SYSTEMS

The electrical work a homeowner may undertake is usually governed by community codes, which vary from one locale to another. Some communities require that all electrical installation be made by a licensed electrician; some require that all electrical repairs be similarly made; and some (usually smaller) communities have no codes at all other than the National Electric Code (NEC).

Before beginning any electrical work, you should check with local authorities to see just which work you are allowed to do yourself and which must be done by a licensed professional.*

HOW TO UNDERSTAND ELECTRICAL TERMS

The three basic codes or standards that relate to wiring and rewiring in older homes are as follows:

LOCAL HOUSING CODES Most communities have regulations requiring property owners to maintain certain minimums of safety and health in electrical service. These regulations relate to safety and not necessarily efficient, convenient, or adequate wiring. Most electrical regulations of local codes are patterned after the NEC, although they often vary to some degree from community to community.

FHA-VA MINIMUM ELECTRICAL REQUIREMENTS If a home buyer applies for an FHA or VA mortgage, the home is inspected by a licensed electrician who completes an "electrical certificate." The home wiring must be brought up to the minimum FHA-VA electrical requirements. These requirements are usually similar to or the same as local housing codes.

NATIONAL ELECTRICAL CODE (NEC) FOR ONE- AND TWO-FAMILY DWELLINGS The electrical code establishes national standards for installing wiring when rewiring an older house or building a

new one. Paperback copies of the NEC report are available from your power company or utility, your state board of electricity, or from the National Fire Protection Association, 470 Atlantic Avenue, Boston, Mass. 02210, which administers the NEC.

A home must always meet any local housing code. It must meet the NEC if wiring is installed or if existing wiring is changed. The local inspector is directly responsible for enforcing these standards.

ELECTRICITY BASICS As a homeowner, you will benefit by understanding the wiring system of

---

*Caution: Safety First. The instruction and examples in this chapter have been reviewed by qualified electricians, and the material is believed to be accurate and up to date. However, the individual homeowner must make the judgment regarding his or her capability to safely work on electrical systems. Most locales require building permits and inspection of any modification to the mechanical systems of the home. Comply with local requirements, and have the final job inspected to be sure electrical repairs and improvements are done safely and in accordance with state building codes. Most building departments and inspection personnel will be extremely helpful in advising you of wiring requirements for code compliance.

your own home. You will have a better idea of whether your system is adequate and not overloaded and dangerous. You can save many times over the cost of outside help by being able to trace blown fuses and by accomplishing simple repairs and replacement of outdated components, as allowed by local code.

A few common electrical terms and their meanings are listed below. Familiarity will make it easy to follow this chapter.

Alternating current The current that in most cases is supplied to the home. It reverses its direction of flow at measured intervals, or cycles, usually 60 times per second. The term *hertz* has come into use recently. It may be used interchangeably with cycles.

Ampere A unit of measure for the rate of flow of electric current passing through a wire at a given moment.

Circuit breaker A device used in place of a fuse to stop the flow of current on an overloaded circuit. Excess current activates a spring to open the circuit. When the cause of the excess current is corrected, the circuit breaker may be reset manually.

Fuse A replaceable protective device that interrupts the flow of current when circuits are overloaded. It contains a short length of soft metal that is melted by heat generated by excess current.

Voltage A unit of measure of the pressure of electric current. The normal household voltage is 115 (plus or minus 5 volts).

Watt A unit for measuring electric energy. One thousand watts equal 1 kilowatt. Electricity used is usually billed in terms of kilowatt hours.

The electrical system in a home is relatively simple to understand.

• The amount of electricity that flows is measured in amps (or amperes). Because some appliances need more electricity, they are said to "draw more amps."

• The force at which electricity is delivered is measured in volts. Some appliances such as electric ranges, dryers, and large air conditioners require more force, or volts, to operate.

• The combined amount (amps) and force (volts) of electricity is measured in watts. For example:

5 amps flowing at 115 volts = 575 watts (5 × 115)
10 amps flowing at 115 volts = 1150 watts (10 × 115)
5 amps flowing at 230 volts = 1150 watts (5 × 230)

Thus, watts measure the combined amp amount and volt force through an appliance, as illustrated in the following table.

WIRING CAPACITY As electricity enters the home from power lines, it passes through insulated conductors that are enclosed in a conduit. Some areas allow service entrance cable.

	Amps	Volts	Watts	
Air conditioner (window)	6 to 11	115	690 to	1,380
Air conditioner (central)	22	230		5,000
Clock	.3	115		3.5
Washer	5 to 8	115	575 to	920
Dryer (electric)	22 to 30	230	5,000 to	6,000
Dryer (gas)	5 to 8	115	575 to	920
Dishwasher	15	115		1,840
Garbage disposal	5 to 8	115	575 to	920
Iron	10	115		1,150
Electric range	35 to 70	230	8,000 to	16,000
Refrigerator	5 to 8	115	575 to	920
Toaster	10	115		1,150
Television (black and white)	3	115		345
Television (color)	5	115		575

Service entrances have many varying requirements, depending on distance from the utility poles, height of the house, and such factors. However, all will have the same basic elements shown here.

Several manufacturers assemble service entrance kits (often also called "mast kits"), which include the essential equipment for installation. Parts included in a typical kit are the service head, roof flashing, gasket, and brackets. Conduit and connections are purchased separately. The kit shown is designed for a mast that extends through the house eave.

From the entrance, the power goes through a meter, which measures the amount of electricity used. The power then flows to the main service panel, which houses the main switches and branch circuits protected by either fuses or circuit breakers. If an individual circuit becomes overloaded because of excessive power drain, the fuse burns out or the circuit breaker trips, interrupting the electrical flow for that particular circuit.

Many older homes, though adequately wired when built, do not provide the amount of electricity needed for common appliances or additional expansion. To be adequate, the wiring system must be able to deliver the amps required by the home's appliances. Wiring systems of the following capacities are typical:

30 Amps This capacity service was installed before 1920 to replace gas lights with electric lights. It can handle only a limited amount of lighting and a few minor appliances. It is not adequate for most families. Additional circuits cannot be added safely or legally. FHA-VA minimum electrical requirements do not allow 30-amp service to remain if the buyer obtains an FHA, FmHA, or VA mortgage.

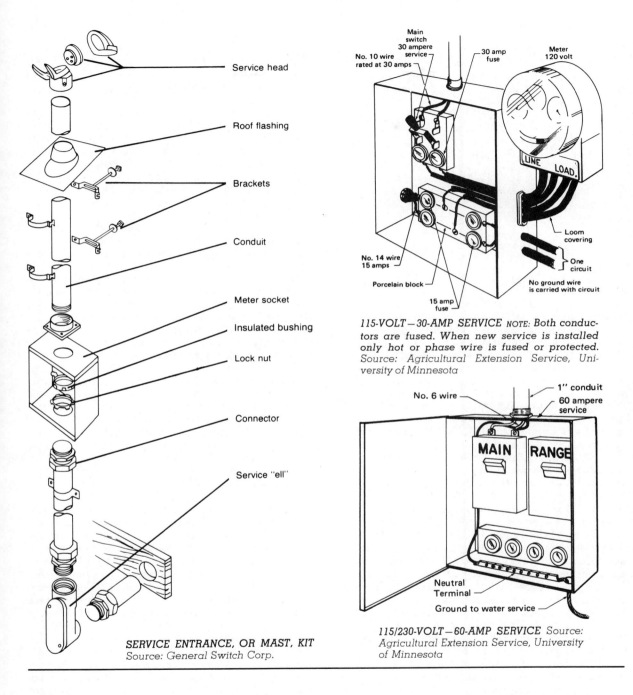

Service head

Roof flashing

Brackets

Conduit

Meter socket

Insulated bushing

Lock nut

Connector

Service "ell"

SERVICE ENTRANCE, OR MAST, KIT
Source: General Switch Corp.

Main switch 30 ampere service

No. 10 wire rated at 30 amps

30 amp fuse

Meter 120 volt

LINE   LOAD.

Loom covering

One circuit

No. 14 wire 15 amps

No ground wire is carried with circuit

Porcelain block

15 amp fuse

115-VOLT—30-AMP SERVICE NOTE: *Both conductors are fused. When new service is installed only hot or phase wire is fused or protected.* Source: Agricultural Extension Service, University of Minnesota

No. 6 wire

1" conduit

60 ampere service

MAIN   RANGE

Neutral Terminal

Ground to water service

115/230-VOLT—60-AMP SERVICE Source: Agricultural Extension Service, University of Minnesota

60 Amps This service may be adequate if only one major appliance such as a range, dryer, or air conditioner is used. This size service is the minimum allowed under FHA-VA requirements for FHA, FmHA, or VA financing or under the NEC if new circuits are to be added. Under the NEC, for example, if you have an electric range, you cannot add a circuit for an air conditioner without increasing the service to 100 amps.

100 Amps This size is the minimum required for

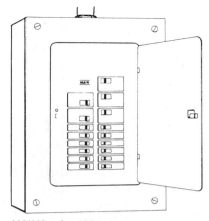

115/230 volt — 100-amp service

new houses and the minimum accepted when re-wiring older houses. It will be adequate for most loads, including electric dryers, ranges, water heaters, and air conditioners. Unusual loads such as electric heating will require a larger service such as 150 or 200 amps.

If you wonder about the adequacy of 60- or 100-amp service, you may wish to check with a licensed electrical contractor or electrical inspector. You can also refer to Section 220 of the NEC to help check the service capacity, considering your likely electrical demand.

ELECTRICAL CIRCUITS. In newer homes a 220/240-volt supply enters the house over three-wire lines, instead of the usual two-wire lines. Two of the three are "hot" wires. The third is called the "return," grounded conductor. In effect, this means that there are two separate 115/120-volt lines, each consisting of the grounded wire and one hot wire. The current enters the house through a box containing cartridge-style fuses or a main circuit breaker and is then connected to provide a number of 120-volt circuits and usually one 240-volt line. This line operates those appliances, such as electric stoves, dryers, and heaters, that are specifically designed for this higher voltage. Each circuit is then fed through circuit breakers or fuses.

In a typical three-wire system, one wire will normally be a black insulated wire, one will be a red or a black insulated wire, and the third wire will be either white insulated wire or stranded bare wire. If the power is taken from the neutral or bare wire and either the black or red wires, you'll have 120 volts. If all three are connected into a circuit, you will have 240 volts.

This system (3-wire, 240 volt) must be grounded

to both a cold water system and a ground rod. The ground rod will suffice if a water pipe is not available. All circuits in the house are connected to a neutral or grounding bus bar in the fuse or circuit box, thereby providing grounded circuits throughout the house.

The wires leading to various parts of the house start just behind the fuses or breakers. Those controlled by one fuse or circuit breaker are said to be on one circuit. To tell where the various circuits lead, you can remove a fuse or manually trip a circuit breaker, then check the house to find which lights and outlets are not working. For future reference, indicate all these units on a chart near the service box.

You generally can tell the number of circuits in a house by counting the number of fuses or circuit breakers. In some cases, however, "dummy" fuses or circuit breakers are installed either to fool the untrained eye or to facilitate future expansion. To determine the actual number of circuits, consult a licensed electrical contractor. He also can tell you the capacity of each circuit, which may also be deceiving to the untrained eye because unsafe overfusing (replacing of burned-out fuses with larger fuses) often occurs in older homes.

The licensed electrical contractor can also tell you what must be done to correct an inadequate number of circuits or overfusing and how much it will cost. The NEC states that a single 15-amp circuit shall not be used to service more than 575 square feet of floor area. Ten lights and convenience outlets on a single 15-amp circuit is a reasonable maximum number.

HOW TO HIRE AN ELECTRICAL CONTRACTOR

The most important consideration becomes how to select one who is competent, licensed, and bonded. To select an electrical contractor, first check with the local electrical inspector or state electrical board to make sure the contractor is licensed. Then ask material suppliers, neighbors, and friends for their recommendations. Check with your Better Business Bureau about the contractor's record. Shop around; charges for the same work may vary substantially.

Request written bids from several contractors. When comparing bids, make sure the contractors were bidding on the same amount of work. Also realize that a low bid may be undesirable if the resulting job is full of problems and delays. Consider the contractor's track record as well as the bid.

It's best to have a written contract specifying the total and itemized costs; that the contractor will obtain all necessary electrical permits in his own name; that the home's wiring will meet or exceed all applicable codes when completed; and that final payment will be made only after approval of the finished job by the electrical inspector and after the contractor has furnished lien waivers from all material suppliers and subcontractors.

HOW TO REWIRE YOUR HOUSE

ARE YOU ALLOWED TO DO YOUR OWN REWIRING OR WIRING? The answer is "yes" for remodelers who own and occupy the single-family home to be rewired. Some local inspection departments require that the remodeler sign an affidavit (before the permit is issued for do-it-yourself work) stating that he or she lives at and owns the single-family home for which a permit is requested, and that he or she will personally purchase all materials and personally perform all labor in connection with the permit.

You can consider doing your own wiring if you know what you are doing, know the code requirements, have the time and patience, have the tools, and respect the power of electricity. Otherwise, a licensed electrical contractor is the best way to go.

When rewiring, evaluate possible future electrical needs, such as electric heat, central air conditioning, electric range, electric dryer, and electric water heater. These needs should be considered before consulting a contractor so the size of the electric service can be established. Normally, 100-amp, 115/230-volt service is adequate, but future needs may dictate larger service. The difference in cost between 100-, 150-, or 200-amp 115/230 volt service is not very great.

SECURING PERMITS A permit is both desirable and legally required before work begins. Even competent do-it-yourselfers and licensed electrical contractors occasionally make mistakes. By obtaining a permit, the consumer is assured that the inspector will do everything he or she can to give help and protection. When the job is completed, the inspector will make a final check to make sure everything is safe.

When rewiring, two separate 20-amp circuits are required: one for servicing the kitchen and one for the laundry. Separate circuits are necessary because of the larger appliances often connected to the kitchen and laundry outlets (lights must be on another circuit). The NEC requires a separate circuit if window air conditioners draw more than 50 percent of the capacity of the general circuit. If your electrical system has any of the following symptoms, individual circuits may be overloaded and the wiring of the circuits may be inadequate:
- Frequently blown fuses or tripped circuit breakers.
- Lights that dim or flicker.
- Air conditioners working at less than full capacity.
- Television picture that shrinks.
- Appliances with heating coils that warm up slowly.

The amount of current required by each electrical device in your home is indicated clearly on it somewhere. It's shown on the large end of light bulbs, on the manufacturer's plates of all motors, and on the plates of practically all heating units. By knowing how much wattage is consumed by each of your appliances, you can help spread the total load used over several circuits.

Most wiring devices, such as receptacles (outlets), have been designed for use with copper wire or conductors. At one time all wiring was copper. In the past few years, however, aluminum wire has been used. Either copper or aluminum wire may be used for wiring or rewiring with switches, receptacles, and connectors tested and listed by a recognized testing laboratory (e.g., Underwriters Laboratory) and designed and listed specifically for use with that type of wiring. It is extremely dangerous and illegal to connect with aluminum wire devices designed for use with copper wire. Although the 1978 version of the NEC accepts aluminum wiring when code requirements are observed, it has been outlawed in certain localities. It's up to you to find out if it's acceptable in your own community.

REWIRING CONSIDERATIONS—A CHECKLIST

All hazardous and illegal wiring (usually improperly installed by nonprofessionals) should, and legally must, be removed. Common unsafe and illegal deficiencies include the items listed in this checklist.

These are minimum safety and convenience standards required by local housing codes and the NEC for rewiring. Requirements for better wiring are greater than these standards.

Existing Condition		Common unsafe and illegal wiring in older homes
OK	Defective	
——	——	Appliances fed from overhead lights
——	——	Open, unprotected splices
——	——	Loose or broken boxes, switches, and receptacles
——	——	Exposed knob or tube wiring within 8' of a floor (often found in garages and basements)
——	——	Octopus outlets serving several appliances (additional outlet needed)

Existing Condition		Common unsafe and illegal wiring in older homes
OK	Defective	

Areas where electrical equipment is used frequently, such as basement shops, without convenience outlets (additional outlets needed)

Overhead wiring within 10' (horizontal) of a swimming pool must be moved.

If a garage is already wired, it should have at least one light and one convenience outlet, both of which must be grounded.

When rewiring, it is desirable, although not required, to provide for lighting and convenience outlets to the garage, entrances, patios, and so on.

When rewiring, new convenience outlets installed in the bathroom, garage, or outside must include ground fault circuit interrupter protection.

Every room, other than storerooms and unfinished attics and basements, should and legally must have:

At least two wall or floor convenience outlets for the first 120 square feet of floor area.

An additional wall or floor convenience outlet for each additional 80 square feet or fraction of floor area. For example, a 10' × 22' (220 square feet) living room would require at least four convenience outlets (two for the first 120', one for the next 80', and one for the remaining fraction of 80').

Kitchens require at least one additional outlet, beyond the 120/80 square-foot requirements, which shall be a 20-amp circuit. Metal light fixtures within 8' above the kitchen sink or 5' to the side of the kitchen sink must be grounded.

Dining rooms, when new circuits are added, must have a convenience outlet serviced by a 20-amp circuit.

Bathrooms must have at least one light fixture and one convenience outlet, which may be in the light fixture if it is easily reached. Metal fixtures in the bathroom must be grounded. (If new convenience outlets are installed, they must be protected by a ground fault circuit interrupter.)

Laundry areas must have at least one convenience outlet serviced by a separate 20-amp circuit.

If ceiling light fixtures (controlled by a separate switch) are provided, the required number of wall or convenience outlets may be decreased by one. For example, the 220 square-foot living room requires as a minimum either four convenience outlets or three convenience outlets and one ceiling light fixture controlled by a separate switch.

At least one light fixture shall be provided in the hall, stairway, laundry room, and furnace room.

Overfused and overloaded circuits must be corrected. The correct size fuse depends on the size of wire used.

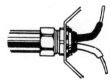

Romex (1972 to present)
—also known as nonmetallic-sheathed cable (with a grounding wire).

Greenfield (1947 to present)
—also known as Flexible Metal Conduit.
—used to carry conductors.

EMT Conduit (1932 to present)
—Electric Metallic Tubing (EMT).
—used as a raceway to carry conductors.

BX Cable (1930 to present)
—also known as Armored Cable (type A.C.).
—used primarily for concealed wiring in ceilings and walls.

Nonmetallic Cable (1943 to 1947)
—nonmetallic cable without a grounding wire.
—used sometimes during the 1943 to 1947 period of metal shortage.

COMMON WIRING
Source: Agricultural Extension Service,
University of Minnesota

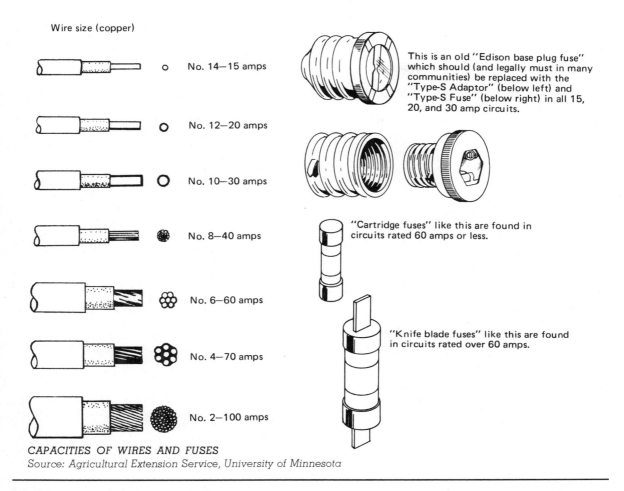

Wire size (copper)

o	No. 14—15 amps
O	No. 12—20 amps
O	No. 10—30 amps
●	No. 8—40 amps
●	No. 6—60 amps
●	No. 4—70 amps
●	No. 2—100 amps

This is an old "Edison base plug fuse" which should (and legally must in many communities) be replaced with the "Type-S Adaptor" (below left) and "Type-S Fuse" (below right) in all 15, 20, and 30 amp circuits.

"Cartridge fuses" like this are found in circuits rated 60 amps or less.

"Knife blade fuses" like this are found in circuits rated over 60 amps.

CAPACITIES OF WIRES AND FUSES
Source: Agricultural Extension Service, University of Minnesota

FUSES AND CIRCUIT BREAKERS Only a fixed amount of electric current (amperes) can flow along a wire of a given size. If this amount is exceeded, the wire gets too hot and becomes a fire hazard. Smaller wires cannot carry as much electricity as large wires. Thus, smaller capacity fuses or circuit breakers are placed on these circuits as safety devices. When too much electricity flows through the fuse or circuit breaker, it stops the flow of electricity to prevent a fire.

When fuses blow or a circuit breaker trips, it indicates something is wrong within the circuit. Before replacing the fuse or resetting the circuit breaker, determine the cause, as outlined on the next page.

To replace a fuse, first locate the switch handle on the side of the fuse box. Pull this handle to the off position before you open the box or touch any fuses. If there's no handle, when you open the door you may find one or two cartridge-fuse holders at the top of the box. Pull both of them out, being careful not to touch the metal ends. If fuses are open to view, use a fuse puller. This turns the current off.

When replacing a fuse, be sure to use one of the proper size, i.e., one that will blow before the current consumption becomes high enough to overheat the line. Do not substitute a larger fuse in place of one that keeps blowing. A circuit breaker works in much the same manner, except you merely have to flip a switch instead of replacing it.

Circuit breakers are available in various amperage ratings, for either 120-volt or 240-volt capacities, and in ½" and 1". A 1" breaker is also referred to as a full-size breaker; ½" are also called half-size. In many cases, breakers by different manufacturers are designed to be interchangeable and can be used in almost any breaker panel. However, ½" breakers, regardless of manufacturer, require special service panels that take notched bus tabs.

CIRCUIT BREAKERS

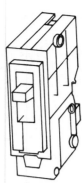

One-inch (full-size), single-pole circuit breaker with a 120-volt capacity for use in general-purpose circuits of 15, 20, 30, 40 or 50 amps.

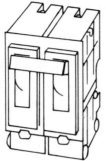

A double-pole circuit breaker, actually made up of two 1-inch breakers, is 2-inches wide and has a 240-volt capacity. Amperages range from 20 to 125, designed for circuits supplying heavy appliances, such as electric ranges, water heaters, and electric furnaces. This type of breaker will trip open through both poles if a fault occurs through either pole.

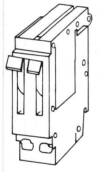

Two ½-inch, single-pole circuit breakers (often called twin breakers) with a 120-volt capacity. Available only in pairs, these breakers snap into the side of the bus tab, rather than into the center. Available in 15/15, 15/20, and 20/20 amp models.

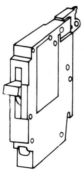

One-half-inch (half-size), single-pole circuit breaker with a 120-volt capacity for use in lighting circuits of 15, 20, or 30 amps. Performs same function as full-size unit of similar rating. Half-size circuit breakers allow more circuits in a given panel size.

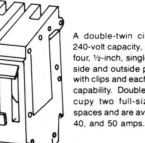

A double-twin circuit breaker with 240-volt capacity, actually made up of four, ½-inch, single-pole breakers. Inside and outside pairs are connected with clips and each pair has a 240-volt capability. Double-pole breakers occupy two full-size circuit breaker spaces and are available in 15, 20, 30, 40, and 50 amps.

Source: General Switch Corp.

To find the cause of short circuits, do the following:
• Disconnect all lights and appliances on the circuit with the blown fuse or tripped circuit breaker.
• Replace the blown fuse or turn on the tripped circuit breaker.
• If the fuse blows or the circuit breaker trips with all appliances unplugged from the circuit, the short is in the wiring itself and the wiring must be repaired or replaced.
• If the circuit is good, reconnect each light and appliance on that circuit, one at a time. Use extreme caution. *Do not* connect suspiciously frayed cords to outlets. When you plug in or turn on the faulty light or appliance, the fuse will blow or the breaker will trip again. Carefully check the appliance for a bare cord, broken light socket, or damaged plug.

Two types of circuit testers can be used to help locate problems in fuse panels, current leakage in appliances, and shorts in line cords and receptacles. One is a small circuit tester with a small line and insulated leads near two metal tips. The other type is the Universal Continuity and Line Tester. This type will also show where current leakage is developing due to shorts in faulty line cords, appliances, and motors. Follow the instructions supplied with the testers.

If your fuse panel is older, you can also use a light bulb to help locate short circuits. If one particular fuse blows several times, shut off all wall switches and appliances on that circuit and remove all line cords from the sockets. Remove the fuse and screw a 100-watt bulb into the fuse socket in its place.

If the bulb lights with all appliances disconnected from the circuit, there is a short in the line. If it doesn't light, connect each of the appliances, lamps, and line cords one at a time with the bulb still in the fuse socket. Now if the bulb lights at the fuse panel, but the appliance *fails to work*, you've located the short. It's in the appliance that caused the bulb to light. Remove the bulb from the panel before disconnecting the faulty appliance.

Ignoring the cause of blown fuses or tripped circuit breakers can lead to fires, excessive power draw, or appliances running below optimum levels. Check the following reasons for circuit failures:
Loose connection in a fused panel After turning off the power, remove the fuses. If the bottom of the fuse is blackened, discolored, or pitted, a loose connection is probably at fault.
Loose connection in a circuit breaker panel After turning off power remove cover from panel. WARNING: The connections where the main wires enter the panel are HOT or LIVE. Inspect the panel for

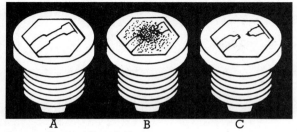

Source: General Switch Corp.

darkened or pitted marks on the bus or circuit breakers. Also check the wires connected to the circuit breakers for signs of excessive heat.

Fuse poorly seated Although the fuse window shows no indication of burnout (Figure A, above) and the bottom is not pitted or discolored, the fuse may not be making contact with the bottom of the fuse holder. Remove the fuse and replace with one of adequate length to make contact.

If any of these conditions exist, look for an unused branch space in the panel. If there is an unused space, move the branch wire from the damaged fuse or circuit breaker to the unused space. Obtain a new fuse or circuit breaker and install it carefully.

If there are no unused spaces, replace the entire panel. The damaged connection could cause a fire. If you replace the panel, consider installing larger service to meet future electrical service requirements.

Short circuits If a fuse is blown, the fuse window appears discolored and the metal strip inside, visible through the window, is broken (Figure B). This indicates a short circuit caused by either two bare wires touching or a hot lead grounding out to a metal object somewhere in the circuit. Cartridge fuses will give no visible indication that a short circuit has taken place. Circuits protected by circuit breakers can be identified by the handle of the tripped circuit breaker being in the "tripped" or "off" position. But the method for identifying the cause is the same for all types of circuit protection.

Overloaded circuits If a fuse blows and the window remains clear, an overloaded circuit is the cause (Figure C). Again, cartridge fuses give no visible indication of an overloaded circuit. Circuit breakers will be in the "tripped" or "off" position. Most circuit failures are caused by either temporary overloads or constant overloads. A circuit with a short should be repaired: constant overload means a new circuit should be added.

Temporary overload Fused circuits can be corrected to handle temporary overloads by using a time delay fuse (also called a "slow-blow") of either 15 or 20 amps. This type of fuse will handle temporary

power drains from start-up of appliance motors. Many electric motors require nearly three times the normal line current for initial starting. Circuit breakers are designed to automatically handle temporary overloads.

Constant overload If one circuit repeatedly fails, there may be too many heavy appliances on that circuit. If removing some of the appliances from the circuit does not eliminate the overload, an individual circuit must be added for the appliance that requires the most current.

WIRING TYPES AND METHODS One of the most common and most dangerous problems in home wiring is an improper connection, especially between wires and switches, receptacles, and connectors. The illustrations below and on page 82 show installations of concealed knob and tube wiring (now outdated, but which was used up to 1930 and during the metal shortage of 1943 to 1947); and nonmetallic-sheathed cable (Romex), on page 82.

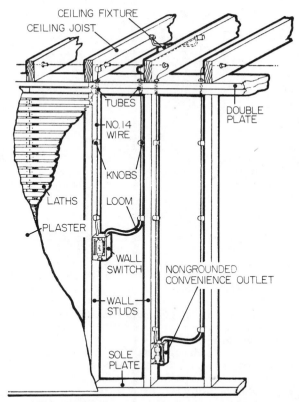

Older knob and tube wiring. *When rewiring, new outlets are generally recommended. When replacing, do not install grounded outlets unless a ground conductor is also installed. Check local code. Illustration: Ron Chamberlain*

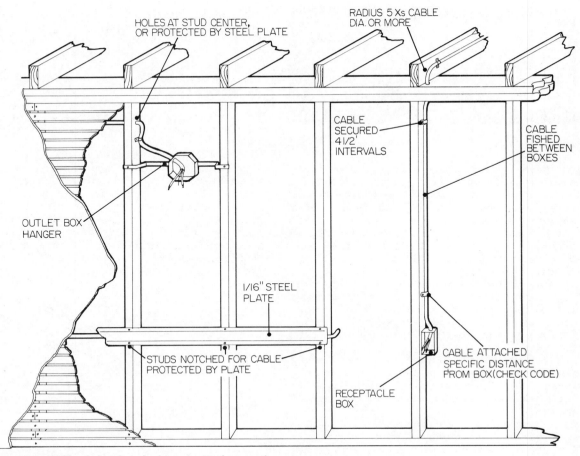

HOLES AT STUD CENTER,
OR PROTECTED BY STEEL PLATE

RADIUS 5 Xs CABLE
DIA. OR MORE

CABLE
SECURED
4 1/2'
INTERVALS

CABLE
FISHED
BETWEEN
BOXES

OUTLET BOX
HANGER

1/16" STEEL
PLATE

STUDS NOTCHED FOR CABLE
PROTECTED BY PLATE

CABLE ATTACHED
SPECIFIC DISTANCE
FROM BOX (CHECK CODE)

RECEPTACLE
BOX

Newer wiring. *Check local code for permitted uses of nonmetallic sheathed cable (Romex). Illustration: Ron Chamberlain*

When connections are loose, fuses and circuit breakers cannot detect the problem. Heat builds up at the fault to the point that a fire may result. Improper connections often are indicated by hot outlet or switch plates, the smell of smoldering insulation, or flickering lights and fluctuating appliance operation. If you suspect this condition, contact a licensed electrical contractor immediately.

Household cable is divided into four basic types (see below), each designed for particular uses. Cables are rated by the diameter of the wires and the number of wires. What is called standard two-wire cable actually has three wires, the third wire acting as the ground. And standard three-wire cable has four wires: one ground, one white neutral wire, and two hot leads — one black and one red.

In new wiring, cable with a ground wire is now

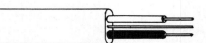

Branch circuit or underground Cable UF: Moistureproof outside jacket allows cable to be used outdoors, underground, or indoors. In many localities, it can be used without a conduit. Usually two-wire cable.

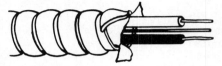

Armored BX cable. For dry indoor areas, and only for hookup to metal receptacles and panels where connectors with locknuts can be used. Extremely durable cable, used primarily to extend existing circuits. Available in two-wire and three-wire types. *Source: General Switch Corp.*

INSULATED OUTDOOR COPPER WIRE SELECTION

Load in Building Amperes	Distance in Feet from Pole to Building	*Recommended Size of Feeder Wire for Job
Up to 25 amperes, 120 volts	Up to 50 feet	No. 10
	50 to 80 feet	No. 8
	80 to 125 feet	No. 6
20 to 30 amperes, 240 volts	Up to 80 feet	No. 10
	80 to 125 feet	No. 8
	125 to 200 feet	No. 6
	200 to 350 feet	No. 4
30 to 50 amperes, 240 volts	Up to 80 feet	No. 8
	80 to 125 feet	No. 6
	125 to 200 feet	No. 4
	200 to 300 feet	No. 2
	300 to 400 feet	No. 1

*These sizes are recommended to reduce "voltage drop" to a minimum. Source: General Switch Corp.

INSULATED INDOOR COPPER WIRE SELECTION

Wire size	In Conduit or Cable		In Free Air		Weatherproof Wire
	Type RHW* THW*	Type TW, R*	Type RHW* THW*	Type TW, R*	
14	15 amp	15 amp	20 amp	20 amp	30 amp
12	20	20	25	25	40
10	30	30	40	40	55
8	45	40	65	55	70
6	65	55	95	80	100
4	85	70	125	105	130
3	100	80	145	120	150
2	115	95	170	140	175
1	130	110	195	165	205
0	150	125	230	195	235
00	175	145	265	225	275
000	200	165	310	260	320

*Types "RHW," "THW," "TW," or "R" are identified by markings on outer cover. Source: General Switch Corp.

required by electrical codes. For existing installations wired with aluminum wire rather than copper (some newer homes have aluminum wiring), all devices used with aluminum wire must have the Underwriters' designation CU/ALR. Aluminum wire and devices with this CU/ALR marking are compatible. If aluminum wire is used, consult your dealer for proper sizes.

When buying cable, tell your dealer how you plan to use it. He will be aware of local codes and may save you money by advising, for example, that you can install a smaller cable than you intended to use.

Selecting the proper size wire is determined by the distance from the outdoor electrical source to the building and the total amperage to be drawn from the wire at any one time.

Interior wire sizes are determined by the same method, first finding the length of the run needed for a circuit from the electrical source (usually the service panel), and the total amperage of appliances to be used on the circuit. To find the amperage of an appliance or light, divide the wattage by the voltage, add the totals of each appliance, and you will have the approximate total amperage needed for the wire. For interior wiring #12 copper wire, which will handle both 15- and 20-amp circuits, is recommended throughout the home.

Tips on installing cable Exposed cable should be strapped at least every 4½' to stud, joist, and wall

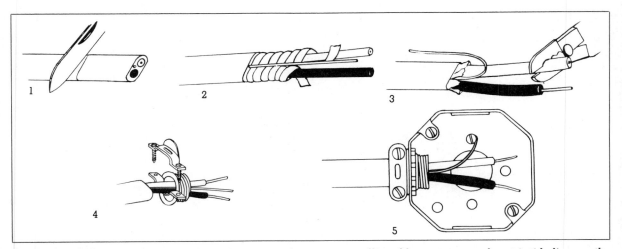

Working with Romex cable. Step 1. *Carefully cut outside fabric sheathing 6" to 8" from end and strip away from inside insulated conductors. Avoid cutting into insulation of conductors on inside.* **Step 2.** *Remove outer wrapping from the insulated conductors and pull back firmly against the outer jacket. Carefully cut the wrapping flush with the jacket.* **Step 3.** *Strip the insulation on each of the conductors one inch from the end, so that the copper wire is visible.* **Step 4.** *Slide the wires through the center of the* nonmetallic cable connector and seat inside lip over the outside cable jacket. Secure top clamp of connector firmly over cable jacket. Screw down connector clamp tightly. **Step 5.** *Insert connector into receptacle box and thread locking nut to connector on the inside of the box. Tighten locknut firmly for solid connection. Attach grounding connector firmly to screw on grounding clip in the box. Follow same procedure for installing into side of circuit panel.* Source: General Switch Corp.

or ceiling surfaces. For long cable runs over open spaces, cable must be supported with a 1" × 2" lumber strip secured to the joists, or the cable can run through holes drilled in the middle of studs or joists for support. When bending cable, be careful not to damage the insulation. Run cable on top of floor joists with nail-in cable supports, or support on roof rafters at least 7' from the floor. Place guard strips over the cable for rafter runs.

To install a new concealed circuit in an older building with plaster walls and ceilings, cut channels in the plaster, and replaster after the work is completed. In many cases, it will be necessary to notch upright studs so that wires may pass over them and replastering will be smooth.

In concealed work, cable should be strapped every 4½' to either studs or joists. Nail-in strapping supports are to be used rather than staples. Where nonmetallic cable is run within 1¼" of the surface, a ¹⁄₁₆"-thick metal strip must be placed over the cable. (If cables are fished in through walls, strapping is not required.)

Staples used improperly may penetrate cable insulation and cause short circuits or weaken insulation. Cables must also be strapped no more than one foot from all receptacles and switches.

CONNECTING AND SPLICING CABLES When cutting wire, make sure cuts are clean and at right angles, especially with stranded wire. Loose strands can cause short circuits and power drains. Clean wire ends before making connections and use wire nuts to hold wires together. Never splice without using a junction box. Unsupported splices are illegal.

When cutting wire, carefully strip away insulation, leaving approximately ½" of conductor showing. With a knife shave down the plastic insulation in pointed fashion.

To splice, firmly twist conductors together in a clockwise direction. Snip any excess wire if the ends are uneven. Screw on wire nut snugly. This connection does not require solder. Fasten cables to box, then tuck spliced wires into box, double-checking that no exposed wire is in contact with the metal box.

GROUNDING ELECTRICAL SYSTEMS All circuits must be grounded by utilizing the bare or grounding wire connected to the grounding screw on receptacles, fixtures, and even to the box itself, which gives a grounded box should the receptacle or fixture be removed for some reason. Bathroom, outdoor, and garage receptacles must be protected by a GFI, as covered later in this chapter.

One cardinal rule must be followed in wiring

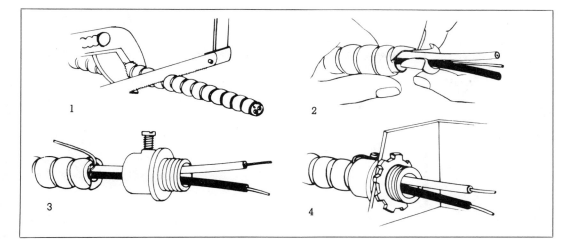

Working with BX cable. Step 1. *Hold armor securely and use hacksaw at slight angle to cut through armor approximately 6″ from cable end. Be careful not to cut into the insulation of inside conductors.* **Step 2.** *Twist armor loose and discard. Strip one inch of insulation away from conductors. Insert fiber insulator around conductors and push inside the armor against the cut. Bend ground conductor back against the cable to lie flat.* **Step 3.** *Slip conductors through middle of BX cable connector, and slide connector over the armor, with grounding wire crimped in between. Tighten locking screw securely against armor. Fiber bushing should be against the front of the connector.* **Step 4.** *Place connector into side of panel or junction box and secure tightly on inside with locking nut. Approximately 6″ of conductor is left for making connections. Source: General Switch Corp.*

circuits: *the white or neutral wire must always run direct from the source, without interruption to the point where the current is to be consumed at 115 volts.* The only time a white wire may be attached to a hot wire is when cable such as BX or Romex is used to connect a switch. White wire is then used as a supply wire and not as a return.

Larger appliances should be grounded Grounding, simply put, is an electrical connection to the earth from the appliance. It usually means attaching one end of a wire to the appliance's frame and clamping the wire's other end to a water pipe.

Electric irons, mixers, clocks, and heating blankets are used under conditions that do not involve simultaneous contact with pipes or other conductors. But larger appliances, particularly washing machines, dishwashers, refrigerators, broilers, air conditioners, and clothes dryers, are used under circumstances that make grounding extremely advisable.

To ground an appliance, connect one end of an ordinary single electrical wire to the frame of the appliance. Make the connection by loosening a bolt on the appliance, turning the bare end of the wire around it, and retightening. Make sure that the bolt and metal surface are clean and free of

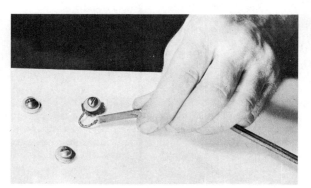

Purpose of grounding is to protect you if electric current enters appliance frame. The machine otherwise will give you a severe shock if you touch it while in contact with an electrical conductor. Be particularly careful to ground appliances in a bathroom.

rust. Connect the other end of the wire to a water pipe by means of a grounding clamp, which has a bolt or other device for tightening around the pipe and a screw for securing the wire. If no pipe is nearby, a ground connection can be made by fastening your grounding wire to a screw on the plate of the electrical outlet where your appliance is plugged in. This is feasible only if your home is wired with conduit and all outlets are already grounded.

Clamp is fastened over pipe; then ground wire is attached by tightening the crimping screws. Clean pipe with emery cloth or sandpaper before attaching clamp.

Never use a portable electric tool unless it is grounded. This is one great way of getting killed. When using an adapter, be sure it is attached properly to a properly grounded outlet. Most of today's quality tools are double insulated, but they should still be used only on grounded circuits. Photo: Graf-Whalen

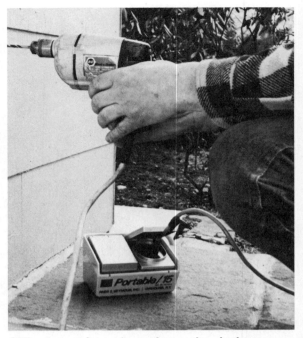

GFI's are mandatory for outdoor outlets, bathrooms, garages, and around swimming pools. Unit shown is a portable one. Photo: Graf-Whalen

Nonarmored cable is provided with a separate grounding wire. Attaching it to each fixture or outlet box by a screw and to the main ground line of the master fuse box will ground these fixtures and outlet boxes, thus providing a system — equipment ground.

HOW TO INSTALL A GROUND FAULT INTERRUPTER

More commonly called GFI's, these safety devices are receiving wide endorsement by safety authorities and the National Electrical Code. The fuses and breakers in your home electrical system provide protection to shut down power in the event of an overload. However, a common breaker or fuse won't react until at least 15 amperes of current is flowing, while a human being can be electrocuted by only $1/100$ of that current.

Before GFI's were developed, a protective system that added a third prong to every metal-cased device's power plug was introduced. The prong mated with a three-contact outlet, providing a separate ground wire that connected the case of the device to a solid, water pipe ground. But because three-wire mechanical grounding methods were not 100 percent effective, two new approaches are used. First is double insulation of tools and electrical devices so components are completely insulated from metal parts likely to be contacted by the user, and enclosing the device completely in a nonconductive plastic housing. Second is the GFI.

A GFI unit may replace a circuit breaker or wall outlet. Or it may be a portable accessory that plugs in between a present outlet and the device you're using.

GFI's monitor the current flowing through the hot wire to a device, and the current flowing back through the neutral wire of the device. If these currents, which should be the same, vary by as little as .005 ampere (about $1/30$th of the current it takes to light a flashlight bulb), the GFI immediately switches off power.

Any excess current is passing to a ground via a pathway other than the neutral wire. That could mean a short or fault in the device you're using, and the path could be through your body. The GFI cuts off current in $1/40$th of a second. There are three basic types of GFI's: circuit breaker, wall-receptacle, and portable.

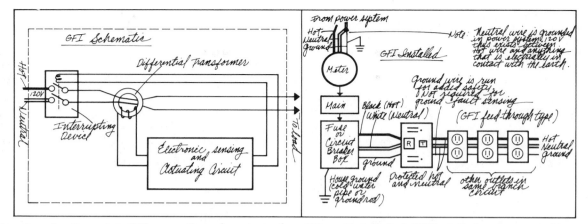

How it works: *Power into GFI passes through contacts of interrupting device and through differential transformer. Currents through hot and neutral wires must be equal. If current through hot wire is greater, circuit trips interrupter before current reaches shock level.*

Where it's installed: *GFI installed as shown provides protection to several outlets in same branch circuit. In typical home power-distribution system, it prevents hot wire from delivering 120 volts to grounded objects not stopped by a fuse or circuit breaker.* Illustration: Terry Redlin

---

Circuit breaker GFI The circuit breaker GFI replaces conventional circuit breakers. It will break on both large-scale overload currents and on ground-fault protection to any outlet receptacle served by the branch circuit fed through it.

The circuit breaker GFI, however, will also sense incidental leakage current paths that occur in the best of home wiring systems. The longer the branch and the more devices it serves, the higher its leakage current. If normal accumulated branch leakage is 4 milliamperes, and the GFI is set to trip out at 5, plugging in a device that has a slight leakage of 1 milliampere will cause the GFI to trip.

The right way to use a circuit breaker GFI is to protect dedicated circuits (i.e., to swimming pool pumps, patio lights, and so on) where the natural leakage of the branch will not reduce the GFI's tolerance.

Replacing a breaker with a GFI may require the services of a licensed electrician, depending on your local electrical code. However, the task is fairly simple. First, find the breaker that serves the electrical branch you want to protect. Note the physical dimensions and the current rating of the breaker. Obtain a GFI breaker with the same current rating and installation dimensions. Install it during daylight hours, by turning off the main power switch, removing the standard breaker, and mounting the GFI breaker in its place. Test after installing, following the manufacturer's recommendations.

Wall-receptacle GFI This unit replaces a standard duplex receptacle. It fits within an outlet box and protects you against ground faults in any device

Circuit breaker GFI combines full functions of overload current tripping plus fault sensing, all in same-size package as standard breaker. Photo: Square D Co.

plugged into it. It ignores natural leakage in the branch circuit leading to the GFI and is resettable at the same location where it trips. Some units may require a deep outlet box.

The wall-receptacle GFI allows maximum protection of a limited area of electrical device use.

Alternatively, you can get a feed-through receptacle GFI. With this type, you gain not only protection at the receptacle you're replacing, but you can also extend this protection to other outlets downline of the GFI receptacle. To make this possible, a feed-through GFI receptacle has two extra wires

---

Outlet-type GFI fits standard outlet and provides two grounding receptacles. Test and reset buttons allow you to check the unit periodically. Photo: Graf-Whalen

Plug-in portable GFI fits standard receptacles wherever you need protection. Photo: Square D Co.

(or terminals) in addition to the normal three (hot, neutral, and ground). These two extra wires extend protected hot and neutral to the next outlets and fixtures in the branch.

The photos show how to install a receptacle GFI. Before replacing the old one, turn off power to the affected branch circuit (by flipping the branch circuit breaker at the power box, or by removing and pocketing the fuse).

If the GFI you're installing is a three-wire type, simply connect hot (black), neutral (white), and ground (green or bare wire) to the appropriate terminals, following the manufacturer's diagram. This type will protect only devices that plug into this outlet. Install into the box, taking care to dress wires carefully, and replace the cover plate. Test as recommended by the manufacturer.

If the GFI you're installing is a feed-through type and you have determined that everything downline is fed through the circuit, connect the feed line hot, neutral, and ground to the GFI. Then connect its protected hot and neutral feed-through wires to the respective wires that feed the down-line branch circuit.

Because of the extra wiring, a feed-through GFI tends to be harder to get back into a snug outlet box. Some manufacturers offer stand-off faceplates that bulge the GFI outward from the wall. Measure

box depth carefully and compare to the physical requirements of a feed-through GFI before installation, especially if the outlet to be replaced is in a highly visible location. After installing, test as the manufacturer recommends.

Portable GFI If you don't have dedicated GFI's protecting outdoor, basement, or garage outlets in your home, you can use a portable GFI with electrical tools where your body is likely to contact ground. The simplest portable is a molded case with a three-prong plug on its back. You plug it into an outlet, then plug the device into the portable GFI.

Extension types plug into an outlet at one end and have the GFI located at the other end, with its receptacle feeding the device you're using. These are well suited to use of outdoor power tools. Portables feature all the test and indicating features of built-ins.

Testing and maintenance The National Electrical Code and Underwriters Laboratories have established the requirement for built-in test provisions to assure that GFI's deliver the protection they should. By testing a GFI once a month, you know you have working protection against accidental ground faults.

Portable GFI's should be protected against physical mistreatment, moisture, and contaminants.

HOW TO INSTALL A GFI OUTLET

To install a modern GFI outlet, shut down the power to the circuit; remove cover-plate screw. *Photo: Graf-Whalen*

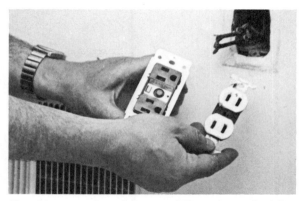

The old receptacle and the new GFI aren't greatly different in size, but the added safety from the GFI adds a new dimension of safety in the use of any device plugged into it. *Photo: Graf-Whalen*

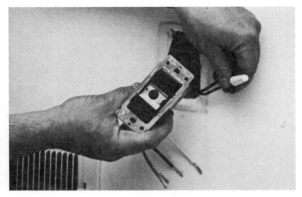

The slightly larger size of a GFI requires extra care in dressing the wires back into the box, especially where a feed-through type is installed to protect other outlets down the line. *Photo: Graf-Whalen*

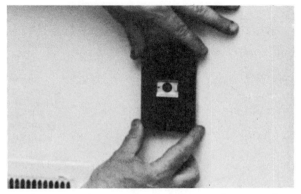

The GFI cover plate stands off wall somewhat, providing added space within the electrical box to accommodate the extra wires that extend its protection to other outlets. *Photo: Graf-Whalen*

ADDING BRANCH CIRCUITS Branch circuit distribution at the main panel must be carefully considered. When wiring additional circuits to an existing system, make sure there is adequate panel capacity to handle the new wiring, and, if existing circuits are being expanded, be careful not to overload them.

In load centers with circuit breakers, new breakers can be snapped into place to expand present capacity without installing a larger main entrance panel. By inserting a circuit breaker, a new circuit is available for adding lights or receptacles, or for connecting an appliance separately.

Some load centers that have fuses may be expanded by connecting conductors to the take-off lugs located between the fuses, and connecting a

neutral lead to the neutral strip. Branch circuits can then be wired into the add-on panel.

The wire used for making the run to an add-on panel should be rated the same as the add-on panel. Wiring appliances to the hot leads will give 240-volt current for running a clothes dryer or range, and wiring to a hot lead and neutral will provide 120-volt power.

Check local codes before adding an underground circuit. Some communities require conduit or lead-sheathed cable, rather than dual-purpose plastic cable. The National Electrical Code requires that some underground circuits be GFI-protected. Using conduit will prevent damage to the cable from digging or crushing. Conduit also provides a permanent ground for your entire electrical

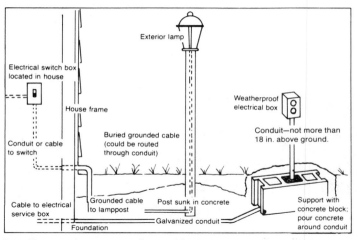

Installing outdoor receptacles and lamppost.
Using a star drill, punch a hole through the concrete block or masonry at least 12″ below ground level. Dig a trench and lay the galvanized conduit along the trench. Connect elbows and use locknuts to secure to outside weatherproof box. Caulk around the hole in the foundation and around the outside box. Secure the cable or conduit to the outside wall with straps. If the outside receptacle is to be free-standing, extend conduit through the center of the cement block vertically about 18″ above ground level. Pour concrete inside the block to support the conduit. Cover the entire block and trench with earth. Fish the wires through the conduit and attach the conductors to terminals. Make final connections to service panel. Illustration: General Switch Corp.

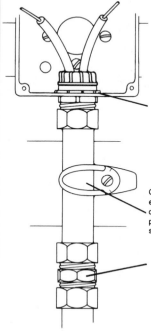

Compression-type raintight connectors fasten conduit to weatherproof box. With knockout plug removed from box, the threaded end of the connector fits through the hole and is secured from the inside with a locknut. Threads are capped with plastic bushing to protect the wires from sharp edges.

Conduit clamps are available in several types for securing conduit to walls or studs. They are either screwed in place or supported with heavy gauge screw nails.

Raintight couplings are used to join conduit in outdoor uses.

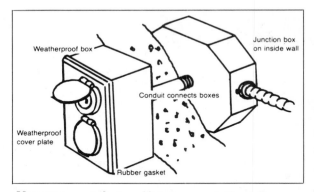

Mounting a weatherproof box on an outside wall.
Use two boxes with a length of conduit to connect them. Drill hole no larger than necessary to contain conduit. Be sure outside box and fittings are all weatherproof, and that you caulk around the conduit before mounting the outer box. Run connecting cable through conduit. Source: General Switch Corp.

Conduit fittings and accessories
Illustration: General Switch Corp.

system if connected to the grounding terminal or the main service entrance.

Underground cable should be placed at least 12" below ground level to eliminate possible damage from freezing. When making underground runs with plastic cable or wires in conduit, be sure to use unbroken lengths of wire to prevent shorting from rainfall run-off. If splices must be made, use special underground boxes with waterproof seals. Where conduit or cable enters an outside wall, or around receptacle boxes located on the outside wall of a building, use caulking compound to seal out moisture.

Each outdoor circuit should have a separate fuse or circuit breaker at the service panel for added protection. Wiring can be made directly to the main service entrance or to an add-on panel used expressly for outdoor circuits. Wire for underground runs should be a minimum of #14 copper or heavier.

HOW TO INSTALL NEW CIRCUITS

Adding new circuits in older buildings often presents a problem because studs and ceiling joists are covered with lath or gypsum wallboard, making wiring runs more difficult than in new construction. When working with existing walls it becomes necessary to break away narrow channels so that wires can be snaked behind the wall or strung over the front facing of the studs. The channels can be plastered over later and sanded smooth for finishing.

Wire runs in drywall construction require using a "fish tape" to bring the wires between the ceiling and the wall. Holes are drilled in ceilings and walls and the wire is pulled through these holes with the flexible steel "fish tape." Using flexible Romex cable facilitates passing the wire through such narrow spaces. It is recommended that long wire runs first be made across open ceilings and floors to reduce the amount of fishing.

Here are the ways to locate a wall stud:
Knocking on the wall A firm tapping on the wall above the nails in the baseboard will give you an idea as to the location of studs. Tap slowly across the wall until a solid sound indicates the presence of a stud. A thin finishing nail or small drill can then be used to verify your find. Drill holes near the baseboard so that when patched later they will be less noticeable.
Removing a baseboard After the baseboard has been removed, check to see where two sheets of plasterboard come together. Where the two boards meet will indicate the center of the stud.
Measuring for centers of studs Although building codes vary with different communities, studs are generally spaced 16" or 24" apart. By measuring out this distance from the corner of a wall, you can usually determine the approximate stud location. When you take a 16" measurement, tap on the wall at that location. If a solid sound is heard, drive a finishing nail through the wall near the baseboard to determine the exact center of the stud.
Using a stud finder A special device with a magnetic pendulum suspended in a clear plastic case will determine stud location. The stud finder is moved across the wall slowly, and when the pen-

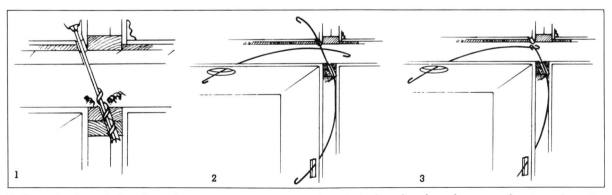

Pulling wire through floor from above.
Step 1. *If pulling a wire from the room above, first remove the baseboard. (When the wire is drawn from the attic, this is unnecessary.) Next locate the diagonal beams that cover the wall area you wish to fish the wires through. Drill a hole with an 18" bit and a brace.* **Step 2.** *Feed one fish tape through a hole in the ceiling where the fix-* ture is to be placed, and run another tape from the room above through the electrical box hole in the wall. Pull both tapes slowly taut until the two hooks catch. **Step 3.** *Secure the wires to the hook on the fish tape at the wall receptacle, and carefully pull the tape at the ceiling fixture hole until about 8" of wire is exposed through the hole. Disconnect the fish tapes.*

INSTALLING AN OUTLET BOX

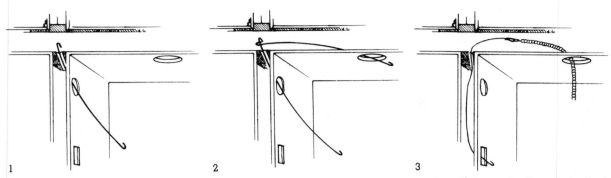

1   2   3

Fishing wire when tapes cannot be used from above.
Step 1. *First locate a point above the wall receptacle hole about 6" from the ceiling. Cut a hole approximately 3" in diameter at this location with a keyhole saw. Using an 18" bit, drill a hole diagonally through the horizontal beams above into the space between the floor and ceiling. Insert the fish tape into the hole and push up into the ceiling cavity.* **Step 2.** *Push the second fish tape through the*

ceiling fixture hole and catch the two hooks at the ends of both tapes. Pull the ceiling tape until the hook of the wall tape appears at the ceiling hole. **Step 3.** *Attach cable to wall tape hook. Withdraw wall tape back down through wall receptacle hole, pulling cable in through ceiling hole for the overhead fixture. Source: General Switch Corp.*

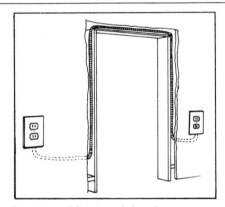

Running cable around door frame.
Carefully remove the door frame trim and the baseboard on both sides of the frame. Using a chisel, notch the spacers between the frame and the jamb. With an 18" bit, drill diagonally through the upright and header into the cavity above the door frame. Repeat the procedure on the opposite side of door. Run Romex cable across the top of the door using a fish tape. Replaster horizontal channels and replace the trim and baseboards.

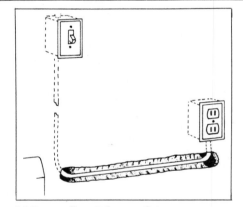

Adding wall switch to outlet.
Cut a channel in the plaster and notch out a hole for the outlet receptacle. Pass the cable down vertically from the switch between the studs, along the channel, and back through the wall to the receptacle. Replaster the channel and finish the surface by repainting. The channel may be hidden entirely if the baseboard is removed and the channel cut behind it. This method can also be used for wiring from one receptacle to another on the same wall. Source: General Switch Corp.

dulum moves toward the wall you are at the center of a stud. The movement of the pendulum is caused by magnetic attraction of the nails holding the wallboard to the center of the stud.
Fishing a wire Fish tapes can be purchased in either 12' or 25' lengths. The hook at the end of the

tape is used to secure the ends of the wire you wish to pull through the conduit, or when Romex cable is used to pull from ceiling to wall. Two tapes are often used when a severe bend is encountered.
Adding an outlet Long extension cords can be

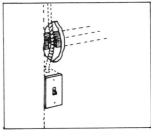

Running wire past door frame headers.
When the partition of your door frame has headers attached to an adjacent stud, notch the outer door frame in two places approximately 6" apart. Run the cable between the two notches, being careful not to put extreme bends in the wire. Wiring around headers may also be achieved by making a 1" diameter hole around the header, centered above the receptacle. The cable can then be passed across the notched header and fished up the wall. Replaster and finish the surface.

dangerous. If your codes allow you to use nonmetallic cable, you can easily add a new outlet.

After the hole is made for the outlet and the hole from the basement is drilled, fish the cable up from the basement through the outlet hole with a stiff metal wire. The illustrations show how to handle door frames, headers, and plaster walls. Only after the outlet is wired and the cover plate screwed in place should you connect the wire to a junction box in the basement.

Shut off the current leading to the box by removing the proper fuse or turning off the breaker. Then remove the cover plate. If you're not positive that you have turned off the proper circuit, either pull the main fuse or flip off the main breaker. To be certain, check the circuit with a small two-prong tester. Then, with the wires inside the box exposed, disconnect them by either twisting off the twist-on wire-nut connectors, or untaping solder joints and clipping them apart (if there is enough wire to rejoin).

One of the easiest methods of rejoining the wires is to use wire-nut connectors. Strip the ends of all wires about ½", hold the black wires together, and twist a new connector on. Make sure you have the next larger connector that will properly hold the three wires. Then connect the white wires, and last connect the bare or ground wires. Replace the

INSTALLING CEILING BOXES

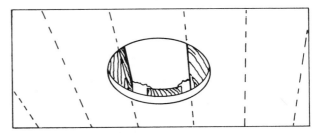

Draw an outline of a box on the ceiling and chip away the plaster, exposing the ceiling joists or lath. Remove the center lath with a keyhole saw and remove any insulation that may be blocking the hole from above.

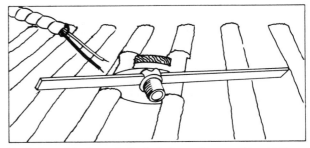

Push the cable through the hole from above and insert the hanger bar across the hole so it rests on the ceiling. The mounting stud nut is removed, and the cable pulled through the outer hole in the box.

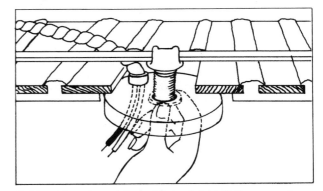

Holding the wires of the cable taut, install the connector and locknut and tighten firmly. Position the box over the hanger mounting stud and push the box into place. Tighten the nut over the stud, pulling the hanger bracket down firmly against the ceiling. Source: General Switch Corp.

cover and turn on the current. Or, if you prefer, you can solder the wires together and retape. (Some local codes do not permit soldered connections.)
CEILING BOXES AND FIXTURES For ceiling mounts, a shallow box is often necessary to fit the

INSTALLING A RECESSED CEILING FIXTURE

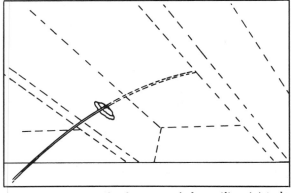

Step 1. *Determine the location of the ceiling joists by lightly tapping the ceiling with a hammer until a solid sound is heard. Drill a small hole and use a coat hanger to find the position of the stud.*

Step 2. *Using a keyhole saw, cut away the area within the box outline positioned between the ceiling joists. Put the wood mounting strips in place and nail them into the joists. Push the cable into the box and tighten the connector and locknut to hold the cable in place. Use a fiber insulating sleeve at the cable connector. Connect the black wire to the brass-colored terminal and the white wire to the silver terminal. Temperature rating of wire must correspond to rating stamped in fixture.*

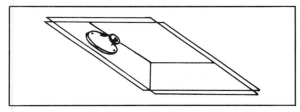

Step 3. *Move the box into place and tighten it into position through the top of the box with the wood screws into the mounting strips. SPECIAL CAUTION: There must be at least 3" separation between any recessed fixture and thermal insulation and a ½" separation from wood members. Source: General Switch Corp.*

narrow air spaces above the box. If the ceiling is not accessible from above, all work will of course have to be performed from below. First, make a template of the box itself and sketch an outline on the ceiling. Drill several holes, and, using a key-hole saw, remove as much plaster as possible. Chip away the remaining plaster covering ceiling joists within the box outline. Pull the cable through the opening. Install the hanger bar. Thread the cable to the inside of the box and secure it with a connector and locknut. The center hanger nut is then snugged up tight so that the hanger bar is pulled firmly against the studs above.

To install a recessed ceiling fixture, begin by tapping the ceiling gently with a hammer to find the joists. When a solid sound is heard you will know the approximate location of the joist. Drill a small hole and fish a coat hanger through the hole to determine the exact position for the box. Screw the box to the wood supports.

WIRING SWITCHES, RECEPTACLES, AND FIX- **TURES** Two-way, single-pole switches can be wired either ahead of or behind the light fixture. The switch is always wired on the hot side of the circuit and the fixture on the neutral side. Thus, current is prevented from flowing between the fixture and ground when the switch is in the "off" position, reducing the danger of electrical shocks. After wires are hooked up to the proper terminals, connect the ground wires to the ground terminal on the box.

In general, three-way switches are used to control one or more lights from different points; for example, at the top and bottom of a stairway or at either end of a hallway.

In some cases three-way and four-way switches are used in combination to control lighting from three different locations. This allows switching one or more lights from three different points. Adding another four-way switch to this arrangement provides a fourth control point, if needed.

To do a particular wiring job, find the illustration on the following pages that is similar to your wiring needs and connect the wires as shown.

Make sure to connect the wires according to their color codes. Match black wires to black and white to white. Use wire nuts to join the two conductors.

Three-way switches have three terminals. Two of them are brass for wiring red and black hot leads. The third terminal is usually colored silver (but is sometimes black) and is for the white neu-

INSTALLING AN OUTLET BOX

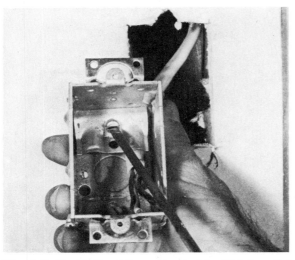

Step 1. *Pull cable through opening and feed it into outlet box. Tighten holding screw in back of box.* Photo: Monte Burch

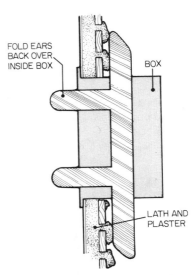

Step 2. *Push box into opening in wall and push ears of box holding clamps in behind wall and against box. Then bend ears back inside box.* Illustration: Ron Chamberlain

Step 3. *Strip wires back a bit.*

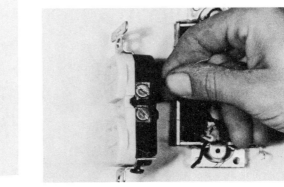

Step 4. *Fasten wires to new receptacle—white to silver, black to gold, and green or ground to grounding screw. Some local codes may also require a jumper wire to grounding screw on box.*

Step 5. *Fasten receptacle in place in box. Install cover plate and turn power back on.* Photos: Monte Burch

tral lead. In three-way switch installation, the conduit or Romex cable must contain three conductors: one white neutral lead, one black hot lead, and one red hot lead. The manner in which these conductors are wired to the switch depends upon where the switch is located in the circuit. Refer to the appropriate diagram on the next page for details.

WIRING SWITCHES

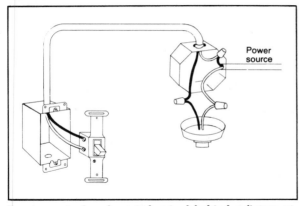

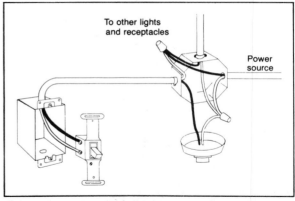

Two-way, single-pole switch wired behind a fixture at end of run.
The power source enters the light fixture and the hot black lead is connected to the switch. The white conductor at the switch should be painted black at the switch terminal to indicate that it is a hot lead.

Two-way, single-pole switch wired to a fixture in middle of run.
Attach black wire from power source to black wire that branches to the other run of the circuit; then attach the white lead of the switch to both of these. White wires at the switch terminal should be painted black to show they are live hot leads.

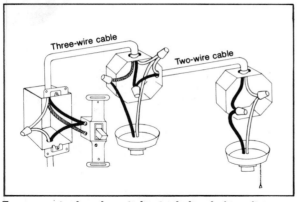

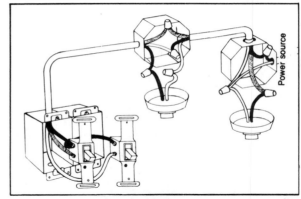

Two-way, single-pole switch wired ahead of two fixtures with separate switching.
The power enters through the switch box and the red and black hot leads are connected to the switch controlling the first fixture. (The second fixture is controlled by a pull chain switch on the fixture itself.) A duplex receptacle may be substituted for the second fixture.

Two switches controlling different light fixtures.
Three-wire cable is used between fixtures and receptacle box; white feeder cable is two-wire. White wire running from fixture to box must be painted black where it is connected to hot terminal on switch. Each switch controls one light fixture.

NOTE: *The switch and receptacle wiring diagrams are shown without grounding wire connections to simplify the illustrations. Remember to connect all bare grounding connections to the green pigtail connection on the inside of each receptacle.*

Wiring of four-way switches is always done in combination with three-way switching. If one or more light fixtures are to be controlled from three or more locations, four-way switches must be installed. Using four-way switches will permit as many fixture control points as needed on a particular circuit. Remember to connect the Romex cable grounding wires to the green pigtail on the inside of the switch and the receptacle boxes. Using BX cable or conduit provides proper gounding when connected to receptacle and switch boxes, completing the grounding through the main panel.

INSTALLING RECEPTACLES Double receptacles, often called duplex outlets, are easy to wire and available in either 15-amp or 20-amp capacities.

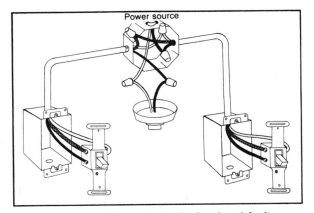

Two three-way switches wired on both sides of the fixture.
The switches are connected with three-wire cable from the fixture, and the fixture is energized with two-wire cable. Each switch can control the fixture regardless of the switch location. This type of wiring allows a switch at each end of a stairway or hall.

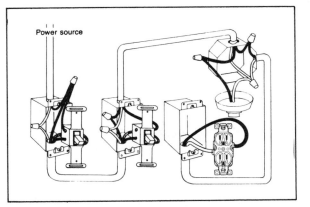

Two three-way switches ahead of fixture and receptacle.
Power source wire and outlet connections are two-wire cables. Four-wire cable between switches may be substituted by two two-wire cables. Wired as shown, light is controlled from either switch; receptacle is always hot.

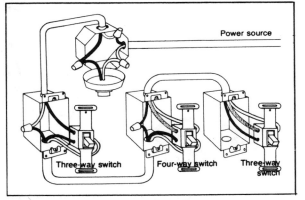

Controlling one fixture from three locations.
Two-wire cable comes from power source to the fixture, and connects the fixture to the first switch. Between switches, use three-wire cable. Two three-way and one four-way switch are the control points. Each additional control point would require another four-way switch.
Source: General Switch Corp.

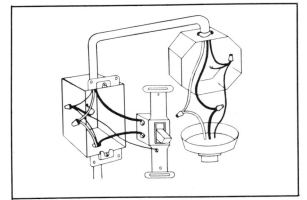

Grounding a switch controlling a light fixture
The bare wire in Romex cable is used for the grounding wire which is connected directly to the switch yoke, with a separate "jumper" wire from the ground conductor wire nut to the receptacle box. The hot and neutral leads are connected in the usual manner.

When wiring 20-amp receptacles, the wiring run from the load center to the receptacle must be #12 copper wire, which will prevent wires from overheating when there's a heavy power drain from appliances. New receptacles are required to be grounded. This is accomplished by attaching a bare or green conductor from the receptacle to the ground conductor supplied with the circuit. A good method is to make a splice that will also ground the box, if it is metal. Run the splice or short wire from the pigtail to the corner grounding lug on the receptacle.

HOW TO REPLACE A LIGHT FIXTURE

Replacing a light fixture is easy if you follow a step-by-step procedure. Before touching the existing fixture, turn off the power to the line upon which you'll be working. Remove the fuse controlling the line or shut off the current to the whole house.

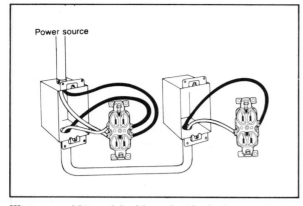

Wiring an additional double outlet (duplex) to an existing outlet.
The power source is connected to the terminals on the existing receptacle, and the hot lead runs from the top terminal to the brass-colored upper terminal on the new receptacle. The white neutral lead is run to the silver-colored lower terminal on the new duplex.

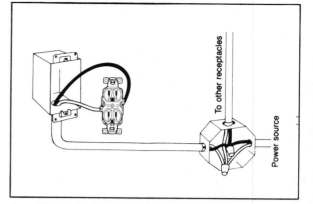

Installing a duplex outlet from an existing junction box.
The hot and neutral leads are tapped to the box and run to the terminals on the new duplex receptacle. The black hot wire is attached to the brass-colored lug and the white neutral lead to the silver-colored terminal.

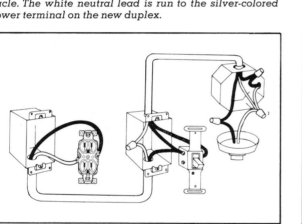

Wiring new duplex and switch from existing fixture.
Three-wire cable runs from the fixture to the switch controlling the light, and a secondary two-wire run is made to the receptacle. The outlet remains live regardless of the switch position.

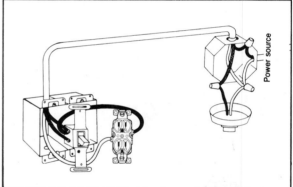

Installing duplex and switch in common housing.
The double receptacle remains live and operates independently of the switch that controls the light fixture. Three-wire cable is required for the run from the fixture to the receptacle box. Source: General Switch Corp.

CHANDELIERS If the new fixture is identical to the old, there's no problem in reattachment. However, if you are changing to a different type of fixture, the way in which it will be attached to the ceiling box depends on both the box and the design and weight of the fixture. Lightweight fixtures, such as those used on stairway landings or entrance halls, may be attached directly to the ceiling box with long machine screws.

However, if the holes in the ceiling box and the fixture do not align, a strap is necessary. Medium-weight fixtures require a metal strap for mounting, regardless of the type of ceiling box. Heavyweight fixtures, such as chandeliers, are usually held in place by a stem, which is attached to the center stud in the ceiling box. A fluorescent fixture is attached in the same way as an incandescent fixture of the same weight.

Holding the fixture, unscrew the crossbar and lower it gently until the weight of the fixture is totally on the wiring. If the fixture is heavy, have a helper support it instead. Next, disconnect the black and white wires leading from the fixture. If they are attached with solderless connectors, sim-

REPLACING A CEILING FIXTURE

1

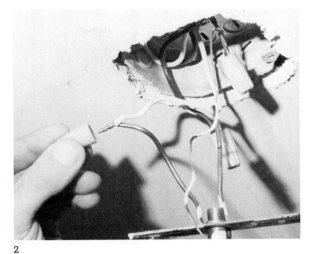

2

3

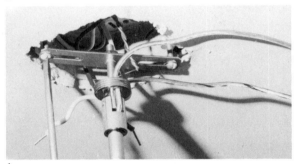

4

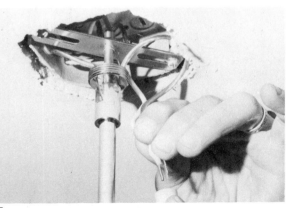

5

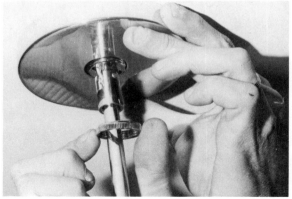

6

Step 1. *Loosen nut holding ceiling cap, then slide ceiling cap down chain. Note threaded nipple and crossbar.* **Step 2.** *Untwist solderless connectors to disconnect wires. Support the chandelier, now connected only by wires.* **Step 3.** *Screw the new threaded nipple and crossbar supplied into the top of the new chandelier.* **Step 4.** *Fasten crossbar to outlet box in ceiling with screws. New fixture hangs from nipple in center hole.* **Step 5.** *Reconnect house and lamp wiring with solderless connectors used for old fixture.* **Step 6.** *Push ceiling cover of new chandelier against ceiling and fasten with threaded ring.* Photos: May Communications

INSTALLING TRACK LIGHTING

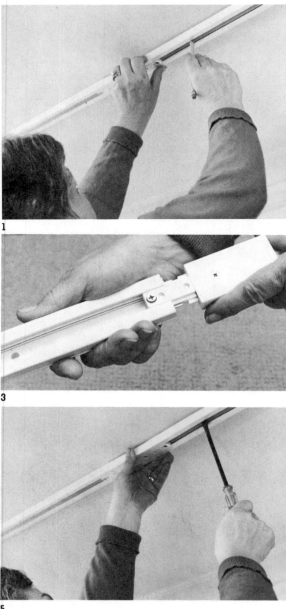

1

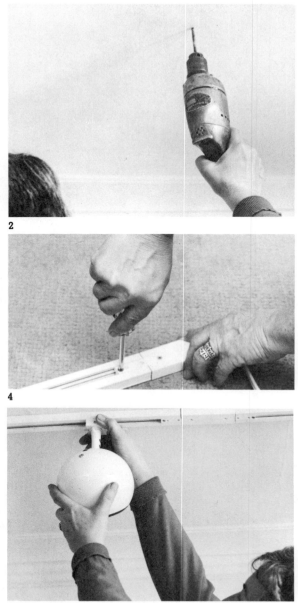

2

3

4

5

6

Step 1. Marks are made in ceiling over joists where tracks will run. Tracks can also attach directly to plasterboard with molly bolts. **Step 2.** From these marks, holes are pre-drilled where screws or molly bolts from the track will fasten to the ceiling (or the wall). **Step 3.** A cord and plug connector fits at one end of the track and carries the connection to an ordinary grounded electrical wall socket. **Step 4.** Connectors are simply pushed in the track and then locking screws are tightened. The connections are made without any splicing. **Step 5.** Next the track is fastened to the ceiling through the predrilled holes. A straight connector joins two pieces of track here. **Step 6.** The lamp is attached to the track with a 4" adapter that touches conductors in the track and permits complete turning.

ply rotate them counterclockwise until they come off. Then untwist the exposed tips of the wires, and your fixture is disconnected from the ceiling.

If the existing wires were soldered and taped, cut the wires just above the splice, leaving as much wire as possible for ease of handling. If cutting leaves too short a wire to work with, cut several inches *below* the splice and use the wire with the splice in it. However, it is safer to eliminate the old splice.

After you have cut the two wires, use a pocketknife or wire stripper to remove the insulation, exposing about $3/4''$ of bare wire.

The new fixture should have a threaded nipple, a strap, and a ceiling plate with a decorative retaining nut. First slide the nut down the stem of the light fixture, then the ceiling plate. Screw the threaded nipple into the top of the stem. Then screw the strap, through its center hole, onto the nipple.

Position the strap on the nipple very carefully. If too low, you won't be able to attach the ceiling plate. If too high, the ceiling plate will not fit against the ceiling. To find the correct position for the strap, slide the ceiling plate up to the top of the stem.

Next, screw the retaining nut halfway up the threads. Screw the strap down the nipple until the distance between the strap and the top edge of the ceiling plate is equal to the distance between the ears on the box and the ceiling surface.

Now loosen the retaining nut and let it and the plate slide back down the stem. Lift the new fixture to the ceiling and have a helper support its weight. Insert screws through the strap and screw them into the ears in the ceiling box.

Join the black wire coming out of the box to the black wire from the fixture, using an insulated solderless connector.

Next attach the white wires in the same way. If a green wire is present, attach it to the ceiling box. Push the connected wires back up into the box until they are neatly above the strap. Slide the ceiling plate up the stem of the fixture and position it over the hole. Screw it in place with the nuts. Lastly, put in the light bulbs and assemble any globes or decorative parts.

FLUORESCENT LIGHTS Fluorescent fixtures can be purchased in many types and sizes. Probably the most common are the ornamental types designed for installation on or in ceilings and walls. The most adaptable type of fixture is the simple "wiring channel," consisting of an enclosed white-enameled metal box containing the necessary wiring, ballast, and lamp holders. The channel is installed the same way as the ornamental fixtures.

Wiring connection If you connect a wired channel to a convenient outlet with a heavy extension cord, it will work. However, such wiring of a built-in (permanent) channel is not approved. It should be wired permanently into an outlet box.

HOW TO INSTALL TRACK LIGHTING

These systems provide lamps that can be aimed in any direction from tracks installed on the ceiling or walls. The lamps may be ball-shaped, cylindrical, square tube, and other shapes. Since the lamps are usually meant for accent lighting, the bulbs used are generally of low to medium wattage — 35, 50, 75, and 100 watts.

The tracks are attached to walls or ceilings with screws through the track into wall joists or studs. Where joists or studs are not accessible, use toggle bolts or molly bolts to hold the track to the plasterboard itself, since the tracks and lamps are very light in weight.

Track lighting systems should be approved by the Underwriters' Laboratories (UL). The photos show the installation of one system. Follow the manufacturer's directions to install the system you choose.

HOW TO INSTALL DIMMER SWITCHES

Installing a dimmer switch is relatively simple. Shut off the power. Then remove the old switch and install the new dimmer switch as shown in the photos. Install the switch plate and push the dimmer switch knob over the spindle.

INSTALLING DIMMER SWITCHES

1   2

Step 1. *To change conventional switch to dimmer, turn off power to circuit and remove cover plate.* **Step 2.** *Remove old switch from box. (Continued on next page.)*

3

5 6 7

Step 3. *Disconnect wires from old switch. On newer switches with push-in wire connectors, a screwdriver is pushed in slot indicated on back of switch to loosen wires.* **Step 4.** *Connect new dimmer switch.*

Step 5. *Fasten in place in box.* **Step 6.** *Install new cover plate.*
Step 7. *Push control knob onto shaft. Photos: Monte Burch*

HOW TO INSTALL SMOKE DETECTORS

There are two kinds of smoke detectors: photoelectric and ionization.

There are two versions of photoelectric detectors and three versions of ionization detectors. Either kind is available in plug-in or wired-in models.

Some communities allow only wired-in models in new construction. The ionization detector is also available in battery-powered models. Each model has certain characteristics you should be familiar with.

Wired-in models These are connected directly into a home's wiring system and are easily installed when the home is being constructed. They are

INSTALLING A PLUG-IN SMOKE DETECTOR

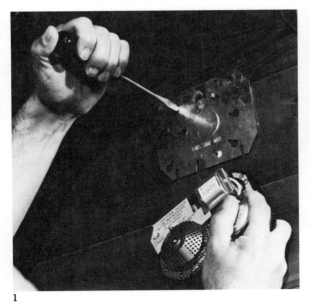

1

2

3

4

Photos here show steps of installing a plug-in smoke detector. Optional cord attachment connects to detector with a snap-in connector. Other end of cord is plugged *into outlet. If you want it permanently wired in, an electrician can attach the device easily to household wiring.*
Photos: Honeywell

more difficult to install in completed homes, since a ceiling or wall has to be opened to get at a junction box.

With a wired-in model, there is danger of a power failure when the detector is needed most. However, some experts consider this possibility a long shot. Wired-in models cost less than battery-powered ones, but are equal in price to plug-in models.

Plug-in models Simply mount these on ceilings or walls and plug into outlets. When buying a unit of this type, keep two things in mind.

First, never connect a plug-in smoke detector to an outlet that is controlled by a wall switch. If the switch is accidentally turned off, the detector won't operate. That wall outlet must be "live" at all times.

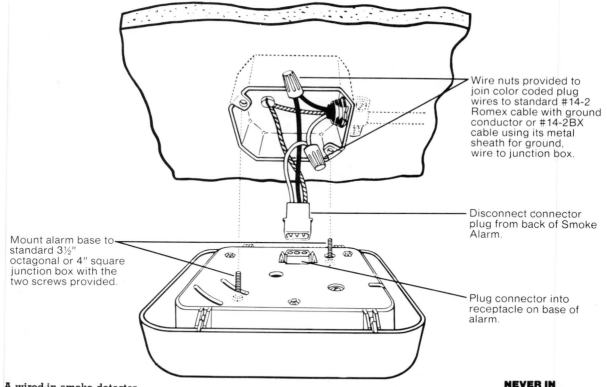

Wire nuts provided to join color coded plug wires to standard #14-2 Romex cable with ground conductor or #14-2BX cable using its metal sheath for ground, wire to junction box.

Disconnect connector plug from back of Smoke Alarm.

Mount alarm base to standard 3½" octagonal or 4" square junction box with the two screws provided.

Plug connector into receptacle on base of alarm.

A wired-in smoke detector.

Second, the plug of the model you buy should have a retainer to prevent its accidental removal from the wall outlet. As with permanently wired-in models, plug-ins have the disadvantage of being useless during a power failure.

Battery models These are powered by a battery with a life of about one year. Except for a connection to an outlet, they are installed in the same way as plug-in models. Completely self-contained, they eliminate the cord hanging from wall or ceiling if this is a consideration. The chief drawback is dependence on a battery, because there is a tendency to install detectors and forget about them. Since batteries must eventually go bad, many battery-powered units have some means of keeping you aware of the battery's condition, such as an audible short beep.

Plug-in and wire-in models are often equipped with a red indicator light that glows as long as power is being supplied to the unit. If the glow ceases, current has either been disrupted or the tiny bulb has burned out.

Choosing detectors It's important when selecting detectors to be sure they bear the Underwriter's

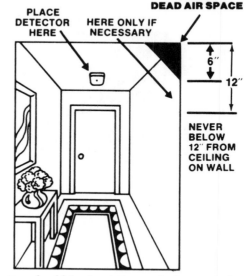

PLACE DETECTOR HERE

HERE ONLY IF NECESSARY

NEVER IN DEAD AIR SPACE

6"

12"

NEVER BELOW 12" FROM CEILING ON WALL

Detectors should be located near bedroom or sleeping area of home. In a two-story house, locate a second detector at the top of the stairwell to the basement. In the bedroom location, the device can be mounted on the ceiling or on a wall—not within 6" of the ceiling, but no lower than 12". Source: Honeywell

REPAIRING DOORBELLS

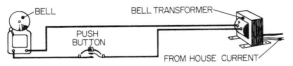

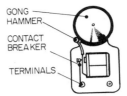

The first step in curing a balky doorbell is to trace all the wires from the push button to the bell and back to the transformer. These wires usually are exposed along the beams in the basement ceiling. But in finished basements, they may be more difficult to find. When tracing the wires, make certain that all connections—at the push button, bell, and transformer—are tight and clean. Tighten any loose screw or bolt as you go along, and sand wire ends clean. NOTE: Case on transformer should be grounded. *Illustration: Ron Chamberlain*

The third step, if the trouble is in the bell itself, is to remove the cover from the bell. Do this only after you are certain there are no wire breaks. Even if you can't get at the wires, do this anyway. Use some emery or fine sandpaper to clean the contact-breaker points. Remove paint or dirt around the mechanism. Also check to see if the hammer touches the gong when the contacts are closed. If not, just bend the hammer slightly; it is pliable and easily adjusted. *Illustration: Ron Chamberlain*

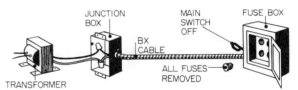

Step four is to check the push button itself. It is exposed to the elements, and sometimes dirt covers the contacts so they won't work, or something causes a malfunction in the spring. Here again, use emery or sandpaper to clean the contacts. Check to see that the contacts touch when the button is pressed. *Illustration: Ron Chamberlain*

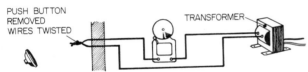

The second step, if the bell still doesn't work, is to have someone push the door button while you listen to the transformer in the basement. If you have no assistance, remove the push button and twist the two wires together. A) If the bell rings when the wires are touched together, your job is almost over. You have a defective push button. (See Step 4 for details on how to fix it.) B) If the bell doesn't ring but you hear a hum in the transformer, then the trouble is between the transformer and bell or in the bell itself. C) If the bell doesn't ring and you don't hear any hum in the transformer, then there is a break in the wiring or a burned-out transformer. *Illustration: Ron Chamberlain*

Step five is at the transformer again. If it's burned out, it must be replaced. Throw the master switch and remove the fuses before you touch any of the wires. Then unscrew the connections to the bell and push button. Disconnect the heavy wires from the house current. Place the new heavy wires in the same manner as the old. Use solderless connectors, or solder and tape, to join this end of the transformer. *Illustrations: Ron Chamberlain*

Laboratories (UL) label. The number of detectors you need depends on the layout of your home.

Every smoke detector comes with installation and maintenance instructions that should be studied and followed.

At least one detector should be installed on every occupied level of the house, and the furnace or boiler level. Detectors are sensitive and can be set off by "innocent" smoke, such as that given off by a fireplace or even by cooking. To shut the alarm off, clear smoke from the area.

HOW TO INSTALL AND REPAIR DOORBELL SYSTEMS

Most doorbells work on low voltage. However, exercise caution at the transformer where two heavy wires connect the system with house current. To work with these wires, shut off the master switch or remove the fuse controlling the bells.

If you replace an old bell or chime with a new one, and it doesn't work, first check the transformer. Many new chimes and bells require a higher voltage than older ones—12 to 14 volts as compared with 6 to 8. The illustrations show how to troubleshoot transformers and the entire system.

HOW TO WIRE MAJOR APPLIANCES

Circuit runs for major appliances are used specifically for appliances and not for lighting. It is best to check local code requirements for these circuits, and compare them with the National Electrical Code, which requires #12 copper wiring with 20-amp receptacles for all major appliance circuits. Heavier appliances, such as electric ranges with greater load requirements, must have special cables and receptacles.

Many 240-volt appliance circuits use three-wire cable. However, some codes insist on four-wire cable; the fourth wire is for grounding. The local codes must be checked before proceeding with your installation.

Before wiring major appliances, determine if the service entrance and main panel are sufficient to handle the loads from clothes dryers, ranges, air conditioners, and water heaters. Consult your local building inspector, a local electrician, or the utility company to determine your present load-handling capabilities. Ask if your local code requires that the neutral entrance wire be connected directly to the neutral terminal on the appliance. Remember that both grounding and wiring must conform to local codes in your community.

The types of plugs and receptacles used with heavy appliances vary widely, as the illustration indicates. Before you buy the receptacle, make an actual-size drawing for the prong arrangement on

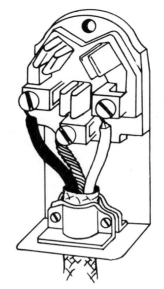

Interior connections for typical appliance receptacle.

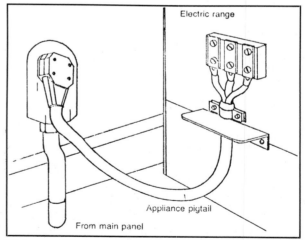

Wiring installation for electric range or clothes dryer. *Appliances such as an electric range require dual voltages. This type of appliance uses a cable of #6 copper three-wire Romex rated at 50 amps. The cable runs directly from the appliance's receptacle to the main panel. If cable is run through floor, it should be enclosed in rigid metal conduit, intermediate metal conduit, or metal pipe extending at least 6" above the floor. Always ground metal frame of the appliance to the neutral terminal. Wiring for a clothes dryer would be similar, except that appliance cord (often called "appliance pigtail") is usually built in. Illustration: General Switch Corp.*

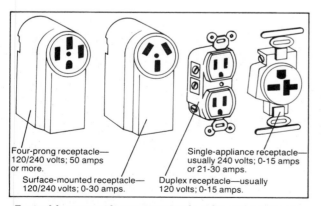

Four-prong receptacle—120/240 volts; 50 amps or more.
Surface-mounted receptacle—120/240 volts; 0-30 amps.
Single-appliance receptacle—usually 240 volts; 0-15 amps or 21-30 amps.
Duplex receptacle—usually 120 volts; 0-15 amps.

Typical heavy appliance receptacle inlet arrangements. Most have two current-carrying contacts, and one grounding contact. Often heavier receptacles (50 amps or more) have four contacts for four-wire connections. Source: *General Switch Corp.*

your appliance plug. Also, write down the amperage and voltage requirements, usually shown on a metal plate on the appliance, near the power cord. Make sure the receptacle you choose has an Underwriter's Laboratories (UL) label or tag.

WIRING A HEAVY-DUTY APPLIANCE RECEPTACLE Take off the plastic cover on the receptacle face by removing the screw between the receptacle plug-ins. Remove about 2½" of the outer insulation, and strip ½" of insulation from each conductor. Twist the bare stranded cable tightly so that no wires are loose. Pull out the knockout plug at the receptacle bottom and push the three conductors through the base so the outer insulation shows above the clamp; then secure the screws on the clamp. Connect the hot red and black leads to the outside terminals and the ground to the floor and receptable back plate secured to the wall at floor level. When using conduit, the receptacle is screwed to the wall and the conduit is strapped at the baseboard.

The illustration shows how to wire for an electric range or clothes dryer. Many water heaters use a dual-element heater rather than a single, to provide greater hot water capacity and faster water heating. Most utility companies specify the method for wiring water heaters, the size of elements allowed, and type of thermostats permitted. Therefore, it is helpful to consult your power company or an electrician before wiring a water heater.

4

HOW HOME PLUMBING WORKS · HOW TO CURE DRIPPING
FAUCETS · CONNECT FIXTURES · UNCLOG BALKY DRAINS ·
KNOW WHAT TOOLS AND FITTINGS YOU NEED ·
UNDERSTAND PLUMBING CODES · UNDERSTAND VALVES ·
WORK WITH PLASTIC PIPE · HANDLE EMERGENCIES · HAVE
A QUIET PLUMBING SYSTEM · PATCH PIPES · PREVENT PIPE
FREEZING · CONSERVE ENERGY · TROUBLESHOOT · INSTALL
A WATER SOFTENER · REPLACE A SUMP PUMP

PLUMBING SYSTEMS

While the home plumbing system seems like a complicated maze, it is actually a logical series of interconnected pipes and fittings that carry water in and wastes away. Fittings are used to make turns, change sizes, change types of pipes, and to control the flow through pipes.

Once understood, the home plumbing system is easy to work with. It will pay you to understand it, for you'll save both time and money by not having to call in a highly paid professional plumber. You'll be saving money, for example, each time you clear out a kitchen sink or bathroom basin drain. A quick repair of a dripping faucet saves water, too. Yet the repair takes only minutes.

HOW HOME PLUMBING WORKS

Your house plumbing system comprises two separate systems, one for bringing water into the house and distributing it to the fixtures, and one for getting it out of the house after use. The first is called, logically enough, the water supply system. The second is called the drain—waste—vent system, often called simply DWV. Water in the supply system is under pressure; the DWV system depends only on gravity flow. Water supply piping, because of its pressurized flow, is much smaller in diameter than DWV piping.

The two water systems are always separate, never interconnected. The reason for this is that any connections between the two systems—called cross connections—might permit contaminated water in the DWV system to enter the potable, or drinking, water in the water supply system. Sickness or death could result. Once water is used in a fixture it may enter the DWV system but it is never permitted to backflow in the other direction.

PIPES Water supply piping varies in diameter from ½" to a maximum of about 1". The smallest is ⅜". The largest water supply pipes are found in what is called the house service entrance. This pipe brings water from the city main or rural well into the house. Municipal water passes through a measuring device called a water meter. From there water branches to the water softener, water heater, and the various fixtures around the house. It also flows to outside garden hose taps called bibbs.

Main shutoff Immediately after the meter is located what's called the main shutoff valve. Closing this valve turns off all water to the entire house. The main shutoff is often located at the lowest spot in the house water supply system. In this case it probably contains a separate drain opening so that the system can be drained if the house is to be left unheated during freezing weather. (See page 134.) Such a valve is called a stop-and-waste valve.

Every family member should know where the main shutoff valve is so the water can be turned off quickly in an emergency. Most often it is located in a crawl space or basement. In a mild climate it may even be outdoors along with the water meter.

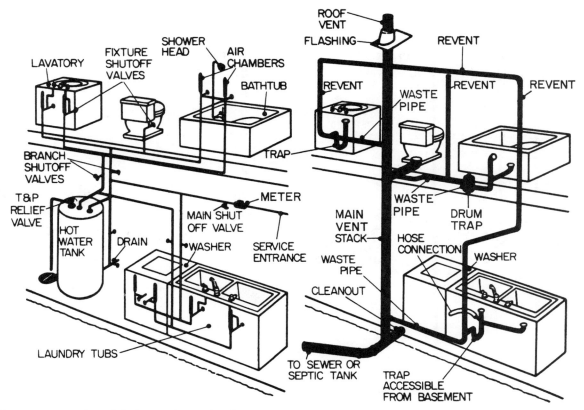

LAVATORY
FIXTURE SHUTOFF VALVES
SHOWER HEAD
AIR CHAMBERS
BATHTUB
ROOF VENT
FLASHING
REVENT
REVENT
WASTE PIPE
REVENT
REVENT
BRANCH SHUTOFF VALVES
TRAP
T&P RELIEF VALVE
HOT WATER TANK
DRAIN
METER
MAIN SHUT OFF VALVE
WASHER
SERVICE ENTRANCE
WASTE PIPE
WASTE PIPE
DRUM TRAP
MAIN VENT STACK
HOSE CONNECTION
WASHER
WASTE PIPE
CLEANOUT
LAUNDRY TUBS
TO SEWER OR SEPTIC TANK
TRAP ACCESSIBLE FROM BASEMENT

Home water supply and drain – waste – vent systems

In a house equipped with a softener, the water next flows through it, except for a supply for outdoor use and toilet flushing. Water for these purposes is usually drawn off before it is softened. There is little reason to treat water destined for such uses.

Hot and cold mains At this point the water supply system branches. One branch continues to the fixtures, delivering cold water. The other branch flows through the water heater, then to all the fixtures that use hot water. Pipes carrying cold water are called cold water mains, carrying hot water, called hot water mains. Branches of these mains that lead to fixtures are called simply fixture branches, hot and cold. Cold water is valved as it enters the water heater. This valve can shut off the entire hot water system from one point.

If there is a solar collector to help heat water, the supply is usually kept separate from the conventional house hot water system. Interconnection is only through the water heater tank's storage. Should the solar system not be working, as on a very cloudy day, delivery of hot water would be uninterrupted through the conventional fuel-using hot water heater.

FIXTURES At the ends of water supply lines are house fixtures. These may also be appliances, such as a hot water heater, water softener, or dishwasher. When the water in one fixture is turned on, it tends to reduce the amount of water flowing to another fixture. For this reason, correct pipe sizing, which will permit no single fixture to steal water from another, is important.

Air chambers Cushions of trapped air inside footlong vertical pipes, air chambers, are located behind each fixture and appliance. Separate capped chambers serve hot and cold water supply pipes. The purpose of air chambers is to stop the flow of water more gently when a faucet is turned off suddenly. Without air chambers, the shock of fast-moving water being turned off abruptly would cause a noise called water hammer. (See page 110.) Water hammer can build up pressure inside the water supply system to the point where it can rupture the system. So air chambers not only prevent this annoying racket they also protect pipes and

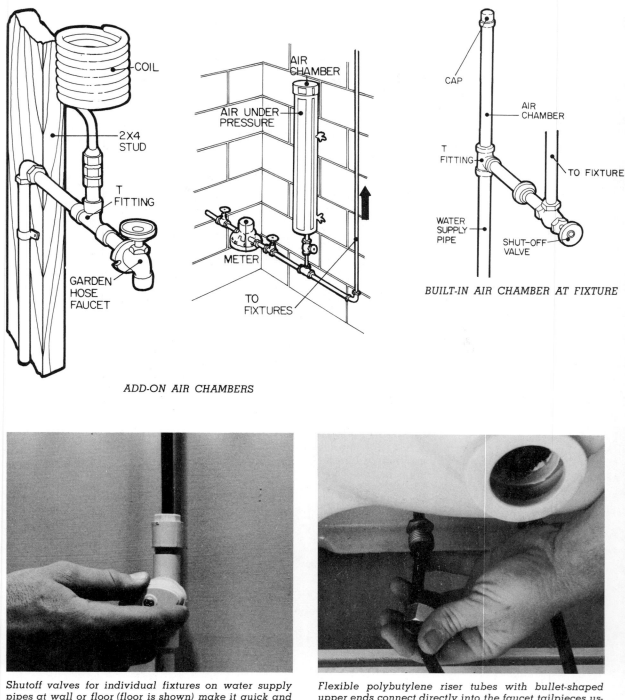

COIL

2X4 STUD

T FITTING

GARDEN HOSE FAUCET

AIR CHAMBER

AIR UNDER PRESSURE

METER

TO FIXTURES

ADD-ON AIR CHAMBERS

CAP

AIR CHAMBER

T FITTING

WATER SUPPLY PIPE

TO FIXTURE

SHUT-OFF VALVE

BUILT-IN AIR CHAMBER AT FIXTURE

Shutoff valves for individual fixtures on water supply pipes at wall or floor (floor is shown) make it quick and easy to turn off the water to a fixture for a repair or emergency. All are designed to accept flexible riser tubes. The risers make easy connections up to the fixture.

Flexible polybutylene riser tubes with bullet-shaped upper ends connect directly into the faucet tailpieces using a faucet nut. Use of riser tubes greatly simplifies awkward underfixture work.

fittings from overpressures. Appliances with fast-acting solenoid water inlet valves, such as dishwashers and washing machines, have a special need for air chambers. Internal pressures as high as 500 psi can develop when the valves shut off the water flow. No fixture or appliance should be without air chambers on both hot and cold supply lines.

Fixture shutoffs As water supply pipes come out of the wall or floor near each fixture, they are often provided with valves to shut off the water to that fixture when repair is needed.

Riser tubes Making the run from the shutoff valve to the fixture faucet are usually bendable pipes called riser tubes, often $3/8''$ in diameter. There is one for hot water and one for cold. Because riser tubes are flexible, connection between the water supply system and the fixture is rather easy. By the same token, quick disconnection is simple, should the fixture or faucet have to be replaced.

Dishwashers and some laundry tubs do not use riser tubes but connect to the water supply system directly.

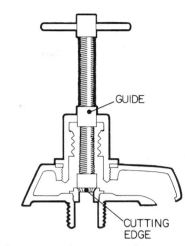

To dress the seat in a faucet, use a low-cost seat-refacing tool. Install the tool in the faucet body using the faucet's packing nut to hold the tool squarely against the seat.

HOW TO CURE DRIPPING FAUCETS

No matter how complex or mysterious it may seem at first glance, any faucet can be taken apart and reassembled. Work step by step, remembering how the parts came apart so you can get them back together again.

The usual order of parts removal is 1) cap screw; 2) handle screw; 3) handle; 4) large nut that holds the spindle housing; 5) the housing; and finally, 6) the spindle.

At the base of the spindle you'll find the washer, fastened by a brass screw. Replace both it and the washer with new ones. Be sure that the washer is just a little smaller than the recess in the spindle into which it fits. The shoulder around the recess can be filed off with a mill file if the washer happens to be too large.

Put a few turns of faucet washer packing around the stem under the cap nut before putting the faucet back together again. This will prevent leakage between the spindle and the nut.

If frequent washer replacement is necessary to stop leaking, it usually indicates a worn faucet seat. Rough seat metal chews up the washers. You can use several techniques to solve this problem. One is to reseat or smooth the faucet seat. Or you can add a new seat or self-contained seat and stem. The latter method has several advantages. A new faucet seat insert—the replacement for an existing seat—not only provides a trouble-free seal, but reduces chatter or water hammer. It also eliminates the need for further washer replacement. Faucet seat inserts are made to fit virtually all types of sink and tub units. They come with

long stems, short stems, chrome plating, brass finish as well as for hot or cold water faucets. Your plumbing supplies dealer should have a selection or be able to order what you need. Be sure to take the old one in with you.

A large hex-head (Allen wrench) or a faucet seat tool may be needed to remove a faucet seat. Turn the seat counterclockwise to unscrew it from the faucet body. Otherwise, the only tools needed for faucet work are a monkey wrench or an adjustable open-end wrench and screwdriver.

Seat dressing Some faucets do not have removable seats. If these become worn or damaged, the only cure is to dress them. For a few dollars you can get a tool made specifically for this. The tool comes with spacers, cutters, and a handle. To use it, all you do is turn off the water, remove the faucet spindle to expose the seat, install the tool, and turn. Use the seat-refacing tool as gently and smoothly as possible. Hold the tool vertically. When you're finished, reassemble the faucet, being sure to install the handle so that it reads properly when the repaired faucet is closed.

Fixing a faucet leak is easily worth the trouble. A leak of sixty drops a minute wastes some 2,300 gallons of water in a year. Forcing a faucet closed to stop a drip only wears the washer and faucet seat excessively. It also wears the threads of the faucet spindle, making them tend to become loose.

Faucet washer If you don't have a washer the right size, you can file down a larger one by chucking it on a bolt in an electric drill. Run the drill at high speed and bear down on the cutting portion of a file until the washer is milled off to the proper size. Don't use a too-small faucet washer.

Faucet packing If the faucet leaks at the packing, try tightening the packing nut. That failing, the packing can be replaced. There is a new kind of packing made with an outer nylon coating that lasts longer and makes the faucet easier to operate than does ordinary packing.

To replace the packing, simply turn off the water and remove the handle and packing nut to expose the old packing. Wrap on the new packing. Reinstall the packing nut and other parts.

Washerless faucets So far we've covered the old globe-type faucets. The new washerless faucets are built and repaired differently. Fewer repairs are needed, fortunately. One type uses a diaphragm valve. A neoprene diaphragm is moved over the valve seat by the thread and spindle. Rotating friction of the spindle is absorbed by a swivel on the end of the spindle. Thus, unlike a faucet washer, the diaphragm receives only up-and-down movement. For this reason a diaphragm will outlast a faucet washer many times over. The diaphragm also keeps the faucet shaft sealed off from the water chamber of the faucet. Thus the shaft can be lubricated for easier action. No packing is needed.

The diaphragm is replaced to cure any problems with this type of faucet. To do it, remove the handle to expose the hex-head bushing. When you unscrew the bushing, the diaphragm assembly may be lifted out. Leaks around the faucet shaft also are cured by replacing the diaphragm.

Single-lever faucets This type of faucet, and push-pull faucets, use water pressure plus spring pressure to turn themselves off. Strainers are built into them to keep debris out of the delicate valve mechanism. The only service usually needed is an occasional cleaning of the strainers.

For installation of a spring-and-seat kit (such as Delta, Peerless) consult the faucet manufacturer's instruction sheet. On the most common Delta and Peerless lever faucets everything needed, including instructions, comes with the spring and valve seat kit. Included is a combination set-screw wrench and spanner for removing the handle and for adjusting the tension collar.

To put in a new set of valves and springs, you simply remove the handle's set screw and pull off the handle. (Be sure to turn off the water.) Then unscrew the cap nut and lift the ball or cap out of the faucet by the spindle. Down inside the body you'll find both seats sticking up on springs. Pick out the old seats and springs and insert new ones. Reinstall the ball or cap and nut. Adjust the tension collar just tight enough so the faucet doesn't leak around it when turned on and off. If too loose there

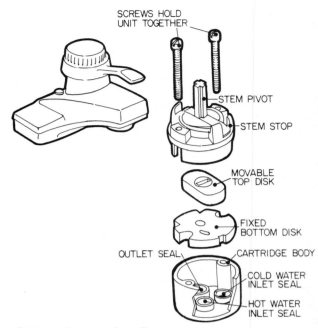

Disk-type faucet without O-ring

will be leaks; if too tight the faucet's action will be stiff.

DISK-TYPE FAUCETS Some of the newer disk-type faucets make use of replaceable cartridges rather than the conventional faucet seats. If one of these leaks (rare) it is fixed simply by installing a new cartridge. These faucets have no packing, and use O-rings instead. One type uses metal-to-metal action. Some come with smooth or serrated cap nuts intended for removal and installation by hand, not with a wrench or pliers. If one is corroded too tight for hand loosening, wrap it with a few turns of masking tape. Then turn counterclockwise gently with pliers. Sometimes you'll also need pliers to pull the cartridge unit out of the faucet. This is because of the resistance offered by the O-ring seals.

REPAIRING A SINK SPRAY HOSE When the water is turned on and you press the button on the spray head, water should come from the spray hose in a good stream. If there is a slight flow from the faucet at the same time, this may be normal. The switch from faucet to spray hose is automatic. It's done by what is called a diverter valve in the base of the faucet at the center.

Sometimes, if you're not getting enough flow from the kitchen faucet, the problem is the aerator

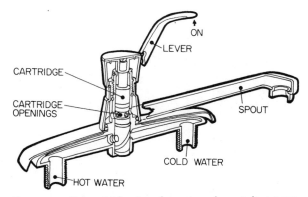

CARTRIDGE

CARTRIDGE
OPENINGS

LEVER

ON

SPOUT

COLD WATER

HOT WATER

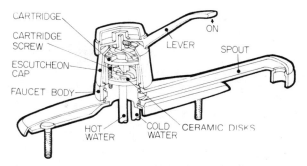

CARTRIDGE

CARTRIDGE
SCREW

ESCUTCHEON
CAP

FAUCET BODY

LEVER

ON

SPOUT

HOT
WATER

COLD
WATER

CERAMIC DISKS

To remove the cartridge in a lever-type faucet, first press
the lever down to "off." Use a screwdriver to pry off the
lever cover. Remove the lever screw. Then the housing
and lever may be lifted off. Unscrew the retaining nut and
take it and the sleeve beneath it off the cartridge. To get
the cartridge out, first remove the clip at its top, using the
tip of a screwdriver. Then grasp the cartridge tightly with
pliers and pull it vertically out of the faucet body. The
new cartridge is pushed into position and the parts replaced in the opposite order they came off.

To repair a single-lever cartridge-type kitchen mixing
faucet, loosen the lever set screw with an Allen wrench.
Lift off the lever and unscrew the escutcheon. The cartridge can then be removed by unscrewing the two long
screws that hold it to the faucet.

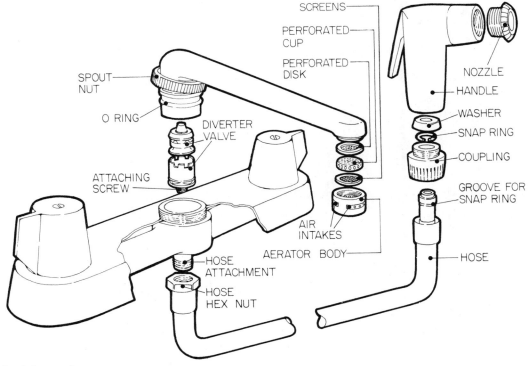

SCREENS

PERFORATED
CUP

PERFORATED
DISK

NOZZLE

SPOUT
NUT

O RING

DIVERTER
VALVE

ATTACHING
SCREW

HANDLE

WASHER

SNAP RING

COUPLING

GROOVE FOR
SNAP RING

AIR
INTAKES

AERATOR BODY

HOSE
ATTACHMENT

HOSE
HEX NUT

HOSE

Parts of a sink spray hose

FAUCET REPAIR: COMPRESSION FAUCETS

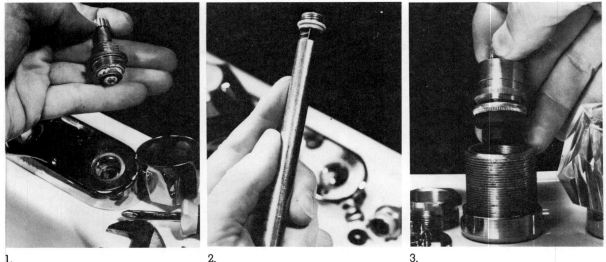

1.   2.   3.

4.

1. *Ordinary washer-type faucet basic repair is made by removing spindle from the body and replacing compression washer. It comes off when the brass screw is removed.*
2. *Diaphragm-type faucet outlasts many washer-types. Diaphragm fits the stem snugly but is not held by screw. To replace, simply peel it off, remove stem, then install new diaphragm. Replace stem in faucet and you're done.*
3. *Compression faucets are often made with removable seats. These let you unscrew worn seat using seat-removal tool that fits a number of seat openings. Sometimes a screwdriver will suffice. If washers are short-lived, seat is likely at fault.*
4. *Some faucets, especially American Standard faucets, contain combination washer-seat units that are replaced with new ones. While these renew all the wearing parts, they cost more than washer-seat repairs. This long unit is from shower faucet. Photos: Richard Day*

at the end of the spout. This may be taken apart and its disk cleaned and replaced. Or a new aerator may be installed. Aerators lose their flow characteristics as their parts become coated with water scale.

Low flow coming from the sprayer hose may mean that the valve or its spray head needs cleaning. If this doesn't help, check the spray hose for kinking. You can inspect the portion underneath the sink with a flashlight. There is also a possibility that the hose is swollen on the inside or pieces of it are chunking off. Then the cure is hose replacement.

To replace the hose, shut off the water supply to the fixture and remove the hose connection at the base of the faucet underneath the sink. Some con-

NONCOMPRESSION FAUCETS

1.

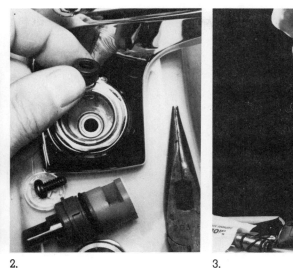

2.

3.

tain several hex nuts. The one closest to the hose is the one you want. Get an exact replacement and install it the reverse of the way it came off.

The final check should be of the diverter valve itself. It may be reached through the faucet body or from underneath. Screw or lift out the valve parts and take them to your dealer so you can get an exact replacement. Some diverter valves are enclosed, and the entire unit is replaced, rather than just the parts of it.

FAUCET REPLACEMENT To modernize an old faucet involves a simple replacement of the old unit. If you're tired of changing washers and redressing seats in your old faucet, it may be time for replacement with a long-lasting, single-lever, or push-pull faucet. Make sure that the new faucet comes in the proper *centers* to match your counter or sink bowl. Lavatories use faucets with 4" centers, usually. Sinks use 8" centers. Sinks with spray hoses often contain four holes each on 4" centers. The deck-mounted faucet uses three of the holes, the spray hose uses the fourth.

The first step, of course, is to shut off the water supply. Open the taps to release all water pressure remaining in the pipes. Then the risers are removed from the faucet's tailpiece using a tool called a basin wrench. The wrench is applied facing one way for loosening and the opposite way for tightening. It is the only special tool required for the job. When its hold-down nuts are removed, the old faucet can be lifted off the countertop or bowl and thrown away.

The new faucet is put in place on the sink top

4.

1. *A variety of repair kits exist for popular ball-type single handle mixing faucets. Some come with seats and springs only. Others have O-rings and other parts. Each contains a hex wrench tool for removing faucet's handle and combined spanner for tightening cap tension.*
2. *Cartridge-type faucets, like this Moen single-handle model, are easy to repair. With upper parts removed and clip pulled out, old cartridge lifts out and the replacement lowers in.*
3. *Faucets with ceramic or plastic cartridges rarely need service. If they do, all it amounts to is replacing tiny rubber seal and spring. You can buy parts in low-cost kits.*
4. *Just as easy to replace is the popular flat single-handle mixing cartridge. Once faucet is apart, take out two screws and lift off old cartridge, positioning the new. Install screws and reassemble. Replacements are color-coded, so get one of the same color. Photos: Richard Day*

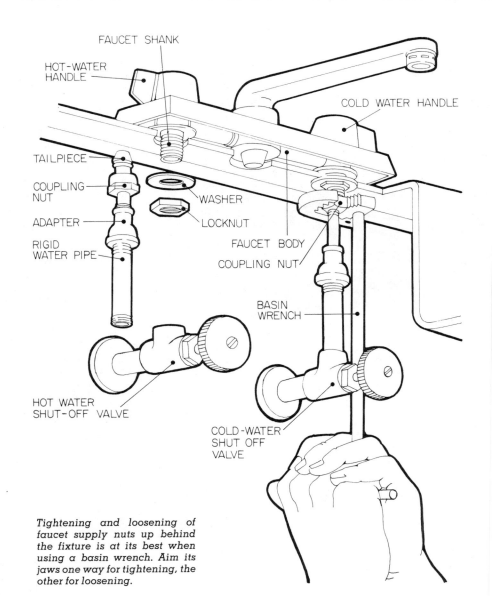

FAUCET SHANK

HOT-WATER HANDLE

COLD WATER HANDLE

TAILPIECE

COUPLING NUT

ADAPTER

RIGID WATER PIPE

WASHER

LOCKNUT

FAUCET BODY

COUPLING NUT

BASIN WRENCH

HOT WATER SHUT-OFF VALVE

COLD-WATER SHUT OFF VALVE

Tightening and loosening of faucet supply nuts up behind the fixture is at its best when using a basin wrench. Aim its jaws one way for tightening, the other for loosening.

and fastened from below with its new bolts and washers. If the old riser tubes won't reach the new faucet, buy new ones and install them. (The riser tube hookup procedure is covered on page 110.) When you tighten the faucet nuts between the riser tube and the faucet tailpiece, be sure that you hold the faucet's fitting, in order to keep it from twisting while the nut is tightened.

When you're all done, turn on the water again and inspect your work for leaks. Then remove the aerator from the faucet spout. Turn on both hot and cold water full force for a few minutes to clear any debris in the piping, which prevents it from becoming trapped in the faucet's valve or aerator.

If you've taken off all collars and bonnets and a spindle still will not come out, look for a clip holding it in. Ease out with a screwdriver.

HOW TO CONNECT FIXTURES

Installing water systems and DWV systems is called rough plumbing. The installation of fixtures is called finished plumbing. The work is very different, too. Finished plumbing consists of fixture connections. Each fixture has two kinds of connections: water supply and waste. Always make the waste connection to a fixture first, because it is the least flexible.

Lavatories, sinks, and laundry tubs hook up similarly through fixture traps, which are purchased separately from the fixture. A trap is a bent tube of metal or plastic 1¼″ or 1½″ in diameter. Traps and trap parts are called tubular goods in the plumbing trade. They come in many forms and materials. The newest are made of beige polypropylene plastic. These are easy to use, lightweight, inexpensive, and resistant to all household wastes. Also, they do not corrode.

When a fixture drains into a wall connection, a P-trap is used. It's shaped like a P. And if a fixture drains into a floor connection, an S-trap is used. It is S-shaped, in case you didn't guess. Some plumbing codes outlaw S-traps because of the contention that they tend to siphon dry of sealing water.

Most common is the ordinary P-trap. It comes in two sections. The first is a J-shaped bend that slips over a tailpiece coming down from the fixture drain. Both tailpiece and drain ordinarily come with the fixture. The connection between the J-bend and tailpiece is made watertight by a jam nut washer compressed by a trap jam nut. The O-ring and slipnut come with the trap assembly. The other major part of a P-trap assembly is the trap arm. This is longer and less bent than the J-bend. The curved end of the trap arm connects with the J-bend using a ground joint that fastens with a jam

Fixture trap parts, known as tubular goods, are available in many forms. These packages hold two different styles of P-traps made of polypropylene. Photos this series: Genova

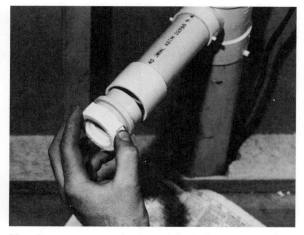

Most fixture traps need some method of connecting them to the DWV system; thus the trap adapter. This street-type trap adapter of PVC solvent-welds into a socket, in this case a coupling. The fixture trap fits it directly.

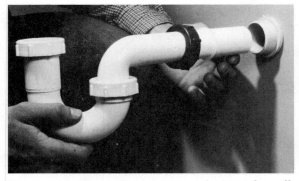

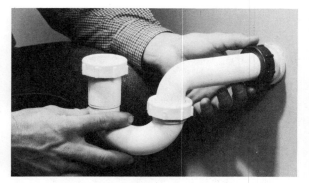

The assembled P-trap slips into a trap adapter at the wall. The white wedge-shaped plastic O-ring is put on the long trap arm after a slip jam nut goes on the arm nearest the wall. The O-ring should point toward the trap adapter.

An easy hand tightening of the slip jam nut onto the trap adapter seals the joint between the trap arm and the trap adapter watertight. A smaller 1¼″ trap could likewise be used in the 1½″ trap adapter by using a 1½″ × 1¼″ slip jam nut.

nut. The trap arm is inserted into a trap adapter at the wall.

Trap parts are adjustable up and down on the J-bend and in or out on the trap arm. This enables a connection to be made even though all fixtures have their waste openings at different distances from the wall. The trap also adjusts from side to

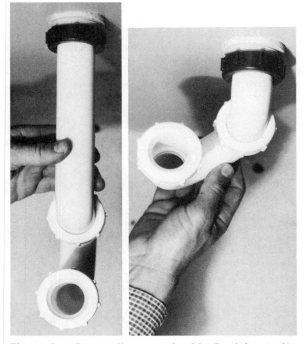

The modern P-trap offers considerable flexibility in fixture drain location. It fits a fixture with its drains centered far out from the wall (left) or a fixture with its drain off-center or close to the wall (right) simply by flexing its joint. Once positioned and the slip jam nut tightened, the trap becomes watertight.

side to permit connection to a fixture drain that is not centered perfectly on its outlet connection.

To install a P-trap, take its two pieces apart, slide a slipnut up onto the fixture tailpiece with threads facing downward, and hold it in place by sliding a washer on after it. If the washer is made of plastic and has a wedge-shaped cross-section, its wedged side should face downward.

Insert two jam nuts onto the trap arm. The first goes on threads-first. The second jam nut goes on threads-last, followed by a washer. Now you can slip the J-bend, right side up, onto the drain's tailpiece and start screwing the jam nut on. Slip the trap arm into the trap adapter at the wall and begin threading its jam nut onto the trap adapter.

If you're using a 1½″ trap for a sink or laundry tubs, use a standard jam nut washer at that location. To use a 1½″ trap with a 1¼″ lavatory tailpiece, install a 1½″ × 1¼″ reducing washer in the J-bend's jam nut. Some traps come with this.

You can now make up the jam nut connection between the two parts of the trap, sliding the trap arm in and out or raising or lowering the J-bend and rotating it until both parts line up.

At this time do not tighten any of the jam nut connections. Leave them loose. Slide and turn everything until the trap fits without strain. Then tighten the three jam nuts using a fixture or monkey wrench.

Fill the sink bowl with water and drain it out all at once. If there are leaks, tighten the fittings more. If leaks persist, remove the trap and apply silicone rubber sealant to all the joints (See photo.) Then put them back together. Silicone sealant may be used on polypropylene, PVC, or metal traps but not on traps made of ABS. Chemical action of the silicone causes intergranular stress cracking in ABS.

DOUBLE-BOWL SINK Although a twin-bowl kitchen sink has two drains, only one trap is used. To do this the drains are connected by a cross-pipe.

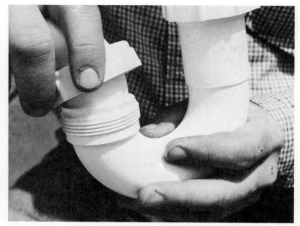

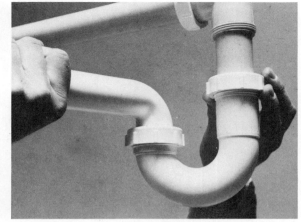

A trap's J-bend and trap arm are joined with a slip jam nut. This connection must be tightest of all, because this portion of the trap is below the water level.

When the trap fits the sink tailpiece and trap adapter both without strain, you can tighten all slip jam nuts. The slip jam nuts on these polypropylene traps are designed for hand tightening. If additional tightening is required to make them leak-free, use a pair of water-pump pliers.

If leaks are a problem or simply to make sure they are not, you can apply silicone sealant to the main trap parts, especially the J-bend trap arm joint. Then assemble as usual with O-rings and slip jam nuts. The silicone will cure to prevent any leakage. Do not use silicone on ABS traps.

This trap, called a Los Angeles pattern trap, solvent-welds directly to 1½" PVC DWV piping. It needs no trap adapter; thus, one slip jam nut is eliminated. The pipe stubout can be made any length to allow the trap to be centered under the fixture drain.

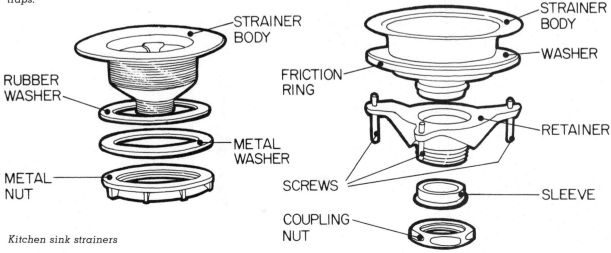

Kitchen sink strainers

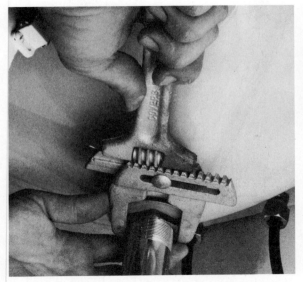

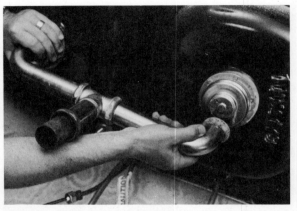

Double-bowl kitchen sink drain with a center trap uses two drainage arms and a slip-coupled T to connect the twin bowls. The single pipe coming down from the T enters the top of the fixture's trap. Thus both drains connect to one tailpiece.

A trap-and-fixture wrench is useful for tightening drain nuts. Its jaws will open wide enough to get even the largest nuts. The jaw ends are designed for turning lugged nuts.

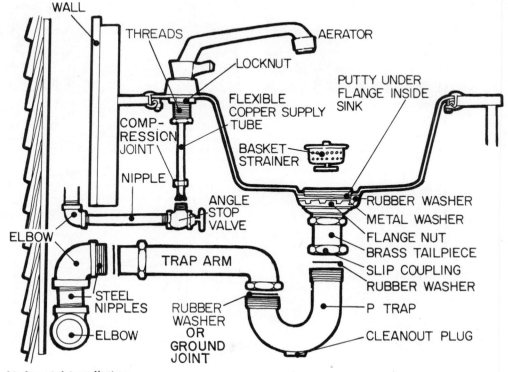

Parts of a kitchen sink installation

The curved end of the cross-pipe connects directly to one drain. Its other end slips into a tee attached to the other drain. The tailpiece below the tee accepts the fixture's trap. All the parts make use of slipnut connections.

This hardware, too, is available in modern plastic or traditional metal. The trap may be placed under the left or right bowl, whichever is convenient. The trap adapter should have been located in the wall centered behind one bowl or the other for an easy-in connection. Normally the trap adapter is centered behind the right bowl so that a food waste disposer may be located there. (A disposer installation requires slightly different tubular goods under the sink.) If the trap adapter is centered on the twin bowls, use tubular parts that provide for this. Double-bowl laundry tubs are often connected to a trap more nearly centered on the tubs. The actual hookup is not so different from what has already been described, using slipnuts.

WATER SUPPLY. Once you connect a fixture's drain to its waste pipe, you're ready to hook up the water supply tubes. In new construction the water supply most often comes from outlets at the wall. Sometimes a water supply for a fixture is located in the floor beneath it. Either way, the outlets should be fitted with riser tube adapters. (See page 134.)

One end of the riser tube adapter fits the water supply pipe stub coming out through the wall or floor. In the case of a new installation using CPVC/PB to water supply tubing, the CPVC fitting would be solvent-welded to the stub-out tube. The fixture side of the riser tube adapter accepts the cut-to-length end of a ⅜" riser tube. Using chromed copper risers, this is what's called a compression fitting. A small brass ferrule fits over the end of the riser and is compressed into a seat by a compression nut. Then the nut is tightened. Flexible polybutylene risers (described in the section on plastic pipe) may be hooked up with a compression nut fitting. Best yet, they're used with a special Genogrip (a registered trademark of Genova, Inc.) riser tube adapter.

Each riser tube is cut to the proper length to reach from the faucet tailpiece and into the riser tube adapter. All bends in risers should be tried before the riser is cut.

Riser and faucet hookup At the upper end of the riser tube, a number of connections may be used. Easiest is the simple faucet nut connection. Many of the most modern faucets are built to accept this. These end in ½" nontapered male pipe threads at hot and cold water tailpieces. A faucet nut—available at your plumbing supplies dealer or home center—is slipped threads-first up onto the riser tube and screwed onto the ends of the tailpieces.

There it holds the riser tube's bullet-shaped end tight and leakfree against the faucet tailpiece. Nothing else is needed except possibly a flat brass washer that is available with the faucet nuts. The washer fits between the faucet nut and the riser tube's shoulder to prevent twisting of the tube as the faucet nut is tightened. With this connection two wrenches should be used during makeup. One keeps the faucet tailpiece from twisting while the other tightens the faucet nut over the riser tube. If your fixture's faucet ends in a different style of tailpiece, you can easily adapt riser tubes to it, for example, as follows:

Copper tube tailpiece The simplest way to connect to a plain-ended copper tube tailpiece is to flare both it and the riser. Then make the connection with a flare coupling and a pair of flare nuts. Even though the riser and faucet tailpiece are different sizes, the hookup can be accomplished using a reducing flare coupling. Of course, the bullet-nosed portion at the upper end of the riser must be cut off so it can be flared. Flare nuts won't go on after you flare, so be sure to install them first.

Bayonet-end pipe tailpiece Common on kitchen sink faucets, the short bayonet-end brass pipe tailpieces usually end in ¼" pipe threads. This style of faucet connection is ideal for a riser tube hookup. Simply remove the faucet nuts, discard the two tailpieces, and install the bullet-nosed riser tubes in their place. You may need to use a reducing washer between the faucet nut and the riser for a surer connection. These are stock items and are sold at most plumbing supplies dealers and home centers.

Threaded faucets Faucets designed to take pipe threads directly are most common in laundry tub installations. Connecting to them is simply a matter of adapting. If they contain ½" threads, it's simple. If the threads are female, screw in a ½" pair of nipples, wrapping the threads with white Teflon plumber's tape before you make them up. The bullet-shaped ends of the riser tubes and faucet nuts can be connected directly. If an angled connection is needed, use a pair of brass ½" street elbows with nipples threaded into them.

A connection between a riser tube and a ½" nipple may be made more leakfree by using a special rubber fixture supply grommet between the two. These are shaped to fit snugly over the bullet ends.

If the faucet's threads are ⅜", you can do the same trick using ⅜" nipples and ⅜" × ½" bell reducers, plus ½" nipples. A better way would be to simply install a ⅜" male flare adapter, cut off the bullet-nosed ends of the riser tubes, flare them, and connect them to the flare adapter with flare nuts. This would also work with the ½" faucet openings, but you'd have to use a ½" × ⅜" reducing male flare adapter, which may not be readily available. At any rate, with some persistence, parts to make the connection may be found.

On laundry tub installations that are plumbed from above, such as in a basement, the plastic piping is often brought right to the faucet without using riser tubes. The final connection is made with a proper-sized transition union. (See page 133.) Pipes are fastened securely to the wall with pipe straps and masonry anchors or masonry drive nails. This is not quite as flexible an installation as one using riser tubes, but—exposed to view—it looks more orderly.

TOILET CONNECTION Sinks, lavatories, and laundry tubs get both hot and cold water supply connections. Toilets need only cold water. Stubbed

Most toilet tanks are furnished with a nut for connecting a flat-ended riser tube directly to the bottom of the inlet valve. Simply cut the riser tube to length, install the nut over it facing upward, and connect the riser at its lower end. Then all you have to do is join the riser to the inlet valve at its upper end and install and tighten the nut.

Sometimes the simplest connection to a faucet—particularly a laundry tub faucet—is by means of a flare adapter. This requires that the supply pipe be flared to fit. Soft copper or CPVC or PB pipes can be flared with a standard flaring tool.

Be sure to put the flare nut on before you make the flare. Then make up the flared tube to the flare adapter, which is attached to the faucet, and you've got a neat but removable connection. Photos this series: Richard Day

out on the wall or on the floor underneath the toilet and to the left of it is the toilet's cold water connection. The hookup is made exactly like that for a sink, except that, instead of using a bullet-nosed riser tube, a flat-ended one is used. No additional faucet nut is needed. Toilet inlet valves usually come with a nut designed to hold the riser tube tightly in the inlet. A toilet supply line should be fitted with a shutoff valve so that the water can be cut off quickly in an emergency.

HOW TO UNCLOG BALKY DRAINS

One of the best places for the home handyman plumber to apply skills is in unclogging a stopped-up drain pipe. When the waste water in a fixture drains slowly or not at all, the reason is an obstacle in the piping between the fixture and the house sewer, usually, restricting or stopping the passage of waste water.

The most common blockages occur close to the fixture in the trap beneath it. Less common are blockages farther along the piping system.

If you knew where the blockage was, you could go right to the cure. A sure sign that the problem is close to a fixture is that it develops quickly when water is run into *that* fixture and no other fixtures are affected. A sure sign that the blockage is farther along the piping system is that much water must be run into a fixture to make it back up. When it finally does, other fixtures back up, too. For ex-

USING A DRAIN AUGER IN WASTE PIPE

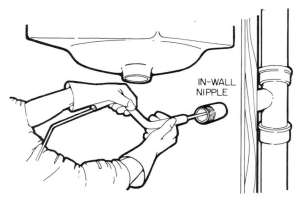

Drain take-apart is an early step in most drain unclogging. Lavatory drain stopper is disconnected first by removing the large nut at the rear of the tailpiece.

ample, when you drain the lavatory and water flows into the bathtub, you can be sure that the stoppage is in a portion of the DWV system that handles the flow from both these fixtures.

If the stoppage is in the main house drain or house sewer, problems will show up most noticeably at the lowest point. Usually, this is a first-floor shower or bathtub, because their drains are at the floor.

KITCHEN SINK DRAIN A plugged kitchen sink drain is one of the most common plumbing problems. It may be a recurring stoppage that quickly breaks up when a drain-opening chemical is poured into the sink. On the other hand, it may be a slow-flowing kitchen sink drain that annoys more than it harms.

Both problems may be due to a faulty drain installation underneath and behind the kitchen sink. If the horizontal waste pipe serving the sink has too little slope, water will only trickle through it, leaving grease and garbage particles behind. As these cool and harden, they build up into clogs. If the pipe has too great a slope, water races away, leaving its solids behind to stick to the walls of the pipe and form clogs.

A pipe that is too small clogs easily. On the other hand, a pipe that is too large becomes "lazy" and may tend to clog, as water flows along its lower surface only.

If too many changes are made in the direction of flow, a waste pipe can become clogged. Right-angle bends are particularly bad. And, if the installing plumber used less expensive water supply fittings instead of smooth-turn drainage ones, these will form catch spots for clogs.

If your kitchen sink has recurring drain stoppage problems, look for one or more of the above faults. To put a permanent end to the nuisance, you may want to take out the old piping and replace it with a proper waste installation.

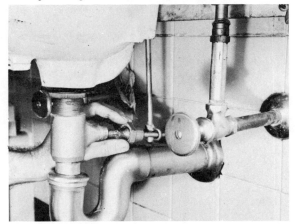

The nut slides off, pulling out the drain-operating lever. Be sure the basin is empty before disassembly of the drain operator.

With the drain-operator lever free, the stopper can be lifted out for removal of lint and other clogging debris.

Chemical cleaning If the drain installation is not what's at fault, you can choose among several methods for breaking up the clog. The first thing to try is chemical cleaning. This is useful only if the stoppage is not complete and there is some flow past it. Chemicals will, in some cases, dissolve grease, a common culprit in balky drains. Some chemicals even state that they may be used on completely stopped-up drains. These are supposed to be heavier than water and settle into the drain, finding their way to the clog to free it. Mostly, chemical drain cleaning is not very effective.

Be sure to follow the directions on the container of drain cleaner. These materials are caustic. Keep them off the skin, out of the eyes, and away from children. And of course do not take them internally.

Plunging More effective at unstopping drains is the plunger, or plumber's rubber force cup. This is sometimes called a plumber's friend. To use it, run some water into the sink, enough to cover the rubber cup. Smear petroleum jelly on the lower edge of the cup and place it down squarely over the drain. Tip it as you go under the water to remove as much air as possible. Then work the plunger up and down vigorously ten or twenty times. At the end of each plunging cycle, pull the plunger sharply up off the drain. This puts tremendous backpressure on a clog, which often breaks it up where ordinary plunging could not.

If the drain is still clogged, try again. If waste water is sucked back into the sink, remove paper, hair, and other solid material that may come with it. Keep the sink's strainer clean. Don't give up easily. Repeat the plunging operation eight to ten times, if necessary. Often it takes some time for plunging to be effective.

You can follow successful plunging with the use of a chemical drain cleaner to try to get rid of anything remaining of the clog. It may help to run hot water down the drain for a few minutes to melt and wash out collected grease.

Trap cleaning If plunging won't start even a slow waste runoff through the drain, the next step is to remove the drain plug from the trap beneath the sink. If the sink drain is one of those built without a drain-cleaning plug, you'll have to remove the trap instead. Either way, all the waste water above the trap will run out as soon as you open it. Put a pail under the trap to catch it. If the sink is full, it can even overflow a pail, so you'd better bail some of it out first. And if any drain-cleaning chemicals have been added to the waste water, remember that they'll be in the flow from the trap. Wear rubber gloves and goggles, and be careful of splashes. If you get any on your skin, rinse immediately in clear water.

If the stoppage is in the trap itself, it's easy to remove. Make a small cleaning tool out of a coathanger wire with a hook-shaped end and clean the trap thoroughly.

Plumber's snake If the stoppage is farther along the drain beyond the trap, the only way to get at it is with what's called a plumber's snake. This is a flexible cable tool. If you don't have one, you can either buy or rent one for the purpose. The handiest of these are self-contained. The snake comes coiled up inside the crank handle. It can be fed out as needed to enter the drain.

Insert about a foot of the snake into the pipe, heading away from the sink. Tighten the clamp screw and crank the snake. Then work it in another foot and crank again. Keep turning as you advance the snake along the sink's waste pipe.

You may be able to feel the clog as a spot that is soft but offers resistance. However, bends in the

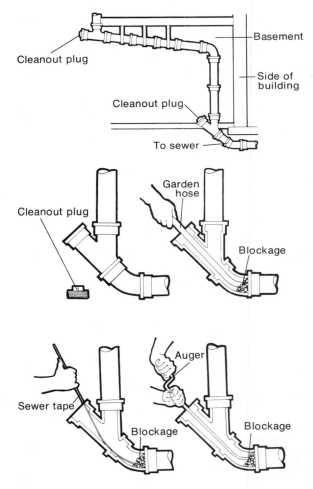

1

2

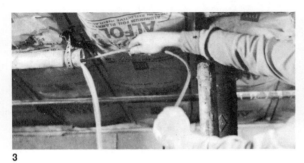

3

4

5

6

7

8

Step 1. *This drain runs from the sink at the left and turns down to the sewer below. The elbow is broken off with a cold chisel and hammer to open the line.* Step 2. *A short length of pipe between the elbow and sink is removed for better access to the stoppage. The stoppage has not been located, so probing follows.* Step 3. *When the drain snake runs into the stoppage between the elbow and sink, backed-up water runs out the pipe. There should be a pail underneath to collect it.* Step 4. *The opened-up pipe from the elbow to the sewer line should next be cleared of accumulations that might cause future stoppage. Vertical lengths rarely plug up, however.* Step 5. *The vertical pipe*

is fitted with a T into which a clean-out plug is fitted on top. A close nipple is added to connect the T to the rest of the line. Step 6. *The distance from the T to the drain is measured and allowance is made for a union, which will permit opening the line easily later.* Step 7. *A short piece of pipe is cut and threaded, attached to the union, and then inserted into the drain line before joining to the nipple.* Step 8. *This collar-type union is sealed around the free end of the pipe with oakum and lead wool tapped in with a caulking tool. Use pipe compound or TFE plumber's tape for all other joints.*

pipe also offer resistance to the snake. These usually feel hard. Rotating the snake will make it jump past them. Always turn in the same clockwise direction as you work the snake in.

If the sharp tip of the snake works into and pierces an object causing a stoppage – a dishcloth, for example – while being turned in one direction, it will hold on better if turned in the same direction while withdrawing. Then you stand a good chance of pulling the clog back out with the snake. Other clogs must be broken up with snake action and flushed down the drain with water, later.

When you've cleared the blockage, pull the snake back out. Replace the sink trap plug or put the trap back together and pour boiling water into the sink. If the runoff is slow, add a chemical drain cleaner. If the water backs up and there is still no runoff, the clog is probably beyond the limit of the snake's reach.

If you're on the second floor or above, you can try working the snake into the DWV system down through the sink's vent stack. Do this by working from the roof. You can run water down the vent stack from a garden hose. If you do this you'd better station someone inside the house to make sure it doesn't back and simply run out on the floor.

If the clog is on the first floor, you can do the same thing. If that doesn't help, trace the sink drain in the basement to the point where it joins the large main building drain to which all fixtures flow. At the upper end of that drain there should be what is called a cleanout plug. Remove the plug and work the snake in from that position. If there is no plug, you can use an electric drill to bore a hole for access. Later you'll have to tap the hole with threads and close it by screwing in a threaded pipe plug.

Sewer tape If you run into a stoppage that's too solidly packed for the flexible snake to go through, rent what is called a sewer tape. This is a flat steel snake that is pushed rather than rotated through a drain line. The clog can be hit over and over again with the sewer tape to break up almost any stoppage.

If there is enough room behind the cleanout plug, you may be able to insert a piece of pipe or concrete reinforcing bar or other solid rod in place of a more flexible sewer rod.

Garden hose method If there isn't enough room to use someting stiff, a garden hose may do the job. The garden hose has the advantage of being able to supply hydrostatic pressure against the clog. Pack some rags around the opening where the hose enters the drain, then have someone turn on the water while you hold the rags tightly in place to prevent most leakage. This method is particularly effective when the blockage is due to sand, often

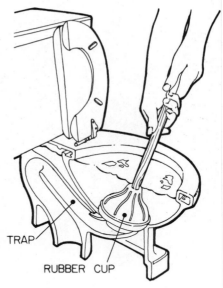

Toilet auger used to remove obstruction

Rubber plunger used on toilet bowl

found in the drains of seashore homes. Once penetrated, let the hose run a while to flush the clog down and out.

BASINS AND BATHTUBS If a bathroom's lavatory, bathtub, or shower stops up, the same plunger/snake methods of clearing it may be used. Both lavatory and bathtubs have overflow pipes that render plunging much less effective. To help the

To reinstall a toilet after taking out the bowl to remove a blockage, rest the bowl upside down on newspapers. Install a special wax toilet gasket around the outlet horn at the bottom of the bowl.

Position a pair of new toilet hold-down bolts (with putty around their bases if they will not stand up straight alone) in the slots of the floor-mounted toilet flange.

Turn the toilet bowl right side up and lower its outlet horn with wax gasket directly onto the toilet flange at the floor. When it makes contact, press down and wiggle the toilet bowl until it rests firmly on the bathroom floor.

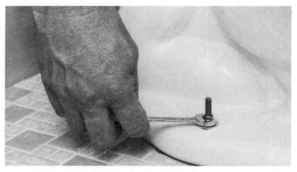

Install the hold-down nuts and washers over the floor bolts and tighten until snug. Do not overtighten, or you may crack the bowl. The excess bolt length sticking above the nut may be cut off before installing the appearance cap.

situation, hold a sopping-wet rag tightly over the overflow.

Some basins have pop-up waste stoppers that are raised and lowered by a handle on the bowl. Remove the stopper for more effective plunging. Some simply lift out, some twist and lift out, and still others must be disconnected underneath and lifted out. Sometimes the stopper itself contains

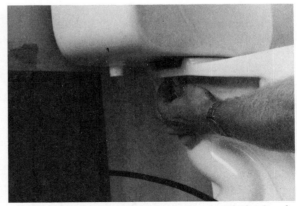

Finally, mount the toilet tank to the bowl with the dough-nut-shaped gasket between; then snug down the tank-to-bowl bolts slightly more than finger tight. Connect the water supply and you're done. Photos this series: Richard Day

the clog. Hair and lint tend to collect below them.

Some bathtubs and showers have drum traps with access covers set even with the bathroom floor or in a basement or crawl space below the floor. The trap's cover is unscrewed for cleaning. Like a sink or lavatory trap, a drum trap can be cleaned with a snake. If there is no drum trap and the bathtub strainer cannot be removed, you'll have to snake through one of the strainer holes. Bathtub traps are generally not very accessible and many do not have trap plugs.

TOILETS If the toilet stops up, first use the plunger. If plunging doesn't work, then switch to a tool called a toilet auger. This is a stiff wire snake that works inside a sharply bent housing that feeds the snake up into the toilet trap. Fill the toilet bowl with water to a point just below the rim — the additional pressure of the water will help to flush out any object you may loosen in the toilet's trap. It will also show you when the stoppage has been cleared. To use the toilet auger, lift the snake wire until its end is touching against the curved end of the auger. Place this up into the curved trap of the bowl. Then, as you turn, force the snake through the auger housing and into the toilet trap by turning and pushing it at the same time. Withdraw it in the same manner, always turning in the same direction.

Next, put about five or six feet of toilet paper in the bowl and let it get wet. Then flush it down with a pail of water. If this makes the toilet back up again, you know that some solid object — a toothbrush, comb, medicine bottle, child's toy — is caught in the bowl's trap passages. Plain water may pass but not water and paper. Try again with the auger.

Toilet bowl removal If the stoppage still continues, you'll have to remove the toilet bowl. To do this, turn off the water in the toilet and flush and bail out the water in the toilet tank. If the toilet is not a one-piece tank/bowl unit, remove the bolts that hold the tank to the bowl and lift off the tank. Wall-mounted toilet tanks may be left in place by disconnecting the tank-to-bowl discharge pipe from the bowl.

Next, work on the two bowl hold-down bolts at the floor. Take off the nuts, or if they are corroded on, cut or saw through the soft brass.

Now the toilet bowl can be lifted from the floor. As you lift the bowl, tilt it forward slightly so that bowl water doesn't drain out through the trap. Pour the trap water into a pail, leaving the bowl dry. Invert the bowl on newspapers and work at the stoppage through the bowl's outlet.

If it helps, carry the bowl outdoors and backflush it with a stream from a garden hose. Once in a while, a toilet must be replaced because none of these tactics succeeds.

If you discover that the clog is not in the bowl but in the piping beyond it, you can now work through the exposed toilet waste pipe with a drain auger, the same as when cleaning a sink drain.

MAIN HOUSE DRAIN If upstairs fixtures back up into downstairs or basement fixtures, you know that the main house drain is blocked. Find the point where the drain leaves the house. Sometimes there is a U-shaped house trap near the wall at that point. Unscrew the trap cover on the street or septic tank side of the trap. If the drain leading outside seems clear, the stoppage may be in the bottom of the trap. You can probe it with a stick, but there's no better way than putting on a rubber

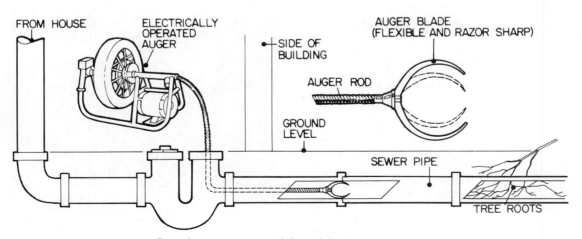

Root-cleaning auger used through house trap opening

glove and reaching in with your hand. If the bottom of the trap is clear, unscrew the other trap cover. If no stoppage is visible there, replace both covers. When you do clear the stoppage, a lot of waste will suddenly gush to the trap and overflow if the covers are not on.

Next, locate the cleanout plug for the house drain. It may be in the crawl space or basement. A flat steel sewer tape is needed. These come 1" wide for heavy-duty use. If you can't reach the stoppage with a sewer tape through the cleanout, unscrew the inside trap cover and work to the stoppage.

Tree roots Roots growing through cracks or defective joints sometimes clog outside drains and sewers. The stoppage can be cleared temporarily with a root-cutting tool. However, to prevent future trouble, the defective portion of the line should be relaid using sound pipe and making sure that all joints are watertight. If possible, sewer lines should be laid out of the way of tree roots. If this is impossible or impractical, make sure that the pipe joints are tight.

All drain-cleaning work is likely to be dirty and wet. Wear old clothes. Wash the snakes and sewer tapes when finished. Spread them out to dry. Wipe them with motor oil before putting them away or returning them to the tool-rental firm. Oiling prevents rust.

HOW TO KNOW WHAT TOOLS AND FITTINGS YOU NEED

Basic tools that you will need for simple plumbing installation and repairs include the following: wrenches, including pipe wrenches, in a range of sizes to fit the pipe, fittings, fixtures, equipment, and appliances in your house system; screwdrivers in the range of sizes to fit the faucets, valves, and other parts of the system; machinist's ball peen hammer; rubber plunger; cold chisel or center punch; cleanout auger or snake; pliers, either slip-joint, channel-locking, or both.

Plumbing installation work also calls for a tape measure, wood saw, hacksaw (32-teeth-per-inch blade), electric drill with wood bits, keyhole saw, carpenter's claw hammer, and sometimes a pipe or tube cutter and reamer.

Another tool you will need, for reaching up behind fixtures, is a basin wrench. This is used to tighten faucet and faucet hold-down nuts where ordinary wrenches cannot reach.

If you're working with sweat-soldered copper pipe, you'll need a propane torch and soldering supplies. To work with threaded pipe, you'll need a pipe cutter, a set of pipe dies, and a pipe vise — quite costly and probably best rented when needed.

Tools you might require for plastic plumbing in-

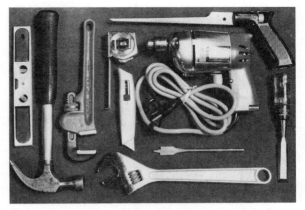

These basic tools will handle most around-the-house plumbing. They are (left to right): level, carpenter's claw-hammer, pipe wrench, measuring tape, knife, ¼" electric drill with wood-boring bit, open-end adjustable wrench, fine-toothed saw, and wood chisel. *Photo: Richard Day*

stallation work include a fine-toothed saw (a hacksaw will do) for cutting plastic pipe and a knife for deburring it.

You'll also need a large monkey wrench or what is called a trap-and-fixture wrench for working on fixture trap slipnuts.

Do not use a pipe wrench on nuts with flat surfaces. They are for pipes and fittings. Use an adjustable or open-end wrench instead. Also, do not use pipe wrenches on the polished surfaces of tubing or fittings. Use a strap wrench instead. This encircles the tube or fitting with a tough canvas strap that permits turning it without marring the surfaces.

If you must use pliers or pipe wrenches on exposed chromed surfaces, be sure to protect them from the wrench jaws with two layers of adhesive tape. Tight nuts or fittings can sometimes be loosened by tapping lightly with a hammer or mallet.

PLUMBING FITTINGS Fittings for water supply use vary from those for DWV use. DWV fittings are called drainage fittings. Drainage fittings are designed with gentle inner curves. When a drain pipe is joined with a fitting, no shoulder is left between the two to trap solids as they flow through. Water supply fittings, on the other hand, may make sharp turns and may contain shoulders when assembled with their piping. (See page 131.)

Fittings that change the direction of a run of pipe are called elbows. Fittings that branch the flow are called tees and wyes (DWV only). Fittings that merely join two pipes in a straight run are called couplings. All come in many different sizes for water supply and DWV use. Elbows vary in the

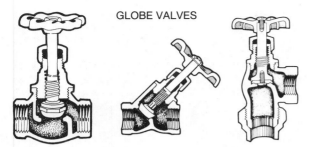

GLOBE VALVES

Types of globe valves, from left, include: Straight-through globe valve (note the large passages for water); Y-pattern globe valve (flow is almost straight), and globe-type angle valve (often called a stop-and-waste valve).

amount of direction change. The most common elbows are 45 degrees and 90 degrees.

Fittings that change from one pipe type to another—for example, from plastic tube to steel pipe—are called adapters. Fittings that change from one pipe size to another, for example, from ¾" to ½", are called reducers. Some fittings adapt and reduce at the same time, as one that changes from ½" threaded pipe to ⅜" plastic pipe. These are called reducing adapters. Sometimes a direction change is incorporated in the same fitting, for example, in an adapting elbow.

Valves Valves of two types—globe and gate—are used in house plumbing. The advantage of a globe valve is that it takes few turns to close it. Perhaps less than a full turn does the job. Its disadvantage is that the internal passages of the globe valve force water to make a 90-degree bend as it passes through, thus often restricting the water flow.

A gate valve is a straight-through flow valve, but it takes many turns of the handle to operate it. Gate valves are also more costly. Normally, the valve used for main house water shutoff is a gate valve and all others are globe valves. (More about valves later.)

HOW TO UNDERSTAND PLUMBING CODES

Almost every local and county government enforces what is called a plumbing code. This is a set of regulations the plumber is supposed to follow in installing a plumbing system. Many of the local codes follow what is written in the plumbing portion of the locally accepted building code—there is no nationally accepted plumbing code. Consult your local building department about what codes you must follow. Although codes are supposed to protect public health, they also have been used in some localities to discourage the homeowner from doing plumbing.

If a plumbing project is part of one that requires

1.

3.

2.

Step 1. *A handy valve called a saddle valve makes tapping water pipe for an add-on spigot quick and easy. Simply install the proper-sized saddle over the pipe with its gasket in place and tighten.* **Step 2.** *Then drill a hole in the pipe, using the opening at the bottom of the saddle as a guide. The water must be turned off before you start drilling.* **Step 3.** *Now all you have to do is screw on a male-threaded hose faucet and you're in business. Turn on the faucet full blast and let it run for a minute to clear any drilling chips left in the water system.* Photos this series: Burt Murphy

a building permit, it may have to be inspected at various stages to see that it conforms to the local code. Work done without a building permit often is not inspected. Some inspections include a water-test of the water supply and DWV systems to make sure there are no leaks.

Because plumbing technology is constantly improving, especially through the introduction of new materials and fittings, a good many local codes have become outdated. For example, systems that work and have been used for years in European countries still are not widely accepted in the United States. However, every home plumber should be aware of the plumbing code and make installations and repairs in line with the health and comfort of his own family as well as the public.

If a restrictive code prevents you from using certain plumbing materials, you may ask the chief plumbing inspector to grant you a variance. Another way, suggested by a master plumber, is to interpret your local plumbing code's provisions as applied to what you want to do and the materials you want to use. Then go ahead as you judge best.

The only thing that is tough about plumbing is learning how to work with some of the antiquated piping materials that professional plumbers once used; for example, lead-caulked cast-iron pipe. The development of easy-do materials for home plumbing has taken the hard work and skill out of the job. If you use compatible materials, you'll find it fairly easy to do your own home plumbing. This means using plastic pipe and fittings to a maximum, avoiding the older hard-to-work-with ones.

HOW TO UNDERSTAND VALVES

Valves are used to control the flow of water within water supply pipes. The proper kind of valve should be used in each valve location. When some kinds of valves go bad, they may have to be replaced. When others go bad, repairs may be possible. Here, for example, are some household uses for valves, along with the recommended valve for each.

Underground sprinkling system When you're hooking up an underground sprinkling system and your water pressure is low, use a gate valve. It offers the least resistance to water flow. And, whether your code requires it or not, you should use a vacuum-breaker valve in addition, to prevent backflow from the sprinkling system from carrying harmful bacteria or chemicals into your house potable water system. This may be purchased where underground sprinkling supplies are sold.

Frostproof valves Outdoor outlets for houses in cold climates can make use of the freezeproof valve. This is a valve with a handle and spigot long enough to be located outside the house but with the actual valve located inside, safe from freezing. When you turn off a freezeproof valve, the water in it drains out by gravity, leaving the exposed part undamaged during below-freezing weather.

Globe valve The globe valve is the most common valve in the house. It operates like the average lavatory faucet. Use it for hose spigots, washing machine spigots, controlling hot and cold water pipes, water supplies to boilers, and hot water tanks.

Globe valves are made in several styles. The two most common are the standard one with inlet and outlet pipes in a straight line. (See page 130.)

Another is the angle-type globe-valve in which the inlet and outlet pipes are at right angles. This valve also serves as an elbow.

A third type of globe valve, patented and carry-

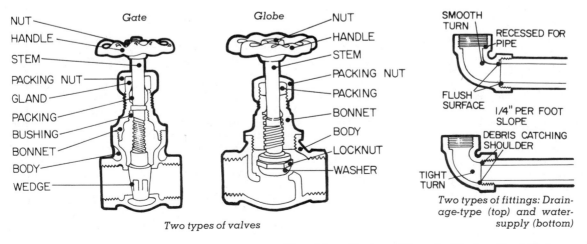

Two types of valves

Two types of fittings: Drainage-type (top) and water-supply (bottom)

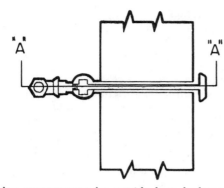

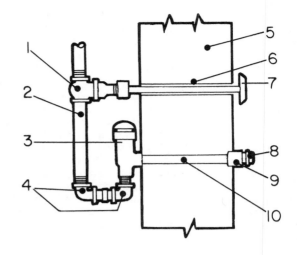

Vacuum-breaker arrangement for outside hose hydrant
1. ½" or ¾" gate valve **2.** ½" or ¾" sch. 40 galv. **3.** ½" or ¾" vacuum breaker. **4.** ½" or ¾" ell M.I. galv. **5.** Exterior building wall **6.** 1" sleeve, sch. 40 **7.** Hand wheel **8.** IPS hose adapter **9.** Coupling M.I. galv. **10.** ½" or ¾" nipple galv.

ing the trademark Full-Flow, is one in which the internal bore elbows up full sized to the valve's seat. The valve body around the seat is enlarged so that the water flow through the valve, when open, is almost as unrestricted as it is in a gate valve. Like the standard globe valve, both pipes serving the valve inlet and outlet are in line. It is made in vinyl for use with CPVC/PB plumbing systems. (See page 134.)

Generally, globe valves may be installed with their spindles in any position. The flow, however, should enter the valve so that pressure is exerted from below the valve's washer (See drawing.) If a valve is in a line that is drained for the winter, the standard-type globe valve should be placed horizontally. Then there is less chance of water freezing within the valve body and damaging it. Some of the better globe valves have an arrow indicating the proper direction of flow.

The flow of water through a valve is affected by the size of the opening inside the valve and the change of direction within its body. It is also affected by the number of changes of direction in some types of valves. Use the accompanying water resistance table as a guide to choosing the proper valve. Note that a standard globe valve offers eight times more resistance to the flow of water than does a 90-degree elbow. It offers 16 times as much resistance as a gate valve. Use an angle globe valve where you want a valve plus an elbow in a line. Because of its lower flow resistance the angle valve is often used for controlling branch risers from the basement up into the house above.

Gate valve Most homes have a gate valve as the main shutoff valve in the house. Since they offer

VALVE FLOW TABLE
(Compared to flow through a same-sized 90° galvanized steel elbow)

Valve Type	Flow Units
Standard globe	¹⁄₁₆
Angle globe	⅛
Full-flow® globe	1.9
Gate	2
90° elbow	1

practically no resistance, gate valves are used where full water flow is important.

Gate valves may be installed in any position. It makes no difference which way the water flows through the valve. In cold climates a gate valve should be installed with its stem upright or at least at an angle somewhat above horizontal. Otherwise the valve bonnet will remain full of water even after the line is drained. Then a freeze-up could split the valve body.

Stop-and-drain valves Some globe and gate valves are made with side tappings that permit draining the water in a turned-off branch line without disconnecting anything. These are called stop-and-drain valves because they stop the flow and permit draining the line. They are often used as shutoffs for outside water spigots. In winter the valve is turned off and the water in the piping beyond it to the outdoor hose connection is emptied from the line by unscrewing the small cap on the side of the valve. (See page 134.)

Check valve A check valve is a one-way-flow valve to prevent backflow in a pipe. Sump pumps should be connected with a check valve in the discharge line. (See page 147.) A flow arrow on the check valve shows the correct installation direction. Installed backward, a check valve will not work. The arrow always should point in the direction of required flow.

A check valve should never be used to prevent the backflow of sewage into a water line. No such connection should be made with any device other than with an approved vacuum-breaker valve (see below). The reason for this is that check valves are seldom completely tight. A little piece of sand between the valve's face and its seat will permit a slight leakage, not permissible between contaminated and potable water systems.

Vacuum-breaker valve The vacuum-breaker valve is used to prevent back-siphonage of polluted water into the potable water supply. It operates automatically, allowing air to enter the line whenever a back-pressure or vacuum occurs in the potable water supply. This can be when a large water-using device is turned on elsewhere in the house. The vacuum-breaker valve breaks up siphon action immediately and prevents any polluted water from siphoning back. These are used on underground sprinkling systems and tankless toilet valves where, otherwise, a cross connection between potable and polluted water would exist.

A plumbing fixture with its faucet (inlet) below the flood rim of the basin constitutes a potential cross connection. So does a laundry tub hose with its end left in the laundry tub. A lawn fertilizer aspirator left connected to a garden hose is another potential cross connection.

A vacuum-breaker valve must be installed so that it is at least 6″ above the overflow level of the fixture it protects. Most vacuum-breaker valves have to be installed so that the valve itself is perfectly vertical, although some models will operate in any position.

One trouble with some vacuum-breaker valves is that they drastically reduce the flow of water. If you live in an area with low water pressure, be sure to use the type that does not restrict water flow.

HOW TO WORK WITH PLASTIC PIPE

Recent advances in materials and connectors make do-it-yourself plumbing with plastic an easy job. Plastic tubes and fittings can be used, if local codes permit, for both pure water piping and for waste water piping.

For hot and cold water pipes, tubes and fittings are available in both rigid and flexible form. Rigid plastic piping is chlorinated polyvinyl chloride, called CPVC. The ½″ and ¾″ CPVC tubes join to like-sized CPVC fittings by easy solvent-welding. Rigid CPVC makes a neat, orderly installation. It is

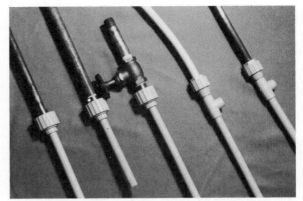

Plumbing adapters (left to right): *three transition adapters connect CPVC to sweat-soldered copper and a threaded steel pipe and fitting; PB/CPVC street adapter; and a Genova Universal adapter, which connects tubing to CPVC street without sweat-soldering.*

Flexible PB tube, which comes in long lengths, is ideal for making joint-free pipe runs beneath concrete slabs. Pipe stubs coming up out of the slab are held during slab construction by wiring them to short lengths of reinforcing bar driven into the ground. Later, connections are made with PB adapters.

CPVC connections—especially on the hot-water side—should be made with a transition union. This permits differential expansion between the metal fixture and prevents the plastic tubing from causing leaks at the connection. To save money, cold-water connections may be made with a simple male CPVC adapter. Photos this series: Richard Day

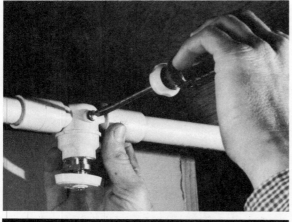

Stop-and-drain valve (top, left) has a side tap. Photo above shows PB Polyriser riser tubes reaching from Genogrip fixture stops on wall to faucet.

Plastic hot/cold CPVC water supply fittings (left) include, left to right, top row: coupling, 90° elbow, 90° street elbow, 45° elbow, tee, male thread adapter, cap. Center row: wing elbow, reducing bushing, reducing tee, line stop valve, boiler drain valve. Bottom row: adapters, including CPVC-to-PB, CPVC-to-sweat copper, CPVC-to-threaded-pipe-fittings (disassembled), CPVC-to-pipe threads, CPVC-to-sweat-copper Universal adapter.

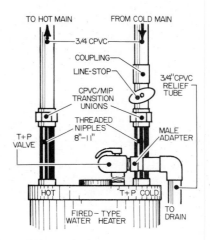

Hookup for fired-type water heater is shown. When plastic water supply piping systems are used with either gas- or oil-fired water heaters, install a pair of 8″ to 11″ threaded metal pipe nipples coming from the heater's inlet and outlet tapping. This protects the plastic piping from excess burner heat. Transition unions, and a line stop on the cold side, join to CPVC tubing. Also protect household piping by installing an air chamber at every hot and cold water faucet and every water-using appliance.

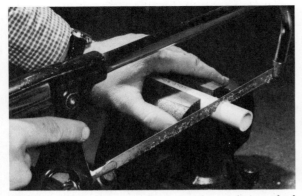

CPVC and PB tubing can be cut with any fine-toothed saw. Make the cut clean and square; remove burr on both the inside and outside edges of the cut.

To solvent-weld CPVC, first wipe mating parts with cleaner. Apply solvent cement inside fitting socket and outside tube end. Join immediately with a slight twist.

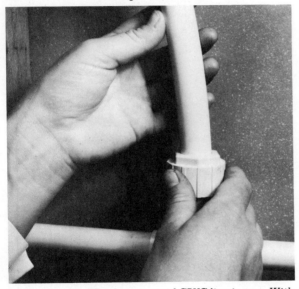

Joining flexible PB tubing to rigid CPVC line is easy. With Genogrip adapter, you simply stab the tube end, after chamfering, into the adapter full depth then tighten.

often used in basements, garages, and utility rooms where pipes are exposed. It's ideal for short runs, such as creating air chambers.

Flexible plastic water supply piping is made of polybutylene and commonly called PB. Polybutylene is available in ⅜", ½", and ¾" nominal sizes. Since it cannot be solvent-welded, PB is joined by mechanical connectors. One of these is a patented Genogrip connector. The PB tube is pushed full depth into the Genogrip connector and the connector is hand-tightened. It makes a quick, leakfree pulloutproof connection. Genogrip fittings join by solvent-welding to any CPVC fitting of the same size.

Flexible polybutylene tubing is best for making long, joint-free pipe runs beneath concrete slabs, for water service entrance runs, and for piping a distant add-on bathroom. Also its flexibility makes PB ideal for remodeling home plumbing, since it can be fished through walls, floors, and ceilings without removal of finish materials.

Both CPVC and PB tubing and fittings are rated for 100 psi pressure at 180°F temperature. Cut them with a fine-toothed saw—a hacksaw or coping saw—and remove any burr around the inside and outside with a knife or sandpaper before joining.

For solvent-welding, a two-step process is recommended. First a primer, or cleaner, should be wiped onto the tube end and fitting socket with a clean cloth. The cleaner ensures grease-free mating parts. Then liberally apply solvent to both the tube end and the fitting socket. Immediately assemble the tube and its fitting with a 5° twist that brings the fitting to its correct alignment.

A uniform bead of solvent around the fitting indicates that enough solvent was used. In practice it is difficult to use too much solvent. Always work with solvent at room temperature. Avoid breathing the vapors for very long. Also, don't solvent-weld while smoking or near an open flame. One advantage in working with plastic tubing over sweat-type copper tubing is that flame isn't required to make joints.

CPVC can be adapted to sweat-soldered copper and threaded metal piping with adapter fittings. The simplest of these is a plain male adapter that has outside threads at one end to screw into a threaded pipe fitting. At the other end it solvent-welds to a CPVC tube. Male adapters sometimes leak at the threads with heating and cooling because plastic and metal expand and contract at differing rates.

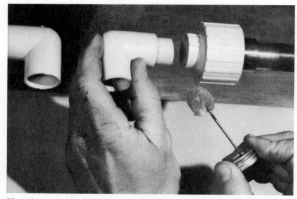

Here's an easy way to tap a water softener into your house cold water main. First cut out a piece of the main and fit the cutoff ends with CPVC adapters. Then solvent-weld in a pair of CPVC street elbows facing downward toward the softener. Complete the hookup (photo at right) with CPVC piping, or else polybutylene tubing and adapters. Connect the other parts of the softener per manufacturer's directions.

For that reason, it's better to make metal-to-plastic connections using a transition union. This adapter is made in two halves. One half is metal and connects to the metal pipe and the other is CPVC to connect to the CPVC tube. When a hand-nut is tightened, a pair of flanges with an elastomeric gasket between them seals leak-free. Transition unions also let a joint be disassembled and put back together as often as needed. Also use them at connections with existing metal pipes, where a metal-to-plastic adaption is needed.

Running flexible polybutylene tubing is slightly different. Start with a CPVC transition union and then solvent-weld a CPVC/PB adapter into that and start your PB run.

When running rigid plastic pipe, it's important to allow space for thermal expansion and contraction. A 10′ length of CPVC pipe expands about ¼″ upon heating. Put foot-long offsets in pipe runs longer than 35′. At the ends of runs leave space between fittings and wood framing. Where riser pipes take off from hot and cold water mains up through a floor or down through a ceiling, make risers at least 8″ long. The main will not bind against its thermal movements. If you use PB for risers, it is flexible enough that even a short length should not restrict the main.

Be sure to protect plastic water supply piping from excessive conducted burner heat in both gas- and oil-fired water heaters. Do it by installing 8″- to 11″-long threaded metal pipes in the inlet and outlet tappings on top of the heater. Adapt to these with transition unions, continuing with CPVC or PB.

Water hammer is tough on all household piping. Protect systems by installing an air chamber at every hot and cold water faucet and every water-using appliance outlet. These cushion the harmful impacts of fast water shutoff. Also support plastic water supply piping every 32″ on centers — at every other joist — with special plastic tubing hangers that permit the tube to slide back and forth with thermal movements, yet secure it to the framing.

When connecting new water supply piping to faucets, be sure to use flexible riser tubes. The newest types are made in beige polybutylene to match the rest of the plastic system. Called Poly-risers, the very flexible tubes come in lengths to 36″ and can be cut to shorter lengths with a knife. Ends are either flanged for direct connection to a toilet tank's inlet valve, or bullet-nosed for connection to most modern faucet tailpieces. Both connections are made with faucet jam nuts, which usually come with the faucet or toilet. The lower end of the PB riser pushes into a Genogrip adapter at the wall or floor and hand-tightens. Both angle and straight-stop valves are available containing the adapter. These permit fast shutoff underneath the fixture in an emergency. See page 134.

Polyrisers may also be used with the common compression adapter valves usually found at the wall or floor behind a fixture. Or a Genogrip valve may be used with a metal riser by replacing the plastic grab-ring inside it with the serrated stainless steel grab-ring. Don't use the steel rings with polybutylene risers.

If any leaking joints are found in a CPVC water supply system turned on for pressure-testing, cut out the affected fitting and solvent-weld in a new one, connecting it with two CPVC couplings.

HOW TO HANDLE EMERGENCIES

Here are some plumbing emergencies that homeowners may be confronted with, and what to do about them. One of your household emergency phone numbers should be that of a plumber who offers twenty-four-hour service.

Burst pipe or tank Immediately shut off the flow of water by closing the shutoff valve nearest the break. If none can be found, head for the main house shutoff valve. Then arrange for repair.

Toilet overflow Do not use that toilet until it is back in working order. As a safety precaution, turn off the fixture shutoff valve beneath the toilet tank. Remove stoppage in the bowl, outlet, soil lines, or sewer or septic tank. (See page 122.)

Overheating hot water tank Signs of hot water heater runaway are boiling noises coming from inside the tank, steam popping from hot water faucets, or hot water backing up into the cold water supply. Cut off the burner immediately. Check the safety relief valve to make sure it is operating. Then use a thermometer to check the temperature of the water in the nearest hot water faucet. If it is above the temperature setting on the water heater, the thermostat that controls the heater may have failed. If resetting doesn't correct the problem, call a professional. (For more on water heater troubleshooting, see page 141.)

Cold house If your house heating system fails in subfreezing weather, completely drain the plumbing system. (How to do this is described on page 139.)

Leak inside a wall When you hear water dripping behind a wall, act fast to prevent damage to the house. Turn off the house main shutoff valve and call a plumber. The repair often involves tearing out a part of the wall to get at the leaky pipe or fitting. The plumber will install a new one.

HOW TO HAVE A QUIET PLUMBING SYSTEM

Most of your home's plumbing is supposed to be unseen. All of it should be unheard.

Chattering and whistling noises are two of the most common and annoying faults of a malfunctioning plumbing system. Fortunately, they are the most easily corrected.

Chattering If you turn on a faucet and hear a chattering noise and feel a vibration in the handle, it's

If the toilet tank refill tube looks like this—that is, aimed into the tank rather than into the end of the overflow tube—a splashing sound will be made as the tank refills. Simply rebend the refill tube so that it is aimed into the overflow tube to correct the problem.

likely the faucet washer or its spindle is defective. The loose parts vibrate up and down in the water flow, causing the noise. This can be caused by a loose faucet washer. In that case, merely tightening the washer will effect a cure. If not, washer replacement will be necessary. Perhaps the washer spindle may need to be replaced.

Whistling A whistling noise results from a poorly closed valve with a worn-out washer. Replacement of the washer or grinding down the old valve seat will usually remedy it.

A whistle in a toilet tank accompanied by splashing and dripping sounds is also likely due to a faulty valve. To fix it, remove the toilet tank cover and watch the water level. If water runs out the overflow tube and disappears down it, the float valve is improperly adjusted, or else it leaks or its float rod is bent. In some cases the valve in the ballcock—the tall rod on which the float arm hangs—is damaged and needs replacement.

If raising the float manually turns off the water, the repair is easy. Bend the rod down to set the float lower in the tank. If this doesn't work, replace the damaged ballcock, first shutting off the water and draining the tank.

Splashing If there is a steady flow from the toilet tank into the bowl, the flush valve is probably defective. The flush ball may be hardened, crusted, or it may be resting on an uneven or worn outlet seat. With steel wool you may be able to rub the seat down for a good seal. Drain the tank first. Or you can replace the valve and ball, at relatively little cost.

If there is a splashing sound in the tank as it refills, lift the lid and see if the refill tube is aiming its water into the overflow tube, as it should, or missing the tube and spraying directly into the tank, which it should not. The repair is easy. Simply bend the refill tube to discharge into the overflow pipe. If the refill tube leaks at its base, it is best to replace the whole ballcock assembly.

Water hammer The loud slamming, banging sound as some faucets are closed rapidly is called water hammer. It can also occur when a dishwasher or automatic washing machine ceases calling for water.

If you have the old spring-type faucets that close automatically when released, water hammer may be reduced by replacing them with faucets that close manually.

The real cure is to install air chambers behind each fixture. Sometimes, lacking them, you can install one large air chamber on the main water line nearest the area where the trouble is found. You can buy add-on air chambers made of a coiled length of copper tubing sealed at the upper end, to install in the water supply pipe beneath the fixture.

Refilling chambers One problem with air chambers is that they sometimes become waterlogged as the water that practically fills them absorbs their air cushion. Gradually, water rises higher and higher in the chamber. The air cushion may be replenished by turning off the main house shutoff valve and draining the water supply system. When refilled, the chambers will contain their full complement of air.

Pressure-control valve If the elevation where you live is much lower than the water pumping station, your water pressure may be too high. This is great for getting good flow from faucets, but it aggravates water hammer. It's also harder on faucets and toilet inlet valves and the solenoid valves in appliances—besides being wasteful of water. Average city water pressure is about 50 psi. If yours runs more than 80 psi, you may want to install a pressure-control valve in the water service entrance line and adjust it to provide the desired pressure.

Water heater boil Pounding and rumbling noises in a hot water line may accompany a surging sound in the water heater. The cause may be a water temperature setting that is too high, generating steam that becomes active inside the system. Tap water for domestic use should not be hotter than 140°F. There is danger of being scalded if this temperature is exceeded. Extreme settings of the water heater's thermostat also are wasteful of energy. Ideally your heater's temperature setting should be at the minimum. This temperature, often

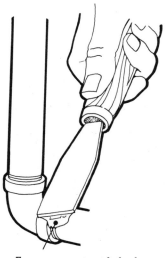

Epoxy cement seals leak

labeled "warm," is 140°F. The "medium" setting is usually 160°F, the "hot" setting often 180°F.

Amplified vibrations Sometimes a slight humming noise comes as water flows through pipes. This is normal and is hardly noticeable unless the pipe is tightly anchored to a floor or wall. Then the floor or wall becomes a sounding board, magnifying the sound out of proportion. The hum can be eliminated by slipping bits of felt between the pipe and wall. This will also reduce vibrations caused by water hammer.

Give all exposed pipelines the same treatment. The screws or nails holding the pipe hangers may have to be backed out somewhat to get the felt in. If the noise still persists, the pipe may be too small or its inner passages may be partially blocked with scale deposits. Pipe replacement, then, is the cure.

HOW TO PATCH PIPES

Leaks in pipes are usually simple to repair. The first step, naturally, is to turn off the water at the nearest shutoff between the leak and the water supply. Open the nearest outlet to bleed off the pressure.

For the easiest repair of leaks at joints or fittings, try epoxy cement. To make it stick, clean dirt, scale, grease, and oil from the fitting and the pipe threads. Get them down to bright metal, using a wire brush, sandpaper, or steel wool. Mix up the epoxy—the five-minute type saves time—and apply it as thickly as possible over the area of the leak. If you get it too thin, the water pressure later will force its way through.

Allow the full time stated on the package for a

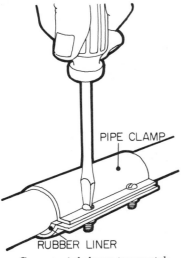

PIPE CLAMP

RUBBER LINER

Commercial clamp-type patch

complete cure, then turn on the water. If the leak isn't fixed, you'll have to remove the fitting and re-join it.

If it's a sweat-soldered copper pipe system, all water will have to be drained before you can melt any solder to get a joint apart. Sometimes the pipe has to be sawed through to drain it completely for unsoldering.

The joint should be taken apart, recleaned, fluxed, and soldered together. A sawed-through pipe opening can be cleaned, fluxed, and soldered together with a copper coupling of the proper size.

Leaky joints in threaded metal pipe can often be stopped by tightening the threads with a pair of pipe wrenches. However, when you tighten one set of threads, you are loosening the next joint in line. For this reason, you have to open up one end of the pipeline. This is done at a union or a terminal point of the line, then by working back toward the leaky fitting. Since it can involve you in lots of work, cutting through the pipe near the leak may be easier. Tighten the loose threads as necessary then install a no-threads slip-coupling across the cutout you've made in the pipeline. No-thread slip-couplings are available from most plumbing supply dealers.

A leaking joint in plastic pipe must be cut out and replaced with new parts. Connect it with pipe couplings on either side. (See the section on working with plastic pipe.)

Hole sealing Small holes in pipe, such as those made by accidental punctures, can often be sealed with self-tapping screws. Make a gasket from an old tire innertube or other piece of rubber. It should fit under the screw head, between it and the pipe.

The gasket should be about twice the size of the screwhead. Punch a screw-sized hole in the center of the gasket and coat both sides with rubber cement. Install the gasket, then drive the screw into the hole. The larger the hole, the larger the screw must be. This method is not recommended for pipes less than 1½" in diameter, since the plug impedes water flow. Nor is it recommended for pipes too thin to form a thread as the screw is driven in.

On smaller pipes you may place a small square of tire innertube rubber over the leak and install a worm-drive hose clamp around the pipe at that point. Tightening the clamp onto the rubber patch should seal off the leak.

A commercial-type pipe patch to seal larger pipe leaks works the same way but covers more area. It is placed over the leak with a gasket and tightened.

Pipes that have been split by freezing cannot be patched and must be replaced. Most pipe repairs are only temporary until the pipe corrodes and must eventually be replaced.

HOW TO PREVENT PIPE FREEZING

When temperatures fall below freezing, the pipes in unheated portions of your home are subject to freeze-up unless you take preventive measures. When water in them freezes it will expand as ice, and the pipes will split. Later, when the ice melts, water will spurt out of the split, soaking everything within reach. This expensive destruction can be avoided by taking some of the following precautions.

Before freezing weather arrives, wrap the affected pipe with electrical heating cable and plug it in. Leave it connected for the entire cold spell to keep water in the pipe warm enough to prevent freeze-up.

If the below-freezing spell is short lived, a pipe may be protected by wrapping it with insulation, which comes shaped to fit around the pipe. All you do is put it on and tape it in place. In time, though, the heat will escape through even the best-insulated pipe and it can freeze.

An old-fashioned kerosene lantern hung under a U-bend or cleanout point along a main drain will prevent freeze-up in this critical area where water sometimes stands. Heat will be carried by metal piping some distance from the lantern. Beware of creating a fire hazard with this method.

HOW TO DRAIN PIPING The most practical protection for frost damage in pipes is to drain them. Draining of all pipes and tanks is a necessity if you plan to leave your house unheated during winter months, or if the house is left without heat due to storm-downed powerlines.

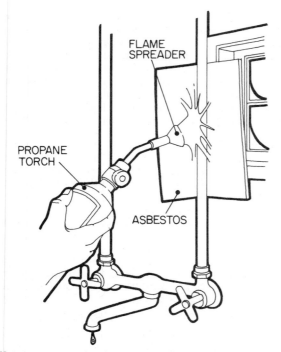

Using a propane torch is a risky way to thaw frozen pipes.

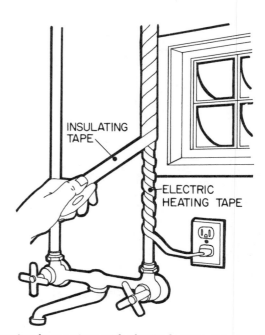

Thawing frozen pipes with electric heating tape is safer.

To drain a house plumbing system, open all valves, including stop-and-drain valves. Be sure that the main shutoff valve is closed, however. Connect a garden hose to the drain bibb on the water heater and run it to a convenient drain below the heater. Then open the heater's drain valve so that all the water in the heater runs out. Hot and cold water taps should be open at this time.

When water no longer flows from any of the openings, insert a hose from an air compressor in an exterior hose bibb with its valve open. Start the compressor and blow compressed air into the house water system. This should expel any remaining water that collects in low points of the system. Make certain also to drain the system boiler, expansion tank, and hot water heat piping.

While the water is turned off, the toilet should be flushed to empty its tank and any water standing in the bottom of its tank should be sopped up with a sponge.

Traps should not be drained, because that would open the house to entry by sewer gases and vermin from the DWV system. Protect water in the toilet bowl and fixture traps against freeze-up by pouring automobile antifreeze/coolant into them. About 4 ounces in each fixture trap and a cup or two in a toilet bowl should do the trick. Don't run any more

water into the bowls or you'll wash out the antifreeze.

Remember, too, that the pump of your washing machine or dishwasher is filled with water. If this freezes, it will split open the pump housing, so be sure to drain that out by opening the snap catch that holds the cover. Drain into a shallow pan.

THAWING PLUMBING If you forget to take the necessary precautions and a quick freeze-up leaves your plumbing solid with ice, you may be able to save it from further damage by proper defrosting. Be wary, though. You may only make things worse. Too much heat can produce steam in a confined area, such as a pipe. The pipe can explode in your face. Avoid thawing pipes with a propane torch.

The best way to thaw piping is to restore heat to the room where the frozen pipe is located. If this is not practical, let it stay frozen until you can warm the area. Otherwise you will only have the job to do over again and the pipes may burst next time.

A frozen pipe is thawed most safely by wrapping it with rags and pouring boiling water over them. No steam pressure can be created by this method. Piping can also be thawed with an electrical heating cable wrapped around it and plugged in.

A hair dryer makes an ideal defroster. It works

slowly but safely in melting all interior ice, and thus prevents explosion and subsequent pipe cracks. When you notice a slight drip of water from the open faucet after this treatment, turn off the blower.

If you don't have a hair dryer, you may have a heating lamp. This works as well as the hair dryer on exposed pipe. Moreover, it will melt out ice from pipes behind walls of moderate thickness, such as plasterboard. The heating lamp takes a bit longer but is just as effective. Be sure to keep the lamp at least six inches away from the wall.

The most serious problem is a frozen home-heating boiler. Thaw its intake pipe first. Next, open the drain and thaw the drain pipe and its fittings. Finally, apply warmth to the boiler. If it was completely filled and has frozen, it probably has been split open. You will see as soon as the ice begins to melt. Whatever you do, don't try to start a fire in the boiler until all the ice has melted inside it.

HOW TO CONSERVE ENERGY

One of the best energy-saving devices is an insulation kit for a water heater. Heaters that were manufactured before energy became so costly are too lightly insulated for today's needs. The answer is to add more insulation. Add-on kits are available to outfit any size gas or electric water heater in minutes. They retail for much less than they will save in energy costs over the years. One made by Johns-Manville should pay for itself in about two years.

No special expertise or tools are required to do the installation. This new fiberglass installation kit includes all necessary tools along with easy-to-follow instructions.

LOWER TEMPERATURE SETTING An easy way to cut your water heating bills is to lower the temperature setting on the heater. Use the lowest setting that will provide your family a sufficient amount of hot water at the temperature you need but not beyond. Use the "warm" setting if at all possible. This not only reduces heat loss through the water heater tank and hot water piping, but lengthens water heater tank life.

PIPE INSULATION Heat loss in pipes leading from the heater to every hot-water-using fixture can save on energy costs. Not only this but insulating these pipes makes the water in them slower to cool when it stands between uses. Thus it takes less time for fully heated water to reach the faucet.

Pipe insulation is made in several types. That of molded fiberglass comes ready to fit around the pipes and be secured in sections with tape. Joints that cannot be covered by these sections are packed with loose insulation, which is then taped

in place. This is the most effective pipe insulation material you can get.

Other kinds of pipe insulation come in strip form and are wrapped onto the pipe and around fittings.

FLOW DEVICES When you cut down on use of hot water, you save water and the energy required to heat it. Cutting down on flow is a job well done by an ultra-simple flow device now on the market. Fitted to faucet or showerhead, it reduces water consumption from an average of 5 to 2 gallons per minute. One type uses a rubber orifice that becomes smaller with increasing water pressure, larger with decreasing pressure. Thus, no matter what the water pressure, the flow is about the same. Soon after the device is installed, the old profligate flow of water will not be missed. Two gallons a minute is ample for showering; one gallon per minute is enough for the sink and lavatory.

Another type of flow device for showers is the hand-controlled valve. This lets you control the flow from a full stream down to a complete shutoff without touching the shower valve's on-off-temperature valve. You can turn on the flow to lather up, turn it off while you wash, then on again to rinse. You can also adjust the flow to the rate desired.

Flow devices are easily installed. Follow the instructions that come with them.

COLD WATER WASH You can save considerably on hot water heating costs by doing the laundry — or most of it — in cold water. While cold water does not do quite as good a job, many families do it anyway to save energy.

HOW TO TROUBLESHOOT

WATER HEATERS Household water heaters are largely self-sufficient. They require little attention. When problems do occur, the homeowner can usually handle them, keep the heater working, and push back the day when a new heater will be needed.

A water heater is basically a storage tank that also has some way to heat the contents — electrical elements or a gas or oil burner. Cold water from the house main enters the tank at the top from a pipe with a valve. It is conducted to the bottom of the heater tank by a dip tube, which keeps cold water from mixing with hot water in the tank. When hot water flows from the tank through another opening at the top, more cold water enters at the same time, so the tank is always full.

Whenever water temperature at the bottom of the tank is below the thermostat setting, the heater is turned on. If the heater's energy should fail to cut off properly, and water begins turning into steam, there is a valve atop the heater called a temperature-and-pressure relief valve (T&P), which would

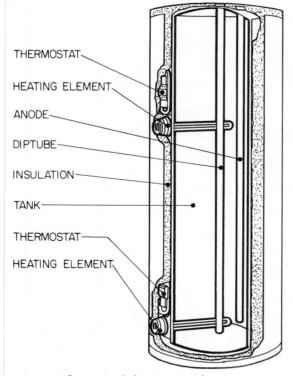

THERMOSTAT

HEATING ELEMENT

ANODE

DIPTUBE

INSULATION

TANK

THERMOSTAT

HEATING ELEMENT

Anatomy of electric water heater

open. Through it, steam would bleed off to keep the heater from exploding. No water heater should be without a T&P valve.

Another feature of hot water tanks is a magnesium anode rod that reaches down into the tank's water to help prevent electrolytic damage to other metal inside the tank.

Here are some common problems with water heaters and their solutions.

Long wait When you have to wait a long time for water flowing from a faucet to become hot, there is probably nothing wrong with the water heater. The faucet is simply too far away from it. At one time, this problem was solved with a circulating hot water system. However, that was before energy costs increased so drastically. Now it's better to waste a little water and wait for the hot water to reach the faucet than to waste all that energy keeping all the water in the system hot.

If the problem is serious, you can put a 5-gallon plug-in electric heater—the kind used in travel trailers—underneath the counter and pipe the hot water supply through it before going to the faucet. This way you would have instant hot water, except that the main water heater would do most

of the heating. Some plumbing codes frown on this. ***Not enough hot water*** If your water heater is too small for the family, you may run out of hot water during the times of heaviest use. This is probably better, though, than having a heater that is too large for the family and wastes energy. If the problem is serious, you can set the water heater's temperature control higher shortly before the periods of highest use. If the thermostat is defective, that's a problem for a professional.

Rusty water Rusty water flowing from faucets could mean that the heater tank is corroding badly. More likely, it means that silt or mud had collected in the bottom of the tank. The cure is to turn off the heat, then drain the tank through the drain valve at the bottom. Refill and turn on the heat again.

Crackling or sizzling noises When the burner is on and you hear a crackling or sizzling sound, the tank may have a leak that drips water onto the burner. It may simply be sizzling of water from tank condensation. If it's a leak you'll likely need a new tank, thus a new heater.

T&P valve drips A check valve somewhere in the plumbing system ahead of the water heater may permit excessive pressures to develop that make the temperature-and-pressure relief valve drip. The drip comes from excess pressure buildup as heater water expands and has no place to go. The answer is either to remove the check valve or to install an expansion chamber—an extra length of pipe capped on one end above the hot water supply near the T&P valve. This gives hot water extra space in which to expand.

If lots of hot water comes from the T&P valve, the water heater's temperature may be set too high. Lower it. If this doesn't solve it, the T&P valve could be bad. Have it checked, or replace it.

Rumbling sound A rumbling sound coming from the water heater is often caused by sediment that collects at the bottom of the tank. Water droplets get under the sediment and, when heated, flash into steam, making the sound. It sounds dangerous but isn't. The cure involves cleaning the tank of these deposits. Usually draining it as described above will do the trick. If that does not work, then a professional cleaning may be required. The same sound can come from an electric water heater with scale-encrusted heating elements. Replacing the elements is the cure.

Heater care In addition to the above, there are a few things you can do to keep a hot water heater working well. Normally a heater's corrosion-protective magnesium anode rod will last three to ten years. On some heaters it is a simple matter, after shutting off the water and fuel supply, to unscrew the anode rod from the heater and replace it with a new one. This can increase heater life significant-

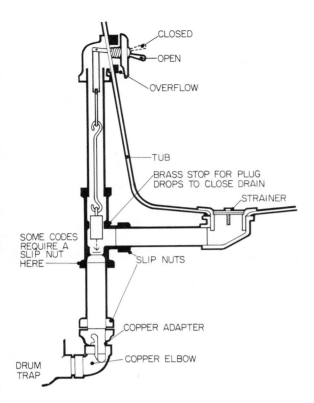

Old-style bathtub drain stopper mechanism

ly. Make sure you have the replacement anode on hand before taking the old rod out. They're not always easy to get.

If you have a glass-lined heater tank, scrupulously follow the manufacturer's recommended temperature settings. While glass-lined tanks are conceded to be best, consistently high temperatures may damage them.

Regular draining Once a month open the drain valve at the bottom of the heater's tank and run out a pail of water. This won't get rid of lime deposits, but it will rid the heater of sand and smaller particles. The more of these you can eliminate the better off your heater will be. They insulate the water from the burner right where you want good heat conduction.

TUB AND SHOWER TROUBLESHOOTING In the vast literature on taking care of plumbing problems, the hardware that is part of the bathtub seems to have been slighted. The following is a roundup of problems that can occur and what you can do to cure them.

Leaky faucet Tub faucets are essentially like sink faucets, but handling their repair is slightly differ-

ent. First turn off the water. Unlike a sink faucet, there probably is not a valve nearby to do this. You may have to look in the basement below the tub for the valve that controls the water supply. In an apartment the valve may be located on the wall, or behind an access panel. If in doubt, you can simply turn off the main house shutoff valve.

Like a sink, the repair should take only a few minutes, so no one will be greatly inconvenienced.

Disassembly of a tub faucet is not unlike that of a sink faucet. Remove the faucet cover. Inside you'll find a retaining ring that holds the spindle. Turn this ring with a wrench, and the whole thing comes out. When the spindle or the faucet shaft is exposed, you will probably find a worn or chewed-up washer. Simply replace it with one of the same size.

If this doesn't solve the problem, try reaming the valve seat. It may be chewed up or nicked. Many old faucets have removable seats. Some older faucets have seats with square or odd-shaped mouths. These may require a special wrench, which is simply a steel bar of the right shape that is thrust into the seat mouth and turned with a wrench. Hardware and plumbing supply stores usually have them.

When the problem is solved, reassemble the faucet in the reverse order that you took it apart.

Balky stopper The classic tub stopper is simply a rubber plug. But many tubs have a short handle that must be flipped up or down to open or close the drain. Sometimes this handle won't stay up or down. The problem is usually corrosion. First, remove the decorative plate by taking out the screws holding it to the tub. To get the stopper mechanism out, just lift the handle upward, gradually snaking it out.

Clean off all corrosion by rubbing briskly with steel wool. Apply a little grease where moving parts meet, and replace the mechanism. If it seems beyond repair, get a new mechanism at a plumbing supply store. Just take the old one along to be sure you get the right size.

Clogged showerhead It can be a pain, literally, to take a shower when some of the showerhead holes are clogged. This makes the water fire out of the unclogged ones, yet feeds too little water to satisfy.

To clean it, first remove the head by loosening the nut that holds it on. Use a wrench or locking pliers, being sure to protect the chrome finish with adhesive tape or by wrapping it with a rag.

With a toothpick and hot, soapy water poke through the holes. Rinse thoroughly. Then hold the head up to the light and look through from the back. All the holes should be clear. Continue until they are.

Diverter This is the device that turns to route water

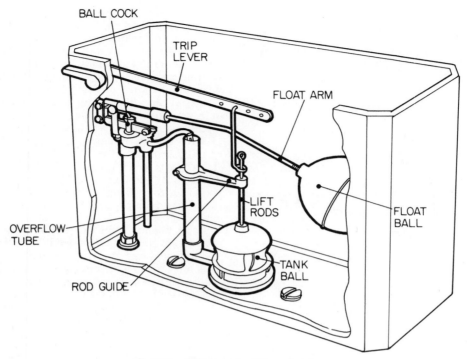

BALL COCK

TRIP LEVER

FLOAT ARM

OVERFLOW TUBE

LIFT RODS

FLOAT BALL

ROD GUIDE

TANK BALL

Toilet tank flush and refill mechanism

either to the showerhead or to the tub spout. It works on the same principle as a faucet. As time goes by, the diverter's washer can wear out and water will run out of both the shower and the tub spout at the same time. Replace the washer.

Blocked drain A stopped-up tub is relatively rare, but if it occurs, you can handle it with a plunger in the same way that you'd plunge a sink. Fill the tub partway with water, then plunge away. Every now and then pull up hard. Keep the plunger under water at all times.

TOILET TANK PROBLEMS *Partial flushing* When you trip the flush lever on the toilet tank but only part of the water in the tank goes out to flush the bowl, chances are the tank flush ball is not being lifted high enough off its seat. The out-rushing water is thus able to pull it back down on the seat before the flush can finish. The cure is to bend the upper lift wire to make it pull the flush ball well up off the seat. (See diagram.) Also be sure that the lower lift wire—the one attached to the flush ball—and the trip lever are working right.

Tank doesn't refill After a flush, if the water flows but the tank fails to refill, it's likely that the flush ball has not reseated itself properly. Check for binding of the trip handle, trip lever, both lift wires and the tank ball's guide arm. Make sure that the

guide arm is correctly centered over the valve seat. Parts may be bent to make them work right, or you can buy new ones from a dealer.

Tank fills but water flows When the flush tank's refill action is all right, but the water fails to shut off, the flush tank float level may be set so high that water flows out over the overflow tube. Lower the level as described below under "Water Level."

Another cause of continual flowing happens when the refill tube is inserted down into the top of the overflow tube with its end reaching below the tank water level. Then the refill tube becomes a siphon, running tank water continually out of the tank. There should be some distance between the end of the refill tube and the water level in the tank.

If the tank float reaches the top of its travel and water comes up around it and runs out the overflow tube, the tank inlet valve probably is defective. Shut off the water. Take the screws from the inlet valve levers, if it has them, and take the valve apart. Pull out the old inlet valve washer with a pair of pliers and install a new washer. Also check the valve seat to make sure it is not damaged. If you wish, the entire inlet valve can be replaced by draining the tank and removing the old valve.

The toilet float ball may develop a leak and fail

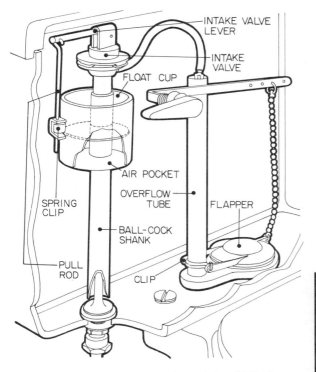

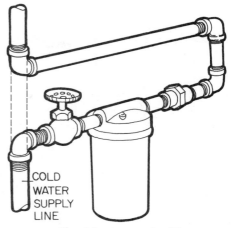

Cartridge-type water filter

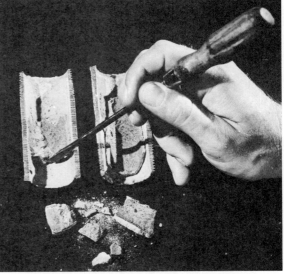

To install a flapper valve in place of the old flush ball, remove all the flush ball parts, slide the flapper down over the overflow tube, then hook its chain to the end of the trip arm. A flapper provides a much more positive seal. More troublefree, too.

to rise to the proper shutoff position. If it does, you can quickly unscrew it and replace it with a new one. A brass float ball can sometimes be drained and the leak soldered.

Many parts are available for repairing toilet tank inlet and flush valves, including whole new valves. If you have many problems with a standard ball-type flush valve, remove the ball, lift wire, and guide arm and replace the flush ball with a more modern rubber flapper. The flapper comes with a lift chain that attaches to the trip lever for flushing. Flappers give far fewer problems than flush balls do.

Tank sweating When cold water enters a toilet flush tank, it may make the tank cold enough to cause condensation of atmospheric moisture on the outer surface. This sweating can be prevented by insulating the tank on the *inside* to keep the temperature of the outer surface above the dew point of the surrounding air. Stick-on insulating jackets or liners are available to fit inside most toilet flush tanks. They also displace part of the flush water in the tank, helping to conserve water.

A sawed-open section of pipe shows the mineral deposits left there by excessively hard water. Water heaters and boilers, too, become coated the same way and eventually will burn out.

Water level If the toilet tank water level is too high or too low, you can change it by bending the float arm. Bend the arm down to lower the level or up to raise it. The correct level is about ¾" below the top of the overflow tube. Sometimes the tank is built with a water-level mark. But you may wish to have it lower than the mark to save water. If the level is too low, the toilet bowl may not flush completely. Your best bet is to experiment with lower water settings until you just get a complete flush but

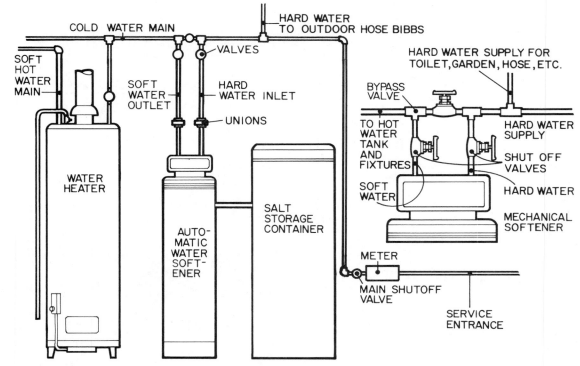

Water softener hookup

without water waste. (For other toilet repairs see the section on plumbing noises, page 141.)

HOW TO INSTALL A WATER SOFTENER

If you live in a hard water area or have water that looks bad, tastes bad, or smells bad, a water-treatment unit may be an answer. Added to your house water supply system, one or more units treat the incoming water to render it better for use. To know exactly what treatment unit you need calls for a water test by a local dealer. He will analyze your treatment unit needs based on test results. He may recommend adding one or more units to your water supply system. You can buy or rent them, install them yourself, or have them installed.

If you install your own water treatment equipment, you will probably want to purchase it outright. In fact, you may have to. Make sure that it is properly sized both for your water quality and your family's water use. One or more of the following units may be added.

Sediment filter Simplest of the water treatment units is the sediment filter. Many of these use activated carbon to remove tastes and odors as well as suspended solids from water. If you have one and

have changed the cartridge, you already know how much junk can be removed from household drinking water. The units cost little. They attach to the cold water supply pipe underneath the sink or in the basement. Since a sediment filter usually supplies only one fixture, that is usually the one from which all drinking water is drawn. Larger models that treat all incoming water are installed in the incoming house water service entrance.

The installation simply involves cutting a piece out of the cold water pipe and installing valves and connectors so that the water is rerouted to flow through the filter. If the supply pipe is vertical, install the filter in the lower horizontal portion of a U-shaped pipe assembly attached to the cutoff vertical pipe by means of elbows at top and bottom. Valves at the incoming supply line let you turn off the water while changing a cartridge. New ones are needed every six months or so.

Hard water contains ions—minerals that react poorly with soap—causing you to use lots of it and leaving a soap scum on everything. A water softener contains tiny beads of resin that remove bad-acting sodium ions from water passing around them and replace these with good-acting calcium and magnesium sodium ions.

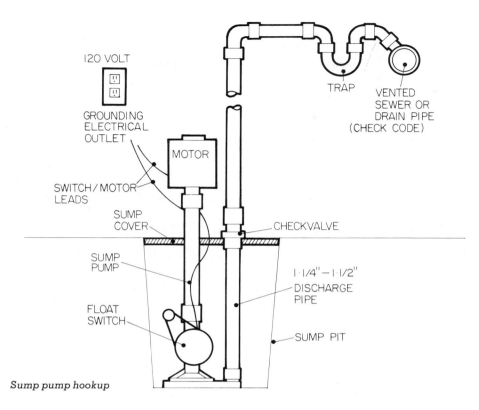

120 VOLT

GROUNDING
ELECTRICAL
OUTLET

SWITCH/MOTOR
LEADS

MOTOR

SUMP
COVER

SUMP
PUMP

FLOAT
SWITCH

TRAP

VENTED
SEWER OR
DRAIN PIPE
(CHECK CODE)

CHECKVALVE

1·1/4" − 1·1/2"
DISCHARGE
PIPE

SUMP PIT

Sump pump hookup

After so much water has passed through the resin bed, its ability to absorb calcium and magnesium ions becomes depleted. Then the beads are said to need regeneration. Regeneration is done by passing salty water—brine—through the resin bed. The resin collects sodium ions from the salty water and gives up its magnesium and calcium ions to it. The regeneration process is done inside the softener while household water is bypassed. When complete, brine flow through the resin bed stops and the brine is rinsed out before the bed goes back into service.

Some water softeners do the whole process automatically; others require some degree of mechanical control. The more automatic the softener, the more it costs.

PUTTING IN A SOFTENER A water softener should be located to treat all the hot water and all the cold water that flows to household fixtures and laundry. Water for toilets and outdoor hose bibbs may be left hard. Try to locate the softener, if you can, after pipes for garden hose spigots have taken off their supply from the cold water entrance, and after toilet supplies branch off, leaving other cold and hot water to be softened.

To make the installation, turn off the water at the

main shutoff valve. Cut through the cold water main in the desired location. Adapt the existing pipe ends on either side to polybutylene plastic tubing. (See page 136.) Supply the softener with flexible PB tubing. Adapt the tubing at the softener's control valve to whatever is found there, usually threads. Valves should be located in both inlet and outlet lines to the softener and a bypass line with valve installed. The bypass lets house water service continue even though the softener is removed for major service.

The softener should be assembled and installed according to the manufacturer's directions. Its brine discharge line should be run to the nearest drain. Softener effluent may be run into septic systems without harm to the system.

To put the softener into service, close the bypass valve and open the inlet and outlet valves to the softener. Fill the brine storage tank with softener salt. Set its regeneration control and follow any other steps that the manufacturer calls for. Your house should then be supplied with soft water.

Iron removers, sulfur removers, chlorinators, pH adjusters, and reverse-osmosis units may be added ahead of the softener. The softener should al-

1. *To install a new sump pump, simply lower it into the sump pit. This Genova Sump Witch™ upright-type sump pump is made of vinyl to keep it from corroding inside the sump.* Photos this series: Richard Day

2. *Connect the discharge pipe through the second opening in the sump cover. It should contain a check valve to prevent backflow of already pumped water. The discharge pipe runs to the house sewer or other suitable drain.*

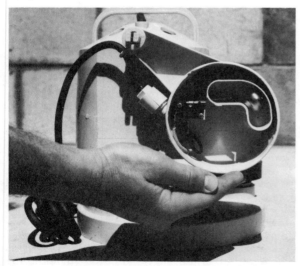

Cutaway view of hermetically sealed switch shows its ball-and-raceway construction. As the floating switch module lowers while water is being pumped out of the sump, the raceway tips, letting the ball fall to the other end of the raceway. As the ball leaves the microswitch arm (center) the switch shuts off the pump's motor. The pump will not turn on again until the float rises, with the rising sump water level and the ball returns to its "on" position.

ways be the last unit in the series before the water is distributed throughout the house.

HOW TO REPLACE A SUMP PUMP

The awful atmosphere a sump pump works in makes its life miserable. If the pump isn't built to withstand these rigors, it may soon fail.

The first sign of trouble is often rising water in the basement. If that happens during a storm, it may be too late to prevent flood damage. For this reason a sump pump should get the best care you can give it according to its service manual. This includes regular cleaning of the sump pit and hosing down of both the pit and the pump. It also includes checking the position of the pump in the pit to make sure that the float switch is not stuck or jammed against the wall of the pit.

To replace a defective sump pump, it must be uncoupled from its discharge line and removed from the pit. NOTE: Be sure to unplug the pump from the wall before you work on it. A plugged-in sump pump, or any of the metal parts connected to it, can deliver a fatal shock, if faulty.

Before you install a new pump, you'll need to provide a modern three-pronged grounding-type electrical outlet for the matching grounding plugs found on all recent sump pumps. (If you don't know how to install the outlet, see page 94, or else hire an electrician to do it for you.) The 120-volt outlet should be fused or circuit-breaker-protected for 20 amperes.

Your new sump pump should be installed with a check valve in the discharge line if there is not already one there. If nothing else, the check valve is an energy-saving device. Once the sump pump has lowered the water level to the cutoff point and switched off, the check valve will prevent the water that remains in the discharge piping from flowing back into the pit. Without a check valve the pump would have to pump an extra gallon of water at the beginning of each cycle. Having no check valve not only causes additional water to be pumped but makes for more frequent pump cycling. Every sump pump should have a check valve.

Another thing every sump pump should have—if you're interested in getting more than brief use out of it—is corrosion-free construction. Some sump pumps are made of brass and stainless steel to be corrosion-free. Others are made of tough vinyl for the same reason. Sump pump switches should be designed to provide up to a million cycles of use without failure. Ideally, the switch is permanently protected from the sump atmosphere.

You'll find there are two kinds of sump pumps—

upright and submersible. Of the two, the submersible type costs considerably more but will keep working even though inundated with water. On the other hand, an upright sump pump has its motor above the basement floor level and is protected from inundation except under the most severe conditions. Having a sump pump is like having a flood insurance policy.

If connecting the new sump pump to the old discharge piping presents an adaptation problem, there's an easy way out. A new-design check valve called a Universal Check Valve is built with a series of stepped shoulders at its upper end. It comes with a flexible rubber coupling that will fit most kinds of discharge piping. This coupling also helps to isolate pump noises from the house plumbing.

If you're making a new sump pump installation, check with local health department officials to see how you must dispose of sump water. In some localities, it is permitted to be piped directly into the building drain via a trap. In others it may enter the building drain but must do so by what's called an air-gap device. (Ask your plumbing supply dealer for details.) In still others, sump water can be pumped out onto the ground, into a drainage ditch, or into a dry well. In most cases, sump water is great for irrigating a garden. On the other hand, you get most of it during rainy weather when the garden least needs irrigating.

5

HOW TO TROUBLESHOOT AND REPAIR ELECTRIC AND GAS RANGES · CLOTHES DRYERS · CLOTHES WASHERS · REFRIGERATORS

HOME APPLIANCES

In a world used to push-button living, we're inclined to the "set it and forget it" approach. We place an expensive appliance, such as a washer or dryer, in the basement, connect it, and forget it's there. As a result the equipment may malfunction prematurely, or a steel cabinet may soon show signs of rust.

Misuse of an appliance is another area that causes early failure and frequent repair bills. Don't overload your washer or dryer beyond the recommended capacity. Apply a coat of wax to the metal exterior of your appliance. (Auto wax is excellent for this purpose.) Keep the equipment and the area around it clean and free of dust. Read the maintenance instructions that come with your appliances, and keep the manual handy in the event of failure. Set up a routine maintenance schedule for all your appliances, including such fixed equipment as furnaces, dehumidifiers, and air conditioners. Clean filters in the air conditioners, furnace, and the lint filter in the clothes dryer frequently, and replace them when necessary.

If your appliances are several years old, you will soon have another figure added to your monthly budget in the form of appliance repair bills. To eliminate this expensive outlay, follow the instructions presented here. Only if these steps fail to remedy the problem should you call a repair man.

HOW TO TROUBLESHOOT AND REPAIR ELECTRIC AND GAS RANGES

ELECTRIC RANGES A surprising number of homeowners are not aware of the ease with which a burned-out electric range burner unit can be replaced with a new one. The truth is that, at worst, it's a simple screwdriver job.

On most electric ranges made within the last ten years, replacing a burner is as easy as plugging in a line cord; it is so easy that many housewives remove all the burners periodically to clean the drip trays beneath them. Basically, it involves only disconnecting three wires from the old burner and connecting them to identical terminals on the new unit.

Late model ranges New burners cost around twenty dollars, depending upon the make of the range and the size of the burner. A replacement for your range should be readily available from the manufactur-

er's service shop in your area, or from a shop stocking universal parts for all appliance brands. It's a good idea to take the old burner with you (plus the make and model number of the range) to be certain that you get an exact duplicate replacement part.

Before replacing plug-in burners on late-model ranges, be sure that the burner control switches are turned to the "off" position. Then raise the burner about 1" above its recess and pull outward (not upward) to disconnect it from its socket, partially concealed beneath the range top.

To install the new plug-in burner replacement, simply align the two prongs with the socket and push them into place. The burner will center itself in the recess, and light downward pressure will snap its supports into slots in the rim of the drip tray.

Older ranges When replacing the older three-wire burners, first remove the fuse or trip the circuit breaker in the range service line. To remove a

REPLACING AN ELECTRIC RANGE BURNER UNIT

1

2

3

4

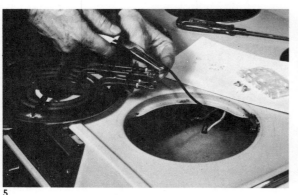

5

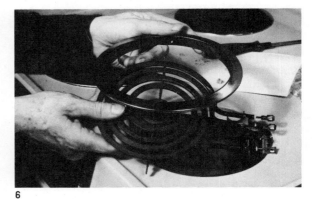

6

Step 1. *Pull burner out to unplug two prongs from socket. On older ranges, lift burner and trim ring to remove drip tray.* **Step 2.** *Continue pulling outward until glass or ceramic insulator is visible, along with three wires connected to the burner.* **Step 3.** *Loosen the hinge screw and slide the slotted hinge bracket from under the screw head to free the burner.* **Step 4.** *Unsnap spring clip to separate and remove the two halves of the insulator. Be careful:* insulators break easily. **Step 5.** *Note the positions of each colored wire on burner terminals before loosening screws and removing. (A sketch will help prevent mistakes.)* **Step 6.** *Remove trim ring from old burner by pressing tabs out of slots at perimeter. Install ring on new burner. Work backward to reassemble.* Photos this series: Arnold Romney

burner from an older range, raise it along with the chrome trim ring about an inch and remove the drip tray from beneath it. Loosen the single screw that fastens the burner hinge to the range top. (It's not necessary to remove the screw, just loosen it.) Then slide the slotted hinge from under the screw head. Now pull the burner outward cautiously until you can see three wires entering a glass or ceramic insulator.

Unsnap the metal clip holding the two halves of the insulator in place over the terminal screws, and make a note or even a sketch to show which color wire is connected to each of the three terminal screws. Loosen the terminal screws and remove the wires.

Snap the burner supports out of the slots in the chrome trim ring and set the old burner aside. Install the trim ring on the new unit by pushing the tabs into the slots. Holding the new burner in the same position as the old one as it was removed, connect the three wires as you noted their positions on the original burner.

If the new replacement unit includes new insulators, install them over the terminal screws and lock them in place with the spring clip. If no insulator was included, install the original insulator halves over the screws to cover them. Push the burner into position, slide the slotted hinge under the screw head, and tighten it securely.

Check to see that the burner tilts easily for access to the drip tray. Slide the drip tray beneath the burner, and press downward on the burner so that the trim ring fits flush on top of the porcelain surrounding the burner opening.

Now replace the fuse, or reset the circuit breaker to "on" and try your new burner. It should make your range function like new.

GAS RANGES Gas ranges are really very simple machines. If yours is old and not working to your satisfaction, you can get it back into working order in as little as an hour.

First thing to do is to remove the grates and the covers around the burners. Next, remove the handles that turn on the gas. These are usually plastic and shaped to fit the flat on the round stem that sticks out from the front panel. To remove them just pull them straight off.

If you find it difficult to remove them, use an old screwdriver to exert gentle leverage. Be careful how you do this or you may break the plastic handle. If you do, however, you can get inexpensive substitutes in most hardware stores and home centers.

Now you are ready to take off the front panel. This is usually held in place by two sheet metal screws, which are easily removed with a screwdriver. With these items removed, you have complete access to everything you can adjust.

To avoid the possibility of burning yourself while working on the range, turn off the pilot lights. Gas to the pilot lights is fed through a ⅛″ pipe that comes out of a fitting at the front, which has a screw in it. This screw regulates the size of the pilot flame and if you turn it all the way down with a screwdriver you will shut off the flame.

Cleaning burners To clean the burners, use a piece of wire to penetrate every hole. Pay special attention to the holes that face the pipe that shoots a jet of gas to the pilot light. If these are clogged, the pilot light will not ignite the burner. Hardened, burned food on the burners can be removed with a wire brush.

Your cleaning task will be made easier if you take the burners out of the range. You can easily do this by lifting them up slightly and pulling them forward. They are not held by any fastening.

Before you remove the burners, disconnect the pipe that shoots gas to the pilot flame. These pipes are anchored in various ways to the burner. In the range shown in the photos, a small hole at the end of the pipe snaps onto a little knob on the burner.

Lubricating the valve After the burners are cleaned, restore them to their positions and turn your attention to the valve mechanism in front of the range that turns the gas on or off. If they are hard to turn they need cleaning and lubricating.

Put a little benzine or lighter fluid into the mechanism. In some models, like the one shown, there is an opening or notch at the top into which you can drop the benzine. In others you may have to spray the cleaning fluid into it.

Wait a few minutes for the benzine to evaporate, then drop a light oil like 3-in-One into the valve. Slip one of the handles back onto the shaft and work it back and forth a few times. If it is still stiff you may have to use a penetrating oil and again work the shaft back and forth until it turns easily. Then add a few drops of light oil and give the valve a few turns.

Connect the pilot flame pipes to the burners. These pipes come in two pieces and are adjustable so that you can easily reach the burners.

Pilot adjustment Now open the screw that admits gas to the pilot and light it with a match. Keep the flame low and turn on the front burner. If the burner doesn't ignite, turn it off again. Then turn the pilot light up a little at a time until the burner lights as soon as it's turned on. Use the lowest flame that will work for both burners. Repeat this operation with the other pilot light and burners.

Put the covers back on, noting that the larger holes go over the front burners. (On some ranges all the holes are the same size.) Try each burner again. It sometimes happens that, with the covers

SERVICING GAS RANGES

1

2

3

4

5

6

Step 1. *Typical gas range with grates removed and pilot lights burning. Extinguish pilots before repairing, to prevent accidents.* **Step 2.** *Disconnect pilot pipes, which are anchored in various ways to burner. Here, small hole at end of pipe snaps onto small knob on burner.* **Step 3.** *Cleaning is easier with burners removed. Lift up slightly and pull forward to release. They are not held by fasten-* ers. **Step 4.** *To clean burners, use short pieces of wire to penetrate all holes.* **Step 5.** *Use wire brush to give burners a thorough cleaning; remove burned, hardened food that has accumulated.* **Step 6.** *Clean and lubricate hard-to-turn valves. Use small amount of benzine or lighter fluid to loosen, then apply light oil.* Photos this series: Herb Pfister

on, one or more may not ignite and you may have to adjust the pilot flame again. CAUTION: Do not leave any unignited burner on for more than a couple of seconds. Accumulated gas can ignite explosively, causing severe burns.

Flame adjustment If any burner has a yellowish flame, it is not getting enough air mixed with the gas. At the front of the range you will find a large hole in the burner pipe with a metal cover held by a screw. Loosen the screw and pull the cover back a little at a time until the flames turn blue. Then tighten the screw.

HOW TO TROUBLESHOOT CLOTHES DRYERS

All at once your automatic clothes dryer doesn't work. Before calling in a serviceman, check to see if you can correct the problem yourself. Troubleshooting isn't difficult, and you may save yourself a pile of money.

Most malfunctioning clothes dryers will show one of the following symptoms:
- The dryer shows no life.
- The motor operates (you can hear it), but the drum doesn't rotate.
- Clothes don't get dry although the machine runs.
- The dryer doesn't shut off after the cycle is done.
- The dryer makes a lot of noise as it runs.

Each one of these problems can be investigated further by following specific troubleshooting procedures. In most cases the cause of a problem may be some simple thing that's easy for you to fix yourself. In fewer cases the services of a professional technician may be needed.

THE DEAD DRYER There are three main reasons why a clothes dryer won't demonstrate any life: incorrect use, electrical failure, and a bad door switch. Before calling a repairman, check to be sure the power cord has not been inadvertently pulled from the electric outlet. Also, check to see if a fuse has blown or a circuit breaker has been tripped.

A blown fuse Check the fuse or circuit breaker in the main electric service box. If a new fuse also blows or the circuit breaker trips again, call a professional electrician. There is undoubtedly a serious malfunction in the electrical system that should not go unattended. It could cause a fire.

In addition to a main fuse or circuit breaker, older model clothes dryers are usually protected by a fuse in the unit. It is normally positioned in the dryer's doorway. If a fuse is not there, check the wiring diagram on the dryer for its location.

The purpose of this fuse is to prevent serious damage if there is an electrical failure inside the dryer, such as a motor malfunction or a strong electric surge. When this fuse blows or fails because of age, one of two things will happen.

First, the dryer may not run. This would be true for either an electric or gas unit. Secondly, the dryer may run, but drying elements won't work and clothes will remain damp. This is true for electric dryers only. Whether one or the other occurs depends upon the way that the fuse is employed to protect the dryer.

In any event, replace the fuse and see if the dryer operates. If the dryer functions properly, but the fuse blows again, there is an electrical malfunction which will probably require a technician's expertise.

Thermal overload A thermal overload (high limit) switch in the motor protects the dryer if it doesn't have a fuse. The following tip regarding this switch could save you money and time.

Suppose your dryer has done one or two loads normally, but fails to run for another load. This malfunction is frequently caused by lint clogging the motor housing vents. The motor overheats, which causes a thermal overload switch to trip.

Clean out the lint by opening the dryer and brushing and vacuuming the rear of the motor housing. To clean the front of the housing, which is more difficult to get to, use your fingers and a small brush. You can check on cleanliness by holding a pocket mirror so you see the housing. Make sure all lint has been removed.

Faulty switch. A faulty switch may also be the culprit. A dryer normally has a door switch that is wired in series with the main power intake line. When the door is opened, the switch interrupts the electrical service, causing the dryer to shut off. When the door is closed on the switch, the dryer starts up as long as the switch is in good condition. If the switch has failed, the dryer won't run.

The door switch is easy to locate. Find the button in the dryer's doorway, and you have found the switch. Getting to the switch so it can be tested is a bit more difficult. The top of the dryer usually has to be raised. This is done either by using a knife to pry the top loose or by undoing screws that hold the top. First, however, *disconnect the power cord from the electric outlet.*

When the top has been raised, reach inside and carefully pull the wires from the door switch. Note which wire goes to which terminal. Now connect a jumper wire, which is equipped at both ends with an alligator clip, between the two wires that were connected to the switch. This completes the circuit.

Reconnect the power cord and turn the machine on. Turn the machine off as soon as it starts (or doesn't start). If the dryer starts, disconnect the power cord and replace the door switch, which may be held by a screw or locking tab to the dryer's chassis. Reconnect wires, and you're set.

The centrifugal switch A defective centrifugal switch is another reason why dryers won't run. The purpose of this switch is to keep the heat turned off until the drum is rotating at full speed. You might want to take a chance that the switch is bad and replace it. The switch is normally near or adjacent to the motor. Consult the wiring diagram.

Replacing the centrifugal switch involves opening up the dryer. The power cord must be disconnected to prevent possible serious injury. If you

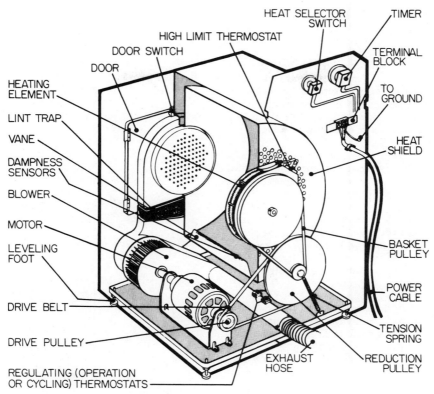

HEAT SELECTOR SWITCH

TIMER

HIGH LIMIT THERMOSTAT

TERMINAL BLOCK

DOOR SWITCH

DOOR

TO GROUND

HEATING ELEMENT

HEAT SHIELD

LINT TRAP

VANE

DAMPNESS SENSORS

BLOWER

MOTOR

BASKET PULLEY

LEVELING FOOT

POWER CABLE

DRIVE BELT

TENSION SPRING

DRIVE PULLEY

REDUCTION PULLEY

EXHAUST HOSE

REGULATING (OPERATION OR CYCLING) THERMOSTATS

Parts of a typical clothes dryer

own a new model dryer, it may have a removable front panel. Undo the screws and remove the panel. This will reveal the centrifugal switch and other major parts.

Most older model dryers have to have the rear panel removed to get at parts. If the dryer is a gas model and has to be pulled away from the wall to do this, you must shut off the gas valve and disconnect the gas line.

NOTE: Do not attempt to move the dryer without disconnecting the gas feed line. You may rupture the line and cause a gas leak.

If you have a gas dryer, your local utility company will probably send a serviceman to repair a malfunction at little or no cost to you, except for new parts. Thus, whenever it becomes obvious that you cannot make a repair or troubleshoot a problem without difficulty let the gas company do it.

Defective timer and defective motor Two more reasons for a dryer not showing any life include a defective timer and a defective motor. Troubleshooting each to make an accurate diagnosis involves the use of a voltmeter. However, there are

indications that will let you pick out one over the other.

The first is a blown dryer fuse (see above). Blown fuses indicate a motor problem. The second indication is a strong odor of scorched insulation. Again, this points to motor failure. In any case, replacing a timer and repairing or replacing a motor are jobs best left to a professional if you have had no experience.

THE DEAD DRUM By "dead drum" we mean one that doesn't turn at all or binds as it rotates. However, the dryer motor is operating, which leaves out an electrical failure as a cause. Reasons for a drum not revolving or binding include a loose or broken drive belt, loose or defective pulley, broken tension spring, or a heavy accumulation of lint.

The belt The belt arrangement from dryer to dryer varies. One type uses a single large belt that extends from the pulley on the motor around the drum. As the motor revolves, the belt, which must be extremely taut, causes the drum to turn.

In this model, there may be another belt, smaller in size, that extends from the motor pulley to a pulley on a blower housing. As this belt turns, it operates the blower, which expels air to blow moisture and heat from the drum through the vent to the outside.

Another type of setup has a drive belt that extends from the motor pulley to a so-called reduction pulley. A second belt is placed between the reduction pulley and a pulley on the drum housing. The motor pulley drives the reduction pulley, which in turn drives the drum housing pulley to rotate the drum.

When a drum won't turn, every belt has to be checked to see if it has broken. Every belt must be as tight as possible, with no more than ¼" of free play allowed when you press on the belt between pulleys.

The pulleys Check the pulleys if the belts are okay. Make sure each is tight by tightening its setscrew. See if pulleys have sustained damage by examining their grooves. If glaze has built up in the groove, it is probably allowing the belt to slip, which is hampering operations. Replace the pulley.

Many dryers have a spring, or springs, between the motor pulley and drum and/or blower pulley that keep parts aligned with each other. See that a spring has not fallen loose or lost tension. Reconnect the spring tightly or replace it with a new one.

Lint Lint may also be a cause of a drum not turning. Try turning the drum by hand. If it is difficult to turn, lint may have accumulated around the drum or some object may be caught between the drum and housing. This will cause the drum to bind.

Some dryers have a removable baffle plate on the drum. Take it off and fabricate a cleaning tool. This can be a metal coat hanger that you straighten out and hook at one end. Use it to pull lint or a binding object from around the drum.

With other dryers you may be able to clean the area around the drum by reaching in from the front panel, rear panel or top lid area. If this doesn't make the backside of the drum accessible, the drum should be removed from the dryer and the area cleaned thoroughly.

INADEQUATE DRYING Inadequate drying is another problem that in nine cases out of ten has a cause easily rectified. Tackle the problem in the following order:

1. Is the drum being overloaded? If so, clothes will not dry as they should. Consult the owner's manual for manufacturer recommendations regarding loading.

2. Are clothes sopping wet when they are put into the dryer? Then the dryer isn't at fault. The washing machine is. Clothes coming out of the washing machine should be damp, not dripping wet.

SERVICING A DRYER

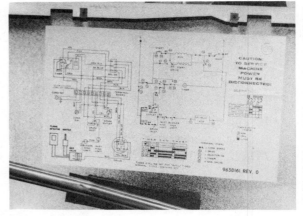

Wiring diagrams help you locate parts, which vary by model.

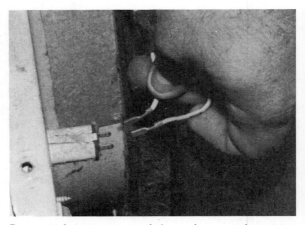

Door switch is easy to reach for replacement by raising the top of the dryer.

3. Is the machine being set properly? Be sure the dryer is being operated in accordance with manufacturer's instructions.

4. Has the fuse inside an electric dryer failed? Check and replace as necessary.

5. Has lint built up to a critical stage? This is one of the primary causes of clothes not being dried as they should.

Lint If lint is the problem, unhook the vent pipe and disassemble it if possible. Clean out the pipe (or separate pipes) by ramming a wad of cloth through. Using the fabricated coat-hanger tool described above, clean lint from the vent connection on the dryer.

Reconnect the vent pipe. Be sure joints between sections of pipe are tightly sealed with duct tape.

Lint causes more problems than anything else. Clean the lint trap before every use. Clean dryer and ductwork yearly.

All dryers must have door switches to obtain UL sanction. Button in door indicates switch location.

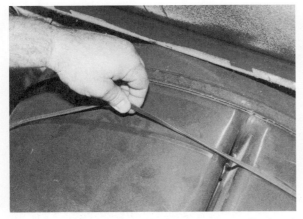

New dryers use a one-piece belt to drive drums. If a break occurs, wrap the new belt around the drum, fit it to motor pulley, and tighten.

Apply duct tape to joints to prevent lint from escaping, and to prevent unnecessary heat loss from dryer.

Also make sure there is no hole in the vent pipe. This is especially applicable to plastic tubing.

Leaks Leaks in the vent system will cause insufficient drying and create a fire hazard in the laundry area by allowing flammable lint to be expelled. Check the outside wall where the vent pipe protrudes for a draft cover. The cover keeps wind from blowing back into the dryer. This wind can extinguish the pilot flame of a gas dryer, preventing the burner from igniting.

In gas dryers with glow coils and in electric dryers, wind that enters the system will reduce drying efficiency.

Other causes If everything to this point is okay, then the cause of insufficient drying is a defective thermostat or heat source problem. If you lack ex-

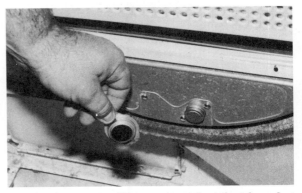

Thermostats are usually easy to reach and replace. Just remove three screws, remove thermostat, replace with a new one. *Photos this series: Mort Schultz*

perience in treating these areas, call a serviceman.

DRYER KEEPS RUNNING This problem may be caused by a defective door switch, which was covered above. Other than this, the cause is either a defective timer, thermostat or electronic dampness-sensor system, or a grounded motor.

The electronic dampness-sensor system is a relatively recent innovation that detects moisture. It allows the dryer to remain on as long as clothes are wet, but it turns the dryer off as soon as clothes are dry. The system, therefore, prevents unnecessary operation.

The electronic dampness-sensor as well as the integrated circuit solid-state controls of some new model dryers are complicated devices that should not be tampered with. Call a serviceman if something seems amiss.

TOO MUCH NOISE If excessive noise isn't being caused by loose objects flopping around inside the revolving drum, then look for a loose drive pulley, loose drive belt, or a loose fan in the blower housing. To repair the last, the blower probably has to be disassembled so the fan-blade setscrew can be tightened.

It is possible, also, that noise is being created because the machine is not level. This may be checked with a carpenter's level. Most dryers are leveled by turning adjustable leveling legs.

Finally, excessive noise can be produced by a worn drum bearing. A new bearing is available from a parts dealer. However, the drum must be removed to make the replacement.

HOW TO TROUBLESHOOT CLOTHES WASHERS

Thirty percent of the calls made by professional service technicians to repair major home appliances are not necessary, because homeowners could have done the fixing themselves. That's the conclusion of a recent study made by the Center for Policy Alternatives at the Massachusetts Institute of Technology.

"With washing machines, the percentage is much higher," says the owner of a major appliance service company in Fort Lauderdale, Florida, which has a twenty-man travel squad repairing every type of major appliance.

Most complaints concerning washing machines, this experienced professional reports, involve a water-related problem.

"Unlike a mechanical problem (transmission, for example), the homeowner should be able to repair a water-related problem himself."

What keeps most of us from attempting repairs is an effective, simple troubleshooting procedure, such as we've outlined below. Following this procedure, it's likely you'll be able to solve 95 percent

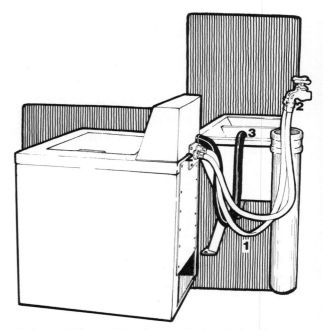

Three possible troublemakers to check include 1) kinks in water-supply hoses, which restrict water flow; 2) plugged filter screens, either in couplings that connect hoses to faucets or in the water-inlet valve nozzles; and 3) improper positioning of drain hose, which can cause either siphoning or water remaining in machine during wash cycle.

of all your water problems with a clothes washer in short order. The only malfunction you may not be able to handle yourself is water pump failure. Before attempting any repairs, be sure to disconnect electricity to the appliance and follow all safety precautions.

WATER VALVES To start with, let's suppose water flows into your machine sluggishly or not at all. The machine's motor is running, so the malfunction is not electrical. First make sure that water valves are opened all the way to assure a maximum output of water. If water valves are closed or partially closed, water won't flow or will flow sluggishly.

Though this sounds academic, servicemen regularly collect service fees from distraught homeowners who have nothing wrong with their machines, except closed or partially closed water valves.

Also, it's important to make sure that water valves are turned off when the washing machine isn't in use for extended periods. Many homes are flooded every year because valves are left on and a hose bursts or a water-inlet valve fails.

WATER HOSES Check to see that hot and cold water hoses from water faucets to the machine are straight. If a hose won't straighten, replace it. Kinks in hoses are sometimes created when a clothes washer is placed too close to a wall. Moving the machine away from the wall may help solve the problem.

If you have to replace a hose, make sure you get one designed for a clothes washer. Do not use ordinary garden hose. It is not made to withstand the high pressure a clothes washer hose must endure.

With water faucets shut off, disconnect water hoses from faucets and machine.

FILTER SCREENS Inside the couplings at each end of a hose you may find small filter screens. If there are no screens in the ends of the hose couplings at the water-inlet valve, the screens will be located in the water-inlet valve nozzles. You can pry them out without removing the valve from the machine. Pry screens out with a screwdriver and clean them under running water, using an old toothbrush to remove deposits.

Test the screens after cleaning to determine if water passes freely. Let water flow into the screens from a tap. If the screens fail this test, replace them.

Never run a washing machine without filter screens. Particles may lodge in the water-inlet valve and prevent the valve from closing. This will cause overflow.

NOTE: New parts are available from a dealer who sells your make of clothes washer and from companies listed in the Yellow Pages of the telephone book.

The procedure you have followed to this point will solve a sluggish water-flow problem in most cases.

INLET VALVE/SOLENOID If trouble continues, check the water-inlet valve and solenoid assembly and the water-level switch. These components can also cause the machine to overflow. Remember, before doing anything, disconnect the power supply cord from the electric wall outlet. Failure to take this step may result in severe electric shock.

In the case of a sluggish flow problem, replacing the water-inlet valve and solenoid assembly will usually solve the condition. Take off the cover plate from over the valve housing and remove wires from the valve's terminals. Make a note of which wire goes to which terminal so the new valve can be connected correctly.

As long as we're discussing the water-inlet valve, there is an easy way to determine if your washing machine is overflowing because particles have lodged in the valve. See that the water faucets are open and that the power cord is unplugged. Turn the control dial to "Fill" position. If

water flows into the machine, the water-inlet valve should be replaced.

WATER LEVEL SWITCH If a sluggish water flow or an overflow problem is not by the water-inlet valve and solenoid assembly, check the water-level switch. Here's how to replace it:

1. The power cord must be disconnected. Consult the wiring diagram on the chassis to determine the location of the water-level switch. In most machines, the switch is in the console that houses the controls. Remove the screws and take off the cover plate to reveal the controls.

The switch can be identified by a plastic or rubber water-level tube connected to the switch. There are also three electric wires connected to the switch's terminals.

In some older models, the water-level switch is inside the cabinet. The top of the machine will have to be released. This is usually done by slipping a butter knife in the seam where the top and cabinet join. Pry up to pop the top loose. You will spot the switch in one of the corners.

2. Before pulling .wires, make a drawing of which wire goes to which terminal.

3. Disconnect wires by pulling them off the switch's terminals. Disconnect the water tube from the nipple on the switch. Tape the tube to the cabinet to keep it from dropping inside the machine.

4. Remove the screws holding the switch. Attach a new switch, reconnect the tube and wires, and close the cabinet.

FINDING LEAKS Another water-related problem you may encounter with a washing machine is a leak. Repairing the problem usually isn't difficult, but finding the origin of the leak can cause a headache, because it can be elusive.

To make the task easier, keep in mind that a water leak will occur either in the water-intake system, in the tub, or in the drain system. With the machine running, examine all hoses and look under the unit (use a flashlight) to try to see the area where water is dripping.

Intake hoses will leak if coupling washers become defective, the coupling loosens or a hose splits. Check couplings at both ends as the machine fills with water.

If water is leaking from a coupling, try to tighten the coupling. If this doesn't help, replace the coupling washer. To test the drain system for leaks set the machine to pump water out. Examine the drain hose, which may be split and should be replaced, and the standpipe as the pumping cycle is taking place. Naturally, replace a bad hose.

If water is dripping from the base of the machine, look for a leaking water-inlet valve or a bad pump. A leak at the water-inlet valve may be caused by a loose hose connection.

Whether the water-inlet valve or pump is leaking, replace the faulty part as soon as possible since water can drip on the motor and cause the motor to burn out. If this happens, you might as well buy a new clothes washer.

WATER BACKUP/SIPHONING If water is backing up and coming out the standpipe, there is a stoppage that should be cleared by removing the drain hose and cleaning the pipe with a plumber's snake.

A complaint frequently heard by clothes washer repairmen is that water siphons from a machine. The most common reason for this is improper positioning of the drain hose. The manufacturer of the

Loose hose couplings can cause leaks. Don't overtighten plastic coupling; turn by hand, or make ½ turn with slip-joint pliers.

Filter screens are in coupling or water inlet valve. NOTE: Screen can be removed without taking the valve from the machine.

On most washers, remove cover plate to gain access to water-inlet valve and solenoid assembly.

Water-inlet valve and solenoid assembly. Number of solenoids attached to valve depends on number of wash-rinse cycles.

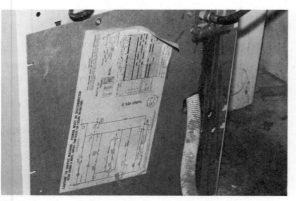

Water-level switch can be located by checking wiring diagram on washer chassis. Turn off current to the machine for safety.

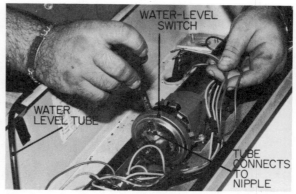

Nipple on level switch is where water level tube is connected. Tube signals water level to the switch.

machine sets limits at which a drain hose should be placed. The limit for many washers is not less than 34″ and not more than 72″ from the base of the machine.

If the minimum height is less than this, water will siphon from the washer. If the maximum drain height is exceeded, all the water may not be pumped from the machine during the washing cycle.

HOW TO TROUBLESHOOT REFRIGERATORS

A professional appliance repairman has estimated that in seven out of ten times, the refrigerator malfunction repairs he is called on to make could have been handled by the homeowner. We'll review some common refrigerator problems and indicate when a serviceman's expertise is needed. Keep in mind that the basic refrigeration system is highly reliable. Most problems requiring a technician's knowledge are concentrated in this basic system. With a little study you can handle all problems outside the main system.

A refrigerator's working parts can be found beneath the unit (accessible from the back) or in the cabinet walls. To get at them, you must remove panels. If the screws holding the panels are not visible, they are often hidden under escutcheons.

DEFECTIVE DEFROST TIMER If your defroster is not functioning properly, the cause may be a defective timer. In some refrigerators the defrost timer is under the unit; in others it is in the walls of the cabinet. You can locate yours by checking the wiring diagram that is usually glued to the refrigerator's chassis. Once you locate it, you can remove the timer and buy a replacement from an appliance repair center.

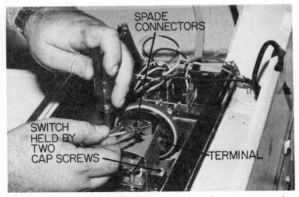

SPADE CONNECTORS

SWITCH HELD BY TWO CAP SCREWS

TERMINAL

Water level switch is attached with spade connectors for easy removal and replacement of switch. Photos this series: Mort Schultz

OBJECTIONABLE ODORS You may smell objectionable odor when you open the refrigerator door. If the model is frost-free, the odor may even be detectable with the door closed. The latter odor is a dangerous one, because it can cause a respiratory infection known as farmer's lung. The odor may be coming from the defroster drain pan. Bacteria may form if the pan isn't cleaned periodically. To clean the pan, remove the toeplate at the bottom front of the refrigerator. Slide the pan from its holder and wash it in warm water containing a disinfectant. Let the pan dry. When you reinstall it, make sure it is properly replaced on the holder track. If the pan is off-center, dripping water can run over the sides and onto the floor. Cleaning the drain pan, a service that should be performed at least every three months, is an easy task for the homeowner.

Objectionable odors inside the refrigerator can usually be eliminated by washing with warm water and baking soda. Keeping food covered helps prevent odors. A container of activated charcoal alleviates persistent odors in the refrigerator compartment. Activated charcoal may be purchased in an aquarium supply store.

If charcoal doesn't work, try putting a few drops of oil of wintergreen on a dish in the refrigerator. It can be purchased in drugstores.

An odor that smells like burning electric insulation means that an electric component, such as a relay or wire, is shorting out. Disconnect the power cord. The defective part may be found and replaced, but the odor may linger indefinitely if it's been absorbed by the fiberglass insulation in the cabinet walls. To eliminate the smell the insulation will have to be replaced, a job for a trained serviceman.

INADEQUATE COOLING If you have adjusted the thermostat control to the setting recommended by the manufacturer and the refrigerator is not overloaded, milk, soda, and other beverages should feel cold to the touch. If not, the first step is to make sure that cooling is indeed inadequate. Place a half-full glass of water on a refrigerator shelf and insert a thermometer. Leave the door closed for eight hours. (The best time to do the test is overnight.) Next morning read the thermometer. A reading higher than 45 degrees is too high.

Improper cooling may be caused by:

Blocked condenser Vaporized refrigerant comes into the condenser from the evaporator and is then changed back to liquid form. In the evaporator, refrigerant is a liquid. As it absorbs the warmth from the cabinet, the refrigerant vaporizes. The vapor then flows through the condenser and is converted to a liquid again. The refrigerant then returns to the evaporator, and the cycle is repeated.

If the circulation of air around the condenser,

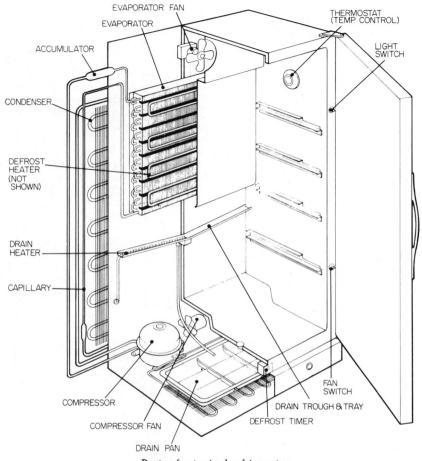

Parts of a typical refrigerator

which is a fin-and-tube assembly, is poor, the refrigerant will remain in a partially vaporized state and refrigeration will suffer.

Normally, two conditions hamper air flow: (a) Dirt is covering the condenser assembly, or (b) The back of the refrigerator is too close to the wall, blocking air flow to the condenser, which is attached to the rear panel of most refrigerators. In some models the condenser is placed under the appliance and is ventilated by a fan. The condensing process will be hampered if the fan stops running.

If the condenser is attached to the back panel, make sure the refrigerator is at least four inches from the wall to permit free air circulation. Fit a vacuum cleaner with a small brush attachment and go over the assembly carefully.

If the condenser is under the refrigerator, remove the toeplate, start the refrigeration cycle by ad-

vancing the thermostat and see if the fan revolves. If it doesn't the fan motor should be replaced, a job a competent handyman can do. A beneath-the-refrigerator condenser should also be kept clean. Condenser tubes are easily damaged, so be careful not to hit them with sharp or hard objects when adjusting anything or cleaning. This would necessitate a major and costly repair.

Air leaks around the door seal The presence of frost or moisture in a frost-free model is a sign that warm air is leaking into the cabinet. This will happen if the door is out of alignment or the seal is damaged. Insert a dollar bill between the door and the seal at several points around the door. Close the door and pull the dollar. A definite resistance should be felt. If there are places where the door isn't sealing, loosen the top hinge screws and readjust the door to attain proper alignment. Retighten hinge screws.

Most models have a rear-mounted condenser. Allow free movement of air around the condenser by setting refrigerator away from the wall.

Replacing a faulty door seal is an easy handyman project.

Some refrigerators do not use a drain tube. Drain in this unit is at back: Water drips down rear wall to drain opening that leads to drain pan.

Some models have the condenser and fan beneath the refrigerator. Unit may be reached via front or rear access panel.

In this model, the evaporator is in the back wall of the freezer compartment. Access is through a cover.

Faulty evaporator defroster heater can be replaced by removing grommet on each end, slipping out the heater coil. *Photos this series: Mort Schultz*

In time, a seal may become brittle or tear and lose its effectiveness. Buy a new seal made specifically for your model. Lift the old one to find the retaining screws. Loosen them, releasing the seal. To install the new piece, turn screws until they're snug, then shut the door to seat the seal. Now tighten the screws securely.

An iced evaporator The evaporator coil assembly is positioned inside the refrigerator so warm air is drawn to it. In frost-free units with the freezer compartment above the refrigerator the evaporator is placed in the bulkhead separating the two compartments or in the back wall of the freezer. There is a cover over the evaporator, which is held by screws (normally found on the freezer side). Remove the screws and cover, exposing the evaporator. If it is covered with ice, warm air will remain in the refrigerator. Examine the ice on the evaporator. If it's hard and clear you can be pretty certain that frost has melted and refrozen because it was unable to drain from the unit. Ice accumulation on the evaporator of a manual defrost model is natural and requires that the unit be defrosted periodically.

The most common cause of hard, clear ice in frost-free models is a clogged drain. This system consists of a drain opening and perhaps a tube that carries moisture from the evaporator to a pan beneath the refrigerator.

Remove the cover over the evaporator and find the drain opening. Pour water down and see if the water flows into the drain pan beneath the refrigerator. If it doesn't, algae which forms where moisture exists is probably blocking the passage. Pouring a tablespoon of ammonia down the tube will kill algae spores.

Sometimes a piece of solid material, such as insulation, may block the drain. This is most likely to occur when a refrigerator is new. You can try to remove the blocking material by injecting water under pressure through the tube, using a large syringe. If this doesn't work, remove the drain tube, which is often attached to the refrigerator's rear panel, and replace it. On some models the drain tube will be inside the rear wall.

Some refrigerators have a small heater that warms the surface of the drain tube, preventing moisture from freezing and blocking the tube. To find out if the heater has failed, locate the heater (consult the wiring diagram) and use a volt-ohmmeter to test the coil. Replace a defective heater.

When the reason for an iced evaporator has been found and the problem has been corrected, all ice must be removed from the evaporator to restore maximum cooling efficiency. Do not use an ice pick or propane torch to remove ice, as the evaporator is expensive to replace.

The safest way to defrost an evaporator is to store food elsewhere temporarily. Disconnect the power cord. Open the doors. Remove the evaporator cover and let the ice melt. White, snowy looking frost on the evaporator of a frost-free model indicates an inoperative defrosting system. Defrost systems consist essentially of a timer, heater, and limit switch to turn off the heater. A volt-ohmmeter is needed to test this system. A weak component should be replaced.

Leak in the refrigeration system One way to determine if this has happened is to feel the condenser, then the evaporator. If there's a leak the condenser will feel cool and the evaporator will feel warm. A repairman is needed to make a definite judgment and repairs.

Standing water When water accumulates on the deck of the refrigerator you can be pretty certain that one of three things is wrong: (a) The refrigerator door is being opened and closed too often. Take care how you use it, especially in warm, humid weather. (b) Air is leaking into the cabinet because of a misaligned door or bad seal. (c) The drain system is clogged.

If water develops on the floor under the refrigerator, look for a drain pan out of position or a misdirected drain tube that is discharging outside the drain. If this is the case, shift it to where it belongs.

Food won't freeze You may sometimes notice that some foods, especially ice cream, won't freeze solid. First check the freezer compartment door for alignment and a tight seal. If the door passes this inspection, the difficulty may be due to overloading of the freezer compartment. The freezer compartment of a refrigerator is not a substitute for a regular freezer. It is intended to hold at most a week's supply of food.

There are two mechanical malfunctions that will impede freezing. One is a defective evaporator fan in the freezer compartment. The other is a defective evaporator heater (in frost-free models).

The evaporator fan directs warm air from the freezer compartment to the evaporator. A malfunctioning fan will hamper the freezing cycle. Check the fan. It is found in the wall of the freezer compartment.

If the evaporator heater of a frost-free model cuts off too soon, frost remaining on the evaporator will impede cooling. In some units a bad terminator thermostat, a small disk that controls the heater, may be causing the heater to shut off prematurely, shortening the defrost cycle. This thermostat can be replaced easily.

Compressor keeps running Another common problem is a compressor that runs too long or won't shut off. As a result the temperature of the refrigerator may get too cold. Testing the temperature of a refrigerator is done with the glass of water and thermometer mentioned earlier. The temperature inside the refrigerator should be above freezing, but below 45°F. The freezer compartment should be at zero degrees Fahrenheit. To test here, put a thermometer between two packages of frozen food and leave it there overnight.

A defective thermostat is often the cause of a compressor that keeps running. The thermostat usually isn't difficult to replace. It is positioned under the temperature control dial. In many units the assembly is held in place with a single screw.

When you replace the thermostat, carefully note the position of the sensing tube or bulb. Make sure the tube or bulb of a new unit does not touch any part of the compartment after you have installed it. Air must circulate freely around the tube or bulb if the sensing device is to do its work correctly.

6

HOW TO BUILD WALLS · COVER WALLS · REPAIR WALLBOARD · INSTALL PANELING · REPAIR PLASTER WALLS · INSTALL CEILING TILE · BEAM A CEILING · FIX FLOORS · LAY HARDWOOD FLOORS · FINISH WOOD FLOORS · LAY FLOOR TILES · INSTALL CARPET SQUARES · INSTALL ROLL CARPET · INSTALL SHEET VINYL · REPAIR LINOLEUM · REPAIR STAIRS · REPAIR DOORS · INSTALL STORM DOORS · INSTALL COMBINATION WINDOWS · REPAIR WINDOWS · PAINT INTERIORS · HANG WALLPAPER

THE HOME INTERIOR

HOW TO BUILD WALLS

Home improvement or remodeling projects are likely to include building an interior wall. It is almost certain to alter the light and heat in the room; and it may make some wiring, plumbing, and heating changes necessary.

The wall will only be a partition and, therefore, bear no load other than its own weight. As a result, relatively light materials may be used. The framework of the wall consists of a sole plate on the floor, a top plate on the ceiling overhead, and studs at regular intervals between them. Use 2 × 4 stock for plates and studs. These will support the "skin," the wall covering on both sides.

HOW TO START   First secure the sole plate to the floor. If the floor is wood, nail down the plate with 10d nails at 16" intervals. If the floor is concrete, bore at least two or more holes through the plate every 3' and matching holes in the concrete. Fiber or metal plugs will hold screws put through the plate. If you plan a doorway, mark its location on the plate. Measure the door width, adding 1" on each side for the frame (or jamb) of the door and 1⅝" on each side for the short jack studs of the rough doorway framework. Cut out the plate where the door will be located after it has been nailed down, since this makes lining up the sole plates on both sides of the doorway much easier. Don't nail the plate where the doorway will be located or the section will be difficult to remove later.

Next, the top plate is cut and secured to the ceiling. Make use of either a plumb bob or a straight piece of wood, trued up with a level, to mark the location of the top plate. You can't use a nearby wall as a guide, since that wall itself may be out of alignment. The method of fastening the top plate depends on the ceiling material and the direction of the joists above it. If your plate is to run at right angles to the joists, it may simply be nailed to them. If, however, the plate is to run parallel to the joists and you have a plasterboard ceiling, it is necessary to plan the wall so that the top plate will be directly under a joist, which will supply the required nailing surface. If your ceiling is good sound plaster, the plate may be fastened to it with anchors.

Studs are cut to fit snugly between the two plates. Although they are generally spaced at 16" intervals, they may also be spaced at 20" or 24" intervals, depending on the sheet size of the wallcovering material that will be used. Studs are toenailed on all four sides into the plates with 8d nails. It's practical to mark off the location of all the studs on the sole plate before any are nailed in. If you plan a doorway, locate the two full-length studs on each side and then mark off the location of those to each side of the opening at the desired spacing. If your wall has an outside corner or a door, start at this point and mark in each direction from it. Regardless of the final spacing, attach one stud to any wall your new wall contacts. Studs may be trued up with a level, their position marked on the top plate, and then toenailed into place. Fur-

1

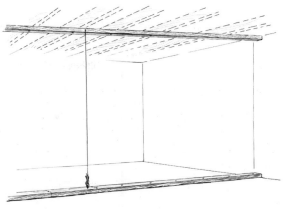

2

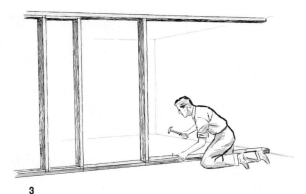

3

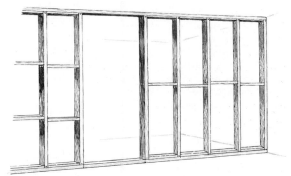

4

5

6

Step 1. Secure a sole plate to a floor with 10d nails. Screw the plate into a concrete floor. **Step 2.** For accurate placement of the top plate, hang a plumb bob to mark the location. **Step 3.** Mark the location of all studs before nailing them in place. **Step 4.** Put center braces between studs to support tongue-and-groove paneling. Center braces are not needed for sheet paneling or sheetrock. **Step 5.** Frame the doorway by cutting two short studs, erecting a header, and removing the sole plate for the door opening. **Step 6.** Three 2 × 4s are joined to form the corner stud if framing makes an inside corner.

ther bracing of the wall is made by horizontal pieces of 2 × 4 nailed between studs. The need and location of these depends on the wall covering to follow. If the covering is to be of full-length vertical boards, a single brace at the center will do. You may stagger these braces their own width so that nailing into their ends through the studs with 10d or 16d nails is possible. This eliminates a lot of toenailing. Use two nails into each end.

FRAMING A DOORWAY Go back to the marked-off doorway and cut out the plate. You can use the two studs as a guide for the saw. Measure the height of the door you intend to use. Standard sizes are either 6'8" or 7' high. Add 1" to this height to allow for the frame, and—if you plan to have a threshold—add 1" more! Cut two short jack studs to this combined length and nail them to the two full-length studs on each side of the opening. Be sure to put one nail through into the cutoff ends of the plate. Cut two pieces of 2 × 4 the width of the opening above these short studs, nail them together, and insert. Keep the narrow dimension of these pieces vertical. Nail through the side studs into this lintel, or header, as it is called.

A short stud, called a cripple, is then erected between the header and the top plate. Other openings in the wall are handled in the same way. If the opening does not extend all the way to the sole plate, as in a pass-through, for example, fit a double 2 × 4 into the bottom of the opening. Short studs extend to the sole plate from the bottom one and from the upper one to the top plate.

GOING AROUND A CORNER For the average short wall, an outside corner post consists of three pieces of 2 × 4 joined as sketched. If the inside surface of this wall is not going to be covered (as in a rough closet, for example), two pieces may be used, joined as an L and put in place on the sole plate. The three-piece post, however, is necessary where both sides of the wall are to be covered.

INSIDE THE WALL At this point, install any wiring that must pass through the wall, or position any outlet boxes, switch receptacles, and light receptacles. If you have to extend heating pipes, ducts, or plumbing facilities of any sort, get them in now. Also, if you plan on making use of the space between studs for any kind of built-ins, mark their location and set in supports for the future recessed items.

HOW TO COVER WALLS

Gypsum-based panels are often used for covering interior walls. The panels consist of a gypsum core sandwiched between two layers of chemically treated paper. With the exception of prefinished gypsum panels, gypsum wallboard lends itself to

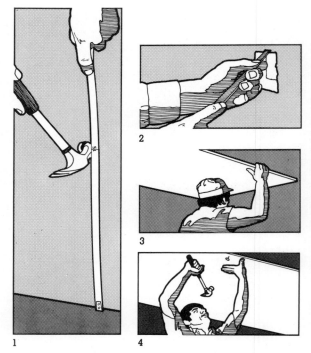

1. *Cutout for electrical box (under panel) is started by the pros by penetrating panel with hammer.*
2. *A keyhole saw is used to complete the cutout by sawing around the perimeter of the box.*
3. *For ceilings, professionals literally use their heads to simplify this part of drywall installation.*
4. *Nailing and finishing of secured ceiling panels is done in the same way as with wall panels.*

almost any finish—paint, paper, fabric, or texture. Commonly available in 4' width, gypsum panels are also available in lengths from 8' to 14'.

The heaviest and most expensive gypsum panels are ⅝" thick. The extra thickness provides increased rigidity and resistance to fire exposure and sound transmission. Panels ½" or ⅜" thick are more common. For new construction where a single layer of gypsum will be used, the ½" thickness is preferred. The lighter-weight ⅜" gypsum is used primarily in remodeling, repair, and where double-layer applications are called for.

Installing and finishing gypsum panels calls for preplanning. You should lay out the room, planning where edges and joints will occur. Use the largest panels you can get into the room: 4' × 12' panels will make less waste, with fewer seams to treat, than will 4 × 8's. Always install panels hori-

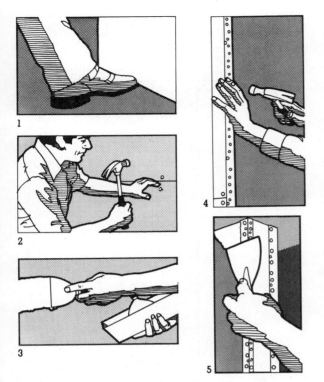

1. *To position lower panel firmly in place with upper panel, you can use your toe, as shown here.*
2. *While nailing, this pro's left hand is firm against panel to assure contact with studs.*
3. *Use a set procedure to cement and tape joints. Joints and nailheads receive three applications.*
4. *Outcorners are covered with metal bead, which prevents joint from separating. Set nailheads properly.*
5. *Areas requiring cement treatment (shown here) include joint between panels, inside corner, and an outcorner.*

zontal to, not parallel with, the framing. Before you begin, mark the location of ceiling joists on the top wall plates with a carpenter's pencil. Mark all outlets, vents, or other openings in the wall by drawing a box with an X in the center on the floor. Make these directly beneath the location of the opening on the wall.

To install gypsum board panels on ceilings, build a scaffold high enough to allow you to touch the ceiling with your head. In this way you will be able to use your head as a sort of third hand to help hold the panels, freeing your hands for nailing. It is much better to have an assistant to hold the panels up. It is feasible but difficult and awkward to use props.

Always use gypsum board of at least ½" thickness; use 1¼" ring-shank nails. It will make a smoother wall if you use adhesives and nails, rather than just nails, where adhesive use is possible.

Cut outside corners square and flush; do not rely on corner bead to hide a sloppy corner. The bead requires a square corner to fit properly. Never force a panel into place; take it down and trim it so it fits. Outlets or other openings may be cut in with a knife along the perimeter of the hole. Cut on the *finish* side of the panel, and knock out the opening with a blow of the hammer.

After starting a nail, hold the panel firmly against the framing with the free hand. Then drive the nail home, until it is slightly below the surface of the wallboard, in a dimple formed by the hammer head. To finish, it is best for an amateur to use the ready-mixed vinyl taping cement. This is recommended because cement of the proper consistency is a major key to good finishing. A good job of taping requires three coats over nails and corner bead, or tape and two coats over seams. The taping cement, containing water, will shrink between coats. Three coats eliminate the shrinkage. Make the taping coat just wide enough to span the recess of the seams—just over 6". The second coat carries the cement beyond the taping to a width of 8" to 10"; the final coat should be 10" to 12" wide. By making each coat successively wider you will eliminate a lot of sanding.

Smooth the final coat with 100 grit production sandpaper. Run the palm of your hand over the job, checking for smoothness. When smooth, it's ready to paint.

Tools needed to install gypsum panels include a square or steel straightedge, wallboard or other sharp utility knife, tape measure, marking pencil, a couple of joint-finishing putty knives (one 10" wide, the other approximately 9" wide), a pan for mixing joint compound, a caulking gun if adhesive is to be used for fastening, sandpaper, and a keyhole saw. The chart on page 170 shows other wallcovering materials and their relative pros and cons.

Some of the materials listed here can be used to construct entire walls in themselves; others will make walls on wooden frames. In either case, they may be left in their original state—or finished to taste.

Insulating value Covers used on outer walls, or as outer walls.

Durability Based on ability to withstand rough treatment without dents or damage.

Sound deadening Covers use on interior walls and the ability of the materials to soften sounds inside the room as well as resist sound transmission from beyond the particular walls.

Wall materials	Insulating value	Resistance to dampness	Resistance to grease and dirt	Durability	Ease in application	Sound deadening	Ease in cleaning
WOOD							
Solid hardwood—unfinished	G	G	P	G	F	F	P
Solid softwood—unfinished	G	F	P	G	F	F	P
Plywood—unfinished	F	G	P	G	E	F	P
Plywood—prefinished	F	F	F	G	G	F	G
STONE AND ARTIFICIAL STONE	F	G	P	E	P	G	F
BRICK	F	F	P	E	P	G	F
PLASTER—BARE	G	F	P	F	P	E	P
WALLBOARDS & PLASTERBOARDS							
Fiberboard—unfinished	E	F	P	F	G	E	P
Gypsum board—unfinished	G	F	F	F	G	F	F
Insulating wallboards	E	F	P	F	G	E	P
Hardboards—prefinished	F	G	E	E	E	P	E
Asbestos board	G	E	P	E	F	G	G
Perforated hardboard	P	G	G	E	E	P	G
CORRUGATED PLASTIC SHEETING	G	E	E	E	F	F	E
PLASTIC BLOCKS	G	E	E	G	F	F	E
GLASS BLOCKS	G	E	E	E	P	F	E

E = Excellent   G = Good   F = Fair   P = Poor

HOW TO REPAIR WALLBOARD

Sooner or later, most homeowners will need to repair gypsum wallboard. Corners can crack as a house settles. Temperature changes can cause expansion and contraction. Plumbing leaks can make it necessary to replace sections of wallboard. And walls can be physically damaged.

Loose ceiling nails can show up either as slight hollows, or dimples, or as protruding nailheads. If you simply bang them back in with a hammer and apply spackle over the blemish, you'll have the same problem later. Generally, you can assume that any protrusion defect in a ceiling is a popped nail.

Dimples, rather than protrusions, indicate an area where the panelboard was never nailed tight against the framing, due to sloppy workmanship or irregular framing. Because gypsum boards are soft, they cannot be pulled tight by nailing alone. On irregular framing, panels must be held tight to framing so the nail does not pull but simply holds the material to the framing.

The probable cause of a popped nail that shows up as a protrusion rather than a hollow is shrinkage in the framing lumber. The panel was probably tight to begin with but came loose from the framing because the lumber shrank.

With both protrusion and dimple defects, it's necessary to hold the sheetrock firmly against the framing and renail around the defect. Keep in mind that as you press back loose sheetrock and renail it, more nails will likely pop along the rows, presenting additional nail pops to repair.

If your ceiling is textured, scrape away the texture around the blemish before starting repairs. Then, using a hammer with a crowned face, drive the ring-shank nail approximately 2" from the pop or hollow. Tap the nail to set it slightly below the surface of the panel, in a dimple.

A dimple of $1/64''$ is enough; don't overdrive the nail or you will crush the core of the sheetrock. Do not use a nail punch to set the nail. If you do, you may cut the face paper of the sheetrock, causing a fracture that will bring problems in the future.

Renail all the sheetrock in this manner. As you

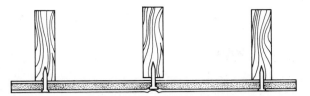

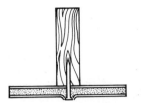

1. *A dimple rather than a bulge indicates that sheetrock was not pulled tight to framing at the time of installation. Press sheetrock tight to framing, renail 2″ from old nail. Redrive old nail after new nail holds sheetrock tight.*

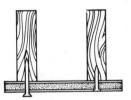

2. *When defect is a bulge or "pop," framing has shrunk. Sheetrock will follow framing. Nail does not move, leaving nailhead protruding.*

3. *The degree of "pop" on the head will be proportional to the length of the nail used. Penetration of nail at left produces severe bulge. Use only 1¼″ nails or ⅞″ screws.*

proceed, press the palm of your hand upward all along the joists to check for any looseness that is not obvious to the eyes. After renailing the loose sheetrock (a) drive old nails below the surface of the ceiling; and (b) scrape away any loose or chipped taping cement that is displaced by either the pops or your repair.

Now refill the dimples around all nails, using spackle or ready-mixed taping cement. Use a broad knife, or scraper, at least 3″ wide to apply the cement. In the case of the taping cement, you will need to use three coats of cement and allow a drying interval between each coat. There is a degree of shrinkage in any patching material that contains water.

Sand the patched areas lightly when the third coat of cement is dry. Use 100-grit, open-coat, aluminum oxide paper. This type of paper will not clog as readily as others.

The next step is to prime the repair spots. If the ceiling was finished with flat paint, you may sim-ply use the finish paint to spot-prime repair areas, then recoat the entire ceiling.

If the surface was textured, you'll need to reestablish the texturing to have it blend in with the existing texture. If it's a ripple texture of the type applied by a roller, you may attempt the spot-texture yourself. If it is a spray-textured surface, you will have to call in a professional if you want to match it.

Once you have renailed all loose paneling by following the correct procedures, the problem should not recur. Shrinkage has already occurred in framing joists. Nail pops will be a thing of the past if you have taken care to get all sheetrock tight to the framing.

Patching holes Small holes, such as those caused by doorknobs, are sometimes harder to repair than large ones. To repair, dampen the edges of the hole with a wet cloth and insert a piece of zinc-coated ¼″ steel mesh behind the hole. A piece of string attached to the mesh will let you pull the mesh tight against the back of the hole. Then tie the string to a stick lying across the hole. This holds the mesh in place. Then cover the mesh with patching plaster. Let the plaster harden overnight, cut the string, and remove the stick. Sand the plaster, spackle, and sand when dry.

Special repair kits for this are available. Most consist of a small bag of patching plaster, corrugated cardboard to provide backing for the patch, and a screw to hold the cardboard in place. Use the kit as described with the photos on the next page.

Major repairs For holes or other damage too extensive to patch, establish the limits of the damage. Square off the area before beginning removal, but plan to remove slightly more than the damaged area. Inspect the framing behind the damaged area, and cut the hole so that the ends of the new piece of panel will fall upon framing members.

Repeatedly score or cut along the outline of the damaged area with a sharp utility knife. A keyhole or saber saw will cut the portions between the framing. Remove the damaged area and cut a matching piece from new material. Insert this piece into the hole, and nail it into place at 7″ intervals along the edges that fall on the framing. (See illustration on page 173).

For damage between two studs or joists, cut away the damaged area back to the center of the stud or joist on both sides of the hole. Again, make your cuts square so that a square patch will fit. Nail this piece into place. You will also have to renail the edges of the existing panel around the hole, as you have probably left those edges unsupported when you cut out the damaged section.

Keep in mind that ½″ thick gypsum board has been the standard in wall or ceiling construction

1

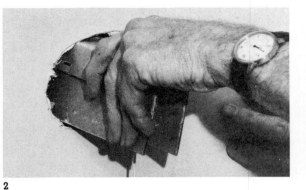

2

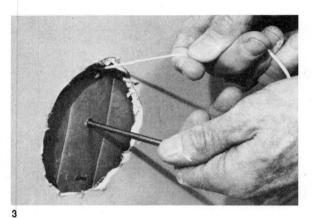

3

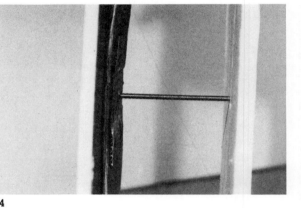

4

5

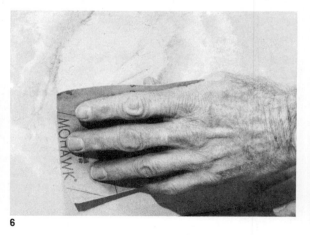

6

Step 1. *Damage to plasterboard walls results from a variety of causes. This familiar damage results from a swinging door without a doorstop.* **Step 2.** *Corrugated cardboard provided is inserted into hole, with string kept accessible.* **Step 3.** *String pulls cardboard up against back of hole. Then screw is inserted into nut held in place by layers of cardboard.* **Step 4.** *Screw is driven in until head touches surface of cardboard. Opposite end of screw presses against back wall, keeping cardboard firmly in place.* **Step 5.** *String is cut. Then the next step is applying plaster to the damaged area of the plasterboard wall.* **Step 6.** *After allowing plaster to dry, use sandpaper to smooth the surface before finishing. Repair is now complete. Photos this series: Arnold Romney*

1

2

3

4

5

Step 1. *Repair of leaking pipe resulted in holes in soffit above kitchen cabinet. Old plasterboard is removed to stud on left and cabinet is removed to get at underside of soffit.* **Step 2.** *Water-damaged section of wall under soffit to right of window is also removed. New plasterboard is applied to front and underside of soffit. (A hole is cut for the outlet box.)* **Step 3.** *Fresh joint compound is applied on both sides of soffit corner with 6" blade. Tape is pressed into compound and smoothed with blade.* **Step 4.** *A second application of compound is used to apply thin coat over tape, after the first application has dried overnight.* **Step 5.** *After second application of compound is dry, it's sanded with fine sandpaper wrapped around flat wood block. Last step is priming with a coat of water-base acrylic paint. Photos this series: Arnold Romney*

for twenty years. Before that, ⅜" thickness was common. Determine which was used in your home before buying any supply for repairs. Mismatches where the repaired area joins existing walls can be difficult to conceal.

Tape the seams where patch and existing wall meet, as described earlier. Spot all nails three times, allowing the cement to dry completely between coats. When no bulge or patch marks are visible after sanding, hold a lamp or drop cord with a 100-watt bulb near the panel but to the side of the repaired area. This light check will magnify bulges or other defects by throwing them into bold relief. Correct these by sanding, or widen the trow-

eling out so that the bulge appears as a smooth rise, rather than a sharp break. Then sand lightly with 100 grit production paper, and apply paint or primer.

The lighting method is used by professionals to check their repairs before decorating. If the work stands up under such harsh lighting, it will be satisfactory under normal room lighting conditions.

HOW TO INSTALL PANELING

Whether used for remodeling an existing room or finishing a new one, paneling is a natural for the handyman. It goes up in a hurry, and it can be

Panels, after you buy them, should be allowed to condition before you install them. Here furring strips are nailed in place.

Panel adhesive can be applied to wall studs with caulking gun. Run a ⅛″ to ¼″ continuous bead.

Try for good fit, but remember that molding will cover small gaps. Never force seams together tightly.

Use a fine-tooth saw for cutting. Face panels up when using a hand saw; face them down when using a circular saw.

A compass or a scribe can be used to duplicate irregular shapes, in corners, and around moldings and trim.

After paneling is installed, finish with moldings and trim. *Photos this series: Masonite Corp.*

attached directly to existing plaster or gypsum-board walls, as well as to wall studs. For installation on concrete block or masonry walls, however, it is necessary to apply wooden furring strips or free-standing wall studs.

Concrete or masonry walls, or other irregular wall surfaces, almost always require the installation of wooden furring strips to provide a flat, even surface for attaching either gypsum board or other paneling.

Manufacturers have made paneling one of the most sought-after wall coverings by producing innovative new designs suitable for rooms from basement to attic. Paneling is two things: exterior finish and base material. Exterior finishes may be stained wood, simulated grain variations printed on a vinyl film that's affixed to a base material, or a grain that's imprinted into a base material. Base materials are divided into three categories: flakeboard or waferboard, hardboard or Masonite, and plywood. Here's how you can recognize each type.
FLAKEBOARD (OR WAFERBOARD PANELING) Flakeboard is a wood composition material glued together to form a flexible panel. It may be shavings, chipcore, chipwood, or other wood byproducts covered with a vinyl wood grain glued to the surface. These materials, vulnerable to moisture, are not recommended for below-grade installations. This is the lowest grade paneling.
HARDBOARD OR PAPERBOARD PANELING Hardboard paneling is recognized by a smooth back in the case of Masonite or a grain back in the

case of Luan. Many panel products in this category are also sold under the trade names of Celotex, Insulite, and Homasote. This category is also subject to expansion and contraction when exposed to moisture, but is attractive for above-grade installations.

PLYWOOD PANELING Plywood paneling offers strength because an odd number of layers of wood crisscross, which gives dimensional stability. Plywood-backed paneling resists moisture well and can even provide support on interior walls when applied directly to studs.

Natural wood finishes today are a small part of the paneling market. However, novel effects, such as a weathered look, are achieved through an etching process that removes soft wood tissue, leaving the hard grain boldly standing out. Natural wood panel finishes are the result of a multistep process where the wood is heated and special sealants and coloring are applied.

Wood finish panels require a limited amount of care, usually only moisturizing oil or polish to retain their original beauty. Easy cleaning, strength, durability, and resistance to scuffs and scratches are characteristics of vinyl covering affixed to hardboard, flakeboard, or plywood panels. Various effects are achieved with the 2-mil vinyl film covering that has an opaque backing to obscure any grain from the base material.

Thicknesses range from $3/16''$ to $5/8''$. Thinner pieces are recommended only for use on gypsumboard walls. The thicker panels may be used to cover studding.

PLANNING THE JOB First, measure all the walls carefully, including door and window dimensions. Find the locations of outlet boxes. Draw out a plan (one for each wall) on graph paper for later use as a reference when you start cutting. Check the wall for any obstructions or major irregularities as you go along.

Measure the linear feet of the walls you intend to panel and multiply this total by the ceiling height. For a full 8' high installation, divide total linear feet of each wall by 4 to get the required number of 4×8 panels. For a 32''-high wainscot, divide the total linear feet by 12 to find the number of panels.

When figuring total square footage, you cannot simply deduct door and window area from your total. This is because the panels will not end evenly along a door edge, for example. You will have to cut out from the full sheet, creating a waste piece. You may be able to use some of these waste pieces above windows and door frames, but most will wind up in the cellar, stored for future projects.

To strike a compromise figure, on the average, you can deduct half a panel for each good-sized window (or fireplace opening). After getting your total square footage, subtract the total allowed for openings. You'll most likely end up with a fraction, so round it off to the next full sheet.

PANEL CONDITIONING Prefinished hardwood paneling, like all wood products, is susceptible to changes in humidity and can be expected to expand or contract slightly with changing moisture levels. For this reason, about 48 hours prior to installation stand your panels up against the wall in the room where they will be applied. Free them of any coverings or packing material so moisture content of the panels will equalize with the room environment as room air circulates around them. Don't try to apply paneling on new construction where conditions are abnormally damp because of drying plaster or curing concrete.

Take the time to plan how the sheets should be positioned. You may find minor variations in tone that can be blended with other panels.

Wall preparation Start by removing the old molding and trim, switch plates, and the like. To support the paneling evenly, the walls underneath should be straight and sound. Regardless of whether you apply it over stud framing, wood furring, or a solid backing with either nails or panel adhesive, the final surface will only be as straight as the wall beneath it.

Many homeowners use paneling to cover walls that seem beyond repair. A serious problem is frequently caused by structural changes, such as stud warping or uneven settling on the foundation. If this is the case, irregular surfaces must be shimmed and furred with 1×2s or 1×4s.

The strips should be nailed directly into the wall studs continuously across the top, bottom, and sides of the wall and spaced not more than 16'' on centers. Place the furring so it is plumb (in the same vertical plane) with the highest spot on the wall. You can find this spot by 'trying' the wall with a straight 2×4, moving it first vertically, then horizontally, noting where it rocks.

Low spots behind the furring can be shimmed by inserting small strips of wood between the 1×2 and the wall. One good way to shim is to use wooden shakes. Split them into 1'' or 2'' strips and insert them (with the tips pointing toward each other) under the furring strip from opposite sides. Tap the shims alternately on each side, overlapping them, to raise the 1×2 away from the surface to the amount desired.

On new construction a 2-mil polyethylene vapor barrier should be applied to stud faces over the wall insulation. Leaks or cracks on masonry walls should be filled and sealed before applying furring, insulation, and a vapor barrier. To be effective, a vapor barrier must form a continuous shield on the warm side of the wall. If seams in the polyethylene are necessary, make sure they overlap 4″ or 5″ and are sealed. Before applying paneling on basement walls, coat the wall with a paint sealer or vapor barrier to prevent moisture from entering behind and warping the paneling.

Cutting and fitting Measure the floor-to-ceiling height at a number of points along the wall. If the variation is ½″ or less, subtract ¼″ from your smallest measurement and cut all your panels to this dimension.

Never force panels into place. Trim will cover the small gap that gives you a little room to maneuver the sheets and adjust them, using a level so that the joints are plumb.

Tools you'll need for the job will include a hammer, drill (for starting holes for interior cutouts), keyhole or saber saw (for cutouts and irregular shapes), level, plumb bob, tape measure, fine-toothed hand or power saw, nail set (if exposed nailing is used), stud finder (if paneling is to be applied over finished walls), miter box (for cutting molding and trim), caulking gun (for adhesive application), and compass (to trace irregular shapes).

Material needed will include the paneling, color-matched nails (or panel adhesive), a color-matched putty stick for touch-ups, and molding for top, base, and openings. Use fine-toothed saws (10 to 12 points per inch on hand saws) to avoid chipping panel finish. The panel should be placed face up when cutting with a hand saw and face down when using a power circular saw. Panel seams should be fitted with moderate contact.

Installing paneling Start the first panel in a corner, taking extra care with the level to make sure that it is perfectly plumb. This first sheet acts as the guide against which the other seams must fit. If it is out of plumb, you'll soon find that the succeeding panels are working their way up or down the wall little by little as you close the seams.

If the corner itself is not plumb (this is quite likely, even on newer homes), position the panel about ½″ from the corner, check it with your level to get it perfectly plumb, and tack it temporarily in place. Then open your compass so the needle end rests in the corner and the pencil end rests on the panel. Carefully run the needle down the entire length of the corner, transferring irregularities to the sheet. Cut the sheet along this line; you should then be able to push it right into the corner, where it should now fit precisely, irregularities notwithstanding. The compass can also be used wherever irregular profiles must be traced, such as around fireplace moldings, window trim, and the like.

Get a good fit, but remember that where moldings are to be used you can afford to leave a small gap. For nail applications, get the panel in position, then tack it, using color-matched, annular-ringed hardboard nails. When the paneling is applied directly over studs, 1″ nails will do. If over wallboard, use 1⅝″ nails.

When nailing paneling to studs, always nail from the middle to the edges, never the edges first. After tacking the sheet in place, double check your dimensions, make sure it's plumb, and make sure that you haven't inadvertently covered an outlet (this happens, even to professionals) before you drive nails home. Begin nailing at the edge of the previously installed panel, working across the sheet. Nailing from opposite sides could lead to buckling in the center. Recommended nailing procedure calls for 8″ spacing. Some manufacturers call for a $1/32″$ spacing between the panels. This leaves room for expansion, but may not look as good as a closed joint. In any case, one panel should not be forced against another tightly. Leave ¼″ spaces at the bottom of paneling that's applied on basement walls. This allows moisture to escape and prevents warping on the bottom edges should condensation occur.

Paneling with adhesives When using panel adhesive, keep in mind that adhesives require careful handling, and the work area needs proper ventilation. Make sure you use an adhesive of the type that is recommended by the panel manufacturer. Follow application instructions on the container faithfully.

Prepare the first panel the same way as for nailing, scribing any irregular edge cuts that may be needed. With steady pressure on the handle of the caulking gun, apply the adhesive to the back edges of the panel and to the intermediate furring strips or studs. Cut the nozzle on the adhesive tube so that the bead it extrudes is between ⅛″ and ¼″ thick.

If using canned adhesive for paneling with a solid backing, apply the adhesive with a saw-toothed spreading trowel. Cover the back of the entire panel with ridges of adhesive. For a tight bond, press the panel into place, then pull slightly away from the wall so that "strings" of adhesive can be seen between the panel and the studs. Then press back firmly, applying pressure to all parts of the sheet. Keep the job neat by having handy the solvent recommended by the manufacturer.

Moldings and trim Your paneling dealer will have a selection of color-matched moldings and trim. Check your wall layout plans for the total number of feet required. There are four specialized types of moldings: inside corner, outside corner, edging (or cap), and seam divider moldings. A variety of baseboard, ceiling, and chair-rail moldings can also be used on the surface. Here's a rundown on each.

• Inside corners. After the first panel is in position, fit the nailing flange (it's concealed behind

TYPES OF PLASTIC MOLDINGS

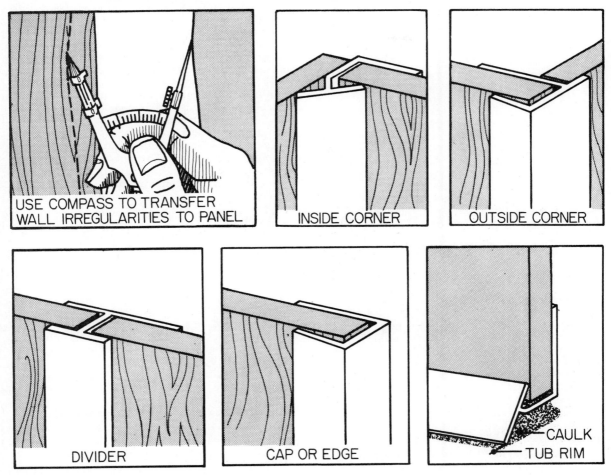

USE COMPASS TO TRANSFER WALL IRREGULARITIES TO PANEL

INSIDE CORNER

OUTSIDE CORNER

DIVIDER

CAP OR EDGE

CAULK

TUB RIM

Illustration: Ron Chamberlain

the sheet) along the edge of the butting sheet. When this sheet is in position, the molding can be adjusted to conceal the corner joint. Nails through the edge of the panel secure the nailing flange to the wall.

• Outside corners. The nailing flange on this molding is applied the same way. In both cases the molding can be fitted onto the first panel before it is placed on the wall, then secured by nailing through the edge of the first panel after the joining panel has been positioned.

• Edge molding. Although not a common situation, you may run into a partition or divider wall where the paneling simply ends without butting up against another surface. In this case an L-shaped cap molding is fitted around the edge of

the panel, in order to conceal the end grain.

• Divider molding. Depending on the groove pattern on the paneling you select, you may choose to join each vertical seam with an H-shaped molding. In this case, insert the divider with the narrow flange onto the first sheet, nail the longer flange directly to the wall, then fit in the next sheet.

Moldings used with special panels for tub and shower applications should be fully sealed with waterproof caulking. Other special effects can be achieved by adding solid wood decorative moldings in box patterns or vertical strips. If natural wood moldings are used, finish them before fitting them in place. Finishing nails can be set slightly below the surface of the wood and covered with wood putty that matches the panel finish.

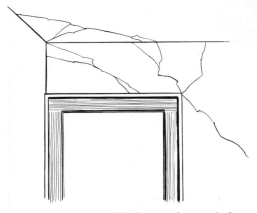

The most common type of failure is the crack that runs diagonally across a wall from a corner or from a door or window opening. Cracks of this type are caused by shrinkage in framing members or house structure; they are called structural cracks.

HOW TO REPAIR PLASTER WALLS

Almost every plaster wall and ceiling develops cracks—if not in the broader expanses, then at least in corners where flat surfaces join one another. Structural expansion and shrinkage, traffic vibration, and household activities all contribute toward weakened plaster. Plaster repair must be done before redecorating.

First, clean away material that appears loose. If it's a fair-sized crack, use a putty knife and open the crack to its deepest part; then undercut it so it's wider underneath than on the outer surface, like an inverted V, with the point of the V facing you. Little cracks can simply be brushed clean. With a spray, a sponge, or a wet rag, *thoroughly* dampen all surfaces of the crack. If this is overlooked, moisture from the new plaster will be absorbed into the wall, leaving the patch powdery and weak.

Mix patching plaster to a thick paste and pack it into the crack with a putty knife. (For thin hairline cracks, use a paint brush.) Press the mix into the bottom of the crack, build up slightly more than necessary, smooth off the excess, and let it dry for two to four hours.

Then use medium-grit sandpaper on a flat block to smooth off the excess. A few strokes with fine-grit sandpaper will finish it off nicely. Before you paper or paint over this patchwork, brush on one coat or more of thinned shellac as a size coat. If there is no "glazed" look to the size coat when dry, apply a second coat.

One word of caution: When the job is finished, don't pour excess plaster down the sink; it will solidly block the drain pipe. Each quantity mixed should be just what you can apply in ten minutes. After that, it starts to harden and has little holding strength left.

The general procedure for patching holes where plaster has fallen from the wall is the same for patching cracks: undercutting, cleaning, dampening, and applying new plaster. Before applying the patch, however, make sure the lath or other plaster base has not come loose from the framing members behind. If it has, nail it back into place.

If the area of the hole to be patched is larger than approximately one square foot, you will find difficulty in doing an adequate repair job with patching plaster alone. One way of repairing large holes is to apply two coats of gypsum plaster and then a third coat of finishing plaster. Another way is to cut a piece of plaster rock-lath to fit the hole, nail it to the lath, and apply a finish coat of patching plaster.

In the case of wooden lath that is broken, you will have to enlarge the hole in the plaster until two adjacent studs or joists are exposed. Then remove the broken laths and replace them with short lengths of new-stock lath nailed to the studs. If the hole is more than an inch or so in diameter, apply the patching plaster in two coats. First, put on a fairly thick undercoat and, before it has dried, score its surface so the next coat will bond to it. After the undercoat has dried and set, dampen the surface and apply the thin finish coat.

To repair a bulge, first create a hole where the bulge appears. Do this by rapping the bulge with a hammer until the loosened plaster falls out. Be sure to knock or pry away any loose material remaining around the hole so as to have sound plaster at the edges of the patch.

HOW TO INSTALL CEILING TILE

You can add new life to any room by covering a worn, drab ceiling with easily installed ceiling tiles. They are available in many colors, sizes, and styles. They may be installed two ways: by fastening to furring strips or by hanging oversize tile sections in the grid framework of a suspended ceiling. In some cases, tile can be fastened directly to an existing ceiling.

In an area with plenty of headroom, you may want to install a suspended ceiling, which affords easy access to the space above the ceiling. The suspended ceiling requires only 3″ minimum clearance below the present ceiling or any obstruction and is ideal for covering open beams, pipes, wiring, and ducts. The furring strip method uses standard 12″ square tiles. They are stapled to the furring strips, which are first attached directly to the overhead joists or to the existing ceiling. First, level the ceiling to place the tiles evenly. Start by

Your room measures this many inches over exact no. of ft. in width or length	1	2	3	4	5	6	7	8	9	10	11
Proper border width is (in inches)	6½	7	7½	8	8½	9	9½	10	10½	11	11½

carefully marking off needed guidelines.

Installing a stapled ceiling system is simplified by the interlocking tongue-and-groove joint on each ceiling tile. The joint conceals all fasteners, permits the tiles to fit together quickly, and simplifies alignment.

Before making the actual installation, take care to measure and lay out the ceiling area. Multiply the room's length by its width to get the number of square feet. Each tile measures 12" × 12", so just add 5 to 10 percent additional cutting allowance to determine how many tiles you need. Tools required are a hammer, fine-tooth saw or very sharp fiberboard knife, chalk line, steel square-edge, and stapling gun.

You'll also need ⁹/₁₆" coated staples, 1 × 3 wood furring strips (100' for each 100 square feet of ceiling), and 8d nails to fasten the furring (1³/₄ pounds per 100 square feet of ceiling).

To apply a tongue-and-groove tile system, first apply wood furring strips at right angles to ceiling joists, using two 8d nails at each joist crossing. The first furring strip is applied flush where the wall and ceiling meet. The location of the second furring strip is determined by the width of the border tile that you decide on for your ceiling layout.

Since few rooms are an exact number of feet in width or length, border tiles are needed. Borders should be at least 6" wide and of the same width at opposite sides of the room for best appearance. The border chart (based on 12 × 12 tiles) will help you to determine the proper border width for your room. Because the length and width of a room have different measurements, the border tiles will also be different on the long sides as against the short. The table above tells you how to measure your ceiling in both width and length so you have border tiles of about even width on edges of opposite walls when using standard 12" tile.

Space the second furring strip so that the stapling edge of the border tile will be centered on it. Work across the ceiling from the second strip, installing furring strips parallel to it on 12" centers (for 12 × 12 tiles). The next-to-last strip will be the same distance from the wall as the second strip, and the last strip is nailed flush against the wall.

Furring strips must be level to provide a smooth, even base for your new ceiling. Check with a straightedge and shim (add thin wood strips as spacers) if necessary to ensure evenness. Snap a chalk line down the center of the second furring strip and across other strips at 90° to serve as a guide in applying tiles.

When applying tiles to the strips, start at the corner of the room. Cut border tiles face up, using a fine-tooth saw or very sharp fiberboard knife. As a precaution, open each carton of tiles at least twenty-four hours before installation so they will adjust to temperature and moisture conditions in the room.

Apply the first tile, placing the stapling edge on the chalk line you marked on the furring strip, staple in place, and nail through the face at the wall, since the stapling edge is cut on border tiles. Nails can later be covered by ceiling molding. Make sure that stapling edges of the tiles face into the center of the room. Provide a small space between the first tile and the wall to allow for possible expansion.

Always be sure tongue-and-groove edges fit snugly, but do not force them. Fasten with three staples in one flange and one in the back corner of each 12 × 12 tile. Make sure that joints in both directions are continuous and straight. A broken-joint effect provides an attractive staggered pattern and is even easier to install, since tiles need be exactly aligned in only one direction instead of two. Application is the same as described except that alternate rows are started with a half tile.

To install a suspended ceiling system, first plan your ceiling layout. Draw an accurate sketch of your ceiling dimensions, including all lights, air openings, posts, alcoves, and so forth. Your dealer will then help you determine the number of 2 × 4 lay-in panels needed, as well as wall angles (10' lengths), main tees (12' lengths), and cross tees (2' and 4').

All components of a grid system can be purchased separately or as a package from your hardware or building supply dealer.

To plan the system, find the center line of the ceiling and space main tees 4' apart to provide

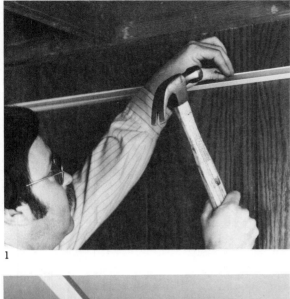

1

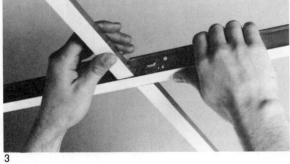

2

3

Step 1. *Determine the height you want suspended ceiling to be, nail wall molding at this height.* Step 2. *Install the main runners by fastening them to hanger wires at 4' intervals.* Step 3. *When the main runners are in place, install cross T's between them. T's have tabs that engage slots in the main runners to lock firmly in place.* Step 4. *Finally, lay the ceiling panels into the grid flanges. Pan-*

4

els are easily removed for access to the space above the ceiling. Photos this series: Armstrong Cork Company

equal-size ceiling panels on outside rows. Next, locate 4' long cross tees at right angles to the main tees at 2' intervals, again providing for equal-size panels on outside rows. To install the grid system and panels, establish the new ceiling height desired and mark a level line with a carpenter's level. Chalk a line around the room at that height. A minimum depth, usually 3", must be allowed to permit maneuvering the ceiling panels into position. Fasten the wall angle with screws or nails spaced every 2'.

Following your ceiling layout drawing, nail or

screw all hanger wires to sides of ceiling joists along the main tee lines; attach the main tee to hanger wires, maintaining an exact level with the wall angle molding.

Snap 4' cross tees into main tees at 2' intervals, making sure the grid members are level. It is important to install 4' cross tees laterally from wall to wall rather than in rows between main tees from front to rear of room, since lateral installation locks the entire grid in place and prevents movement of main and cross tees.

Cut the final main tees and cross tees with snips

or hacksaw so they rest on top of the wall moldings. The grid is then finished. Now you only have to fit the panels into the grid by tilting slightly, lifting and dropping them into place. You may have to tuck some of the panel edges in to ensure a neat and clean appearance. The photos on the facing page show installation of one of the available suspended-ceiling systems.

USING ADHESIVES If the existing ceiling is sound, not badly cracked or peeling, and if it's level without hills and valleys, tiles can be applied with special adhesives. Work a thin priming layer of the adhesive into the four corners of the tile with a putty knife. Then apply several dabs over the primed areas, about 1½" from the corners of the tile.

Place the tile against the ceiling in approximate position, along the nearest guideline to a wall. Then slide the tile back and forth slightly. When good contact is made, and the adhesive is holding, slide the tile into position. If the ceiling is slightly uneven and the tile being installed is deeper than the one next to it, remove the tile. Dab on more adhesive, using the adhesive as a shim and again press it into position.

Continue placing tiles along the guideline across the room. After one row is finished, start at the beginning corner and install another row of tiles. After all full tiles have been placed into position, measure and cut the remaining tiles needed to fill in at the end of the wall.

HOW TO BEAM A CEILING

Few interior projects result in more eye appeal than a beamed ceiling. Better yet, installing beams is an inexpensive do-it-yourself project. A dining room ceiling can be fitted with two full rough-sawn cedar beams, with half beams at each outside wall for under $100.

For box beams, use 1 × 4s and 1 × 6s. You only have to cut the pieces to length with a hand or circular saw. In addition to a saw, you'll need a square, a pound of 6d nails, stain and sealer, and sufficient wood to make the beams.

BEAM LAYOUT If you're building a new house, and intend to beam a ceiling, you can nail 2 × 4 blocks across, and flush with, ceiling joists, so you can later place your beams without regard to joist position. If the ceiling you want to beam is already finished, you will have to position the beams so they fall under existing joists. In this case, you may have a slight variation in the spacing. An inch or two difference will not be noticeable, but keep the spacing as even as possible.

Half beams are usually used at outside walls. Full beams are run the width, rather than the length, of the room. Plan out the approximate spacing of the beams, then mark these points lightly with a pencil. Now, using a 16d nail, "fish" for the location of the joist to nail into. In most cases, measuring 16" in from an outside wall will give you the location of the first joist. Once you have it located, the others should fall at 16" intervals across the ceiling.

If your beams are parallel to existing joists, you need only mark for the beam width between the beams at the interval you have chosen (4' spacing is common). But if your beams are to be installed at right angles to the ceiling joists, you will need to locate all the joists, in order to attach your beams to the ceiling at 16" intervals. A good way to locate joists is to drive a test nail through the ceiling plaster to be sure the joist is actually there.

BUYING LUMBER Cedar boards tend to split for a few inches at their ends. For this reason, make sure your supplier knows that the lumber you are about to buy is to be used for beams and will be highly visible. Ask the dealer to select unsplit boards or, if not possible, to sell you boards sufficiently long to cut a few inches off each end, thus getting rid of the split.

You will need the following pieces of lumber for each full beam: one 2 × 4 pine or fir; two 1 × 6 pieces of rough cedar, and one 1 × 4 in rough cedar. If you plan half beams at the walls (they make a better looking installation), have the lumberyard rip 2 × 4s, 1 × 6s, and 1 × 4s as needed for each outside wall. Buy these boards long enough to make the beam in one continuous piece, without splices. If your beams across the width of the room will be 9'6", buy 10' material; if 11'6", buy 12', and so forth.

First, 2 × 4s After cutting the lumber to length at home, you'll be ready to install the beams. If they are to be in line with existing joists, follow this procedure: Locate the center of the joist you will nail into, make marks on each end 1⅞" back from the center of the joist, and snap a chalkline across the ceiling. (The 1⅞" measurement is half the width of a 2 × 4. You want the chalkline to be at the edge, where you can see it, not at the center where the 2 × 4 will cover it up.)

Now cut your 2 × 4 to length. It does not have to fit tight; the cedar will. Nail the 2 × 4 onto the joist at 16" intervals, using 16d nails. Be sure the nails are hitting the joist underneath.

If you are installing beams at right angles to the joists, choose your interval, then measure out from the wall at each end, and use a chalkline for a guide.

Next, place a 1 × 6 cedar board down each side of the 2 × 4. Press it against the ceiling to see if it lies flush. If the ceiling is uneven, tack the 1 × 6 at the center so a gap appears at each end and "split the

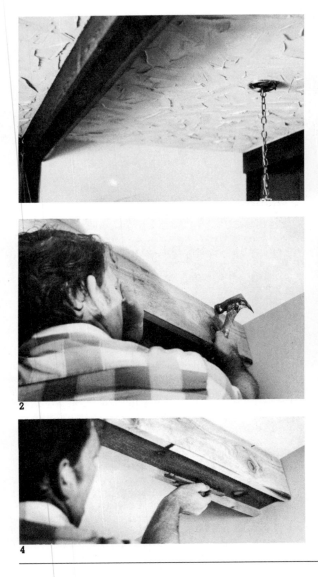

This beamed ceiling can be a one-day project for the handyman. **Step 1.** *Nail 2 × 4 to ceiling at each beam location.* **Step 2.** *Nail 1 × 6 sides of beam onto 2 × 4 support.* **Step 3.** *For uneven ceiling, use ⅜" block of wood as guide to scribe.* **Step 4.** *Use ⅜" block as guide to maintain even lip at bottom of beam.* Photos this series: Gary Branson

difference." Drive the 6d finish nails into the 2 × 4 far enough to hold the 1 × 6 into position. Now check the width of the gap. Normally it won't be more than ⅜". Using a ⅜" to ½" block of wood for a guide, lay the block against the ceiling, with a pencil laying over the block and the lead against the 1 × 6. Slide the block and pencil along the 1 × 6 to scribe it to fit. Cut along this line with your circular saw and you'll have a fit that's watertight.

Story pole helper To avoid cutting the cedar lumber too short, use a story pole — two pieces of wood (1" × 2" is a good size) whose combined length is greater, but are individually shorter than the room

width. Two 7' 1 × 2's (combined length 14') make a good story pole for a 12' room, for example.

It takes two people to hold both pieces of 1 × 2 (with ends overlapping) at the ceiling where the beam will be. Slide the two pieces until the ends touch both walls. Then, with a pencil, mark where the overlapping end of one falls on the other. Clamp the two together at this point. Total length end-to-end will be the length of your beam.

Because few walls are perfectly straight and plumb, you will need to measure separately for each beam (on very crooked walls, each board). Be sure to erase the pencil mark from the last mea-

TYPES OF BEAMS

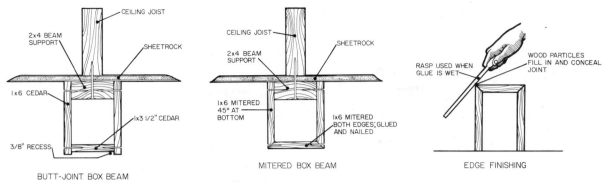

BUTT-JOINT BOX BEAM

CEILING JOIST
2x4 BEAM SUPPORT
SHEETROCK
1x6 CEDAR
1x3 1/2" CEDAR
3/8" RECESS

MITERED BOX BEAM

CEILING JOIST
2x4 BEAM SUPPORT
SHEETROCK
1x6 MITERED 45° AT BOTTOM
1x6 MITERED BOTH EDGES, GLUED AND NAILED

EDGE FINISHING

RASP USED WHEN GLUE IS WET
WOOD PARTICLES FILL IN AND CONCEAL JOINT

Illustrations: Ron Chamberlain

surement before making a new one, so you don't cut by the old mark.

ASSEMBLING THE BEAM   When you have cut the two side 1 × 6s, nail them to the 2 × 4. Space the nails at about 8" intervals, and use 6d finish nails. Set them just below the surface of the wood. Now cut a 1 × 4 for the bottom of the beam and inset it between the edges of the two 1 × 6s. Use a ⅛" wood block for a guide and tap the 1 × 4 up ⅜" inside the two 1 × 6 sides of the beam. Now nail through the side of 1 × 6s, at 12" to 16" intervals, into the 1 × 4 bottom of the beam. Set these nails, too. Build all full beams likewise.

For half beams at wall edges, nail 2 × 4s ripped to 2 × 2s at the corner where ceiling and wall meet. Use 16d nails into the top plate of the wall. Drop the other 2 × 2 down until its bottom is 4⅛" below the ceiling.

IMPORTANT: This mark is 4⅛" *down from the ceiling,* not the bottom of the first 2 × 2. If you've had to scribe your 1 × 6s by ⅜" or whatever amount to get a fit at the ceiling, subtract the scribed amount from the 4⅜" figure. (The 4⅜" is the 5½" width of the 1 × 6, less the ⅜" inset of the 1 × 4 from the bottom of the 1 × 6, less the ¾" thickness of the 1 × 4.)

Nail the 1 × 6 into the top 2 × 4s as with the full beams. Then put half the ripped 1 × 4 on the bottom of the lower 2 × 2. Nail the 1 × 4 into the 2 × 2, then nail the 1 × 6 side into the 1 × 4 bottom.

Staining rough-sawn cedar overhead can be rather difficult work. It's far easier to stain and seal it on the floor, after it's cut but before nailing it up. Then you only need to putty the nailholes.

MITERED BEAM   If you're in the advanced handyman class, and want to build a box beam that looks like solid wood, buy all 1 × 6 material rather than 1 × 4s for the bottoms of the beams. Then rip the bottom edge of the 1 × 6 sides at a 45° angle on a radial arm or table saw. Rip both edges of the bottom piece, at the same 45° angle so that the

board measures 5⅛" wide on one side and only 3⅝" on the other where the angle cuts reduced its width. (See illustration.) Run a bead of Elmer's Glue along the angled faces and nail the two sides and bottom into a U-shaped box, using 6d finish nails. While the glue is wet, run a wood rasp over the apex, or point of the corner, where the pieces join. This will rough up and fill the joints, hiding small imperfections.

Now, with a helper, push the box up over the ceiling 2 × 4. If the ceiling is uneven, tack the beam as tightly as possible to the ceiling line, then scribe (both sides) as directed earlier. When you've trimmed it to fit, push it up over the 2 × 4 again, and nail in place with 6d nails into the 2 × 4.

You'll get the best appearance if the beams fit wall-to-wall without a gap at either end. If you do miss slightly, all is not lost. Center the beam, splitting the difference so you have a small crack to fill at each end, rather than a single large one. Fill the cracks with a latex caulk of a shade to match your stain.

BUYING BEAMS   The cheapest route is to build beams yourself. But you can buy fiberglass beams that are already channeled to fit over and fasten to a 2 × 2 nailed to the ceiling. They may be nailed or glued. Their cost is something like $2 per linear foot. Available, too, are premitered wood beams that you easily fit together.

The dining room beams shown here were built in only four hours. But if you take the time to miter corners on your beams, expect a day-long project.

HOW TO FIX FLOORS

Proper floor maintenance begins with a solid, level underfooting. Sagging floors may indicate a serious weakness developing in the structure of the house. Sometimes the only satisfactory way to restore the floors in an older home is by thorough overhaul. Extra supports may be needed; the com-

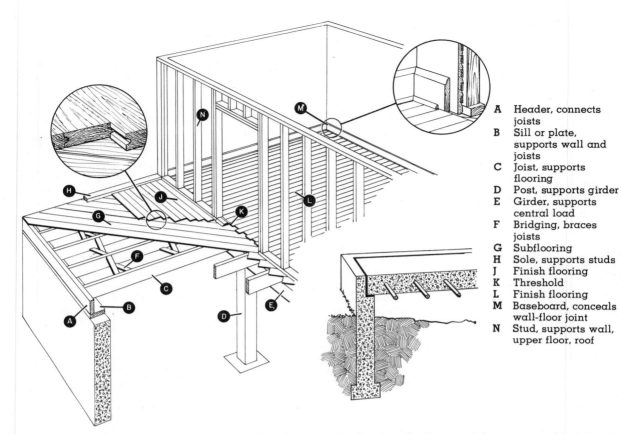

A	Header, connects joists
B	Sill or plate, supports wall and joists
C	Joist, supports flooring
D	Post, supports girder
E	Girder, supports central load
F	Bridging, braces joists
G	Subflooring
H	Sole, supports studs
J	Finish flooring
K	Threshold
L	Finish flooring
M	Baseboard, conceals wall-floor joint
N	Stud, supports wall, upper floor, roof

While this cutaway drawing shows a typical floor, there are many variations. Subflooring may be laid at right angles to the joists instead of diagonally, for example, and bridging may be omitted from your floors. In some houses, the supporting wall over the girder may be placed directly on the girder instead of on the subflooring. Flooring is not necessarily laid in two different directions as shown here, in which case a threshold or saddle is not needed, as its function here would be to cover the

joint between the flooring of the two rooms. In any event, these are the most likely details you will uncover when you lay a new floor in your home.
Lower right view is that of concrete-slab floor with radiant-heating tubing exposed. This type is common in one-floor ranch-style homes. Floor may be covered with wood flooring nailed to furring strips or covered with asphalt tiles.

plete removal of boards (or other flooring material) that are no longer serviceable may be necessary, and this in turn will mean laying a new floor.

On the other hand, some older floors can be made as good as new by the simple replacement of a few damaged boards or even the application of a new finish coat. Concrete floors are usually cold, but a basement with a concrete floor can quickly become a useful family room with an overflooring of wood. Stairs that are too steep can be widened and the steps replaced. You may even have room to make an extra landing.

Floors that squeak when you step on certain spots can be a great annoyance. What causes

squeaks? Often the upper layer of hardwood strip flooring separates from the softer fir planks or plywood of the subfloor. When a hardwood strip floor is laid, a wedge-shaped nail with a blunt point (called a cut nail) is driven through the tongue of the oak strip at a slant into the subfloor. The next oak strip has a groove that covers the tongue of the previous strip and the head of the nail. The drying effects of household heating, plus the humidity of summer, cause alternate expansion and contraction of both floor layers.

A squeak may also result as two pieces of flooring rub together at the joint, as a loose nail moves in the wood, or as hardwood slides against the

Floor squeaks can be silenced by driving a screw from below through subfloor and halfway into hardwood floor above, as shown in large photo. Squeaks are some- times caused by cross-pieces of bridging rubbing against each other when floor flexes. Cutting with a saw where pieces touch, as shown, may solve the problem.

A hardwood floor, if it can't be reached from below, must be nailed from above. As in photo left, drill hole with bit only slightly smaller than the diameter of the nail, to

avoid splitting. Then drive the finishing nail at a slant into predrilled hole through finished flooring and into subfloor as shown in photo center. Use nail set (photo right) to drive

nail home last ¼" to avoid hammer marks. Set or countersink nail head about ¹⁄₁₆" and fill with wood putty tinted to match floor color. *Photos this series: Arnold Romney*

subfloor plywood. Each time you step on the loose area, one of these problems can make itself heard. The wood-rubbing-wood squeak is the reason building paper is laid over subfloor before hardwood flooring is laid.

There are two ways to stop squeaks. One is from below when the floor is just above a basement or crawl space. The other way, when the floor cannot be reached from below, is to renail the finished hardwood flooring with concealed nailing.

Working from below, you must first locate the squeak. The easiest way to do this is to have somebody walk around while you listen. Once the squeak is located, drill a pilot hole for a 1" wood

screw up through the subfloor and no more than halfway in the hardwood layer. The person above should remain standing on the squeaky area to keep the two floor layers together while you are driving the screw. You may have to use two or three screws several inches apart before you succeed.

Sometimes the noise is caused by movement of the bridging—the diagonal braces that form an X between the floor joists to prevent them from moving. A simple saw cut between these braces to provide a space so that they will no longer touch each other may be enough to prevent further rubbing and squeaking.

Sagging, bouncy floors can be helped by driving 2 × 6 or 2 × 4 braces snugly between joists against subfloor. Toenail at each end to joists, then drive screw nails down from above into brace.

Warped boards—particularly wider ones—can be flattened by first soaking them, then setting countersunk screws or screw nails through their outer edges into subfloor. Sanding is the only other method.

Boards that have cracked along grain may be helped by forcing glue into the cracks with a putty knife. This treatment stops cracks from lengthening. Use glue-and-sawdust mixture for wide cracks.

New floor laid with green or wet lumber develops cracks as wood dries. Fill cracks with glue-and-sawdust, plastic wood, or wood-fiber putty if floor is to have clear finish. Otherwise, use putty under paint.

Rotted or damaged section requires replacement. Process involves several steps. First, cut length of flooring to size of piece to be removed. Bevel one end of replacement piece at a 45° angle.

Mark length of replacement piece on section to be removed. Using large bit, cut hole in each corner of section right up to edge of board and marked line. Do not cut into subfloor.

Split damaged piece end to end between holes along grain. Use a sharp 1" chisel and hammer or mallet. Be careful not to damage tongue and groove of adjoining piece.

Undercut the remaining piece of the damaged board at a 45° angle. The beveled end of the replacement board will fit snugly under it and make a smooth, tight joint.

Plane off underside of groove on replacement piece so it can be fitted over the tongue of the adjoining board. If not cut away, replacement board can't be fitted.

Insert beveled end of replacement under beveled end of old section, then press into place carefully. Tap down, using a block to avoid marking new piece.

Drill at least four pilot holes for screw nails or finishing nails. Without pilot holes, flooring would be split. Use drill slightly smaller than nail size. Do not drill in center.

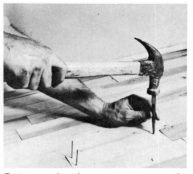

Drive in finishing or screw nails, then countersink heads. If replacement board is thicker than old flooring, plane or sand down flush with rest of floor.

If new piece is lighter, or of a different grain pattern, you may make it match by darkening with stain, orange shellac, or crayon rubbed in with alcohol.

Any noticeable space between the top of a joist and the underside of the subfloor should be filled with a wedge. As long as there is room for the subfloor to move, it will eventually separate from the upper hardwood layer and cause squeaking. Drive in a wedge or a piece of wood that just fills the space. If it is too thick, it may create a bump in the floor above.

What about squeaks in floors you can't reach from below? One thing you can do is to face-nail the hardwood floor to the subfloor. But before nailing loose flooring down, try spraying powdered graphite into any open cracks in the squeak area. The graphite is available from auto supply and hardware stores and will lubricate the wood so squeaking will stop.

If this doesn't work, drill a hole slightly smaller in diameter than a 1½" finishing nail. If you don't do this first, the nails may split the wood. Counter-sink the finishing nail with a nail set. Drive the head about 1/16" below the surface.

To avoid disfiguring the floor with hammer marks, start using the nail set when the nail head is still ¼" above the surface. As shown in the photo, the hole/nail should be driven at an angle, not straight down.

HOW TO LAY HARDWOOD FLOORS

The beauty and durability of a hardwood floor is unmatched, but its cost may at first appear prohibitive.

After you measure the floor and determine the square footage, price various floor coverings. Tell your dealer how many square feet you wish to cover; with some wood flooring you must increase your area by a certain percentage.

Hardwood floors, you will find, are affordable, especially if you do the work yourself. Laying a hardwood floor is possible for the handyman.

To begin, check the condition of the existing floor (which is to become the subfloor). Correct any problems first.

A cracking floor may be corrected by methods already described. If a floor is buckled, renailing may restore it. If not, the floor may have to be trimmed. Rotted subflooring must be replaced. Carefully take off the baseboards and brush or vacuum the floor. Locate the joists and mark each of their positions at the very bottom of the wall — these marks will be covered by the baseboards when replaced.

Cover the entire floor with good quality building paper, not tar paper. (The floor must breathe.) Snap chalklines on the paper, indicating where the floor joists are located. Remember to lay hardwood strips across rather than parallel to the joists. Snap a chalkline on the paper the length of one wall

Open several bundles of flooring and separate the flooring into graduated lengths. Place against wall.

Lay flooring out several rows ahead, cutting end pieces for length. This will speed installation and nailing.

End view shows how tongue-and-groove flooring fits together. Be sure to drive flooring up tight to eliminate cracks.

Side view of flooring. Ends are also tongue and groove, and should be fitted tightly together using a pry bar.
Photos this series: Jack Cascio

perpendicular to the joists. Do not place the first strip against the wall. Instead, leave at least ½" (but no more than the thickness of the baseboard) for expansion between the strip and the wall. Use long strips for the long course (to ensure as straight a row as possible), placing the grooved edge toward the wall, with the tongue facing the center of the room. Be sure to stay on the chalkline. This strip will have to be face-nailed into the floor joists. Drill a hole first, if you find nailing difficult.

Although this step may take a little time initially, it saves considerable work in the long run. Open about one-half of the bundles of various lengths, and place them perpendicular to the wall (as shown in the photo) in order of length. This system holds searching and cutting to a minimum.

Another timesaver is to place strips in rows prior to nailing. You may facilitate nailing by renting a portable nailer. Should you decide to do the nailing yourself, get a block of soft wood, a 20-ounce hammer, and case-hardened nails that do not bend easily.

When fitting the applied strips make sure the end-to-end and edge-to-edge fits are tight. Snug up the applied strip by tapping the block of softwood with the hammer against the nailed strip. Next toe-nail the applied strip through the corner so the tongue meets with the body of the strip. When laying the next row, keep all end-to-end joints a minimum of 6" away from the end joints of the preceding rows. Continue laying and nailing the strips in this way.

You may have a room layout that requires laying a section of strips backward from the original direction you were working. In this case you will be forced to butt the grooved edge of the applied strip up to the grooved edge of the nailed strip. Since there is no tongue to hold the strip down, insert a spline (purchase from your dealer) into the groove of the nailed strip, thus forming a tongue for the next strip. Then proceed as described above.

As you approach the far wall, you will begin running out of pieces you originally placed against the far wall. Open the remaining bundles and place the pieces in graduated lengths on the completed floor. Toe-nail the remaining rows, approaching as close to the far wall as possible. When you no longer have adequate room to swing the hammer, you will once again have to face-nail the strips. If you have trouble snugging up the applied strip as you approach the wall, take a crow or pinch bar and lever the strip in. Again, remember you may have to drill the holes for face nailing.

The last row may have to be ripped (sawed lengthwise) to fit in the remaining space. Do not forget to leave the ½" space for expansion between the last nailed strip and the wall.

Now either plug or fill the holes and reinstall the baseboard. Measure the vertical door casing pieces and cut off the thickness of the floor you just added. You may want to sand the floor before reinstalling the baseboard. The floor is now ready for finishing.

HOW TO FINISH WOOD FLOORS

No matter what type floor you intend to finish, two basic rules must always be observed: a) Prepare the surface carefully to assure good results; and b) Be sure that wood floors are firm, sanded smooth, and thoroughly dry.

Wax is possibly the worst problem in finishing floors. No finish will dry satisfactorily over it, so make sure all wax is removed with turpentine or a commercial wax remover. Floor polish should be completely removed. All loose boards must first be fastened, broken or badly split boards replaced, and protruding nail heads set.

If the floor is covered with varnish, paint, or shellac, using a sander is the easiest method of removal. Don't try to save time by skipping the sanding operation. And be careful when handling the sander. Careless use of this machine will gouge your floors. Three "cuts" are suggested for sanding: a coarse grit (3½) for the first sanding, a medium grit (1½) for the second, and a fine grit (2/0) for the final operation.

Always sand *with* the grain, *lengthwise* with the floor boards, except where it is impossible, as in the case of parquet floors. Use only finer grits here and take special care. Three sanding operations are recommended with new floors as well, but use finer grits—medium-coarse, fine, and extra-fine.

In areas inaccessible to the big drum sander, such as along baseboards or on stair treads, use an edge sander. All dust must be removed from the floor, ledges, and baseboards with a vacuum cleaner or dry mop before applying a new finish.

A filler is a pastelike substance painted on *along* the grain, wiped off *across* the grain with a cloth, using a light touch to leave behind a deposit of the filler in the pores of the wood. Most fillers dry rapidly. Some are wiped off immediately after application; others are allowed to set about five minutes first. Commercial fillers are available either neutral (colorless), or in a variety of pigmented tones.

If you cannot use a power sander, the old finish may be removed with a solvent type of paint and

Before sanding on a floor prior to refinishing, go over it carefully with a hammer and nail set and countersink all visible nailheads. They'll ruin sander and paper.

To make sanding your room edges easier, remove shoe molding along the baseboards. You can then sand all the floor without damaging either the baseboard or shoe molding.

If there are areas where the floor is high or bulged upward, plane them smooth. The sander might ride over such areas without reducing them to a level with the rest of the floor.

Power sander, rented, is run from end to end of the wood flooring, never across the boards. Never stop sander in one spot with sandpaper in contact with the floor!

Edger, also a rental tool, gets up close. Guard protects shoe molding. Your disk sander on a drill will also do this job. Use medium grit paper for the main work, then fine.

No round sander can get into a square corner, so eventually you get down to hand work. Sandpaper on a block will do the trick if you don't have an orbital sander.

For super-smooth floor finish, use a disk sander to remove "trees"—short, treelike fibers thrust up from the first sanding. Floors treated in this way need less seal.

varnish remover. Provide plenty of ventilation in the area where you are using solvent removers, and turn the furnace thermostat down so fumes are not cycled through the house.

The solvent remover is easy to use and does not raise the grain. Brush on a heavy coat and let it stand undisturbed until the finish softens. Then remove it with a stiff putty-knife and #2 steel wool. Several applications may be necessary if the old finish is particularly heavy. Wash the surface thoroughly with turpentine and wipe dry with clean cloths.

If the floors are dark with age and wear, an alkaline remover and bleach will be more effective. But it must be made up in a solution of hot water (and applied hot). This will cause the grain to raise, entailing later sanding. With the solvent type of paint remover there is also always some danger that the wax generally found in these liquids will remain in the floors; hence, it's a good idea to scrub them afterward with a strong floor cleanser. Rinse with clear water and wipe with a clean cloth. Do not attempt painting or finishing until the surface is thoroughly dry.

If you want to retain the beauty of the grain of your floors, but wish to add color to them, use an oil stain. Apply it to the bare wood as the label directs, brushing it on a few boards at a time with the grain. The longer the stain is allowed to remain on the wood, the darker it will become. The depth of color is easily controlled by wiping off excess stain when the desired shade has been reached.

Varnish stain will do the job of staining and varnishing in one operation. It is faster and easier than staining and varnishing in separate steps but

Applying finishes

Penetrating floor sealer may be applied with cloth or brush. When pigmented, it adds color. Penetration is ¼" deep. Final finish is floor wax.

The penetrating sealer finish is waxed. To simplify the job, use the disk sander with brush attachment. Similar wax application may be made over shellac-varnish finishes.

Two coats of a good plastic finish will cover the floor, also. This is a clear, hard finish requiring no wax and lasting many years without refinishing of any kind.

does not produce the beauty and clarity obtained by using varnish on an already stained surface. It will, however, with a minimum of effort, bring new life and color to old, worn, and discolored floors. Also, you may on occasion wish to change a darker finish to a lighter one. This can be done without removing the old finish. Simply apply a coat of ground color, and, when this is dry, apply one or two coats of the lighter varnish stain in the exact color you want.

The polyurethane varnishes provide the best finish for wood floors. They are very tough, scuff resistant, and impervious to water. Any moisture spilled on the floor may be wiped up without the usual blackening of the oak that is found with other finishes. They are relatively fast drying, but try to keep the area free from dust and drafts until the finish has hardened, as with any finish material.

HOW TO LAY FLOOR TILES

Replacing old carpet or tile with a vinyl asbestos tile floor is a do-it-yourself project. The adhesive-backed tile is easy to install, reasonably priced, and a constructive project that can also be a creative one.

Putting down a single pattern of tile is so simple any novice remodeler can handle the job. Creating a "custom designed" floor requires a little more planning but no more technical expertise for the installation. Graph paper and colored pencils or crayons can be used to draft your special design. Since tile is 12" × 12", each square of the graph can represent a tile.

Be wary of using too many *colors*. Remember, you'll be living with this floor a long time. Most successful custom floors are usually two or three colors—the field in a pastel or neutral shade, the design in solid colors: black, brown, or any bright color.

First prepare the subfloor. Vinyl asbestos tile (unlike some resilient floor coverings) can be put over almost any kind of subfloor. But whatever the subfloor, it should be smooth and even. If not, the tile will eventually show every imperfection beneath it.

If the floor has holes, bumps, or cracks that cannot be eliminated, put down underlayment panels of plywood or hardboard. There is an exception: if you wish to use tile as a short-term cosmetic and don't want to bother with underlayment, a heavily embossed tile will help mask subfloor irregularities.

Installation begins in the middle of the room. You do a quarter of the floor at a time. Find the center via chalklines between midpoints of each wall. When measuring, ignore bays, alcoves, and minor

Before

After   Photos: GAF

HOW TO LAY FLOOR TILES

1

First a chalkline is snapped from the middle of one wall
to the middle of the opposite wall to meet at right angles.

2

Then the tiles are temporarily laid in place to check for
equal spacing from end of rows to wall.

3
Next, crossed rows are permanently placed.

4
Fourth photo shows the first quarter of the floor filled in.

HOW TO HANDLE EDGES

1

2

3

4

An open strip is left next to the wall to be filled in later with tile cut to fit. Full tile (Tile A, photo 1) with protective paper is placed over tile in last row, as shown above. This allows you to use an easy measuring system of cutting tile to fill open strip. Tile B (photo 2) is pressed against wall

and positioned on top of Tile A. Next, Tile A is scored with knife (photo 3) using edge of Tile B as guide. The scored Tile A (photo 4) snaps clean. Section in right hand fits open strip.

irregularities in the wall line. Lay a test row of tile without adhesive from the center point to one side wall and one end wall—making a big L. If the space between the last full tile and the wall is less than 6″, shift the chalkline. This will give you a better proportioned row of border tile. Every package of adhesive-back tile contains explicit instructions on how to handle the border, or ask your dealer for a folder with easy-to-follow instructions.

Once the borders and center point have been established, you can begin laying tile from the point where the chalklines cross. Remove the backing papers from one tile at a time. Put the backing paper in a wastebasket as you work because they are slippery when stepped on. Position each tile very carefully—you cannot slide it into place—and press down. The bond is instantaneous.

HOW TO FIGURE TILE REQUIREMENTS

Square Feet	Number of Tiles Needed			
	9″ × 9″	12″ × 12″	6″ × 6″	9″ × 18″
1	2	1	4	1
2	4	2	8	2
3	6	3	12	3
4	8	4	16	4
5	9	5	20	5
6	11	6	24	6
7	13	7	28	7
8	15	8	32	8
9	16	9	36	8
10	18	10	40	9
20	36	20	80	18
30	54	30	120	27
40	72	40	160	36
50	89	50	200	45
60	107	60	240	54
70	125	70	280	63
80	143	80	320	72
90	160	90	360	80
100	178	100	400	90
200	356	200	800	178
300	534	300	1200	267
400	712	400	1600	356
500	890	500	2000	445
600	1068	600	2400	534
700	1246	700	2800	623
800	1424	800	3200	712
900	1602	900	3600	801
1000	1780	1000	4000	890

	1 to 50 sq. ft.	14%
	50 to 100 sq. ft.	10%
Tile waste	100 to 200 sq. ft.	8%
allowances	200 to 300 sq. ft.	7%
	300 to 1000 sq. ft.	5%
	Over 1000 sq. ft.	3%

HOW TO INSTALL CARPET SQUARES

Installing wall-to-wall carpeting is no longer a job that must be left to the professionals. Good quality carpeting is now available in 12″ squares mounted on ¼″ foam backing with a pressure-sensitive adhesive on the back of the foam.

In the better grades, the pile is a deep-sculptured shag continuous filament 100 percent nylon, anchored to a woven polypropylene scrim, which is then glued to a synthetic foam.

Still others, which are somewhat less expensive, have less nylon to the square and may be tufted or sheared.

Another group is made of dense, highly durable bonded polypropylene. These less expensive propylene types, which look like felt, are good for door entrances, corridors, children's playrooms, and recreation rooms that are subject to hard wear.

The new carpet squares come in packages of ten squares, which covers ten square feet. The top of each package is wrapped in clear plastic that reveals exactly what you are getting.

The installation system is designed to be as easy as possible for the homeowner and is modeled directly on that used for vinyl and vinyl-asbestos tile.

The first thing to do is to remove the shoe molding. This is often simply a quarter-round molding that you can easily pry up together with its nails without breaking or cracking if you are careful.

Remove all floor wax. Get a commercial wax remover from your carpet dealer. Then sweep the floor to be sure it is free of dust and dirt.

Divide the room into rough quarters by snapping a chalkline from the midpoint of one wall to the midpoint of the opposite one, then do the same to the two remaining walls.

With the room arranged in quarters, lay a row of squares (without removing the protective paper from the back of the foam backing) from the midpoint of the room along the chalkline to both the short and long walls in an L-shape. This tells you how much space there is between the last squares and the wall. If the space is much less than half a square, move the chalklines so that the end squares which will have to be trimmed to fit will at least be approximately equal.

Now, beginning at the midpoint again, turn the first square over and remove the protective paper from the foam back. Press it down firmly on the floor exactly where both chalklines meet. Repeat this procedure till you have filled one-quarter of the room, taking care to place each square so that the arrows on the back of each square (which are revealed when the protective paper is removed) all point in the same direction. If you do this faithfully, pressing each square firmly against the previous one already laid down, no line or crack will show between them and all the squares will look like

1

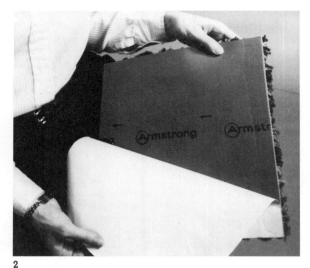

2

3

4

5

Step 1. Divide the room area into quarters. Locate the center point between opposite walls and connect the points by snapping a chalkline down and across the center of the room. Use a square to be sure you have 90° angle. **Step 2.** As you peel the protective paper off the back, note the direction of arrows. As you lay carpet, be sure all arrows are pointed in the same direction, either toward or away from you. Press squares firmly in place; cover entire ¼ of the room except for border trim. **Step 3.** To fit carpet at wall, place a loose tile paper-side up exactly over the last tile in any row. Be sure arrow is pointed in same direction. Then place another square over the upside-down square, and slide the top square till it butts the wall. Mark and cut the bottom square; fit at wall. **Step 4.** To fit around pipes or other irregular objects, make a pattern on a 12″ × 12″ piece of paper, tracing the pattern on the back of a carpet square. Cut with scissors and fit. **Step 5.** Carpet tiles go down quickly, requiring only a pair of sharp scissors to apply. Tiles make carpeting a do-it-yourself project. *Photos this series: Armstrong Cork*

one solid piece. Leave the space between the last row of squares and the wall unfilled.

The last row of squares must all be trimmed to make them fit against the wall. Take a full-sized square—let us call it Square A—and turn it over with the white paper uppermost. Lay it on one of the squares in the last row.

Now take another carpet square (called B) and lay it bottomside up on A so that the far end is against the wall and the lower end partly overlaps A. Draw a pencil line on A using the bottom of B as a guide. Cut A along the pencil line with sharp scissors. You will find that the larger piece fits perfectly in the space between the last row of squares and the wall.

With the last row filled in, the final job is to restore the shoe molding. A word of warning about the shoe molding: do not drive nails through the molding into the floor or carpet squares. The nails should be driven into the base molding.

HOW TO INSTALL ROLL CARPET

The advent of foam-backed carpeting has placed carpet within the realm of the do-it-yourselfer.

Since this product incorporates both carpet and pad, placing it becomes largely a matter of proper fit. Carpet comes in rolls 12' wide, and is cut to the appropriate length by the dealer.

Measure carefully when you order the carpet. Lengths and widths should be rounded off to the next highest foot when computing the yardage of carpet needed for your job. If the room is 12' or less in width, you need only measure for length. For example, if your room is 14½' in length, buy a piece 15' long.

It's best to empty the room of furniture, then unroll the carpet, allowing the edges to overlap the walls.

Leave the carpet there for a few hours, or overnight, to settle. Kinks or wrinkles will flatten if the carpet is simply left alone, without fastening, and this will make it much easier to get a smooth job.

You can secure foam-backed carpet to the floor with latex glue, staples, carpet tacks, or double-faced adhesive tape. Often rooms carpeted with this product appear to have a wall-to-wall installation, in spite of the fact that the carpet is secured to the floor only at the doorway. There the double-

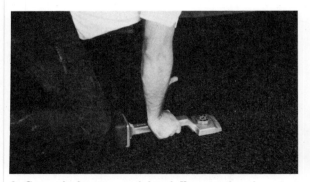

1. Cut the carpet, as described in text.

2. Start the job by laying factory-cut edge of carpet against one wall. Here the baseboard was left in place.

3. Carpet kicker is a useful tool. Knee is placed against pad; opposite end has teeth that grip carpet without ripping it.

4. When carpet is pulled flat to unsecured side, it can be trimmed in place. Be sure blade used is sharp.

5. *This installation involved making a seam between living room and hall. It is best to butt factory-cut edges.*

6. *With kicker holding carpet, seam is secured. You can use staples to tack carpet in place.*

7. *Secure cut ends of carpet to floor with binder bars or saddles. Original pieces can often be reused.* Photos this series: Tom Philbin

faced tape is often used, or a binder bar, to prevent the carpet from curling.

To install, remove the shoe moldings, which are ¾" quarter rounds nailed to the lower part of the baseboards. A sharp utility knife will break the paint film where shoe molding and baseboard meet. Pry gently only where the base and shoe are nailed. Now adjust the carpet on the floor so that no trimming is necessary along one end and one side. Secure this end and side temporarily with a few staples or tacks.

Then tug the carpeting to stretch it and be sure it lays flat. If you have let the carpet settle, only a minimum amount of stretching will be necessary. You can rent a kicker, a device padded on one end, with hooks on the other, to help in this stretching. Place the hooks through the carpet, and bump the kicker with your knee to move the carpet.

To cut the carpet, use a sharp linoleum knife. Once the carpet is stretched into place, a metal straightedge, such as an aluminum yardstick, can be used to ensure a straight cut. Lay the straightedge as tightly as possible to the wall, and cut along it with the knife. Often repeated cutting is

necessary, since the carpet is quite tough. The carpet can be held in place with a few tacks, until the shoe molding is replaced. The shoe molding will hold the carpet easily. There is no need for many fasteners, which may only serve to cause wrinkles in the carpet.

To fit around pipes or other obstructions, cut from the nearest edge to the center of the hole you need, then carefully trim out the hole with a knife or heavy shears. Trim very carefully where carpet meets carpet, to be sure the edges lie together tightly. As long as the edges are cut to a tight fit, especially on long-nap or shag carpets, you can conceal the point where the two meet by running the vacuum cleaner in a "swirling" motion, over the joint. This will cause carpet nap to intertwine, and the joint will not be visible.

If your room is more than 12' wide, you can use the double-faced tape to join the two pieces together. Roll the edges of the carpet back, and stick one side of the tape on the floor at the point the seam will occur. Then peel the top side of the tape and fit the two edges of the carpet onto them. A slight touch with a steam iron will help the tape and carpet stick together tightly.

A binder bar can be used at such high-traffic points as doorways, where carpet tends to come loose and curl if not firmly anchored.

The key to carpet installation is to move slowly. Cut and fit at corners, doors, and edges with deliberate care. There is no way you can go wrong, except to badly miscut the carpet. This will not be a problem if you cut the carpet in place, on the floor, and use care.

HOW TO INSTALL SHEET VINYL

In the past, installing sheet flooring was considered a job for professionals who knew how to handle awkward 12' rolls without cracking them. Today any do-it-yourselfer can do the job and come up with professional results.

Foam-cushioned vinyl flooring is positioned in room. Excess material is allowed to curve up on walls.

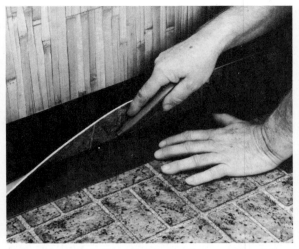

Excess material is bent into joint where wall and floor meet. Cut with sharp knife using straightedge as a guide.

Vinyl flooring is stapled close to baseboard in this installation. Quarter-round moldings conceal staples. Photos this series: Armstrong Cork

Modern sheet vinyl flooring is light, easy to handle and cut, and so flexible that it can be bent at a sharp angle without cracking. Available in 6', 9', and 12' widths, it can be installed without seams in most rooms. For rooms over 12' wide, you can make seams that are practically invisible.

PREPARING OLD FLOORS Floors to be covered must be clean, dry, smooth, and free of wax. Fill all holes and cracks with a latex floor-patching compound. Either sand or cut down high spots with a plane, and drive down all protruding nails. If old wooden floors are in such bad condition they can't be patched, cover with a ¼" underlayment hardboard, ⅜" particle board, or ¼" smooth sanded underlayment-type plywood.

You can buy special kinds of hardboard and plywood made specifically for vinyl flooring in 4' × 8' sheets. They should be fastened with threaded or ring groove flooring nails spaced 6" apart ½" in from the edges. Nails inside each sheet should be spaced 8" apart.

You can install sheet vinyl flooring over old tile or sheet flooring, even over terrazzo and concrete. Usually old embossed or foam-cushioned flooring must be removed, although some types may be installed over it. No resilient flooring of any type should be laid on concrete that generates moisture or alkaline salts.

REMOVING MOLDINGS The next step is to remove the small shoe moldings. Lift the moldings gently, using the thin edge of a pry bar. Work your way along the length of each molding, exerting a little bit of pressure at a time.

Try to remove each molding intact. To minimize paint chipping, insert a sharp knife where the molding meets the baseboard and run the blade the length of the molding to break the paint seal. Remove the rubber or vinyl cove base by working one corner loose and pulling it away while breaking the adhesive bond bit by bit with a scraping tool.

CUT SHEET FLOORING Make a sketch of the room showing fixed built-ins, closets, and other features that will affect the size and shape of the floor. Transfer measurements to the new vinyl sheet, but allow an extra 3" around the perimeter.

Now cut the sheet with scissors or a sharp utility knife.

TIP: If you had sheet flooring that was never cemented, you can use it as a cutting pattern for the new flooring.

TRIM TO FIT Leave clearance of at least ⅛" between the edge of the sheet and the wall to allow for expansion and contraction of the wood subfloor. Now butt the new flooring against the longest, most regular wall and unroll it, allowing excess material to curve up the other three walls. Adjust the butt edge for proper clearance before trimming the other edges. At each of the other walls, bend excess material into the joint where the baseboards meet the floor, and cut with utility knife. Use a metal straightedge or carpenter's square to help keep cuts straight.

At this point you can install the moldings or cove base, leaving the new sheet uncemented. However, with some types, all the edges are stapled to the floor. The staples are covered by shoe moldings. The exception is when this type of flooring is applied to concrete or in areas where a staple gun can't be used because of overhanging floor cabinets. In such cases cement is used.

MAKE SEAMS WHERE NEEDED For rooms wider than 12', a second piece of sheet must be used. It must be large enough to overlap the edge of the first sheet by 3" or 4" so you can match its pattern. Tape it or hold it in place with weights so it won't move. Using a straightedge, cut through the two layers in the overlap area. Hold the knife straight up and down. Fold the top piece back and remove the upper and lower cutoff strips.

Next, mark a line on the floor, along the edge of the other sheet, and fold back. Spread a 6" band of adhesive (centered on the line) on the underfloor with a notched mastic trowel. Press the two pieces of sheet flooring into the wet adhesive; wipe up excess with a damp cloth. Then trim the other three edges of the second sheet at the wall perimeter.

The choice of adhesive depends on the backing of the sheet flooring and the type of underfloor. Some manufacturers offer different adhesives for sheet floorings with mineral fiber or vinyl foam backing. Special adhesives are also provided when applied to concrete.

With more than one seam in a room, cement the entire sheet and use plywood underlayment or level with floor patching compound. All seams in sheet flooring with a clear vinyl wear surface should be sealed with special clear solvent cement.

REPLACE MOLDINGS Allow for a ¹⁄₃₂" clearance between the vinyl flooring and wood shoe moldings. Nail wood moldings to the baseboards, not to the floor, with finishing nails. Countersink nail

heads and fill holes with wood putty. (Rubber or vinyl cove base can be cemented back to the wall without clearance.) Install metal or plastic moldings on all other exposed edges. The moldings should not restrict movement of the sheet.

HOW TO REPAIR LINOLEUM

When linoleum wears thin around the kitchen sink, the back door, or under the table, you can patch it, choosing your color and design so that the patch becomes an attractive decoration in the room. All that is needed for this small job is a ruler, a hammer, some small nails, a putty knife, a linoleum knife, the linoleum patch, and paste. Then follow the photos shown.

Make desired pattern and use it as a guide to cut old linoleum with a knife. Take piece to dealer; use it as guide for thickness of replacement. Buy new piece about 1" larger than worn sample.

Use 4 or 5 small nails to hold patch in place; do not drive nails all the way in. Cut along edge and remove extra old linoleum. Clean out space. Use paper underneath to raise new linoleum level with old, if necessary.

Remove nails and linoleum; apply the cement generously to floor or both sides of paper, if used. Fit patch in position. If linoleum is warm, it will lie flat; otherwise, use weight to hold it down while cement is drying.

When cement is dry, some edges may be higher than the rest of linoleum. Hammer them down or sandpaper lightly. Fill any large holes with fine chips of linoleum added to varnish; small spaces will be filled as linoleum spreads.

Putting down floor tiles is easy, but removing them is often another matter. In removing one tile for replacement, a second might be damaged. The easiest and quickest way is to use the broad-flame nozzle of a propane torch and play the flame, held about 6″ away from the tile, over the center area of the tile. The heat softens the adhesive underneath, and then a putty knife or scraper will pry it loose easily. Work from the center to the edges and stop there so the adjoining tiles will not be damaged. The adhesive under these adjacent tiles may be softened, but if pressed tightly against the floor, they'll be firmly resealed. Then you can lay a new tile in the open space and press it into the still-soft adhesive.

HOW TO REPAIR STAIRS

A two-level house with a basement and attic will probably have three sets of stairs. Complaints of squeaks can be dealt with here, too, but the more important concern is safety.

The first-floor-to-second-floor stairs receive the heaviest use and are the least accessible, being finished on the underside and, perhaps, carpeted on the steps.

Look first at the moldings, noting any separations at the stair edges and the walls. Gaps or spaces do not necessarily mean the stairs are faulty, but like everything else in the house, the stairs will settle, too. Periodically, test each step with body weight, rocking on the edge to determine if there is looseness or play on the board step. Apply hand pressure to the risers and note if there is any looseness. If steps are carpeted, do not confuse the "give" of the fabric (especially on the risers) with structural looseness.

To silence noisy stairs on the first to second level, drive in nails diagonally at the step ends, in the direction of the wall (if a fully enclosed stairwell). If a portion of the stairs—or one complete side—is open, then nail down at the step ends, into the stringer. Additionally, nail along the long edge, into the edge of the riser directly below the tread.

If carpeted, check the tread-to-riser corner and make sure that there is no loose covering that could cause unsure footing when using the stairs.

Unfinished or open basement stairs are easy to inspect and repair. Loose treads or risers can be treated in the same way described above. Since most basement stairs have rubber treads, it is important to watch for wear and tear. Tread edges crack and peel and flake off; they should be replaced without delay. Minor tears can be stapled and restored to use—but don't overdo it.

HOW TO REPAIR DOORS

There are three main causes for stubborn doors. The first and most common is improperly adjusted hinges. The second is distortion of the door so that it no longer fits the frame. And the third, more prevalent in older houses, is distortion of the frame so it no longer fits the door.

To determine the cause, stand on the side away from the doorstop and close the door. Check the space between door and jamb all the way around. Where this space is only a hairline crack, the door fits too tightly and sticks when opening or closing.

If there is such a tight spot, and a contrastingly large crack appears on the opposite side, the trouble is probably in the hinge setting. If the door fits too tightly all around, it has swelled from dampness. If there are telltale cracks in the plaster

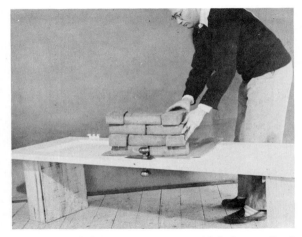

1. *Lay warped door across supports with bulge up. Stack bricks for weight on center, allow sufficient time for the door to straighten.*

2. *Doors can also be pulled straight by use of a bridge and turnbuckle. Insert a screw eye into each end—top and bottom—and attach wire. Tighten turnbuckle over bridge until door is straight.*

around the door frame, the house has settled from shrinkage in the framework, distorting the frame until it presses on the door at one or several points.

To correct the trouble, first remove the door. With the door closed, knock out the hinge pin with a nail set and hammer, then lift the door from the frame. If the screws are loose in either half of the hinge, they must be tightened. If the holes have become enlarged, try longer screws or plug the holes with putty or plastic wood. When this has dried, reset the screws. Tightening them in this manner will often correct the trouble. If it doesn't, readjustment of the hinges is needed. If the sticking spot is located on the lock stile opposite the hinges, set the hinges deeper by increasing the depth of the undercut, or mortise, in which the hinge leaf is recessed. It may be necessary to deepen the mortise on both door and jamb. When the sticking spot is found on the hinge stile, hinges set too deeply are the probable cause. Raise them by setting a sheet of cardboard under the leaves of the hinge.

Heavy doors, tending to sag at the lower outside corner, can be raised by deepening the mortise of the upper hinge. When the screws here are tightened, it tends to pull the door up. You may also insert a piece of cardboard under the leaves of the lower hinge to push the door upward from the bottom.

Occasionally moisture will so swell a door that it no longer fits the frame. In such a case, remove the door and the hinges, then plane down the hinge stile. Usually the part of the door that needs to be planed does not extend full length. Mark the sticking area while the door is in place, then plane to the mark. Don't be overzealous in planing. A little

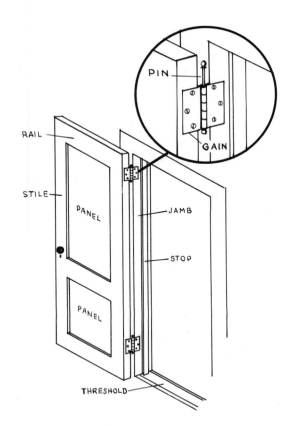

HANGING A DOOR

1. *Determine which side of door is to be hinged. Locate top of hinge 7" from top jamb. Allow 3/16" clearance to door stop. Outline hinge on jamb, cut out mortise to depth of hinge-leaf thickness with a sharp chisel. By holding the chisel flat, the mortise will be cut smooth and level.*

2. *With hinge pin up, attach leaf of hinge to jamb with three screws. Insert door in opening and wedge upward. Allow 7/8" clearance over a carpet, 1/2" over a linoleum or tiled floor. If door fits, mark hinge location. Mark the areas to be trimmed away if the door does not fit.*

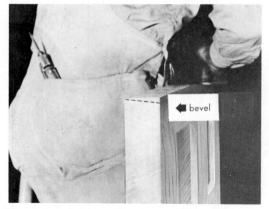

3. *Trim sides of door with jointer plane, working with grain. Latch side is beveled slightly inward to prevent binding.*

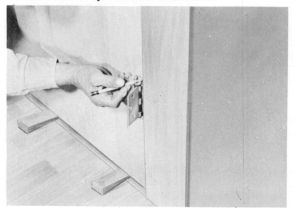

4. *Place the trimmed door back in the frame, blocked up to the necessary clearance, and mark the exact location of top and bottom of hinge. Only a sharp pencil will do this job accurately. Locate bottom hinge 11" above the floor.*

---

may be enough. Frequently, a rubdown with Number 1 sandpaper will suffice, but take care not to bevel the edge of the door.

When a door sticks at the bottom, either the threshold has become warped or damaged or the door itself sags. If the sagging condition cannot be corrected by hinge adjustment and the threshold is in good condition, the door itself must be trimmed to shape. Remove the door and plane the surface.

Planing across the grain of the stiles will be difficult, and unless care is taken the wood may splinter. Sandpaper is better than a plane on these surfaces. Occasionally the bottom rail alone is at fault, because of swelling. This can be remedied by reducing it with a plane. If the threshold is damaged, it must be replaced.

If a door is repeatedly exposed to moisture on one side and the other side is kept dry, it may

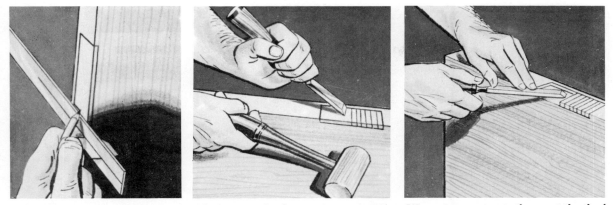

5. *Remove the door again and cut out the mortises for the hinges. By making horizontal cuts across the grain, scrap can be removed with a sharp chisel without cutting below* *the marked line. All mortises are cut to the exact depth of the thickness of hinge leaves.*

warp. One side swells, the other shrinks, and the door is pulled out of shape. The photos show two ways to straighten out such a bowed door. To prevent recurrence of the trouble, be sure to double-coat the top and bottom with sealer and then prime and paint both faces of the door, covering every corner and joint. This will keep out moisture.

A door that sticks at the top results from a settling house. Since the frame cannot be made "true" without dismantling it, the door must be made to fit. A plane does this job quickly. Frame distortion may also cause sticking at other points, and in such cases either adjustment of the hinges or planing the door to fit is necessary.

One more point: In curing the sticking door, the latch may have been thrown out of line. The door no longer sticks, but it won't stay closed. Note first the polished mark on the striker plate where the latch once fit. Partially close the door and mark the point where the latch must now fit. From this mark, relocate the striker plate in outline. Then, with a chisel, cut a new mortise for the plate. With the plate reset, fill in the old mortise with plastic wood, sand smooth when dry, and touch up with a finish to match surroundings.

REPLACING A DOOR If your back door has gone bad after exposure to rain, snow, ice, and summer heat, it has to be replaced. First, measure the width and height of the old door. Measure the width in at least two places, 6″ from the top and 6″ from the bottom, as there may be slight differences in the measurements if the door was ever trimmed to make it fit. Measure the height 2″ from the right and a similar distance from the left.

You may also need new hinges and a lockset but be sure the old hardware is too worn to use before you buy another set.

After the old door is removed, the new one is placed in the door opening and marked so that the recesses for its hinge leaves line up with those already on the door jamb. A new hinge leaf is laid on the marks and outlined in pencil. When struck with a hammer, its edges cut into the wood as deep as the thickness of the hinge leaf, marking it clearly.

The wood inside the penciled outline is removed with hammer and chisel, leaving a shallow recess for the hinge leaf. Check the fit of the hinge leaf to make sure it fits flush with the surface. Holes for screws are then marked and drilled. This operation is then repeated for the other hinge. The new hinges are then screwed into the recesses in the doorway jamb previously occupied by the old hinges. To make it easier to drill the new holes for the lockset, the door is temporarily attached to its hinges.

Most locksets come with a paper template to guide the installer. One hole is drilled through the front stile for the drum that connects the inside and outside handles. A second, smaller, hole for the latch mechanism goes through the front edge of the stile and meets the first hole at right angles. A recess is chiseled out around the smaller hole in the door front for the rectangular latch plate. Then the two screws for the latch plate are driven in. Both handles are inserted to see if they operate the latch properly. The lockset is temporarily removed so the door may be given a primer coat of paint, followed by a second coat of semigloss exterior enamel.

When the paint is thoroughly dry, the lockset is installed permanently and the door is hung on its hinges.

REPLACING A LOCKSET Sticky locks, knobs that bind, keys that catch—the homeowner need not

Problem	Cause	Cure	How to Prevent
Lock frozen—can't get key into the cylinder	Moisture in lock expands when frozen, thus binding free movement of cylinder	Warm key; insert in cylinder gradually; alcohol on key will speed process	Keep inside dry; best to spray with graphite; or use fine typewriter oil but not ordinary lubricating oil
Bolt stuck—key turns but bolt won't move open or closed	Door out of line puts pressure on bolt	Check door alignment; see pages 200–202 for details on how to cure faulty doors	Check door alignment regularly, especially when it shows signs of jamming
	Bolt blocked by paint over end	Scrape clean with knife; use paint remover to assure full removal of paint	Use extra care when painting edge of door to avoid going over bolt or plate
Key binds—goes into cylinder but won't turn	Improper mounting so that cylinder is out of line with lock housing	Remove lock; check all parts to see that they're aligned	Make certain to follow instructions when installing a new lock; use the templates or pattern included with lock by the manufacturer
	Cylinder in upside down; tumbler springs won't work properly	Remove cylinder; replace it in proper position	
	Poor duplicate key fails to line up tumblers inside of cylinder	Use original key to check if door works; have duplicate key checked at locksmith	Don't buy poor quality blanks for duplicate keys; stick to top names
	Outside elements affected metal inside cylinder or housing	Remove cylinder; a new one undoubtedly will be needed	Make cover to fit over cylinder; use thin coated metal; cut to any decorative shape
Key breaks—part of key remains inside the cylinder	In 9 out of 10 cases, key not in all the way before it was turned. Wrong key used; did not line up tumblers and therefore cracked when turned	Remove cylinder; use long, fine pin to push key out from shaft end. Or slide long crochet hook along top of cylinder, lower hook over end of key and pull out. If no spare key available, tip of screwdriver can be used to open or close lock if cylinder is turned properly	Lubricate cylinder with graphite; insert key fully before turning. Mark keys for easy identification; better yet, have one key to work all locks

put up with these annoyances any longer than it takes to visit a local hardware store and buy a new lockset.

Periodic lock maintenance—resetting strikes, tightening set screws, and applying graphite in the slot—is a good practice when operation continues unhindered. When replacement becomes necessary, keep the following steps in mind.

After removing the old set (it may not be necessary to remove the strike on the jamb), slip the latch assembly from the new set into the hole at the edge of the door, making sure the beveled end of the bolt faces the direction of the strike. Secure the latch with two Phillips screws.

Next, the exterior knob assembly is positioned upright (key should enter the lockset with cuts in the "up" position) and slipped into the door, threading the spindle through the latch's bar, and aligning the stems correctly through the latch holes. This done, it is pressed firmly against the door.

INSTALLING STORM DOORS

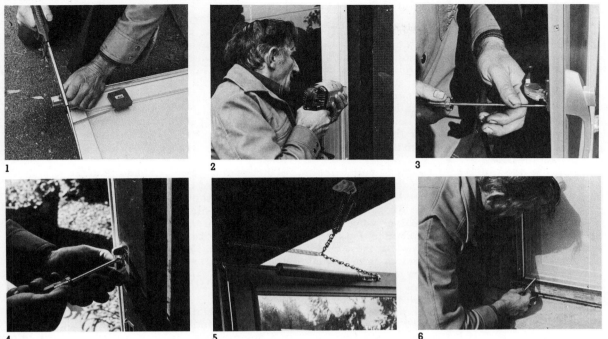

Step 1. Measure height of exterior door frame. Cut side rails on the storm door to proper length. **Step 2.** Place storm door into wood frame. Secure storm with screws into wood. **Step 3.** Drill three ¼" holes, attach lockset. Inside lock plate is used for a template to locate holes. **Step 4.** Attach door latch, making sure set height will match door lock. Shim is supplied if needed to shim out the latch. **Step 5.** Door closer, retaining chain, and spring-mounted in proper position. Check closer with door open. **Step 6.** Attach metal or vinyl weatherstripping at bottom of door. Slotted screw holes allow adjustment. *Photos this series: Gary Branson*

The interior knob comes next. The spindle of the exterior knob and the screw holes at the end of the stems will show on the interior side. All that's necessary is to place the interior knob on the spindle and align screw guides with the screws. This done, push flush against the door. Insert the screws and tighten them until the whole assembly is firm. Test the action of the latch by closing the door; it should click into the strike's slot easily, yet without play. Opening the door, the action should be smooth; there should be no binding of the latch on the edge of the strike.

An old door may be rejuvenated quickly by the use of replacement lockset pieces. For instance, an oversized escutcheon plate that fits around the knob can completely cover all the holes left by removal of the old knob and lock plates. Or, around the corner on the door edge, a two-piece lock-together latch plate will conceal the gaping hole left by mortise-lock extraction. And the screws that hold it have new wood to grip and hold fast. Anoth-er solution is that the strike plate for the new latch can be long and broad enough to cover the gap in the door frame left by old strike plates. No new hole is needed for the latch, and there will be no trace left of the former damage.

A brace, two sizes of bits, and one screwdriver are all that is needed for new lock installation.

HOW TO INSTALL STORM DOORS

Tight-fitting storm doors are valuable in saving energy. They are not difficult to install. If you are replacing an existing storm door, take a Polaroid shot of the lock, latch, and closer so you can refer back to it. Your new installation should look the same.

New wood doors have slightly oversize rails. You must measure the wood frame of the existing door, and cut the rails to the right measurement with a hacksaw if needed. There are metal clips attached to the edge of the door; they hold it square until it's fastened in the wood jamb with the screws provided. Just drive the screws into the predrilled holes you'll find. A variable-speed drill and Phillips bit will make this an easy task.

When the door is secure, remove the clips. The door will now swing open on the hinges. You must drill three holes through the door to install the lock. Use the old storm door for a guide so the lock will not interfere with the exterior door knob. You will need two holes for the screws that secure the inside and outside portions of the lock. The third hole, midway between the screw holes, allows the plunger rod to fit through the door. Use the interior portion of the lock as a template to find the proper position for the holes.

Install the door latch at a height to match the lock. The latch is screwed into the wood door frame. An extra metal shim is provided so the latch may be adjusted outward if necessary.

Drill two holes at the top of the door, using a ⅛" bit, and secure the door side (the shaft) of the closer. Now, with the door open to 90°, screw the frame-side bracket into the top of the door frame. The retaining chain fits onto the closer to prevent accidental override, and subsequent door damage. There is a spring that merely holds the retaining chain up, so that it won't interfere with the closing of the door. The spring is fastened about midway into the chain, then into the top of the wood frame with a nail.

Slight adjustments may have to be made at the latch, closer, or retaining chain. Open and shut the door, and note and adjust for any misfit.

The bottom of the door is sealed by adding a metal door shoe with a rubber gasket to both sides of the door. On some models there is an adjustable rail that seals by loosening screws, slipping the rail tight to the sill, then retightening the screws.

Check to make sure door strips and insulation are in top condition to prevent drafts. Insulation that has lost its resiliency will not be effective, even when snug. To test insulation strips, run your hand along them. If they're soft and do not snap back, replace them. Similar material is available in rolls at hardware stores. Be sure when tacking up new strips that the door is firmly closed and the strip is tacked against pressure—the pressure that will become the seal against drafts.

Metal weatherstripping may become crimped, torn, or ripped off. A missing piece of weatherstripping, no matter how short, is the equivalent of a hole in the wall. Available in packages to do one door, weatherstripping is inexpensive. The package contains small nails for installing the stripping, plus a small section that fits behind the strike plate.

Door molding and trim is often responsible for draft problems also. Spaces can become quite wide, so don't delay reseating them and caulking the crack line.

Door saddles will also become dislodged in winter, as a result of contraction. These hardwood thresholds must be exactly positioned, especially when they're integrated with the door's weather-stripping. It is easy enough to nail them in place, following the old outline against the floor. Holes will have to be predrilled before nailing in order to avoid cracking.

When repositioning other types of door saddles, just make sure that the felt or rubber strips on the bottom edges of doors hug the saddles when closed.

Latches and locks for windows and doors, if not installed or used correctly, won't hold these important elements shut, allowing drafts to enter. Therefore, examine all of the closing actions to determine that there is no play after the click. If so, this slack can be taken up by moving the latch bar or strike plate, as indicated. When the door clicks shut after that, it will be firmly closed.

HOW TO INSTALL COMBINATION WINDOWS

You can install aluminum combination storm and screen windows to cut winter heating bills and summer air conditioning costs. These windows have a triple-track frame that lets the glass and screen panels slide up for storage and tilt for removal. Dealers carry them in stock sizes to fit most stanadard windows or will custom-make them for odd-sized windows.

MEASURING Measuring the opening is your first step. The "W" width is between the side casings, the "H" between the head and sill. Do the measuring carefully and use the proper dimensions when you order.

INSTALLATION Installing the windows is easy. Begin by standing the window upright against the outside wall and removing the protective cardboard. IMPORTANT: Don't remove the glass or screen panels or the shipping clips (at the center of the window) that lock them in place until the window is completely installed.

Trimming the sides or bottom This may be necessary to fit the window in the opening. If the window is too wide or too high, scribe along one of the V grooves on the side or bottom fins with a sharp tool and break off whatever width is needed with pliers. File off the burr that remains and check the fit of the window in the opening.

Caulking the opening This is your next step. Lay a narrow bead of caulk on the outside of the blind stop on the head and the stops on the sides; its purpose is to seal the window in the opening and prevent air leaks. The blind stops are the wood strips that hold in the rear sash of a double-hung window and form the outer ridge of the channel in which it moves. The new windows are installed on the outsides of these strips.

Installing the window Do this now, keeping glass, screen, and shipping clips in place. Check the fit of the window in the opening to make sure it bears snugly against the blind stops.

Fastening the window Next, using the aluminum wood screws that come with it fasten the window. Drill ⅛" holes for these—located ⅛" from the outside edge of the frame. Fasten a screw on both sides of each corner and one in each side of the frame, clustered from top to bottom. Use two screws at the bottom of the frame to hold it to the sill.

Removing the shipping clips Use a screwdriver to remove the shipping clips, and the installation is done.

HOW TO REPAIR WINDOWS

If you have old, loose, wooden double-hung windows that let drafts in whenever it's windy, there is an easy, permanent cure. Install aluminum channels on each side of the window opening to serve as new tracks for the sash. The new channels will also eliminate such troublesome mechanisms such as sash weights and worn-out spring balances.

The channels do not require any ordinary devices to hold the sash in position. Instead, the parting bead (the center ridge separating the tracks) presses against the sides of the sash so that they stay put, wherever you leave them. Here's how to install the new channels.

First, pry off the inside stop strips on the sides and top that hold the sash in place. Using a 1" wide chisel, start at one end of a strip and gently pry it up ¼" at each nail until you come to the end of the strip. Then work back the other way, prying the nails out ½". By the time you reach the end of the strip, it should come away easily, undamaged, for reinstallation later. If you have an old-type window with parting strips, remove these; also, remove excess paint buildup. You can then remove the two sashes, first disconnecting them from the sash weights by removing the chains or cutting the cords. The weights will then drop down into the pockets. If you wish, you can open the pocket doors and remove them, but this isn't really necessary.

Next, remove the pulleys. You may simply unscrew them. If they balk, simply hammer them into the pockets. The new channels will cover the holes they leave. If there are spring balances and metal tracks, remove both.

Also, cut ½" recesses on both sides, in the top parting strip where it butts against the sides of the

window opening. This enables the channels to fit snugly against the top of the window opening.

Now, stand the two sashes on a flat surface. Then push the channels onto their sides. The parting bead in each channel will cause the channels to lock firmly to the sash sides. Pick up this assembly and place it in the window opening. Insert the bottom section first, so that it butts against the outside stop strip, then ease in the top.

See if the windows work properly. Push the sash up and down. If they stop when you take away your hands, they're okay. If they don't move freely enough, gently pry along the length of the flanges, or channel lips, to push them outward slightly. If too loose, push in the lips, along their full length, using the handle of the knife.

Secure the channels. Leave about ¹/₃₂" clearance between the outside stop and the channels. First, nail in the top of the channels, then lift up the sash and nail the channels at the bottom. Replace the inside stops or trim, again leaving about ¹/₃₂" clearance, to allow further adjustment if needed.

The channels can be installed so they can be later removed, allowing the sash to come out for easier painting. Use Number 6 flathead screws, two for each channel, one at the top and one at the bottom. Trim can also be installed with screws. On the side stops, put one 8" from the top and another 8" from the bottom. Use two screws for the top stop.

STUCK WINDOWS To repair a stuck window, examine the upper and lower sash. The flat wooden molding on the inside of the window that holds the lower sash in place is called the inside stop. The square-looking piece between upper and lower sash is called the parting strip. Find the spot where the lower sash is jammed against the inside

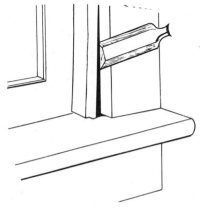

Use broad chisel or screwdriver to pry stop strip from window frame, starting at bottom.

Above: Block of wood, cut to window-groove width, is gently tapped along groove to expand frame. Below: Remove T strips, working down from top with sash closed; slide sash to top, free lower end of T strip.

stop and hammer in a floor or glazier's chisel about ½" at this point. Then rock the handle of the chisel back and forth several times. Only a slight pull is needed. Repeat the chisel-inserting process in at least two places on each side of the sash or wherever it appears to be tightly jammed. This will pry the sash and the stop apart and should break the window free of any paint bond.

When the lower sash is free, slide it up to the top of the window. If it jams on the way, insert the chisel again, and repeat the procedure. The upper sash can be made to move in the same manner. Never use a screwdriver instead of a chisel.

When you know that a window has been immobilized by paint, insert the chisel under the bottom of the sash. It is also good, especially if enamel has been used, to cut through any paint binding the sash to the stop with a sharp, pointed knife.

Another technique is to expand the window frame itself. Lay a small block of wood in the groove above the sash, then tap the block sharply with a hammer. Slide the block along the groove, tapping as you go. Repeat on the opposite side. The fractional amount of space you may gain is often enough to free the sash. You may be able to jar the sash free by laying a block of wood against the sash itself and moving it slowly up and down

while tapping the block lightly with a hammer. Use caution: Limit the force of your blows, or you may crack a pane or two.

If none of these methods works, it may be necessary to remove the sash from the window frame entirely. Work from the bottom with your chisel. Pry out ⅛" of the stop strip at one side, then move on to the next nail. Do not try to pry it all out at one place. Do it little by little.

With the strip gone, you can easily pull the sash out of the opposite groove. Lift out the sash, and then remove the sash cord from both sides.

Plane the sash lightly, frequently testing it for fit by putting it back into the groove. When it has been made to fit well, push it to the desired position, then reset the strip slightly farther from the sash than it was before. Nails should be pulled through the back of the strip to avoid damaging the finish. Treat the newly bared edges of the sash with a wood preservative or linseed oil. Sandpaper the interior of the groove and immediately apply a preservative there too, and follow with a treatment of floor wax or melted candle wax as a lubricant.

Occasionally a window fitted with metal weatherstripping will stick. The cause may be damage to the strip or it has come loose from the frame. To remove the sash, it may be necessary to first remove one of the metal T strips on the groove of the frame. Handle the strip gently to avoid kinks. Pliers can straighten it, and new nails will hold it fast.

When removing a window from its frame, take firm hold of the sash cord, remove it from the slot into which it fits, and lay aside the sash. Then tie the cord around a stick of wood and let the rope gently slide into its socket over the pulley. Remember that the weight is substantial. If released suddenly it will snap the rope into the pulley socket beyond recovery.

REPLACING GLASS Putting in a new pane of glass is relatively simple. The importance of a good glass cutter cannot be overemphasized. Buy one that makes a steady sound as it scores a line on the glass. Keep your cutter in good condition by storing it in a glass jar resting on a pad of cloth or felt, soaking in kerosene that extends about 1" over this pad. The pad protects the wheel from nicks, and the kerosene prevents rust.

Before cutting glass, clean it. Dust or grit will interfere with the cutting wheel. Cover your working surface with a single layer of blanket or rug, or several layers of newspaper. A china marking crayon or a piece of sharpened soapstone is ideal for marking a guideline on the reverse side of the glass.

You need a metal straightedge for a cutting guide. A good method to anchor it is to drive two brads into the table and set the guide against them.

When cutting heavy glass or mirrors, prepare path of cutter by painting on kerosene to cool glass at point of cut, to increase life of cutter.

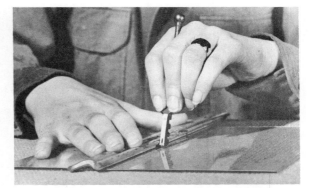

For scoring line, hold cutter at right angles to glass and slant in direction of cut. Use even pressure. A good cut makes a ripping sound.

Place glass over guide, or pencil, and snap with a gentle downward pressure. Long pieces of glass can best be separated over a straightedge. Press down firmly and confidently.

To remove narrow strips, score, then fit notched edge of cutter over glass and snap downward. Slivers too thin to be grasped are separated with chipping teeth after cutting.

Hold the glass cutter firmly, in a more perpendicular position than you would hold a pencil. Keep the cutting wheel away from the body. The cutting line starts just inside the far edge of the glass. Use even pressure and draw the cutter toward the near edge slowly and deliberately, so that the cutter makes steady sound, which indicates the quality and depth of the cut. You will gradually learn to cut by the sound of it as well as the feel.

After the line is scored, gently tap the underside of the glass near the edge, below the cut. Use the reverse end of the cutter. This will start the cleavage, or split. The split will continue through the entire length of the glass if the break is forced by pressure. Another way to complete the break is to place a pencil or guide on the table under the scored line on the glass and press gently down on

each side of the line. Cut only one line at a time.

The cutting procedure is the same with heavier types of glass, such as mirrors and plate glass — with this exception: Apply a thin film of lubricating oil on the line to be cut. In the case of mirrors, do not apply oil to the backing side, as it may damage the reflective material.

To replace a broken window pane, the first step often proves to be the hardest: removal of the remaining shreds of glass and the old putty from the frame. The glass can usually be lifted out by hand (protected with heavy gloves), but only very old putty will come away easily. A soldering iron or electrical paint remover will often provide enough heat to soften the putty. If you work fast, you can scrape it away before it cools and resets. Take out the old glazier's points along with the putty.

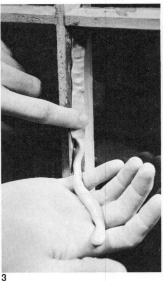

1

2

3

4

5

1. *Remove broken bits of glass with glove-protected hands. Remove old putty by softening with heat, then scraping off.*

2. *Paint groove of frame with linseed oil, then lay in a bed of putty or glazier's compound about ⅛" thick all around. Layer of putty cushions glass and seals out air.*

3. *Putty should have the consistency of thick, dry dough. To soften, add linseed oil and knead on a piece of glass.*

4. *Run small ribbon of putty inside opening all around and press glass into putty. Insert two glazier's points at each side to hold glass in position and tap them halfway into wood.*

5. *Insert glazier's points about every 4". Start points with finger pressure, then drive them in about halfway with chisel. Slide chisel along surface of pane.*

HOW TO PAINT INTERIORS

Because no single type of paint works well on all surfaces, a variety of special-purpose paints is available. Choosing the right type for the job is very important. Many paints acquire their name from a pigment-carrying liquid vehicle base. Three of the most common vehicles are alkyd, latex, and oil.

Alkyd paints, available in both enamels and flats, produce tough, durable, and quick-drying paint films. They have good gloss retention and produce strong, tight paint films for use in areas where surface moisture, caused by high humidity conditions, is common.

Alkyds are excellent for kitchens and bathrooms, have very good leveling properties and exceptional resistance to yellowing. They need no primer,

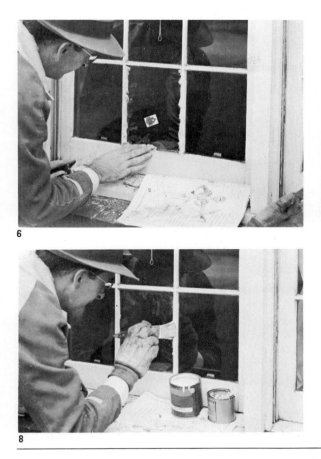

6

7

8

6. *Roll putty into a ½″ thick rope and lay it along all four sides. The easiest way to apply putty is with the fingers, pressing it against wood and glass.*
7. *Your putty knife now takes over and smooths out fingerprints, stripping off excess putty. Putty surface should be smooth, unbroken, and firmly sealed.*
8. *Any exterior grade, oil-base paint can be applied over the putty immediately.*

leave no lap or brush marks, and may be applied by brush, roller, or spray. Their washability and marring resistance are excellent. Alkyds may be thinned with mineral spirits or a similar solvent. Read labels for proper thinning directions.

Enamels use a varnish vehicle rather than raw oil and produce a smooth, hard film. There are various types of enamels, each having different properties. With all enamels, a smooth undercoat is necessary to obtain a first-class finish. This undercoat is a flat paint, specially formulated to flow out smoothly and leave no brush marks.

Interior enamels and their finish lusters are termed *high gloss, semigloss* and *flat.* The difference between high gloss and semigloss lies in the relative proportions of pigment and binder. The greater the proportion of binder, the higher the gloss. Flat enamel produces a dull, soft finish and is sometimes used as an undercoat for high-gloss enamel.

Exterior enamel, much tougher than interior enamel, is used for porch floors, boats, machinery, outdoor furniture, and other outdoor surfaces.

Latex paints are favorites with houseowners. In addition to being tough and durable, they are easy to apply and cleanup is just a matter of washing with soap and warm water. Some latex paints are specially formulated for exterior use, others for interior application.

Perhaps the easiest of any type of paint to apply, latex flows well when applied with rollers, brushes, or guns. It adheres to plaster, old paint, wallpaper, wallboard, brick, concrete block, wood, or primed metals. Latex paints dry very quickly; a second coat may be applied in a couple of hours, if needed. The emulsions in the latex paints provide a tight, impervious film that will not permit dirt to become embedded. Latex paints may be applied over fresh plaster (don't attempt to do this with oil-base paints); you can touch up spots that were missed without leaving marks, and lap marks don't show.

SPRAY CAN TECHNIQUES

1

2

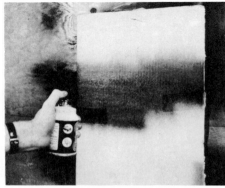

3

4

5

6

1. *Test spray pattern against cardboard before starting work. Measure distance from target, and note the spread of the sprayed pattern.*

2. *Start coverage of surface at left and work to right evenly. Carry spray on past end of work, and then release button to stop it.*

3. *Second stroke overlaps the first by about one-third. Maintain equal distance from work at all times for uniform application.*

4. *If spray is tilted at an angle while spraying, paint piles up and runs badly. Right-angle position is best for flat work.*

5. *After spraying, turn can upside down and press button once or twice. This frees feeder tube and valve, prevents clogging of orifice.*

6. *Removable trigger on some cans ensures nonclogging, since trigger can be cleaned after use. Thinner or solvent will clean it.*

7. *In spraying a chest of drawers, open drawers about ¼" so that all the edges are completely painted.*

8. *Turn chairs upside down to spray inner surfaces of legs and rungs, then outer edges. Then spray upper portion.*

PREPARATION TECHNIQUES Some people love painting the inside of a house. But often the same homeowners who tackle other do-it-yourself tasks with relish will shy away from the brush or roller. They may have good reason. A bewildering number of products are available to choose from. Plus, both preparation for painting and clean-up can be drudgery unless you know the best way to do it.

The "tricks of the trade" from professionals shown here won't make painting like going to the movies, but they will make the job easier, and your results more professional.

Set up the night before Painting can be tiresome. One way to make it easier is to set up the room properly the night before, if you can. If you start moving furniture the morning you're going to paint, you'll be tired before you dip the brush. Try to clear the room of furniture. If you can't, clear out all the portable items and move all heavy stuff to the center of the room. You should be able to reach the center of the room from your ladder. Test before you start putting down dropcloths. Cover everything and don't forget to make dropcloth paths— newspapers work well—wherever you expect to walk during the job. Otherwise paint is sure to fall on a dropcloth and your shoes will carry it into other rooms.

Cover up to save time It's much easier to cover up than to clean up paint splatters. Masking tape in widths of ½" and 2" will handle most masking jobs. You can also buy pregummed masking paper in 3" widths, wide enough to cover modern trim and

In spraying a finish on wicker work, spray is held at a 45° angle so that paint is not forced through the crease opening.

base. Consider investing in a canvas dropcloth. A 9' × 12' size sells for about ten dollars. The canvas will soak up paint spills and won't stick to your feet or slip as plastic will.

Also buy a roll of 1 mil poly plastic, 8' wide, to

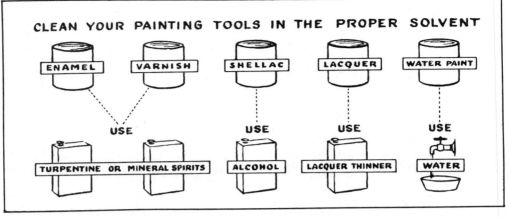

CLEAN YOUR PAINTING TOOLS IN THE PROPER SOLVENT

ENAMEL | VARNISH | SHELLAC | LACQUER | WATER PAINT

USE | USE | USE | USE

TURPENTINE OR MINERAL SPIRITS | ALCOHOL | LACQUER THINNER | WATER

Proper cleaning of painting tools will keep them in shape for the next job.

use as a covering. For ceilings, cover the floor completely with dropcloth, old sheets, or newspapers. Then mask around the ceiling edge, using 2" masking tape. Tack tape lightly at the top edge, leaving the bottom loose. Then slide poly plastic sheets under the tape and press firmly. Allow the 8' width of the plastic to drape over walls, woodwork, and furniture.

SELECT GOOD EQUIPMENT For average jobs, you'll need a couple of nylon bristle brushes, one 1" to 2" wide for small jobs and trim, one 3" to 4" wide for walls and large areas. If you plan to use varnish or enamel, buy a brush with pure hog bristles—they won't leave brush marks on shiny finishes. Buy a 9" wide roller frame rather than the smaller 7" model. Pay attention to the roller covers. Quality covers with a medium-to-long nap will carry more to the wall and leave fewer roller marks than the roller with a short nap. If you intend to roll enamel or varnish, you can buy a mohair roller cover to do the job right.

MATCH PAINT TO THE JOB Latex paints provide a finish that's flatter but generally less washable than oil-based paints. Problem walls or ceilings look better with flat finish paints. Sheen or gloss collects more light and magnifies, rather than hides, defects. High gloss in a ceiling, usually the largest unbroken surface in the house, emphasizes harsh lighting. This is why ceilings are spray textured, or painted with specially formulated paints called ceiling flat whites. Latexes offer easy application and cleanup with water. Flat oils provide low gloss, are washable, and must be thinned and cleaned with mineral spirits or other solvents. Enamels are highly moisture resistant, clean easily, but lack the ability to hide defects as well.

CONSIDER EFFECTS OF COLOR Recent studies show you will feel several degrees warmer in a room that is decorated with warm colors, wood tones, and furnishings. For example, tests at Kansas State University show persons in a room with wood paneling, red carpeting, comfortable furniture, and pictures on the walls felt warmer by 2½°F. than those in a room with white walls and spartan furnishings. Keep in mind that reds, yellows, and oranges are considered warm; blues, greens, and white are cool tones, no matter where you live.

THE EFFECTS OF COLORS

How to choose colors

Light Colors reflect more light; seem lighter in weight; make things seem farther away; make you feel cheerful.

Dark Colors absorb light; seem heavy; make things seem smaller; make things seem closer; depress you if used on surfaces too large.

Bright Colors seem larger in area than they actually are; attract the eye—are sometimes used to draw attention away from unattractive features; are distracting.

Warm Colors (reds, oranges, yellows, yellow-greens) seem to advance toward you; convey the feeling of warmth; are stimulating.

Cool Colors (blues, violets, blue-greens, blue-grays) make things seem cooler; seem to retreat from you; are subduing.

Darker color on walls pulls them together, creating feeling of intimacy. Large rooms can be made smaller, in effect, with this simple treatment.

Spaciousness is created by light background along side wall and a dark end wall. Note dark background for display pieces on shelves.

The light reflectance of various colors

Do you wish to make the most of the natural and artificial light within a room? Or do you wish to soften the sky glare that sometimes enters through large glass areas? Remember, dark colors absorb light, while light ones reflect it. This chart will help determine the colors that reflect the most light.

White	80%	Salmon	53%
Ivory (light)	71%	Pale apple green	51%
Apricot-beige	66%	Medium gray	43%
Lemon yellow	65%	Light green	41%
Ivory	59%	Pale blue	41%
Light buff	56%	Deep rose	12%
Peach	53%	Dark green	9%

KNOW HOW TO DOCTOR PAINT A drop or two of black pigment such as lampblack added to a white paint will make it appear whiter. But if ceilings, for example, are badly soiled, you can "gray down" the white paints slightly by adding as much as 1 ounce of lampblack. The lampblack is available at your paint dealer in 1 ounce tubes. You can gray a white paint with as much as 1 ounce of lampblack per gallon, and the ceiling will still look white when it dries.

For texture, you can add Perltex to latex paint. Perltex, an aggregate similar to fine sand, is available in small packages. The amount you add depends on how heavy a texture you want. Test by rolling a sample on cardboard or a scrap of wallboard. You can also buy powder textures to mix with latex. Among the more widely available brands are Dramex and Textone. For a light stipple finish, the powder is mixed with water, then latex is added. A little Water Lox transparent sealer

added to latex gives a more washable paint. It's a tung oil sealer you can also use on masonry, stone, cement drives, or walks.

MAKE REPAIRS BEFORE YOU START Fill nail holes and small cracks with spackle. Patch plaster and renail and finish any popped nails in drywall. If you have ridged seams in dry walls, you can minimize the ridging by troweling a thin coat of ready-mixed taping cement or spackle down each side of the ridged seams. Sand all repair areas lightly, and prime before starting the finish paint coat. NOTE: Patch plaster normally has a working life of about ten minutes. To retard the setting time, add a little vinegar to the plaster after it's mixed. The vinegar will give you thirty minutes extra time before plaster hardens.

CLEAN SURFACES THOROUGHLY Most dirt and grease on surfaces to be painted will yield to household detergents. If you have a particularly tough cleaning job, ask your paint dealer or building supply outlet to suggest a good cleaner. One is called Triko. If you can't find it, write the Proko Co., P.O. Box 15766, Dallas, Texas 75215. It will do a good job of cleaning difficult surfaces where dirt and grease have built up for years. If you're repainting enameled woodwork, sand the old finish lightly to destroy the gloss finish of the paint. Wipe the sanded surface with a tack rag, and coat it with a "liquid sander" before applying new paint. This provides a superior base for the new paint, and helps eliminate peeling.

USE PRIMERS AND SEALERS These products provide *hold out* of the finish paint. A wall that is porous will have what professionals call high suction, which is an unusually high rate of paint absorption. The absorption rate may vary over a sin-

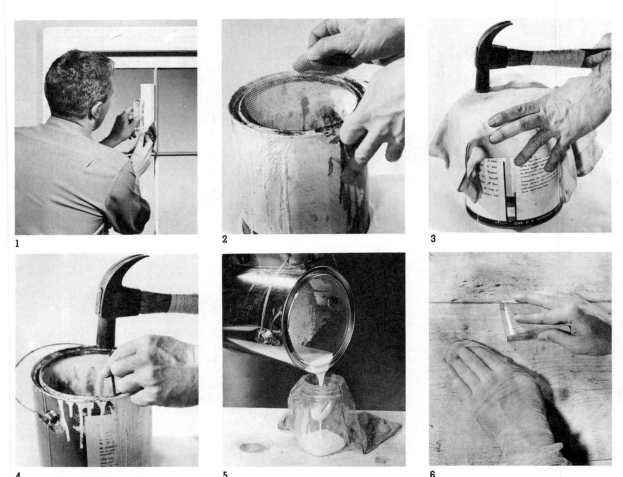

1. *Shields of metal, wood, or cardboard are useful in keeping paint where it belongs when you are painting windows, woodwork, or trim and save tedious cleanup.*

2. *With old paint that has become lumpy this is a real boon: Cut a piece of wire screen to fit can. Mix paint, drop in screen. It sinks, carries lumps with it.*

3. *To avoid splattering when you hammer back the lid on a paint can, drape a cloth over the lid. You'll save yourself, and clothes, from a dosage of paint.*

4. *A series of holes punched around the bottom of the lid groove will enable paint to drop back into the can. Paint will not splatter or run over when lid is replaced.*

5. *Cheesecloth is good for straining paint, but an old nylon stocking makes the best strainer. It is lintless and ideal for this job and may be used for varnish, too.*

6. *Here is another use for old nylons. Slip one over your hand to detect any roughness (which will snag the stocking) so that you may sand it down for a glasslike finish.*

gle wall or ceiling. If painted unprimed, the paint is absorbed into the wall unequally and the finish will appear thin or patchy. Finish paint should not soak in, but lie on the surface evenly as a film. Latex paints are in some instances self-sealing, allowing you to paint new gypsum wallboard with two coats. You should use a latex or vinyl sealer as a first coat on gypsum wallboard if you intend to use an oil-base paint such as an alkyd or an enamel for the finish coat.

TREAT NEW WOOD RIGHT If you're finishing new wood, stain it, apply a sanding sealer, then putty the nail holes. Seal the wood before puttying because the oil in the putty will soak into the wood around the nail hole, leaving what looks like an irregular wet spot. When the sanding sealer is dry, sand woodwork lightly with the grain, then apply varnish. Safety note: The fumes from lacquer and some varnishes and enamels can be highly volatile. Be sure to turn down the thermostat so the furnace doesn't suck the fumes into the heating system.

7 **8** **9**

7. You'll find that drilling a few large holes in a paddle used for mixing paints helps to stir them thoroughly. Enamels, particularly, must be very well mixed.

8. Glue a paper plate to the bottom of a paint can to catch drippings. You can then move the can anywhere while on the job without cleanup, after you're through working.

9. To prevent skin forming on paint, pour a little turpentine over paint, making sure it floats on the surface. Stir turpentine in when you're ready to paint.

INTERIOR PAINTING METHODS

Flat paint used on walls will give rooms a soft, pleasing appearance. It has no shine or gloss and is by far the most popular finish for bedroom, living room, and dining room walls. Semigloss and eggshell enamels have a slight sheen and are popular for woodwork and for walls that are frequently washed. Since semigloss is its own best primer, two coats will provide an excellent finish if one coat doesn't do the job. Kitchens and bathrooms, which receive a lot of scrubbing, are usually painted with high-gloss paint or enamel for a hard, washable finish. If you use enamel, you might encounter difficulty with a roller; most handymen will find it easier to use a 4" to 6" brush on ceilings and walls. However, flat and semigloss paints are adaptable to either brush or roller.

Left: *Dip paintbrush about half the length of the bristles. If paint is allowed to run back into the heel of the brush, it will harden and be difficult to remove.*

Center: *Lightly wipe off excess paint against the side of the can. Deeper dipping is a waste of paint, leads to splattering; hold brush so loaded bristles are down.*

Right: *Keep all painting strips on the wall narrow so that you are always working with a wet edge. Failure to observe this rule will result in unsightly lap marks on wall.*

Lay on paint with short, slightly curved strokes, lifting the brush gradually at the end of each stroke. Do not apply paint by using brush in just one direction.

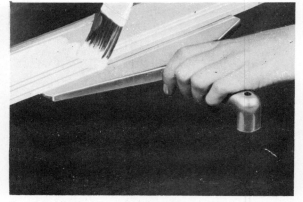

A paint shield will protect your floors when painting the baseboard or the bottom of a door. If any paint splatters on floor, wipe it off immediately with a rag.

The task of painting a room is speeded up considerably if one person "cuts in" around woodwork, and so on, with a brush and a second uses a roller for large wall areas.

Rubber-base paints are self-sealing and usually require no prime coat. With other paints, new plaster may absorb oil from top coat and leave an uneven appearance.

Provide adequate ventilation to allow fumes to escape.

PAINT WHAT YOU CAN REACH When you stretch you strain, and when you strain you'll miss spots. This rule also applies when painting windows. If you aren't tall enough to paint the top of a window without straining, use a ladder. It will make a surprising difference in how fast a job goes. You can roll ceilings, after proper cover-up, using a 4' extension handle screwed into the handle of your paint roller. Set the roller pan on the floor, dip paint, and roll. Remember to leave protective plastic in place until paint dries sufficiently to be sure you've gotten full coverage.

Keep in mind it's much easier to paint a straight line at corners or trim with a wide brush than with a narrow one. Use a 3" to 4" brush at corners, and paint with a bold, even stroke. Set the brush at the

edge of the corner or trim, and move along with a single flowing motion. You'll get a straighter, cleaner edge.

PAINT FROM DRY INTO THE WET Most people start a new brush stroke from the wet edge of the previously painted area. This is wrong. Dip your brush in the paint and start your stroke about a foot or so from the wet edge of the previously painted area, and paint back toward it until you overlap. In this way you cover the maximum dry area with each stroke. If you start from the wet edge you will have a tendency to go over the same area again and again. This wastes paint, time, and energy. The idea is to cover the most dry area with the fewest strokes possible. This also applies to using rollers.

LEARN TO HANDLE ROLLERS Paint rollers have a tendency to dump their paint load in the first

TO PAINT A DOOR

TO PAINT A WINDOW

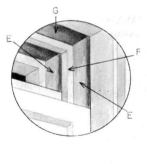

1. *Remove as much of the door hardware (A) as possible.*
2. *After window panes have been masked for protection, paint the muntin bars (B). These are the small wood trim pieces holding the glass in place. Paint the horizontal ones first.*
3. *The molding edges (C) around any inset wood panels in the door are painted next. If any paint overlaps the edges, wipe it off with a turpentine-dampened cloth.*
4. *The inset panels (D) are painted by using long vertical brush strokes over the entire panel.*
5. *The wide horizontal parts of the door (E), called the rails, are now painted, working the brush across the door.*
6. *Complete the job of door painting after you have applied the paint to the vertical end pieces (F), the door stiles.*

1. *Move the bottom section of the window all the way up and pull the top sash part of the way down. Paint the check rail (A), that is, the bottom horizontal piece of the top sash.*
2. *Protect the window panes and paint the muntin bars (B), using the same technique as for the door. That is, cover the horizontal pieces first.*
3. *The stiles (C), the vertical sides of each sash, are painted next.*
4. *The top rail (D) of the upper sash is painted, and so is the top rail of the bottom sash.*
5. *The side jamb (E) and the parting strip (F) are now painted, as is the head jamb (G).*
6. *Raise the bottom sash until the bottom rail (H) just clears the apron (K). Paint the bottom rail and apron.*

area of contact with the wall. First, with a full roller, paint a 3' or so wide W on the top third of the wall. Come back and fill in with horizontal strokes, then go up and down over this small area with an undipped roller. You should only have to load the roller once during the operation.

With the top third filled in, do the middle third of the strip, then the bottom third. After you finish each 3' wide strip, go back to the previously painted strip and make floor-to-ceiling vertical strokes with an unloaded roller. This rolls out excess paint and catches any "holidays" (missed spots). The same procedure can be used for ceilings.

DON'T BE AFRAID OF GLASS Painting windows neatly and quickly is not only a matter of experi-

ence; there are some tricks that can help. Don't be afraid of getting paint on glass. Rather, paint boldly. Get a good amount of paint on the bristle tips, wipe on the edge of the can very lightly and paint. TIP: Position your body at an oblique or off-to-the-side angle when painting mullion. This lets you see more wood surface than if you stand directly in front. If you get paint on glass—and you will—simply wipe it off with a rag while it's wet.

SAVE ON CLEANUP TIME If you're going to paint the next day, you can save time by using a paint stick or scraper to squeeze excess paint out of a roller or brush, and wrapping it tightly in clinging plastic wrap. The tools should stay soft until the next morning. Once you're done, store cleaned

PAINTS, SEALERS, AND COATINGS—WHAT PAINT TO USE—AND WHERE

Surface	Coating
Plaster walls and ceilings	Flat, latex, emulsion paints, sealer, or undercoater
Wallboard	Flat, latex, emulsion paints, sealer or undercoater
Wood paneling	Flat, latex, interior varnish, shellac, wax, stain, wood sealer, floor varnish, sealer, or undercoater
Kitchen and bathroom walls	Flat, semigloss,* enamel,* latex paints, wax, sealer, or undercoater
Wood floors	Interior varnish, shellac, wax, stain, wood sealer, floor varnish, floor paint or enamel,* sealer, or undercoater
Concrete floors	Floor paint or enamel,* sealer, or undercoater
Rubber tile floors	Wax, floor varnish
Asphalt tile floors	Wax, floor varnish, floor paint, or enamel
Linoleum	Wax, floor varnish, floor paint, or enamel
Stair treads	Interior varnish, shellac, wax, stain, floor varnish, wood sealer, floor paint, or enamel,* sealer, or undercoater

Surface	Coating
Stair risers	Flat, semigloss,* latex paints, interior varnish, shellac, wax, stain, wood sealer, floor varnish, sealer, or undercoater
Wood trim	Semigloss,* enamel,* latex paints, interior varnish, shellac, wax, stain, wood sealer, floor varnish, sealer, or undercoater
Steel windows	Enamel,* metal primer
Aluminum windows	Shellac, metal primer
Window sills	Semigloss,* enamel,* latex paints, interior varnish, shellac, wax, stain, wood sealer, floor varnish
Steel cabinets	Semigloss,* enamel,* latex paints, metal primer
Heating ducts	Flat paint, aluminum paint, metal primer
Radiators and heating pipes	Flat paint
Old masonry	Cement base paint, sealer, or undercoater
New masonry	Cement base paint, sealer or undercoater

Primer or sealer may be necessary before finish coat, unless previously applied

brushes by wrapping the bristle with the cardboard wrap the brush came in, to keep bristle from spreading. Hang brushes from a hook through the hole in the brush handle. To keep yourself free of paint spatters, wear a long-sleeved shirt and a paint hat. It will be much easier to clean the paint off your hands if you apply a hand cream before painting. A lanolin-based hand cream product is effective in removing dried paint from skin.

FLAT OR GLOSS? Flat paint will give rooms a soft, pleasing appearance. Semigloss and eggshell enamels have a slight sheen and are popular for woodwork and walls that are frequently washed. Semigloss is its own best primer, and two coats will provide an excellent finish if one will not do the job.

Kitchens and bathrooms, which receive a lot of scrubbing, are usually painted with high-gloss paint or enamel for a hard, washable finish. If you use enamel, you might encounter difficulty with a roller; most handymen find it easier to use a 4" to 6" brush on ceilings and walls. A flat-nap roller cover has been found to work acceptably on some enamels also.

Flat and semigloss paints are adaptable to either brush or roller application.

INTERIOR PAINTING CHECKLIST

1. Determine the color scheme, amount, and type of paints to be used.
2. Remove all lightweight furniture and also light fixtures, switch plates, etc.
3. Cover the floor and remaining furniture with dropcloths.
4. Prepare the surfaces to be painted, as fully as possible:
   a. Patch plaster and cracks.
   b. Sandpaper woodwork and trim; wash with strong ammonia solution to remove gloss.

TIPS FOR FAST, PROFESSIONAL PAINTING

1. *Cover up to save time.*

4. *Match paint to the job.*

6. *Make repairs before starting.*

2. *Set up the night before.*

7. *Clean surfaces thoroughly.*

3. *Select good equipment.*

5. *Know how to doctor paint.*

8. *Use primers and sealers.*

c. Remove hardware from doors and windows, curtain rods and other obstructions, and all other removable objects not to be painted.

d. Clean ceilings and walls of calcimine, glue, and dirt with soap and water or detergent and water.

e. Remove old wallpaper completely. If wallpaper is to be painted over, test first to see if paper color bleeds through.

5. Dust entire room carefully, paying special attention to the top edges of doors and door frames.

6. Apply wall primer and sealer to unpainted plaster surfaces. Start on the ceiling and at the window end. Start walls at left side of main window frame or left-hand corner of window sills.

7. Apply enamel undercoat to woodwork. Start by applying paint to the inside of closet doors, allowing the brushes to be worked in. Make finishing brush strokes in the direction of the grain of the wood.

8. After twenty-four hours, apply finish coat to ceiling and walls if the first coat is completely dry.

9. Lightly sand enamel undercoater on woodwork and trim. Then apply finish coat. Avoid overlapping where woodwork contacts walls and floors.

PLASTIC WALL COVERINGS Extraordinarily resistant to household stains, particularly oils and greases, vinly plastic is one of the most practical materials available as a wall covering. Upkeep for a wall of vinly plastic is at a minimum. Made in the form of yard goods, tiles, simulated stone or brick, and other designs, it easily conceals wall defects and irregularities.

FABRIC WALL COVERINGS Cracks in the plas-

9. *Paint "from dry into wet."*

10. *Paint what you can reach.*

11. *Learn to handle rollers.*

12. *Don't be afraid of glass.*

13. *Save on clean-up time.*

Photos this series: **Gary Branson, Tom Philbin, Gene Schnaser**

ter, uneven ceiling lines, and spaces in the corners where the walls have settled can all be brought under control with a fabric wall covering. Available in pretrimmed 24″ widths, all you have to worry about is cutting it to the right length. The straightedge makes it easy to do a perfect butting job instead of overlapping the strips, as is done with ordinary stock. The procedure for hanging fabric wall covering is exactly the same as that for any other wallpaper.

HOW TO HANG WALLPAPER

Because of its variety, attractiveness, and ease of application, many homeowners each year turn to wallpaper when redecorating. Washable papers, many already trimmed, offer a handsome finish with long-lasting surface. Ceiling wallpapers create interesting decorative effects, and the fabric-supported type of paper not only hides imperfections in the ceiling but, as the house settles, the paper stretches and conceals minor cracks.

You can easily improvise a long table for pasting by putting a panel of plywood right over a ta-

ble or laying it between two sawhorses. You will also need a 6′ stepladder, seam roller, scissors, sponge, and razor and handle. One particularly useful tool is a metal straightedge. An aluminum yardstick or the blade of a 6″ scraper works well.

All surfaces to be wallpapered should be dry, smooth, and even. If the wall was previously papered, remove all loose paper and edges, and sand along seams to avoid ridges later. Lapped seams should be stripped with a razor, then sanded. If the wall is of plaster, check carefully for holes, bulges, and cracks; mend any defects, remembering to apply wallpaper size to new spots of plaster and any unpainted, dry, porous plaster. If the wall was enameled or finished with a glossy paint, roughen it slightly with sandpaper before papering.

If your paper is not pretrimmed, mark matching guidelines with a light pencil at both ends of the roll. Then trim off the edges, using a straightedge and razor or scissors. To cut wallpaper to size, measure the distance from ceiling to baseboard molding and add 3″ to 4″, always watching the pattern to make certain of matching edges. If a length

1

2

3

4

5

6

1. *Before starting, use a square to make sure molding falls square with the plumb line on the wall.*

2. *Level is used to establish a plumb line down the wall. Plumb line will be needed as you start each wall.*

3. *Using a rule, measure the wall for height. Paper will be cut at height of wall, plus drop in pattern.*

4. *Wallpaper is checked to determine drop in paper pattern. Paper drop is the interval at which the pattern is repeated.*

5. *Paper here has been glued, folded, or booked, at top and bottom. To book paper, fold bottom ⅓ up and fold bottom ⅓ down.*

6. *Top ⅓ of the paper is unfolded, matched to plumb line. Leave bottom ⅓ folded until top of paper is in place.*

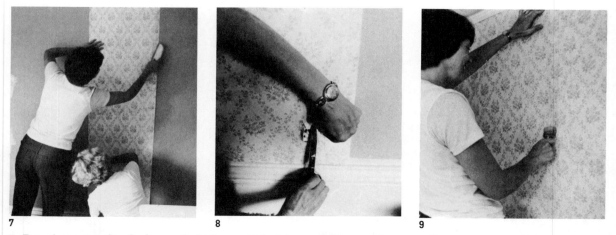

7   8   9

7. *Top of paper is brushed smooth, bottom matched to plumb line. Note which area at left is primed plaster patch.*

8. *Cut an X in paper over electric outlet. Then use scissors to cut the paper to match the edge of the outlet.*

9. *Use a roller on wallpaper seams. This step ensures a good bond at the edges of the paper. Photos this series: Gary Branson*

of wallpaper does not fit properly, it can be removed easily by just lifting it off. The paste remains pliable and doesn't dry for a few hours.

Wall preparation Prepare walls carefully. All cracks should be repaired, using fiberglass resin patch kits available, or by taping and troweling cracks as you would wallboard seams. Fill all holes and voids with patch plaster. Prime the repair areas after sanding lightly.

If you plan to apply wallpaper to new gypsumboard walls, a good sealer used by professional paperhangers is the sanding sealer designed for sealing wood. A perfect seal on the wall is an important aid in removing the paper later.

If the walls were previously oil painted or enameled, they could be washed down with a potash solution (which used to be called "pearlash"), if your dealer carries the product. A light sanding will also help. If the walls were previously waterpainted, calcimined, or whitewashed, they should be gone over with a wire brush and a strong detergent. This will assure a good clinging surface for the new covering. If the walls were previously unpainted, scrape them with a wire brush to remove all loose particles and wash with a strong detergent to remove any grease and dirt. If walls were previously papered, make sure there are no loose edges or peeling paper, and apply a coat of glue size, allowing it to dry thoroughly before applying the vinyl.

When selecting paper for a given room, keep the condition of the walls in mind. Wavy plaster walls

that are not plumb will not look well with stripes on them—the stripes will be difficult to match and will accent the wavy condition. Shiny papers also tend to accent wall imperfections.

Calculating wallpaper needs To determine the amount of paper you'll need, measure the combined distance around the room, and multiply this total by the height of the wall. Subtract the area of all doors and windows. Your wallpaper dealer will figure the number of rolls you'll need. Coverage per roll varies. To some extent it depends on the pattern and whether the rolls are single or double. The dealer will also tell you the amount of paste needed. If walls are wavy or crooked, select a paper that helps conceal the defects, and one that will be easy to match.

Hanging wallpaper Cut several sheets of paper at a time and spread them over the plywood table face down. This way any glue brushed off the edge of a sheet is spread onto another, thus keeping the work surface and the faces of the other sheets clean. Be sure edges are well covered with the paste, so that they do not come loose on the wall.

If you hang prepasted paper, you need only pull the paper through a plastic tray filled with water. The trays are available at your paper dealer.

To carry the paper to the wall, fold the paper into thirds (see photo 5, page 223). Position the top edge of the paper, align the vertical edge against the preceding piece or the plumb line, and smooth the top third onto the wall with the brush. If you get a wrinkle in the paper, just pull it away from the wall and smooth it out again.

Start papering at a corner. Establish a plumb line on the wall. Its distance from the corner should be the width of the paper, less ½″. This excess ½″ of the first strip of paper will wrap around the corner. The paper will be straight and plumb, and the ½″ is enough to allow for any irregularity at the corner. You will start the first sheet of paper plumb, and line each succeeding sheet against the first. When you turn a corner in the room you will automatically establish a new plumb line on the wall.

Trim paper by folding it at the corner, or at trim or base molding lines. Press the paper tightly into the fold, and use a metal straightedge such as a 6″ paint scraper as a guide. Cut along the guide with a paper knife, or the type of linoleum knife that uses a razor blade. Keep a fresh blade in the knife. A dull blade snags and tears.

At electric outlet boxes or heating vents, cut an X at the center of the opening, fold back the points of paper and trim along the edges of the box or vent. Leave enough paper so that the outlet or vent cover will hide the edges of the paper.

For window or door openings, hang the paper so that it extends past the trim or opening. Then carefully cut it back to the corner, at a 45° angle, and fold the paper against the wood trim. Now trim the paper as above.

You will need a special paste to hang vinyls. You may substitute a roller for a brush to apply the paste. Take care not to get paste on the face of flocked or heavily embossed papers. It will be difficult to clean up.

Keep a sponge and a pail of warm clean water handy, and wipe away extra glue from facepaper or woodwork as you proceed. You should test a small scrap of paper to be sure the dyes are colorfast before sponging them.

Don't throw away extra pieces of wallpaper. They may be useful later to cover switch and outlet plates. A screwdriver, scissors, some rubber cement, and ten minutes are all that are needed. First, take out the fuse that controls the current to the light switch box where you plan to work. Then remove the two small screws holding the plate. Line up a piece of wallpaper over the open switch box, match the paper pattern, and cut a piece 1″ larger all around than the opening. If the paper is not washable, spray it with clear plastic so that fingerprints can be easily removed.

Apply rubber cement to the back of this paper and lay it with pattern side down. Now place the plate over the back of the paper face down. With a sharp knife or razor, cut out an opening for the switch toggle. Puncture holes for the screws which hold the plate to the wall, with an ice pick or the tip of a knife. Trim corners diagonally so that there will be a smooth surface when the ½″ fold of the wallpaper is pressed over the back of the plate. Apply rubber cement liberally to hold the side pieces in place. The plate is now covered and can be put back.

You may also use leftover scraps of paper to patch any tears in the paper later. Just place a scrap, being sure you have a pattern match, over the tear. Cut through both the patching scrap and paper on the wall. Then soak the cut section around the tear loose, and carefully remove it. Put in the new piece, lightly glued, and wipe in place with a sponge. Since you cut the old and new paper together, they will be a perfect fit.

7

HOW TO: REPAIR A ROOF · REPLACE A ROOF · MAINTAIN
GUTTERS AND DOWNSPOUTS · MAINTAIN EXTERIOR
WALLS · REPLACE SIDING · CURE WET BASEMENTS · PAINT
THE EXTERIOR · MAINTAIN AND REPAIR SIDEWALKS AND
DRIVEWAYS · BUILD AND REPAIR OUTDOOR STAIRS ·
BUILD AND REPAIR FENCES · BUILD STURDY GATES ·
PATCH PIERS AND POSTS · BUILD AND REPAIR RETAINING
WALLS · SOLVE YARD FLOODING PROBLEMS · USE
GARAGES FOR STORAGE · CARE FOR YARD TOOLS
AND EQUIPMENT

THE HOME EXTERIOR

This chapter deals with the outside of your house, from top to bottom. The old adage "You can't tell a book by its cover" doesn't hold when judging a house. You can tell a good deal about a house from its roof, outer walls, and foundation.

You can tell whether the house has been well cared for or whether it's been allowed to deteriorate; whether it's watertight or damp; and whether its foundation is good and sturdy or apt to crack and let the house sag. In addition to learning about year-round maintenance and repair, you'll find in this chapter what you need to know to prevent damage and deterioration and eliminate major repairs.

HOW TO REPAIR A ROOF

Although the greater part of the roof is hidden from view, it's important that you know just how it's put together. The accompanying diagram will serve as a preliminary guide to roof terminology and maintenance.

The proper care of gutters and downspouts prevents water damage to walls and saves what may later become serious expense. Snow and ice on the roof don't have to be hazardous; safety measures are simple if they're taken in time. Effective water-repellent flashing will add years, not only to the life of the roof, but to the entire house.

ROOF LEAKS A leaky roof can cause serious damage to your house and its furnishings. A damp and discolored ceiling spells trouble, as joists can rot and ceilings can sag or fall. The first step toward effecting a cure is to locate the leak. Careful inspection of the underside of the roof above

the wet ceiling area will reveal the major leaks.

If the house has an open attic, trace trickling water to its source by the trail it leaves on the underside of the roof or along rafters. Water may run along a sheet of sheathing, down a rafter, and then along a joist. The leak may originate in the shingles, but often it is somewhere in the flashing. After finding the leak, drive a thin nail up through the shingles (unless they are slate or tile). When you are on the roof, the nail will show where the leak is.

If the house design does not allow indoor inspection of the rafters, it will be necessary to climb onto the roof and locate the leak from the outside. Look for cracked, torn, curled, and missing shingles and for openings in the flashing or other defects that could contribute to a leak. Often a leak can be located by pouring water on the suspected source of the leak while someone inside the house watches for the moisture to appear.

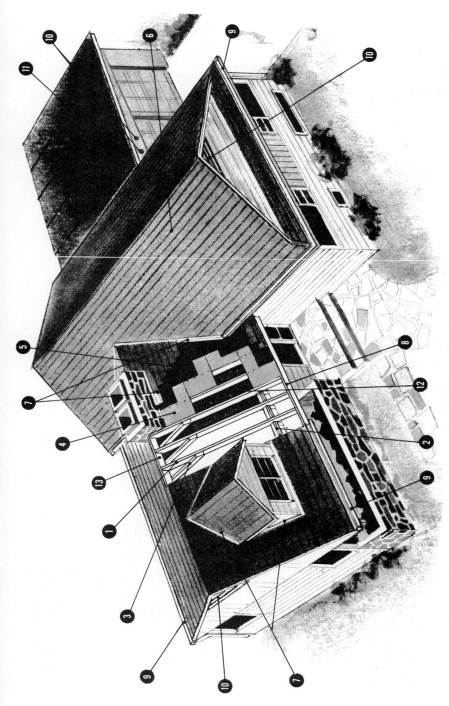

An X ray of the roof

1. Rafters—main roof supports.

2. Top plate of walls—on which rafters rest

3. Collar beam—prevents outward thrust of rafters, which would push walls apart.

4. Sheathing—covers rafters, joins them rigidly, provides support for roofing material.

5. Felt—waterproof barrier to any rain penetrating through shingles.

6. Shingles—the outer roof covering.

7. Flashing—metal lining for joints around chimney, at junctions of walls and roof, and at junction of two sections of the roof.

8. Fascia—trim strip at eaves covering rafter ends.

9. Gutters—to conduct rain from the roof to rain spouts.

10. Louvers—used to provide ventilation to the underside of the roof, and to spaces directly under the roof.

11. Roll-type roofing material—used on flat roofs and those where pitch is less than 23°, where shingles would admit rain.

12. Insulation—placed between rafters and over collar beams to keep artificial heat inside.

13. Ridge—board between upper rafter ends, joining sets to each other.

Small breaks in shingles can be patched with asphalt roof cement.

To remove broken shingle, pry up next one above to get at shingle nails.

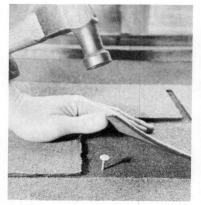

Nail down new shingle by carefully raising edges of shingle above.

If old shingles are brittle, press nail in with thumb, then drive it as shown.

To repair hip covering, apply asphalt liberally as a base under new shingles.

Overlap the new shingle pieces at least 2", nailing down all four corners.

REPAIRING ASPHALT SHINGLES Minor cracks and splits in asphalt shingles can be repaired easily with roofing cement. However, these repairs are usually short-lived unless reinforced with fiberglass screen. Fill all cracks and splits with black sealer, using a small putty knife or trowel. The cement should fill the cracks and overlap slightly onto the surrounding surface. Then press fiberglass into the cement. If the crack extends under the next higher shingle, raise the shingle and repair the entire crack.

Where shingles are torn, nail down loose pieces, cover the edges of tears with cement, and dab cement over the nail heads. Shingles that have been lifted by the wind should be pressed into place and flattened. If the shingle is unbroken, put a few dabs of cement under it and press it down. If the shingle is cracked, raise its overlapping neighbors, put cement on the crack, and reposition the overlapping shingle or shingles.

Asphalt shingles that have slipped down probably have been torn loose from the nails. Raise the overlapping shingle as much as possible, reposition the loose shingle, and drive new nails—preferably in the area of overlap by the shingle above. Cement any breaks and cover the heads of the nails with cement. Replace missing or badly damaged shingles. Start by raising the next good shingle above and drawing out all the nails you can reach. Slip the new shingle into place and secure with nails under the overlap.

Shingles sometimes break in winter where they are bent over the hip of a roof. Remove the broken pieces and replace with new ones cut from whole shingles. Overlap pieces in the same manner as they were first laid, using plenty of cement be-

Slate shingles can be held down by asphalt under lower edges, with joints painted with asphalt. Knock out broken shingles with hammer.

Cracks in slate roofs can be patched with roof cement.

You may have to make a slate puller by bending and notching a piece of strap steel as shown.

To remove a slate, slide the puller under the slate and hook the notches over the nails. Then draw nails out by driving the puller with a hammer. There are two nails per slate.

If a slate must be cut to fit, first score both sides deeply with a screwdriver or cold chisel.

neath the patching pieces. Small breaks in asphalt shingles can be patched with roofing cement.

To remove broken shingles, carefully raise the good shingle above and pull out all nails that can be reached. A slotted pry bar works well here. Rustproof, broad-headed roofing nails should be driven under the area of overlap from the shingle above. Cement should be applied liberally as a base for new shingles, overlapped as shown.

SLATE ROOF REPAIRS If a slate shingle is broken, remove it by using a slate puller. If you don't have one, you can make your own from strap steel, as shown in the photos. Slide the puller under the shingle, and draw the nails out. Cut the slate by first scoring both sides, tapping lightly with a hammer, and breaking by hand. Use a drill or punch to make nail holes. Cover the area with roofing cement and secure with slate roofing nails.

REPAIRING FLASHING LEAKS Flashings—the metal sheets used to close gaps between the roof and protruding elements like chimneys and vent pipes—are usually sealed at their edges with roofing cement. Sometimes because of aging of the cement, weathering, or settling of the house, gaps open between the flashing and the surface to which it is attached. The easiest way to treat these gaps is to apply liberal amounts of roofing cement, which can be purchased in caulking tubes. Nails can be used to close the gap enough so it can be sealed with roofing cement.

Hold the scored slate against a solid edge and tap lightly along scored lines with a hammer. This deepens the scoring.

Next, lay the slate flat and break along the scoring. It will break evenly, but with a ragged edge.

The ragged edge can be smoothed by tapping the edge with a hammer while holding the slate at an angle on a masonry surface.

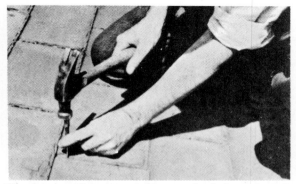

Slip the new slate into position to check fit, and mark where nail holes are to be drilled.

A drill or punch can be used to make holes for the nails. If using a punch, a single sharp blow from the hammer, while supporting the shingle, will do the job.

Finally, cover the area with roofing cement, insert the new slate, and secure with special slate roofing nails.

Vent pipes often have wraparound collars as flashing. Gaps here can usually be sealed with roofing cement. If the collar is too far gone to be repaired, replace it with a new one. If the new collar is made of metal, it can be fastened with nails and cement. Cement alone will work for vinyl or asphalt collars.

Large cracks around chimneys and pipe vents can also be mended with fiberglass cloth and roofing cement, an asphalt-asbestos mixture.

Trouble in the heavy roll roofing used for flat roofs is usually indicated by blisters that ultimately crack. Here, a blister has burst and a chunk of the roofing material has blown away.

With a linoleum knife, cut away all loose roofing surrounding the break.

Spread a liberal amount of roofing cement over the hole and uncovered edges.

Cut a new section of roofing to overlap the hole by about 4" on all sides.

Place the patch over the hole and press into the roofing cement firmly.

Spread a generous amount of roofing cement around the edges of the patch to make a good seal.

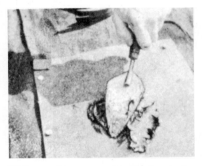

If the roof is exposed to high winds, it's also a good idea to anchor the patch with roofing nails, covering the heads with cement.

When you've finished patching, spread dry sand over the new asphalt. It helps to protect the roof from the elements.

If chimney flashings buckle and cause edges to collect water, nail gaps and seal with roofing cement. To repair long cracks in the flashing, use fiberglass screening and roofing compound.
FLAT ROOF REPAIRS A flat roof covered with heavy felt is subject to leaks just as is any shingle roof. Potential trouble is indicated by blisters in the roofing material; these blisters ultimately crack, and then a leak is in the making. See the illustrations for repair methods.

HOW TO REPLACE A ROOF

You may have enough experience to do a reroofing job yourself, or you may leave the big jobs to a contractor but make repairs and take care of maintenance yourself. In any case, you should know what materials are available and how they're applied.

How can you tell if your roof needs to be replaced? Some of the telltale signs include shingle edges that are curled or brittle; many corners may have broken off and, patches of black asphalt may show where most of the protective mineral granules have been worn away by the weather. Depending on the climate in your part of the country, you may notice some of these signs on a roof after seven to ten years.

A fifteen-year-old roof is a prime candidate for reroofing. The life expectancy of modern shingles ranges from about fifteen up to twenty-five years for thicker, specially rated types, so reroofing is not a job you have to do too often.

CHOOSING THE ROOF By far the most popular roofing material today is asphalt strip shingles. They cover more than 80 percent of the houses in the United States. Within this category there is a wide variety of color, texture, patterns, weight (or thickness) and, consequently, fire and wind resistance ratings.

Asphalt shingles The typical asphalt shingle is a square-butt strip shingle, rectangular in shape, with three sections called tabs along the lower half that are exposed to the weather. The solid upper half is spotted with asphalt which "self-seals" the tabs of the next course (or row) of shingles. They are made with either an organic (cellulose fiber) or inorganic (glass or asbestos fiber) base that's saturated and coated with asphalt and surfaced with mineral granules.

Shingle thickness is classified by weight. For instance, a 240-pound shingle means that enough roofing to cover one square (the standard measurement for roofing, which is 100 square feet) will weigh 240 pounds. A heavier shingle is not automatically better, since some of the weight may be due to a particular texture or overlapping design. But within one particular category, say a standard organic three-tab shingle, a heavier weight offers better protection, will last longer, and therefore costs more than a lighter shingle.

Aside from weight, shingles are also classified by their resistance to fire and wind. Generally, fiberglass shingles carry better fire and wind ratings as well as a longer warranty from the manufacturer. Tests for the ratings are conducted by Underwriters' Laboratory (UL), and their seal should appear with the fire rating on the shingle bundles. Ratings can range from Class C shingles, which will not readily ignite or support the spread of fire over the roof area, up to Class A fiberglass shingles, which are recommended for high fire-risk areas.

A UL wind-resistance label is attached to the bundle if the shingles can withstand at least a sixty-mph wind, continuously for two hours, without lifting. This factor is crucial in areas frequently hit by hurricanes or tornadoes. And if you live in a particularly warm and humid region, you should consider shingles made with algae-resistant granules so that your heat-reflecting white roof will stay white longer.

Other roofing materials There are many other roofing materials that can be used in place of strip shingles: wood shakes, tiles, slate, and metal sheeting (called terne roofing). Applying these materials takes more building skills and experience than most homeowners have.

Roll roofing, on the other hand, is another asphalt-based material that is used more frequently and can be mastered by the do-it-yourselfer. The 3'-wide material comes in 36'-long rolls and, like strip shingles, is available in different weights from 55 to 90 pounds per square. It is used primarily on roofs with a very small pitch (or slope), even as little as 1" per foot. Single-coverage rolls are applied with a 2" to 3" overlap. Double-coverage rolls (only the lower half of the strip has a granular coating) can be used so that the roof is always covered with two layers of the material for more protection.

This type of roofing requires less figuring, measuring, and nailing and it can be applied in less time than shingles. Although it's available with granular coatings of various colors, it is generally considered less attractive than shingles and is often relegated to an inconspicuous area.

Totally flat roofs can certainly be maintained and repaired by the homeowner, but installing a built-up roof, where layers of roofing are sandwiched with layers of hot tar, requires special equipment and is a job best left to a professional roofer. New cold-applied layer roofing is now available but still somewhat difficult to apply properly.

BASIC TOOLS AND SKILLS Before you scramble up on the roof, seriously consider whether you should tackle the job yourself. The amount of time it takes you and the risk involved may not justify the money you could save on labor costs. Use common sense. For instance, if your roof is not easily walkable (so steep that you'll need equipment on the roof for support) and if you don't have experience with ladder brackets and roof jacks, it doesn't make much sense to start experimenting.

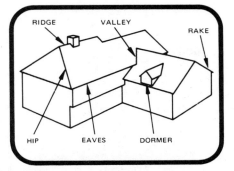

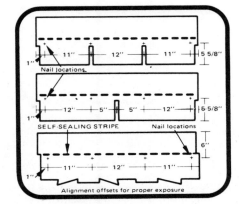

Alignment offsets for proper exposure

INSPECTION

Inspect your roof spring and fall. If you decide to reroof yourself you'll need a good ladder, chalk line, carpenter apron, utility knife, tape measure, hammer, and pointed trowel. Other tips: don't roof below 40°F or in wet weather. Keep roof surface clean, wear rubber-soled shoes for good footing, don't touch power lines or conduits, and lift only easy loads. Before reroofing, take care of loose or lifted shingles, protruding or loose nails. Repair or replace flashing, then sweep surface clear.

NAILING

Check the nailing information on each bundle of shingles. Never drive the nailhead into shingles. Always drive the nail straight with the head flush with the shingle surface. Place nails just below sealing stripe.

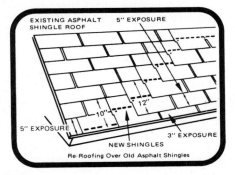

Re-Roofing Over Old Asphalt Shingles

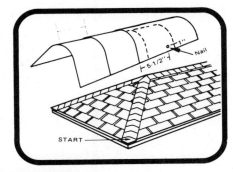

STARTING

For roofing over standard square butt asphalt shingles, proceed with starter course by cutting off tabs and trimming head portion equal to exposure of old roof, usually 5". For first row, cut 2" from top edge and align this cut edge with butt of old shingle in above course. For second row use a full shingle, aligning top edge with butt edge of old shingle in next course. For third and additional rows, use full-width shingles and align with butt edges of old roof.

HIPS AND RIDGES

You can buy special hip and ridge shingles or cut them from shingles used for roof. Cut 3 ridge shingles per 3 tab shingle and 4 from a two tab or no cutout shingle. Bend each shingle down center. Start on end of ridge opposite prevailing wind. Expose shingles 5" using two nails each, 5½" from exposed butt end and 1" from side edges. Start hips at bottom and apply ridge after hips are installed. Finish with last ridge cap piece set in black plastic cement. Don't leave nails exposed.

Check your ladder carefully before starting any job. To make nailing a little easier you might try attaching a hammer holster (either a metal or leather loop assembly that holds the hammer at waist level) to a nail apron. This way your hands are free to manipulate the shingles, and your nails and hammer won't slide down the roof.

To lay out shingles or roll roofing you should also carry a steel measuring tape and a chalkline, which is simply a long string wound up in a chalk-filled container. To align the rows of shingles parallel to the roof edge, measure equal distances up on each side, tack the line at one side, stretch it tightly across the roof, and snap it against the surface to mark a parallel guideline. For new roofing, it's a good idea to do this every four or five courses. For reroofing, follow the illustrations.

For cutting and trimming you can use a utility

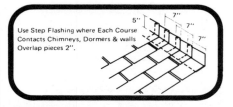

STEP FLASHING

For sides of chimneys, dormers, and walls, cut metal flashing pieces 7" × 10" and bend in half, 7" × 5" each side. Nail each flashing piece to roof at top edge with two roofing nails. Apply shingles on top of metal, set in black plastic cement. To allow for possible roof movement, don't nail flashing to wall or chimney. Carry metal cap or the wall siding material down over the step flashing.

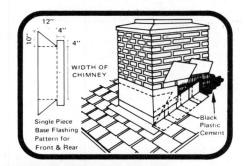

MASONRY WALLS OR CHIMNEYS

Apply shingles up to base of wall or chimney using step flashing. For chimneys, cut base flashing as shown for upper and lower side. Apply both set in black plastic cement. The lower flashing only goes on top of shingles. Insert a metal counter flashing into the mortar joint, as shown, and bend down over the step and base flashing.

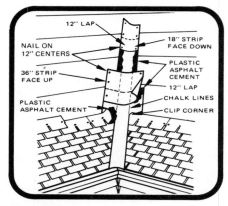

OPEN VALLEYS

First lay an 18" wide strip of mineral surfaced roll roofing, surface down, in center of valley from eaves to ridge. Nail outer edges and apply 2" wide strip of black plastic cement along edges. Then apply 36" wide piece, mineral side up. Snap chalk line down each side of valley, 6" apart at ridge, spreading apart ⅛" per foot down to eaves. Lay shingles to chalk lines, cut to fit. Cut upper corner off each valley shingle diagonally about 1" to direct water flow into valley. Set each shingle edge in cement, nail firmly.

VENT PIPES

Apply shingles up to vent pipe and cut hole in next shingle to go over pipe. Set shingle in black plastic cement. Cut flashing flange or mineral surfaced roofing or metal and place over shingle and vent pipe, set in black plastic cement. Cut rest of shingles around pipe, set in black plastic cement.

---

knife with roofer's hook blades. Make sure you have some extra blades or a small file to touch up the edge occasionally, because the granular coating wears it away quickly.

Finally, you should expect to run into some areas around chimneys, for instance, where you'll need to waterproof joints or edges with roofing cement. You can use cement in tube form, applied with a caulking gun, but in most cases a gallon can of asbestos-filled roof cement (not roof coating, which is liquid), and a small trowel will be the most useful. Here are the usual steps in a reroofing job.

PREPARING THE SURFACE   There are only a few cases where the existing shingles should be removed before you reroof. If they are so deteriorated that they are literally crumbling and falling off the roof, you might have too much patching and preparation work to make leaving them on worthwhile. If there is significant damage from algae, tree

branches, or even vines that have worked their way under the old shingles, you should uncover the problem, treat the area with an algicide, and check the roof deck for structural damage.

Typical preparation consists of removing any loose nails and using new shingles to level out any areas where sections of the old ones are missing. The layout of the new roofing will be guided by the courses of the existing shingles. However, you can improve the appearance of your new roof (and add to its wind resistance) by removing enough of the old shingles along the eaves and rake lines to make way for new 1 × 4 wood strips.

An aluminum drip edge should be installed on these strips, creating a solid and neat border. The strips replace those areas where your old shingles are most likely to be in the worst condition.

INSTALLING THE NEW SHINGLES
The starter course Measuring down from the top of

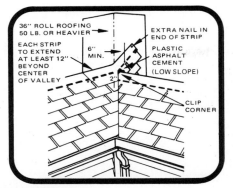

36" ROLL ROOFING 50 LB. OR HEAVIER

EACH STRIP TO EXTEND AT LEAST 12" BEYOND CENTER OF VALLEY

6" MIN.

EXTRA NAIL IN END OF STRIP

PLASTIC ASPHALT CEMENT (LOW SLOPE)

2"

CLIP CORNER

CLOSED VALLEYS

Lay a valley liner of 36"-wide mineral surfaced roofing, nailing outer edges only. Lay all shingles on one side of valley and across center line of valley a minimum of 12". Nail 6" away from center line on each side of valley. Strike chalk line 2" from center line on unshingled side, then apply shingles on unshingled side up to chalk line and trim. Trim upper corners of these shingles, nail and cement, keeping nails a minimum 6" away from valley center.

the shingle, make a mark (you can score the shingle with a utility knife for this purpose) at 2" and at 7". The 5" strip between the cut lines leaves the self-sealing strip near the bottom of the starter shingles so the first full course will be properly sealed down.

The first course Trim 2" off the top of the next course of shingles. You can use another shingle as a straightedge guide for your knife. These 10" shingles should butt against the third course of old shingles, completely covering the starter strip and overhanging the roof edge by about ½".

The second course To stagger the butted shingle joints from course to course, the first shingle in each successive row must be cut back. For two tabs and no cutout shingles, the simplest method is to cut each course back 9" (allowing for about ½" overhang along the rake edge). There are many other stagger patterns. With a standard three-tab shingle you could, for instance, cut back 6" of the starter shingle for each new course, creating five courses with successive starters of 36" (a full shingle), 30" (half of one tab removed), 24" (a full tab removed), 18" and 12" before repeating the sequence.

Working up the roof Professional roofers often complete one section from bottom to top, leaving a staggered pyramid pattern of shingles behind them. Shingles from the next section are then laced into this pattern. For less experienced do-it-yourselfers, it's usually easier to complete four or five courses at a time. It's recommended to go three or four rows across to limit possible color variation.

Roofing the valleys A valley, created where two sloping roofs meet at an angle, can be covered using either the open or closed valley method. On older homes the shingles may be trimmed about 3" back from the valley centerline on each side, exposing a continuous trough of metal flashing. Fill in the old valley first. An exposed valley can be protected by nailing down an 18"-wide strip of 90-pound roll roofing (granular side down) and covering this with a full, 36"-wide strip (granular side up) again, centered over the valley and nailed along the edges. Snap two chalklines, 6" apart, to guide the angle cuts on your shingles.

Closed valleys are made by laying shingles from one roof section across the valley and 12" up the other side. Shingles from the other roof can be laced across the valley in an over-and-under pattern or simply run straight over the top to a chalkline 2" short of the valley center line. In this case, the top valley-side corners of the covering shingles should be clipped, angling away from the valley, and set in roof cement. In all cases, no nails should be driven within 6" of the valley center line.

Capping off the roof Ridge shingles are trimmed from full, 36" shingles. You should have quite a few left over from cutting back shingles to stagger the butt joints. To make more, divide full shingles into three equal pieces by cutting from the top edge to the center of the keys (the spaces between the tab sections). These shingle sections are bent over the ridge center line and laid with 5" exposed to the weather and the bottom edge facing away from prevailing winds. Use one nail on each side about 6" up from the bottom and 1" in from each edge. The last trimmed tab should be set in a layer of roof cement without nails.

Flashing check Areas with metal flashing around chimneys or vent pipes can be sealed with roof cement. When fitting shingles around these obstructions apply a heavy coating to the old roof and to each course of shingles as they are cut to fit.

Nailing tips Every time a nail is driven into your new roof it makes a hole and therefore a potential leak. It's important that you follow the nailing instructions on the shingle package. They are designed to combine maximum holding power with maximum leak protection.

As a general rule, the nails you use should penetrate ¾" into the roof deck, have a hot-dipped galvanized coating, and an oversized head at least ⅜" in diameter. Occasionally you may find that a nail meets no resistance. Left in place it will likely work loose and possibly cause a leak. In this case, where the nail may have been driven into the seam between roof boards or a knot hole, you should carefully remove it, lift the shingle, and patch the hole with layers of roofing cement.

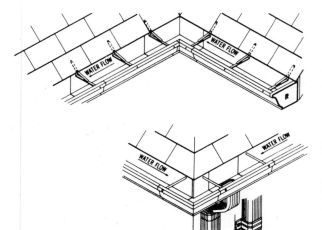

Properly sloping gutters drain away from valleys and toward corners where downspout insertions are made.

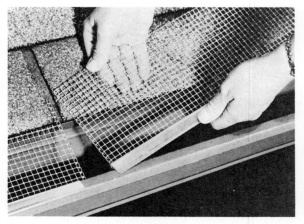

Keep gutters free of blocking debris by covering with gutter screens; these slip under shingles, over gutter, diverting debris over edge.

HOW TO MAINTAIN GUTTERS AND DOWNSPOUTS

Keeping gutters functioning properly is an important part of house maintenance. Otherwise they may become a major problem and expense.

UNCLOGGING GUTTERS Of all the problems gutters develop, clogging is the most common. Waste material such as leaves, twigs, and weeds build up regularly. The result is that water overflows and saturates the ground around the foundation and ultimately seeps into the basement through the foundation or through cracks. In winter, a clogged gutter can also lead to overflow. With the help of ice, water can back up under roof shingles and seep into the house. Or, if enough blocked water turns to ice, the sheer weight may rip your gutters off the house.

Check gutters every few months for debris, especially in the fall and spring. Use a small trowel to scoop out the material. Follow by flushing with a hose equipped with a "jet stream" nozzle. If the downspouts are clogged, an ordinary plumber's snake can be used.

CORRECTING PITCH Gutters should be pitched, or slanted, a minimum of 1" for every 30' of length to a maximum of 1" every 10'. In short, the difference in height between the ends of a gutter should be at least one inch for each 30 feet of gutter length, proportionately less or more as the length varies. If the pitch isn't correct, water can overflow or become trapped. Don't trust your eye to tell if the gutter is pitched properly. After a rainfall see if any water is standing in the gutter. Or, pour in a bucket of water at the high end and see how well it flows.

To determine correct pitch, it is first necessary to establish a level line on the fascia, the trim board on which the gutter is mounted. This line will then serve as a reference point to correct pitch. The house itself is of no use as a guide, because it is never perfectly level.

Mark a 1" line below the gutter at the downspout end, and another mark 1" below the high end. Drive nails into these points and draw a line tightly between them. Raise or lower the line until a bubble level shows that the line is truly horizontal. It is best to hold the level under the string without touching it. When the line is in fact level, mark the ends of the fascia accordingly, establishing two points, both at equal height.

Next, check the gutter at the high end (the non-downspout end), to see that it is touching the shingles, as it should be. If so, raise the line, refastening it a fraction of an inch below and parallel to the gutter bottom. Then refasten the line at the opposite end so it runs at the proper pitch.

EXAMPLE: If the bottom of the gutter at the high end is ½" above the level mark, and the gutter is 30' long, the line should be reset ½" below the level mark at the downspout. This would yield the required 1" pitch for every 30'. Or, if the high end of the gutter is 1" above the level mark, the mark at the downspout end would yield the necessary 1" pitch.

Resetting gutters Once the guiding string is set, the idea is to loosen the gutter, and reset it so that the bottom of the gutter is parallel to the string. There are various methods used to secure gutters.

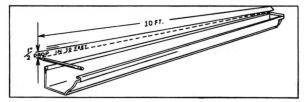

Pitch gutters no less than 1" every 30'; no more than 1" every 10'. Here it drops ½" in 10'.

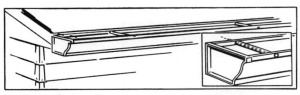

Spikes are secured through gutter outside, ferrule, other side of gutter, and into rafter end. One every other rafter is fine.

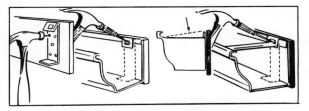

Hangers are used to secure some gutters. When replacing, first nail brackets to fascia, slip gutter into bracket, and depress top flange with screwdriver and hammer. Insert strap hanger under front lip of gutter, place strap in bracket hook, and depress bracket hook locking gutter in place.

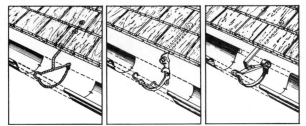

Some gutters have hangers with metal strips extending under shingles. Nails secure strips to roof. To free, pry up roofing and pry out nails. Or use the claw on a crowbar or hammer to sever nails and slip hanger out. Fill nail holes with roof cement to guard against leaks.

One popular method is with large spikes and ferrules (aluminum tubes). Building supply stores and lumberyards sell them.

Begin at the high end. Using a hammer and small pry bar, tap the inside of the gutter to knock out the head of the end spike, enough to slip the claw of the bar under it. Now rap the bar with the hammer to remove the spike completely. Using this procedure, knock out three or four more spikes, enough so the gutter can move to the pitch it needs. Then drive new spikes through the gutters into the rafter ends, as follows.

First, carefully lift up the shingles to locate the rafters. Next, position a ferrule inside the gutter pointed at the rafter end. Punch a starter hole in the outside face of the gutter with an awl. Drive the spike through the hole, then through the ferrule, and into the rafter end. Throughout, make certain the gutter remains parallel to the string or pitch line. Do this for the entire length of the gutter.

NOTE: If the high end of the gutter was not touching the shingles, reset it before establishing a level line. If your measurements indicate that everything is so far out of level that the low end of

REPAIRING A GUTTER

Coat inside of gutter with asphalt, using a paintbrush and smoothing as much as possible.

Cover with fiberglass cloth, pressing smoothly with a brush. Add second coat of asphalt.

REPAIRING A GUTTER (continued)

Cut length of identically shaped gutter, and flare beaded outer edges with pliers.

Coat area with asphalt, fit metal patch over coated area, and press down firmly.

Crimp outer beaded edge over lip of old gutter with pliers. Caulk edges with asphalt.

the gutter will have to run below the edge of the fascia if it is to be properly pitched, then either replace the fascia board or add a piece to it to gain the extra width you need.

FIXING LEAKS Leaks are a common problem with gutters, usually where pieces join together. This is caused by open joints facing flowing water rather than away from it. The joints must be reversed, which is easier to do with the gutter removed. When reconnecting the gutter sections, use ½" Number 6 or 7 sheet-metal screws. Use one on each side and the bottom.

Before refastening, apply a generous bead of sealer between sections. Hardware stores carry sealant that works well on aluminum. Remove all excess sealer inside the gutter because it will impede water flow.

If a downspout leaks, it is usually because of improper outlet installation—the lipped fitting on top that connects the downspout to the gutter. The lip should be located outside the gutter. If it is located inside, remove the piece and secure it with sheet-metal screws and an ample bead of sealer, outside the gutter. If the end pieces of the gutter leak, seal and refasten them with sheet-metal screws.

The bottom of the downspout should be a few inches above ground level, unless it enters an underground drain. A splash block—a formed piece of plastic or concrete—set under the end will prevent damage to sod and shrubbery by routing water away.

Patching kits are available to repair holes in a gutter. One that gives good results uses fiberglass mat and liquid plastic that hardens into a durable, waterproof patch.

REPLACING GUTTERS Years ago, when gutters were made of wood, replacement was a major task. This is no longer the case with today's metal and plastic gutters with simple slip-joint connectors and ready-made fittings.

Metal gutters come in four varieties: galvanized steel, unfinished aluminum, enameled galvanized steel, and enameled aluminum. Galvanized steel is the least expensive. For the sake of appearance and long life, plain galvanized gutters must be carefully cleaned with mineral spirits to remove contaminants such as oil. They are then coated with a special galvanized iron primer, then painted. Care must be taken to paint all exposed areas and cut edges, or corrosion will occur at these points. This type, or unfinished aluminum, lets you color-match the gutter to the house.

The long-lasting, baked-enamel finish on steel and aluminum gutters lasts many years. Buying prepainted replacements speeds up installation, and they look better than brush-painted types. However, steel gutters will rust if the paint is scratched deeply enough to expose bare metal.

Aluminum gutters offer better corrosion resistance than steel; and will not leave rust stains if scratched. Aluminum gutters are lighter and easier to install than steel, but they are less strong and therefore more easily damaged.

Vinyl plastic (PVC) gutters are the latest entry in the field. Plastic neither corrodes nor requires painting. A drawback of PVC is its high coefficient of thermal expansion, calling for special engineering to prevent sagging on hot days. PVC's lack of stiffness is a problem when a ladder must be placed against the gutter. But if the ladder is laid against gutter hangers, the problem is solved.

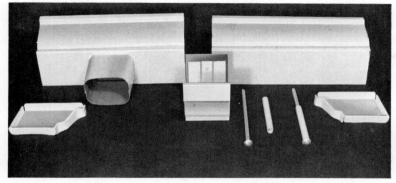

Modern gutters, such as the aluminum ones here, have preformed fixtures and go together with mastic and special connectors—a far cry from the soldering job of yesterday.

This is an exploded view of all components necessary to install PVC gutters. The job is simple and the material maintenance-free. To save on scrap pieces left over when buying gutter components, make a diagram to calculate exact gutter and fixture needs.

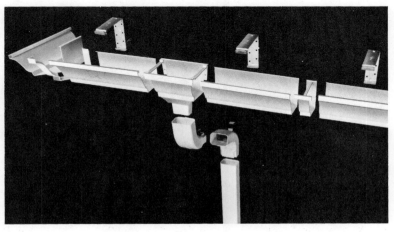

Assembling new gutters With the old gutter on the ground, line up parallel to it the appropriate fixtures and the required number of gutter lengths. Use a carpenter's square to mark the cutting lines on the new pieces.

The best cutting tool for metal gutters is a hacksaw, or a power saw fitted with a metal cutting blade. PVC may be cut with a coarse hacksaw blade or a crosscut saw. To prevent either material from bending during sawing, reinforce it with a short length of 2 × 4 lumber. Another piece of lumber located under the gutter gives saw clearance from the ground. Cut with the gutter upside down—with the trough facing down. Remove rough edges on metal and PVC with a file. Dab metal edges with rust-preventive primer. Its color doesn't matter, as the edges will not be visible after assembly.

Metal gutters are frequently fastened with large spikes. Locate spikes about 30" apart on ordinary gutter runs. Also locate spikes on each side of a fixture, such as a corner, to assure proper alignment. Another good method of hanging gutters is to use metal hangers. Sickle shaped, they are fastened to the fascia every 30", with the gutter laid on top. This method doesn't require holes in the gutter, but the hangers are more expensive than spikes.

When ready to assemble gutters, begin by applying mastic to the inside of one end cap, then slip it over the gutter end. Also, apply mastic to the lip of each connector. Assemble and join one run of gutters on the ground and carry it up the ladder for spiking to the fascia. Joints of angled sections can be strengthened with sheet-metal screws or pop rivets.

Corners, downspouts, and downspout outlets are not a problem. These preformed fixtures slip-joint together. Apply mastic first to prevent leakage. These fixtures are installed once the gutters are up and in place.

Connectors for PVC are cemented to the gutter. Rivets can be added for extra strength. These connectors fit inside and reinforce the trough. Cement combines with PVC chemically to unite the gutter sections. The finished joint is leak-free and almost invisible. End caps are installed in

To assemble metal gutters, use old ones as a guide for cutting and fixture placement. Just line up new sections next to old.

Next, use a hacksaw to cut the gutter where necessary. Insert a 2 × 4 inside gutter near cutting line to avoid bending metal.

After cutting, carefully file all burrs from cut edges. This will make it easier to insert cut ends into slip-joint connectors.

One way to attach metal gutters to house is with spikes. Use a 2 × 4 as support as shown, and drill spike holes 10" apart.

Apply mastic at all joints before assembly. Then join components by slipping them into connectors. Check for leakage.

After you have joined the various sections, bend over the tabs on the connectors. Now the gutter is ready for installation.

nearly the same manner as metal gutters, except that they are cemented in place. The drop outlet portion is built right into the gutter by cutting a hole in the bottom of the trough and cementing the fixture in place, on the outside of the trough. While the cement at the joints is drying, install the special gutter hangers.

On hip-roofed houses that require gutters on all sides, a separate collector box that allows thermal expansion of the PVC is used. The collector box fits outside the gutter and is not cemented in place.

Using whatever hanging method is desired, plan the correct pitch by following the procedure discussed earlier. Begin by driving one spike near the high end of the gutter, with a helper supporting the free end. Then locate the proper height for the other end and spike it in place. Have a helper on the ground to provide alignment guidance.

EXTERIOR WALLS—TYPICAL FRAME STRUCTURE

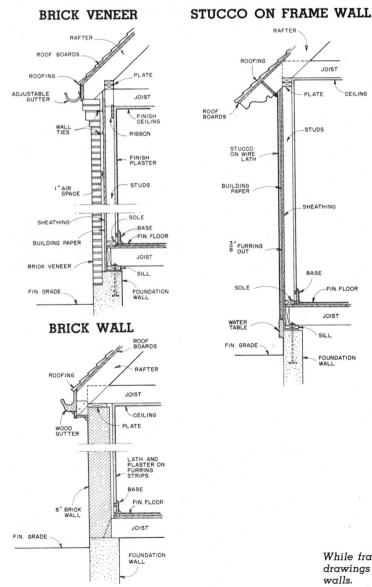

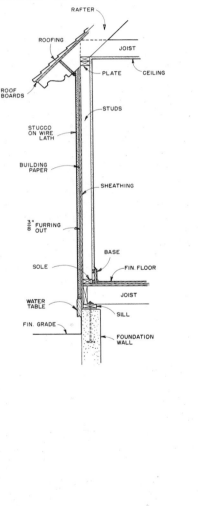

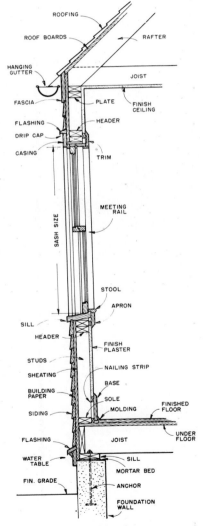

While framing styles vary considerably, these sectional drawings are a guide to what you'll find in your own walls.

Cap trim piece on outside corner has separated but can be resecured with a few finishing nails.

A screwdriver can be used to check for suspected loose or damaged shingles in this house siding.

1. Mending a split board—if not mended immediately, a split board allows water to penetrate and induce rot.

2. Pry up loose portion and spread waterproof glue along the split with a putty knife.

3. Slip board back into place and drive finishing nails beneath, directing them upward to force the split edges tightly together. Let glue set hard before removing nails and plugging nail holes. If necessary, plane thin inserts to size, glue in place.

HOW TO MAINTAIN EXTERIOR WALLS

An exterior wall of your house must be made from material that will meet the rigors of extreme climate. And if it hasn't been properly installed, it won't protect the outside or inside of your house.

ROUTINE MAINTENANCE Routine maintenance of exterior walls, performed seasonally, should begin at the roof line, under the eaves. Examine the trim and look for separations at joints of siding and eaves. Loose strips may be found; these can be nailed down with finishing nails. Gaps that look as if they could take water in a driving rain should be filled with caulking compound. Look for signs of loose shingles or soft clapboard. Slip the shank of a screwdriver under the shingle and test gently for looseness. Use an awl or an ice pick to probe boards for softness.

Examine all inside and outside corners of the

house siding. Outside corners often have individual shingles that have separated. Wood corner trim may have separated and cap trim may have worked loose. These can be resecured with finishing nails.

Shingles at inside corners may have buckled slightly under pressure from slight shifting of the house. If openings have been created where rain can enter, drive these back into place. Check for deterioration from water that may have got into the fracture. If there is deterioration, a shingle replacement is required. Use the previously described method of replacing a shingle. Wood trim on inside corners may be concealing irregular joints. Be sure this trim is sound. Where there are minor separations, lay a bead of caulk.

Examine all fittings around windows, including drip cap flashings. Probe this trim all around to be sure there is no softening. Look for rust staining at the joint where the siding meets the window trim. If there is any, examine the darkest section carefully for a source of water outlet; trace this, if possible, to a shingle or wood trim member that may be allowing water to enter.

CLAPBOARD SIDING   A battered and unpainted clapboard wall may appear hopeless at first glance, but patching a few boards is usually sufficient. Clapboards are overlapped and nailed together, so remove only one clapboard at a time. Others can be mended on the spot without removal.

Split boards Nail down individual sections of split boards, but first drill pilot holes for the nails, or the split will only worsen. Gently pry the lower end outward, just far enough to spread glue along the edges of the split; then push the board back together. To hold the glued joint firmly, drive finishing nails under the bottom edge and bend them upward. This will force the glued surfaces tightly together. Use waterproof glue, remove nails when dry, and plug nail holes with putty.

If a wide board has curled or bulged outward without splitting, it may be flattened by boring a few small holes in the center of the bulge for screws and pulling it back by tightening them. Once screws have taken hold, soak the board well before driving them all the way. This is done to avoid splitting the board as force is exerted by the screws. Countersink screws and fill holes with knife-grade caulking or exterior spackling compound.

Replacing boards When a clapboard is beyond repair, remove the damaged section as the photos illustrate. Make vertical cuts as high as possible in several places along the damaged area. Using a chisel, reach under the next board above without disturbing it, or use a hacksaw blade to cut the nails holding the upper board. Then carefully insert a wedge under the edge of the board. The remaining section can be removed with a chisel. Patch any holes in the tar paper covering the sheathing. Use roofing asphalt or apply patches of tar paper over large gaps with the same material used as adhesive.

Finally, cut a length of matching clapboard so that it fits tightly in the opening and push it in place under the upper board. Nail it and any loose ends of adjoining pieces in place. Replace the cut nails in the strip above the replacement clapboard.

MAINTAINING CLAPBOARD SIDING

1. *Cut bad section vertically with back saw as close as possible to overlap.*

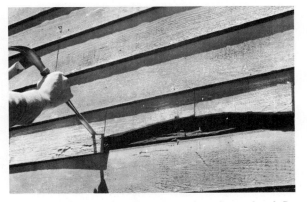

2. *Cut out chunks of cut lengths with a sharp chisel. Do not cut into tar paper.*

3. *Where possible, remove nails from edge of upper board to free the cut length.*

4. *If need be, insert wedge under upper board and cut nails with keyhole hacksaw.*

5. *With upper board wedged, chisel out ends of cut length even with saw mark.*

6. *To avoid splitting good section, hold chisel at angle and cut short pieces.*

7. *If upper board can be wedged outward far enough, cut with hacksaw.*

8. *Patch nicks in tar paper, cut new length, and nail in place top and bottom.*

STUCCO SIDING The most common damage to stucco walls is the development of fine cracks near doors and windows. Settling framing and water seepage and subsequent freezing are only a few causes of these cracks. All are easy to repair and should be taken care of before cold weather sets in.

First, remove all loose stucco to form a proper base for patching. Ready-mixed concrete is convenient for small patches. A homemade mixture also works. A mixture of 1 part portland cement to 2½ parts fine sand is best. Add a waterproof compound at the same time; it will make the cement easier to work with and will ensure a lasting bond. If much stucco needs replacing, it may be necessary to remove all the damaged stucco and apply new material. The photos show both types of repair.

HOW TO REPLACE SIDING

Time and weather combine to batter your house, and eventually, in spite of the best maintenance efforts, you may be forced to consider recovering the exterior walls. New siding can change the entire appearance of your house. It is an expensive job, so, unless you are an expert with tools and the house has simple, clean lines, it may pay to have a professional do the job.

First, consider trends in siding. Smooth sidings are losing their popularity; textured sidings are more popular. These are prefinished and unfinished. The latter can be stained or painted. The textures, regardless of material, generally copy wood grains or the weathered textures of years ago. The patterns have been around for centuries — the lap or bevel, board and batten, kerf, groove and channel, rough sawn. Here is a rundown on the types of siding available.

HARDBOARD SIDING This is made from logs that have been shredded and reduced to fibers. The fibers are permanently bonded together under

PATCHING STUCCO

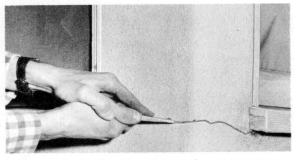

1. *Use a cold chisel to dig out all the loose cement; open the crack to about double its existing depth. Undercut the crack to provide a key or slot for the new cement to hold.*

2. *Wet the crack thoroughly with a brush or cloth, or use a hose. Fill crack, using a putty knife, and overlap each side about 1", smoothing cement into the existing surface.*

3. *If your stucco is colored, buy matching colored stucco, called sand-finish, and dab a wet sponge in the material. Dab the material over crack filler, applying in circular motion.*

4. *This is the way the repaired crack should look. In 3 or 4 days the sand-finish will dry — it fades as much as 70 percent and should nearly match the old stucco finish.*

REPLACING STUCCO

1. *Remove damaged stucco down to the wood underneath. Cover area with tar paper, then nail securely 1" mesh wire or wire lath. Mix plastic cement (one shovelful) with sand (three shovelfuls) and spread on upward to cover the wire.*

2. *You can make your own scratching tool from a piece of heavy-gauge scrap metal, or buy the professional type shown here.*

3. *Scratching is done while the first coat is still soft and workable. Hold scratching tool lightly; press just hard enough to score, but not hard enough to take off stucco.*

4. *Allow first coat to dry 7 days, then spray area with fine mistlike spray to soak it, then apply a second coat, using same mix.*

5. *This second coat must be smoothed off level. Use a straightedge. A metal bar is best, since it won't warp and bend.*

6. *It's a good idea to work this second coat with a trowel while still damp. You can make a trowel from a wood shingle by putting on a handle. Float surface until sand grains show.*

heat and pressure and formed into panels usually $7/16'' \times 4' \times 8'$. It is also supplied as individual planks $7/16''$ thick in widths of 8", 10", or 12", and lengths of 16' for lap siding. It may be prefinished or unfinished, and range from smooth to very rough in texture. It is easy to install, weathers well, and its low cost makes it attractive.

VINYL PLASTIC Vinyl plastic is usually made of

polyvinyl chloride. It's strong and tough, and under ordinary conditions it will last for years. Colors penetrate the plastic, so it will never need to be refinished, and most are warranted for ten years. Newer vinyls have better resistance to cracking in extremely cold weather or if struck by a hard object. They are highly resistant to dent marks such as those made by hail. This type of siding should be considered if you want to keep costs down.

PLYWOOD Plywood is the most popular siding in use today. It comes in many textures and patterns and the 4' × 8' panels make it economical and easy to install. Plywood is somewhat lighter than hardboard panels of the same size. Plywood varies widely in quality, depth of texture, finish, and price.

ALUMINUM Aluminum is the most popular choice for remodeling jobs because of its great durability and freedom from maintenance, especially painting. The average house with wood siding must be repainted every three to five years, depending on weather conditions.

On the other hand, the acrylic resin paint that covers most aluminum siding is guaranteed for twenty years or more. Some companies also have aluminum sidings with a vinyl-fluoride plastic film permanently attached to the exterior, which is guaranteed for forty years. The film is available in a variety of colors and withstands solvents such as kerosene, cleaning fluids that are used to remove paint and ink, and even strong acids that remove rust and concrete smears. A big selling point is

Plywood siding designed for interior or exterior use makes an interesting pattern under a wide roof overhang.

Plywood has the advantage of rapid installation and fewer joints; it is also totally waterproof. It may be prefinished before installation.

Aluminum siding with a built-in plastic foam insulation is applied over old. Corner trim locks the two siding pieces together in a rigid, weathertight joint.

An easy way to cover a wall is to nail special thin bricks up with metal clips, right over the old wood siding.

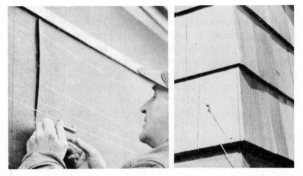

Left: Rugged shakes or smooth shingles are applied after a wall is covered with tar paper, chalk lines drawn with a level, courses with even exposure calculated. Nail each piece twice. Right: First course is double, following courses are single. If corner trim is not used, a staggered overlap provides a neat and finished appearance.

that it can be cleaned with soap and water. Care must be taken not to use metal sidings where abuse can cause scratching of the surface paint coating. The back of aluminum siding is often coated with epoxy resin to prevent corrosion.

The outside surface may be plain or embossed to resemble wood grain. The style may be clapboard or lap type, vertical V-groove, or vertical board and batten.

Aluminum siding is usually applied directly over the old siding. Reflective foil, which has tiny "breather" holes to allow water vapor to escape and evaporate in the spaces between the siding, is installed prior to aluminum siding. It also acts as a form of insulation, reflecting heat back into the house. Another insulation, polystyrene foam, is glued to the back of the siding panels. Check your area to see if codes require grounding of the aluminum siding.

SHAKES Shakes, which look like shingles, have a rustic look that makes them popular for vacation homes and for homes in contemporary architecture. Styles include individual cedar and redwood shakes, hardboard, mineral composition, vinyl, and prefinished aluminum. They're attractive, are more expensive than other sidings, and installation costs are higher than other types.

STEEL Steel is the newest type of siding. It is strong, tough, durable, and expensive. Since it comes prefinished, it needs no further attention unless scratched. It should be grounded to avoid electrical fires.

SOLID WOOD Solid wood is still the standard against which all other sidings are measured. The wood can be cedar, fir, redwood, or pine. Most is lap siding. Other types of materials try to copy the interesting grains and patterns found in wood siding, but if you want the true character and beauty of wood siding, there is no substitute.

MINERAL FIBER Long established and known as asbestos-cement in the past, mineral fiber siding is fireproof, rotproof, and immune to carpenter ants, termites, and other insects that eat wood. It is among the most durable of siding materials and is relatively inexpensive. It is brittle and tends to crack if struck. It also is available with ceramic or hard plastic coatings that make its colors fade-resistant. It is usually not more than ⅛" thick, but deep shadow lines can be achieved by raising the lower edges of the shingles with concealed strips of treated wood.

PATTERNS AND STYLES Siding patterns have remained the same over the years. There are five basic patterns:

1. Lap or bevel is the leading horizontal pattern. It will make your house look longer, lower and wider. It comes in different widths and thicknesses. Viewed from a distance, a wall faced with this pattern has shadow lines that are pleasing to the eye.
2. Board and batten is a vertical pattern. It increases the height of low buildings. It can be used to accent different sections of a house.
3. Grooved can be either a V groove or a straight channel cut into the siding. These grooved patterns are mostly vertical. The grooves give pleasant relief to the walls of the house and provide interesting shadow lines.
4. Kerfed pattern is a narrow groove, about the width of the kerf of a circular saw blade. It is usually found in vertical siding. Distances between the kerfs vary to give different effects.
5. Rough sawn is more a texture than a pattern. It is used mostly on plywood siding. Whether stained or painted, rough sawn patterns give a rustic, pleasantly soft appearance to the house. To achieve a similar effect, sometimes wood sidings are reversed and mounted with the rough portion facing outward.

SPECIALTY TEXTURES These sidings can be used on any style or type of single house, apartment, modular, or mobile home.

1. "Stuccato" is a hardboard panel siding that looks like stucco and must be applied by skilled craftsmen. The embossed hardboard closely resembles and feels like the skip-trowel texture of real stucco. It is available in standard panels that can be mounted in either vertical or a horizontal position.
2. Moonspot has tiny indentations resembling a rough cement finish. It is used for accents or on buildings that feature Tudor architecture. It is a hardboard panel developed by Masonite.

3. Wood shakes in panels are a line of red cedar wood shakes in assembled panels. These cut construction costs and are easy to mount.
4. Bayside is a hardboard lap siding that looks and feels like wood shakes but comes in strips rather than individual pieces.
5. Stone on plywood sidings are also known as Sanspray. Plywood is coated with a strong epoxy coating and stone chips are embedded in it. The textures and colors are pleasing and practical. The panels can be sawed and mounted like ordinary plywood.
6. Aluminum and plywood sidings are now available with a tough, long-lasting surface. A polyvinyl fluoride film is heat bonded to the aluminum or plywood. Manufacturers guarantee these sidings for thirty years. They are supplied in most patterns and shades.
7. Fine line textures are being introduced by plywood manufacturers. These give interesting effects, especially at close range. They can be mounted in the horizontal as well as vertical positions. They're often used as accent points.

COLORS AND FINISHES More sidings are being introduced with finishes that resemble natural weathered wood. Less painting is being done because new textures lend themselves to penetrating or heavily pigmented stains. Sometimes manufacturers attempt to preserve or simulate the wood grain. Others stain it the deeper color of the particular wood or the blue-gray appearance of wood that has weathered for many years.

HOW TO CURE WET BASEMENTS

The foundation is seldom regarded as an exterior wall. But an exterior wall it is—and a very important one at that—because the foundation has the job of dealing with house-destroying things like dampness, dry rot, and termites.

COMMON CURES If water seeps into the basement, watch for cracks in poured concrete, loose or crumbling mortar between cement blocks and brick walls, openings around pipes and electrical conduits, window openings, and floor cracks.

Small openings around pipes and electrical conduits should be filled with a hydraulic cement formulated for plugging holes in concrete. The joint between the window frame and concrete foundation should be filled with concrete. If water is seeping at the wall-floor joint, chisel away cement until you have a crack that is ¾" wide and ¾" deep. Fill the crack with a nonshrinking hydraulic

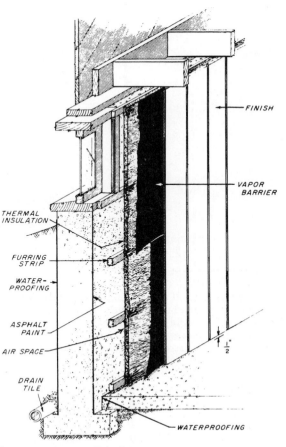

Keeping water out of the basement.

Filling around pipe openings will keep out water. Trowel in a mix of 1 part cement to 3 parts sand.

All cracks outside around windows should be filled in. Pitch sill away from the frame.

Waterproofing the outside is effective. Note the shoring (timbers) used to prevent cave-in.

Waterproofing mastic is applied to exterior wall with a brush and covered with 4-mil polyethylene sheeting.

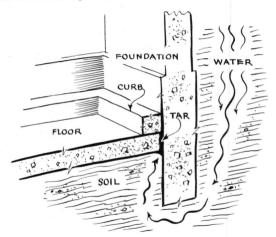

Water seepage through the wall – floor joint is a frequent cause of dampness. Here the joint is filled with asphalt and a curb, made of concrete, is added above the joint.

patching cement. If a wall is free of visible cracks or other defects, but moisture is present, use a waterproofing compound. Apply only to clean, unpainted masonry, never to painted or white-washed walls. Choose a product that is alkali- and mildew-resistant. Use a stiff-bristle brush and work the compound into wall pores.

Channel water away from the outside of the foundation wall. Downspouts or leaders from gutters should not dump water next to the foundation. Place a splash block under the leader to direct the flow of water away. Or, if the ground is spongy and absorbs water readily, connect the leader through clay tiles to a dry well.

EXTERIOR WATERPROOFING The most effective and permanent cure is to dig a trench along the outside walls so the foundation can be water-proofed down to the footing. Remove shrubs and walks and dig a trench wide enough to work in, without danger of the trench collapsing. Next, put clay or plastic drainage tiles in the trench bottom just below the footing, allowing a gap of 1", with a tar paper covering between adjoining tiles. Run the tile line to a dry well.

Apply a waterproofing mastic to the clean foundation walls. While the mastic is wet, apply a 4 mil polyethylene sheeting over it. Allow the 8' wide plastic to drape the wall from the grade line, at the

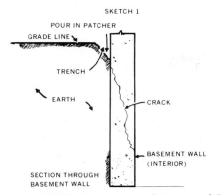

SKETCH 1

POUR IN PATCHER
GRADE LINE
TRENCH
EARTH
CRACK
BASEMENT WALL
(INTERIOR)
SECTION THROUGH
BASEMENT WALL

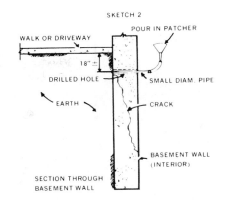

SKETCH 2

WALK OR DRIVEWAY
POUR IN PATCHER
18"
DRILLED HOLE
SMALL DIAM. PIPE
EARTH
CRACK
BASEMENT WALL
(INTERIOR)
SECTION THROUGH
BASEMENT WALL

How to apply patching when ground is exposed (left) and when it is covered (right).

1. *A chip or knock-out at a corner is easy to repair, and gives a straight corner when the job is complete. With a stiff wire brush, remove all the loose particles.*

2. *Prop a 2 × 4 against the corner and wet the area thoroughly. Fill the crack with patching cement, smoothing it off with a trowel so that the patch is flush with the wall.*

top, to the bottom footings. Backfill the trench, making sure you don't tear the protective plastic coating on the wall.

SEALING CRACKS Another way to stop basement leaks that are difficult to locate or reach is to use liquid patcher. It is usable with cracks, provided they aren't on the floor or at the floor-wall joint. Liquid patcher is a latex solution with a consistency of paint. To make a watertight repair, pour the patcher into the ground directly above where the crack starts. The solution makes its way down, following the microscopic channels created by the water that found its way into the basement, and finally flows into the crack. As it flows, it sets and fills both channels and cracks until they're closed off completely.

SUMP PUMPS If there is high water or subterranean springs under your home, or if the sewer periodically back flows, you may need a sump pump. The pump and motor should have a capacity at

3. *Now prop the 2 × 4 against the outer side of the corner. Use the edge of the trowel to slice off any excess cement sticking out of the corner. Leave the 2 × 4 in place for at least 4 hours.*

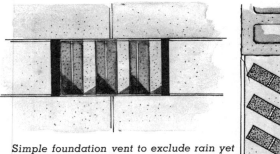

Simple foundation vent to exclude rain yet permit ventilation in crawl spaces can be constructed by removing one block or series of bricks and inserting bricks as shown.

least equal to the greatest possible flow of water that may be encountered. Your plumbing dealer will help you select the proper size.

Check the pitch of the cellar floor; it should slope toward one end. Dig a pit 3' to 4' deep in the lowest part of the floor. Line the sides of the hole with concrete. Make a plywood form to hold the mix until it sets. Install a sump pump so the water flowing into the pit can be removed through the wall, into a dry well.

CHIPPED FOUNDATIONS Chipped corners can be fixed with patching cement, a trowel, and a 2 × 4 prop, as shown in the photos on page 251.

SMALLER PROBLEMS Musty odors and mildew problems can be solved if these steps are taken: Make certain that there is no water penetrating the basement foundation. After a heavy rainstorm, inspect the understructure for signs of water. Increase basement ventilation. Keep a window open, add louvers, or use a ventilating fan. If these methods fail, use special moisture-absorbent chemicals or an electric dehumidifier. Cover sweating pipes with felt tape and pipe wraparound material. Leave valve control wheels and stems exposed.

Finally, seal the wall with a cement-based material such as Thoroseal. This type of concrete sealer is formulated to moistureproof, provide alkali and mildew resistance, and ensure good adhesion on wet or dry unpainted concrete.

CRAWL SPACES Crawl spaces—partial basements or additions over unexcavated areas—are apt to be problems during winter.

When space under the floor, or the floor itself seems damp, check for inadequate cross-ventilation. Foundation vents may be needed. With these, the crawl space is rarely damp, but it may be cold, resulting in cold floors.

To prevent cold floors, add 6" of batt-type insulation between floor joists. Insulation is stapled flush with the lower edges between joists, forming a dead air space between insulation and subfloor. Further insulating and moistureproofing can be done by stapling a layer of 4 mil polyethylene sheeting over joists. By attaching it to sills on all sides, a perfect seal results.

If dampness and dank odors are a nuisance, cover the ground of the crawl space with plastic sheeting. Spread a 2" layer of dry sand over the plastic. Moisture from below cannot penetrate the crawl area and the floors stay dry and warmer.

TERMITES AND DRY ROT Termites and dry rot thrive and spread where the moisture content of wood is generally high. Termites are visible and the paths they leave apparent. Dry rot, on the other hand, is invisible. It is a microscopic, plantlike fungus, capable of multiplying with amazing speed in moist wood. Left untreated, dry rot will destroy wood quickly.

Typical invitations to dry rot and termites are homes with one or more of these situations.

1. Improperly cleared land with remaining stumps, roots near the house; scrap lumber from construction tossed into crawl spaces, under porches, or into the backfill.
2. Wood siding low to the ground or covered with earth during leveling and landscaping.
3. Open downspouts splashing water onto and under low siding boards.
4. Concrete slabs and block foundations full of cracks and damaged mortar points.
5. Paint on clapboards badly peeling or blistered.
6. Damp crawl space poorly vented, with moisture rising to sills and joists above.
7. Wood steps outdoors with their stringers touching the ground, and wood fences nailed to the corners of the house.

Probe sills with ice pick. If pick can be thrust deeply into timbers, either an infestation of termites or dry rot is present.

Removal of lowest siding board reveals damage done to house sill. Close contact with masonry stop kept wood damp — an ideal invitation to termites or dry rot.

8. Excessive moisture inside the house with windows sweating all winter and paper peeling from walls.
9. Basement windows in contact with masonry, and wood often damaged by rain.
10. Joists adjacent to sills that are open to attack.

If your home has even one of these defects, check for dry rot or termite infestation. Probe suspected wood with a sharp tool or ice pick. If hand pressure forces the tool into the wood over 1″, saw out a length of wood. If the center is badly tunneled, it is probably the result of termites. If the wood appears sound but spongy, and close inspection shows countless tiny open cells, dry rot has been at work.

In either case, replacement of the damaged wood is necessary. Termites sometimes leave cellulose-and-mud tubes running from wood to earth along foundations. Break these up and examine carefully the wood where they start; it's probably been infested.

The same measures taken to eliminate infestation of dry rot or termites also offsets further invasion. Moisture elimination will also help avoid dry rot development.

Effective prevention of dry rot is achieved by treatment of the wood before construction. Preparations forced into wood under pressure are the most effective. Dipping works, and paint-on coatings are fairly effective, particularly when introduced into the end grain. When planning any new construction, make use of treated materials. The pressure treatment increases the cost of materials but assures against dry rot and termite infestation.

If termites have invaded your house, poisons placed in the soil will eliminate them. Professional exterminators can get rid of them with special tools and techniques.

HOW TO PAINT THE EXTERIOR

A good application of paint will do more than add beauty to your house. It will also preserve and weatherproof your home, protecting it against the effects of weather, dry rot, and decay.

Before proceeding with the painting itself, consult the table on page 258 to analyze the nature of your paint problems.

PREPARATION Preparation before painting requires close attention. Most paint failure problems can be traced to incomplete or improper preparation of the surface.

The first step should be a close inspection, followed by repairs to prevent entrance and entrapment of moisture. Nail heads that have not been set and puttied properly may rust out entirely. Or, they may bleed through the paint, leaving rust-colored spots.

Caulking to seal out drafts and moisture is easy to do. It pays off in fuel savings and adds to the life span of the house. Caulk cracks around window and door frames, butt joints of siding, and corner boards. Sashes are a major problem area, so they should be kept well caulked and tight.

Replace loose and rusted nails. Tighten down boards that have warped and pulled loose to leave cracks between clapboards.

Before painting, caulk open cracks. Don't count on paint to do it for you. Caulking compounds can be painted over.

Fill nail holes, loose knots, depressions, and cracks with putty or a good wood filler. Let dry, spot prime with exterior wood undercoater, then paint.

Check the condition of masonry for cracks and crumbling—even hairline cracks should be attended to, since they enlarge in time.

Paint failures around windows, such as peeling, can often be traced to deteriorated flashing, or the complete absence of flashing because the builder neglected to use it. The tops of all doors and windows should be protected by flashings to prevent moisture from getting in. The bottoms of windows should also have a flashing. Flashing should begin at the sheathing under the building paper and extend past the drip cap of the window or door.

Paint properly applied to a good surface will last for years. Chalking of the old paint is evidence the paint is wearing away, a natural and desirable process. Simple sanding and washing is all that's required on surfaces that are only chalked. (Make sure you read all label instructions before buying and using any coating.) Others call for application only on new wood or masonry.

A wire brush will remove dirt along with scaling paint or any other loose material that would adversely affect the adhesion and appearance of primers and finishes.

Masonry surfaces also require treatment before painting. Wire brush knocks off old paint, loose scale, and dirt.

Stucco surfaces should be carefully checked before painting, all cracks and breaks patched with fresh stucco.

A chemical paint remover may be used to soften several layers of paint. Use the semipaste type for vertical surfaces, then scrape away loosened layers.

REMOVING PAINT Professionals use flame to burn and soften old paint, but this is a tricky business. Electric paint softeners work well for amateurs, but they use a lot of electricity. Make sure you use a heavy-gauge extension cord. Chemical paint removers cost more, but do a good job of removing many coats of old paint. Let the chemical remain in contact with the paint for the suggested time, longer if necessary. When the layer of paint comes loose, it is ready for scraping. Some chemical removers are designed to be washed off with a garden hose. If used, protect shrubbery from damage.

Wirebrush the surface after it is free of all loose paint, all the cracks are filled, nail holes are puttied, loose boards are nailed down tightly, and all structural defects corrected. All uneven spots should be sanded smooth. When the surface is smooth, dry and clean, you can begin the actual painting.

WHEN TO PAINT Check the weather forecasts for the days you intend to paint. Look for days with a temperature range from 55 to 90°F. Above or below this paint will not dry properly. A direct, hot sun will blister new paint, so try to work in the shade as much as possible. Don't paint if you expect a sudden drop in the temperature within several hours, avoid painting on hot, humid, or windy days.

Because the moisture content of the air is usually highest in the early morning, start to paint only after the sun has had time to dry some of the moisture. In general, you should never paint during damp, rainy weather, but when using latex paint on hot days, it is desirable to paint on slightly damp surfaces.

Mask the windows or use a paint shield to protect them during painting. Tie shrubbery back, away from the house. Spread dropcloths over anything else you don't want painted.

PAINTING METHODS Start the paint job at the top of the house so drips will fall on unpainted surfaces. Work on a strip about three feet wide. Once it has been covered completely, lower the ladder and start another three-foot section.

Paint the edges of the wood first, then the flat areas in between. Always paint with the flat surface of the brush, never the edge. This helps avoid streaking and wearing the brush down at the edges, which reduces its effectiveness. Cover as much of the surface as possible with a brushful of paint. Don't try to "stretch" paint coverage, however. This can cause streaking. Always brush the paint out well at the edges to prevent lap marks. Lap marks will show up if the next day's painting starts in an unbroken surface (i.e., one wall), so try to complete sections in one day if possible.

Observe manufacturer's recommendations regarding drying time between coats. Otherwise, the paint may crack or wrinkle because the base coat

When painting the side of a house, begin at the highest point and apply paint in horizontal strips about 3" wide. Paint above the top of the ladder, when possible, as you can reach a wide area. Do not stop in the middle of a strip for any length of time. The distance between the house and the base of the ladder should be about ¼ to ⅓ of the ladder's length.

1. *Load your brush, then apply two or three dabs of paint along the joint of the siding. You will find this will help to distribute the paint quickly and easily.*

2. *Brush the paint out well and be careful to coat the underedge of the clapboard. If possible, paint only after a week of dry weather.*

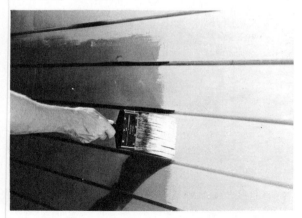

3. *Feather the ends of your brush strokes so that the coat will be smoother where one section joins another. A 4" or 5" brush is most often used for this job.*

did not dry sufficiently. If the weather is cold or damp, allow several days' additional time before applying the second coat.

Painting trim The trim and shutters of your home should be painted last. Clean and prime any new wood or metal trim before starting to paint. If possible, take shutters down and place them over sawhorses or scaffolding for easier painting.

Many paints are made with "controlled chalking" or "self-cleaning" properties, an advantage when painting clapboard houses. These paints, however, should not be used on white trim or shutters of houses with brick or masonry finishes. They might wash onto the masonry surface below, causing white streaks that would be difficult to remove.

Other exterior surfaces New wood roof shingles should be the predipped variety, if possible. The finish coat should be brushed or sprayed on after the shingles have been laid. For best effectiveness, shingle penetrating stains should be used, but not over painted shingles. For floors, railings, and steps—for both priming and finishing coats—use only porch or floor quality enamel. This finish resists effects of constant wear, weathering, and scrubbing. Latex floor enamel can also be used very effectively on concrete floors.

Metal surfaces When preparing metal surfaces for painting, make sure all traces of oil, rust, and grease are removed. Paint will not adhere to greasy or oily surfaces. Oil and grease may be removed by using common household detergents or thinners such as turpentine or naphtha. Remove all rust with steel wool, a scraper, wire brush, sandpaper, or emery cloth.

If the metal was previously painted, and the old coat is not cracked and there is no rust, you may skip the primer coat. If signs of wear are evident, sand all chips and cracks smoothly, remove any rust, and prime before applying the finish coat. Galvanized steel, tin, and iron will eventually rust and deteriorate if not adequately protected against moisture. Copper, although it will not rust, will give off a corrosive wash that can stain adjacent surfaces. Aluminum will never rust or corrode, but it will tarnish.

Masonry Masonry must also be clean before painting. Remove any dirt and loose paint with a wire brush, then wash the surface with clean water.

Salts, found to some degree in all masonry products, cause efflorescence by rising to the surface and drying, leaving a thin white film. Never attempt to paint over such material, because the paint will not adhere. Scrub the efflorescent material with a solution of one part muriatic acid and five parts water, and rinse well. Muriatic acid is caustic and should be handled very carefully. Wear protective goggles, rubber gloves, and old

Do not use a chalking exterior paint on siding above a brick or masonry wall. Chalked paint will wash down on the masonry surface and mar its appearance.

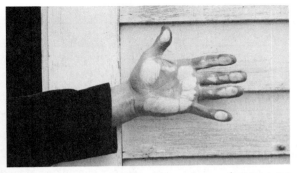

Chalking normally is desirable, and manufacturers try to incorporate this feature in paint formulas. Excessive chalking may be due to improper application.

clothes. Allow the masonry to dry completely before repainting.

Both latex and alkyd masonry paints are good topcoats for outdoor surfaces. Others include several types of cement water paint, resin-emulsion paint, and oil paint. Rubber-base paint, polyvinyl acetate emulsions, and silicone sealers also work well on foundations, gate posts, fences, and enclosures.

Use only latex or specially formulated masonry paints for covering masonry floors. Cement water paints are specially suited for damp concrete walls. Use pretinted commercial brands if color is desired. Apply cement water paints in two coats, with less than twenty-four hours between coats. These paints adhere best to surfaces that are not completely dry. Applying fine sand to the first coat will help cover small defects that may exist in the surface.

Use a short, stiff brush and scrub the first coat into the surface. Keep the first coat moist with a fine mist for at least twenty-four hours. The final coat should be kept moist for at least forty-eight hours to aid in proper and complete curing.

Resin-emulsion paints are applied by brush or spray and dry in a few hours to a smooth, opaque, flat finish. Do not wet the walls before or after applying this type of paint. Two coats, applied with either a brush or sprayer, are recommended. When working on surfaces that are open textured, first use a cement water paint with fine sand added, before finishing with resin-emulsion paint.

Polyvinyl acetate paints must be used on unpainted masonry or on masonry that has been painted with the same type of paint. Easy to apply,

It is easy to apply silicone masonry water repellents with just a brush. Simply apply one full flooding coat. These sealers give good protection, can be used over cement-base paints, and will retain texture and color of the masonry.

they will usually cover well in one coat, resist alkali, and provide a waterproof film.

Silicone sealers provide an excellent water-repellent seal, yet retain the original color and texture of the masonry wall. These sealers should not be applied over oil- or resin-based coats.

Natural exterior finishes Use of redwood and cedar siding has created the demand for "natural" finishes that allow grain to show through while still protecting the wood. Three types of natural sealers and finishes are available: varnish, sealer, and drying oil.

COMMON PAINT PROBLEMS

Problem	Cause	Cure
Peeling paint	1. Paint applied over dirty surface, mildew.	1. Scrape, sand, or burn peeled paint away. Prime all bare wood. Wash exterior with scrub brush, detergent to ensure dirt-free surface. Remove mildew as below.
	2. Moisture through siding plus inadequate venting.	2. Install adequate venting in roof, attic, soffits, and siding.
	3. No moisture barrier in exterior walls.	3. Apply oil base primer/paint, or aluminum foil/vinyl wallcovering to interior side of exterior walls.
	4. Lack of caulking around doors, windows, etc.	4. Latex caulk around window/door trim, all vertical cracks in siding.
		5. Use "breathing" latex paint finish for all problem peeling surfaces.
Mildew	1. It's a fungus. Spores grow on dirty, moist, shaded, warm surfaces.	1. To test if "dirty spots" are mildew, wash with bleach. If "spot" washes away, it's mildew.
	2. Inadequate venting of interior moisture. Trapped moisture in soffits, porch ceilings, or siding permits moist conditions that support mildew growth.	2. Install vents in areas where mildew recurs.
		3. Trim trees, shrubbery to allow air, sunlight to reach affected area.
		4. Apply detergent to house exterior, spray with hose nozzle each spring. This removes dirt that supports mildew growth.
		5. Chlorine bleach will kill mildew; detergent will wash it away. Mix 1 tblsp. dry detergent, 1 qt. chlorine bleach, 3 qts. warm water. Scrub mildew area with this solution and a stiff brush. Rinse with clear water.
		6. Apply primer and paint that contain fungicides to affected areas.
Stains (rust, rusty nails, wood sap, oils bleeding through paint)	1. Exposed siding nails, excessive wood sap or oils in siding.	1. Drive popped siding nails. Wirebrush or apply naval jelly to remove rust. Seal with shellac sealer such as B-I-N.
Peeling, efflorescence of salts on masonry surfaces	1. Masonry surfaces exude salts (alkaline) when new (for about 1 year).	1. Allow masonry to cure fully before painting. Clean/wash masonry surfaces, use specially formulated (alkali-resistant) paint finishes.
Peeling gutters	1. Improper preparation of new metal surfaces.	1. Wipe new galvanized metal surfaces with mineral spirits or vinegar to remove oil and metallic contaminates. Rinse with clear water. Allow to dry.
	2. Improper paint finish.	2. Sand, scrape, burn, or wirebrush peeling paint away. Use specially formulated metal paints (Galva-Grip, etc.) to paint metal surfaces.
		3. Try this pro tip: use oil-based exterior wood stains on metal, or for a recoat after cleaning peeling gutters. Also, clean and apply oil stains to all metal chimney flashing, roof vents, and valley flashing used in roofing.

Problem	Cause	Cure
Scaling, "popping" of concrete drive walk or patio surfaces. Popping of brick face on chimneys, brick trim, common where bricks are "soldiered" (laid with ends, rather than sides, exposed) at window sills.	1. Common in cold areas where water penetrates flat concrete surfaces, brick trim around sills. Freezing water expands, "pops" surface.	1. Apply concrete sealers (Water Lox, Thompson's Water Seal) to flat (horizontal) masonry/concrete surfaces, to prevent moisture penetration. 2. Vertical brick or stone walls, fireplace chimneys are constructed to shed water. Exception: in cold climates, seal masonry cap and entire brick chase on brick chimneys above the roofline.
Rusty metal surfaces	1. Metal improperly finished.	1. Sand or wirebrush loose paint, rust, and scale away. Wipe clean with rag soaked in lacquer thinner. 2. Spray/brush gloss metallic-finish paint on all exterior metal surfaces.
"Alligatoring" (crazed or cracked paint surface)	1. Many coats of paint on an old surface. 2. Paint applied over dirty, improperly prepared surface. 3. Latex paint applied over gloss oil. 4. Inferior siding material.	1. Sand, scrape, or burn old paint off. 2. See cure above. 3. Sand glossy surface to dull finish. Use proper primer for base coat under latex. 4. Some fiberboard siding made in early years was soft, dimensionally unstable. It will not hold paint. Replace siding.

A marine-grade spar varnish produces a natural finish that has long life expectancy. Varnish is usually chosen for smaller surface areas, such as doors and trim, rather than large expanses of siding. Varnish does have its drawbacks, however. It may craze, develop milky spots, or become opaque in some areas. And after several applications, varnish must be stripped before it can be effectively reapplied. Don't use shellac as an undercoat for varnish because it will ruin the finish.

Pigmented sealers offer the most promise of all natural finishes. Adequate protection is offered by applying two coats and merely retouching them every few years, or by renewing the finish completely by adding a fresh coat. Use of pigments in this type of finish gives it lasting power. The pigments repel the harmful ultraviolet and infrared rays of the sun.

Other types of natural finishes include oils, waxes, stains in clear gloss or clear flat compounds, and penetrating and semitransparent stains. No matter which type of natural finish you decide on, it is best to:
1. Apply a penetrating, waterproof preservative to the wood.
2. Make sure the finish contains mildewcide. If not, add one before applying.

3. Make sure the finish will seal in any tannins or other poisons contained in the wood. If it doesn't, these materials will later spoil the appearance of the finish by working their way to the surface.

Here is a good example of the old coat bleeding through the new one. The use of a stain-blocking primer will generally prevent this from happening.

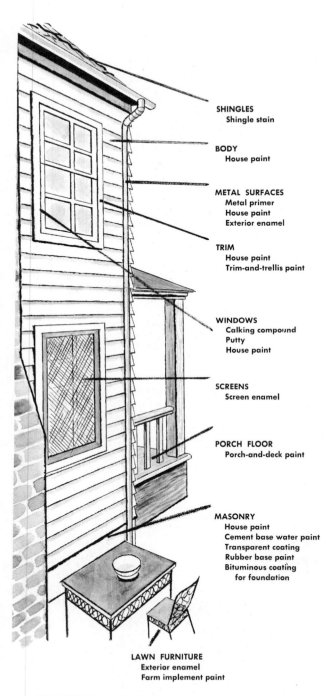

SHINGLES
Shingle stain

BODY
House paint

METAL SURFACES
Metal primer
House paint
Exterior enamel

TRIM
House paint
Trim-and-trellis paint

WINDOWS
Calking compound
Putty
House paint

SCREENS
Screen enamel

PORCH FLOOR
Porch-and-deck paint

MASONRY
House paint
Cement base water paint
Transparent coating
Rubber base paint
Bituminous coating
    for foundation

LAWN FURNITURE
Exterior enamel
Farm implement paint

USE THE RIGHT PAINT

CHOOSING PAINT Some confusion exists with names given to various types of paints, such as "latex," "water thinned," or "enamel." Since each type of surface has its own special requirements, choosing the correct paint often determines success or failure.

Paint is composed of two major ingredients: the pigment and the vehicle. The pigment gives the paint its color, and the vehicle is the carrier for pigment. Three of the most common vehicles from which many paints take their names are alkyd, latex, and oil.

As a rule, pigments are mineral or metallic in origin. The most common is titanium dioxide, which because it is quite costly is supplemented with other elements.

One particular supplement, calcium carbonate, chalks readily. It powders and drops off or washes off the surface. To a degree this is desirable, because dirt also washes off at the same time. However, if the process is too rapid, the surface is soon left unprotected and the house wall and the ground below are stained. The relative percentages of titanium dioxide and calcium carbonate must be regulated to ensure proper chalking.

Special purpose paints Paint manufacturers have been keeping pace with new building materials and their paint needs. While many well-known house paints have been used for years to cover clapboards and shingles, newer houses with newer materials — vertical siding and predipped shingles, for instance — require special protection. Some of the specially formulated paints on the market today are discussed below.

Redwood finishes are used where vertical boards and other parts of the structure are made of redwood. Here the finish must be clear, yet must preserve the color under strong sunlight. A treatment of water-thinned polyvinyl acrylite has been developed which combines a sealer and a natural redwood color. It is applied to the bare wood in two coats, one right after the other.

Specially formulated shake paints are available to cover predipped shingles with another color. A six-month weathering period should be observed before dipped shingles are painted. Test their readiness for painting with a stiff brush and water. If water collects in small droplets, as it does on a new-waxed surface, withhold painting for a longer period of time. After sufficient weathering has taken place, shake paints will adhere without bleeding through. Shake paints may also be used on asbestos shingles.

Alkyd Alkyd paints are available in enamels and flats, and derive their name from synthetic resins. Alkyd-type finishes produce tough, durable, and quick-drying paint films. They have good gloss retention and produce strong, tight films for use in high-humidity areas. They have very good leveling properties and exceptional resistance to yellowing. They need no primer, leave no lap or brush marks, and may be applied by brush, roller, or spray. Their washability and resistance to marring is excellent. These paints may be thinned with turpentine or a similar solvent. Read the label on the can for correct thinning methods.

Enamels Enamel produces a smooth, hard film. There are various types of enamels, each having different properties. With all of them, a smooth undercoat is necessary to obtain a first-class enamel finish. This undercoat is a flat paint, specially formulated to flow out smoothly without brush marks. Exterior enamel is much more durable than the interior type and is used for porch floors, decks, boats, lawn furniture, and other outdoor projects.

Latex Latex paints are favorites with millions of house owners. They are tough, durable, easy to apply, and they clean up with soap and warm water. Some are specially formulated for exterior use, others for interiors. Latex paints are water-thinned emulsions with a synthetic base.

Perhaps the easiest to apply, latex flows well when used with rollers, brushes, or guns; and it adheres to plaster, old paints, wallpaper, wallboard, brick, concrete block, wood, or primed metals. Latex paints dry very quickly and a second coat may be applied in a couple of hours, if needed. The emulsions in the latex paints provide a self-sealing finish.

Polyvinyl acetate (PVA) PVA emulsions are used chiefly for exterior masonry. They are easy to apply over brick, stucco, and concrete. They are resistant to alkali in masonry, to fading under sunlight, and to fumes and acids. Use a brush, roller, or gun for application. They are fast drying and require only simple soap-and-water clean-up.

Stains Because of trends in building in recent years, the "natural wood" look is very popular. Stains allow the wood grain to show through the finish, while enhancing its eye appeal. Semitransparent stains contain enough pigment to color raw wood without concealing its natural grain. These penetrating stains, either water- or solvent-thinned, leave the wood with a dull, flat finish. Although stains do not flake or peel as paint does, weathering is a problem. Eventually the stain will require recoating. Stains come in a wide assortment of colors and finishes. For best results, test the stain on a small, concealed portion of the surface. Follow the manufacturer's instructions for proper application.

Primers A coat of primer will increase the durability of a finish coat of paint. Primers are so called because they prime the wood or other material to

EXTERIOR PAINTING CHECKLIST

1. Analyze present condition of the surface.
2. Estimate material requirements.
3. Do preparatory work before painting:
   a. Erect scaffolding.
   b. Remove shutters and screens.
   c. Do preparatory repairs.
   d. Replace broken glass, reglaze windows.
   e. Clean and repair gutters.
   f. Remove loose and scaling paint.
   g. Remove rust from any metal surfaces.
   h. Clean and sandpaper surfaces.
4. Undercoat bare surfaces and any other, as needed, with primer.
5. Complete final preparation.
   a. Caulk with quality caulking compound.
   b. Sandpaper.
   c. Touch up any defects in first coat.
6. Apply finish coat to dormers, cornices, and roof metal work.
7. Apply finish coat to body of house.
8. Apply finish coat to windows and porches.
9. Apply finish coat to doors and shutters.
10. Apply coat to floor of porch and steps.

receive the finish coat of paint. Primers seal the surface and provide holdout so that the finish coat lays as a thin film on the surface of the wood. They provide good adhesion to receive and hold finish coats. Unprimed surfaces allow the paint to penetrate the wood. This penetration will result in an uneven finish, because of the unequal rate of absorption of paint on the surface. All new materials, and all repair areas, should be primed to provide equal absorption and holdout.

ESTIMATING PAINT NEEDS In addition to the size of your house and the number of coats required, certain other conditions should also be considered when estimating paint needs.

1. Very rough or heavily textured surfaces will require more paint.
2. Narrow lap siding requires 10 percent more paint than wide siding.
3. Corrugated metal surfaces need 33 percent more paint than smoother metal surfaces.
4. The first coat on concrete block, used to fill the pores, requires 50 percent more paint.

When estimating the amount of trim paint needed, allow one gallon for each five gallons of body paint. You can cover roughly between 400 and 500 square feet with a gallon of paint. To estimate the number of gallons of paint needed, measure, in square feet, the area to be painted and divide by 400, the smaller of the two coverage estimates.

Advances in paint chemistry have made special coatings for any surface available to the homeowner. Take your paint problems to your dealer, and explain what materials the paint will be applied on. He will provide you with a proper finish for the job. Follow the directions of the manufacturer implicitly. Major paint companies conduct extensive experiments to determine such paint qualities as ease of application, durability under difficult conditions, and life expectancy of their products.

The salt air of a seaside home will require a different formulation than will a home on a mountain top, and major manufacturers recognize this. No manufacturer will stand behind its product unless its specifications have been followed. Do not try to "improve" on the manufacturer's research and experience by substituting your own. Most paints are made to be applied as they come to you, with little or no thinning.

HOW TO MAINTAIN AND REPAIR SIDEWALKS AND DRIVEWAYS

The appearance of your home depends upon its setting and its upkeep. Outdoor maintenance hits a peak in spring and fall. Cracked, crumbling pavements must be mended and asphalt driveways waterproofed. The following are some of the most common outdoor maintenance projects requiring work with masonry materials. Before you set to work on any of them, you might want to refer to Chapter 9, which covers masonry work in general.

CRACKED SIDEWALKS When grass and weeds begin to grow up through a sidewalk, it's high time for action. Rain entering the crack will wash away the fill under the slab, and eventually at least one side of the walk will sink. Then the repair is twice

REPAIRING CONCRETE

1. *Widen crack with cold chisel to about 2" width and clean out broken masonry and dirt down to the bottom of the crack.*

2. *Wet the interior of the crack with water, or, better still, paint with a bonding chemical, which will assure adherence.*

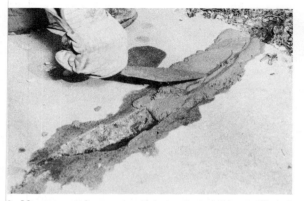

3. *Mix prepared cement and water thoroughly until batch is uniformly plastic. Then trowel into crack and press down.*

4. *Level off and let stand 30 minutes until surface is watery, then smooth with steel float. To roughen, use wood float.*

as difficult. By using the following method, there will be no broken concrete to haul away, no new concrete to mix or pour. The only cost is the price of a chisel and a little cement.

First, cut out the crack with a cold chisel to a width of about 2″. (Wear goggles.) Scrape out all loose earth and broken masonry and remove any other loose material with a wire brush. Wet the inside thoroughly with water or, for an even better patch, with a bonding chemical such as may be purchased at any building-supply yard. Mix cement to a rather stiff consistency and, with a trowel, pack it tightly into the crack, forcing it down to the very bottom of the joint. Then level it with the walk on each side. Keep the patch moist for two or three days to help it cure properly.

If you started this job too late and the two sections adjoining the crack are no longer level with each other, you have two choices: either pry up the sunken side with a crowbar and block it there while you pack crushed stone under it, and then mend the crack, or break up the sunken section, excavate the area to a depth of about 4″ to 6″, and use the broken pieces of walk as fill, then cover with new concrete. This requires a form board on each side, and the surface is made level with adjacent sections of the walk.

Most concrete walks are poured in one piece, with a fiber separator about every 15′. Obviously, you cannot hope to lift an entire 15′ length. If the sunken section has not already cracked free at a score or cross line, you can crack it there. Raising a single square can then be readily and safely done by one man.

TREE-LIFTED SIDEWALKS Often a tree growing close by a sidewalk may lift a portion of the walk with its expanding roots. Usually the cement slabs crack evenly along the expansion lines. These slabs can be raised with a heavy crowbar or an auto jack fitted with a lift hook at the bottom. Raise each piece of slab until it clears the ground at one side, block it there, and then lift the other side and block it up. Next, use a mason's broad chisel and a heavy hammer to score straight lines each way across the center, dividing the slab into four parts. Make successively heavier blows with the hammer and chisel along the lines until the slab suddenly breaks at the scored mark. These easier-to-handle pieces can then be moved aside while the roots, which caused the trouble, are cut down to size with an ax. Level the ground, then replace the four section, chipping off the edges, if necessary, to pro-

LEVELING OLD CONCRETE

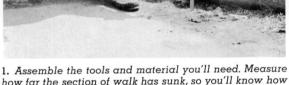

1. *Assemble the tools and material you'll need. Measure how far the section of walk has sunk, so you'll know how far you'll have to raise it.*

2. *Check the level of the adjoining walk. If its slope is too great, you may have to raise it, too, for a satisfactory appearance.*

3. *Use a cold chisel and follow the score mark, chipping carefully and slowly until you have cracked the concrete all the way across at this point.*

LEVELING OLD CONCRETE (continued)

4. *Using a pick or shovel, loosen the soil along the edges of the sunken slab. Clear a strip a few inches wide, to a depth below the concrete.*

5. *Using a pick, crowbar, or other lever, carefully and slowly pry up the edges of the concrete square. Make certain it is free all the way around.*

6. *With a crowbar or other lever, raise one edge of the slab on blocks, working it up higher and higher until you have it raised about a foot in the air.*

7. *With a shovel, spread enough cinders underneath the slab to raise it to level. Gravel or crushed rock may be substituted for cinders.*

8. *Use your rake to make certain the supporting layer of cinders conforms to the uneven bottom of the slab. One high point may cause the slab to crack.*

9. *Lower the slab and go to the other edge. Raise this edge as in Step 6. A longer length of lever would have made this handyman's work even easier.*

10. *Shovel in some more cinders and rubble. Note the rough bottom of the slab and make sure supporting bed you prepare conforms to these irregularities.*

11. *Use the rake to get in under the slab. Make absolutely certain no single clod of cinders or rubble is raised above the rest.*

12. *When bed is properly spread, lower the slab and sweep it clean. Use edge of broom to sweep all loose dirt from the crack between the squares.*

13. *Spread asphalt into the crack. It will permit the slab to shift slightly without cracking. Sand on the asphalt prevents its sticking to shoes.*

vide an even crack between them. Then with a mortar mix of 1 part cement and 2½ parts sand cement the slabs to each other, to the adjoining walk, and to the curb or building, if necessary.

COLD MIX ASPHALT FOR SIDEWALKS For building new walks or driveways or for mending old, the cold-mix method is highly efficient. Cold mix can be purchased in 60-pound bags, but it is more economical to buy it in bulk and haul it yourself. Store it on a double layer of tar paper to protect the ground under it. By all means, buy in bulk for such large jobs as patios, tennis courts, and play areas.

For heavy traffic areas, a 2″ deep ballast of rock is best, topped with 2″ of cold mix. Drives should have more ballast, depending on the weight of the

cars or trucks using them, but for garden paths 1″ of each (rock and cold mix) will do on firm soil.

Redwood is best for the header boards since it doesn't rot and is very attractive. Locust also will not rot and is as hard as iron when thoroughly dried out. Or you can use impregnated lumber of other types, but the harder the better.

Before beginning the job, cover all tool surfaces with a film of motor oil to prevent adhesion of the cold mix.

For cold-mix patchwork on old blacktop surfaces, clean out all holes deep enough to allow the addition of 2″ of crushed rock and 2″ of cold mix. Then follow the same procedure as for new work, as detailed in the photographs on page 266.

COLD-MIX ASPHALT

1. Remove weeds, grass, old roots, not only from the site of the new path but alongside it, too; such growths can crack the walk.

2. Sprinkle a weed killer over the site, according to the label, to kill off sprouted seeds and roots.

3. Rake in the weed killer, wet down, and then roll the area thoroughly (about 30 minutes) to compact soil. This is good insurance against cracks.

4. Set corner stakes and lay off path with heavy twine. One stake every 3' is good. Inner edge of stakes should just touch line.

5. Set headerboards against stakes and nail them there. A concrete block against the stake makes the nailing easier. Use rustproof nails.

ASPHALT DRIVEWAYS Even a driveway that is in good shape, but hasn't been sealed in the past two or three years, can benefit from the application of sealer. Asphalt, although an excellent low-cost paving material, is surprisingly vulnerable to weather, oil and grease drippings from your car, and even sunlight. Water, which penetrates cracks and holes and goes through repeated cycles of freezing and thawing, is a major cause of asphalt paving breakup.

Oil and grease are solvents that soften asphalt, loosening its fine gravel and mineral fillers so holes result. Salt and ice-melting crystals also have a damaging effect on asphalt. Wind, heat, and weathering gradually reduce the amount of oils that give the asphalt its binding strength.

Over a period of time, the sun and air make asphalt brittle. The result: surface gravel breaks loose and falls out, leaving small holes and cracks. Unlike asphalt, coal-tar-emulsion driveway seal-

6. *Make frequent use of your level and measuring tape. Keep sides level unless you plan to slope the whole walk to one side for drainage.*

7. *Bank the outside with earth and tamp it down to add more strength to headerboards. They have to support the ballast and the cold-mix.*

8. *Use ¾" crushed rock for ballast. This should come to within 2" of the top of headerboards; the remaining space will be filled with cold-mix.*

9. *Level off ballast and then roll both lengthwise and crosswise to compact and force into the earth beneath. Don't dislodge headerboards.*

10. *Apply the cold-mix at the rate of 22 pounds per square foot. Pour into piles at short intervals and then rake out, adding more as needed.*

11. *Use the back of a rake to level off. Cold-mix should be piled on until it is ½" above the tops of the header-boards, enough to allow compacting.*

ers are not affected by oil and grease, sunlight, salt, or ice-melting crystals. They are waterproof, so the damage caused by water that freezes in cracks and holes simply doesn't occur here.
Preparation Your driveway should be free of all loose material and oil. All holes should be patched before applying the sealer. Start by sweeping away loose stones and dirt with a stiff broom. Then large holes should be filled with a suitable patching mix and tamped down firmly until the patch is flush with the surface surrounding it.

Such patching material is available in most home centers and hardware stores. Allow patches to cure for the time stated on the package before applying the sealer. Small cracks can be filled with latex sealers. This dries fast and cures overnight. A coal-tar-emulsion sealer with mineral filler used on the entire driveway will take care of hairline cracks.

Oil and grease Use a shovel or steel trowel to re-

COLD-MIX ASPHALT (continued)

12. *A lawn roller filled with water is used to compact the cold-mix. Roll for at least 30 minutes to 1 hour. Your footprints can be rolled out later. Keep at it!*

13. *Dry cement, of a selected color, can be spread over the top at the rate of 10 pounds per 100 square feet, then broomed into pores of the cold-mix.*

14. *Final rolling lasts 15 minutes. Afterwards, take a wet brush and dust off the tops of the headerboards. Conceal stakes at sides with earth fill or sod.*

MAINTAINING ASPHALT DRIVEWAYS

Left: Sweep driveway clear of loose stones and dirt with a stiff bristle nylon or natural fiber broom. Right: Scrape away built-up deposits of oil/grease and dirt with a shovel or sharp tool.

Left: Thoroughly scrub remaining oil spots with strong detergent or use TSP mixed with water. Right: Hose down the driveway with maximum water force to clear away all dirt and debris.

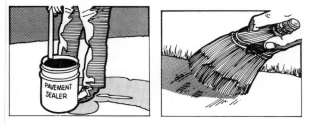  

Left: Mix the blacktop emulsion in pail thoroughly to a smooth fluid before beginning application. Right: You may want to make an 8" border around driveway to avoid pushing blacktop into grass.

Left: Pour a small quantity of blacktop from the pail each time and spread it around. Right: Spread sealer, working it into all minor cracks and voids.

move built-up deposits of oil or grease drippings that are mixed with dust and dirt. Scour the spots with a detergent and a stiff broom or brush. Don't use gasoline, benzine, paint thinner, or solvents to clean the oil and grease spots. They will damage the asphalt. The last step in preparing your driveway for sealer application is to thoroughly wash it with a hose, using as much water pressure as possible to remove remaining dirt from the surface.

Application Before applying the coal-tar-emulsion sealer, check the weather. Don't apply sealer if there is a prospect of rain within twelve hours. You will need about twenty-four hours of dry weather for thorough curing. Do not allow any traffic on the driveway during the curing period.

If your driveway surface is rough or has hairline cracks, use a coal-tar-emulsion sealer with mineral filler. Sealers with fillers cause minor depressions to vanish. If your driveway is smooth after being repaired, you can use the thinner type of coating. Several manufacturers offer both types.

You will need two kinds of tools to spread the sealer: a long-handled push broom with stiff nylon or coarse fiber bristles, and a squeegee, which has a flexible rubber-faced blade.

The push broom or brush is used for working the sealer into the surface of the driveway and filling cracks and small voids. The squeegee is used mainly for spreading; it is available wherever sealers are sold. The 5-gallon pail in which most sealers are sold will cover about 500 square feet in one coat on a relatively smooth driveway. Thick coats are not desirable. Immediately before application, stir the contents of the can thoroughly to a smooth consistency.

The driveway should be damp when you start. Keep it damp with a fine spray from a garden hose, but avoid making puddles. You may find it advantageous to make an 8" border all around the driveway with a small brush to avoid pushing sealer into the adjacent grass areas.

Pour a thin ribbon of sealer from the pail across one end of the driveway and pull the squeegee through it, spreading it out in a thin coat. Use the broom in cross patterns, working back and forth to fill small holes and cracks. Repeat this operation as you work your way down the driveway, pouring from the pail and then spreading the sealer. For the best appearance, your finishing strokes should be made in one direction. Wear boots to protect footgear from the sealer.

Cleanup Rinse your broom, squeegee, and boots as soon as you have finished. Hardened sealer can only be removed with a coal-tar solvent like Tolunol, which isn't always easy to obtain. Your driveway will be protected for at least a year, perhaps several if traffic is light.

HOW TO BUILD AND REPAIR OUTDOOR STAIRS

By making use of durable materials—concrete, flagstone, and stone, for instance—you can make outdoor steps that will last indefinitely. Such masonry work can be done by almost any amateur. It's simple and inexpensive, and the results remain attractive over a period of many years.

There is actually only one "rule" to follow. That is, first make a sound footing for the stairs you intend to build. Otherwise, they might be undermined later by heavy rains or unsettled by frost upheaval.

When building steps, the first thought is for the ease with which they can be climbed. The two parts—the treads on which you step and the risers (the vertical distance between steps)—must be of correct dimensions. Treads should have a minimum width of 10" but 12" is even better, and 16" will make a particularly wide and attractive stairway. Risers should never exceed 8", and they may be trimmed down to 6" or 7" for added comfort. Steps leading to a door should be at least 4' wide to allow space on each side of the door.

In calculating the riser-tread figures, measure first the distance from ground level to door sill (or other point of arrival). Divide by units of 6, 7, or 8 (depending on the riser height you choose) to decide how many equal risers will be needed. Then count the number of treads needed (calling the ground level one tread and the sill another) and lay out the plan of the whole stairs.

ONE-STEP RISE Suppose you have a simple one-step rise from the ground to a door sill, patio, or stoop. It's best to provide a footing of about 6" of crushed rock below grade, for which you'll need an excavation. Then lay out the outline of the step with brick-on-edge mortared together. The center is then filled with cement (or waste mortar) and a capping of brick or flagstone is applied on top. Coat the tops of flagstones (but *only* the tops) with floor wax before setting in place and before pointing up the joints between them. This prevents mortar staining and keeps them clean and bright. After an hour, brush away any excess mortar with a stiff, dry brush.

CONCRETE STEPS The simplest form of concrete step construction is that of making one step at a time. Box in the lowest step to size with heavy lumber (2" stock), braced by stakes driven securely into the ground. Fill with a concrete mix of 1 part portland cement, 2½ parts sand, and 5 parts gravel or crushed stone. Compact with a float, then level off the forward portion, which will become the lowest finished step, leaving the back section rough. When this has set, repeat the process for the

How to construct progressive form for pouring one step at a time with concrete. Attach each added form to the one below with securely anchored cleats.

Stone mason's double-edged ax will cut virtually all types of stone to shape.

next step, pouring directly over the rough part of the first. Repeat again for each higher step. For higher sets of steps (more than three or four), cut out two stringers to tread-riser size and use these as a form for the sides, nailing on wood riser boards to contain the concrete. Then pour all the steps at once, smoothing off after compacting across each tread. After forty-eight hours, remove the forms. Don't be discouraged when you first see the results. The sides will be rough, the tops of the treads flaky. In some cases, rock from the concrete mix will be exposed. All this is natural. The next step is to cover this concrete base with cement, at the same time waterproofing the steps and adding color if you wish.

Mix cement of 1 : 2½ mix, adding a waterproofing chemical to the water used in making the cement. Color may be added by including an additional ingredient in the mortar mixture. Prepared dry color in powder form can be added to a maximum of 10 percent of the volume of the portland cement used. The use of smaller quantities results in lighter shades. Dry color may also be sprinkled on the surface of the mortar immediately after it has been applied. It is then scrubbed into the mortar's surface with a stiff bristle brush (not wire), after which the surface must be troweled smooth.

Wet down the concrete steps thoroughly with a hose. Then trowel on ½" of the cement mix, starting at the base and working up the sides, up the risers, then over the treads. The use of a steel float glazes the surface and also cuts the angles sharply for neatness. But if safety is an important factor (concrete or cement may become slick when wet), use a wood float.

CONCRETE BLOCK STEPS Concrete blocks can be stacked up and used for steps. However, since the average block is approximately 8" × 8" × 16", the 8" tread is not wide enough for comfort. On the other hand, if blocks are laid with the square 8" × 8" end toward the riser end, the extended 16" surface makes a good tread. Lay a series of blocks side by side, cement them together, and the steps are easily and quickly made. To bind sections together for greater stability, scrap pipe can be run through the voids of adjoining blocks and a flange can be screwed to each end before the voids are filled with cement.

STONE STEPS Cutting stone is an art quickly learned. Don't try to break a large stone by hitting it dead center with a sledge. Dangerous splinters may fly, and if you do succeed in breaking it, the fragments will probably be useless. Wrist work, rather than arm-and-back muscle, will reduce even the toughest stones to the size you want. A length of twine tied to stakes may be of help in laying out your steps, but you may also go by eye. If you wish, set in a few double-length steps to vary the effect. Your stone stairway need not be a straight drop but may be curved gradually down the slope. However, the straight drop uses the fewest stones.

Stone steps on earth are best laid from the top down. Make a smooth spot for the top step and set it in place. With a shovel, cut straight down to the position where the next step will be, adding the thickness of the stone to your cut. By scraping the removed earth forward and tamping it into place, another shelf is created for the next stone. The process is repeated down the grade until the stair is finished.

The beginning and ending of the stair may be given a touch of grandeur by adding larger border stones, by rounding off the last step, or by flaring

Cut into the hillside to form a shelf on which to rest the next step down.

Tamp down the new shelf evenly and smoothly to serve as seat for the next rock.

Massive borders, with flat edges toward the steps, make a formal though rustic stair.

Where earth is inclined to crumble, use small stones to support front edges.

Alternate wide and narrow steps create a pleasant pattern, make climbing easy.

Large slabs on smaller stones make cutting into the hillside unnecessary.

the borders apart toward the lower end. On extremely loose soil, it may be a better plan to support the forward ends of each step with smaller upright stones to prevent undercutting by rain rather than to leave this riser area bare. Just remember that in placing these supporting stones, they should not tilt the step upward. This would cause rain to collect and seep into the soil, loosening it further, and eventually causing the stones to settle deeply into the earth. Tilting them slightly downward allows the rain to run off. Eventually all stones will settle somewhat, but rarely will any have to be dug up and earth replaced beneath them.

FLAGSTONE AND BRICK STEPS Often a facing of flagstone, particularly on treads, is needed to

KEEPING BRICK STAIRWAYS IN CONDITION

1. *Cracks in mortar need immediate attention to prevent water penetration which would widen crack and rot mortar.*

2. *Cut out all mortar from damaged area, exposing bare brick; use cold chisel and hammer.*

3. *Clear away all loose material and scrub the surfaces with wire brush. Don't settle for half measures on this part of job.*

4. *Rinse out cracks with hose and soak brick thoroughly to prevent absorption of moisture from new mortar before it sets.*

5. *Mix only small quantities of mortar (1 part cement, 2½ parts sand) at one time so that mix will not harden as you work.*

6. *Lift mortar into cracks carefully to avoid staining bricks. Wipe up spills at once, as mortar stains are hard to remove. Pack mortar tightly into every crack with your trowel, then smooth off level with adjoining brick surfaces.*

match an adjoining patio. In this case, allow for the thickness of flagstone in making the concrete steps (usually about 1½"), and when the concrete forms have been removed, wet the concrete and set the flags in a ½" bed of cement. To make brick steps, make allowance for the brick thickness on both the risers and treads and then set the bricks with mortar flat against the two surfaces, using the technique required for flagstones.

REPAIRS FOR OUTDOOR WOODEN STAIRS Outdoor wooden steps take a beating during the winter. They should be checked over carefully for any signs of weakness or decay.

First inspect the stringers—they're those side pieces that hold up the steps. In some cases, they're saw-toothed with the steps nailed across. In other cases, they're merely straight with a step support nailed to them and the steps nailed in between.

If there are any cracks along the grain, these sides can be strengthened by bolting a 2 × 4 along the full length. Use bolts, as nails in old wood only split it further. Use ¼" carriage bolts spaced at 1' intervals. It's best to drill a ⁵/₁₆" hole through the side support and the 2 × 4. Then insert the bolt with washers around the bolt head and under the nut.

With those saw-toothed stringers, if the step support shows signs of weakness, remove the step first. Do this by tapping up lightly a little at a time on each end of the step. Next, cut 2 pieces of wood

to match the shape of the saw tooth out of 2" stock or stock as thick as the original stringer.

If the stringer is still in good shape, cut off any weakened saw tooth. Replace it by bolting the new piece as noted in the sketch. But if the stringer is supported by a 2 × 4, just add a new supporting angled piece to it in the same way. Then renail the step in position.

Maybe the steps need attention. Some may be worn uneven in the center; if so, they can be turned over. With others it may be necessary to visit a lumberyard to buy replacements.

If your steps are the saw-tooth stringer type, it's easy to remove a step. Simply tap upward on each end, as noted before.

With the other type of step construction, where the steps are nailed in between the side supports, the job is somewhat more exacting. The step, despite the side nails, is removed by tapping upward at each end. You have to hit a little harder but the step will come out. After the step is removed, hammer the exposed nails back through the supports.

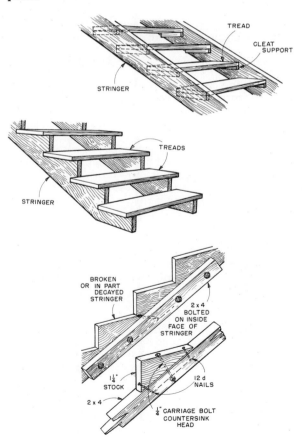

7. *Use trowel tip to indent mortar in joints to shed water rapidly. After mortar is cured, apply masonry sealer paint.*

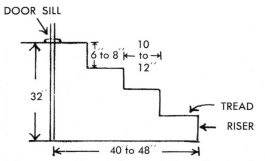

Calculate size of risers by measuring distance from ground to doorstep sill and dividing it into units of 6", 7", or 8" plus fractions necessary to make the total. Then measure from house outward in units of 10", 11" or 12" for treads.

If the step supports attached to the stringers are worn, replace them. They pry up easily. Attach new ones with ¼" carriage bolts the same way as for the saw-tooth stringer supports.

Nail new steps first to these step supports. Then drive nails through the stringers into the step.

HOW TO BUILD AND REPAIR FENCES

You'll find fencing easy to do, rewarding work. Privacy, rather than security or boundary definition, is often the chief function of fencing. Fences can be used as walls to enclose outdoor living areas, isolate a service yard, or cut off an undesirable view. Before building a fence, check with your local building department as to possible restrictions and permit requirements. The top height allowed for a home fence in most coded communities is 6'.

The materials used and the way they are put together determine how long your fence will resist the forces of the elements. Some types of lumber, such as redwood and cedar, resist exposure very well in their natural state. Others, among which are Engelmann spruce, the Western pines, and Douglas and white fir, are easy to work, straight-grained, and accept finishing readily. With proper treatment, these too will last for years.

Poorly built fences just don't stay built for long. Wind and weather wreak their havoc. Undersized lumber soon sags. Flimsy gate hardware gives way, and out-of-plumb posts lean even further. Damage can sometimes be patched, but faulty basic construction and the deterioration that follows mean more work. In the long run, it's better to do the original job correctly.

Low, light fences don't blow over easily, but the posts can be lifted by frost. High, solid fences offer areas large enough for wind to work against. If posts are too short or are loosely set, they may not be able to resist pressure. Examine a tottering or loose post by excavating around its base. If the post is set in the earth, it may be rotted or the soil so loosened around it that there is inadequate support. If set in concrete, the entire mass of concrete may have shifted, taking the post with it; the post may have rotted in its concrete jacket if water seeped in between it and the masonry.

Probably the most common disease of fences is rot, which may result when no preservative is used or when rusting nails provide water pockets. Rot can also stem from poor painting techniques and end-grain absorption of water. There is just one thing to do when rot is discovered. Remove the rotten pieces and take steps to prevent recurrence. The sketches suggest patchwork steps to take at the various points where rot starts. As a rule, it is the end of a rail that rots first. Nails rust out and rain is carried into the end grain through these openings. If not more than an inch or two of the rail ends is damaged, you may make an attempt at salvage and repair. Cut off the rotted end of upper and lower rails equally and nail a length of 2 × 4 to them, then nail the 2 × 4 to the post.

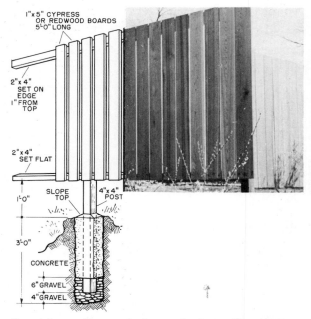

Board fence offers a maximum of privacy. Open bottom helps air circulation, allows shielding where it counts most, and makes a third rail unnecessary. A third rail is usually required for any fence over 5' high.

MAINTAINING FENCE POSTS

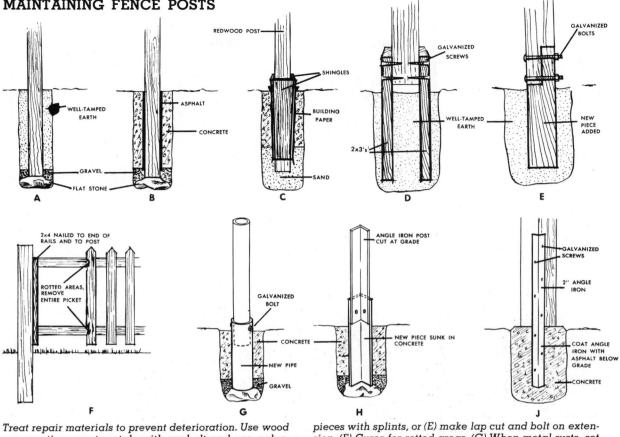

Treat repair materials to prevent deterioration. Use wood preservatives, coat metals with asphalt and use galvanized screws. (A) Post in tamped earth and (B) with concrete collar. (C) Surround redwood post with shingles and building paper before pouring concrete. Remove when concrete sets and fill gap with sand. (D) Replace damaged pieces with splints, or (E) make lap cut and bolt on extension. (F) Cures for rotted areas. (G) When metal rusts, set old post inside larger piece, bolt together. (H) Replace rusted angle iron with new piece bolted on. (J) Bolt wood post to angle set in concrete. Leave gap between to prevent rot.

Before planting any posts or, for that matter, any other parts of a fence, they should be treated with preservative to retard decay. Even those woods listed above as being weather resistant will benefit from this treatment. One of the best liquid preservatives is pentachlorophenol. To apply, soak post ends for two to eight hours. Other surfaces may be painted with a generous coat. Do this before assembly of the fence so that surfaces that may be hidden inside joints are adequately protected.

The length of the below-ground portion of a post should equal half the height of the fence above the ground. And length alone won't help if the post is improperly set. In such cases, new holes must be made and a flat rock or brick dropped into the bottom of the hole on which to reset the post. Tamp the dirt solidly around the post. In firm soil or clay, it's not generally necessary to use concrete, but in looser soil use 1 part portland cement to 3 parts sand and 5 parts gravel or crushed rock. The concrete should form a collar around the post. With rock and gravel in the hole, brace the post in position (see page 274). Compact the concrete well and bring it 1" above grade. Trowel off the top so that it slopes away from the post for drainage. When the concrete sets, seal the space between post and concrete with asphalt.

Rusted steel or cast iron posts may be salvaged by cutting a piece from a spare and splicing it to the old piece with carriage bolts. Pipe-style posts can be mended by slipping the old post into a pipe

HOW TO ANCHOR A FENCE POST TO CONCRETE

1. Pour concrete posts at least 8″ deep on a rock fill and insert upended bolt in wet concrete. Let base set 48 hours before erecting posts.

2. Drill holes in ends of posts to fit over anchor bolts. If patio concrete is already in place, drill hole in masonry and insert lag screw in post end to fit into the hole drilled in the concrete.

3. Before putting posts in place, coat the grain end with asphalt paint as a seal against water penetration. This will check possible rot and insect invasion.

4. Slip post over anchor bolt in concrete. This type of anchorage resists side pressures and heavy winds.

1   2   3

1. If your fence posts have been pushed over or have pulled up, reset them, using a posthole digger to make holes as small as possible. **2.** A good wood preservative is of greatest importance when mending fences. Treatment with this chemical assures a long life for the posts. **3.** When it comes to replacing pickets, a good spacer is quickly found in a spare picket placed between the others for uniformity.

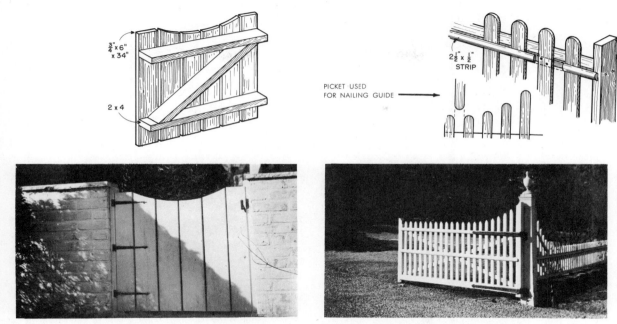

1. *Wide board gate, 2 × 4 supports on back, top curve made with straight-line cuts.*

2. *Picket fence gate, supported on long strap hinges, makes a graceful picture anywhere.*

of larger diameter. Apply protective coatings to metals, using red lead for above ground and asphalt compounds for below grade.

Broken or rotted pickets are best replaced individually, using an old one as a model for forming new ones. They can be cut quickly from standard stock obtainable in your lumber yard.

HOW TO BUILD STURDY GATES

The simplest gate of all is one built of boards using only lap joints, a process of nailing one board to another. The first sketch shows the Z-shaped frame of 2 × 4's that joins the boards and adds strength. The boards are ¾" × 6" stock.

Gate Number 2 is a combination of a picket fence with the pickets increased in length to form an upward curve at the hinge end. The strength of this gate lies in a solid footing for the post, plus the extra-long strap hinges on which it swings.

Gate Number 3 requires only one complex joint, a cross lap joint in the center, which can be completed with a hand saw and chisel but which adds greatly to the strength of the gate. All the joints are nailed; strength can be gained by the use of angle irons screwed to the inner surfaces of the joints.

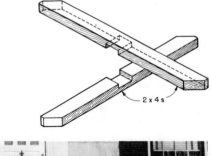

3. *Simple but substantial gate of heavy material requires but one cross lap joint.*

For rustic fencing, make a simple gate as shown in photograph 4. Here, of course, the homeowner can let his own talent have free rein, since there are no hard and fast design rules to follow.

4. *Rustic fence, with beveled ends in slots for added strength, cannot be moved unless both hinge supports are turned at once.*

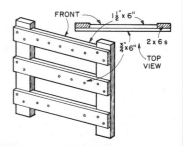

6. *Three-rail gate with seemingly mortised joints is easily constructed of overlapped boards, which add strength as well as beauty.*

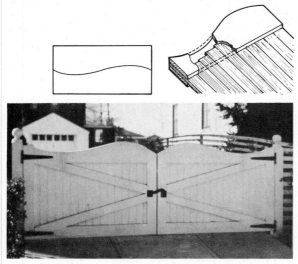

5. *Seemingly massive gate is made entirely of ¾" or 1" boards, tongue-and-grooved stock. Top curve is cut with coping saw.*

Gate Number 5 is a major project. It will look solid from all angles and—properly built—be solid. The body of this structure is tongue-and-grooved stock, which adds rigidity. Bracing is all of 1" stock, the same as is the body part, and the bracing is duplicated for both sides. The monotony of the pattern is relieved by the upper curve, which requires a band or saber saw (power), or coping or keyhole saw (hand). Cutting a curve can be accomplished for all needed pieces in a single cut, using the system shown. Nail two wide boards together, mark the curve, and cut an identical curve matching both sides and right and left gates. After the cutting, you'll have four pieces, each with the same curve. Assemble as shown.

The sixth gate, although plainer in appearance, is more complicated to construct but has added rigidity. The two uprights are 2 × 6 timbers; the cross members—visible from the front side only—are 1½ × 6's set flush on the rear side and covered over by ¾" × 6" boards. The latter, in overlapping the uprights, give the appearance to the visible cross members of having been set in mortises.

HOW TO PATCH PIERS AND POSTS

Out of sight and frequently concealed by shrubbery, therefore likely to be overlooked during periodic house check-ups, are those piers that support porches, girders, and parts of the house foundation. In the case on page 279, a brick pier under a porch corner was the culprit. Once cemented over, cracks developed in the cement and water penetrated to the brick, which in turn crumbled. Many bricks were defective, and replacement of the entire pier was the only economical and safe procedure.

First clear a space for a temporary footing for a house jack, which may be borrowed or rented. Broad boards and heavy timbers are necessary for ground supports under the jack. Proceed carefully with the jack, raising the building only 1/32" above the pier; this should be just enough to remove the defective material.

Since the new pier will not be ready to receive

MAINTAINING POSTS AND PIERS

1. *Investigation reveals a badly worn and weathered pier, stucco peeled away, and bricks no longer sound and safe.*

2. *Both eye and level show the house has not dropped and rebuilding the pier to the same size is possible and practical.*

3. *A building jack needs a firm footing before it can hold the house load. Long planks and large blocks are pyramided as a base.*

4. *A borrowed screw-type jack is tried for size and the block footing adjusted to dimensions of the jack.*

5. *Jack bar is turned until the load rests on jack instead of footing. One more half turn is enough to lift house from pier.*

6. *Paper slips between house sill and pier. Jack now carries the load and the pier may be removed with safety.*

7. *Pier comes apart easily, as most of the mortar has decayed and turned to sand.*

8. *A new footing for a new pier is the first step undertaken. Cement square is ready to receive brick at ground level.*

9. *New pier doesn't fit, so a concrete filler between pier and house is constructed to fill gap. No form is necessary.*

10. *Final touch is new stucco coat over the new brick pier. Stucco is brushed smooth, then troweled over.*

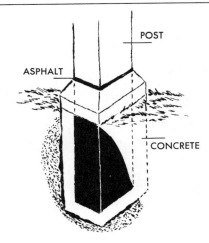

the weight of the building for at least twenty-four hours, provide additional props as a safeguard. A hydraulic jack may not be able to hold the weight that long, particularly if it has a slight leak. Also, the base under the jack may be on soft ground.

After removal of the defective pier, the all-important footing should be checked. Frost action, roots, and animals may have undermined it. Concrete is the best material to use here. With a mix of 4 parts gravel, 2½ parts sand, and 1 part cement, rebuild the pier as illustrated. The core of a brick pier may be filled with rubble or concrete to form a solid masonry unit.

If, as will probably happen, the new pier does not exactly fit under the sill, the space between should be filled either with mortar, forced into the space to fill it completely, or with wood wedges (preferably hardwood) inserted all around and the protruding ends sawed off.

POSTS SET IN A CONCRETE PORCH

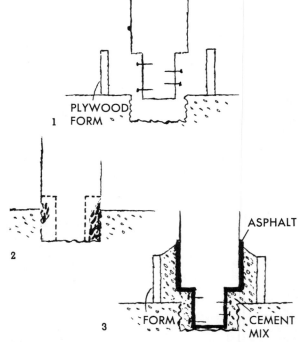

1. *When a wood post set in a concrete porch rots at the base, remove the rotted portion with a saw. Cut as sketched to form two rabbets for new base.* **2.** *Drive several nails into lower part of the post where new base is to be added. These nails will hold post securely in the cement which is to be poured into the form.* **3.** *Coat exposed underpart of post with asphalt, and compact 1 part cement to 2 parts sand plus bonding agent and water into form. Bevel top to shed rain quickly.*

POSTS ON A WOOD-FLOOR PORCH

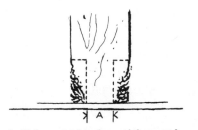

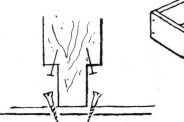

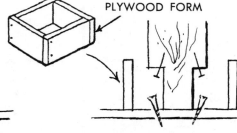

PLYWOOD FORM

1. *If the outside edges of the post have rotted, rabbet cut the post with a saw and remove the excess with a chisel. The center part A must be at least half the thickness of the post.*

2. *Drive several coated nails into this center base and into the underside of the exposed part of the post. Also set several large screws into floor within cutout area.*

3. *Make a form of ½" plywood to fit around the four sides of the post. This form should be about 2" wider and longer than the size of the post. Coat the inside of the form with oil or grease.*

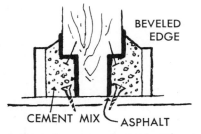

BEVELED EDGE

CEMENT MIX — ASPHALT

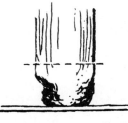

4. *Coat the exposed wood with asphalt. Then mix 1 part cement, 2 parts sand, and water, and compact into form. Bevel the upper edge of the cement mix. Let cement harden, then remove form.*

5. *If, however, most of the base has rotted through, it is necessary to cut across the post about 2" above the rotted area. Hold post securely while sawing so as not to disturb the upper part.*

6. *Make a base out of several pieces of wood, beveling the edges so that it sheds water easily. Nail pieces together with aluminum or coated nails that won't rust.*

Cement must set twenty-four hours before the jack is removed and the building's weight placed on the new masonry. Whether the brick pier is left bare or cemented over, it's best to protect it from water penetration by means of a masonry-sealer paint after the cement has cured for a week or two.

The proper way to set a post in the soil is to use a concrete form around the base. (See sketch.) If you have this type of post, chances are that you will not encounter rot — as long as you maintain a protective coating over the exposed section of the wood.

If this type of post does develop rot, it is best to remove the entire post and concrete block base. Set a new post into the ground, cover the undersurface part with asphalt, then add a concrete mix of 1 part cement, 2 parts sand, and 4 parts gravel, with enough water to make it a slow-flowing mass.

Methods of setting other types of posts are detailed in the accompanying drawings.

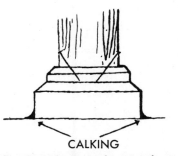

CALKING

7. *Slip base between bottom of post and wood floor of porch. Nail in position with coated finishing nails. Use caulking compound or asphalt around base to keep out water.*

HOW TO BUILD AND REPAIR
RETAINING WALLS

A retaining wall is a masonry fence that holds back earth. While it may be ornamental to enhance the landscape, its primary purpose is one of utility. Its construction differs considerably from that of a simple fence. Retaining walls permit drastic changes in your present landscape. For instance, a steep, unusable slope where not even grass can gain a foothold may be divided into a series of ter-

Selected flat fieldstone joined with mortar, with larger stone keyed in, supports earth base of this terrace, encloses stairs.

Low cut-stone wall, laid up dry, creates a formal effect. Similar stone, also laid up dry, is retaining wall for broad stone-capped step. Flags and wall cap are similarly cut.

Large blocks of stone, laid up dry, make level spot around the house, divide the playground area from wooded slope.

races with low retaining walls. The terraces may then be planted to grass or flowers.

Erosion, which covers graded walks and drives with silt during each rainfall, can be stopped by setting up retaining walls. Then, too, outdoor living requires flat areas for patios and playgrounds. The sloping lot, not naturally adapted to such pastimes, may be leveled by means of a retaining wall of the necessary height behind which the flat area may be constructed.

All retaining walls begin at a point below frost level. Since water in the ground expands on freezing, it will lift anything upward, including a masonry wall. With thawing, the heavy wall sinks deeply and irregularly into the soft ground. Cracks will develop, or the wall may even tumble. To avoid any of this, build the wall on a footing below maximum frost depth, generally no more than 24" in most areas.

The base is the widest part of a retaining wall. The footing it rests on is at least 6" wider than the base, and the wall may taper toward its top. This is possible since the greatest pressure of earth on the uphill side of the wall is at its base. The exposed face of a retaining wall should be slightly inclined toward the uphill side. If it were truly vertical, it would appear to be toppling forward. The slant is approximately 1" for each foot of height. Before backfilling behind a retaining wall, lay a row of field tiles along the footing, sloping ¼" per foot toward either end. Then fill to at least half the wall height with loose gravel and scrap masonry to provide quick drainage. At 6' intervals along the wall's base, leave weep holes 2" in diameter to prevent water from accumulating behind the wall.

Masonry materials for wall construction include irregularly shaped fieldstone, cut stone for more formal effects, concrete and cinder blocks which may be faced with cut stone or brick, concrete blocks cast in decorative patterns, and common and face brick. Common brick and concrete blocks may also be faced with simulated stone. It is wise to choose a material suited to the architectural style of the home as well as to the general appearance of the planned landscape. Formal gardens deserve cut stone or formal brick patterns. Rustic scenes and backgrounds are enhanced with retaining walls of fieldstone, laid up dry or mortared together. In contrast, an informal gathering place, such as a patio with a grill, might appear to best advantage against a wall of common brick.

In planning to control a slope with a wall or with a series of walls, first consider the soil characteristics. Heavy clay slopes with slow water penetration should not exceed a rise of 1' for each 3' horizontally. A greater slope will result in erosion, and the surface will deteriorate into a series of gullies.

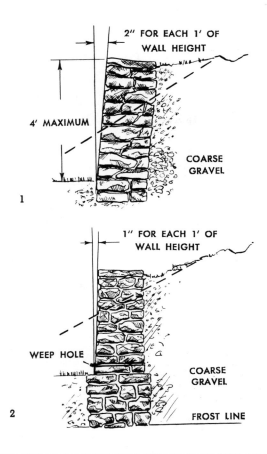

2" FOR EACH 1' OF WALL HEIGHT

4' MAXIMUM

COARSE GRAVEL

1

1" FOR EACH 1' OF WALL HEIGHT

WEEP HOLE

COARSE GRAVEL

FROST LINE

2

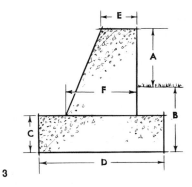

3

Wall Height	Depth to Footing	Footing		Wall	
		Thickness	Width	Top	Bottom
A	B	C	D	E	F
12	12	6	14	6	8
24	18	8	24	8	16
36	24	10	36	10	24
48	30	12	48	12	32

Sketch 1. *Where stone is laid up dry, entire wall is inclined toward retained earth. Fill is the same as for mortared wall.* **Sketch 2.** *Proportion of cut-stone retaining wall laid up with mortar. Face inclines at less of an angle than with dry wall. Footing begins at frost line. Note gravel fill behind wall.* **Sketch 3.** *Measurements indicated in inches.*

BUILDING A RETAINING WALL

1. *In laying a block or stone wall, the footing below grade is most easily made with poured concrete onto which block or stone is cemented.*

2. *When laying concrete or cinder block or cut stone, check work frequently with level to assure strength and even appearance.*

4. Rear of block wall is not finished with pointed joints. All should be tight, however, and scrap masonry used as fill.

5. This block wall is built up with scrap brick and mortar on "fill" side. Inclined brick discourages juvenile wall-walkers.

3. Where a slope is to be established, use a level and a rule to form the triangle indicated in Sketches No. 1 and 2 on the previous page.

6. Visible mortar joints are carefully pointed with concave stone beader, excess mortar being brushed away when partly dry.

7. Filled in behind wall and planted to lawn and shrubs, the new terrace, created by means of the wall, adds new attractiveness to property.

Grade accordingly uphill of the wall. Sandy soil or deep loam, where water penetrates quickly, may be graded for a 1' rise in each 1½'. Start the excavation on a slope so as to follow land contours if at all possible. This will keep the footing of the wall reasonably level and will produce the maximum amount of usable land when the wall is finished and the ground graded behind it.

For walls up to 2' high, where the ground levels off at the wall-top point, an 8" thick wall may serve the purpose. For higher walls, and those where the ground rises above wall level, the base is made thicker in proportion. General wall proportions are indicated in Sketch 3 (page 283). For stone walls, consult Sketches 1 and 2, which show forward slope and other proportions.

So-called dry-wall construction means that stone is gathered and selected by shape—preferably flat—stacked up and keyed together without any mortar at all. In a wet wall, masonry is joined with mortar. The mortared wall is obviously stronger, since the masonry is combined into a solid mass and individual stones or blocks cannot be pushed out. Where earth is level at the top of the

1. *Dig a hole 38" square and 28" deep. From it, dig a foot-wide trench for a run-off pipeline, if desired. Make certain pitch of trench is away from well by pouring water into it.* 2. *For a small well, a depth of two blocks is sufficient. If there is no run-off line, you should make it at least three blocks deep. You may have to cut a block or two for staggered joints.* 3. *Run the bell end of your drainpipe line into the well, as close to the bottom as possible. Use ce-* *ment and rubble to fill in to level of other blocks.* 4. *Drain line is made of 6" vitreous tile, and joints are filled with mortar. Connect into regular city storm drain line, using a "Y" fitting.* 5. *This is the way the well looks before the cover is added. You do not have to worry about packing joints with a lot of mortar. There is little or no strain on them. (Continued on next page.)*

wall, dry construction may be followed, but if the hillside continues upward above the wall, mortar the materials together for greater strength.

Pointing (shaping) of masonry joints on a retaining wall has much to do with the wall's appearance. With stone in particular, interesting effects may be produced. Where mortar is raked out to a depth of an inch or more, a deep shadow pattern results. Brick is usually pointed in a manner similar to that on house walls and chimneys. Concrete blocks may be pointed with concave or convex mortar joints, or you can allow the mortar squeezed out to harden without pointing.

HOW TO SOLVE YARD FLOODING PROBLEMS

If your rainspouts periodically flood your yard, or if you're the recipient of downwash from your neighbor's property, a dry well or catch basin will solve the problem of excess water. A dry well alone will handle most ordinary situations. However, if the soil is of clay, hardpan, ledge, or otherwise very poorly drained, a dry well alone may not suffice. A drain-tile line may be needed in addition to carry the water from the well to your sewer line, storm drain, or a slope where runoff is possible.

A small grill can be used to cover the well or basin if the volume of drain water is never too great. If the problem is that of an occasional flash flood, a large grate is a wiser choice.

In the well illustrated above, 6" wide cement blocks were used in two courses, laid directly atop a 2" floor of cement. A 6" vitrified tile line carries the water from the well into the regular city sewer. The large, barred cover was made with lengths of 1" pipe butt-welded to two lengths of ⅜" by 1½" strap iron. The grill was painted thoroughly to prevent rust. Many hardware stores or building supply dealers carry a variety of stock-size grills, if you would rather not make one (see next page).

6. *The cover, in this instance, is made of 1" pipe welded to two bars of heavy strap iron. You can buy any of a variety of covers at your local building-supply house.* **7.** *A wood frame is nailed around the edge of the well. This frame serves as a guide for the pouring and molding of a* cement border around the cover. Trowel cement smooth. **8.** *The cover is removed carefully, and the supporting surface is troweled smooth with cement. Finally, the cover is replaced and the cement border is given a last touch-up.*

HOW TO USE GARAGES FOR STORAGE

Most garages are either square or rectangular in shape, and since cars don't match such shapes, there are vacant corners, spaces overhead, and room all around the car that can be used for extra storage.

THE OVERHEAD AREA By far the largest space available is found in the gable-roof garage, with a hip-roof structure second in line. Except for large multicar structures where a small apartment may be built overhead, this space is often entirely wast-

ed. With a two-car garage, the entire space may be utilized. A second floor may be built and, except for an entrance into it, the whole floor can be used for storage. The sketch showing joists indicates the manner in which such a floor is supported. Where possible, the new floor joists, which are run across the shortest dimension, can rest on the top plate of the walls. Where there is no room because of the construction of the roof, the joists can be set below the plate and rested on blocks attached to the wall studs. For average lightweight storage, 2 × 6 joists spaced 16" apart will do. If heavier materials are to be stored, use 2 × 8's. Just be sure to provide clear-

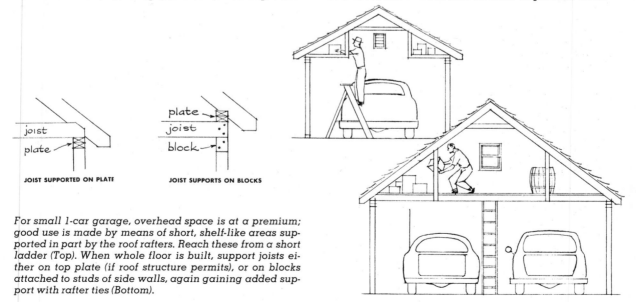

For small 1-car garage, overhead space is at a premium; good use is made by means of short, shelf-like areas supported in part by the roof rafters. Reach these from a short ladder (Top). When whole floor is built, support joists either on top plate (if roof structure permits), or on blocks attached to studs of side walls, again gaining added support with rafter ties (Bottom).

ance for the car. Partial flooring over the area is also a very good idea—in fact, it may even be preferred in order to provide easy entrance from below by way of a folding stairway. With a one-car garage of limited width—and, consequently, limited headroom above—a partial floor along both walls, leaving a triangle-shaped storage area on each side of an open center section, is a good alternative. Small items can be stored this way and access easily made by a removable ladder.

ALONG-THE-WALL STORAGE A storage wall in the home is a popular feature, and the same idea, but with a fraction of the cost, can be adapted to the garage. The shelves are the easiest part—regular sheathing or shelving supported on 3″ strips along the wall and cross pieces connecting the two vertical 2 × 3's in front (one in the middle, the other set out ½″ to serve as a stop for the panels; a 2″ furring strip the length of the opening is nailed to the floor to serve as an anchor for the vertical 2 × 3's and also as a guide for the bottom edge of the panels). The sliding panels are two standard 4′ × 8′ pieces of hardboard, cut down slightly to fit the space exactly and to provide an inch overlap at the center. One of the pieces cut from the hardboard serves as a valance to hide the edges of the hanger rails.

INSIDE-THE-WALL STORAGE Where the walls of the garage are open and the studs visible, innu-merable small articles can be stored on small shelves between studs. Set a ¼″ × 1½″ strip along the outer shelf edge to keep articles from sliding off. The variety of such shelves is almost endless, with spacing between them determined by the items to be stored.

In some parts of the country, this "open" storage might well be objectionable owing to dust accumulation or insect invasion. A cover of transparent plastic in the form of a weighted drop curtain will, in the majority of cases, handle this problem.

HOW TO CARE FOR YARD TOOLS AND EQUIPMENT

HOSES Sooner or later almost every garden hose springs a leak. An unseen kink causes a break when the water is turned on, or the constant rubbing of the hose against a rough wall wears it thin. Hose-mending is a simple process and requires only a few minutes, particularly if you keep a garden hose first-aid kit handy. This should include several splicers or mender tubes and pipe clamps, one or two male and female coupling-splicers, some hose washers and, if you have a rubber hose, a tube of black rubber-base cement (not the ordinary household rubber cement) and a roll of friction tape. When you buy the splicers or mender tubes, make certain to get the right size for your hose.

When you use a splicer, insert one end flush into

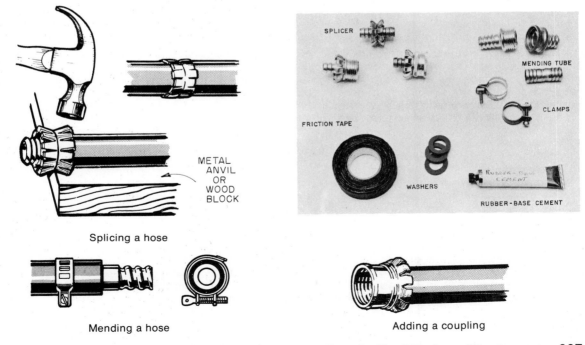

Splicing a hose

Mending a hose

Adding a coupling

INSERTING A FORCE-FIT COUPLING

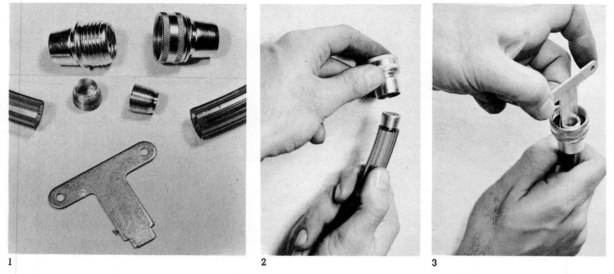

1   2   3

1. *Special force-fit fittings for plastic garden hose come with locking key used for assembly. Both male and female units are available.* 2. *Insert threaded bushing into the plastic hose; it's tapered for an easy fit. Slip male or* *female coupling over outside of hose.* 3. *Special key fits into slots inside the bushing. Turn clockwise to tighten until top edge of bushing is flush with edge of hose.*

the garden hose. Tap the prongs gently and gradually, working your way around all the prongs until they are firmly set into the hose. Make certain the prongs grip the hose tightly; then insert the splicer into the other end of the hose and repeat.

If you use a mender tube, insert one end of the tube into the hose. Slip a pipe clamp over so that it's about ½" away from the edge of the hose and tighten the nut and bolt with a screwdriver. Then slip on another pipe clamp and slide the mender tube into the other section of garden hose so that the two hose ends are touching. Push the second clamp so that it's about 1" from the first and tighten the nut and bolt.

The same method is used to add a new coupling to your hose. Couplings are available in brass, rubber or plastic.

It is easier to repair a rubber hose that has sprung a small leak than a plastic hose. To fix a rubber hose, clean the damaged area thoroughly and dry with a clean cloth. Apply a thick coat of the rubber-base cement and let it dry from five to ten minutes. Then apply a second thin coat and wrap a single layer of friction tape around the hose. Hold the tape securely for a minute or so and then let it dry. To fix a small leak in a plastic hose, add a splicer in the same way as you would if there were a large leak.

To repair a large leak, cut out the defective section of the hose with a sharp knife, making certain the ends are square or straight up and down. If you're repairing plastic hose, dip the ends in hot water to soften the plastic, thus making it easier to work.

In the fall, before you store your hose for the winter months, separate each length of hose and drain any water out of each. Lay them flat or on a slight slope to dry out. Remove all old washers and disconnect any automatic coupling attachments. Roll each length of hose separately without kinks or twists and store them in a bushel basket or on a hose reel. Use a brush with detergent or soap and water to clean the nozzles and couplings, then rinse several times and wipe dry.

YARD TOOLS Tool handles usually break because of dry rot, caused by being left out in all kinds of weather, alternately to soak and dry. Repairs are seldom effective for a long period of time. However, a split handle can be temporarily mended by spreading waterproof glue the length of the split, bringing the two sides together, and taping the handle tightly. Then drill one or several holes through the handle at right angles to the split and insert round-headed carriage bolts, adding a washer and nut on the opposite side.

Shovels and spades often turn up corners by

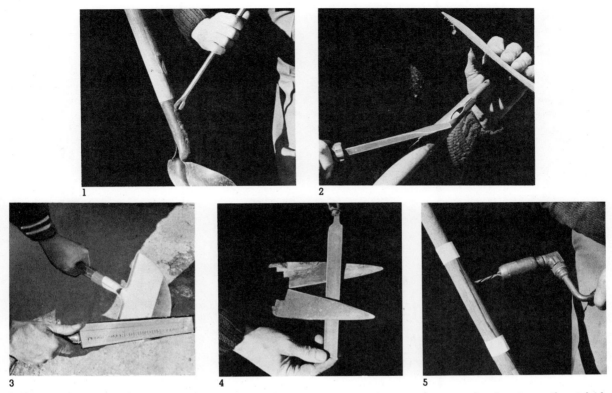

1. *To remove unusable handle, file off rivet head on one side, then pull remainder through with nail puller or pry.* 2. *Some socket-type handles have a hole where wedge can be used to loosen them.* 3. *Sharpen to original bevel.* *Long bevel gives sharper edge but is easily nicked.* 4. *Follow original bevel in sharpening cutting tools and clippers. Thirty degrees is right.* 5. *Split handles can still be used if taped and glued, then bolted through split.*

banging into unyielding rock. These can be hammered flat, then a new edge filed on the dull surface. Use a mill file or a grinding stone. Sharpen spades from both sides. Hoes, on the other hand, are sharpened only from the outside face — that is, the edge toward the ground is filed toward the user. A long, thin edge will work more easily. A blunt edge lasts longer but doubles your work on weeds. It's a good idea in sharpening tools of this sort to follow the lines of the original edge. This applies particularly to assorted grass and pruning clippers. Those joined by pins can readily be dismantled for sharpening and oiled for reassembly.

Steel rakes with missing teeth are best replaced. Wood and bamboo rakes, however, can be given new life with little effort. Replacements can be made from sawed strips of hardwood, shaped with pliers after soaking in boiling water.

Before storing tools away for the winter, clean all working edges. Use steel wool or a wire brush on shovels, rakes, and hoes. Use kerosene to remove dirt. Paint linseed oil on all wood handles to help preserve the wood. Apply a protective coating of grease or oil over metal parts. For grass shears and pruners, wash in kerosene and use sandpaper on tough spots. Sharpen cutting edges on a whetstone; loosen tension on all springs; replace worn or rusted nuts and bolts and coat with grease or oil.

Any sprinkler needs a complete postsummer checkup. Remove and clean all nozzle tips. Then clean the sprinkler itself, discarding old washers. After drying all the parts, lubricate bushings and bearings with a waterproof grease and coat all metal surfaces with a thin layer of oil.

SHAPING UP YARD TOOLS

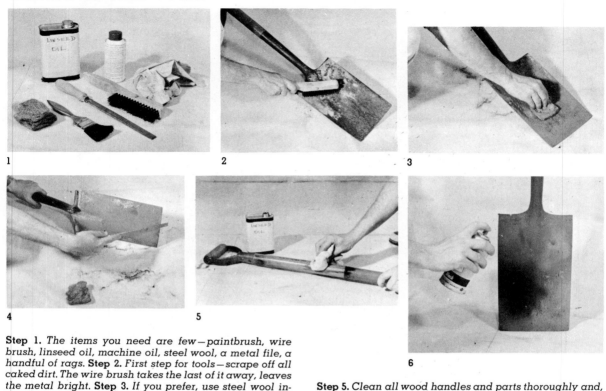

1 2 3

4 5

6

Step 1. *The items you need are few—paintbrush, wire brush, linseed oil, machine oil, steel wool, a metal file, a handful of rags.* **Step 2.** *First step for tools—scrape off all caked dirt. The wire brush takes the last of it away, leaves the metal bright.* **Step 3.** *If you prefer, use steel wool instead of the brush. This does as good a job unless the metal is pitted by long wear and rust.* **Step 4.** *File cutting edges sharp now. Spring may come fast, giving you no time later for putting the lawn equipment in good shape.*

Step 5. *Clean all wood handles and parts thoroughly and, unless they are protected with a coat of paint, apply coating of linseed oil.* **Step 6.** *Spray cleaned metal surfaces with a good grade of penetrating oil, or, if you prefer to distinguish your tools by color, paint the metal.*

8

HAND TOOLS:
HAMMERS · SCREWDRIVERS · PLIERS · WRENCHES · HANDSAWS · FILES AND RASPS · PLANES · CHISELS · DRILL BITS · AWLS · RULERS · LEVELS · SQUARES · VISES · CLAMPS · HAND TOOL CARE
POWER TOOLS:
CIRCULAR SAWS · SABER SAWS · DRILLS · SANDERS · ROUTERS · TABLE SAWS · RADIAL ARM SAWS · BANDSAWS · DRILL PRESSES · WOOD LATHES · THE PLANER-MOLDER · HOW TO CHOOSE POWER TOOLS

THE HOME WORKSHOP

Tools have been used by man since before recorded history. While much progress has been made in tool development and design, basic hand tools are still an important part of the workshop.

Skilled use of hand tools can be personally satisfying. This chapter deals with the use and care of hand and power tools commonly found in the workshop.

HAND TOOLS

HAMMERS

Hammers come in a wide variety, each designed for a specific purpose.

The claw hammer is the most common in workshops and homes. Shapes and weights vary, as well as the quality of construction. The head of a claw hammer is made of forged steel, the handle made of wood, metal, or fiberglass. The claws may be either curved, designed primarily for pulling nails, or nearly straight, for separating boards or splitting wood along the grain.

Claw hammer heads range in weight from 7 to 20 ounces. The most common are 13 to 16 ounces.

The face of the hammer—that part used to strike the nail—is smooth and crowned, which means the center is slightly raised. Crowning of the head allows setting nails flush without marring the surrounding surface.

The face and edge of the hammer are hardened to prevent marring and to resist wear. To prevent chipping of the rim, the edge of the face is beveled; on some hammers, it is specially hardened.

Flying chips are an ever-present hazard when hammers are used, threatening injury to the eyes and face. Always wear protective devices, such as goggles or a face mask.

Claw hammers are designed for driving nails and should be used for this purpose only. Because most nails are of relatively soft metal, it is unlikely that chipping or damage to the hammer will occur if claw hammers are used correctly. Claw hammers should not be used to drive cold chisels, star drills, brick chisels, punches, or heavy-duty all-steel wood chisels. The heads of these tools are made of specially hardened steel that can damage the face of the hammer and present a chipping hazard. However, some types of nails, such as cement nails, are specially hardened and should not be driven with claw hammers either.

The V of the claw is sharpened on the inside edges to grip nails and aid in their removal. When pulling nails, pull on the handle until it is almost vertical. If the nail needs more pulling, relocate the hammer to get a second hold on the nail, nearer the surface. Attempting to pull nails with the handle past the vertical stage causes problems. The force it exerts lessens as it passes the vertical posi-

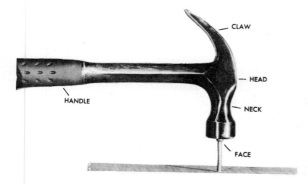

CLAW

HEAD

HANDLE

NECK

FACE

tion. There is also the chance of bending the nail or marring the surface.

Hammers have definite balance points. Maximum impact is provided if the hammer is held properly—at the indentation in the handle, near its heavy end—and swung freely. Allow the face of the hammer to meet the head of the nail squarely, and drive nails with five or six light blows of the hammer, rather than one or two hard whacks. Strike the head of the nail squarely and direct the blow in line with the direction of the nail.

BALL PEEN HAMMERS Ball peen hammers are considered an all-around mechanic's hammer, having crowned faces that are hardened, beveled rims, and a full, round ball. They vary in head weights from 2 ounces to 48 ounces, with the most commonly used sizes being 12 to 16 ounces. The peen was originally designed for hammering rivets flat, a specialty no longer needed in most workshops.

The ball peen hammer is valuable to the average handyman mainly because of the versatility of its hardened head. It can be used to drive cold chisels, star drills, and hardened concrete nails. Ball peen hammers are also useful for shaping and straightening metal, especially in the heavier head weights.

RUBBER MALLETS Rubber mallets are useful when joining two close-fitting pieces of wood, since they will not mar the surface through accidental contact. Rubber hammers are also good choices for driving wooden dowels without mashing their ends.

PLASTIC-FACED HAMMERS Such hammers allow you to work on metal surfaces without marring them. They are available in various head weights, intended for fine to heavy use. Some are available with threaded ends or faces that are interchangeable.

TACK HAMMERS Tack hammers are made of high-quality steel and weigh from 5 to 8 ounces. Small, magnetic tack hammers save wear and tear

on the fingers when driving the small tacks used to hold carpet and upholstery, as well as fine finishing nails. The magnetic end of the hammer is used to pick the tack up and start it in place with a quick, light blow. Then simply reverse the hammer and finish setting the tack.

SMALL SLEDGE HAMMERS The best kind of hammer for pounding star drills when boring holes in masonry are short-handled hammers with double-faced heads that have crowned and beveled faces. The head is of hardened steel, varying in weight from 2 to 4 pounds. This tool is also useful in driving hardened nails into cement—the extra weight will drive the nails more efficiently and with less chance of injury than the common claw hammer. Other uses for this hammer include driving chisels, punches, and wedges.

SLEDGES AND MAULS Sledges and mauls are larger than the drilling hammer, weighing from 6 to 30 pounds. The smaller sizes are useful for driving stakes, splitting firewood with a metal wedge, bracing concrete forms, and the like. The larger sledges are used for heavy demolition work, such as breaking up concrete floors or walks.

Many hammers still retain the wooden handle even in this age of synthetic materials. Handles made of wood (usually hickory) loosen with age. If one shows any such signs, tighten it immediately. If neglected, the head may fly off the handle, causing injury or damage. Loose heads may be tightened by driving a small metal wedge into the area where the handle comes through the head flush with its upper surface.

Hammers are also available with fiberglass or steel handles, the latter generally covered with rubber to make the hammer comfortable to use. The wood handle is quite sufficient in strength, is

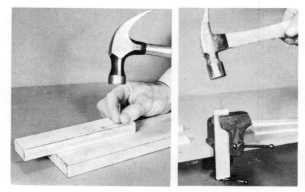

Two types of claw hammer: (Left) the standard claw used for withdrawing nails; (Right) the straighter claw, which can also be used to separate boards or as a splitting wedge.

Wedges driven into end grain of handle secure head in place so it can't fly off.

Extra weight of sledge drills faster.

Light sledge goes hand in hand with cold chisel.

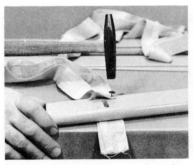

Lightweight tack hammer has dozens of uses for driving small fasteners.

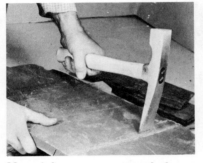

Mason's hammer scores mark, deepens score to split stone. The square end chips points.

Machinist's ball-peen hammer can be useful on jobs such as this, because of its extra weight.

comfortable to the hand, and will last many years. Remember, if the handle and the hammer separate, you have probably abused the tool, either by overstressing it in pulling or prying, or by using the hammer for a purpose for which it was not intended.

If you have one of each of the following types of hammers at your disposal, you are ready to tackle any hammering job:

1. A claw hammer, for general carpentry, 16 ounce head.
2. A tack hammer, preferably magnetized, for driving tacks and brads.
3. A ball peen hammer or 2-pound sledge for hand drilling in masonry or other heavy work. The broader face of the sledge offers more protection to the tool-holding hand.
4. A small sledge hammer for working with masonry, brick, or stone.

SCREWDRIVERS

The screwdriver is one of the most useful tools you can own. Good ones have a tip and blade of high-grade steel, with sides that are nearly parallel. The steel tip is hardened so it will not burr easily.

Screwdrivers are designated by their length and type of tip. The correct screwdriver for the job is one that correctly fits the head of the screw. This makes it easier to drive the screw and reduces the chance of the screwdriver slipping off the head.

Screwdrivers are available in a very large assortment of styles and sizes, some with blades that ratchet, some with interchangeable tips and many other styles. Heavier-tipped screwdrivers are intended for heavier jobs, lighter ones for more delicate work. Using the longest screwdriver possible will increase your leverage and make the job easier.

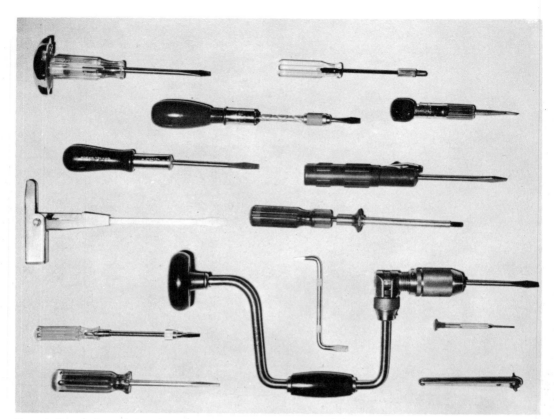

From left to right and down: *palm-grip ratchet screwdriver, screw-holding screwdriver, spiral ratchet, ratchet handle (plastic) screwdriver, ratchet handle (wood) screwdriver, insulated handle with flashlight, T-handle screwdriver, split shaft screwdriver.* Lower left: *Flexible shaft and standard screwdrivers.* Lower center: *Ratchet brace with screwdriver bit, and, pictured inside, offset screwdriver.* Lower right: *jeweler's and offset ratchet screwdrivers.*

The four basic types of screwdrivers most commonly used include:

1. The common flat-bladed screwdriver. Available in a wide assortment of sizes, the width and thickness of the tip should fit the screw exactly. If it is too wide, it will mar the surface around the screw; if too narrow, it may slip.

2. Spiral ratchet and ratchet screwdrivers may be used with blades of various sizes. The ratchet allows the blade to turn in one direction while the handle turns in both directions. They can be used to drive or remove screws. Their semiautomatic action allows them to do the job much faster than ordinary screwdrivers.

3. Phillips screwdrivers are designed for screws with Phillips heads, having two slots that cross at the center of the head to guide the blade of the screwdriver.

4. Offset screwdrivers fit in tight places, where

room isn't sufficient for a regular screwdriver. One type of offset screwdriver has two blades at opposite ends, set at right angles to the handle.

Accessories available to do a neater job with screws include various types of countersinking bits used in a drill or a brace, and a plug cutter. Plugs are cut of the same type of material that the screws are placed in and are used to conceal the hole.

There are heavy-duty screwdrivers with square shanks. When extra force is needed you can use a wrench on the shank to turn and loosen large, rusted screws. The handle of the screwdriver should be held firmly in your right hand, the head of the handle should be against your palm, and your thumb and fingers should grasp the handle near the ferrule.

A screwdriver does not have to be sharpened, but when required, it can be ground on an emery

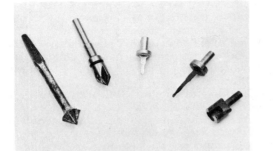

These are various types of countersinking bits (for sinking screws) and a plug cutter for making plugs of wood to conceal screws.

wheel or the sides can be filed with a flat file. Never bevel the tip of a screwdriver. When filing the blade, use a good vise, and make the tip straight across the end. It must be at right angles to the sides and shank. Make certain that the faces of the blade near the tip are parallel to each other. This is a vital point; if it is neglected, the blade will slip often and jump out of the screw slot.

It is possible to repair damaged screwdriver tips, with careful grinding or filing. This may, however, draw the temper out of the metal tip, rendering it soft and useless. It is better to replace the screwdriver than to attempt much repair work on the tip.

PLIERS

Pliers are designed to hold materials better than can be done by hand. They do a wide variety of jobs, such as bending metal, stripping the coating from electrical wiring, grasping hot material, and insulating either for protection against electric shock or for greater comfort.

Pliers can be divided into three general categories based on their intended use: gripping, cutting, and reaching into cramped places.

PLIERS FOR GRIPPING For gripping, use the most common type of slip-joint pliers. Add a larger pair as a supplement and you'll probably find it doing double duty as a vise or wrench. A needle-nose pliers, useful when doing electrical work, will round out the basic groups of pliers you will use most often.

PLIERS FOR CUTTING WIRE Wire-cutting pliers are more varied in their design and intended use. End-cutting nippers and combination wire-cutting and wire-stripping pliers are a valuable aid to the handyman. The wire-stripping device is a notch inside the jaws through which wire is drawn to remove the insulation.

PLIERS FOR CONFINED SPACES Pliers designed for holding generally have long, thin tips that allow you to reach into confined areas. Some are needle-nosed to pick up tiny objects, others are flat or duck-billed, and work well for holding flat ob-

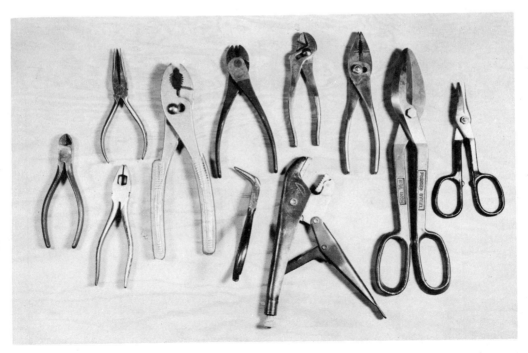

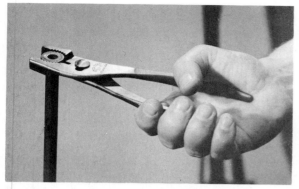

Heavy-duty slip-joint pliers are useful in holding materials with firmer grip than fingers provide.

jects firmly and securely. Do not use them for pulling nails or the finely finished jaws may spread in opposite directions, making them useless. There are also pliers with angled noses, some of which are designed for reaching into the confined areas often encountered when repairing television sets and radios.

Pliers generally require little care, aside from a light coat of oil to prevent rust. Misuse, however, will result in broken tips, dulled edges, and loosened pivots. Some pliers may be renewed by grinding, if the damage is not severe. Dip the pliers into water frequently, to prevent drawing the temper out of the metal. Grind one side at a time, then level out both sides until the nose is restored to shape.

This fine pair of spring-back pliers will be ruined if used to cut heavy-stranded cables.

Hold pliers with handle in palm of hand, using thumb as a cushion. Little finger opens pliers.

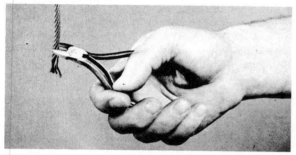

Certain pliers are suited to the job of nail cutting. Others are not designed for it and will nick or break.

End-cutting pliers will snip through wire of all kinds, cut nails off flush with surface.

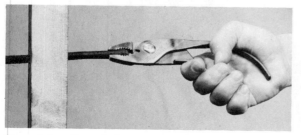

Curved handles of this type provide added gripping strength for forearm, do much extra work.

Duck-billed or flat-nosed pliers are ideal for holding fine or flat bits of metal when heated.

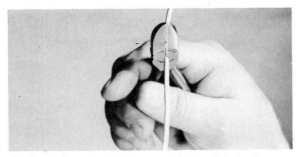

Combination wire-cutting pliers and insulation strippers; wire is being slipped through a hole to clean it of insulation.

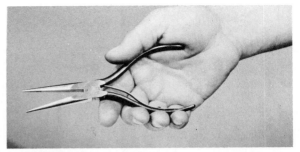

Needle-nosed pliers—handy for getting into tight corners, picking up delicate objects and parts.

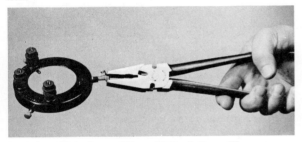

Long-handled pliers with multiple duties will prove useful on many handyman chores and electrical work.

Bent-tip needle-nosed pliers work well in particularly confined areas.

WRENCHES

Although an entire collection of wrenches isn't needed around the house, your tool kit should include at least four types: an adjustable, open-end wrench; a monkey wrench with its flat, smooth parallel jaws; a Stillson wrench for turning pipe (or better still, a pair of them, one to hold and one to turn); and a set of nonadjustable, open-end wrenches. You'll also find the Allen wrench (for recessed-head screws) and parallel-jawed pliers of value.

The majority of wrenches are used to turn square or hexagonal nuts. The first requisite of the wrench is that it fit snugly against opposite sides of the nut. Unless it does, turning will wear off the corners of the nut quickly.

In working with pipe, a Stillson wrench is used. This tightens up under pressure and the teeth of the wrench bite into the pipe. Since turning a pipe tightly into a fitting can also turn the fitting and cause damage to extensions of the line, one wrench should be used to hold the fitting rigidly, and the other to make the turn. If greater leverage is needed to open a stubborn pipe joint, a length of pipe may be slipped over the Stillson handle to lengthen it. Do *not* use a Stillson on chrome fittings, where the teeth may cause damage.

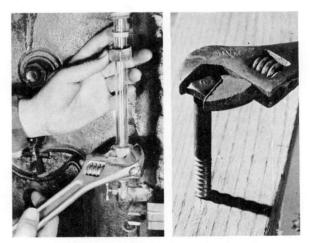

The adjustable open-end wrench is a timesaver, fitting an assortment of nut sizes on the job. Works as well on hexagonal nuts as on square types when tightened.

The plumbing trade has developed a number of special wrenches, such as basin wrenches, the internal pipe wrench, the offset hex wrench or adjustable wrench, and the strap or chain wrench. All are designed for specific purposes and most have rather limited applications.

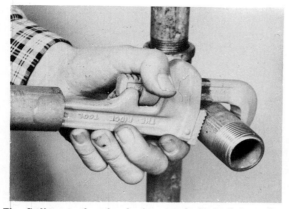

The Stillson is the plumber's wrench, fit for heavy duty. It slides around a pipe, its teeth grip firmly. In places where a joint is "frozen," pipe length slips over handle for leverage.

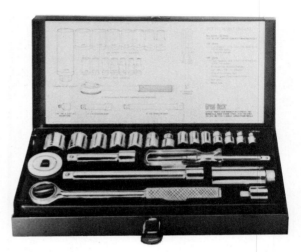

Socket set is combination ¼" and ⅜" drive.

To increase the effectiveness of nuts and to make sure they stay put even under vibration, special aids have been developed. One, the lock washer, is a specially designed washer that is split and offset on one side. As the nut is drawn down, tension is placed on the lock washer's split portions, which keeps the nut tight.

Liquids have been developed to serve the same function as lock washers. When applied to the threads before the nut is put on, they effectively bind the nut to the bolt. They allow the nut to be removed with a wrench, however.

When tightening a nut into wood, the wood may easily be damaged. As the wood shrinks, the nut is left free and its hold is reduced. To prevent this, a metal washer should be placed under the nut.

Keep a can of penetrating oil near the wrench rack in your tool shop. Fed into a rusted nut-bolt combination, it will penetrate and free the joint of rust, and you can loosen the nut then without twisting the bolt out of shape. Also, use the same lubricant on moving wrench parts to keep your wrench in top condition.

A socket wrench set contains a handle, or drive, and detachable sockets of various sizes. Sockets have six and twelve points to grasp the nut. A square hole is in the back, into which various handles can be inserted. Handles have a protruding square stud that fits into the hole. The studs and sockets come in three sizes: ¼", ⅜", and ½". A ratchet handle increases the versatility of a socket set. It is easy to operate, has a reversing lever, and is unbeatable for quick work on nuts and bolts.

With long and short extensions and universal joints, sockets can fit hex nuts and bolts almost anywhere. However, do not try to force open a tightly frozen nut or bolt with a ratchet. The mechanism can be damaged when used for the wrong purpose. To remove stubborn nuts or bolts, use an accessory available with socket sets, called a breaker bar. The breaker bar has a stud that can be swiveled at almost any angle and a long handle for maximum leverage.

HANDSAWS

The handsaw is one of the most basic of all workshop tools and one of the most frequently used. It is generally the first tool to start any job involving wood, once the measuring is done.

There are many different types of saws, each intended and designed for a specific use. With the correct saw, it is generally much easier to do any job and the results will also look better.

The first one you acquire should be a good quality crosscut saw. You will need to use it often. Later, you can add the specialty saws, such as a rip saw.

You can learn quickly to identify the type of saw you are using by looking at the teeth. The number of teeth per inch of saw blade and the manner in which they are set are used to differentiate between crosscut and rip saws.

Crosscut saws—they cut best across the grain—have from 6 to 12 teeth per inch. The more teeth per inch, the finer the cut. An 8-point saw is a good choice for all-around work, and it may, on occasion, be used for ripping. The teeth are bent outward from the plane of the blade, alternately, by the set applied to them. Each tooth of the crosscut saw is beveled on both its forward and rear edges.

Cutting angle determines ease and accuracy. The cutting technique of sawing by hand determines the ease, accuracy, and condition of the tool blade. A crosscut should be held at a 45° angle for most efficient cutting. When sawing, keep the line of sight clear, make long, smooth strokes, and position the body above the cutting surface as shown.

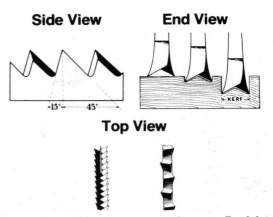

Crosscut saws are for cutting across the grain. Teeth bent to alternate sides make the cut, or kerf, wider than the blade thickness.

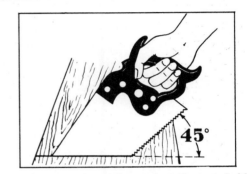

Crosscutting is easiest and smoothest if saw is held at a 45° angle to work. Extend forefinger along side of handle for better control of saw and greater accuracy.

The rip saw, designed to cut wood with the grain, has from 4 to 5½ teeth per inch. The teeth are also offset outward, alternately, but the teeth are not beveled. Rather, they are sharpened straight across on the short forward and longer tapered sides. The blade of a rip saw is tapered slightly from the toothed edge to the back, to prevent binding of the saw while ripping.

When marking work to be cut with a saw, decide first how you will use the mark. That is, will the cut be made *through* the mark or to its side? While this may not seem to be of much concern, it can change the finished dimensions of the piece. The kerf, or saw cut, will take about 1/16" of the stock and, depending on whether you take the mark or leave it, the piece could be short, just right, or too long.

When cutting, hold the saw at a right angle to the face of the stock to be cut. The knuckle of the thumb of your guiding hand may be used to keep

the saw blade perpendicular. This may result in a few scrapes at first, but you will soon get the knack of guiding the saw and keeping your skin.

Push the saw forward with the entire arm, not the hand or wrist. Most important, don't force the saw; let it do the work. *Use the full length of the blade.* The return stroke is made without downward pressure on the blade. If the saw is forced it will most likely leave the guide mark and start a curved cut on its own.

If the saw wanders from the guideline, withdraw it and start over at the point where it left the line. You may need to apply a little side pressure or twist to the blade to get it back onto course. Support the piece while cutting, including the piece that is being cut off. If the waste portion is allowed to fall freely, it may tear the wood unevenly near the end of the cut.

If the wood being cut is green or still contains

Side View   End View

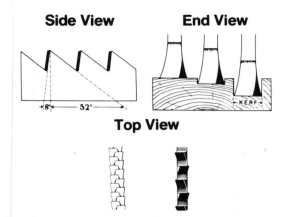

Top View

Rip saws are for cutting with the grain. Rip-saw teeth are set evenly to about ⅓ the thickness of the blade; crosscut teeth are evenly set about ¼ the thickness of the blade. Illustrations: Disston

Ripping is usually done on sawhorses. Use the saw at a 60° angle. If saw binds when cutting long sections, insert wedge in cut to make cutting easier.

This is the saw you need for accurate cutting in cabinet work. The back saw has anywhere from 18 to 32 small teeth per inch, and they are not sharply set. The cut edge is almost smooth, always straight. The big brother of the back saw is known as a miter-box saw from 20″ to 30″ long. Use these saws for cutting moldings to angles, for mitering, for accurate joints. A good trick when cutting moldings or miters is to cut 1° less than the desired angle. The pressure necessary to force the two pieces together will make a tighter joint.

Keyhole and compass saws are tapered so they can enter a drilled hole and move about in all directions from that point. Their purpose is to make cutouts in the center of a piece of wood without cutting the edges. The compass saw, a rugged 8-pointer, tapers to a point, while bigbrother keyhole, finer-toothed at 24 points, is longer and not always sharply pointed at the end. There is an assortment of interchangeable blades available. Use the bigtoothed shorty for plywood cutouts, the finer-toothed blades for cutting plastics.

The coping saw is a thread-thick, spring-steel-tough blade held in a rectangular frame. It can be held at any angle, can work its way along a straight line, turn a right-angle corner, or cut circles. It is useful in face-matching molding cuts. The blade has 17 points, which produce a fairly smooth surface. Breakage of blades is high owing to forcing, so keep a supply on hand. Tension on the blade is produced by turning the handle. The blade may be set to aim the teeth in any direction—an aid to circle-cutting.

Small, resembling the keyhole and the hacksaw, the utility saw has multiple uses all around the house and shop. It cuts metal as easily as a hacksaw. Its fine teeth make it ideal for cutting plastic. It does passably well cutting curves and will do as well as the coping saw on some intricate cuts.

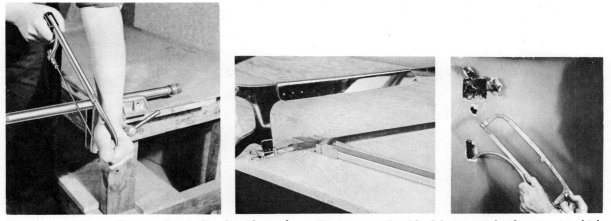

A hacksaw blade can fit into a No. 11 shoe, but it's tough enough to cut through steel. In fact, cutting metal is its principal function. No other tool will cut the armor from electrical cable as easily.

Blades are fitted with from 18 to 32 points per inch. Use the coarse variety on armored cable, copper tubing, soft metals. Use the fine-toothed type for cutting plastics of all kinds or for smoother edges on metals. Keep an assortment of blades on hand.

There is considerable debate over the direction in which the teeth should point when the hacksaw is in use. The usual method is to aim the teeth away from your hand, toward the work. Pressure is applied on the forward stroke. Since this causes the blade to skid on rounded metal surfaces, many prefer the teeth aimed the other way to take pressure on the "pull" stroke. A neat compromise is the use of two blades, one aimed each way. This speeds up cutting but makes the cut far wider.

sap or pitch, coat the saw blade lightly with machine oil to prevent binding and sticking. Paraffin, used for the same purpose, will not mar the finish as oil will.

The back saw is needed for accurate cutting in cabinet work. It has from 18 to 32 small teeth per inch and they are not sharply set. The edge it cuts is almost smooth, always straight. The big brother of the back saw, known as a miter-box saw, is longer and usually used with a miter box of some sort. The back saw is 12″ to 20″ long, the miter-box saw from 20″ to 30″ long. Use these saws for cutting moldings to correct angles and for cutting miter joints accurately.

Compass and keyhole saws have very specialized jobs. They are tapered so they can enter a drilled hole and move about in all directions from that point. Both are used to make cutouts in the center of a piece of wood without cutting the edges. The compass saw, a rugged 8-pointer, tapers to a point, while big brother keyhole, finer-toothed at 24 points, is longer and not always sharply pointed at the end. Many makers include an assortment of interchangeable blades to fit a single handle. In some cases the handle also rotates, making circle-cutting easier from a given position. Use the big-

toothed short blade for plywood cutouts and the finer-toothed one for cutting plastics.

The thin, strong blade of the coping saw is held rigid in a rectangular frame. It can be held at any angle and the blade may be reversed, which makes cutting circles easy. Tension on the blade is maintained by turning the handle. Breakage of blades is a problem encountered when the saw is forced; keep a supply of replacements on hand.

HACKSAWS The hacksaw is designed to cut hard materials, primarily metal. A number of special blades are available that allow the hacksaw to be used to cut glass, plastic, and other material.

Blades break easily when they are forced into the material faster than they can cut or if they are twisted or bent while cutting.

There is considerable debate over the direction in which the teeth should point when the hacksaw is in use. The usual method is to aim the teeth away from your hand, toward the work.

Pressure is applied on the forward stroke. Since this causes the blade to skid on rounded metal surfaces, many prefer the teeth aimed the other way to take pressure on the "pull" stroke. A neat compromise is the use of two blades, one aimed each way. This speeds up cutting but makes the cut far wider.

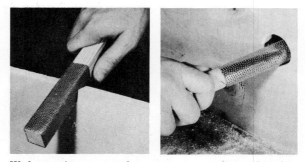

A wood rasp is far more coarse than a metal file. It takes away wood particles at a rapid rate. Yet its shape — a square edge, a flat back, and a curved face — makes it adjustable to almost any desired surface. Once you have used a rasp, you will never be without one again. The double-ender has one end coarse, one much finer for real smoothing. Next time you are making wood joints, cut a tenon slightly oversize, then shape it to a snug fit with a rasp. Or polish off poorly cut dovetails the same way. For rounding edges in simulation of aged colonial pieces the rasp is also handy. In addition, it will dress up scrolled pieces of trim.

With a surface as rough as a coarse wood rasp, but thin enough to be pliable, this piece of tough metal is wrapped around a block or stick and put to work. The pliable rasp shapes surfaces as readily as a rasp — and the holes keep the surface free from clogging.

Right: Not quite a rasp, yet close enough to be a cousin, is this planelike device. It removes strips like shavings instead of particles. Yet it is used on the same jobs as a rasp, while it has all the control of an oldtime plane.

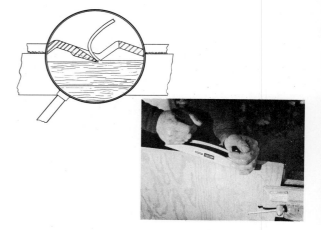

FILES AND RASPS

Files are used mainly to remove material from the surfaces of wood or metal. Those intended for use in shaping and smoothing wood are called rasps. True files are intended to be used on metal.

Being much coarser than a metal-cutting file, wood rasps remove much more material from the surface than metal-cutting files do. Rasps come in a variety of shapes and sizes, making them easily adaptable to almost any surface.

The rasp has many uses, such as fitting tenons in joints, smoothing edges, cleaning, and shaping. A combination rasp, with both a smooth and a rough surface, is a good choice for the workshop.

Rasps are intended to be used in the finishing process, after the sawing has been done. They work very well for removing saw marks and the sharp edges from pieces of stock.

A few light strokes remove saw marks, imperfections, and errors. Cutting notches, rounding edges, and shaping irregular curves can be done quickly and accurately by use of the rasp, with no other tools needed. The roughing-out is done with the heavy-toothed end; then the rasp is reversed and the job finished with the finer teeth. Virtually no sanding is needed on such work if the rasp is properly used.

Small pieces should be clamped in a vise, the outline of the cut carefully marked, and the rasp drawn with even strokes across the wood surface. Freehand work becomes possible as practice with the rasp creates confidence and skill.

A combination rasp is a good type to have around the home workshop, with both rough and smooth surfaces on the same tool. These are called wood cabinet combination rasps. An assortment of rasps for the average home workshop should include a middle, or halfway, in round and triangular shapes; a smooth-grade square file; a coarse half-round; a second-cut flat; and a smooth file of

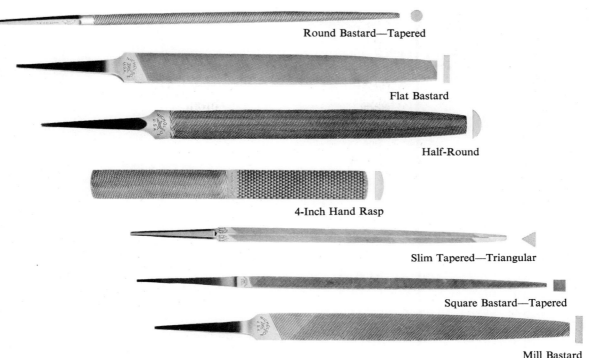

Round Bastard—Tapered

Flat Bastard

Half-Round

4-Inch Hand Rasp

Slim Tapered—Triangular

Square Bastard—Tapered

Mill Bastard

any obtainable shape. These should be adequate for your usual needs.

More intricate metal work requires a wider range of files, with different degrees of fineness to their cutting surface. Files are available in any length, cut, and shape to handle all jobs that may arise.

The home handyman will find a set of files worth a dozen other implements. Constant use of files will keep all other cutting tools in working shape,

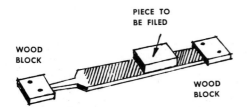

When working on small metal pieces, a bench vise is indispensable. A good light, proper elevation of the work, and a steady hand contribute to a good job. For one not skilled in draw filing, it may be better to secure the file on a bench with blocks and draw the work over it. Move work toward the tang (handle) end of the file, then lift up and start over.

putting keen burr-free edges on plane, chisel, saw, hatchet, drawknife, and axe. Gardeners will work faster and with less effort when the edges of such tools as hoes, spades, mowers, and clippers are kept sharp by filing.

In repair work, there are dozens of jobs where the file will serve as no other tool will. Among them are such simple tasks as smoothing the ends of pipe cut with a hacksaw, cutting through bolts that have rusted in place, substituting for a hacksaw in cutting BX electric cable, reaming holes in metal for larger bolts, shaping scrap metal for patchwork. Again, when soldering and welding, the file is the first tool to use to remove rust and clean surfaces for a good bond between metals.

Files are made in a wide assortment of shapes. There are rattail, square, and triangular files; there are flat, half-round and combinations of these. There are files with flat edges and others with sharp edges used for cutting. While the full complement may not be needed by every handyman, at least seven should be kept available: rattail or round, triangular, half-round, flat, square-tapered, the mill file, and the wood rasp. Files, graded by the spaces between the teeth, are classified as rough, coarse, middle, halfway, bastard, second-cut, smooth, and superfine. These will be found in

Metal files may clog with bits of plastic and very soft metal. This is easily cured by brushing along the scored lines with a stiff-bristle brush. After using any file, coat it lightly with fine machine oil. This stops rust — the one thing that can dull a file faster than the hardest steel.

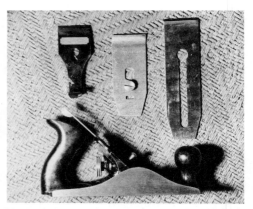

Steel-bodied plane with its three removable parts. Adjusting wheel and lever are not removed for sharpening.

two forms: those with a single set of parallel lines of sharp edges set at about 25° across the file face, called mill files; and those with two sets of lines crossing each other, the second set of lines set at about 45°.

Your files and rasps can be kept in top shape if you protect them from rust by light oiling and keep the teeth free of debris by wirebrushing.

Metal-cutting files tend to clog easily when used on soft materials, such as aluminum or plastic. If these clogged bits of metal are not removed they will mar the surface on the next stroke of the file. Remove clogs with a file card or a stiff wire brush, brushing along the scored lines and across the file at an angle. After using a file, coat it lightly with oil to protect it from rust. Rust damages files easily.

PLANES

A plane basically consists of a knife blade controlled and directed for width and depth of cut. This controlled cutting ability is essential in operations such as smoothing, trimming, and shaping pieces of wood. Effective use of a plane requires practice and patience.

Selection of the right plane for each job of carpentry is shown in the illustrations. The average workshop should have at least three: jack plane, smooth plane, and block plane. For good joinery, add the dado plane, rabbet plane, and plow. If you anticipate intricate, fancy woodworking, you might consider investing in a combination plane, which accepts a wide variety of blades.

A combination plane in skilled hands will do almost all the jobs that a jointer-planer machine or a router will handle. A combination plane can be used for making window frames and fancy moldings, for example. Aside from the combination

plane, most planes are of a basic design. Each plane size is intended for a specific use, although the medium-sized jack plane is a good choice if you own only one.

To cut properly, a plane must be sharp. Remove the blade and check its edge for nicks or burrs, as well as rounding. Hitting knots or nails with a plane is the quickest way to ruin its cutting edge. Formerly, plane blades had to be sharpened on a stone, with only the hands and eyes to guide the blade during the sharpening process. While this is fine in the hands of an experienced person, more than one blade has been ruined by incorrect sharpening.

There are guides for sharpening plane blades. One such device is designed to produce a consistently sharp cutting edge on plane iron, spoke shave, or wood chisel blades when used with a sharpening stone. It will accommodate blades of widths ranging from ⅛" to 2⅜" and is equipped with nylon rollers and a snap-out gauge that ensures the correct honing angle. Once the blade has been sharpened, it is removed from the holder and the burr is removed from the back side of the blade.

CHISELS

While wood chisel blades are uniform in shape, the edges of the larger ones are beveled to reduce their weight. The blades are ground off to a slant of 25°. Beginners need a set of four: ¼", ½", ¾", and 1" widths. These will handle most jobs.

One of the most common uses of the chisel is cutting a mortise for the recessed leaves of hinges. After marking the hinge outline, hold the chisel vertically, beveled side toward the scrap, and tap it down into the mark. Score all around. Then turn the chisel so the bevel side rests on the wood and

USING A PLANE

Use jack plane for making bevels, as its length will guide the plane to an even stroke along the marked lines.

Combination plane with its variety of knives permits forming numerous shapes along edges and surfaces in one operation.

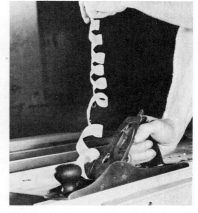

Sharp plane, properly adjusted, will peel off a shaving of equal thickness the full length of the planed board.

To plane down an uneven surface, first use short strokes across the raised portion only, before reducing the rest.

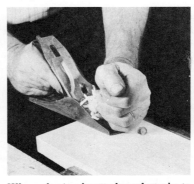

When planing knotty board, stroke to knot from opposite sides to prevent gouging adjoining wood and knot itself.

When planing end grain, stroke from each end toward center to prevent ripping edges. Note bevel to mark depth of cut.

tap it along the grain, removing very thin slices of wood at a time. Continue until the exact thickness of the hinge leaf has been removed. When making a mortise in a plywood veneer door, cut out the soft wood of the stile first, then remove the thin veneer strip. This method prevents marring the veneer with too deep a cut.

In cutting a mortise for a cabinet-door hinge, first check the wood grain carefully. If it is not truly even, cut the mortise as shown. The first vertical cuts are made to outline the hinge, then a number of scored cuts are made through the scrap at equal distances. Remove part of the scrap with the bevel side down, then smooth off the surface with the chisel laid flat on the wood, bevel side up. This last step is done without the use of the hammer.

When cutting plywood with a chisel, cut only the

Cutting a mortise

depth of one ply with vertical cuts. Remove that layer and cut the following layers in the same manner, one at a time.

Many beveled edges can be made more easily with a chisel than with a plane, especially if they are not required for the full length of the piece. With a penciled guideline and a steady hand, the bevel can be cut as neatly with a chisel. Keep the beveled side of the chisel on the wood and, using hand pressure only, cut along the grain.

OTHER CHISELS Masonry can be cut quite easily, provided the right chisels are used. The concrete chisel, also called the bull point, has a pointed end and is used for cutting shallow grooves in concrete. The purpose of the groove is to hold the broader blade of the masonry chisel when cutting concrete block.

The brick chisel is also a handy tool. It has a broad blade, fully as wide as a brick, which widely distributes its cutting impact. This chisel is mainly used to trim bricks to size without shattering them.

Cold chisels can be used in place of a concrete chisel, especially for chipping concrete and cinder blocks. Cold chisels should not be used on brick, as they tend to shatter the brick, rather than split it evenly.

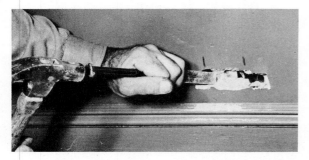

Cold chisels are used to cut metals and masonry. These chisels are of unusually tough steel and are less easily broken. Wear heavy gloves. When cutting masonry, goggles are also advisable.

Cutting through veneer

DRILL BITS

Properly drilled holes are necessary for many handyman projects, from installing electrical cable to making dowel joints.

Drill bits can be broken down into two classifications, depending on their method of operation. Slow-speed, auger bits are designed to be used in a brace, and high-speed bits are intended for use in electric drills and drill presses. These two broad classifications can be further broken down according to the specific uses.

Generally speaking, sharply pointed or tapered bits are used for the rapid piercing of soft material. With soft material, the size and angle of the flutes and rake are designed to carry away the scrap material rapidly, so the hole is kept clean. The bit can stall if the hole becomes clogged.

Blunt-point drill bits are designed for cutting through hard materials. When these bits are used on metal, for example, only tiny fragments of material are removed with each pass of the bit. Therefore, the angle and size of the bit are designed accordingly.

Each manufacturer develops drill bits according to its own idea of good design. This results in considerable variation from one to another. Groups of drill bits are available for ceramics, concrete, and masonry, and plastic. The intended purpose of each bit can be determined by its shape, especially the point. A drill bit must do more than merely make a hole. The hole should be of the correct size and be correctly located. If two pieces of material are to be joined, the holes must be aligned and the centers must match perfectly. If the two materials are of equal density, they can simply be clamped together and a single hole drilled through both at the same time. If the hole to be drilled must be at

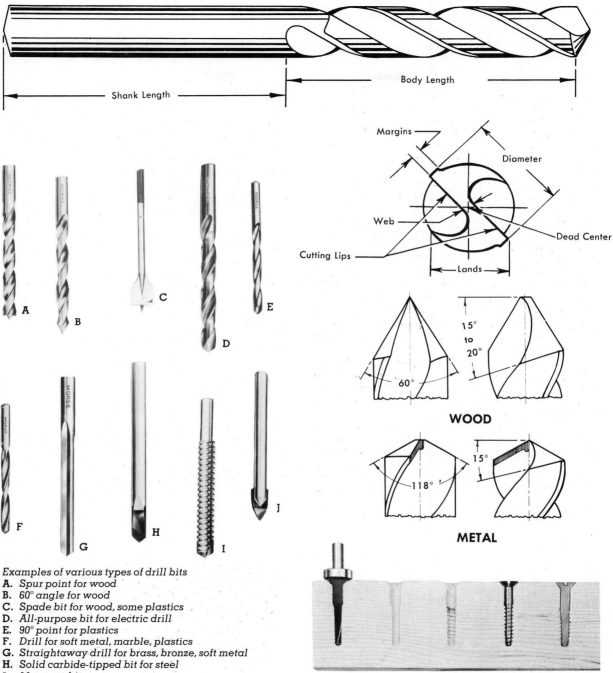

Examples of various types of drill bits
A. Spur point for wood
B. 60° angle for wood
C. Spade bit for wood, some plastics
D. All-purpose bit for electric drill
E. 90° point for plastics
F. Drill for soft metal, marble, plastics
G. Straightaway drill for brass, bronze, soft metal
H. Solid carbide-tipped bit for steel
I. Masonry bit
J. Spear point for glass, tile, porcelain

WOOD

METAL

Pilot holes for screws
Drill bits may be used to match screw shapes—particularly useful in hardwoods. Bit makes hole to fit screw, also provides for countersetting, can make recess for plug-in hole.

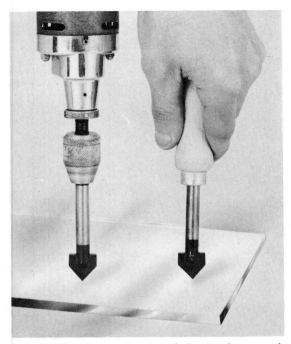

Drill specially designed to bore holes in glass may be operated by hand or in electric drill chuck. Bit will also drill concrete, brick, cinder block, tile, and hard plastic.

AWLS

The scratch awl, a useful tool around the shop, is shaped like an ice pick and is just as sharp. It sticks into wood and can be used to mark and hold measuring devices. An awl is also good for indenting holes for starting nails and screws, or to anchor taut string lines on stakes for leveling foundations, floors, and decks. It can also be used in combination with a chalkline for laying out guidelines for cutting and nailing.

RULERS AND TAPES

There is an old carpenter's saying, "Measure twice, cut once." With the rising price of materials, it pays to measure correctly. The ruler or yardstick, the folding or carpenter's rule, and the roll-up steel tape measure are the most common measuring devices. All have advantages and disadvantages.

The ruler or yardstick (soon to be replaced by the meter stick) can double as a straightedge. However, it must be relocated to measure distances longer than its length, increasing the chances of error.

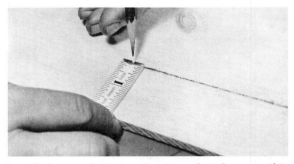

Straight-line mark, for rough cut, needs only a pencil in the indent of the rule, and a finger held at the mark and run along board edge.

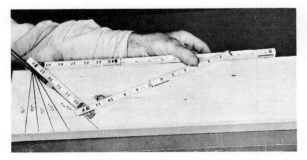

Folding rule can be used in place of framing square for various angled cuts, but it lacks accuracy, owing to flexibility of rule joints.

right angles to the material, don't trust your eye to align the bit to the surface. Use either a drill press or a drilling jig, to assure perfect alignment.

In determining the hole size, consider the material. If it's rigid, such as steel, the fastener cannot expand or bite into it. The hole must therefore match the size of the fastener. In the case of wood, however, where a screw is to be fitted into the hole, the hole itself must be smaller than the screw so that its threads have something to grip. A bolt with a diameter of 3/16", for example, requires a hole of the same diameter or slightly larger in steel, whereas a hole in softwood may be as much as a third smaller than the diameter of the screw. In hardwoods, it is best to use a drill bit which outlines the shape of the screw. (See page 307, bottom right photo.) In soft metal, the hole may be made slightly smaller and a self-tapping screw used, since this type threads the hole by itself.

For cutting holes larger than 1½" in diameter in wood, there are saw bits that can be used with an electric drill. These hole saws are available in sizes from about 5/8" up to 6". The very large hole saws may require more power than your electric drill can deliver. If so, a saber saw should be used to cut the hole.

No question about locating the center of a circle when this device is employed. Two legs, resting on circumference, indicate radius line, and any two intersecting lines mark the center.

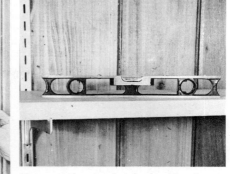

Not even the simple job of putting in preformed shelves can be done correctly without use of a level to check the vertical as well as the horizontal lines. If the supports (left) are not true, shelves cannot be level.

Any try square usually has a small level in one leg. Fine for short distances, it is not practical for wide spans.

The folding or carpenter's rule is something of an engineering marvel in itself. One of the legs is exactly 2″ shorter than the rest, providing instant reference to that length. Measurements of 4″ and 6″ are built into the carpenter's rule, in addition to the regular dimensions that can be laid out with the graduated markings on the rule. The carpenter's rule will not, because of its many joints, take too much abuse. Also, it is not rigid enough to span large gaps without support.

Roll-up tape measures are the wise choice for any handyman. They come in a variety of lengths, from 6′ to 100′. Most are of the 6′, 12′, and 20′ length. The smaller tapes retract into a housing that is exactly 2″ long, a handy reference measurement. The lip on the end of the roll-up tape can be hooked over the end of a board or surface. The larger tapes, in a 1″ width, are rigid enough to be extended vertically without support.

LEVELS

A good level is an invaluable aid when remodeling or building. Without it, it is impossible to establish true vertical and horizontal dimensions as starting points. Levels come in basically three varieties: carpenter's level, line level, and those incorporated as part of another tool, such as a combination square. While their purpose is the same, each is designed to do a job that the other cannot do as well.

The level built into the combination square works well for short spans and in confined spaces. It is not accurate enough for long spans and should not be used for such.

A good carpenter's level is essential for construction work. Better ones are made with a metal housing that will stand some abuse. The metal frame is not affected by moisture and therefore will not warp if left outside overnight. Carpenter's levels are available in lengths from 2′ to 4′.

A good carpenter's level should measure both horizontal and vertical angles, on separate dials. You may want to consider buying one that registers 45° angles as well.

To use the carpenter's level, simply place it on the surface to be checked and note the placement of the bubble within the glass tube (midpoint of the glass). If the bubble is not there, raise one end or the other of the level, to determine which way the surface must be adjusted to be brought into line.

Line levels are actually a miniature version of

the carpenter's level. They are intended to be accurate for use over long spans. The line level is attached to a line stretched taut between two points, by means of hooks on the level. It is then merely a matter of reading the level and making the necessary adjustments.

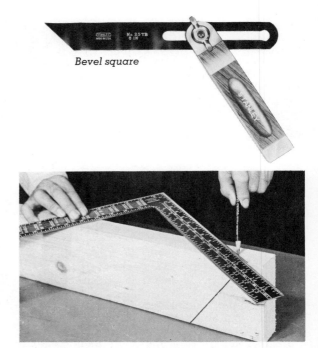

Bevel square

SQUARES

A square is an absolute necessity for building or remodeling. As the name implies, it is intended to be used to square up edges and joints. Squares will also perform many other useful functions, if you know how to use them correctly.

Squares are available in a number of styles and sizes. The try square is a simple tool that gauges 90° angles from any point on a surface. It is small, simple to use, and many persons prefer it to the larger combination square.

THE COMBINATION SQUARE The combination square is a unique tool. The blade can be slipped out of the handle so it can be used as a straightedge or ruler. The small level built into the handle of the combination square allows it to be used for accurate leveling within its limitations. It should not be used for long pieces or over long spans, where a carpenter's level is the better tool.

The combination square, with its sliding handle, can be used to check inside square corners, as well as outside corners. The blade can be adjusted so that the combination square can be used as a marking gauge with an infinite number of possible settings.

THE CARPENTER'S SQUARE Various versions of this tool go by different names. They are all basically the same. The main differences include markings on the blades and information inscribed on the metal. Most handymen settle for a framing square. Framing squares are available in different sizes, the most common being 24″ by 16″.

When using a square, hold the shorter leg, called the tongue, in your right hand (assuming you are right-handed) and the longer portion in your left hand. The heel, or the right-angle portion of the square, should point away from the body. When the square is in this position, the side of the square that is up is called the face; the opposite side is called the back.

To mark a large area, hold the long portion of the blade firmly against the surface, with the tongue of the square extending across the surface. Draw marking lines, using the tongue as a guide. Using the longer portion here, rather than the tongue, on the surface improves accuracy.

Be sure to hold the longer portion of the blade firm against the surface to avoid moving the tongue when drawing a line.

The instruction booklet that comes with a car-

A steel square is an invaluable aid in laying out angles to be cut in rafters.

penter's square explains how to use its many scales and tables. The following is a brief rundown on what the various tables on the square are used for.

1. The Essex, or lumber, scale is used to calculate the number of board feet in a piece of lumber. It is also used to determine how much lumber will be needed for a specific job.
2. A scale for squaring a foundation, especially for an addition to a house; it is an adaptation of the 3:4:5 right-triangle theorem of plane geometry. A triangle with leg lengths in precisely these proportions must be a right triangle, a useful method of checking right angles in construction.
3. Markings for estimating the amount of shingles needed for a surface, either the roof or sides of a house.
4. A formula for determining the correct pilot holes for screws and the drill sizes needed to make them.
5. Points for figuring the number of nails by size, either common or finish, per pound.
6. Conversion of meters and inches.
7. Aids for determining the distance between studs and beams according to their size. There are also other building estimate guides available.

VISES

There is no substitute for a good vise. Selection of the vise depends on the type of work being done. Primary requirements are that it be strong, firmly mounted, and accurate in the meeting of its jaws. It must also grip firmly and hold fast without marring the surface. It should operate smoothly and rapidly. Some vises are mounted with turn screws; others are mounted with wood screws or bolts; still others are mounted in a recessed surface in the face of the workbench itself. For multipurpose duty, those vises with a variety of holding positions and surfaces are best for all-around needs.

Woodworking vise for end-of-bench use is handy for home workshops.

Some bench vises may be converted by adding special jaws to hold pipe.

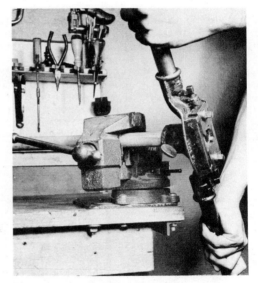

There is no substitute for a pipe vise when threading pipe ends.

CLAMPS

Clamps, although they have many uses, are primarily meant for holding wood for gluing or planing. The major difference between vises and clamps is that clamps are portable. Both serve the same function of applying equal pressure from opposing ends toward the center.

For major gluing jobs, such as building up a large board from several smaller ones, bar clamps are indispensable. Bar clamps consist of a long bar, either flat or round, with a movable tail stop held to the bar and a sliding head equipped with a screw, turned with handle or knob.

It is a simple matter to provide yourself with a supply of these pipe or bar clamps simply by purchasing the head and tail portions and a supply of

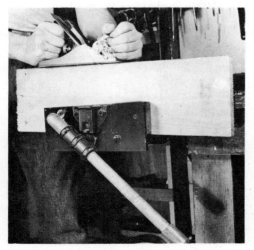

When board is held in vise for planing, the workmanship improves.

pipes to fit them. The pipes should be of correct diameter and straight and smooth. It is a good idea to buy the pipes in a variety of lengths to increase the usefulness of the clamps. Shorter clamps may be used where longer ones won't fit or are inconvenient.

Hundreds of other styles of clamps are available, but the addition of two will meet most of your needs. C clamps come in many sizes and are useful for applying a large amount of pressure over small distances. Hand screw clamps are used extensively for gluing wood and for holding pieces of stock. They should be adjusted simultaneously and evenly to apply correct pressure across the entire surface.

When using clamps and vises, remember that they are harder than the wood you are working with and will crush most softwoods quite easily. Draw them up only enough to bring the surfaces into close contact.

Use scrap stock to guard against crushed wood. These pieces, preferably of hardwood, are inserted between the wood and the clamp and will distribute the pressure over a wider area than the face of the clamp itself. A supply of blocks of various sizes can keep a project from being damaged during assembly.

To provide the same protection when using a vise, pieces of plywood can be cut to fit the jaws of the vise. Plywood is strong and resists cracking. Wood-lined jaws on a vise also permit the holding of metal objects without ruining them.

OTHER CLAMPING DEVICES

Lightweight, portable worktables provide a combination work surface and clamping device. This device holds objects firmly, at comfortable heights, leaving hands free to maneuver tools and providing access to all sides of the material. It can be set up almost anywhere in the workshop, garage, or at the worksite. A built-in vise opens to 5¼" and, used with pegs, can firmly hold objects up to 21" in place. Special attachments can hold irregular and round objects and tubular materials. Such units fold for easy storage and transport.

Photos: Black & Decker

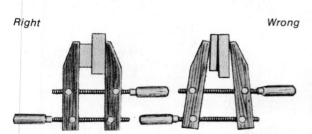

Right   *Wrong*

Hand-screw clamps require care in applying pressure. Turn both screws at once.

On large work, pipe clamps stretch as far as your lengths of pipe.

When gluing little boards to make big ones, bar clamps are a real asset.

Entire pieces of furniture may be glued if you have enough clamps.

HAND TOOL CARE

It makes sense to protect your investment in hand tools with proper care. Protect tools from abuse and rust by storing properly. Store tools so they don't come into contact with other tools, not loosely in drawers. Tools banging into one another quickly lose cutting edges. Store in separate compartments or hang them on a wall. If stored hanging, make certain they cannot accidentally be dislodged.

Rust will form on tools in almost any environment, especially in damp areas such as basements. Corrosion on metal tools is also easily in-duced through contact with the hands. Coat tools with light machine oil or any of a variety of specially prepared commercial rust inhibitors. It takes little time and will go a long way toward protecting your tools and keeping them serviceable.

SHARPENING HAND TOOLS For cutting tools to do their jobs, and do them well, they must be kept sharp. Dull tools will mar the surface, take more time to use, and make drudgery of simple tasks.

The basic sharpening tool is an abrasive. It may be a file, a sharpening stone, or emery paper. If the sharpening surface becomes clogged with bits of metal removed from the tool, it will not function well. Files can be cleaned with a file card or a stiff

Before applying any protective coating, rust must be removed.

Steel wool is often used to remove rust from tools; as you rub, add cutting oil.

Rust may be removed from hand saws and other tools by using emery cloth. Later, apply a protective rust-preventive coating.

Pitch must be removed with special removers from saw blades before applying oil or petroleum jelly.

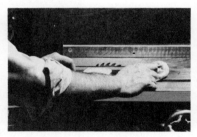

A small block of paraffin can be used for coating saw tables to prevent rust formation.

Paste wax also prevents rust. Surfaces must be clean before applying.

Petroleum jelly is an excellent rust preventive. Light grease is just as suitable.

You can use a pressurized oil spray on tools not handled often. Acrylic sprays may be used as well as oil.

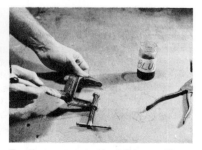

Brush or spray metal bluing (Prussian blue, die-maker's blue) on tools not handled constantly.

A bench grinder, to sharpen knives and hatchets, drill bits, mower blades, chisels, etc. Photo: Black & Decker

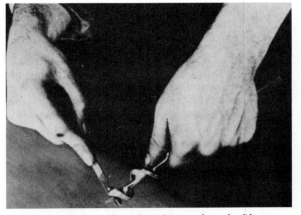

Augers may be kept sharp by a few strokes of a file across the bevels.

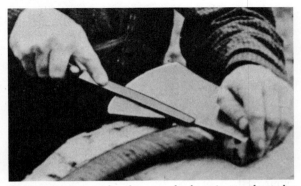

Outdoor cutting tools, also, may be kept in top shape by filing.

wire brush, stones with a powerful magnet or commercial cleaners. Discard emery paper when no longer serviceable.

Sharpening stones should be used with a coating of either oil or water, depending on the type of stone. This coating helps keep metal particles from building up in the surface of the stone. A grinding or emery wheel can be used for a quick sharpening job but requires care. Most are available with a movable sharpening rest, which can be adjusted so the proper edge is maintained on the cutting surface. Take care to prevent overheating when sharpening tools on a grinder. Cool the tool either in water or oil to prevent the temper being drawn out. This softens the metal and reduces its ability to hold an edge. Avoid grinding continuously, trying to remove too much metal too fast, or allowing the tool to become so hot it turns color.

Grinding wheels will become clogged with metal, especially if they are used on such soft nonferrous metals as aluminum or bronze. They can be cleaned with a tool known as a dressing wheel, the head of which is of very hard metal. This wheel, harder than the stone, removes stone as well as the material clogging it. Use it sparingly to prevent damage to the grinding wheel.

A good file or two can also be used. Unless there are large nicks or bumps to be removed, a file can quickly put a good edge on almost any cutting tool. Some tools, such as plane blades, are so hard that attempting to cut them can ruin the file. To check hardness, lightly pass the file across the metal. If no metal is removed, or if it comes off reluctantly, switch to an alternate.

Tools sharpened on a grinding wheel or with a file will generally have a burr or rough edge. Remove this with a stone to make the tool as sharp as

possible. Lightly pass the tool over a stone, maintaining the proper angle. Sharpening aids are available that are designed to be used in combination with a stone to sharpen plane blades and chisels. The blade or chisel is clamped and held at the proper angle to the stone. The tool is then passed over the surface until the blade or chisel is sharp. The burr is removed by passing the back edge of the blade over the stone, parallel to the surface of the stone.

Drill bits can be sharpened with a grinding wheel if there is a proper guide to maintain the angle on the tip. There are also electric grinders, similar to an electric pencil sharpener, for sharpening drill bits.

Broken bits can also be salvaged with these types of sharpeners. Most require no lubricant on the drill bit and do an excellent job of sharpening. This type of sharpener will be ruined if it is used for carbide-tipped bits, since these are much harder than the stone.

Sharpening stone, guide for sharpening plane blade.

Sharpen tools carefully. Never attempt to force a tool into an electric grinding wheel faster than the grinder can handle it. The tool can slip and your hand may come into contact with the wheel.

Also use caution when filing. Files can slip, especially if the metal is hard. Whenever possible, work away from the cutting edge when filing, rather than toward it.

POWER TOOLS

CIRCULAR SAWS

Few tools will get as much work as the portable electric handsaw. You will do many times the work of a manual handsaw with a minimum of effort on your part.

There is a wide range of electric handsaws available, each with an assortment of blades. They vary in their intended use and the type of material they will be used on. Which type you purchase will depend upon your specific needs. There are some general guidelines that you can follow. The saw should be capable of cutting through a 2 × 4 at a 45° angle and a 90° angle. To do so, the blade diameter must be slightly larger than 7". Because of this requirement, many saws on the market today feature blades of 7¼" in diameter.

The depth of the blade should be set so that approximately ¼" protrudes through the other side of the workpiece.

The saw should have adjustments for depth control, which is a must when you don't want to cut all the way through a piece of lumber.

You should also make certain the saw is fully adjustable for bevel cuts up to 45°.

For accurate ripping, a rip gauge is handy, although not required. Rip guides are available for ripping large panels or long boards.

Nearly all electric handsaws are equipped with an automatic blade guard. Without it, the tool is

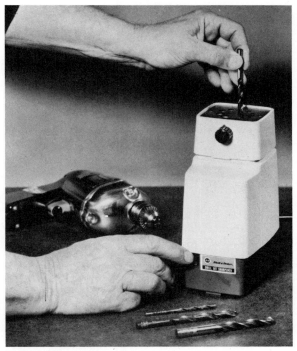
Drill-bit sharpener.

extremely dangerous. Don't buy or use one without it.

The blade guard is spring-loaded and retracts as you cut. When the cut is completed, the guard automatically snaps back over the blade. Once the cut is finished and power to the motor is cut off, the blade will still continue to rotate for some time. For

Combination rip and crosscut circular saw. Photo: Black & Decker.

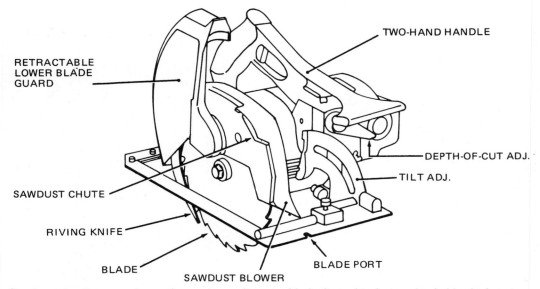

RETRACTABLE LOWER BLADE GUARD

TWO-HAND HANDLE

DEPTH-OF-CUT ADJ.

TILT ADJ.

SAWDUST CHUTE

RIVING KNIFE

BLADE

SAWDUST BLOWER

BLADE PORT

Size for a circular saw refers to the maximum-diameter blade the tool is designed to hold, which, in turn, determines the maximum thickness workpiece that can be sawed through. However, the motor hp and the no-load blade rpm can be equally important for determining the type of work a tool will do. It takes power to saw through heavy or high-moisture-content timbers, and there is small advantage to having a big 7½" blade if the developed motor power is insufficient to keep it cutting when the work is tough. On the other hand, very little motor power is needed to operate a saw designed especially for cutting panels (which are thin and dry)—and the compactness and light weight of a small motor is, therefore, more desirable. Also for such a tool, a higher rpm assures a cleaner, smoother cut.

this reason, a blade guard is essential. An additional feature on many better circular saws is the "dynamic" brake, which stops the rotation of the blade immediately on releasing the trigger. Make sure the trigger is easily accessible and working smoothly.

Beyond these specifics, make certain the saw you buy is one that you can handle well, possibly for extended use. Since portable electric saws vary in weight from 8 to 18 pounds, choose one you can handle accurately and safely.

An optional feature is a knob, positioned at the front of the saw. This second handle increases your control over the saw and allows more accurate sawing.

When operating a power saw, always wear goggles to protect your eyes from flying wood chips and sawdust. Practice using the saw to make sure you can maintain a straight, even, forward stroke. Any amount of weaving with the saw not only results in a sloppy cut but also presents a safety risk.

Support the workpiece as firmly as possible.

Rip guides can assure accurate rip-type cuts on large panels. This device can save many dollars by reducing waste. Photo: Sears

Always support work being cut—the first rule in handling a portable power saw.

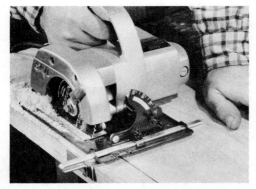

Rip cut—made along the wood grain—in this case with cutting guide attached to saw.

Bevel cut—on this cut a diagonal—is cut through the wood by tilting the saw blade to the desired measured angle.

Crosscut—cut across wood grain.

Pocket cut—this is used to cut a section from the center of a board. Rest saw on its forward edge and press rotating blade slowly into wood. Remove saw and repeat on all four sides.

Compound miter—this is a miter cut at a diagonal across the grain, plus the bevel cut. The miter is made on the line, the bevel by tilting the saw blade.

Stringer cutting—here, cuts meet at right angles. Follow marked lines only to their ends, then complete cuts with a hand saw—circular blade will cut beyond marked line and weaken the stringer.

Cutting corrugated nonwood stock—fiber-supported plastics are cut with abrasive disk substituted for saw blade.

Left: Combination rip and crosscut blade. Right: Plywood blade. Photo: Black & Decker.

Cutting while the material is moving might result in binding the blade.

The motor on your portable power saw is very powerful. Treat it with respect.

Be sure the saw blade is turning at full speed before you begin the cut. Otherwise the motor will be overloaded and may bind.

There is a notch on the base plate of most saws. Its purpose is to indicate the position of the blade, as a guide to the user when operating the tool. It shows the cutting line. Guide the saw along the line, letting it cut at its own speed. Forcing it into the material may result in binding. If you continue to overload the saw, motor damage will occur.

Take every precaution not to cut the power cord.

Maintain even pressure while making the entire cut, especially when nearing the end of the cut. Don't allow the blade to drop or tip just as you fin-

ish the cut. At the end, allow the blade to come to a complete stop before removing it from the stock. Be certain the blade guard has snapped into position before setting the saw down.

As a general safety precaution, unplug the saw whenever working on it, such as changing the depth of the cut. Always disconnect the power cord when changing blades or after you have finished a job.

Make certain the blade you are installing is pointed in the right direction. Circular saws with the blade on the right side of the saw are designed so the blade revolves counterclockwise. If you are in doubt how to install the blade, look for a directional arrow on the saw and the blade.

There are many different types of blades, some intended for very specific purposes, others for more general work.

COMMON CIRCULAR SAW BLADES

Combination crosscut and rip blade. *Most popular blade, good for all-around work, suited to both operations and for use on plywood.*

Rip blade *Best when a lot of ripping along wood grain is to be done. Teeth are larger, specially set for this job.*

Crosscut blade *Best for all crosscut work, excellent for plywood. Also a good blade for cutting hardboards and similar composition materials.*

Combination miter blade. *For smooth cuts, miter work, interior trim, this blade is best. Teeth are not set, width of cut is small, edge of cut is smooth.*

For general, all-around cutting, a combination cross-cut and rip blade is a good choice. It does an acceptable job on most types of lumber and works quite well on plywood. For cutting large amounts of plywood, or when a smooth cut is important, as in cabinetwork, a crosscut blade is recommended.

Ripping blades are for cutting lumber along its grain.

The smoothest cut of all is made by the hollow-ground blade. It consists of groups of a few teeth separated by a deep notch or groove cut into the blade. The cut it makes requires little or no sanding.

Carbide-tipped blades have long life and cut smoothly.

Keep extra blades on hand to replace dull or worn blades. Don't attempt to sharpen old blades yourself unless you know how.

SABER SAWS

The saber saw will do all the work of a coping saw plus other jobs that a coping saw can't do, such as cutting metal pipe. It cuts fancy scrollwork and trims very well. It has a slender blade, which moves up and down at very high speed, allowing very fine, intricate cuts as well as cuts on a tight radius.

You may also find a saber saw useful when putting up paneling or wallboard. The saber saw works well for cutting holes for electrical boxes and switches. It's also a valuable aid when fitting wallboard or paneling against a wall or in a corner that isn't absolutely true. Hold the piece against the wall and run a compass down the panel. The

Continuous variable-speed saber saw is useful in cutting various materials. Speed is controlled by varying the trigger pressure. This allows you to increase or decrease the power and speed instantly to overcome difficult-to-cut areas and knots. Other less expensive saws may have two or three speeds selected by a switch in the same position as the knob in this model. Photo: Sears

pointed leg follows the contour of the wall. Then use the saber saw to make the cut along the pencil line.

A saber saw will handle much larger pieces of stock than a coping saw, and will also make cuts that may not be possible with a bandsaw. When using a saber saw, make certain the stock is well

COMMON TYPES OF BLADES

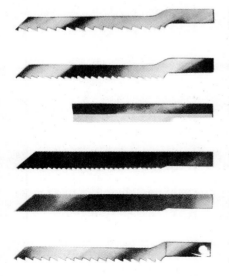

Coarse-toothed blade for wood cutting. Cuts rapidly, has some set. Best where rough edge or cut surface is not objectionable.

Fine-toothed wood-cutting blade. Less set and finer teeth, not so apt to rip grain of plywood, leaves softwood edges ready for final sanding.

Knife blade. This has no teeth, but is designed primarily for cutting such materials as leather, rubber, linoleum, Celotex, and other fibrous composition.

Nonferrous-metal cutter. This one cuts aluminum, brass, copper, and most other metals (not iron and steel). Also cuts Masonite, Formica, asphalt tile.

Heat-treated blade cuts steel and iron—in effect, converts the saber saw to a power hacksaw. Best, too, for plastics, since it leaves smoother edges.

Taper-ground blade for wood has no set. Leaves absolutely smooth edges ready for jointing or final finish. Cuts more slowly but saves time.

The scroll saw allows you to maintain the most comfortable position, yet allows the blade to follow the line of work. This eliminates most difficult and tiring positions when sawing. *Photo: Sears*

With a little practice, you will get the knack of holding saw properly; then try the one-hand method, holding work as required on any substantial support. Model here cuts ¾" ply.

One of hundreds of practical uses of the saber saw—cutting into baseboard without making a pilot hole, for the purpose of inserting a new outlet box.

Saber saws are provided with blower device that clears marked line of sawdust. V-notch in shoe also aids in guiding tool along straight lines or curves.

supported. There is no need to make an entry hole with a drill; it will make its own starting hole. Hold the saw so that the toe of the shoe rests on the work surface and the blade is parallel to the wood. Switch on the motor and slowly pivot the saw on the toe until the point of the blade begins to approach the work. Tighten your grip, because it may vibrate, while continuing to pivot it. The blade will bite into the surface when it finally makes contact.

Eventually it will pierce the work, and when the saw finally rests on the work surface, normally at the end of its pivot, you may proceed with the rest of the cut as you would any other. It sounds more complex than it is. It takes less time to do than to describe. Do not force the blade; let the saw do the work.

Some saber saws are designed for use in conjunction with a table. The saw is clamped under

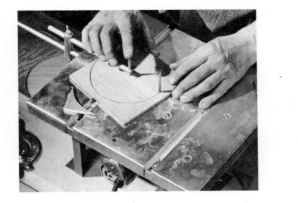

A saber saw, mounted upside down under table, becomes a jigsaw, which can be handled in the usual manner, only feeding stock into the saw instead of saw into the stock. Photo, right: Sears

the table, with the blade protruding through the top. The work is guided into the blade. Installing and removing the saw from the table requires no special tools. Using the saw in this manner allows extra control, moving the stock instead of the saw. Large, heavy, or awkward pieces are better cut without the table, by moving the saw and clamping the stock firmly in place.

When using the saw, be sure to hold the tool firmly, but not with a "death-grip" that makes movement awkward. Make certain the saw is running before it is moved into the work. Gently push the saw forward along the guide you have marked out. Let the saw do the work. Too much force may break the blade or the saw may vibrate excessively and wander. Use both hands for operation.

Some saber saws have variable speeds, a help when cutting harder materials that require a slower speed. Match the speed of the saw to the material being cut. This saves time and saw blades, and produces better results.

DRILLS

Electric drills are one of the most popular of portable tools. As the name implies, the main function of this tool is to drill holes. With accessories, the drill can do almost anything, from mixing paint to turning wood like a lathe.

The drill's components include a gearing system, motor, housing, and chuck. They vary in size, power, and cost. Prices range from $8 to $80 and even higher for the larger industrial drills.

The less expensive drills are usually ¼", and have a speed of about 2,000 rpm. Such drills are for light use only. They will easily drill up to 1" in wood and ¼" in steel, sheet iron, or aluminum. They will also drill holes in such material as ma-

A drill press stand adds much stability and versatility to the portable electric drill. The table may have V grooves for drilling round stock such as dowel rods and pipe. Photo: Sears

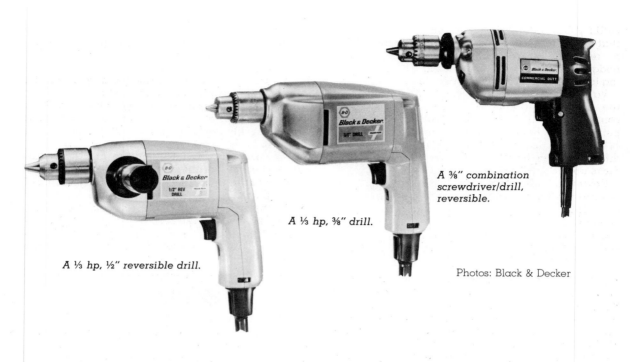

A ⅜″ combination
screwdriver/drill,
reversible.

A ⅓ hp, ⅜″ drill.

A ⅓ hp, ½″ reversible drill.

Photos: Black & Decker

sonry and plastics with the correct bit. They can also drive small sanding disks, wire wheels, and grinding stones. In the $15 range, you can buy a higher quality ¼″ drill, with the added feature of variable speed. Other improvements may include a more powerful motor, stronger cord, and an improved trigger. The chuck will have larger jaws, for a better grip on the bit.

Like a saber saw, the major advantage of a variable-speed drill is the ability to match the speed of the bit to the material being drilled. You can use the variable-speed drill on harder materials without damaging the bit. It isn't the material that damages drill bits, but the heat generated by friction. If the bit is slowed, the chance of damage from friction is reduced.

The next range in ¼″ drills is those priced around $25. They feature beefed-up construction in the gearing system, housing, and motor. They also have a reversing function, which allows you to remove screws as well as drive them. Reversing is also useful when drilling through very hard materials, where it is necessary to back the bit out.

In higher price ranges, drills designed for semi-professional use have needle or ball bearings, and a better chuck with hardened jaws capable of closing to 0 degrees. Heavy-duty construction throughout allows drills in this category to be used in hard service with a longer life and less danger of burn-

ing out. They will also accept larger attachments and power them without hesitation.

Many drills in this range also have infinitely adjustable speed controls, usually by varying the trigger pressure.

Drills costing more than $45 are heavy-duty, commercial, or industrial quality. If you have extensive use for a drill, the heavy-duty model might be the best choice, since it will outlast less expensive models many lifetimes.

The most popular electric drill on the market today is the ⅜″. It is similar to the ¼″ drill in size but is geared down to 1,000 rpm, and has a larger chuck to accommodate a ⅜″ bit. Double-reduction gears in a ⅜″ drill give this size twice the power at half the speed. They are more powerful than their ¼″ counterparts and not much more expensive.

The largest drills used by the homeowner and light industrial market are usually the ½″ size, much more powerful than their smaller cousins. They are intended exclusively for heavy work where slow rpm's are necessary. The ½″ drill speeds are from 350 to 700 rpm. Most models come with (or can be adapted to) another handle for two-handed use.

Drill bits are available for materials from wood to hardened steel, from glass to ceramics. The most important point to remember when drilling is to select the correct bit for the material and use it at the proper speed.

DRILL ACCESSORIES There are drill accessories that can turn wood, grind, sand, pump water, drive or remove screws, mix paint, saw wood, trim hedges, and even raise scaffolding. The only limiting factors for drill use are speed and power.

Variable-speed drills let you match the drill to the power requirements of various tools. Two commonly used accessories that illustrate this point are the hole saw and the sanding disk. Any ¼", 2,000 rpm drill will handle a 1" hole saw without difficulty. With the same drill, you can use sanding disks up to 5" in diameter.

However, larger hole saws or sanding disks will require the power and lower rpm of a larger, ⅜" drill. The larger tools will require a ½" drill as a power source.

One very useful and inexpensive drill accessory is the drill press stand, which adds much versatility to hand-held drills.

There are three easy ways to tell if your drill is overworked. Any one or a combination of the following are warning signs:
1. The job is not getting done.
2. The drill is straining, turning too hard. It may be groaning, turning slowly, or twisting.
3. The drill motor is heating in your hand. When a portable tool of any kind gets too hot to hold comfortably, stop working and check for the cause.

There are ways to overcome the problems indicated by these warning signs. First, if the accessory has a cutting edge, make sure it is sharp, free of nicks, burrs, gums, and resins. The accessory should be in good working order and well-oiled. Second, slow up on the feed or pressure if the motor is working too hard. A light-duty ¼" drill is designed for just that—light duty. Don't expect too much.

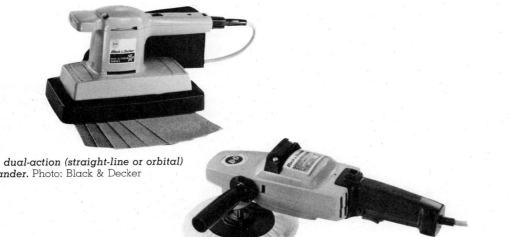

A dual-action (straight-line or orbital) sander. Photo: Black & Decker

A sander/polisher. Photo: Black & Decker

SANDERS

Portable power sanders are ideal for removing stock, stripping off old finishes, smoothing down rough surfaces, or fast smoothing and polishing operations. Three types of electric sanders are available: disk, finishing (orbital), and belt sanders.

DISK SANDERS Disk sanders are designed for removing paint, trimming down rough edges, and cleaning off rusted metals. They should never be used on interior paneling, furniture, or cabinets.

They work fast to remove blistered or cracked paint. They also, when equipped with the correct pads, do an acceptable job of polishing and buffing. Be sure when using this type of sander that you do not "burn" the finish by applying too much pressure.

Disk sanders usually consist of an arbor that is chucked into an electric drill with a semiflexible hard rubber disk mounted at the end. Sanding disks are secured to the face by a recessed nut and washer in the center or, in some cases, by cement.

The major drawback to this arrangement is lack

The sander/polisher is an ideal tool for polishing and buffing cars and boats as well as sanding on wood, metal, and plastics. *Photo: Sears*

A straight-line/orbital sander. *Photo: Sears*

of power. The sideways thrust generated by the revolving disk often proves too much for a ¼" drill. However, some multipurpose portable tools are well built and can take a limited amount of this type of abuse. These consist of a heavy-duty drill with bearings designed to withstand the heavy sideways thrust. The disk is attached by removing the chuck and threading the disk directly onto the spindle, rather than insetting the arbor into the chuck.

There are sander/polishers made for light-duty use in the home and on commercial jobs.

There are also commercial grade sander/polishers available, similar to those used by auto repairmen. These often have a variety of speeds and are easier to handle because the disk is mounted at right angles to the motor body. There is a second handle near the working end of the tool.

For best results, always hold a disk sander so the disk contacts the surface at a slight angle, with the outer edge of the disk doing most of the work. Keep the disk moving continuously as long as the motor is running, sweeping it back and forth in an arc. Apply only a moderate amount of pressure, so the edge of the disk doesn't gouge the surface.

FINISHING SANDERS Finishing sanders are the most popular and probably the most practical of all portable sanders. They utilize flat sheets of paper clamped onto a pad at the bottom of the machine. This pad is equipped with either a felt or rubber surface, which cushions the paper and also protects against gouging.

The machine is designed to propel the pad in a straight-line motion, back and forth, or in an orbital, oval motion. Straight-line motion with the grain gives the smoothest finish but is generally slower.

Orbital action cuts faster, but the motion of the paper occasionally crosses the grain. This cross-grain sanding is usually minimal because of the short stroke.

Most finishing sanders are the orbital variety. However, some models combine features of both orbital and straight-line sanders. They can be switched from one type of action to the other. This lets you start with the orbital action for fast surface preparation, then switch to straight-line for the smoothest finish.

Most finishing sanders are powered by a universal electric motor. Smaller, less expensive sanders may be driven by a magnetic-vibrator mechanism. Although these cost less, they have shorter strokes and work slower. Better quality vibrating units are handy for small smoothing and finishing jobs. They will not prove practical for large jobs that require extensive surface work, such as paint removal.

Sanders are available in either shockproof or double-insulated versions. Most feature a high-impact plastic housing that will stand up to abuse.

Another feature of finishing sanders is a dust catcher. Some have an apron fitted down over the sander, reaching the surface. Then a standard vacuum hose is fitted to the outlet and attached to a vacuum cleaner. While this does an effective job, it is not advised for tight quarters. A better dust catcher is the type that's built into the machine with an attached bag. The power of the machine provides suction for the dust catcher, without the need for hooking up to an external appliance.

ABRASIVE PAPER GRADES AND USES

Descriptive name and old rating no.	Grit nos. or grain sizes	Principal uses for this grade
Very fine 6/0 to 10/0	220 to 600	Light sanding between coats; extra-fine finish on raw wood; final sanding of sealer coat; finishing metal that will not be painted (not garnet).
Fine 3/0 to 5/0	120 to 180	Final finishing or bare wood prior to painting; finishing metal before painting (not garnet).
Medium ½ to 2/0	60 to 100	Average sanding to remove minor imperfections and light scratches; light stock removal before final sanding; removing thin coats of paint and rust.
Coarse 1 to 2	36 to 50	Heavy sanding to remove deep scratches; heavy stock removal; removing many coats of paint on inside surfaces; removing heavy rust and scale on metal (not garnet).
Very coarse 2½ to 4	12 to 30	For smoothing extremely rough wood; first sanding of bad floors; for use with power tools in removing heavy coats of paint and varnish from exterior of houses and boats.

NOTE: Above grades apply to aluminum oxide, silicon carbide, and garnet papers. Flint papers usually carry only name designations or may use old-style numbered ratings. Floor papers also still carry numbered ratings in many places. References to metalwork are for aluminum oxide papers only.

When using a finishing sander, do not press or push the sander into the surface. Let the machine rest on the surface, guiding it back and forth across the work. Let the weight of the machine provide the contact between the paper and the surface. Pressing too hard will slow the machine down and reduce the amount of material being removed, not increase it. You may also overload the machine, thereby overheating it and causing premature wear.

BELT SANDERS Belt sanders are the fastest and most powerful of the three commercial types of sanders. They are preferred by experienced woodworkers and cabinetmakers. They work best on large, flat surfaces for removing paint and finishes and for doing a fast job of smoothing or removing material from rough, uneven surfaces.

Two types of dust catchers for sanders. Photos: Sears

The belt sander employs a continuous belt of abrasive that revolves on two rollers or drums at opposite ends of the machine. A flat, spring-mounted plate between the rollers provides the necessary firm backing for the belt, keeping it in contact with the surface.

Belt sanders are chosen by the size or width of belt they accept, varying from 2″ to 4″. The 3″ model is most common for home use. A belt sander usually supplements a finishing sander, but will also do a good job of finish sanding with the correct abrasive. Special nylon mesh belts, impregnated with a fine abrasive, produce an excellent finish.

Belt sanders, because of their weight and speed,

A 1 hp router. Photo: Black & Decker

Some routers now have a much-needed dust-collection system that can be very beneficial in home workshops where airborne particles can be a problem.

cut very fast and must be handled with great care to prevent surface damage. Never stop moving the machine while the motor is still running, or it will cut deeply into the surface. When working near the edge of stock, don't let the machine run over the edge or it will round it off and ruin what may have been a perfectly square corner.

All belt sanders have a built-in tracking adjustment that lets you center the belt on the rollers. If the belt is not centered, make the necessary corrections. An uncentered belt will either work itself off the edge of the roller or run to the inside and cut into the housing, damaging it.

Belt sanders are also available in dustless models. These usually have a bag attached to the machine. On most models, the bag is constructed so it can be swung in a 180° arc, keeping it clear of machine operations.

ROUTERS

Routers are simple mechanical tools that consist of a high-speed vertically mounted motor and a base. The motor can be adjusted up and down to control the depth of the cut. In some routers this adjustment is controlled by a rack-and-pinion gearing system, in others by a spiral cam.

Scale markings, to set the depth of the cut, are usually in sixty-fourths of an inch. A collet chuck on the shaft of the motor holds the cutting tool.

Routers operate at speeds of 20,000 to 28,000 rpm, producing a finished edge that usually requires no further sanding. The base of the router is equipped

The Dremel Constant Torque Moto-Tool router will shape edges and cut rabbets, dadoes, mortises, tongues, and chamfer. Used freehand, it carves out lettering, figures, and patterns for signs and wall plaques. Photo: Dremel Tool Co.

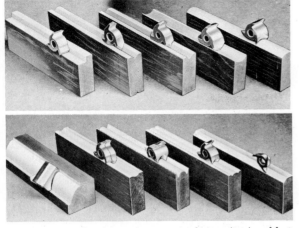

Some of the jobs these cutters can do are (top): rabbet, V-rabbet, spindle bead, concave cut, convex face, (bottom): thumb-mold, combined concave-convex, surface bead, corner bead, chamfer.

For the beginner, a guide clamped over the work guarantees straight cuts across wide boards.

with a smooth-surfaced, circular sub-base that protects the work from being scratched. The edge of the base also acts as a guide.

To change the bit on a router, the collet chuck is loosened with a wrench and the new bit inserted. On some models there is also a wrench for holding the motor shaft, to prevent it from turning when loosening the collet. Whenever you change bits on a router, disconnect the power supply. Another safety consideration is to keep a firm grip on the machine because there is considerable torque generated when the machine is first turned on.

First, select the proper bit for the work you are doing and clamp it firmly into the collet. Make certain the bit has been "bottomed-out" in the shaft and is tightened down securely. A loose bit tends to "walk" across the surface and out of the chuck. This not only ruins the work but is also dangerous.

To set the depth gauge, first set the motor in the base so the tip of the bit is flush with the base. Then zero the depth gauge. Once the gauge has been zeroed, adjust the depth of the bit.

Aside from the sharpness of the tool, another factor that will dictate the cutting smoothness is the amount of material removed in one pass across the surface. Clean, smooth routing is accomplished when the machine is set close to the no-load limit.

Too deep a cut or feeding it too fast into the material will slow the bit down, allowing it to take bigger bites of material. This results in a jagged, rough edge. Feeding speed depends on the size and shape of the bit being used, the power of the router, and the hardness and moisture content of the wood.

The direction of the cut can be controlled and is very important. Always feed from the left to the

For wider dado cuts, make repeated cuts alongside one another until desired width is attained.

Guide for circle cutting attached to router steers it in perfect circle. By cutting through stock, disks and wheels can be formed as well as grooves.

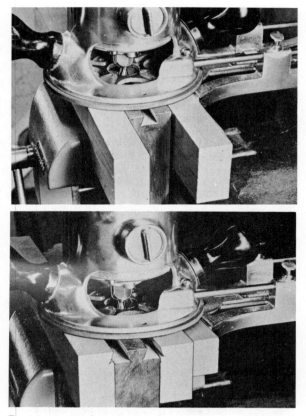

For joining two boards to make a wider one, a dovetail on edges to be joined assures permanent joint. Cut groove along one edge of the boards. Then make a tongue on the edge of the second board, clamping it between scrap stock as shown. Same cutter is used.

right, across the edge. This lets the router produce a smooth cutting edge. As end grain tends to split, use the router across the end of your stock first. The wood may split, but usually as you complete the cut on the side of the stock going with the grain, the chipped portion will be removed.

The simplest way to guide the router across the work is to clamp a straightedge to the edge of the surface and let the edge of the subbase run against it. This allows accurate routing along a straight line. Be sure the material you are using for a straightedge is in fact straight.

Accessory edge guides are available for all routers and may be a worthwhile investment. They guide the router when cutting dadoes and rabbets or for cutting ploughs and grooves several inches from the edge. More complex guides make evenly spaced parallel dadoes, pivot about a point, or plane edges.

Piloted bits can also be used as guides. Unless they are the ball-bearing variety, they may burn the edge of the wood if the machine stops. With a piloted bit you can easily follow the edge of an irregular surface.

Templates also help when routing irregular patterns. The best material for making a template is ¼" hardboard. A template guide bushing is screwed into the center hole of the router base and is used to follow the template.

Freehand routing opens up new vistas to the router fan. With little practice, satisfactory results are easily possible. Freehand lettering and carving are just two of the many interesting things you can do, once you have mastered the basics.

TABLE SAWS

The bench, or table, saw is one of the primary stationary power tools that most handymen add to their workshop. The variety of cutting operations that can be performed with this saw is limited only by the imagination and skill of the operator.

The table saw can rip, crosscut, miter, and bevel one piece at a time, or duplicate a cut over and over. However, cutting boards to length or width is only one simple function. With the addition of accessories, it can cut grooves, rabbets, and most common woodworking joints. By adding a molding head, almost any type of fancy molding or trim can be produced.

A typical motorized table saw. Photo: Sears

The table saw can also be adapted to sanding with the addition of a sanding disk. With selected blades, you can cut materials other than wood.

A table saw is a flat cutting surface with the upper portion of a circular saw blade protruding through it. A motor and drive mechanism are located in the housing under the blade. The blade can be adjusted to cut at 45° to 90° angles.

The size of the table limits the size of the material that can be cut comfortably. Auxiliary tables can be added to increase the size.

All table saws have two guides to help control the course of the work and to maintain accuracy. One is the rip fence, an adjustable flat metal bar that is used when making rip cuts, molding, or rabbet cuts. It can be adjusted away from, or toward, the blade, but is always parallel to it.

The other cutting guide is the miter gauge, which fits into a groove in the table surface, usually one on each side of the blade. The upper portion of the miter gauge can be adjusted to and locked at any angle from 0° to 45° allowing stock to be cut at that angle.

Table saws, as any other power tool, can be dangerous if misused. Bench saws come equipped with a removable saw guard that covers the exposed portion of the blade. Made of light metal or plastic, it helps protect fingers from accidental contact with the blade. Be safe; obey all safety rules and be familiar with your saw.

When using a table saw, always stand a little to one side instead of directly behind the blade so

Always measure the size of the cut by allowing for the saw kerf, the thickness of the blade while it is rotating. Measure from inside the blade to the rip fence. Most table saws have a scale on the rip fence guide bar that eliminates the need for measuring for each different cut. Make certain switch is off or motor disconnected from outlet.

Adjust height of blade to thickness of wood being cut. Keep approximately ¼" above top surface of wood.

Periodically check to see that blade is tight on the arbor. Do not jam blade when tightening. Instead, hold belt to prevent arbor from rotating,. Always disconnect motor from outlet when working on blade.

Keep control knob in working order. When finished working, brush dust off mechanism. Periodically—every 60 days for the average homeowner—lubricate wheel controls with graphite.

you will be out of the way of kickbacks caused by work being twisted or squeezed between the blade and the rip fence, and thrown back by the force of the saw. Another good rule is to avoid pushing a narrow piece of wood into the blade with your fingers. Use a pusher stick—a block shaped to hold the work to the table—to move it along from behind. You can make a pusher stick yourself.

One more rule: Never try to rip short pieces of lumber by using the molding fence unless the fence is faced with a smooth board running its length and bolted or clamped to it. Any object between the blade and the fence may be pulled into the saw if the work binds against the fence. Your fingers may be pulled in with it or the wood being cut may be hurled back in your face. Like every machine, the power saw has its quirks and characteristics. The average 10″ blade saw is driven by a 1 to 1½ hp motor, at about 3,450 rpm. As a result, the saw packs a terrific wallop. The following are techniques that make professional work not only possible but commonplace.

RIPPING   This is one of the simplest operations of all. The wood is fed to the saw blade, which cuts along the grain and reduces it to the desired widths. The fence is set in advance, so the distance between fence and blade is the width of the finished piece of the work. You may wish to allow approximately ⅛″ more for finishing on your jointer or planer. Operate the saw with the guard in position and feed the lumber smoothly with both hands until nearing the end, when only the hand on the fence finishes the run-through. Where the board is longer than the table, use a sawhorse or other suitable support to assist in holding the work flat on the table.

CROSS-CUTTING   Square cross-cutting is done with the use of the miter gauge for applying pressure toward the blade. Gauge and work are advanced at the same rate. If the board is so wide that no room is left on the table for a gauge, reverse the gauge. The wood held against the gauge must be straight or it will twist the blade and be thrown back.

MITER CUTTING   The miter gauge has a swivel setting to obtain any angle of cut. For greater accuracy and to eliminate "creep" (a sideways sliding of the work due to the angle at which it meets the blade), use special clamps fitted with points to hold the work tightly in place.

DADO CUTTING   There are several ways this operation may be performed with a power saw. A group of cutters set in place of the standard saw blade and equipped with special outside blades permits you to cut grooves and rabbets of varying widths. Special washers for use with the standard blades are also available. These rotate the saw at

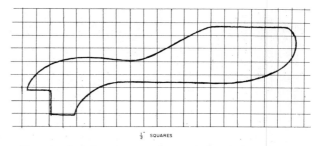

¼″ SQUARES

Here are the plans for a pusher stick. Draw this pattern to scale on any piece of 1″ stock and then cut to shape with a coping or jigsaw. Sand edges smooth and keep pusher handy next to your circular saw.

When ripping narrow pieces of wood, keep your fingers away from the blade. Use a pusher stick to guide and push the wood through between the saw blade and rip fence. The stick is easy to make. Photo: Sears

an angle that cuts a wider-than-normal groove—actually a dado. When cutting a dado groove with the grain, wood is held against the fence. When making this cut across the grain, the miter gauge is used. The depth of the dado groove is governed by adjusting the height to which the saw teeth protrude above the table.

RABBETING   A rabbet is a groove cut along the edge of a board. It can be made by taking two saw cuts at right angles to each other at the edge, or with a dado blade. With a pencil, mark the stock that is to be cut away. If using a table saw, set the fence and saw depth to the pencil marks. Set the board on edge and make the first cut. Then reset the fence to make the second cut. Lay the board flat and cut away the stock with the second cut. If using a dado blade you need only mark the stock to be removed, set the blade depth and fence to match the pencil marks, and cut away the rabbet in a single pass.

When ripping (cutting along the grain) a wide piece of wood, protect yourself and increase the accuracy of your cut by straddling the rip fence with the fingers of your hand as shown.

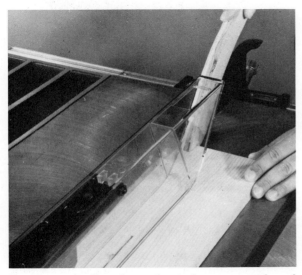

For ripping small stock, use the rip fence as a guide and a push block to keep fingers away from the blade. Keep the blade guard in place while working. *Photo: Sears*

For greater accuracy in crosscutting (cutting against the grain), add a wood fence to your miter gauge. It gives you more support, greater protection, and results in more accurate cutting of lumber.

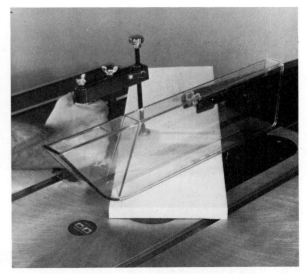

Accurate miter cuts are easily accomplished by using hold-down clamps. *Photo: Sears*

Dado blades are set to thickness and depth of desired cut. When cutting with grain, hold stock against fence. Use miter gauge for cross-grain dado cutting.

SPECIAL CUTTING Taper ripping, tenoning, cutting box joints, tongue-and-groove, panel raising, cove cutting, and cutting molding shapes are all operations requiring special skill and the use of extra safety precautions. They should not be undertaken until considerable experience has been gained. The table saw, in addition to sawing, dadoing, and molding, is also capable of performing sanding operations by using a sanding wheel.

Photos this series: Sears

Dado blades used for rabbeting edge of board.

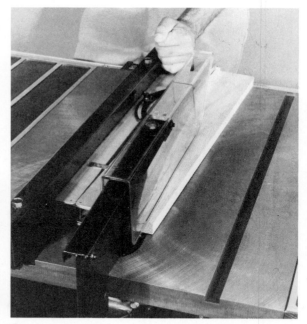

Taper ripping can be easily accomplished by using a taper jig available commercially. You may wish to make your own for a given job by "precutting" the jig.

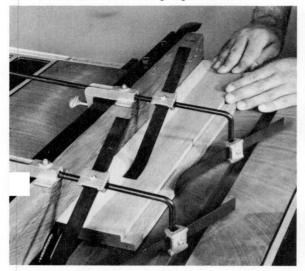

Rabbet cut in long end of board. Clamp an extra length of squared lumber against fence if it is too close to blade.

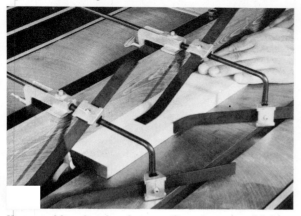

Use a molding head and an auxiliary fence to add decorative moldings to the edge of your workpiece. Photo: Sears

Tenoning is easiest done with the use of a jig that holds the wood firmly in position and vertical to the table surface.

Cutting a box joint for a drawer on a table saw.

Construct a twin fence jig like this one to assist in panel raising for decorative panels and drawer fronts. Tilt the blade 5° to 10° to give the desired bevel angle.

Using a molding head to cut a tongue-and-groove joint for flooring and paneling.

Construct a jig to achieve the cove cut shown here. The blade must be sharp and the stock fed slowly. You may need to repeat the cut, taking a greater cut each time.

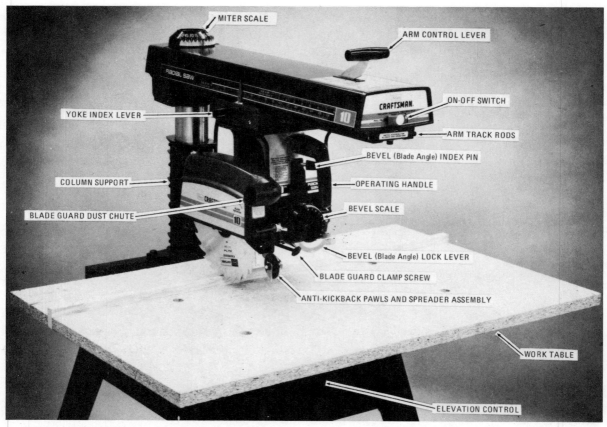

MITER SCALE

ARM CONTROL LEVER

ON-OFF SWITCH

ARM TRACK RODS

YOKE INDEX LEVER

BEVEL (Blade Angle) INDEX PIN

OPERATING HANDLE

COLUMN SUPPORT

BEVEL SCALE

BLADE GUARD DUST CHUTE

BEVEL (Blade Angle) LOCK LEVER

BLADE GUARD CLAMP SCREW

ANTI-KICKBACK PAWLS AND SPREADER ASSEMBLY

WORK TABLE

ELEVATION CONTROL

Parts of a typical radial saw. Photo: Sears

RADIAL ARM SAWS

With the attachment of a "portable" power saw to an overhead arm, a new idea in shop-tool safety was created: the radial arm saw. It can be used to perform all the normal cutting operations, such as cross-cutting and ripping, mitering, and beveling. In addition, the radial arm saw can be equipped with dado heads or molding heads, be used as a sander, grinder, router, shaper, planer; and it will even do limited drilling operations.

The basic difference between a radial saw and a table saw is that when operating a radial saw, the workpiece is held in a stationary position on the table when cross-cutting, mitering, beveling, and when making certain dado cuts. This is very convenient, especially when cutting or dadoing long boards. The saw blade or dado head is pulled forward through the workpiece to make the cut. When making these cuts on a table saw, the workpiece must be moved into the saw blade or dado head.

When ripping long boards on a radial saw or performing molding or dadoing operations along the length of a board, the cutting head is swiveled 90° from the crosscut position and the workpiece is then moved along the guide fence. When making these cuts on a table saw, it is only necessary to position the rip fence.

While many users of power-shop equipment are inclined to consider this all-purpose tool useful for sawing wood only, it is practical to learn all the unit can do. In the right hands, it becomes what it was originally intended to be — an all-purpose tool.

While upward of twenty cuts may be made with the saw in its different positions, the addition of a few supplemental knives and devices makes the radial arm saw capable of virtually any shop job.

Crosscutting at 90° is the most common and simple operation on the radial saw.

Miter crosscutting at 45° is a form of crosscutting and on most saws this operation can handle angles from 0° to 60° right and left.

Ripping is done on a radial saw by moving the workpiece through the stationary blade.

Compound cuts are ideal for shadow-box-type picture frames and crown molding.

Many other operations add to the radial saw's versatility, such as edge molding with shaft of motor vertical.

Surface molding with motor in the bevel-up position.

The basic machine consists of a table with a rip fence to hold the material, an upright column at the back of the table, which supports a radial arm track, and the saw and motor assembly which is suspended beneath the radial arm on a track. Most models have a single arm, but others are equipped with a double arm. Both work the same way.

The weight of the saw is carried on the arm on which it slides back and forth. The arm, too, is movable. And the blade, plus its motor and shaft, can be revolved on an axis. This triple movement gives the saw complete mobility in any direction. At the same time, the operator of the saw doesn't have to hold any weight. Also, the action of the blade itself when cross-cutting holds down the wood. This last is the ideal safety feature, since kickback and upthrust are eliminated.

The size of a radial arm saw is determined by the diameter of blade it will accommodate. They vary in size from 8″ to 16″ contractor's saws. A 10″ model, which develops between 1 and 2½ hp, is the standard size found in most home workshops.

Buffing.

Drilling.

Drum sanding.

Photos: Sears

Disk sanding.

Surface planing.

Routing with a collet chuck.

BANDSAWS

For all-around work, such as building closets, cabinets, shelves, and rough construction, the radial or table saw is the primary tool. But if you plan fancy work such as valances, lawn furniture, toys, and novelties, the bandsaw is a better choice.

The bandsaw is an excellent choice for making almost any irregular, curved, or straight cut in wood or other materials. Also, it will handle thicker wood faster than any other cutting tool in the shop.

The bandsaw can be used to make compound cuts, intricate curved cuts, or for ripping a piece of material to thinner dimensions. Additional blades will allow the bandsaw to be used for cutting pipe or other metal, Styrofoam plastic, or even foam rubber.

The bandsaw is equipped with a frame that

supports the upper and lower wheels, a work-supporting table, drive mechanism and motor, and a continuous blade. The larger the bandsaw, the greater the distance from the throat of the saw to the cutting blade and the deeper the cut allowed. An average bandsaw will have a throat from 10″ to 12″ deep and will cut material up to 6″ thick.

Better quality bandsaws have a tilting table and provisions for ripping fence and mitering gauge, as well as a more powerful motor. With a tilting table, the bandsaw will cut bevels and compound miters as well as its specialty, curves.

The saw should be properly set up before work is begun. Its cover is first removed, then the long blade fitted over the top wheel. The tension-adjustment knob is loosened and the saw slipped over the bottom wheel. The blade passes through a slot in the table top and between two guides. The teeth must always point downward from the upper wheel to the table. Then the tension is restored to its maximum by means of the tension knob, then loosened slightly. There should be a slight give when the blade is pressed between the fingers. Now, rotating the lower wheel by hand, check the blade to see that it rides properly on both upper and lower wheels.

The bandsaw blade passes between two sets of guides, one located above the work, one beneath the table. The purpose of the guides is to prevent the blade from twisting, which would distort the cut. Guides are adjusted by first loosening the setscrews, then bringing the guides back to the blade to a point where the clearance is that of a piece of stiff paper. By holding a slip of paper against the saw blade and slowly bringing up the guide on each side, the adjustment can be made easily. It is always best to follow the manufacturer's manual for all setups.

Check the clearance each time you use the saw, in case the guides become loose in operation. If the clearance is too great, the blade will twist and cut poorly. If it is too small, the blade will strike the

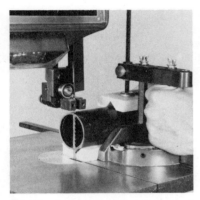

Equipped with a speed reducer and proper blades, the bandsaw can cut ferrous and nonferrous metals, pipe, and even conduit.

The deep cutting capacity of most bandsaws allows the operator to cut materials like this Styrofoam block up to 6" thick.

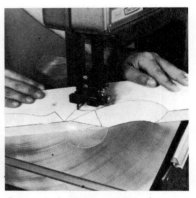

Compound cutting is made easy when the table tilts. These operations are best used for making valances and other decorative workpieces.

The bandsaw is a very versatile tool, especially when it comes to compound cuts where more than one side is cut as on this table leg. This is done by drawing the desired pattern on two sides and making the cut. Before cutting the second side, tape the original piece onto the leg to give you a smooth surface.

Drum sanding is an excellent way to handle curved and contoured surfaces.

Buffing and polishing is easily accomplished with a buffing wheel.
Photos: Sears

guides in running and the teeth will be ruined.

Unlike the circular saw, lumber can be fed to a bandsaw freehand, without a fence. For curved work, the pattern can be scribed directly on the wood or on paper pasted to the work. Since the bandsaw will cut up to 5″ or 6″ thicknesses of material, you can cut identical pieces by clamping lumber together.

To make long, narrow slots, first drill a hole at one end, cut in along the side lines to clear away excess right angles. Use narrow ¼″ or ⅜″ blades for sharp radius turns and the more rigid ½″ and ¾″ blades for straight ripping and cross-cutting.

DRILL PRESSES

A precision tool capable of doing many jobs quickly and accurately, the drill press is as much at home working on wood as on metal. An example is the ordinarily tedious job of wood joining. With a drill press, you can make mortise-and-tenon and dovetail joints, or precisely drill dowel holes. The drill press uses special attachments and accessories for routing, shaping, milling, tapping, polishing, planing, sanding, grinding, fluting, and buffing. Unlike most other workshop tools, a drill press has no particular specialty. You can use it to drill glass and marble, cut keyways in metal, or mix paint.

This all-around tool consists of a thick, round column mounted on a heavy iron base. This column has an adjustable head at the top, holding the motor in the back and the drilling assembly in front. These are connected by a belt on multistep pulleys. Also mounted on this column is the iron work table, which can be clamped on any position on the column.

The typical motor for workshop use is rated at ⅓ hp, 1,750 rpm. The pulleys, known as cone pulleys, allow drill speeds from approximately 600 through 1,300 and 2,400 to 4,000 rpm. Some drill presses have an 8-step pulley for speeds up to 8,550 for routing and shaping. The motor should be a capacitor type with sealed-bearing shafts.

A spindle, which holds the drill chuck or other tools, is fitted and locked inside a movable sleeve called a quill. A feed lever at the side of the head moves the spindle down to the work at any desired pressure. A coil spring returns the spindle upward when the lever is released. The quill can be locked in any position.

For regular wood boring, the drill press uses many styles of bits and twist drills. Holes are bored through the work at any desired depth by a gauge built into the press. They may be drilled at an angle by using a device called a set square, which is a tilting device clamped to the table. By using a

Mortising a chair leg for a strong, sturdy glue joint can only be handled on the drill press (left). The drill press can double as a shaper with a fence and chuck to hold the bits (right). *Photos: Sears*

stop pin as a guide, holes can be drilled in series. A special V block holds round work, and straight holes can be drilled to 8″ or more deep, depending on the capacity of the drill. Expansion bits are used for drilling holes 2″ or more in diameter.

Mortising is done with a mortising bit set inside a hollow square chisel attached to the quill with a special adaptor. A fence clamped to the table guides the work for accurate cutting. A hold-down bracket, a part of the fence, lets the work slide along the fence but keeps it in place when you raise the spindle. The cut is started at the end of the mortise, then continued with successive strokes of the chisel, each cut being slightly overlapped. A depth gauge is essential to keep the bites uniform.

Routing is done with small bits in various shapes that cut on the side to form grooves and notches and that will do rabbeting and pattern curves, fluting, and carving. The press is run at high speed, and a fence or guide should be clamped to the table to prevent sudden twisting. Freehand work can be done only with extremely small router bits not over ⅛″ in diameter.

The shaping operation requires the same cutters used in a standard shaper, operated at about 5,000 to 8,000 rpm. The press can be operated in regular position, or the head can be inverted so the spindle comes through the center hole from below the table. Work must always be carefully supported with a fence or jig and hold-down during a shaping operation. Only moderate side pressure is used, so several passes along the cutters are necessary.

Dovetailing to make a drawer joint. Photo: Sears

Most drill presses have a tilt table accessory that helps to drill angle holes for miter joints. Photo: Sears

The table is raised as close as possible to the quill.

Glass is drilled with either a brass tube slotted at the end, or a triangular file ground to a long, tapering point. With the brass tube, the abrasive (carborundum) is held with a circular dam of putty. Turpentine or kerosene is the cutting lubricant.

Dovetail joints are cut with a ¼" dovetail router. Both sides of the work are mounted together in a dovetailing fixture. The bit will cut into both a

drawer front and side at the same time, so the attachment is designed to offset one section of the work the width of a single cut. The parts then can be lined to and will join perfectly if the calculations and settings are correct.

Planers, sanding drums, and polishing and buffing wheels are similar to those used in other tools. Such work is done at slow speeds and can be held without a fence or guide.

WOOD LATHES

There are few tools a handyman can own that will give as much satisfaction and pleasure as a turning lathe. Wood turning is an old and fascinating art. And, like all art, the only limit is that of talent and experience.

The primary purpose of the wood lathe is to make round forms out of wood stock. With adaptations, wood lathes can also be used for drilling, boring, filing, sanding, and even some light metal work. By simply changing the running speed of the lathe and utilizing the various chisel points and shapes, every step of the forming operation, from beginning to end, can be done without removing the stock from the lathe.

A big feature of the wood lathe that appeals to most owners is the individual creativity that can be put to use with this machine to turn out unique objects, from candleholders to table legs. With the addition of a duplicating accessory, any piece can be copied, from chessmen to legs for beds. A faceplate accessory will allow the operator to make bowls and dishes.

The basic lathe consists of a metal track or bed, with a stationary headstock. The adjustable tailstock is located on the opposite end of the bed. The material being turned is supported between centers of the head and tailstocks. An adjustable tool rest holds the chisels and other forming tools during the operation.

The material is clamped firmly between the headstock and tailstock and locked into place. The speed of the stock is regulated by a series of step pulleys located on the headstock. Slower speeds are required for rough pieces, but it increases as the piece nears completion.

Lathe sizes are always given in two dimensions—the swing and the distance between centers. The swing is twice the distance from the center of the drive spindle to the top of the lathe bed; this limits the diameter of the pieces being turned. The distance between centers limits the length of those pieces.

Once you have learned the art of wood turning, you can move up. For instance, you can turn larger diameter pieces on the outboard side. And you can overcome the handicap of short lengths by joining

USES FOR YOUR LATHE

Face plate turning. Photo: Sears

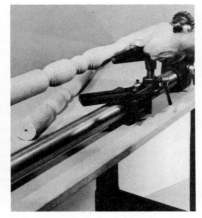

Spindle turning. Photo: Sears

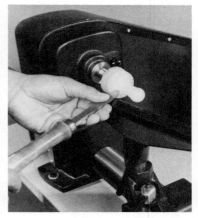

Turning plastic pieces such as this chessman is done using the screw center. Photo: Sears

Some lathes have an automatic index for making equal spaces for such projects as this captain's wheel. Photo: Sears

Turn tail and spindle until work is firmly in position; rotate wood by hand to test firm hold, then position tool rest.

two or more pieces dowel-fashion, making the end of one piece a dowel and drilling a hole to fit it in the next piece to be added. The implements used to cut the wood are mainly chisels of assorted shapes and perhaps a wood rasp and sandpaper for finishing touches. The chisels are held on a rest and slipped slowly forward for contact with the wood.

All work that is turned between centers is called spindle turning. A candlestick, a baseball bat, a bowling pin and a chair leg—all are called spindles. For this type of turning, use clear, knot-free wood a bit longer than the finished piece is to be. Cut both ends square. Mark, then lightly score both

ends with a back saw, forming an X on each end. Set one end against the spur drive so the teeth of the spur match the notches you cut; then tap the wood into the teeth. Center and set the other end and pull up tight. Then turn the wood by hand a few times to see that it is firmly held between centers. Move the tool rest parallel to the wood and allow about ⅛" clearance. The top of the tool rest should be about ⅛" above the center line of the wood. Turn by hand to be sure that no part of the wood stock touches the tool rest. Use a gouge to rough-round the stock. Keep a firm grip on the gouge and all other chisels used. Do not try to turn the piece

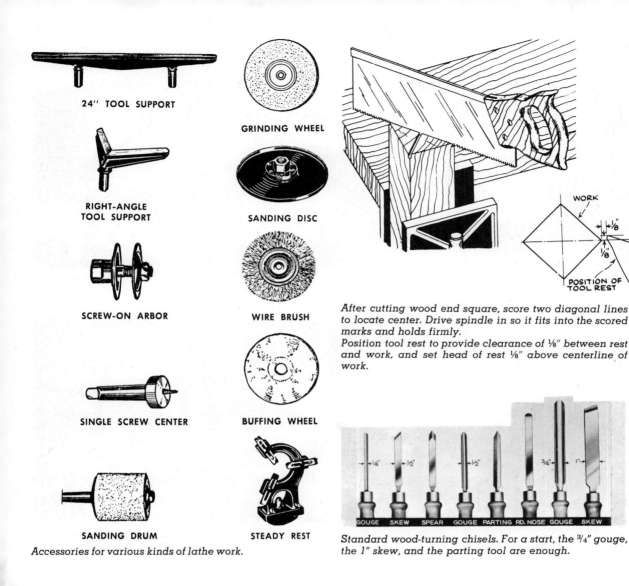

24" TOOL SUPPORT

RIGHT-ANGLE TOOL SUPPORT

SCREW-ON ARBOR

SINGLE SCREW CENTER

SANDING DRUM

GRINDING WHEEL

SANDING DISC

WIRE BRUSH

BUFFING WHEEL

STEADY REST

Accessories for various kinds of lathe work.

After cutting wood end square, score two diagonal lines to locate center. Drive spindle in so it fits into the scored marks and holds firmly.

Position tool rest to provide clearance of ⅛" between rest and work, and set head of rest ⅛" above centerline of work.

GOUGE SKEW SPEAR GOUGE PARTING RD. NOSE GOUGE SKEW

Standard wood-turning chisels. For a start, the ¾" gouge, the 1" skew, and the parting tool are enough.

down to its intended size all at once—take off a little at a time. Reset the tool rest closer to the work— maintaining the ⅛" clearance—as you reduce the diameter of the stock. It's much safer to work with the rest near the work.

The large gouge used for rough-rounding is intended to do the hard work—that of cutting sharp corners off blocks of wood. Start about 3" from the tail end of the stock (away from the drive end) and work left, up to the end. Start the next cut about 3" from the tail end and work to that end. No rough-cutting should be done in one continuous movement. Make short cuts and merge them. The wood

can split if you don't, or the chisel may grab and be torn out of your hand. The marking of patterns on the wood and the proper selection of chisels for cutting and finishing are easily learned.

Simple finishing is fun on a lathe and, with a little experimenting, can be varied considerably. The easiest, of course, is a wax finish. Apply paste wax to the work and let it dry about ten minutes. Then start the lathe and at slow speed hold a soft cloth against the work. If a higher finish is desired, apply a second coat and repeat. Beeswax or paraffin gives an even higher gloss when handled this way. By using mahogany paste wax or a little

Diameter of Work	Roughing Off	General Cutting	Finishing
Under 2″	900 to 1300 rpm	2400 to 2800	3000 to 4000
2″ to 4″	600 to 1000 rpm	1800 to 2400	2400 to 3000
4″ to 6″	600 to 800 rpm	1200 to 1800	1800 to 2400
6″ to 8″	400 to 600 rpm	800 to 1200	1200 to 1800
8″ to 10″	300 to 400 rpm	600 to 800	900 to 1200
Over 10″	300	300 to 600	600 to 900

brown paste shoe polish added to paste wax, you get color as well as finish. A satin-smooth finish without high gloss is obtained with linseed oil, painted on, then buffed as the wood turns slowly. For salad bowls, use salad oil or olive oil in which a garlic clove has been crushed.

For a shellac finish, apply one coat with a brush as you turn the work by hand. Let it dry for ten minutes. Then sand lightly with worn finishing paper (fine garnet is best) and rub with a cloth pad (lint-free, such as an old sheet) about ½″ thick, moistened with shellac thinned 3 to 1, adding 2 or 3 drops of machine oil. Apply to slowly revolving work and when polished to the desired finish, rinse with water.

Don't be afraid to experiment with a lathe. For instance, try using a wood rasp on the rough-round operation. Tear strips from a belt sander abrasive belt and shoe-shine the work as it turns. Strips from aluminum oxide open-coat abrasive paper will do as well. Or, for a more permanent finishing tool, glue a whole sheet of abrasive paper to a strip of hardboard and use it to smooth cylindrical work that has no beading. A length of wire held between the hands and pressed firmly on the work will make a clear, sharp line on a fast-turning spindle. Repeat at marked intervals for fine design effects.

THE PLANER-MOLDER

The planer-molder is a power tool that—by a change of its cutting knife or head—can perform an unlimited number of wood-working functions. The planer-molder reduces wood to the exact thickness and shape desired.

Since it can perform so many varied functions, the tool itself is known by a great many names. You may already know it as a molding cutter, a thickness planer, or a planer-molder, but they're all the same tool. Among its many accomplishments are jointing (making edges interlock or preparing them for gluing), surface planing (smoothing wood or reducing its thickness), rabbeting, bevel cutting and taper cutting, shaping moldings, and edging cutouts.

Jointing, one function of this tool, is a great time-saver. It eliminates hours of hand planing and, in effect, makes a motorized plane of the tool. The jointer smooths the surfaces and edges of wood for joining with glue, and it prepares lumber for a final sanding on exposed surfaces. In many jointers, the wood is pushed along a divided table and over rapidly turning cutters that protrude a measured distance above the tables. The in-feed table, on which the wood starts its trip, is separated from the out-feed table (which is elevated above the in-feed table) by the whirling knives. The cutter head is usually cylindrical, and the knives are inserted into it. As the blades wear down, the blades can be adjusted to compensate.

All jointers have a fence, or guide, which can be set at any desired angle. Auxiliary fences can be added, which will help when jointing wide boards on the edges. A spring-tensioned guard protects the operator from the knives. Don't remove the guard!

In making use of the machine, never cut deeper than ⅛″ for one pass of the wood, particularly on

The planer-molder

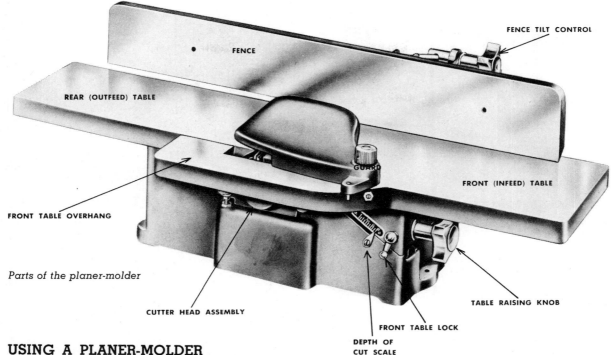

FENCE TILT CONTROL

FENCE

REAR (OUTFEED) TABLE

GUARD

FRONT (INFEED) TABLE

FRONT TABLE OVERHANG

Parts of the planer-molder

CUTTER HEAD ASSEMBLY

DEPTH OF
CUT SCALE

FRONT TABLE LOCK

TABLE RAISING KNOB

USING A PLANER-MOLDER

Jointing an edge on a piece of stock in preparation for gluing. Photo: Sears

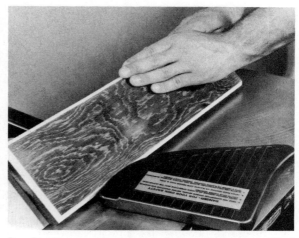

Bevel cutting or chamfering is done with the fence tilted to the desired angle. This operation adds a finished look to the corners of a workpiece. Photo: Sears

softer woods. A setting of $1/16''$, or even as little as $1/32''$, does a better job — just as hand planing is better done with fine rather than deep strokes.

The most common function of this power tool is edging for jointing. The fence is set square to the table at 90°. The depth of the cut is set — $1/16''$ to $1/8''$ — and the best face of the wood is set against the fence. Press the wood against the fence and lightly upon the front table. Hold the wood with both hands and move it forward across the cutter head.

In cutting a rabbet, cutout section is on underside, and fence side of piece being cut.

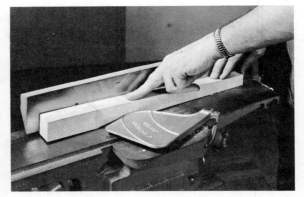

Long taper needs no block, runs through from high to low end, is repeated on all sides.

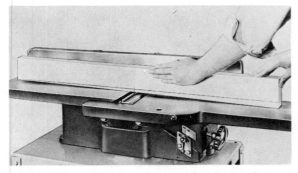

Full-length long taper (guard removed to show technique). Note halfway mark on work.

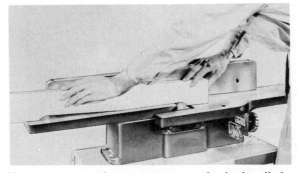

More intricate work on tapering can also be handled — here is a cutout made as a taper.

As the wood passes over the knives, hold it with the right hand, then advance the left without passing it directly over the heads, thus covering the entire board surface. Make the first two passes on the outer 3″ of the two sides, then the center passes.

For bevel cuts, instead of tilting the table, tilt the fence to the desired angle. Lock the fence in place securely. Wherever possible, tilt the fence to a closed angle — less than 90°. You'll have better control of the work when feeding it into the closed angle. In most cases, this work will require several passes across the cutter heads, reducing the stock a little more each time across, until the full depth of the bevel is reached.

Rabbeting is the only operation where the guard must be removed. Remove the guard and set the fence for the width of the rabbet and the front table for the depth of the rabbet. Hold the wood firmly and feed it slowly. If the cut is to be deep, make several passes across the cutters. In making rabbets across the end grain — a common form of jointing — lay the edge to be cut down and against the fence. For safety, use a pusher if at all possible.

Taper jointing is one of the most interesting jobs your jointer will do. Though it's possible to cut a 9″ taper on a 9″ piece of wood, it's better to start out with wood longer than the taper. All taper cuts start with one end of the piece of wood resting on the rear table, which is raised above the front (infeed) table. The height of the rear table is set to produce the desired angle of taper. When the length of the taper to be cut is shorter than the infeed table, use the following method: to taper 9″ of a 15″ table leg ¼″, mark the work and set the infeed table ¼″ lower. Clamp a stop block to the infeed table 9″ from the cutter. Then rest the end to be tapered against the stop block, press down on this end and feed in. If more than one side is to be tapered, as with a table leg, repeat on all the sides to be tapered. Eventually, as you become more proficient, you can omit the stop block and start from the marked line without it. If you see the taper is going to end up longer than the front table, do the following: Divide the taper into two equal sections — each 10″ long for a 20″ taper. Supposing the taper is to be ¼″ deep, lower the feeding table half the depth of the taper — in this case, ⅛″ only. Make the first cut, starting at the 10″ marker point, toward the end of the marked area. Make the second cut, starting this time at the 20″ mark and running the full 20″ length. Repeat for the other sides of the taper.

The jointer will also, with selected cutter heads, convert plain stock to tongue-and-grooved boards. And, with combination cuts, you can make other interlocking joints for connecting two pieces of wood permanently with the addition of glue.

Molder planers can be converted to other uses, such as jointers, by the addition of other blades. They can also be used to make moldings of various types with these knives. Basically, however, the molder planer is a thickness planer, a small machine to pass boards through rather than over, in order to reduce thickness. A curious feature of the molder-planer is that its opening is twice its rated capacity, so that, by reversing the board and passing it through twice on opposite sides, a double-width board may be handled. It can create from raw stock such materials as door and window casings, baseboards and their trim, tongue-and-groove boards, knotty pine and other ornamental panel stocks (such as V grooved boards for random width work) and similar, well-known shapes. All of these can be created from rough stock of irregular thickness and shape. The main limitation is in the amount of wood removable in a single pass.

The thickness planer, similar to the others in many respects, is used almost exclusively to smooth wide boards. One use is salvaging wood. If all nails are removed, you can salvage second-hand lumber with this device. Remember that old paint is partly metallic and may dull the blades. Remove old paint and old nails before reducing the wood to the desired thickness.

JOINTER SAFETY The jointer is very safe to use, but these rules should be followed:

1. Never, for any reason, run the jointer with the guard removed. It is there to protect your hands from moving parts.
2. Use the jointer only on new wood. This is to prevent nails and other material that might be in the wood from contacting the knives. If the knives hit metal, they may be ruined, and may tear the wood from your grasp, which could cause an injury.
3. Always, whenever working on the knives or changing them, disconnect the power source.
4. Use a pusher stick to guide material through the jointer where there is the slightest possibility the wood is thin enough to allow possible contact by your hands with the knives.
5. Check the grain on the wood before you push it into the knives. Cutting into hard knots or tough end grain may force the stock from your hands.

Take your time when running material through the jointer. Forcing the stock into the machine may result in damage to the knives or the stock being torn from your hands.

Keep loose clothing away from the power source of the jointer, and all power equipment. Wear goggles or safety glasses.

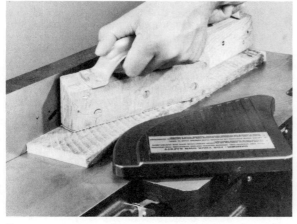

Correct positioning of hands, guard, and fence in surface planing of boards.

In pushing material over cutters, all parts of hands and fingers should be above the table. *Photos: Sears*

Belt Sander

$40 to $50: Fast removal of stock, smoothing rough surfaces.
$60 to $100: Do-it-yourselfer use, boat owner, cabinet maker.

1/4" Drill

$10 to $20: Occasional ¼" holes in metal, small masonry holes, pilot holes for screws, buffing and sharpening, light sanding with sanding disc, paint mixing.
$25 to $40: Boat building, cabinet making, hole saws up to 1½", light sanding.

3/8" Drill

$15 to $25: Metal work, as well as wood, drilling in hard woods, ceramics, glass, holes up to ⅜", light sanding.
$30 to $45: 2" hole saws, masonry, metals, driving screws.

1/2" Drill

$20 to $30: For the man who has a ¼" and ⅜" drill and is an ardent do-it-yourselfer.
$35 to $50: Holes in concrete, hard materials, big holes in wood.

Finishing Sander

$15 to $20: Do-it-yourself use, refinishing, smoothing wood, spackling.
$25 to $45: Smoothing wood for staining and paint. Sanding varnish, lacquer, shellac, urethane and other finishes.

Router

$30 to $40: Inlays, woodjoints.
$50 to $100: ⅞ and 1 and 1½-hp, general cabinet work.

Circular Saw

$18 to $30: (7½" to 8" blade) — building outdoor furniture, finishing basements, building a small garage, cutting tile or brick.
$35 to $50: Cutting out and building a dormer, fence building, boat building, fast rough cuts in wood.

Jig Saw

$10 to $25: Do-it-yourself use, building children's toys, making small signs, fretwork, wall paneling, cutting ¼" sheet plywood.
$30 to $50: 2x4's, thick plywood, curves in wood.

HOW TO CHOOSE POWER TOOLS

The average life of most low-priced power tools is between 7 and 12 hours, depending upon how you use or abuse them. Drills, for example, take only 3 to 4 seconds to bore a ¼"-hole in a 2 × 4, less than 1 second to drill an ⅛"hole in ¼" plywood. That averages out to about 20,000 holes in the life of a low-priced drill.

If you are planning to drill only 20,000 holes in the next 10 years, the low-price drill is the one for you. But you will probably wear the drill out sooner than you like if you plan to use it with a 5"-disk sander to sand all the paint off your car, a 3" hole saw to change the locks on your doors, or a wire brush to take the rust off the railing on your porch.

The difference in drills boils down to the type of construction and the quality of its internal parts.

Two types of construction are commonly used: a) clam shell body casting and b) machined body casting. This holds true whether the tools are made of plastic or metal.

The clam-shell tool is easy to recognize. There is a seam line that runs down the center of the tool that separates the two casting halves. These two halves are usually mirror images of each other and fit together like the two shells of a clam. In most cases, all the screws that hold the tool together are put in from only one side.

This type of construction, used almost exclusively on the low-priced power tools, costs less because it does not require any machining, tapping, pressing of bearings, or skilled handwork. The internal parts are dropped into one shell. When the other shell is screwed down (with self-tapping screws), the tool is finished.

But what makes the clam-shell type less of a tool than a machine-cast tool? The main reason is that it may become somewhat less accurate when it gets hot, particularly when overused or strained under a heavy load beyond its capacity.

The working parts inside the casting actually have to float so they will not bind. The oil-impregnated bronze bearings are usually spherical in shape so they can align themselves to the shafts that go through them. The bearings, brush holders, field coils, and switches are held in place by rubber plugs inserted into grooves in the clam-shell body.

Manufacturers cannot be expected to put high quality parts into a low-cost tool. However, this type is widely used by homeowners and is perfectly satisfactory as long as it isn't overused to the point where it becomes hot.

The next step up in quality is the light-duty commercial tool that has precision machine-body castings. You will find it has a better armature (more power, heavier weight, more segments on the commutator, and more windings) a heavier field coil, better bearings, harder gears, and a better cord and switch.

In the case of a drill, the light-duty commercial tool will have a better chuck with hardened jaws. A circular saw of this type will have a better blade, a thicker shoe, and a better guard. Oscillating sanders will weigh more and have paper grippers for better sanding, speeds of 10,000 rpm, which conceal scratches under staining, and better bearings.

Some light commercial tools use all oil-impregnated sleeve bearings. Some use a combination of sleeve and ball bearings, with the ball bearings in areas that take most abuse.

A light commercial tool is worth considering for two reasons. First, you can use it for more than just small do-it-yourself jobs, such as building a small boat, cabinet work, storage space, closets, partitions, finishing the interior of an attic, or basement. Second, you can afford this better tool because it will last longer, require fewer repairs, and give you more satisfaction as a craftsman.

The next step up in tools brings you into the heavy-duty range. These tools are always all ball-bearing and machined castings, heavy-duty motors, brushes, gears, cords, and switches. Generally these tools will weigh much more than light commercial and homeowner tools, and it takes a pro to use them properly and safely. If you are the kind of homeowner who likes to buy expensive, professional quality equipment, these are for you.

HOW TO: WORK WITH WOOD · SELECT AND USE GLUE· SELECT AND USE NAILS AND SCREWS · WORK WITH MASONRY · WORK WITH METAL

MATERIALS

The large majority of home repairs and maintenance involves wood. Before beginning any woodworking job, first familiarize yourself with the varying grades of this material. Living room built-ins made of No. 4 common boards, for instance, will be woefully disappointing, for no amount of sanding and polishing will ever result in a high-gloss, smooth finish.

This section provides information on grades and types of wood and how to gain professional finishing effects. Correct joinery often means all the difference between success and failure. And even the most accurate and sturdily built job will not be attractive unless the finish is even, smooth, and thoroughly dry. With careful treatment and application, less expensive woods can have a glowing satin finish or be made to take a coat of enamel that's as smooth as glass.

HOW TO WORK WITH WOOD

BUYING LUMBER Buying the right type of wood and the proper grade for the job you plan will not only save money but will also help you do better work. All lumber is divided into two categories — hardwoods and softwoods. Any broad-leaf tree — maple, oak, walnut — is classed as hardwood. All trees with needles or scalelike leaves — pine, fir, cedar, spruce — are softwoods. Hardwoods and softwoods are both used for trim, molding, cabinets, and furniture. Softwoods also are used for general construction.

Lumber is graded according to its various qualities and characteristics but not usually for appearance. An approved grading-agency stamp on the lumber will reflect the quality control in manufacturing and identify the grade, species of lumber, and whether the piece was surfaced dry or green.

There are two classes of lumber — boards (1" thick and up to 12" wide) and dimension (2" to 4" thick and up to 12" wide).

Boards are divided into *select* and *common* grades, with select being used when appearance and finishing are important. Common grades, with noticeable growth characteristics and milling imperfections, are used for construction and general purpose projects.

The grades of select boards are B & Better, 1 & 2 Clear, C Select, and D Select. In B & Better, many pieces are absolutely clear, but others may have a few minor faults that do not detract from their appearance or high quality. C Select is one of the most sought after products. It is from the clear portion of the log, ranking only slightly less than B & Better in appearance and usability. It is widely used for quality trim and cabinetwork with natural, stain, or enamel finishes. D Select is less restrictive than C Select, and may have a quality finish appearance on one side and limiting characteristics on the other.

Common boards are graded differently. The most widely available grades are No. 2 & Better, No. 3 and No. 4. Board grades are not always stamped on the face of the board, for to do so would limit use of part of the piece for finish work. No. 2 & Better is often specified in housing and light construction for paneling, shelving, and other uses where a knotty type of lumber with a fine appearance is required. No. 3 is used where appearance and strength are both important. It can be good for shelving, paneling, and siding, and also for fences, boxes, crating, and sheathing. No. 4 is usually restricted to general construction uses, such as subfloors, sheathing, forms, and fencing. It is not often found where it is exposed to view.

Dimension lumber products are divided into light framing, studs, and structural light-framing grades. They bear grading stamps applied at the time of manufacture. Light framing grades in all the softwood species include Construction, Standard, and Utility. Stud grade is a comparatively recently named category. It is limited to pieces 10 feet and shorter, for use in load- and nonload-bearing walls. The three grades of light framing lumber allow varying combinations of knots and other growth characteristics, and therefore the lowest grade costs the least. It always pays to assess the requirements of the lumber needed and purchase the lowest grade that will do the job.

Structural light framing grades are Select Structural No. 1, No. 2, and No. 3. This lumber is used for engineered applications where higher strengths are required.

It is necessary to point out that lumber used in the United States comes from the western states, the South, and Canada. Because of this diverse distribution system, a growing reliance on second-growth timber, and limited availability of timber from federal lands, not all sizes, species, and grades are always available everywhere. You may have to shop around or even accept substitutes. Or you may have to place a special order if the materials you want can't be obtained by any other means.

Lumber is usually sold by the board foot, which is equal to a square foot of lumber one inch thick, all dimensions being nominal rather than actual.

The table of wood characteristics will guide you to the right selection of the type of wood for the job you plan. Although basswood, gumwood, and poplar are identified on the table as "easy-to-work," this is merely a relative term. It means they are somewhat easier to work with hand tools than are other hardwoods. Actually, all hardwoods are difficult to work with hand tools; the best results are achieved with sharp power tools. Large solid pieces of cherry, mahogany, and walnut are difficult to obtain, therefore most hardwoods are available only as face veneers on plywood and particle board and in small dimensions for cabinet trim and legs on furniture. Solid maple and oak are available mostly for residential flooring.

Lumber sizes When you purchase lumber, check its actual size against what you asked for. Dressed lumber is smaller in actual dimension than its nominal size, due to losses in planing, seasoning, and kiln drying. In general, actual dimensions under 8″ will be ½″ less than nominal, and dimen-

WOOD CHARACTERISTICS

Type of Wood	Easy to Work	Resists Shrinking, Warping, Swelling	Unusually Strong	Resists Decay
Softwoods				
Cedar	X	X		X
Cypress	X	X		X
Douglas Fir	X		X	
Redwood	X			X
Spruce	X	X		
White Pine	X	X		
Yellow Pine	X		X	
Hardwoods				
Ash			X	X
Basswood	X			
Birch			X	
Cherry		X	X	
Gumwood	X			
Mahogany		X	X	X
Maple		X		X
Oak		X	X	X
Poplar	X			
Walnut		X		X

SIZES OF DIMENSIONAL LUMBER*

What You Ask For	What You Get
1 × 3	¾ × 2½
1 × 4	¾ × 3½
1 × 6	¾ × 5½
1 × 8	¾ × 7¼
1 × 10	¾ × 9¼
1 × 12	¾ × 11¼
2 × 2	1½ × 1½
2 × 3	1½ × 2½
2 × 4	1½ × 3½
2 × 6	1½ × 5½
2 × 8	1½ × 7¼
2 × 10	1½ × 9¼
4 × 4	3½ × 3½

*Plywood, hardboard, particle board (also called chipboard and flake board) are actual size in thickness, width, and length. Hardwoods are usually available in nominal or asked-for sizes.

sions over 8″ will be ¾″ less than ordered. There may be slight variations between different lumberyards. Measurements in the table above are expressed in inches.

Prefinished lumber If you are short of spare time or tools, ready-made items at your local lumberyard can help. For example, a variety of ready-made shelves and turned wooden spindles can be as-

Lazy man's lumber. Ready-made, prefinished shelves and spindles can be assembled without glue, nails, or screws. Special invisible fasteners hold everything together firmly. Photo: Emco Industries

Invisible fasteners do the job. Threaded hardwood fastener holds finials, shelves, and prefinished spindles together. Some fasteners are made of plastic, others of metal. Photo: Royal Oak Industries

Eight-foot turned spindles with square ends are strong enough to hold up a balcony or form the balusters of a railing in shorter sizes. Photo: Nord Co.

sembled into a variety of self-supporting shelf furniture. The shelves, spindles, finials, and feet have holes for special invisible fasteners and come prefinished or unfinished. Many prefinished shelves have laminated surfaces. Turned posts with square ends ($2'' \times 2''$, $3'' \times 3''$, $4'' \times 4''$) are available in lengths from 12″ to 8′ and can be made into room separators or stair railings. In addition to standard moldings used around windows and doors, many carved or embossed ornamental moldings can be used as shelf edgings or on flush cabinet doors or room doors.

HOW TO CUT WOOD Lumber is not cheap, so measure and mark carefully before you start cutting. Plan the layout on paper, since it is often difficult to erase pencil lines from wood, and remember to allow for the saw kerf when marking your lumber. Clamp a straightedge such as a board along the guideline to ensure straight cuts, and keep the side of the blade against the board until finished cutting.

When planing the end of a board, work toward the center. Angle the blade toward the center line of the wood. Press the plane against the finished side first and use short strokes. To prevent splinter-

ing, do not try to pass through the center to the outer end. A small block plane is the handiest tool for trimming ends, preferably one with a 12° angle of blade elevation.

Use a circular rip blade to cut solid lumber with the grain. It doesn't cut finely but is fast and effi-

HOW TO CUT PLYWOOD WITHOUT DAMAGE

In cutting plywood with a handsaw, hold the saw nearly flat to the surface and score the first ply (or laminate) with forward strokes only. Then cut through with saw at normal angle. Cut until end of scored line is reached, then repeat the operation.

Tablesaw teeth rotate in direction of operator, enter top surface first. Therefore, place wood with finished side upward. This applies to plain plywood, veneers, or any form of plywood with laminates attached.

Cutting with a portable power saw (circular type) finds teeth entering wood on the underside. Place the finished side down. If using a saber saw, note direction of teeth points and have these enter wood on underside.

Where both sides of wood are finished, use fine-tooth blade without any set at all, or use a cabinetmaker's hollow-ground saw blade with teeth without set. Saw blade can then enter either side.

To make a smooth bevel cut or a miter cut, first set blade at the desired angle and retract saw until teeth points are just flush with the wood surface. This applies to both table and portable circular saws.

On a table saw, the fence is fitted with a wood runner strip for bevels and miters. Teeth, pointing toward the fence, barely protrude above the cut. Either side of wood may be up; damage is very slight.

To smooth a rough-cut end with a plane, press blade against finish side first and angle plane toward center line of wood. Use short strokes and avoid forcing blade out to opposite side or grain will be split off.

cient. Combination chisel-tooth blades can be used for crosscutting, ripping, and general purpose work, but even when sharp cause some splintering. The best blade for very fine smooth cuts in ripping, crosscutting, and mitering is the hollow-ground combination planer blade. It produces cuts so fine that sanding is practically unnecessary. Also, saber saw blades are available in a great variety. For fast, rough work, use a blade with 7 teeth to the inch. For smooth cuts, use a blade with 10 teeth to the inch at medium speeds. Scroll work, circles, and other work where very fine edges are desired require blades with 10 teeth to the inch and fast speeds.

Portable circular saws have a retractable, spring-loaded shield that springs into place and covers the teeth when the saw is pulled from the work. Never tie the shield back or use the saw if the shield is not operating properly. Also, never change blades while the saw is plugged in.

Do not wear loose clothing when using table saws. If you are cutting a narrow strip of wood and the saw is close to the fence, use a notched stick with a long handle to push the workpiece past the blade. Don't operate the saw without its transparent safety cover over the blade. Watch for knots that may jam the blade and cause a backlash. Always wear a safety mask or goggles. And in general, a sharp saw minimizes splintering.

To keep splintering and damage to a minimum when cutting plywood with a handsaw, hold the saw blade nearly flat and score the first ply or laminate on forward strokes only. Then cut through the plywood with the blade at the normal cutting angle to the end of the score mark. A trick to remember when using power tools is to place the wood so the teeth of the blade enter the finished surface first.

When using a portable circular saw, put the finished surface down because the teeth enter the underside of the plywood first. The teeth should be almost flush with the surface they first strike. On the other hand, when using a table saw or radial arm saw, put the finished surface up, because the teeth strike the upper surface first. Where both sides of plywood are finished, splintering of both sides is to be avoided. Use a plywood and veneer blade. Its tapered ground rim and very fine teeth with no set makes it ideal for precise, smooth cuts.

If you use a saber saw on plywood or solid wood, always cut with the finished or smooth face down, because the saw teeth always point upward, entering the wood from the bottom.

FINISHING PLYWOOD EDGES It is not necessary to use special moldings to cover unsightly edge grain of plywood, nor is it necessary to fill the grain, sand it, and hope to get a near-matching finish. There is special tape that conceals the unfinished edges neatly. The tape is real wood, about $1/32$" thick, with a pressure-sensitive adhesive back. It comes in ¾" wide strips. Many popular species of wood, such as birch, fir, oak, walnut, and red or white Philippine mahogany are available. The tape can be cut with scissors or trimmed with a razor blade to fit ¼" or ½" plywood. Here are some rules to follow.

1. Before you use the tape, remove it from its sealed package. Let it stand overnight in the same room with the plywood. This equalizes the moisture content of the tape and plywood.
2. Secure the tape to the plywood edge with moderate heat. You can use an ordinary household iron (make certain the bottom is clean) or a special bonding iron that is sold with the tape or which may be rented from some dealers.
3. More heat is needed for some woods than for others. A temperature of 300°F is right for bonding birch, oak, and walnut; but only 250°F is required for fir and mahogany.
4. Heat alone will do the job. Additional gluing, clamping, or nailing is unnecessary.
5. When applying tape to curved surfaces or inside-circle cutouts in a sheet of plywood, the special bonding iron will do a better job than the conventional household iron. Because it's so small, it can get into tight spaces and may be used around curves with less difficulty.
6. Sanding should be done with fine sandpaper, preferably 150 grit aluminum oxide.
7. To prevent tape edges from lifting off or chipping, use the same kind of sandpaper to feather the edge of the tape slightly where it joins the plywood.

If you can't get the preglued type described, many lumberyards stock rolls of wood tape in widths of 1" or more that can be applied with any contact glue. Place the glued shelf edge face down on newspaper on a bench and trim away the excess tape. Then sand.

WOOD JOINTS Wood joints vary—from the simple butt joints to complex dovetails and mortise-and-tenon joints. The type you choose depends on whether you use a clear or paint finish, the strength needed, and the amount of time you want to spend.

Butt joint The butt joint is the simplest joint, where ends meet at right angles. It is usually held by nails or screws and can be reinforced with glue.

Rabbet This joint is stronger than the butt joint because it allows for more glue surface, and it looks professional when well fitted.

Miter This is a corner joint, in which pieces meet at a 45° angle to conceal end grain. Because of its good appearance it is always used for picture

Strip the protective paper backing off the pressure-sensitive adhesive side of the tape, using your thumb as a guide to prevent the accidental tearing of the protective paper.

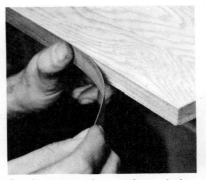

Set the tape in place so that it slightly overlaps the edge grain of the plywood. Press tape into place by applying light finger pressure and keeping the adhesive side toward the wood.

Light heat is necessary to bond the tape to the plywood. An ordinary household iron will do, or you can use a special bonding iron for just this purpose. Keep iron moving.

With the tape firmly adhered to the plywood edge, sand off the excess that protrudes above and below the plywood surface. Fine sandpaper on a block will do a neat job.

When bonding two adjoining edges, cut the second strip of wood tape somewhat longer than the side. Leave about 1/16" to 1/8" overhang at each corner. This will make for a perfect joint.

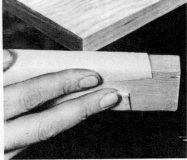

Using fine sandpaper and a sanding block, remove the excess of the second piece of wood edging for a perfectly square corner. Bevel the edge of the corner slightly.

FINISHING PLYWOOD EDGES

To prevent any disturbance because of moisture in the air, seal the tape by applying a coat of shellac, varnish, or any other finish. This should be done within 8 hours of applying the tape.

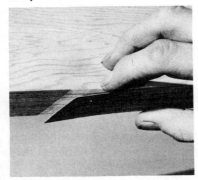

Where an individual length of tape is not long enough to cover the entire edge, butt two pieces together. However, do not use a right-angle butt — cut the pieces at an angle of 45°.

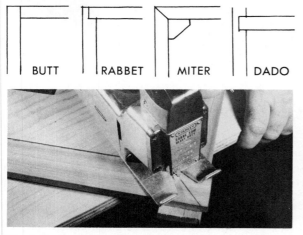

BUTT	RABBET	MITER	DADO

The fastest way to make a miter joint in thin stock is to overlap the two pieces at right angles, hold with a brad, and run saw down miter line as shown.

This is the actual miter. It is perfectly square and has to fit, even if the saw cut is crooked.

frames and often for furniture corners. Basically a weak joint, it is strengthened with glue and (in picture frames) with brads or dowels. Furniture corners (dressers, chests of drawers, and so on) are glued and reinforced on the inside by wood glue blocks or metal braces and screws.

Dado This joint is a groove into which the end of a board fits. It is a favorite for fixed shelves in cabinets and bookcases and makes a strong joint if properly glued and clamped. The groove is best made with two saw cuts across the stock. Then remove the material between the cuts with a router. Finishing nails, driven through the dadoes into the ends of the boards, and glue add strength.

Dovetail The dovetail joint is commonly used in better grades of furniture to fasten drawer fronts and backs to sides. The joints have interlacing wedge-shaped fingers that mesh at right angles.

To make dovetails, you can use hand tools, a saber saw, or, for a very fast and perfect job, a dovetail fixture for a router, which router manufacturers sell as an accessory. (See page 357.) The fixture firmly holds two pieces of wood at right angles. The router is equipped with a guide and a dovetail cutter. By pushing the router and its guide between the fingers of the fixture, matching dovetails are cut simultaneously in both pieces of wood.

Mortise-and-tenon This truly professional joint is widely used in doors, furniture, and cabinets. The tenon (or tongue) fits into a square hole called a mortise. The four faces of the tenon and mortise afford ample area for glue, which makes for an unusually strong joint. The tenon should be one-third (hardwoods) to one-half (softwoods) the thickness of the mortised piece. You can make this joint with hand tools, if you are careful (see page 358). However, with a router, cuts can be made faster, smoother, and more precisely than with a saw.

Lap joints Usually used for narrow pieces such as 1 × 2's, 1 × 3's, the lap joint is made by notching the opposite faces of both pieces so that exactly one-half the thickness of each piece is removed. When joined, the two pieces are flush with the surrounding surface.

If the two pieces cross at right angles, the joint is called a cross lap. End-to-end joints are called half laps. T-shaped joints are known as T laps. Where two pieces meet at a corner, the joint is known as an end lap. (See page 359.)

Dowel joints Dowels are round hardwood rods ranging from ⅛" to ½" in diameter. They come in 3' lengths, which are sawed to length as desired. Dowels used in gluing ¾" stock are usually 1½" long and ⅜" in diameter. Ready-made dowels are available in this size with chamfered ends and spiral grooves. Dowels are used mainly with butt joints for reinforcing connections and providing additional glue area. Miter joints are also often reinforced with dowels.

Either the "open" method or the "blind" method can be used for doweling. In open doweling a hole is drilled completely through one piece of wood and deeply into or through the one to be joined to it. The dowel is coated with glue and pushed through the drilled holes, joining the pieces. Excess dowel is sawed off flush with the outer surface. In the blind method (see page 359) holes are drilled partway into each piece from the joined faces, and a piece of dowel is cut to the combined length of both holes. The rod is then glue-coated and inserted in one hole. The second piece is pressed onto the protruding dowel end. In most joints, two or more dowels are used to prevent the pieces from twisting out of line.

To ensure adequate glue on a snug-fitting dowel, some dowels are spiral- or straight-grooved.

MAKING A DOVETAIL JOINT WITH HAND SAW AND CHISEL

Trace pattern on matching ends of sides, invert pattern for opposite ends. Number matching pieces.

Make a cardboard pattern for corner dovetail joints, to ensure the accurate cuts required for a neat job.

Cut on vertical marks with back saw. Follow line with care, stop even with base line of dovetail.

With sides of dovetail cut made first with saw, the scrap can be removed easily with a sharp wood chisel.

Use cutout ends of side pieces as a pattern to mark matching cuts on end pieces, and number corners.

Apply glue liberally to all the surfaces of the dovetail cuts that will be in contact.

When filled with glue, these indentations assure a firm grip.

In open doweling, the problem of aligning the drilled holes does not occur. Even when poorly centered, the holes match and the dowel can be driven through. In the blind system, however, two separate holes must be drilled—and here trouble can develop unless a jig is used. A doweling jig is a device that can be mounted on two different pieces of wood so holes for dowels can be drilled in mating faces. Both pieces of wood are measured and

Align the parts to be joined and tap each joint together, using a block under the hammer for leveling.

MAKING A DOVETAIL JOINT WITH A SABER SAW

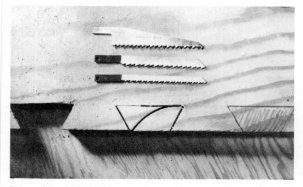

Draw dovetail outlines and mark cutouts to avoid error. Cut as shown in center to remove scrap. Set blade full depth for this.

Guidelines are easy to follow since fan inside case blows sawdust out of its path. Hold saw firmly against stock at all times.

Hold cutout on edge of piece it is to mesh with and mark outlines. Even if the first cuts were poor, this method will match them.

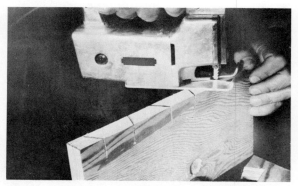

Clamp stock and set saw blade to exact depth of cut. Then follow marked lines exactly, removing lines with the saw cuts.

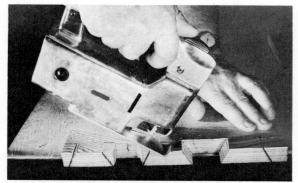

Remove center stock as before, then hold saw nose at angle to cut out corner stock, setting blade at full depth for job.

Assembled joint is firm, interlocked. This joint has been power-sawed with plywood to show the fit possible with saber saw when finished.

DOVETAILING WITH A ROUTER

Dovetails cut the fast way. Fixture holds drawer front and side at right angles ready for cutting by router with dovetail cutter. Photos this series: Rockwell

Drawer front and side now have matching fingers and openings. Add glue and the joint is unbreakable.

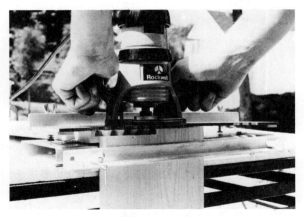

Router cuts through drawer front and side at same time as it is pushed between fingers of fixture.

marked for holes. The jig is then placed over the marks and clamped in position. Then holes are bored.

The jig may have a revolving drum for different sized bits or a number of guide tubes that keep the bit straight. A stop on the bit allows you to drill only to a certain depth into the wood.

If you have a drill press or a portable drill mounted on a drill stand, you don't need a dowel jig, but you must still measure and mark the location of the holes on the mating faces.

For further insurance against the dowel turning or loosening, drive small finishing nails or brads through the wood surfaces into the dowels. Should you need to remove the dowels and reinforce the joint, there is but one possible method: drill out the old dowel, enlarging the hole by ⅛", and replace with a new dowel of a larger diameter, adequately glued.

Boards sometimes have to be joined edge to edge to obtain a greater width. Mark the location of the holes on one edge and drill them with the aid of a jig or drill press. If you use dowel points, further measuring is not necessary.

Dowel points are metal disks of a diameter that matches common sizes of dowels. They have a sharp point in the center and an overlapping lip around the edge that prevents them from falling into the dowel hole. Line up the two edges face to face with the sharp points of the disks in contact with the face of the unmarked piece. A quick mallet blow will push the points of the disks against the unmarked piece, leaving small dents to mark the location of holes to be drilled.

USING MOLDINGS One of the earliest materials used in dressing up the home—wood molding—is still one of the best. Drab areas may be rid of monotony, windows converted into attractive frames enhancing a garden view, or the boxiness of a high ceiling subdued with this easy-to-use material. Wood moldings can add length, height, or grace to any wall, door, or cabinet.

Long lengths of molding should be cut slightly longer—as much as ¹/₁₆"—than the measuring tape dictates. To install, bow the strip, placing the ends in position first. When the center of the strip is nailed, you have a very snug fit. To measure lengths of molding to go around an object against a flat surface, such as a door casing, mark exact dimensions to obtain well-mitered joints at the corners. Here's a good method: Hold the strip to be measured in place. Mark it at the corner with a sharp blade or pencil held flat against the intersecting surface. The mark represents the short side of the miter. Your saw cut should just graze it. To

TWO MORTISE-AND-TENON JOINTS

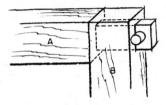

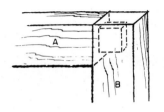

Key mortise and tenon—mortise or square hole in B goes all the way through. Tenon of Piece A extends beyond outside edge of Piece B. Hold tenon as with blind mortise or with dowel peg set through tenon.

Blind mortise and tenon—tenon of Piece A extends part of the way through Piece B. Secure with glue; if stronger joint is needed, dowel or finishing nail is set through Piece B into the tenon.

MAKING A MORTISE-AND-TENON JOINT WITH HAND TOOLS

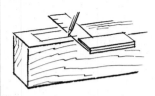

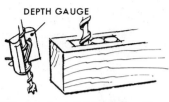

DEPTH GAUGE

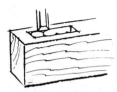

Measure and mark location of mortise, using a square to make certain of perfect alignment.

With brace and bit, drill series of holes in area. For blind mortise, use a depth gauge set for proper depth.

Clean excess wood out of mortise with a sharp chisel. Make sure corners are cut square and even.

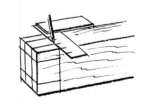

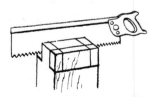

Mark tenon, drawing all lines square with edge of board. Mark on all sides to avoid error.

Use back saw to cut shoulder of tenon. Cut across board first to exact depth, keeping saw perfectly aligned.

Turn board in vise and cut down edge to the two points cut in previous step to form a square corner.

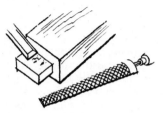

The other parts, called cheeks, are cut in the same manner as the wide sections. Add guide lines down sides before cutting.

With sharp chisel and rasp, smooth surfaces of the tenon and check fit in mortise. Sandpaper smooth afterward.

TYPES OF LAP JOINTS

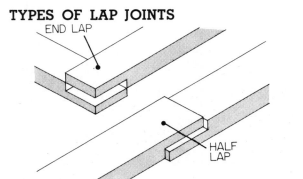

BLIND DOWELING

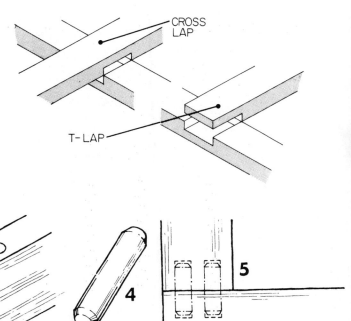

Five basic rules for blind doweling

1. *The diameter of the dowel used should not be less than ⅓ nor more than ½ the thickness of the boards to be joined.*
2. *The depth of the hole should not be less than ¼ nor more than ⅔ of the width of the narrower board.*
3. *When drilling a hole near the end of a board, the hole should be the thickness of the board away from the end.*
4. *Always chamfer the ends of the dowels to prevent them from splitting when being inserted.*
5. *The total length of the dowel should be the combined depth of the two holes less ⅛".*

measure the correct length of long pieces where a tape is awkward, use two overlapped pieces of straight, stiff molding or other thin lumber. A pencil mark on one piece where the end of the other falls, gives you an exact gauge to mark the molding. When two or more pieces are required to fill a given space, do not join ends with a butt or square joint. In time, the best of wood will shrink, and an open butt joint is very noticeable. Make a simple scarfed joint by cutting each piece at 45° to match. Shrinkage then is unnoticeable.

The most important cut in joining moldings at corners is the miter, best done in a miter box. Manufactured boxes may be purchased with or without a saw. The best ones are adjustable to any angle. With care, you can also build your own. If possible, always cut into the face of the molding, since saw teeth tear wood more where they emerge than where they enter. A very fine-toothed saw, such as a cabinet saw, is preferred to cut molding—even a hacksaw with a fine-toothed blade cuts well.

The technique of joining inside corners is called a "cope cut," since it may be made to fit even when the corner is slightly out of square. This is a method in which a coping saw cuts one piece to fit the profile of the other. The photographs show you how it's done. Use this method to put moldings around a room at the ceiling line for decoration, or below for baseboard trim.

To go around a room, square both ends of the first piece of molding. One end of the second strip is coped to fit the first strip and squared into the opposite corner, and so around the room to the fourth piece of molding, which must be coped to both the first and third strip.

At times one molding must be blended, or joined, to the middle of another. How to do this with flat, simple moldings is seen in the photos on pages 362–63. Moldings higher and narrower in cross-section are almost impossible to mark for such a cut. They may be blended by a modification of the coping method. First, the point of the intersecting

HOW TO USE DOWELS

Mark exact position of each hole to be drilled with scriber and square. This enables you to center the dowel in the piece of lumber.

Use doweling jig, where possible, to obtain a perfectly aligned hole. Different-sized tubes are used to match different drill bit sizes.

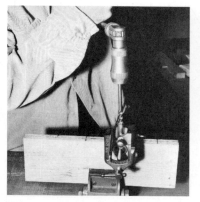

Hold piece to be drilled rigidly. Use auger bit or twist bit through jig, and resultant hole will match with companion piece to take dowel.

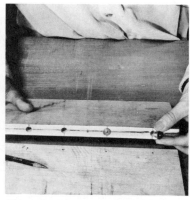

Place dowel pins in drilled holes to align two narrow boards when making a wide one out of them. Pins mark centers of holes.

Mark center of hole accurately and let the drill press do the rest of the job. If board is held properly, the hole will be perfectly vertical.

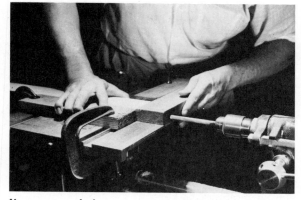

If you own a lathe, you can convert it into a drill press handy for doweling. Use a built-up wood-block jig to assure positioning.

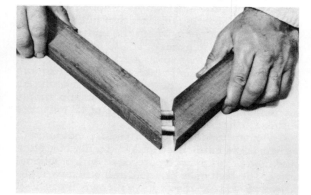

Make miter joints strong by using two dowels at each corner. Use blind method as shown in photo in center, above: dowels fit inside miter.

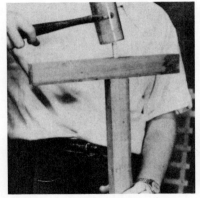

Open doweling method requires a hole drilled completely through one piece into the next; the glued dowel is then driven into both holes.

Eliminate drilling through wood surface by using blind dowel method. It protects the surface of the wood and assures a good finish.

Force dowel and glue into drilled hole. Some dowels have grooves to hold glue for tight joining. Wipe excess glue off after dowel is in.

TYPES OF MOLDINGS

CROWN   BED   COVE

SHOE

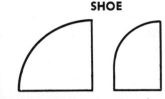

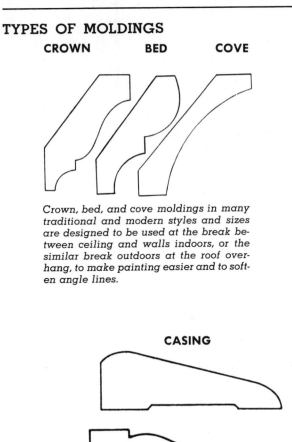

Shoe moldings finish off the baseboard at the floor and are flexible enough to compensate for slight deviations in the level of finish floor surfacing as they hide its edge and also protect the baseboard from scuffing.

Crown, bed, and cove moldings in many traditional and modern styles and sizes are designed to be used at the break between ceiling and walls indoors, or the similar break outdoors at the roof overhang, to make painting easier and to soften angle lines.

BASEBOARD

A baseboard serves the practical purpose of keeping floor-cleaning preparations off walls and also hides the edge of wall-surfacing materials. Often base and casing (used around doors and windows) are identical.

CASING

Casings come in a number of designs, both modern and traditional, with a wide variation in size. When casing and base are the same in cross-section, you know they match. When they differ in size, select something similar in shape, using either a modern or a traditional style but not both.

WORKING WITH MOLDINGS

Irregular wall and floor surfaces cause perfectly cut 45° miter to gap. Crack, being deep, is hard to fill.

Irregularity in purchased stock, not exactly true to measure, shows up when ends are miter-joined.

For turned or coped joint, cut one strip flush and butt against wall, nailing it into place.

Mark outline of free end of butted piece on back of piece to be cut with coping saw.

Holding saw at 45° angle, cut along marked line. Resulting crescent-shaped surface fits against butted strip.

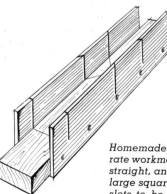

Homemade miter box depends on accurate workmanship. Be sure base is square, straight, and the sides are parallel. With large square, mark both faces of sides for slots to be sawed. Lay out 90° cutoff in same manner. Cut slots from top to base.

Turned corner, even though separated by ⅛" gap, still does not show as unsightly crack, and gap is easily filled.

On more intricately shaped moldings follow same procedure, marking pattern on back of piece before coping.

To blend low, symmetrical moldings, point the first molding 45° each side of center.

Trace cut onto molding to be intersected; carefully make two cuts to remove V.

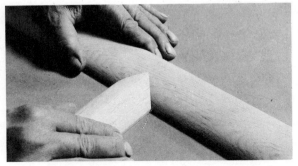

First molding will now fit easily into second if you have worked accurately enough.

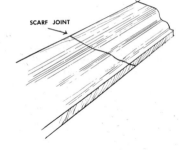

SCARF JOINT

Shrinkage on a slant is less noticeable than a butt joint that opens. Use your miter box to cut the meeting ends at 45°. Use it, too, to joint high-contour molding that is to join another piece at right angles. With 45° cuts as guides, remove stock.

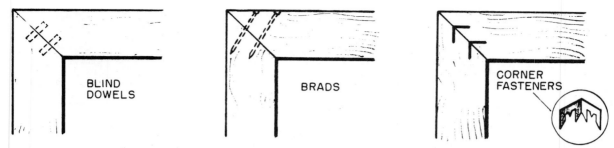

Blind doweling is very strong and is recommended for very large frames. For added strength, you can use small brads to hold the corners together. Counterset nailheads and fill holes with wood filler. Sand when dry. Corner fas- *teners are another way to make picture-frame corners more secure. Special countersink attachment with these fasteners can be used for a concealed joint.*

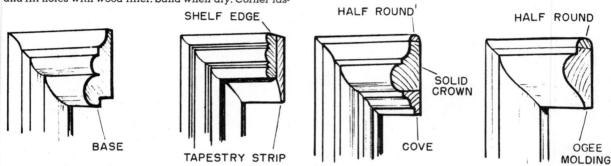

Four attractive patterns that can be made easily by combining various interior moldings used as trim in a home.

member is to cut to a 45° mitered point as above, then stock is cut out with a coping saw, using both edges of the bevel as guide lines. The other strip is not cut at all.

Decorative effects can be obtained with embossed or carved molding on shelf and furniture edges and on room and cabinet door surfaces. They can be attached with 1″ brads, and glue and nail holes can be filled with wood putty. Ordinary interior trim moldings make attractive picture frames with mitered corners fastened with dowels, glue, and brads, or corner fasteners. Combinations of two or even three ornate moldings can be used for trim around windows and doors rather than the very plain clamshell varieties popular today.

INSTALLING SHELVES Few built-ins are constructed without shelves of some sort. Installation may be completed in various ways; which to use should be indicated by the nature of the project. The permanently fixed shelf is usually supported on a wood cleat, a narrow strip of wood attached to vertical pieces with nails or screws on opposite sides of the space. With this type of shelf, it is only necessary to cut matching cleats and check their placement with a level so the shelf lies flat. The shelf may simply rest on the cleats or be anchored to them with brads.

When installing shelf cleats, the weight to be carried by the shelf is the factor that governs the size of the cleat and the way in which it is attached. Shelves that will hold only a small weight may be supported on light quarter-round or cove molding. For heavier weights and broader shelves, cleats may be made of stock as heavy as ¾″ × ¾″, or even up to 1″ × 2″ stock.

If supporting materials are ¾″ thick, as is usual in cabinetmaking, 1¼″ screws are best for holding cleats, because they will reach almost through the supporting stock. The more delicate type of cleats may be attached with 1″ brads spaced about 2 to 3″ apart.

Permanent shelves can also be installed by driving finishing nails through the sides of the cabinet and into glue-covered shelf ends. Nail heads are countersunk and the holes filled with wood putty. Fixed shelves can also be installed in dadoes in the sides.

Methods of installing adjustable shelves are shown in the illustrations on the next page.

Prefinished, ready-made shelves are available in 8″ and 10″ widths and in 2′, 3′, and 4′ lengths. Slotted steel wall channels, or standards, accept the brackets that support the shelves. Standards have holes for screws that are driven through plasterboard into wall studs.

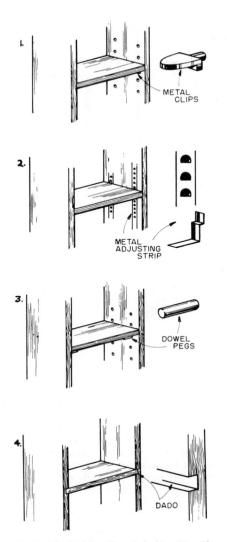

1.

METAL
CLIPS

2.

METAL
ADJUSTING
STRIP

3.

DOWEL
PEGS

4.

DADO

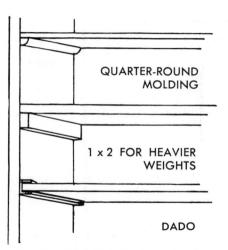

QUARTER-ROUND
MOLDING

1 x 2 FOR HEAVIER
WEIGHTS

DADO

Fixed shelves. Light loads can be supported by quarter rounds as small as ¼", but heavier weights may require cleats as big as 1 × 2's. The best looking and most secure fixed shelves are those that are glued into dadoes (below, left).

Making adjustable shelves. Special clips (1), either metal or plastic, are used to support shelves. The clips can be shifted to any of the holes drilled into the sides. Another method is to use metal adjusting strips on the sides and metal clips that fit the holes in these strips (2), a combination that can take somewhat heavier loads than just clips in wood (3). You can make your own system of adjustable shelves by drilling ½" holes in the sides about ½" deep and placing pegs (dowels) in them that project no more than 1". The shelves should have shallow grooves where they rest on the pegs so that they do not move or slip. (4). Dadoed shelves are more solid.

Ready-made shelving is prefinished in walnut grain in widths of 8", 10", and 12" and in lengths of 24", 36", and 48". Shelves are supported by thin metal brackets that fit into slots in vertical metal channels or standards. Photo: Stanley Hardware

Miniature decorative hinges lend a novel touch to cabinets, display cases, jewelry boxes—anything that needs a little dressing up. They install quickly and easily to add an attractive touch to small items, including craft and découpage projects. A popular variation is the decorative hasp and turn-button combination that provides firm closing for small cabinets and boxes. Many sizes and styles are available.

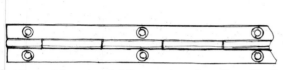

Continuous (or piano) hinges are a favorite with the hobbyist and do-it-yourselfer for boxes, louver doors, cabinets, chests, and the like. They can be fitted to the full length of the work, providing extra strength and more fastening area, especially important for thin wood doors. They also help prevent door warping. Hacksaw cuts to length.

DOORS AND HINGES Except for built-ins with specific types of wood exterior where cabinets and doors must match, doors for all built-ins may be made of plywood. To avoid warping, use ¾″ stock for doors up to 2′ wide and 3′ to 4′ high. The selected plywood may be fir or have a hardwood-veneer finish. As an alternative, a frame may be constructed of ¾″ × 1¼″ stock with mitered corners and a ¼″ ply or hardboard surface attached. Since the hardboards have many types of finishes, the selection is almost unlimited.

The variety of hinges is great. Some of the many types used in cabinetwork are shown. Door handles and pulls should be selected to match hinges, if the latter are visible. But it is also important that the hardware match the spirit of the built-in and the decor of the room. Door latches on cabinets and built-ins are a personal matter. You have the choice of magnetic, friction, or touch latches, the latter opening from a slight inward pressure on the door, which releases a spring that thrusts the door outward. Latches are attached to the cabinet base or to a shelf, preferably on the underside.

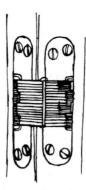

Invisible hinges for doors and cabinetwork allow greater design freedom; no portion of the hinge is visible when the door is closed.

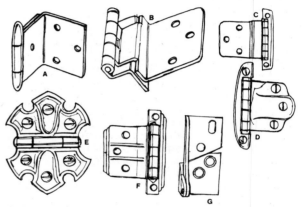

Cabinet hinges are available in many shapes: concealed (A for flush doors; B for lipped doors), on which only the barrel shows; semiconcealed (C) for lipped doors; full-surface (D and E for flush doors; F for lipped doors); pivot (G) for flush overlay doors. Finishes include aluminum plated, chromium plated, nickel plated, aluminum, brass.

HOW TO SELECT AND USE GLUE

Do-it-yourselfers see more advertisements announcing tremendous advances in modern adhesives than ever before. However impressive the ads are, no one glue can serve all your needs. Here's why.

Most modern glues work best on a single material or a single class of absorbent or nonabsorbent materials. Thus white glue is excellent for woodwork but can also be used for paper, leather, and fabric—all of which are absorbent (porous) materials. On the other hand, white glue won't hold glass to metal, or steel to plastic, and so forth. Cyanocrylate is great for nonabsorbent materials like ceramics and metals but won't work with softwood or other absorbent material.

There really aren't as many adhesives on the store shelves as it seems to the occasional buyer. Often the same glue appears under different names. For example, aliphatic glue is called "Titebond" by Franklin Glue Co., "Carpenter's Wood Glue" by Borden (Elmer's), and "Aliphatic Resin Glue" by Wilhold. Cyanoacrylate appears under such names as Eastman 910, Flash, Duro's, Superglue 3, Quickfix, Speedweld, Zip Grip, and others. It's therefore a good idea to acquaint yourself with trade names if you are looking for a particular glue.

In some cases, however, trade names plainly identify a particular adhesive. The words "epoxy" and "contact" are good examples. Similarly, adhesives used to fasten paneling to walls or studs usually have the words "panel" or "construction" in their names or descriptions.

Many manufacturers now produce a water-based version of contact cements. The flammable types dry faster because solvents evaporate faster than water. Both types are nearly equal in effectiveness as adhesives. However, the nonflammable types eliminate both the fire hazard and the dangers of "fume sniffing." Also, tools used with water-based glues can be cleaned with soap and water while the glue is still wet.

For the do-it-yourselfer and home handyman, some of the most important adhesives are those used in woodworking: the epoxies and their combinations, cyanoacrylate, contact cement, and panel cement. A knowledge of these will make your gluing jobs more successful.

WHITE GLUES One of the most commonly used adhesives for woodwork in the home, white glue comes in plastic bottles with a convenient nozzle. White glue has moderate grab and sets in about 30 minutes, after which it becomes translucent. It should be clamped for about an hour, but you'll get the best results by keeping it in clamps overnight. Surplus glue should be wiped away with a damp rag. It is nonflammable and does not give off dangerous fumes.

ALIPHATIC GLUES Growing more popular, this glue is pale yellow in color and works very much like white glue. However, it has faster initial tack and sets in 20 to 30 minutes. It makes very strong joints, needs clamps for only half an hour, and cures in 24 hours. While not waterproof, it is resistant to water, has good heat resistance, and is not affected by varnish, lacquer, and paint. When dry it is translucent and hard and can be sanded without clogging sandpaper. It's available in plastic squeeze bottles and is easy to use. Hands and tools can be cleaned up with warm water while the glue is wet.

PLASTIC RESIN GLUES A tan powder that is

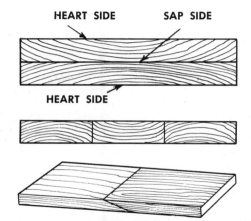

Gluing to minimize warping. By alternating heart sides of lumber, you can reduce warping. In gluing boards edge-to-edge or face-to-face, always place the pieces so the grain does not run in the same direction.

Newer water-based adhesives, such as Elmer's acrylic latex contact cement for the do-it-yourselfer, offer advantages over solvent-based products.

mixed with water, this is one of the strongest types of glue used in woodwork. Once mixed with water, it becomes a loose, chocolate-colored paste. It is best clamped overnight in snug-fitting joints at a temperature not less than 70°F. It will not stain wood and is resistant to water, mold, and rot. When mixed with wheat or rye flour, and water in recommended proportions, it provides an easy way to

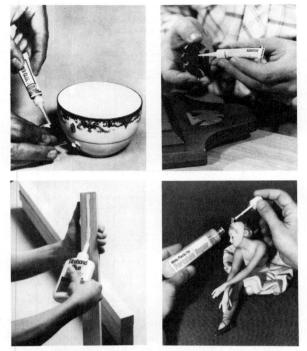

Panel adhesives, available with solvent or latex base, are used to bond materials in light construction work. Hot melt glues (right) come in solid rods and are used in electric glue guns. Here Swingline's solid-stick glue is used to repair table.

Types of glues include newer super glues (top left); cyanoacrylates (top right); aliphatic glue (bottom left); and special glues, such as Duro's white plastic glue for porcelain repair (bottom right).

glue veneers at relatively low cost. Plastic resin glues are odorless and nonflammable.

RESORCINOLS This is the only truly waterproof woodwork glue and is widely used for outdoor furniture, or wherever glued wood is exposed to weather. It is a two-part adhesive, packaged in double cans. One can contains a cherry-colored liquid resin, the other a tan powdered hardener, or catalyst. The result of the mix is a dark brown, loose paste with a pot life of about an hour. When the mixture gets too thick to spread, it must be discarded. It cures in 3 to 4 hours and provides a tough yet flexible bond. Resorcinol glue withstands freezing, boiling water, heat, fungus, and mild acids and alkalis. Wood parts must be firmly clamped until the glue is dry. It cleans off easily with water while still wet.

CONTACT CEMENTS A thin liquid adhesive, contact cement bonds dissimilar materials such as wood, leather, linoleum, synthetic rubber, and plastics to each other and to practically any other material. It is especially well suited to bonding large sheets of material to broad surfaces of wood or even nonporous substrates. Decorative plastic laminates are usually fastened to the tops of kitchen counters with contact cement.

It's applied to both surfaces, then allowed to dry. When the cement is dry to the touch (about 15 minutes), both surfaces are brought together with firm pressure. The glued surfaces grip immediately. The grip is so firm that pieces cannot be pulled apart, so pieces must be properly aligned before contact. Contact cement is ideal for vertical surfaces and areas where clamping is impossible. Where it is used in larger sizes than just a tube, it is best to use the nonflammable type and avoid the hazards of fire.

CYANOACRYLATES In many ways this is a remarkable adhesive. All you need is one drop per square inch. Instructions often warn you not to use too much. The thinner the glue line, the stronger the bond. No clamping is required, since it sets in half a minute and is highly effective on surfaces such as metal, jewelry, glass, china, many plastics, ceramics, and leather.

It does not work well on soft or absorbent surfaces such as fabrics, paper, or softwoods. It does resist temperatures up to 160°F, continuous immersion, water, and many chemicals.

Cyanoacrylate works only with closely matching surfaces. To use it on china or porcelain that has been broken, all chips or pieces should be used. For effective storage, keep the tube upright in a cool, dry location. Light, high temperature, and humidity reduce its effectiveness. Beware of getting this glue on your hands; it can join fingers so tightly that acetone nail polish remover may be needed to separate them. It is also a severe eye irritant.

EPOXY ADHESIVES This two-part adhesive must be thoroughly mixed before it can be used. Epoxy has retained its popularity with repair-conscious consumers for good reasons. It is extremely strong—one square inch can hold a ton. It is oil, gas, and water resistant, and in some formulations, waterproof.

Although mainly for bonding nonporous materi-

HOW EPOXIES WORK

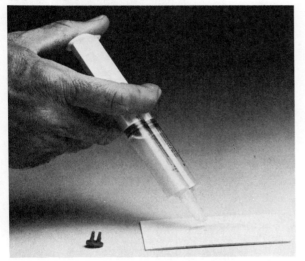

Epoxies are two-part adhesives, resin and hardener, which must be mixed properly. Devcon 2-in-1 dispenser above measures out proportions with push of thumb. Duro's E-Pox-E "5" (photos) uses premeasured glue packs, while E-Pox-E ribbon (top of next page) is a two-part putty.

al such as glass, ceramics, metals, plastics, and china, it is also effective on wood and other porous materials, but isn't used much here because other less expensive glues are readily available.

Epoxy comes in two tubes. One contains the epoxy resin, the other a hardener. Read instructions for proper quantity. If both resin and hardener are not in proper proportion, the bond will be weak and may fail.

Some companies now solve the measuring problem by packing hardener and resin in rigid, transparent plastic tubes joined by a single nozzle. A double plunger at the top of both tubes squeezes resin and hardener through the nozzle in equal quantity. Epoxy will set in about five minutes to one hour, depending on the type you use. On vertical surfaces, objects should be taped into place until the glue sets, because epoxy has no grab. Unlike other adhesives, epoxy has no solvents or water base to evaporate before it sets. Instead there is a chemical reaction between the two parts. It is not flammable, but can be dangerous to skin and eyes.

Epoxy also comes with resin or hardener mixed with fillers to form a putty for various kinds of patching jobs, such as filling holes in gasoline and water tanks, or sealing leaking pipe joints. Once the material hardens, it can be drilled, filed, sanded, or painted. Plastic steel combines atomized steel (80 percent) with epoxy resins and modifiers to form a putty for many kinds of metal repairs.

PANEL ADHESIVES Panel adhesives are packed in cartridges that fit inexpensive caulking guns. They are used to attach sheets of hardboard or paneling to walls or studs. A little of this adhesive goes a long way. It has strong initial grab. A ⅜" bead around the perimeter of the back, plus two diagonal beads from corner to opposite corner, are enough to hold a 4 × 8 panel to a wall. Drive a few finishing nails at the top and bottom of the panel to

1. With premeasured glue packs, contents of both are squeezed into mixing area and mixed well.

2. After mixing, epoxy is applied to damaged area and pieces are squeezed until firmly attached.

3. Tape is used if needed. Epoxy bonds in 5 minutes and repaired item can then be used.

1. *With Duro's E-Pox-E Ribbon, you simply cut the amount you need from the ribbons; there is no waste.*

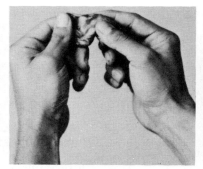

2. *To mix, you knead the two parts of epoxy ribbon together until the mixture becomes green in color.*

3. *Mixture can be used to bond, fill, or seal to make minor repairs, such as fixing water-pipe leaks.*

hold it in place until the cement takes hold. Panel adhesives can be used for drywall (plasterboard), hardboard, furring strips, and almost any other material that must be bonded to surfaces found in light construction and repair work. They are available in a fast-drying solvent base or nonflammable latex base.

HOT MELT GLUES Designed to be used in an electric glue gun, this unusual glue comes in the form of a solid rod ½″ in diameter and 2″ and 4″ long. The glue stick is inserted into the back of the gun and extruded through the nozzle by either pushing with your thumb or pulling the trigger, depending on the tool. Hot melt glue provides a strong permanent bond in just 60 seconds but remains flexible indefinitely.

Hot melts are odorless, nontoxic, resilient, and not affected by moisture. Hot melt glue has an open time of 15 to 20 seconds and sets in 60 seconds, eliminating the need for clamps. Hot melts will bond most porous materials (i.e., wood, leather, cardboard, and some plastics and tile). They provide the same results as many of the other adhesives listed, but in less time and with greater ease and safety. No toxics are given off, and contents are not flammable.

A hot melt caulking/sealer is also available. It's ideal for tough, flexible waterproof caulking around windows, sinks, and tubs. However, don't use hot melt glues where the bond will be subjected to high heat.

When working with adhesive products, it is extremely important that you follow the label directions implicitly. Some adhesives contain materials which produce toxic fumes and should be used only in well-ventilated areas. To get a proper bond, use only as the label directs. Many people, thinking "more is better," use far too much adhesive. In most glues and adhesives the thinner the glue line,

the stronger the bond. Even panel adhesives, which are applied in relatively large amounts, work far better with a ¼″ bead rather than with a thicker bead.

HOW TO SELECT AND USE NAILS AND SCREWS

Most wood joints are made stronger by any combination of glue and nails or screws. Finishing nails are ideal for cabinetwork, because their small heads are easily countersunk and hidden with wood putty. Finishing nails can even be used on veneered surfaces if a walnut or other dark stain is applied.

Where it doesn't matter if they show, use common nails or, if possible, box nails, which have smaller heads and slimmer shanks and are less likely to split the wood.

If you are nailing plasterboard to studs or hardboard underlayment to floors, use nails with threaded or ring groove shanks. They almost never pop or loosen because wood fibers interlock with the grooves.

Screws hold better than nails in wood and come in lengths from ¼″ to 3½″. Screw heads may be round, flat or oval. Diameters are identified by gauge numbers. The usual screw gauge that's used with ¾″ cabinet stock is #8. Flathead screws can be made flush with the surface by countersinking the hole. Where it is not objectionable that the heads be seen, use round-head or oval-head screws.

The easiest and best way to drive screws is to drill a pilot hole with a special ¼″ shank bit that can be used in an electric drill. Each pilot hole bit is stamped with the size of the corresponding screw. Some pilot hole bits also cut a ½″ or ⅝″ hole in which flathead screws can be concealed under a wooden plug. Plug cutters with ¼″ shanks for

NAIL SIZES

Penny Number	Length in Inches	Number per Pound		
		Common Nails	Box Nails	Finishing Nails
2	1	876	1010	1351
3	1¼	568	635	807
4	1½	316	437	548
5	1¾	271	406	500
6	2	181	236	309
8	2½	106	145	189
10	3	69	94	121
12	3¼	64	87	113
16	3½	49	71	90
20	4	31	52	62
30	4½	20		

electric drills are available in many hardware stores.

CHOOSING NAILS Nail sizes are designated by pennies, the symbol for which is "d". Use of this term goes back hundreds of years. It related to the cost of nails. Now penny, or "d," is used to refer only to the length of the nail.

The table lists nails by penny size, shows nail length, and the number of nails per pound of that size. Most nails, with the exception of finishing nails, are now usually sold by the pound.

A rule of thumb for deciding the length of the nail to use is to set the nail two-thirds of the way into the second piece of wood to be joined. Use the thinnest possible nail in thin wood to prevent splitting. In hardwood it may be necessary to predrill holes for large nails.

The common nail takes its name from the fact that it is the most common method of joining two pieces of wood together quickly, inexpensively, and easily.

Although other fastening methods have advantages, nails are the most common wood fasteners in use today. Well over 90 percent of the homes in the United States are nailed together. Nails are quicker to use and easier to handle than other types of fasteners.

There are literally hundreds of types of nails, and each type comes in assorted sizes. They range from massive railroad spikes and shipbuilding nails down to the finest brads, a thousand of which may weigh less than a pound. Despite this bewildering variety most households get by quite well with perhaps a dozen types and sizes of nails and are able to meet the needs of any fastening job.

Proper selection and driving of the nail determines how well the finished work holds together. The holding power of nails depends on friction or the pressure of the wood on their surface. Exactly how well a nail holds depends on a) condition of the wood; b) shape and texture of the nail; and c) the size of the nail in relation to the wood used.

The condition of the wood is of primary importance. Rotted, split, or cracked wood will not hold together well, regardless of what is used to fasten it. If the wood is soft, nails will drive very easily. But the easier it goes in, the easier it will come out.

Nails grip much better in hardwood, but splitting can be a problem. Dry wood splits much more readily than wet, which sometimes will not split at all. But when wet wood dries, it often shrinks, causing the nail to loosen its grip. When a nail thick enough to be driven without bending is also thick enough to split the wood, pilot holes must be drilled. In a situation where pilot holes are a possibility, consider switching to screws.

The second consideration in selecting the proper nail is intended use. Nails are available with different coatings, surface textures, and shapes, each designated for a specific purpose.

The greater the surface area of the nail in direct contact with wood, the greater its holding ability. Some nails, such as the ring-shank type, are textured to increase holding power. However, texturing also increases the chances that the nail will split the wood.

A long, thin nail goes into wood well and has a large percentage of surface in contact with wood, but it also tends to cause a split. Blunt-pointed nails drive somewhat less easily, yet have more holding power. Diamond-pointed nails, usually available, are an excellent compromise between these two types.

So-called coated nails have a special glue on them that melts from the friction of driving. Since the glue seizes almost instantly, you must drive them all the way into the wood without stopping. Trying to drive such a nail later will almost always end up with the nail bending. Nails coated with powdered resin react much the same way.

The last criterion in selecting a nail is its relationship to the thickness of the wood to be nailed. Generally, the nail should not penetrate more than two-thirds of the last piece of wood being joined. This rule of thumb can be applied to all ordinary household chores, with the exception of laying hardwood flooring and some types of trim work.

Correctly placing the nail is also important. It is usually driven across the grain, providing more holding power and reducing the chance of splitting the wood. When driven along or with the grain, the nail is easily pulled out. Any shearing stress placed on the nail will split the wood.

Nails driven too close to the end grain will split out, as will any placed too near the edge of a

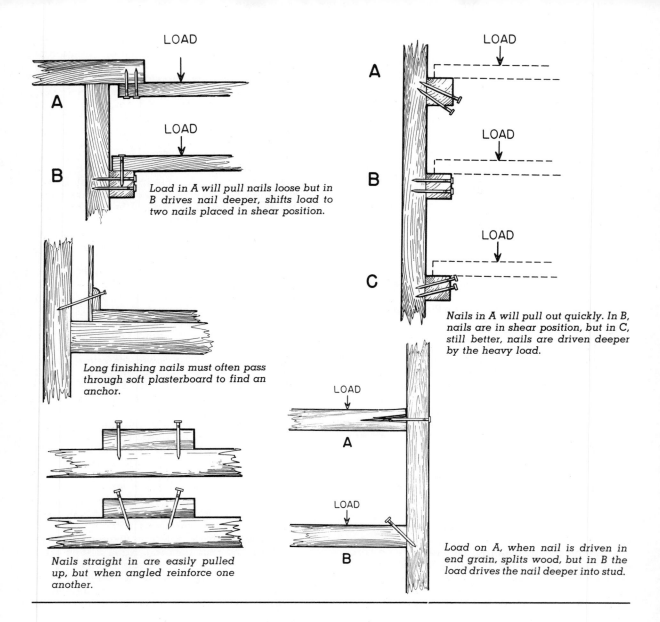

Load in A will pull nails loose but in B drives nail deeper, shifts load to two nails placed in shear position.

Nails in A will pull out quickly. In B, nails are in shear position, but in C, still better, nails are driven deeper by the heavy load.

Long finishing nails must often pass through soft plasterboard to find an anchor.

Nails straight in are easily pulled up, but when angled reinforce one another.

Load on A, when nail is driven in end grain, splits wood, but in B the load drives the nail deeper into stud.

board. A single nail will permit a certain amount of movement in a joint. But two nails not in the same grain will hold fast and more than double the strength of the joint.

Nails should never be selected for their holding ability alone. Always remember to place them so the strain is *across* the nail, not along its length. Although a nail can be pulled out fairly easily, it is very difficult to shear one off. Position as many nails as possible in your construction to take advantage of this fact. With the exception of trim, which doesn't carry much weight, make all structural joints so live load and weight tend to drive nails deeper or force is applied against the shear angle of the nail. Where this is not possible, you should consider using angle irons, joist hangers, bolts or other means of gaining additional strength.

SAFE LOADS FOR SCREWS

Screws are used instead of nails when greater holding power is needed. The power referred to is outward, opposite the direction in which the screw point is aimed. In other words, outward pull against the threads is holding power.

The quality of the wood into which the screw is driven affects its ability to hold. Hardwoods are best. A glance at the table shows the differences.

This table also indicates safe loads for each 1″ of screw thread driven into the *holding* piece of wood. If a screw is driven in only ½″, reduce the safe load figure by 50 percent. Remember that the threads of a wood screw represent ⅔ the screw's total length. When the screw is set *with* the grain of the wood, use 60 percent of the indicated load.

Screw Number	4	8	12	16	20	24
In Oak	80 (pounds)	100	130	150	170	180
In Yellow Pine	70 (pounds)	90	120	140	150	160
In White Pine	50 (pounds)	70	90	100	120	140

EXAMPLE: A No. 20 screw set with threads 1″ into the cross grain of oak will hold 170 pounds; set into white pine, it will hold 120 pounds; set into the end grain of white pine 1″, it will hold 72 pounds; but if only ½″ into the end grain of white pine, it will hold only 36 pounds. To increase load limits, use additional screws.

CHOOSING SCREWS Screws with flat heads may either be countersunk so the head is flush with the surface, or the head may be buried deeper and hidden by putty or wood filler.

When selecting a screw, remember that its number indicates thickness only. Length must also be specified. Use thin screws for hardwood, those with thicker shanks for softwood. A flat-head screw is measured by its overall length; a round-head screw from its point to the base of the slot in the screw head. Select a length that will not pass entirely through the wood. At the same time, remember that, as with nails, the more wood fiber gripping the screw, the more its holding power.

Consult the table above to determine the safety limit to be placed on a single screw.

While 90 percent of all carpentry can be completed by the use of common nails, the remaining 10 percent requires some special fastening device and, in most cases, it will be wood screws that are called on. Screws are specifically recommended in the following instances: a) when the work may have to be taken apart at some future date; b) when greater holding power is required of the joint than

nails can provide; and c) when it is important that the finish be unmarred.

Screws should always be used when the pull of the load is to be directed along the length of the fastening devices. A nail in such a position may pull out, but a well-chosen and properly driven screw will hold tightly.

There are literally hundreds of types of screws from which to choose. Selecting the right one is important. Unlike nails, screws are not identified by length alone. Screws have two dimensions: The diameter of the shank just below the head is indicated by the number of the screw, and the length is indicated in inches.

In choosing a screw for a specific purpose, first select the proper style head. Round heads will remain exposed and can actually become a part of the decorative scheme; otherwise they must be used where they will remain unobtrusive.

DRIVING SCREWS In softwood, a small indentation is sometimes enough when starting screws. Your wrist action with the help of the screwdriver and the threads of the screw make it relatively easy to set the screw. Larger screws require a pilot hole, both to facilitate setting them and to reduce

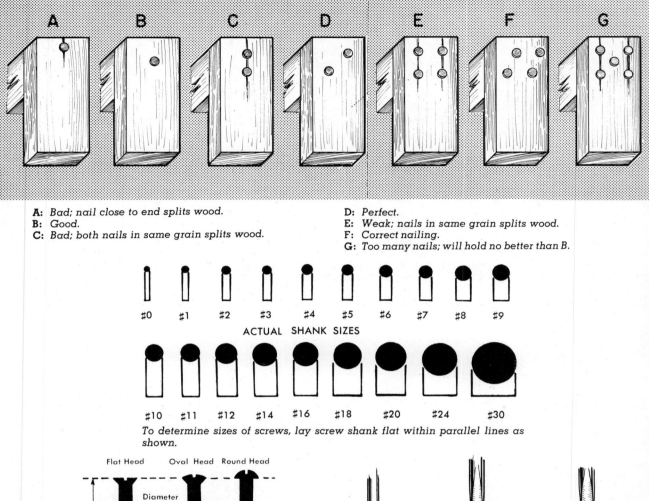

A: *Bad; nail close to end splits wood.*
B: *Good.*
C: *Bad; both nails in same grain splits wood.*

D: *Perfect.*
E: *Weak; nails in same grain splits wood.*
F: *Correct nailing.*
G: *Too many nails; will hold no better than B.*

#0 #1 #2 #3 #4 #5 #6 #7 #8 #9

ACTUAL SHANK SIZES

#10 #11 #12 #14 #16 #18 #20 #24 #30

To determine sizes of screws, lay screw shank flat within parallel lines as shown.

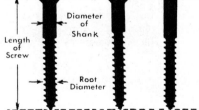

Flat Head   Oval Head   Round Head

Diameter of Shank

Length of Screw

Root Diameter

Unlike nails, which are measured only by length, wood screws are measured by length and by the diameter of the shank, which is not tapered. In ordering screws, therefore, specify the length wanted. Choose screws long enough so that ⅔ of the threaded portions will penetrate the second of the two pieces to be joined. Also check the gauge number, which will determine the diameter of the shank.

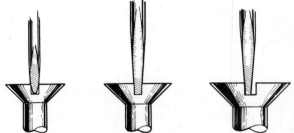

In setting screws, choice of a screwdriver is important. Unless the blade of the driver matches the slotted head of the screw, the head will be torn by the force of the blade. The screw cannot be fully set in, nor can it be easily withdrawn. Make sure the screwdriver bit fits the screw slot (center). At left the screwdriver (used too often as a chisel) cannot turn the screw without shredding the head or slipping out of the slot.

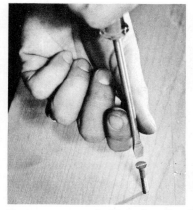
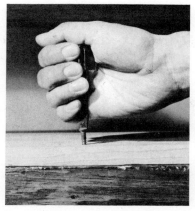
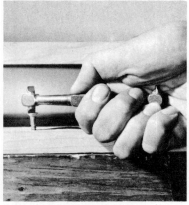

To drive a screw, hold the handle of the screwdriver firmly in your right hand; use your left hand to grasp the blade just over the screwdriver tip.

For removing or driving a screw in confined areas, you will find that a common screwdriver of the "stubby" type is ideal for the job.

In extremely confined areas, it may be impossible to use any screwdriver but the offset type. This has two blades, both at right angles to the handle.

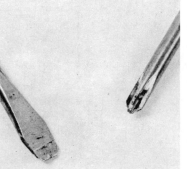
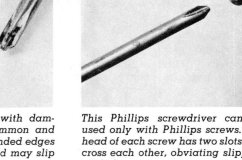

The spiral ratchet type considerably speeds up driving a screw into a predrilled pilot hole. Simply set the blade in the screw slot, steady the blade, and push to drive the screw.

Never use screwdrivers with damaged tips like these (common and Phillips types). These rounded edges will chew up any slot and may slip and injure you.

This Phillips screwdriver can be used only with Phillips screws. The head of each screw has two slots that cross each other, obviating slipping of blade.

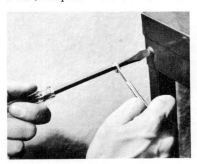

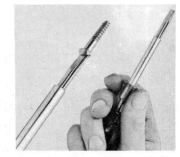

For removing a tight screw, it may be necessary to use a heavy-duty screwdriver with a square shank. Use a wrench on this shank to turn screw.

Do not tap on the handles of common screwdrivers. Use the type favored by mechanics; it has a shank that goes all the way through the handle to the top.

Special screwdrivers help out in a tight spot. This one makes a one-hand operation possible. Tension of split blades holds screw while you guide it.

When driving screw into end grain, use a dowel across grain to hold screw threads.

Old screws with battered heads can sometimes be salvaged by recutting the slot in the head.

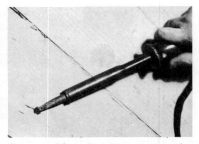

It is possible to free frozen screws by applying heat to the head. This causes the screw to expand, breaking the contact bond between the screw and wood.

the chance of splitting the wood. For softwoods, such as pine and spruce, drill a hole only half as deep as the length of the screw. For hardwoods like oak, maple, and birch, drill a pilot hole as deep as the screw is long.

When using exceptionally large screws in hardwoods, it is best to drill two holes. One should be the length of the screw and slightly smaller than the diameter of the threaded portion of the screw. Drill out this hole about a third of its depth to the same diameter as the unthreaded portion of the screw, enlarging the original hole at the top.

To make it easier to drive screws, it has long been customary to coat the screw with soap. While this does help ease the driving of the screw, it also can cause problems. The soap eventually turns to a form of glue and effectively cements the screw to the wood. Soap also causes rust on steel screws and corrosion on brass screws.

As a result, it is almost impossible to remove these screws later. It's better to coat screws with wax or graphite. Don't use oil, since it will slowly penetrate and discolor the wood for some distance around the screw.

Screws are often used with the intention of later removing them. Remember that, when withdrawn, a screw will leave a much larger hole than a nail. Before the screw can be replaced, it must be provided with a firm gripping area. The hole can be filled with wood putty or plastic inserts, which are driven into the hole. Then the screw can be reset successfully. It is also possible, in some instances, to use a replacement screw longer than the original.

To remove a tight screw, be sure to use a correctly fitted screwdriver, with perfectly parallel sides. If turning the blade counterclockwise doesn't loosen the screw, try turning it clockwise and then back again. While this tightens the screw, it also helps to break the contact bond between the screw and the wood.

HOW TO WORK WITH MASONRY

Working with masonry is simple enough for the handyman who learns the rules and then follows them. No shortcuts here, for the ingredients of concrete, mortar, and cement must be mixed in the proper proportion. Otherwise the results will be dusty, crumbly, or leaky, and the job will have to be done all over again. In the same way, every brick wall needs a strong footing below the frost line, and hurried construction without the proper footing will only lead to quick collapse of the wall.

Portland cement alone, and the finished mixture it makes with sand, are both loosely termed *cement*. To define these terms further, here are the differences:

1. Portland cement is a manufactured product. It consists of limestone, chalk, clay, and other natural products finely ground or fired in kilns to a clinker state, after which it is pulverized and bagged. The usual bag contains 94 pounds and is sold by hardware stores, lumberyards, and building supply dealers.
2. Mortar, as used on stucco, sidewalk, and masonry patching, is a mixture of portland cement, sand, and water.
3. Concrete is the same as mortar — portland cement and sand — with gravel added for extra bulk and strength.
4. Masonry mortar, in the general sense, is a mixture of portland cement and sand with the addition of about 10 percent by bulk or volume of hydrated lime. This keeps the mix fluid longer and makes it easier to handle. It also adds to the hardness of the mix when dried.
5. Grout is the same as 2 or 3 above — cement, or cement and sand — with enough water added to make it a flowing paste. It is used to fill holes or is poured into confined spots where a stiffer mix would not flow, or utilized to bind two masonry pieces together.

Whatever you use, it is necessary to mix the ingredients properly. Always measure the amounts used. If you have no measuring box—use 4 boards to form a 12″ square 12″ deep—then use a shovel. As a guide, remember that one shovelful of portland cement is equivalent to (a) one shovelful of damp sand; (b) two shovelfuls of dry sand; and (c) two shovelfuls of gravel. After all the parts have been mixed in the right proportion for the job (see table) add water until the mix is uniformly damp. When the entire mix assumes the same consistency, it's ready to use.

Under average conditions you should use the specified number of gallons of water per sack of portland cement for the following concrete work about the home:

Basement floor	5½
Cast posts, forms	5
Driveway	5
Stairs	5
Patio floor	5
Sidewalk (light traffic)	5
Sidewalk (heavy traffic)	4½
Topping for house floor	4½

Because sand is seldom thoroughly dry, you must make an allowance for its moisture content. Deduct the following from the amount of water to be used, depending upon the condition of the sand:

1. If the sand is slightly damp to the touch, but leaves only a slight amount of moisture on your hand, deduct ¼ gallon per bag.
2. If the sand is damp and leaves your hand wet and covered with some grains of sand, deduct ½ gallon per bag.
3. If the sand is very wet and drips water, deduct 1 gallon per bag.

WORKING WITH CONCRETE The gravel used in concrete may be either screened riverbed gravel (round) or crushed stone. It is ordered by diameter. When ordering or using gravel, its maximum size should never be more than one-third the thickness of the form. For example, in a 4″ concrete slab, use gravel screened to 1½″—the nearest to the required size.

With time and a few precautions, you can form, pour, and finish a slab for sidewalks, driveways, or patios. After the area for the project is selected, carefully consider water runoff. A slab built against the house or pool should slope *away* from the existing structure, allowing water to drain off. You can use temporary stakes and string or household flour to mark the perimeter tentatively.

Form boards or materials should be clean and smooth to prevent discoloration and marring. For a straight side, use 2″ thick lumber; an inexpensive form for curved sides is scrap paneling ripped in 4″ sections. Start by digging about 2″ around the in-

THE RIGHT MIX FOR THE RIGHT JOB

Cement

Use	Portland cement (bags)	Sand (cubic feet)
Setting flagstones	1	2½
Masonry surfacing	1	2½
Stucco	1	2½
Filling tree cavities	1	2

Use	Mortar cement (or add 10% lime to portland cement)	Sand (cubic feet)
Brick and block laying	1	2½
Repointing brick	1	2
Stucco (in place of cement)	1	2½
General masonry patching	1	2 to 2½

Concrete

Use	Portland cement (bags)	Sand (cubic feet)	Gravel (cubic feet)
Foundation footing	1	2	4
Floors	1	2	3
Foundation walls	1	2½	4
Walks (heavy traffic)	1	1½	3
Stairs	1	2	4
Cast posts, lintels, and other forms	1	1½	3
Setting posts	1	2½	4

side of the perimeter you have already marked. Drive pointed stakes in the ground until they are secure enough to nail through. Make sure you have stakes at least every 1′ to restrain the forms from bowing when the heavy concrete is poured. Brace the stake as you nail the form to the proper height.

After setting the forms with the proper slope, take care not to bump them. You can mound dirt along the outside of the forms to further firm them up. Stretch a string from side to side and use it as a reference point from which to measure the depth you dig. You have to remove all vegetation and firmly tamp loose earth so no voids are left by decompose or settling. The minimum depth for any slab is 3½″, and garage slabs are 4″ to 5″ thick. You can buy gravel cheaper than concrete to fill in voids. Gravel 1″ or less in diameter makes an excellent subbase. You can also use bank-run gravel spread in 6″ layers and tamped.

Use a premade asphalt-treated fiberboard expansion joint, if you have parallel walls on two sides of the slab. The expansion joint contracts and expands to absorb the change in dimension of the concrete due to temperature changes. If the slab is going to butt up against some rigid body, use Styrofoam or plastic film to break the bond where these two surfaces meet.

Concrete is sold by the cubic yard from ready-mix companies. Most companies have a two-cubic-yard minimum load, but for an extra charge are usually willing to deliver a smaller amount. If you need less than a half-yard, it will be worth your while to mix your own, or use ready-mixed dry concrete in sacks, to which you only add water.

If you buy dry ready-mix, be sure it is good quality (not damaged by having previously been wet). Then be sure to use the minimum amount of water to mix it (1 gallon per 94 pound sack). Too much water makes concrete weak. Concrete finishers refer to consistency as the slump. The thicker it is, the less it slumps or spreads when poured in the forms. If you are placing concrete on a steep slope, a stiff, low slump mix will hold best.

Final preparation and check of the forms before the truck arrives assures a successful job. Check the forms for proper slope with a level. See that they are firmly secured and have not moved. So that the forms are not disturbed during placing of the concrete, build a ramp over the form if you have to wheel in the concrete, or just leave off one end of the form until it is needed. Have some kind of dropcloth to catch the spillage from the truck to avoid messy clean-up.

Have two to three helpers: one for pushing the wheelbarrow, one for screeding, and one for finishing. Wet forms and the earth thoroughly. If they are dry, they will absorb water from the concrete, causing the mix to dry too quickly, which tends to weaken it. If the discharge chute of the ready-mix truck cannot reach your form you will have to move the concrete by wheelbarrow, one load at the time. If you are placing the concrete on a slope, keep the concrete from segregating by starting at the bottom and working up hill. The wheeler should deposit his load as near to its final position as possible.

As soon as the form has been filled, strike or screed off the surface by resting a straight 2×4 across the forms and pulling with a sawing motion. Take care to ensure proper consolidation. You may tamp (push a 2×4 on end through the concrete) along the forms, or tap the outside of the forms with a hammer to avoid honeycombs.

If the area is larger than sidewalk width, use a "bullfloat" to rough finish after screeding. A bullfloat is a large flat surface (approximately 6" by 36") with a handle used to press down the larger particles and prepare the surface for final finishing.

Final finishing must not begin until the watery

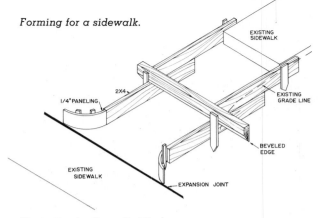

Forming for a sidewalk.

Illustration by Barry Goldfarb

sheen disappears from the surface. Round edges with the special edging tool to prevent chipping and to make a pleasing border. Control joints or grooves across the face of the concrete allow cracks to be masked in the grooves. Control joints are put in sidewalks about every 3'. Remember to cut the joint with the jointer tool to a sufficient depth to form a plane of weakness for the cracks to break along.

By the time the joints and edges have been finished, the concrete should have set enough to be floated, preferably with a wood or metal floating tool 12" to 14" long. This helps consolidate the concrete and prepares the surface for the final finishing process.

All wet spots must be permitted to dry before any troweling starts. Troweling makes the top layer dense and durable. You can vary surface textures and patterns by selecting tools, timing, and method of finishing. In walkways where you don't want slippery surfaces, a final float or a broom dragged across the slab will roughen the surface. In all finishing steps, exercise care not to overwork the freshly placed concrete.

When final finishing is done, don't allow moisture to evaporate too rapidly from the concrete. One easy way to cure a slab is to lay wet burlap over it and after a day leave a sprinkler on. Do not allow the surface of the slab to dry for at least seven days. Concrete gains strength not through drying in the usual sense, but through a chemical process requiring water. If water evaporates out, the strengthening process ceases and cannot be renewed even by rewetting.

Anchor bolts can be set into concrete before it hardens. If you want to attach wood to cured concrete, see the photos on page 380. First drill a hole in concrete slightly larger than the diameter of

POURING A CONCRETE SLAB

Stake and splice the forms securely. *Photos this series: Barry Goldfarb*

Measure from the bottom of the 2 × 4 screed to gauge the slab thickness as you dig.

Leveling the surface by screeding is the first step in finishing the slab.

Tip the leading edge of the bull float as it is pushed and pulled across the slab.

Use the jointer twice—once early in the finishing stage and once for a final touchup.

Use a back-and-forth sweeping motion when you float or trowel the surface. You can roughen the surface with a broom if desired.

Setting a lead anchor in a concrete wall or floor is accomplished by first drilling a hole in the concrete. Use a masonry bit with an electric drill, or a hammer and a star drill to make this hole in the concrete.

After drilling the hole so that it is slightly larger than the diameter of the anchor and about ⅛" deeper, slip the lead anchor into the hole. Some anchors require a setting punch to secure them in place in the concrete.

Place the wood to be attached over the hole and mark its position. Lift wood and drill a hole through it. Then replace and line up holes, using a pencil as a probe. A lag bolt through the hole into the anchor secures the wood to the concrete.

HOW TO ANCHOR TO CONCRETE

Furring strips, 1" or less in thickness, can be anchored in the same manner as a stud or plate. However, steel-cut nails will do the job faster. Hold wood firmly and drive nail through wood into concrete.

If you do not wish to break into the concrete, you can use adhesive fasteners. Spread adhesive on concrete and set anchor in adhesive. When dry, hammer the board onto the nail and then bend the tip over.

the anchor and ⅛" deeper. Insert the lead anchor. Lay the wood over the hold, mark and drill the hole, and fasten with a lag bolt. Furring strips on concrete walls may be attached in the same way, or with steel-cut nails or adhesive.

Adding color to cement Color can be added to cement and concrete in either of two ways: by including it in the cement as part of the mix, or by dusting it on the surface afterward. There are two types of pigments, natural and synthetic. Color brilliance of the synthetic type is better and it is also less likely to bleach out or fade into blotchy areas.

Pigments are added by weight, not by volume. A bag of cement weighs 94 pounds net. That would mean not more than 9 pounds of pigment per bag of cement, since the pigment should never exceed 10 percent of the mixture. If you plan to color your

mix, it is better to use white portland cement since it needs less pigment and does not reduce the color brilliance. Lighter shades of the same color are created with less pigment. Weigh the cement, then the pigment, mix them thoroughly, and put the mixture through a sieve for even blending. Then add 2½ parts sand to the cement – pigment mixture.

Add water sparingly. Too much will wash out the pigment, or create a blotchy effect. Pour enough of the colored cement mixture onto the concrete slab to add 1" to its height. Level with a straight board and trowel smooth with a wood float for a rough finish. If you prefer a glossy surface, glaze with a steel trowel while the cement is still wet. Avoid overtroweling with either tool, or the surface may develop dark spots known as trowel burns.

The dust-on method may be used with a concrete

slab after floating the concrete (if the surface isn't so large that it will set before you are finished), or you may add the pigment into a cement paste topping to the concrete slab. Mix the pigment with dry portland cement, then add 1 part of this mix to 1 or 1½ parts mortar sand (not the coarse concrete sand) and spread over the wet concrete surface at the rate of 1¼ pounds per square foot. Scrub into the wet concrete with a stiff bristle brush and trowel smooth at once. In dry weather the slab may appear to lose color, yet after a rain it may appear fresh again. Clear concrete sealers such as Thompson's sealing products will help maintain an even color through all kinds of weather. When soiled, apply liquid soap, leave it on overnight, then scrub and rinse thoroughly the next day.

CAUSE OF FAILURE Failures in a concrete or mortar job are usually due to any one or a combination of the following:

1. Too much water in the mixture; it flows away from the surface, carrying with it much of the cement and leaving the sand behind. Weak cement is the result.
2. Too much sand in the mixture. It crumbles, pits, dusts, and falls apart. The beginner is better off measuring very carefully until he learns to tell a good mix when he sees it.
3. Freezing of the concrete or mortar, causing it to crumble. This can be overcome by adding to the mix any one of various air entraining admixtures made specifically to prevent such failures.
4. Inadequate curing. It's best to keep the surface damp for several days. Either spray lightly at

regular intervals or cover with a waterproof material such as tarpaper or damp burlap. The idea is to keep the concrete from drying too fast.

5. Mix too old. Don't let any mixture of concrete or mortar stand for more than half an hour. Anything unused after that time should be discarded and a fresh batch prepared.
6. Using color to judge the mix. Color is not a good guide. Since portland cement is made in many parts of the country, of locally obtained ingredients, you can never be certain just what color your particular mix will be when it dries. Colors range from almost pure white to a dark slate blue-gray.

REPAIRING CONCRETE When concrete is cracked only slightly—up to ½" wide—you can use one of the prepared concrete patchers that, like mortar, comes in a cartridge. Following directions on the cartridge, just snip the nozzle, press the nozzle in the crack, and squeeze the trigger of the caulking gun.

Smooth it out with a trowel or scraper frequently dipped in a dish of water. The patcher is latex based and is easy to smooth. As with a mortar crack, you should clean out all loose, unsound material before you begin, and douse the crack with water.

If the concrete has a big hole in it, a premixed powdered concrete patcher is the best bet for repair. Like mortar mix, it comes in various size bags up to 90 pounds. It contains aggregate for strength and will do a generally good job in repairing various size holes.

REPAIRING CONCRETE

All concrete and cement patching starts the same way. Clean out any loose material, dirt, and plant life. Use a wire brush where possible, and an old screwdriver for getting into deeper crevices.

Next step is thorough soaking of old masonry. Every part to be repaired must be wet. If you can't manage it with a hose, use a sponge. Just be sure the full depth of a crack is sopping wet.

Fill crack with cement—a mixture of mortar cement (1 part) and sand (2 to 2½ parts) and water. Add waterproofing agent for a better bond. For vertical cracks, make mix stiff so it won't run out.

REPAIRING CONCRETE (continued)

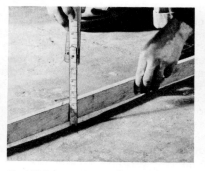

After cement has partly set and appears sandy on the surface, take a wire brush and remove excess cement. If you can't do this now, you'll have trouble doing so when the cement is hard.

To fill depressions where water collects, first check depth of hollow. Figure the area (length times width) and multiply by half of depth for an average. This determines quantity of filler needed.

Important on this type of patch is roughening surface. Light sledge does a good job, but don't crack the slab. Remove debris, then soak surface. Seep away any excess water in hole.

Mix material on the spot. Two shovels of sand, 1 shovel of portland cement, and ½ pail water make only two shovels of mix. (Both cement and water disappear in mix without adding to its bulk.)

Mix until the whole mass is one color and one consistency. There should be no dry portions, no streaks of clean sand through the mixture. Adding a waterproofing agent makes cement stick better.

Use straightedge to level off patch even with surrounding area. Remove all excess cement from the surface now. Later, when it sets, you won't be able to remove it at all.

Smooth new surface with pointing trowel or steel float. Because of sand in mix, you won't be able to feather edges, so mix cement and water to a paste and apply to edges to smooth off evenly.

The first step, again, is to thoroughly clean all debris and loose material from the hole. Use a cold chisel, hammer, and a stiff bristle or wire brush as required. Then flush the hole with water.

Mix the concrete patcher according to instructions on the bag. To facilitate matters, use a piece of plywood for a mortar board. Empty the dry mix on the plywood, then make a crater in the center. Fill the crater with water, then fold in the mix. Pack the patcher into the hole with a trowel or scraper, poking at it to remove all air bubbles.

Then use a rectangular trowel to finish the patch. Use semicircular strokes, slightly raising the leading edge of the trowel as you go. Take special care where the patcher meets the edge of the crack.

Let the patch stand for an hour or so. Then come back and give it some more finishing sweeps with the trowel. Finally, cover the patch with a piece of burlap or cloth and keep the fabric wet for a few days. This allows the concrete to cure slowly and properly.

WORKING WITH BRICK Common brick—a baked clay slab that measures approximately $2'' \times 4'' \times 8''$, usually various shades of red and often faced on the exposed side with a variety of patterns—is one of man's most beautiful and durable building materials, found all over the world. Any handyman can successfully work with brick if he keeps in mind the following basic requirements:

1. A strong foundation below the frost line.
2. Sound brick, new or second-hand.
3. Well-mixed mortar in a proper proportion.
4. Well-filled mortar joints between bricks, able to resist water penetration.
5. Careful placing of each brick.
6. Proper pointing of mortar joints.
7. Curing and protection of the masonry.

Concrete foundations for full-height walls require experience, knowledge of blueprints, heavy excavation machinery, equipment for setting up forms, and so on. But if you are going to build a barbecue, outdoor planter, or a low brick wall, you can dig trenches by hand for poured foundations with footings that go below the frost line. In any case consult your local building inspector about exact foundation requirements for the brick structure you intend to build.

Choosing brick Common brick, without center holes, is usually $2\frac{1}{4}'' \times 3\frac{3}{4}'' \times 8''$ in size. Smooth-faced brick will measure $2\frac{1}{4}'' \times 3\frac{7}{8}'' \times 8''$. Fire brick is $2\frac{1}{2}'' \times 4\frac{1}{2}'' \times 9''$. In various parts of the country and among manufacturers, brick will be found to vary somewhat from these figures. The important point in selection is that the brick be clean, uncracked, and free of surfaces weathered from exposure to moisture.

Before beginning any job, measure the brick you have chosen so that you can accurately figure how many courses, or layers, will bring you up flush with sills, the tops of proposed openings, and against the frames of doors and windows. Measure so that no piece smaller than a half brick need be used at the end of a row to finish any given distance.

Brick patterns Once you have chosen your brick, decide what style of bond you want—common, (American), English, or Flemish. Bond, in this case, means the style in which the bricks are laid. Where you have two parallel rows of bricks to form an 8" thick wall, some courses are laid crosswise at right angles to the length of the wall to bind the two rows of bricks together. These crosswise bricks are called headers. Bricks laid with one side showing following the length of the wall are called stretchers.

In common, or American, bond every sixth course consists of headers. English bond has headers in every other course. Flemish bond is characterized by alternate headers and stretches in every course.

In all brick walls, corners are built up first and

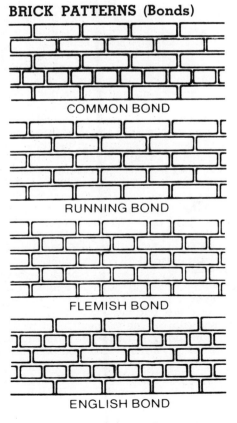

BRICK PATTERNS (Bonds)

COMMON BOND

RUNNING BOND

FLEMISH BOND

ENGLISH BOND

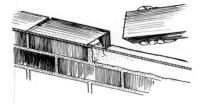

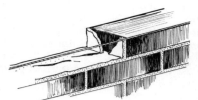

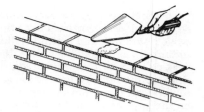

Mortar forced into joint from side cannot properly join bricks.

Mortar forced into space from both sides cannot reach center line.

Spread on top, mortar still cannot penetrate to mortar line below.

Buttering end of brick is quicker, guarantees a mortar-filled joint.

Closing a course with brick buttered on both sides is correct.

bricks are laid toward the middle. The final gap is closed with a cut piece of brick called a closure. To cut brick, use a brick chisel and a heavy hammer. Or chip a line around the brick and strike the line sharply with the edge of the trowel.

SCR brick You can buy larger brick, which makes possible a single width of brick wall. The resultant wall is still of sufficient strength to stand alone without any backing material or ties to a frame wall. This type of brick measures 2¼″ × 5⅝″ × 11⅝″ and is known as SCR brick. It weighs only 8 pounds, owing to two rows of holes down its length and a ¾″ slot cut vertically across one end. The holes lighten the weight of the brick, make it easy to handle, and improve the bond between bricks. The vertical slot not only adds strength to the joints but makes window and door framing much easier, as it provides a groove for insertion of the framing members. This brick speeds construction many times over other methods and permits walls to be built to a height of 9′ without additional bracing or departure from standard construction.

Mortar Since you are going to hold the bricks together with mortar and that mortar must be expected to last as long as the bricks, its ingredients and consistency are particularly important. In most cases, you can get mortar cement in which lime has been included in the correct proportions. Use 1 part of this cement, from 2 to 3 parts clean, sharp sand, and enough water added slowly to the ingredients to make a mass that will slide readily from the trowel. First mix the dry cement and sand together, then add the water. If you have both sand

and gravel on the job, keep them separated, for one pebble in the mortar mix can be very annoying. When working with mortar, mix ⅙ to ¼ parts of lime to 1 part of water, and add a little of this liquid occasionally in order to keep the mortar moist and workable for a longer period of time.

To check the proper consistency of a mortar mix, make a ball and hold it in your hand. It should not fall apart—and it should be able to hold a brick or block in place without compacting.

Joints Successful bricklaying, which means an attractive and durable wall, is the result of care and attention to seemingly minor details. Since it is porous, a dry brick wall is apt to draw moisture from the mortar before it sets, leaving a sandy, crumbling bond. Therefore, the bricks themselves should be damp, when the time comes to bond

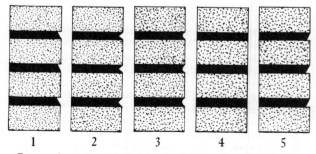

Types of mortar-pointing joints: 1. Weathered; 2. V-joint; 3. Concave; 4. Flush; 5. Struck. All but 5 will shed water. 1, 2, and 4 are done with pointing trowel; 3 with a rod.

Laying wall with large brick is speeded by 11⅝" brick length and by laying single courses without necessity of header coursing.

them together. Fill every joint completely with mortar. Since bricks are closely set together, it is impossible to squeeze mortar between them after they are once placed. For this reason, a system of "buttering" is used. Mortar is spread on the brick before it is placed, to make certain that every joint is completely filled. In a single-brick wall (such as a veneer), the ends are buttered. In a two-brick wall 8" thick, one end and one side are buttered and the brick pushed into place. Once placed, leave the brick alone. Trying to squeeze mortar into a crack will invariably leave a hollow space somewhere else and dislodge the brick. Heavy tapping to get a brick into line will produce similar trouble and may also dislodge other bricks where the mortar has begun to set.

Brick placement The first, or starter, course placed on the footing must be level and square at each corner. It must not bulge outward or curve inward. Constant use of level and steel square will be necessary, and a white guide cord strung from corner to corner should be followed. After the starter course is laid, the square can be put aside and a plumb line put to use, for a third dimension must now be observed: The wall must be plumb at every point. These measuring devices should be kept handy and a constant check made as work progresses.

If you find you've laid a brick or two incorrectly, remove them. They cannot be pushed into place after the mortar has been spread for as little as five minutes. Moving the brick will result in hairline cracks in the joints, through which water will ultimately filter and destroy the wall. If this means removing an entire course or two, do it. Better a little extra work now than much regret later.

Pointing There are several types of mortar joints that may be used on a brick wall. Study the illustrations of these and the values of each. A metal rod, bent to form a handle at one end, will make a good joint-finishing, or pointing, tool. Whatever style you prefer, start finishing the joints as soon as you've laid two or three courses. Later, the mortar will begin to set and you will cause cracks. By finishing each joint while the mortar is still workable, you will seal every crack against penetration by rain. Once water penetrates in cold weather, freezing results and the expansion rips the mortar loose in small chunks. Repointing will then be necessary if the wall is to stand.

Masonry protection Once the wall is up and the mortar has set and cured, it is sound economy to coat the wall with a masonry sealer. This penetrates the porous brick and mortar and fills the spaces with a colorless liquid that hardens into a water-repelling surface that remains weathertight for years. Instead of gradually crumbling and weathering, with loose mortar that needs repointing at intervals, the wall will remain the same in appearance as the day you finished the job.

Care of brick Since brick is composed of clay scooped from the ground, it contains the impurities of the basic clay. After years of exposure to weather, brick faces allow water to seep in deeper and deeper. And when the moisture in a brick freezes, the expansion chips off the face of the brick in small flakes and efflorescence results. This is a white substance that forms on the outer surface of bricks, caused by the release of soluble salts in the bricks or the mortar when water penetrates the masonry.

In many cases, it can be removed with a wire brush and water. A really stubborn case may require a solution of 5 parts water to 1 part muriatic acid. Apply it with a wire brush and wash it off with ammonia and water as quickly as possible or it will etch the brick and soften the mortar.

When mortar in the joints of brickwork crumbles and disintegrates or cracks, it must be removed and new mortar applied, a process known as repointing. First, clean away all loose or cracked mortar by chipping with a cold chisel and hammer or by raking out with some other sharp tool. A nail through a 2 × 4 can often be used for such raking. Then thoroughly moisten all the brick on the sides of the cracks and, with a pointing trowel, force a new mortar mix (fairly stiff) into the spaces between the bricks. Finish the joint to match the rest of the masonry.

During this operation, you may come across bricks that are loose or broken. Remove them by carefully clearing the mortar around them with a chisel or pick. Soak the replacement brick in water

BASIC PROCEDURE FOR TUCK-POINTING BRICK

1. To tuck-point brick, first knock out all loose, crumbly material. A cold chisel and hammer work well.

2. Use brush and stream from hose to remove crumbs.

3. Stuff the joint with mortar mix. Cardboard catches mix spillover.

4. Run over mortar with jointer. Smooth to match adjacent joints.

for a short time before placing it in the opening with new mortar.

Cleaning brick Exterior or fireplace brick blackened by smoke deposits can be restored to virtually the original appearance. If the brick is smooth, simply rub it down with an ordinary carborundum rod or block such as is used for sharpening knives. If common brick, rub it with coarse steel wool dipped in water and a grit-containing mechanic's hand-cleaning compound. After cleaning off the soot, bring back the color of the brickwork by painting it with raw linseed oil.

Even the most persistent paint smears on brick will usually prove no match for a pound of common caustic soda dissolved in three or four quarts of hot water. Keep applying this potent fluid to the paint spots, washing them off each time with clean water until they disappear. Remember that caustic soda is dangerous. Wear waterproof gloves and goggles to protect your eyes when working with it.

A brick appearance is particularly effective in a setting that combines traditional "used" bricks with modern furnishings and in an area below window and wood paneling. Imitation bricks are lightweight, easy to apply, and come in a variety of styles.

To lay out the job, draw a vertical line down wall on each side of area to be covered. Draw small horizontal marks on the vertical lines to represent bottom line of each row.

Spread adhesive about 1/16" thick with putty knife.

ARTIFICIAL BRICK Textured walls are great favorites in home decoration. Brick is surely the favorite. It is an old American tradition to use white-washed brick. One of the most attractive examples of colonial architecture is the Georgian style, combining brick with white woodwork. Since the use of real brick in the home often requires the skills of a professional mason, many homeowners use light-weight, 1/4" thick imitation brick. They come in a variety of styles—from thin, flat Roman to so-called "used" bricks with their clever imitation of brick with white salts (efflorescence) on them.

The advantage of using imitation brick, in addition to its good looks, is that there is no need to have a specially braced floor, because the imita-

INSTALLING ARTIFICIAL BRICK

On floor next to wall, lay out single row of bricks with about 3/8" space between to give you spacing guide when you apply first row at top of installation. Adjust spacing so row ends with whole or half brick.

Starting at top left of installation area, press first brick firmly into wet adhesive.

For an inside corner, leave mortar space between half brick and corner as shown.

tion variety weighs so little. The casual visitor can hardly tell a pseudo-brick wall from the real thing. Even the mortar—usually a tan or gray mastic—fools the eye. In addition, practically all brands of imitation brick have L-shaped pieces for outside corners, which give it a more realistic appearance. Imitation bricks can also be snapped or broken so you can apply them in a unique, individual pattern.

The material in false bricks used to be styrene, vinyl, or urethane. But now plastics are no longer cheap, and imitation brick is generally of lightweight minerals and binders, and comes in a vast variety of brick colors. The method of application is very easy. The only tools needed are a saw, a level, a 3″ putty knife and a measuring tape.

Preparing the wall First make sure that the wall is clean and dry. Remove loose wallpaper or paint and level bumps or hollows with patching plaster or by sanding. If the wall surface is paint, roughen it with a medium grit sandpaper, scratching through the paint to the subsurface material. On the other hand, if the surface is new plasterboard, it should be primed with a water-base primer. Place newspaper or a dropcloth below the wall area to catch dirt or dust.

Laying out the job If the installation is to extend to the ceiling, use the top of the wall as your starting reference line. From there, draw a vertical line down the wall on each side of the area to be covered. Use either a carpenter's level or a plumb line to make sure the lines are truly vertical.

Starting at the top, draw small horizontal marks at equal intervals on the vertical lines down to the bottom of the area to be covered. The space between these marks represents the width of the brick you are using plus an allowance for the mortar lines. If necessary, adjust marks slightly so the bottom row coincides with the bottom of the installation area. The mortar line between rows is approximately ⅜″ wide.

Now you are ready to do the horizontal or left-to-right layout. On the floor next to the wall, lay out flat a single row of bricks with approximately ⅜″ space between each. By slightly increasing or decreasing these spaces, make the row end either at the end of a whole brick or at the middle of a brick. Cut a brick in half if the row ends in the middle of a brick and face the cut end to the side where it is less obvious. Avoid ending a row with anything other than a full or half brick. This gives you the spacing you will use when you apply the first row of bricks at the top of the brick area. Mark off at the top of the area the position of each brick in this row. This will be your guide to placing the first row.

Applying the adhesive Starting at the top of the area (so any spillage does not fall on finished work), spread adhesive with a 3″ putty knife to a thickness of about ¹⁄₁₆″. Take care not to cover the two vertical lines at either side of the installation. You will want to use these lines to check each row as it is applied. They may be covered with adhesive after the job is completed. Irregularities in the adhesive improve its appearance, so don't worry about getting it absolutely smooth. Don't spread adhesive over too large an area at one time. It begins to set in about 15 minutes, so apply the bricks to this area before it begins to harden.

Applying the bricks If your installation includes an outside corner and you wish to cover both walls, start your installation with the corner bricks. Use a full brick and a half brick around the corner.

If your installation includes an inside corner and you wish to cover both walls where they intersect, leave a mortar space between the half brick and the corner as pictured. The full bricks, which occur in alternate rows, should be butted against the corner without leaving a space. If you are not working with an outside or inside corner, however, start at the top left of the installation area, press the first brick firmly into the wet adhesive, positioning it according to the marks you made. Avoid sliding the brick as it is pressed into place.

Apply the second and successive bricks the same way, pressing them into the wet adhesive coating. Do the entire top row first to be sure your spacing is correct. Complete the installation using the same method. One final hint: Check frequently to see that the rows are level and the spacing between rows uniform.

HOW TO WORK WITH METAL

USING METAL SNIPS You need a metal cutting snips to cut into a warm air duct in your cellar for a register or to install aluminum gutters and leaders or to do any jobs with sheet metal. There are two types of snips, inlaid and solid alloy steel.

Inlaid snips, used by professionals, have high carbon steel welded to cutting edges and long handles for extra leverage. Those made of solid steel, often called aviation snips, look somewhat like pliers and have additional small levers that greatly increase the leverage of their relatively short, plastic-coated handles. Aviation snips are marked either L (left), R (right), or S (straight) cutting.

Straight-cutting snips can cut to the left or right in a very wide circle, but to make a very tight turn use appropriate snips.

It is always best to make relatively short cuts, because you have the most cutting power at the point where the blades cross. Never let the blades close completely; this makes distortion of the metal more likely and it will be difficult to resume cutting. It is usually necessary to drill a hole to get started unless there is an outside edge.

Special pipe and duct snips have double cutting edges and a sharp point on the lower jaw that starts holes. This type cuts without distortion and turns out a waste strip 3/16″ wide. It can also cut

Pipe and duct snips easily cut this sheet-metal air conditioning duct. Compound action levers give this aviation-type snips added leverage despite short handles. *Photo: J. Wiss & Sons*

HOW TO USE POP RIVETS

straight or to either side. It is ideal for trimming or cutting aluminum gutters and leaders, sheet metal up to 18 gauge, and warm air or air-conditioning ducts. There is also a general purpose aviation-type snips that can make straight cuts in metal and cut wire, leather, plastics, and fiberglass.

FASTENING METAL WITH POP RIVETS Pop rivets are easy to handle, and rivets and pliers that are used to set them are readily available. Pop rivets are available in 1/8″, 5/32″, and 3/16″ diameters and in lengths of 1/8″ to 5/8″. The pop rivet, available in steel but usually made of aluminum, is tubular with one preformed head. Going up through the center of the rivet and protruding from the hole in its head is a mandrel that looks like a steel nail.

To use the rivet you insert the nail-like end into an opening in one jaw of the plierlike tool that sets the rivet. The handles are squeezed just enough to grip the nail, and the rivet is placed in a predrilled hole in the work. As handles are squeezed together the nail is pulled upward so that its head stretches the body of the rivet and tightens it against the inner surface of the duct or leader. The tool then snaps off the shank of the nail, leaving its end inside the body of the rivet.

Pop rivets can be used to join sections of gutters and leaders, pieces of sheet metal, and make attachments to metal and plastic tubes.

Rivet tool has attachment on lower jaw that swivels to adjust to three different sizes of pop rivet mandrels. *Photo: Swingline Corp.*

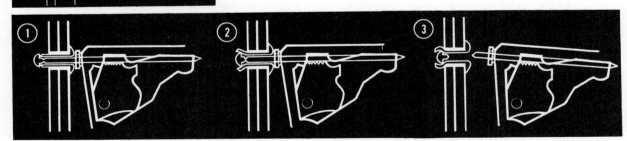

Top: Pop rivets have a tubular body, preformed head, and a nail-like mandrel that goes through the rivet and protrudes from the head.
How to use pop rivets. Mandrel is inserted into rivet tool (1) and rivet goes into predrilled holes. Handles of rivet tool are squeezed together, drawing mandrel head into

rivet body and expanding it against inner surface until both drilled pieces are tight (2). A few more squeezes of the rivet tool handles and the mandrel shaft breaks off, leaving its head (3) inside the pop rivet. Special pop rivets are available with a closed end for watertight uses. *Illustration: Bostick Co.*

Pop rivets used to fasten part of bicycle seat to tubular steel seat support. *Photo: Swingline Corp.*

HOW TO SOLDER

The first step in any soldering operation is to "tin" the iron. Clean it with steel wool, dip in flux, and apply a thin coat of solder to iron.

WORKING WITH SOLDER Soldering is the joining of two pieces of metal by means of a low-melting alloy called solder. It can be either soft soldering or hard soldering, better known as brazing. Soft solders melt at comparatively low temperatures, below 700° F, and are the type generally used in the home workshop. Soft solders make good joints between metals such as copper, brass, tin, aluminum, and steel. They are made of lead and tin with the proportion of each varying between 48 percent and 52 percent—usually called "half-and-half." This type of solder melts at 370° F, a temperature low enough to join the metals mentioned above.

Hard solders are alloys of gold, silver, copper, lead, tin, and bismuth. These melt at much higher temperatures—from 1050° F to 1300° F. Often their melting points will be quite near those of the metal—in thin stock—to be joined.

Soldering flux prevents oxide from forming on the metals to be joined. Oxide interferes with successful soldering. An acid flux is generally used

for heavy-duty soldering, such as sheet metal and roof repair work. A resin solder is used for electrical connections. Fluxes for hard soldering are formulated for the particular metal they are used on.

Soft soldering Propane torches with soldering tips or electrical soldering guns may be used. The first step is to clean the soldering tip with steel wool or sandpaper, then wipe off with a clean cloth. As soon as the tip is hot enough to melt solder, dip in a flux paste or sal-ammoniac. Apply the solder to the tip until it is completely covered. Wipe off excess with a rag, leaving the tip bright and shiny with solder.

The soldering tip is used on smaller jobs and electrical connections. For larger jobs, such as drainpipes, a pencil flame burner on a propane torch can be used.

Surfaces to be soldered must be thoroughly clean. Apply sandpaper or steel wool, followed by a thin coating of flux. Heat the surfaces to be soldered with the tip of the iron. When a face of the tip

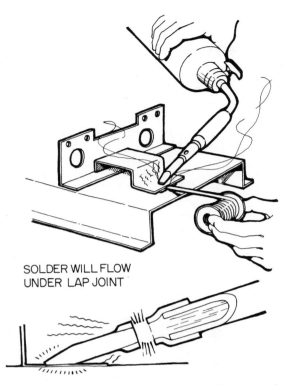

SOLDER WILL FLOW
UNDER LAP JOINT

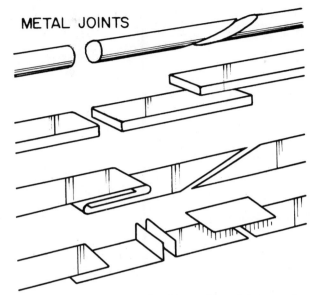

METAL JOINTS

Small lap joint can be soldered with the soldering tip; the flame is not required. Wipe off excess flux while the joint is still warm.

Some of the many ways that lap and butt joints can be made with metal. Fit should be tight; don't depend on the brazing to fill any gaps. Illustrations this series: Bernz-Omatic

is held flat against the work surface to preheat the metal, there is maximum heat transfer to the work. Apply the solder to the work — not to the soldering tip — when the work is heated enough to melt the solder.

Types of common joints The drawing (above, right) shows common types of metal joints. Generally, butt joints are the most difficult (they are impossible with soft solder) and lap joints the strongest. Regardless of anything else, proper preparation of the metals to be joined is the single most important part of the job.

Brazing Brazing or hard soldering on such metals as silver, gold, steel, and bronze makes a much stronger — and neater — joint than soft soldering.

Newer propane torches or high heat brazing torches such as the BernzOmatic Super Torch should be used.

As in soft soldering, the first step is to clean the pieces to be joined. If possible, clamp them together so they will remain stationary. Apply proper flux

to the metal — there are more than a dozen different types of fluxes and brazing rods.

Use a brazing rod that matches the color of the work to be joined. If you are joining silver, for example, use silver solder. This is an alloy of silver (8 parts), copper (3 parts) and zinc (1 part). If the job involves soldering gold, use a rod containing gold, silver, and copper.

An inexpensive flux for really large jobs consists of powdered borax mixed with water to the consistency of cream. Heat with the hottest part of the flame — the tip of the inner core of the flame — until the solder starts to melt when it is applied to the metal. Many brazing rods are flux coated or flux cored, and require no additional flux.

The melted flux left behind when the job is finished is a dark brown residue. It can be removed by immersing the item in a solution of 1 part sulphuric acid to 2 parts water. IMPORTANT: Always add acid to water, never water to acid. Wear rubber gloves and goggles when doing this job. Allow

CHOOSING THE RIGHT SOLDERING AND BRAZING RODS

Type of Solder or Brazing Rod	Stainless Steel & Flux	General Purpose Acid Core Solder	All-purpose Rosin Core Electrical Solder	Aluminum Brazing Alloy & Flux	Silver Solder & Flux	Aluminum Bare Brazing Rod	Flux Coated Nickel-Silver Brazing Rod	Flux Coated Bronze Brazing Rod	Copper Phosphorous Brazing Rod
Apply Solder or Brazing Rod When:	Solder flows freely on contact with heated metal.	Solder flows freely on contact with heated metal.	Solder flows freely on contact with heated metal.	Flux becomes a clear liquid.	Flux becomes a thin, clear liquid & forms dull red.	Brazing rod puddles on contact with heated metal.	Brazing rod flows freely on contact with heated metal.	Brazing rod flows freely on contact with heated metal.	Brazing rod flows freely on contact with heated metal.
For metals below, use solders or alloys marked "X" at right.									
Aluminum — For strength in joining sheets, sections, etc.				X		X			
Chrome Plate — For trim, when on steel, brass, copper or nickel alloys. (Not on die castings.)	X						X	X	
Copper — For electrical equipment.			X						
Copper or Bronze — For fittings, tubing, utensils, etc.		X					X	X	X
Galvanized Iron or Steel — For cans, buckets, tanks, eavestroughs, etc.		X			X	X	X	X	
Silver and Silver Plate — For jewelry, flatware, etc.	X				X				
Stainless Steel — For appliances, kitchen equipment or wherever strength is needed.	X				X		X	X	
Steel — For utensils, pipes, sheets, tool sheets, motors, etc.	X				X		X	X	

UNLIKE METALS such as steel to brass
Unlike metals with X's in the same vertical column can be joined. For example: copper and galvanized iron with general purpose solder

(Table courtesy BernzOmatic)

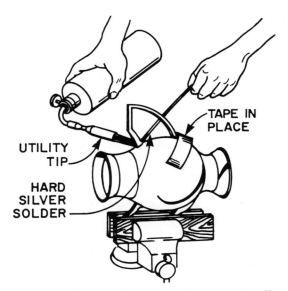

UTILITY
TIP

HARD
SILVER
SOLDER

TAPE IN
PLACE

Mending handle of a silver pitcher with soft solder. Note how handle is kept from moving by taping the lower end to the body of the pitcher.

the work to soak in this solution for about 20 minutes. Flux can also be removed by immersion in boiling water, provided this is done before the joint has cooled.

The rod used in brazing is always of a nonferrous metal with a melting point above 800° F, but always below the melting point of the parts to be joined. As the rod melts, it flows by capillary action between the parts to be brazed. A typical example is the brazing of copper pipe into a T or elbow. The rod becomes a filler under the action of the heat and flows between the pipe and the elbow, making a strong, waterproof connection.

Braze welding—also called bronze welding—uses a rod as a filler too, but involves joining parts by means of fillets, grooves, and butt joints. Capillary action is not a factor here.

Torches for brazing operations are often used with Mapp gas, which delivers a 3,700° F flame, more than 500° F hotter than propane gas can deliver. The chart shows the choice of brazing rods to use depending on the metals to be joined and the joint strength required. Generally, bronze brazing is the most versatile and provides the strongest joint. When done properly, bronze brazing is as easy as soldering and produces a bond as strong as welding.

Follow carefully the metal preparation steps. Note that bronze brazing rods often are flux coated. No further fluxing is required. Heat the metals to

be joined until they are cherry red. Try to keep the flame in one place. Moving the flame will allow the metals not in direct contact with the heat source to cool. The tip of the flame should be held about ½" from the metal.

When the base metal is thoroughly hot all the way through the joint (not just at the surface), introduce the brazing rod into the torch flame, touching the joint at the hottest point. Rub some flux from the end of the rod onto the joint. When both joint and rod are hot enough, the rod will melt and flow easily and quickly into the joint. Now move the torch along the joint, repeating the same sequence as required.

When using either the copper-phosphorus or aluminum rods, the procedures are similar. However, the metals will be heated to lower temperatures. Copper-phosphorus rods are used frequently in plumbing and air-conditioning work. They allow pipes to be joined even though some water may be in them. When using copper-phosphorus brazing rods, heat the metals until they are a dull red color, then follow the procedures described for bronze brazing.

Aluminum brazing is a bit more difficult, since the melting point of the brazing rod is quite close to the melting point of aluminum. For this reason it is best to practice a few times on scrap aluminum before trying a repair job. Use aluminum flux and clean parts to get a good joint.

When brazing aluminum, heat the joint for about 6 seconds. Apply the brazing rod. As soon as the rod begins to flow, remove the heat. Repeat this procedure as needed to complete the repair.

Sweating "Sweating" is another form of soldering for uniting the work. In this operation it is most important that the mating surfaces of the items be as smooth as possible and make a good mechanical fit to each other. Clean surfaces to be joined, flux both surfaces and coat each surface with solder—this is a form of tinning. Assemble the two pieces and clamp them together if possible.

The next step is to apply the torch until the solder within the joint remelts and unites the pieces. Hold the joints in position until the solder is cool. Additional solder can be added, for the sake of strength, around the outside of the joint, forming a fillet of metal. Any flux that has oozed out can be wiped away with a rag while the metal is still warm. But don't do any wiping while the metal is hot; otherwise you may disturb the solder and loosen the joint.

Sheet-metal work Solder itself is not a strong material. You can't make a good joint simply by bringing two metal edges together and running a ribbon of solder over the seam. Instead, use either a lap joint, or when an assembly will be subjected to stress or vibration, a lock joint made by folding back the edges of the stock into two U sections and interlocking them.

With lap joints, spread flux over the metal areas to be mated and coat them with solder. Then lap the parts and run either a soldering tip or direct

flame of a burner over the top of the joint to fuse the coatings. To solder lock joints, clean the contacting surfaces before folding, and apply flux. Then, with the parts interlocked, flow solder in, just as you would to sweat a pipe joint.

Handling rod and wire When bonding the ends of rods and heavy wire, use a lap joint made by filing halfway through each end section. Apply solder to the resulting flat areas, place these "tinned" sur-

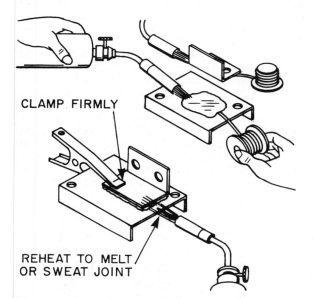

CLAMP FIRMLY

REHEAT TO MELT OR SWEAT JOINT

When sweating, make sure mating surfaces are as smooth as possible. Flux each surface and coat each surface with solder. Clamp firmly.

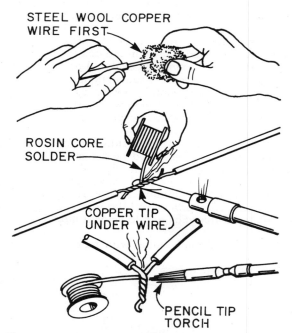

STEEL WOOL COPPER WIRE FIRST

ROSIN CORE SOLDER

COPPER TIP UNDER WIRE

PENCIL TIP TORCH

The soldering tip on the torch will allow soldering where no electricity is available. Clean wires with steel wool, and use rosin-core solder.

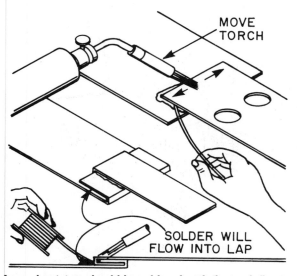

MOVE TORCH

SOLDER WILL FLOW INTO LAP

Large lap joints should be soldered with the torch flame. Solder, because of capillary action, flows to the hottest part of the joint.

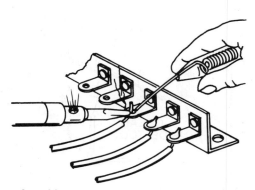

Using the soldering tip to make electrical connections on a subassembly. Always use a rosin-core solder—never an acid type—for all wiring work.

faces together, and sweat them with the flame. Where rods cross, notch both at the point of intersection and sweat-solder the resulting lap joint. Or, if considerable strength is needed, give each rod or wire a half turn around the other and flow solder into the connection.

Electrical connections Remove all traces of insulation and oxidation for a good electrical and physical connection. To splice wires, wind the ends together and bend the tips back. Then, holding rosin-core wire solder against one side of the joint, apply heat to the other until the solder melts and binds the whole connection.

Terminals for soldered connections usually have a hole, or eye. Bend a hook in the end of the wire, place it through the eye, and solder. A pencil flame is good for large electrical connections. For jobs in crowded quarters, a small soldering tip is the right tool. Work fast. Prolonged heat will break down the flux, weaken the wire, and possibly damage nearby electrical components.

WELDING Welding is a metal-joining process that uses the heat generated by a combination of oxygen and a fuel gas to actually melt the metals so that they flow together and are integrally joined when cooled. Unfortunately, this is true in theory only, but in actual practice a filler or a welding rod is used to fill the gaps and to smooth the finished joint.

Welding requires a flame with an exceedingly high temperature. It is for this reason that oxygen is always part of the gas welding process. Simple welding can be done quite easily with torch units that use propane or Mapp gas in combination with oxygen.

Copper tubing Working with copper tube is a great deal easier than working with threaded pipe. For example, if a new length of pipe has to be installed between an existing pipe run, no union is required as with threaded pipe.

To make a connection The first step is to cut the copper pipe to the required size. Use a hacksaw with a fine-tooth blade with a miter box, or a tubing cutter. Next, use a half-round file to remove the burr on the inside of the pipe. Clean about 1½" of the outside end of the cut pipe with steel wool or fine sandpaper. Do the same with the inside of the required fitting. Apply a light coat of soldering flux to the inside of the cleaned coupling or fitting and the outside of the cleaned pipe.

Push the fitting over the pipe (or the pipe into the

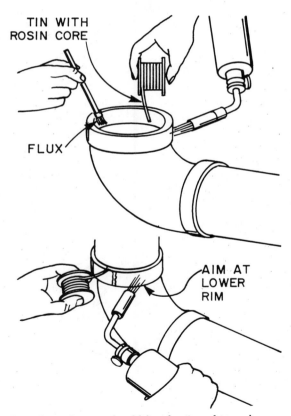

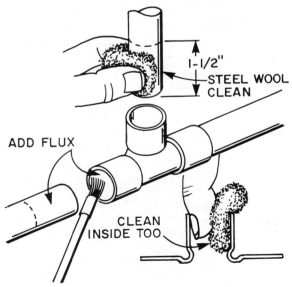

The first step in doing any plumbing work involving the torch is to clean the outside of the pipe and inside of fitting it is to engage.

Extra-large fittings should first be tinned to make sure a good bond will be effected during the subsequent soldering operation.

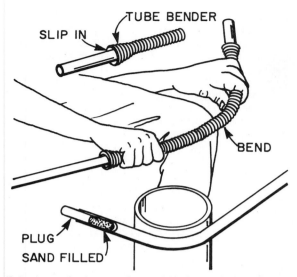

SLIP IN

TUBE BENDER

BEND

PLUG

SAND FILLED

Tubing can be bent with an electrician's hickey, with a spring-type tubing bender, or bent around a cylinder after first filling it with dry sand.

fitting, depending upon the layout of the work) until the pipe makes a positive contact with the shoulder of the fitting. Make sure the pipe and its fitting are secure and will not be subject to movement.

With a torch, heat the tubing about ½″ distance from the end of the fitting. Keep playing the flame at right angles to the tubing—and keep the flame in motion, gradually heating the fitting as well. After the pipe and its fitting have been thoroughly heated with the torch, apply the solder. If the metal is hot enough, the solder will melt freely and will be drawn into and around the joint by capillary action. The solder will flow into the fitting even if the pipe and its fitting are in a vertical position. Flow solder all around the joint so that the solder will make a fillet around the fitting.

Excess flux or discoloration can be removed by wiping the joint with a rag while the connection is still warm.

When more than one connection is to be made at one point, at a T connection, for example, all the joints should be made at the same time. However, if this is impossible, make up the first joint and wrap it with a damp cloth so the nearby heat will not affect it.

An improperly made-up joint can be dismantled by heating the joint and gently tapping it or by pulling at the pipe while the solder is being melted.

Never try to make up a connection with water in the pipe, since the water will dissipate the heat. If there is a little water in the pipe due to a faulty shutoff valve that allows slight leakage, you can stuff the pipe with enough white bread to absorb the water. When the connection is finished and the water is turned on, the bread will be flushed out through the faucet without harm.

FIXING GUTTERS A common gutter problem is a loosened joint between two sections. To fix, clean out the gutter, including all moisture. Sand thoroughly, or use steel wool for about an inch or so on each side of the break in the joint. As soon as you clean away this area, apply the flux, acid, or paste. Bar solder is best for this job, as it costs less than the solder in wire form. Apply flame to the work, wait, and apply the solder. If the solder flows freely, the metal is hot enough. If the solder wrinkles, the metal is not hot enough. When doing this work, make certain that the two ends of the gutter will not move during the soldering. When soldering aluminum or galvanized steel gutters, use a special flux and solder especially designed for use with those metals.

Valley flashing Flashing is usually sheet copper used wherever a roof meets the chimney, a wall, or an adjacent roof. In the average home it will always be found in the valley between two roofs. Valley flashing leaks are often found near the low part of the valley. Small holes in flashing can be easily repaired by filling the hole with solder.

Clean the area around the hole by sanding and apply flux. Use a torch to fill the hole with solder

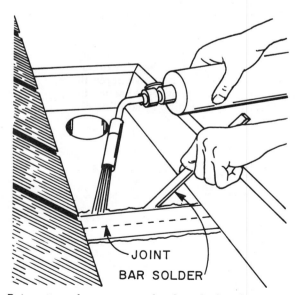

JOINT

BAR SOLDER

Rain gutters always seem to develop a leak at the joints—where else? Clean and sand thoroughly before attempting to solder the leaky joint.

INDEX

maintaining heating systems, 44–52
midwinter maintenance, 51
radiant heat, 42
steam systems, 41–42
summer shutdown, 50–51
supplementary heating, 52–53
high-limit (furnace) switch, 40
hinges, cabinet, 366
hose, garden, repair and splicing, 287–88
hot-air heating systems
correcting common problems, 38
hot-melt glues, 370
humidifiers, 30
how to install, 53–55
size needed, 56
types, 55–56

insulation, 2–5
blowing in, 13, 15
choosing contractor, 15
estimating quantities, 8–9
for hot-water pipes, 141
for pipe, ducts, 16
for water heaters, 16, 17
installation methods, 8–15
materials, descriptions, 7, 8
R-values, 8
isocyanurate insulation, 8

jigsaw, 321, 346
jointer-planer. See planer-molders
jointer safety, 345
joints, wood, 352

kilowatts (kilowatt hours), 74
kitchen ranges. See appliances
knob and tube wiring, 81
kwh. See kilowatt hours

lap joints, 354, 359
latex paints
exterior, 261
interior, 210 ff.
lathes, wood, 339–42
accessories, 341
chisels, 341
speeds, 342

lawn, flooding, 285
lawn sprinkler systems, 131
lawn tools and equipment, 287 ff.
levels, 309
lighting, electrical consumption, 27
reducing energy costs, 2–5, 25
linoleum, repair, 199 ff.
liquid foam insulation, 8
locks
replacing, 203 ff.
troubleshooting, 204
loose-fill insulation, 7
LP-gas heaters, 53
lumber
characteristics, 349
grades, 348
hardwoods, 349
how to buy, 348
prefinished, 349
sizes, dimensions, 349
softwoods, 349

masonry, working with, 376 ff.
insulating masonry walls, 11
painting, 256, 257
PVA paint, 261
protecting, sealing, 256, 257, 385
retaining walls, 282 ff.
mast kits, 74, 75
metals
brazing, 391 ff.
cutting with hacksaw, 301
cutting with bandsaw, 337
cutting with snips, 388
painting, 256
pop rivets, 388, 389, 390
sheet metal, 393 ff.
silver soldering, 392, 393
soldering, 390 ff.
sweating, 393
types of joints, 391
welding, 395 ff.
meters, electric, 74, 75
mildew, 258
mineral fiber siding, 248
mineral wool insulation (or rock wool), 7, 8
mirrors, cutting, 209
miter box, 300, 362
miters, cutting

with miter box, 300
with radial arm saw, 335
with table saw, 330
miter gauge, 329, 331
miter joint, 352, 364
moisture
in basements, crawl spaces, 57
condensation checklist, 62
excess in home, 56
molding head for table saw, 333
moldings, plastic, for paneling, 176, 177
moldings, wood, 357 ff.
cutting with radial arm saw, 335
types of, 361
working with, 362, 363
mortar mix, for brick steps, 272
mortise-and-tenon joint, 354, 358
mortising, 305, 338

nails
nailing techniques, 372, 374
selecting and using, 370 ff.
sizes, 371
types, 371
nail pops (in wallboard), 170, 171
National Electrical Code (NEC), 73
National Fire Protection Association, 73
nonmetallic cable, 78

oil burners, cleaning and maintenance, 47, 48, 49
oil-fired room heaters, 53

painting, exterior
chalking, 257
choosing paint, 260 ff.
common paint problems, 258, 259
estimating needs, 261 ff.
exterior painting checklist, 261
masonry, 256, 257
metal surfaces, 256
methods, 253 ff.
preparation, 253 ff.
removing old paint, 255
stains, 261
painting, interior, 210 ff.
around glass, 219
checklist, 220